Encyclopedia of Law and Development

To Marielle Franco
and countless other defenders of a more just world

Encyclopedia of Law and Development

General Editors

Koen De Feyter

Chair in International Law, Law and Development Research Group, University of Antwerp, Belgium

Gamze Erdem Türkelli

Post-Doctoral Fellow, Research Foundation Flanders (FWO) No: 12Q1719N, Law and Development Research Group, University of Antwerp, Belgium

Stéphanie de Moerloose

Swiss National Science Foundation (SNSF) Post-Doctoral Fellow, Humboldt University of Berlin, Germany; Affiliated Professor, Austral University, Argentina

Associate Editors

Philipp Dann
Humboldt University of Berlin

Celine Tan
University of Warwick

Elina Pirjatanniemi
Åbo Akademi University

Avinash Govindjee
Nelson Mandela University

Cheltenham, UK • Northampton, MA, USA

Published by
Edward Elgar Publishing Limited
The Lypiatts
15 Lansdown Road
Cheltenham
Glos GL50 2JA
UK

Edward Elgar Publishing, Inc.
William Pratt House
9 Dewey Court
Northampton
Massachusetts 01060
USA

Paperback edition 2022

A catalogue record for this book is available from the British Library

Library of Congress Control Number: 2020950848

This book is available electronically in the **Elgar**online
Law subject collection
http://dx.doi.org/10.4337/9781788117975

ISBN 978 1 78811 796 8 (cased)
ISBN 978 1 78811 797 5 (eBook)
ISBN 978 1 0353 0022 8 (paperback)

Typeset by Servis Filmsetting Ltd, Stockport, Cheshire
Printed and bound by CPI Group (UK) Ltd, Croydon, CR0 4YY

Contents

Contributors

Foluke Adebisi, University of Bristol

Titilayo Adebola, University of Aberdeen

Siobhán Airey, University College Dublin

Mayowa Ajigboye, Nelson Mandela University

Alessandra Asteriti, Leuphana University

Vincent Bellinkx, University of Antwerp

Justine Bendel, Vienna School of International Studies

María Valeria Berros, CONICET, National University of the Litoral, Argentina

Kinnari Bhatt, Erasmus University Rotterdam

Joanna Botha, Nelson Mandela University

Deborah Casalin, University of Antwerp

Diogo R. Coutinho, University of São Paulo

Lilla Crouse, Nelson Mandela University

Philipp Dann, Humboldt University of Berlin

Daria Davitti, Lund University

Koen de Feyter, University of Antwerp

Julia Dehm, La Trobe University

Julien Dellaux, French National Museum of Natural History, UMR 208 PALOC

Stéphanie de Moerloose, SNSF, Humboldt University of Berlin; Austral University, Argentina

Deval Desai, Graduate Institute of International and Development Studies, Geneva

Diego A. Dolabjian, University of Buenos Aires

Thomas Dollmaier, Humboldt University of Berlin

Gamze Erdem Türkelli, Research Foundation (FWO) Flanders No: 12Q1719N, University of Antwerp

Juan Bautista Etcheverry, CONICET, Austral University, Argentina

Michael Fakhri, University of Oregon

Octávio Luiz Motta Ferraz, King's College London

Christine Frison, Research Foundation (FWO) Flanders, University of Antwerp

Lila García, CONICET, National University of Mar del Plata

Julie Gibson, University of Strathclyde

Morag Goodwin, Tilburg University

Avinash Govindjee, Nelson Mandela University

Lívia Gil Guimarães, University of São Paulo

Mikaela Heikkilä, Åbo Akademi University

Vitor Henrique Pinto Ido, University of São Paulo

Anna-Liisa Heusala, University of Helsinki

Giedre Jokubauskaite, University of Glasgow

Markus Kaltenborn, Ruhr University Bochum

Nadia Latif, Georgia State University

Yong-Shik Lee, The Law and Development Institute

Helga María Lell, CONICET, National University of La Pampa, Argentina

Liliana Lizarazo-Rodríguez, University of Antwerp

Ntemesha Maseka, Nelson Mandela University

Daniel Mathew, National Law University, Delhi

Glancina Mokone, Nelson Mandela University

Nitish Monebhurrun, University of Brasília

Maija Mustaniemi-Laakso, Åbo Akademi University

Felix Mukwiza Ndahinda, Aegis Trust, Rwanda

Sheila C. Neder Cerezetti, University of São Paulo

Obiora Chinedu Okafor, York University

Jeremmy Okonjo, Queen Mary University of London

Ada Ordor, University of Cape Town

Alberto Pecoraro, University of Antwerp

Juliana Krueger Pela, University of São Paulo

Raquel de Mattos Pimenta, University of São Paulo

Amita Punj, National Law University, Delhi

Ikboljon Qoraboyev, M. Narikbayev KAZGUU University

Thando Qotoyi, Nelson Mandela University

Michael Riegner, Humboldt University of Berlin

Jeannette Francesca Rodgers, University of Birmingham, funded by Midlands4Cities Doctoral Training Partnership

Ignacio Sabbatella, CONICET, University of Buenos Aires

Rafael Lima Sakr, University of Sheffield

Mavluda Sattorova, University of Liverpool

Devanshi Saxena, University of Antwerp

Martin Scheinin, European University Institute

Martin Skladany, Penn State Dickinson Law School

Ajla Škrbić, Freie Universität in Berlin

Urmila Soni (Govindjee), North West University

Paul Stacey, Roskilde University

Yusra Suedi, University of Geneva

Celine Tan, University of Warwick

David M. Trubek, University of Wisconsin-Madison

Janine Ubink, Leiden University

Arne Vandenbogaerde, University of Antwerp

Wouter Vandenhole, University of Antwerp

Amaka Vanni, University of Leeds

Andreia Costa Vieira, ACV International Law Institute, Brazil

Leonardo Villafuerte Philippsborn, Universidad Católica Boliviana "San Pablo"

Patrick H.G. Vrancken, Nelson Mandela University

Attiya Waris, University of Nairobi

Abbreviations

AAAA United Nations 2030 Agenda for Sustainable Development, and the Monterrey Consensus and Addis Ababa Action Agenda

ABS Access and Benefit Sharing

ACHPR African Commission on Human and Peoples' Rights

ADB Asian Development Bank

AfDB African Development Bank

African Women's Protocol Protocol to the African Charter on Human and Peoples' Rights on the Rights of Women in Africa, 2003

AHRD ASEAN Human Rights Declaration

AIIB Asian Infrastructure Investment Bank

AR5 IPCC Fifth Assessment Report

Banjul Charter African Charter on Human and Peoples' Rights, 1982

BCBS Basel Committee on Banking Supervision

BEPS Base erosion and profit shifting

Berne Convention Berne Convention for the Protection of Literary and Artistic Work, 1886

BIS Bank for International Settlements

BIT Bilateral Investment Treaty

BMGF Bill and Melinda Gates Foundation

BRI Belt and Road Initiative

BWI Bretton Woods Institutions

CAC Collective actions clause

Cartagena Biosafety Protocol Cartagena Protocol on Biosafety to the Convention on Biological Diversity

CBD Convention on Biological Diversity

CBDR Common but differentiated responsibility

CDB Caribbean Development Bank

CDC Commonwealth Development Corporation

CEDAW Convention on the Elimination of all Forms of Discrimination against Women, 1979

CESCR UN Committee on Economic, Social and Cultural Rights

CGD Centre for Global Development

CHM Common Heritage of Mankind

CIL Customary international law

CITES Convention on International Trade in Endangered Species of Wild Fauna and Flora

CMS or Bonn Convention Convention on the Conservation of Migratory Species of Wild Animals

COIDA Compensation for Occupational Injuries and Diseases Act 130 of 1993

COP Conference of the Party

CPI Transparency International Corruption Perceptions Index

CRA Credit Rating Agency

CRC Convention on the Rights of the Child, 1989

CRPD Convention on the Rights of Persons with Disabilities, 2006

DAC Development Assistance Committee

DDR Doha Development Round

DES Dietary energy supply

DRR Disaster risk reduction

DSS Dispute Settlement System

ECOSOC United Nations' Economic and Social Council

ECtHR European Court of Human Rights

EIA Environmental impact assessment

EIE Enabling international environment

EITI Extractive Industry Transparency Initiative

ES Earth System

ESCR/ESC rights Economic, social and cultural rights

ETO principles Maastricht Principles on

Extraterritorial Obligations of States in the area of Economic, Social and Cultural Rights, 2011

EU   European Union

EXCOM   Executive Committee of the UN High Commissioner's Programme

FAO   Food and Agriculture Organization of the United Nations

FAO Seed Treaty   International Treaty on Plant Genetic Resources for Food and Agriculture

FDI   Foreign Direct Investment

FfD   Financing for Development

FfDO   Financing for Development Office

FGM   Female genital mutilation

FP2020   Family Planning 2020

FSB   Financial Stability Board

FTA   Free trade agreement

G30   Group of 30

GA   General Assembly

GATT   General Agreement on Tariffs and Trade

Gavi   Global Alliance for Vaccines and Immunisation

GC   Geneva Conventions

GDP   Gross Domestic Product

GHG   Greenhouse gas

GIs   Geographical Indications

GSG   Global Sustainability Goal

HLTF   High-Level Task Force

HRBA   Human rights-based approaches

HRBAD   Human rights-based approaches to development

IAC   International armed conflict

IACtHR   Inter-American Court of Human Rights

IADB   Inter-American Development Bank

IAEG-SDG   Inter-agency and expert group on SDG indicators

IATI   International Aid Transparency Initiative

IBRD   International Bank for Reconstruction and Development

ICA   International commodity agreement

ICC   International Criminal Court

ICCPR   International Covenant on Civil and Political Rights, 1966

ICERD   Convention on the Elimination of All Forms of Racial Discrimination, 1966

ICESCR   International Covenant on Economic, Social and Cultural Rights, 1966

ICJ   International Court of Justice

ICPD   International Conference of People and Development, 1994

ICSID   Convention on the Settlement of Investment Disputes between States and Nationals of Other States

ICSID   International Centre for Settlement of Investment Disputes

ICT   Information and communication technologies

ICTR   International Criminal Tribunal of Rwanda

ICTY   International Criminal Tribunal for the former Yugoslavia

IDA   International Development Association

IDL   International disaster law

IDRL Guidelines   Guidelines for the Domestic Facilitation and Regulation of International Disaster Relief and Initial Recovery Assistance

IEL   International economic law

IFI   International Financial Institution

IFR   International Financial Regulation

IFRS   International Financial Regulatory Standard

IHL   International humanitarian law

IHRL   International Human Rights Law

IIA   International investment agreement

IIF   Institute of International Finance

ILC   Indigenous and local community

ILO   International Labour Organization

IMF   International Monetary Fund

Implementing Agreement   Agreement relating to the implementation of Part XI of the United Nations Convention on the Law of the Sea of 10 December 1982

INDC   Intended nationally determined contribution

IO   International organization

IPBES   Intergovernmental Science-Policy Platform on Biodiversity and Ecosystem Services

IPCC   Intergovernmental Panel on Climate Change

IPN   Inspection Panel

IPPC   International Plant Protection Convention

IPR   Intellectual Property Right

ISDA   International Swaps and Derivatives Association

IsDB   Islamic Development Bank

L&D   Law and Development

LDC   Least developed country

LDRN   Law and Development Research Network

LFI   Legal framework and institution

LNG   Liquefied natural gas

LOSC   UN Convention on the Law of the Sea, 1982

MDBs   Multilateral development banks

MDG   Millennium Development Goal

ME   Mother Earth

MGRs   Marine genetic resources

MNC   Multinational corporations

MoI   Means of implementation

MSP   Marine spatial planning

MSP   Multistakeholder partnership

Nagoya Protocol   Nagoya Protocol on Access to Genetic Resources and the Fair and Equitable Sharing of Benefits Arising from their Utilization (ABS) to the Convention on Biological Diversity

NDB   New Development Bank

NDC   Nationally Determined Contributions

NGO   Non-governmental organisation

NIAC   Non-international armed conflict

NIEO   New International Economic Order

NTBs   Non-tariff barriers

ODA   Official Development Assistance

OECD   Organisation for Economic Co-operation and Development

OOF   Other official flows

OPEC   Organization of Petroleum Exporting Countries

Paris Convention   Paris Convention for the Protection of Industrial Property, 1883

PB   Planetary boundaries

PDP   Productive Development Partnership

PFII   Permanent Forum on Indigenous Issues

PIL   Private International Law

PPP   Public-private partnership

PSNR   Permanent sovereignty over natural resources

QuODA   Quality of ODA

R2P   Responsibility to Protect doctrine

Ramsar Convention   Convention on Wetlands of International Importance especially as Waterfowl Habitat

RBA   Rights-based approach to development

RCEP   Regional Comprehensive Economic Partnership

RON Tribunal   Tribunal de Los Derechos de La Naturaleza - Rights of Nature Tribunal

RTD   Right to Development

RTWS   Right(s) to safe and clean drinking Water and Sanitation

SAP   Structural adjustment program

SDG   Sustainable Development Goal

SEA   Sexual exploitation and abuse

SERAC   Nigeria-based Social and Economic Rights Action Centre

Sexual Offences Act   Sexual Offences and Related Matters Amendment Act

SIDS   Small island developing state

SPF   Social Protection Floor

SRHR   Sexual and Reproductive Health Rights

SRSG   UN Special Representative of the Secretary-General

SSC   South-South cooperation

STI   Forum on Science and Technology and Innovation for the Sustainable Development Goals

SUNFED   Special UN Fund for Economic Development

SYR   Synthesis Report

TCC   Troop contributing country

TFA   Transnational Financial Association

the „P5"   the USA, France, China, Russia and the United Kingdom

TK   Traditional knowledge

TOSSD   Total Official Support for Sustainable Development

ToT   Transfer of Technology

TPP   Transpacific Partnership

TrC   Triangular development cooperation

TRIPS   Agreement on Trade-Related Aspects of Intellectual Property Rights

TRIPS   Trade Related Aspects of Intellectual Property Rights

TWAIL   Third World Approaches to International Law

UBI   Universal basic income

UDHR   Universal Declaration of Human Rights, 1948

UN   United Nations

UN Draft Norms   Draft Norms on the Responsibilities of Transnational Corporations and Other Business Enterprises with Regard to Human Rights

UN GA   UN General Assembly

UN OCHA   UN Office for the Coordination of Humanitarian Affairs

UNCCD   United Nations Convention to Combat Desertification in Those Countries Experiencing Serious Drought and/or Desertification, Particularly in Africa

UNCLOS   United Nations Convention on the Law of the Sea, 1982

UNCTAD   UN Conference on Trade and Development

UNCTAD   United Nations Conference on Trade and Development

UNCTC   UN Commission on Transnational Corporations

UNDG   UN Development Group

UNDRIP   United Nations Declaration on the Rights of Indigenous Peoples, 2007

UNEP   United Nations Environment Program

UNFCCC   Framework Convention on Climate Change

UNFCCC   United Nations Framework Convention on Climate Change, 2016

UNGA   United Nations General Assembly

UNGP   United Nations Guiding Principles on Business and Human Rights

UNODC   United Nations Office on Drugs and Crime

UNWGIP   United Nations Working Group on Indigenous Populations

UPOV   Act of the International Convention for the Protection of New Varieties of Plants

USA   United States of America

USAID   United States Agency for International Development

USP   State University of São Paulo

WASH   Water, Sanitation and Hygiene

WATSAN   Water and Sanitation

WDR   World Development Report

WEF   World Economic Forum

WHO   World Health Organisation

WIPO   World Intellectual Property Organization

World Heritage Convention   Convention

Concerning the Protection of the World's
Cultural and Natural Heritage

WSSD   World Summit on Sustainable
Development

WTO   World Trade Organization

WWAP   UNESCO World Water Assessment
Programme

1. Future of Law and Development Research: An Introduction to the *Encyclopedia of Law and Development*

When the General Editors started discussing this introduction, our first idea was to attempt a history of law and development. We decided against it – not only because the entries in this Encyclopedia provide ample historical material – but primarily because there are not one, but many histories of law and development. These histories are located, and inevitably informed by particular understandings of the relationship between law and development.

In developed countries, law and development historically referred to development cooperation aimed at legal reform in developing countries. In a post-colonial context, it implied continued involvement by the former colonial powers in the design of the legal systems of the newly independent States. In a Cold War context, it meant ensuring that the legal systems in developing countries reflected the economic and political zone of influence of which they were (made) a part. As a result, the US history of law and development differs significantly from the Soviet or European histories of the same.

At the receiving end of development aid for legal reform were developing countries attempting to mobilize law to both reflect and direct their own societies. In this context, the terminology of 'law and development' was used less frequently; the emphasis was on how law could be used to foster economic growth, tackle poverty, deal with inequality and the like.

In our own research, perhaps coincidentally, the General Editors have been mostly engaged with yet another dimension of 'law and development', i.e. the role of global institutions. Here, the perspective is different again: the emphasis is not on bilateral relationships between donor and recipient countries, or on legal reform in the Global South, but on how international law and international organizations impact – for better or for worse – on development within and among countries. Law and development scholarship tends to focus on the (dis)connect between development objectives promoted through global legal and institutional reform projects and the results they achieve on the ground in developing countries.

It is striking to note how many of the terms used to describe 'law and development' historically – and in the preceding paragraphs – have now become contested not only among States, but also among law and development scholars. The language of development cooperation between donor and recipient countries is now largely avoided in policy circles; it has been replaced by talk about global partnerships and global engagement. Development has become 'sustainable' development and, as a concept, is meant to apply equally to both developed and developing countries. The term 'development' itself is rejected by some, as it suggests a process of transformation imposed by one actor on another deemed less developed. The usefulness of categorizing countries as 'developed' or 'developing' is increasingly questioned, as modalities of differentiation between countries multiply. On the other hand, it is argued that maintaining the term 'developing countries' remains politically relevant, in order to maintain a sense of unity between countries that shared an experience of colonial domination. The North is in the South and vice versa; the Global South can now also refer to underprivileged neighbourhoods in the geographical North. The Third World was invented when there was an East and a West. The concept of law (in development) has opened up to informal, customary and private forms of regulation.

The terminological shifts demonstrate an unease within current scholarship about the past: about how law and lawyers facilitated colonialism, imposed conditionalities reflecting the preferences of hegemonic countries and global institutions, authoritarianism and acculturation. The legitimacy of law and development as an ongoing scholarly venture thus hinges on avoiding the replication of injurious past practices.

It is clear, however, that today, law and development research remains plural, both in terms of how the functioning of law with regard to development is envisaged; the areas and levels of regulation that are prioritized, and in how it views the extent to which scholarship should direct policy and law reform. The entries in the Encyclopedia reflect this variety. Our authors, for instance, do not necessarily agree on the suitability and or feasibility of the Sustainable Development Goals. As Editors, we have not sought to address contradictory positions, nor do we necessarily agree with all positions taken in the book. These contradictions are part and parcel of the field. Having said this, law and development scholars are well advised to consciously situate themselves within the field. The personal identity and experience of the writer is not disconnected from the history of law and development, and it is certainly useful to reflect on what that position means for one's own work and the dialogue with others that are differently situated.

In crafting the Encyclopedia, we have sought to build on insights from discussions that have taken place over the last few years within the law and development research community. They may be summarized as follows:

Law and development research stands in need of a dialogue between law and other disciplines, given that development is not primarily a legal concept. In this area of scholarship, inevitably the social functioning of the law, and its impact on development objectives, come to the fore. Engagement with research from other disciplines, even if it is methodologically complex and may require a team of researchers, is therefore to be welcomed. Given the particular concern within development studies with those among and within societies facing inequalities, transdisciplinarity, inspired by the experiences of those most affected by inequality, is also to be encouraged. Transdisciplinarity requires researchers to take responsibility for ensuring that the products of their research benefit those who have contributed to it.

The law in law and development is not limited to a specific area of the law. Most legal researchers, including those contributing to this volume, have an expertise in a specific area of the law or focus on a particular level of regulation. The areas covered in law and development research are vast: economic law, environmental law, labour law, administrative law, private law, human rights. . . . Law and development scholars may self-identify as international, regional or domestic lawyers, comparatists, legal anthropologists, legal theorists and so on. What a legal approach to development as a minimum requires, however, is an identification and acknowledgment of all legal norms that are relevant to the development issue under review. The legal norms are as interconnected as the different dimensions of development.

Consequently, it makes sense that even if the emphasis of the researcher is on a particular area or level of the law, the plurality of applicable norms at other levels of regulation or in other areas of the law, and their interplay should be taken into account.

Knowledge from the Global South is insufficiently accessible and valued within current law and development research. The obstacles are well documented: researchers based in the Global South have little access to local funds for research (including field work); they often work in environments where research is not prioritized; and they face the prohibitive cost of accessing internationally published material. When quality research in law and development, or more broadly in the social sciences, does get generated, it is not necessarily produced in English. If no financial resources are available for translation, valuable, original work may never reach the global audience it deserves. Many a manuscript based on data generated in the South by Southern researchers has been rejected because funding for language review is absent. In practice, research produced at institutions in the North but based on data gathered locally in the South may stand a better chance of international publication, resulting in a particular brand of extractivism. In addition, publishers tend to cater for the interests of affluent markets where they can sell. The production and publication of knowledge replicates global inequality. The challenge then is how to ensure a truly equal bi-directional flow of knowledge between scholars located in the Global South and the Global North.

Finally, given the ambivalent role law has played over the years in development relationships between North and South and in dealing with domestic inequality, law and development research should be critical of the law, i.e. reflect on to what extent the law under review supports power dynamics that maintain established privileges, and is able to achieve its stated objectives.

The Encyclopedia emerged from the Editors' collaboration in the context of the Law and Development Research Network (LDRn). This Network was established in 2017 in order 'to enhance knowledge and understanding of the role of law, both domestic and international, in relation to development and governance, as perceived globally and locally' and 'to engage in fruitful discussions from both orthodox and critical perspectives on the role of law in

KOEN DE FEYTER, GAMZE ERDEM TÜRKELLİ AND STÉPHANIE DE MOERLOOSE development'. The idea of an Encyclopedia intended as a reference book for those interested in acquainting themselves with this area of research originated from discussions at the LDRn annual conference in 2017 and 2018 and steering committee meetings. Our publisher, Edward Elgar, attended activities organized by the Network from the start, and expressed a keen interest in publishing research produced within its fold.

The Associate Editors are all affiliated with LDRn institutions. Each of them contributed to a specific sub-theme on: Actors (Philipp Dann, Humboldt University of Berlin), Economic Law (Celine Tan, University of Warwick), Governance and Human Rights (Elina Pirjatanniemi, Åbo Akademi University) and the Sustainable Development Goals (Avinash Govindjee, Nelson Mandela University). In addition, the General Editors took responsibility for the 'Environmental Law' and 'Concepts' sub-themes.

The Associate Editors contributed to identifying the entries for their respective sub-theme, and contacted potential authors. During the drafting process, the sub-themes served as a vehicle for the division of labour. They have disappeared from the final book, where entries are simply listed in alphabetical order. All entries, including this introduction, are limited to approximately 2,000 words and ten references, which allows authors to interpret the essential debates in relation to a topic from their perspective. Any choice of entries will always be subject to debate. We attempted to strike a balance between issues that were topical at the time of publication and others that are more foundational, and perhaps also perennial. The Editors were supported at the Law and Development Research Group of the University of Antwerp by PhD researcher Alberto Pecoraro, who maintained communication with all authors throughout the complex drafting and double peer review process.

The majority of the authors contributing to the Encyclopedia are from the Global South. About one-third of the authors are based at institutions in the Global South. Some are early career researchers; others, senior authorities in the field.

The Encyclopedia is therefore not a Handbook of authoritative scholarly essays comprehensively dealing with the issue at hand, but it does show a variety of voices writing from very different perspectives, differing sensitivities and in different styles. It offers a picture of the diversity of the field today and perhaps, also of the direction into which it is bound to evolve. For these reasons, the General Editors hope the book may also be useful for supporting law and development curricula, regardless of where they are located.

We acknowledge that the accessibility of the Encyclopedia remains limited for researchers based in the Global South. The publisher offers the Encyclopedia material in the schemes run by EIFL and GOALII, which give free of charge or low-cost access to institutions in the Global South. We were, however, unable to simultaneously establish an Open Access Repository on request.

In conclusion, our sense is that reports on the death of law and development as a field of inquiry were greatly exaggerated. The field has a future, but it also has a past. In our view, law and development has a future if it is understood as an equal exchange of knowledge between scholars in the Global South and the Global North on how law impacts on societies in the Global South, as well as on marginalized and underprivileged communities in the North. This can be done, but it requires scholarly self-awareness rather than estrangement, and a conscious self-critical effort. We hope the Encyclopedia can make a contribution in this regard.

KOEN DE FEYTER, GAMZE ERDEM TÜRKELLİ
AND STÉPHANIE DE MOERLOOSE

2. Academy and Law and Development: The United States and Beyond

Academic research on law and development emerged in the United States (US) in the 1960s as an outgrowth of development assistance. It was created in part by people with hands-on development assistance experience and supported by development agencies. Gradually the field moved away from direct contact with the agencies and dependence on their financial support to emerge today as a semi-independent academic specialty. But the evolution of the academic field has not been linear and it has gone through several phases in its 50 year history.

The First Wave – lawyers seeking ideas

Academic work in the US started in the 1960s as an offshoot of reform projects supported by the Ford Foundation and USAID. A few agency officials thought law was important for development and recruited lawyers and academics to lead reform projects. When US lawyers recognized they lacked an intellectual framework for planning reforms and designing projects, they sought support from USAID, the Ford Foundation and the International Legal Center (a Ford spin-off) to create academic centers and launch ambitious research and education projects. The law and development (L&D) pioneers, who lacked training in empirical research and socio-legal theorizing, teamed with social scientists and socio-legal scholars in their effort to craft a new interdisciplinary field.

One notable example was the Yale Program in Law and Modernization which was the first US effort to create an interdisciplinary center for the study of law in development. Launched in 1969 and lasting about seven years, the Program was supported by a $1 million dollar grant from USAID. It supported interdisciplinary research and trained scholars from the US, Europe and the Third World. Some of the founders had field experience in development assistance but no one had been prepared intellectually for the challenge. To figure out how to study and reform legal orders in the Third World, the Program's founders drew on classical social thought, contemporary social science, and the nascent field of Law and Society. It worked with Yale's social scientists, brought well-known legal and social science scholars to campus, sought conceptual tools to link law with economic, social and political change in the Third World, and developed new courses. It supported field research in many developing countries, and worked on the reform of legal education in Africa and Latin America.

For a while, the US academic field flourished, nourished by major grants to universities like the one to the Yale Program, another by USAID to a sister program at Stanford, and Ford-supported initiatives at Wisconsin and Harvard. But by the late 1970s the field faltered because it lost outside support before it had built a sustainable place in the academy. When outside support from USAID and Ford dried up, efforts were made to get the law schools to pick up the costs. But these largely failed: even affluent law schools like Yale were unable or unwilling to pick up the cost. However promising its beginnings, L&D was still in its infancy and had not been accepted by the academy. At the same time, given the need for empirical research and in-depth training, the field was an expensive enterprise which bore little direct relation to a US law school's primary mission of preparing students to practice law in the United States. So it is no surprise that by 1977, with the founders gone and the grant expired, the Yale Program in Law and Modernization was closed down and activity at other early L&D centers slowed.

It is ironic that intellectual developments in the field, rather than strengthening ties with the aid agencies, actually weakened them and may help explain why external funding dried up. Many of the founders of the field were originally influenced by Cold War-inflected "modernization theory" and the reform agenda of aid agencies related to it. But over time they sought to make the field more independent, critical, and academic. This was real progress for the field but also may have been a cause of its decline in the 1970s. As the field evolved, scholars from the Yale Program and elsewhere began to question assumptions behind the very projects they and the agencies had developed.

Critics questioned the efficacy of transplanting law from advanced countries, realized that legal reform might strengthen authoritarian regimes, and doubted some strategies they initially supported. Some L&D trained scholars like Bonaventura de Sousa Santos went even further, arguing that the way the Program conceptualized law and development fostered US imperialism. The founders reacted to all these critiques by calling for better theory and more empirical study, which they hoped would help them resist the "pull of the policy audience", escape the influence of the agencies, and create an autonomous academic field.

This rethinking led to one of the most important essays on the future of the field: "Scholars in Self-Estrangement: Reflections on the Crisis in Law and Development Studies in the United States" published in 1974 and written by David Trubek and Marc Galanter, both former participants in the Yale Program. While the authors sought to strengthen the field by giving it a more academic and independent basis, their critique of prior efforts was very strong and some believe the essay was one reason the field declined in the 1970s.

In its short life, the first L&D wave had repercussions in some parts of the developing world. Probably the most active region was Latin America. Many of the early reform projects involved law schools. US L&D pioneers worked closely with scholars in countries like Colombia, Peru, Chile, and Brazil, some of whom studied in the US. Interchange between scholars in the North and South contributed to the increasing sophistication of the field. But as agency support declined, the L&D wave in Latin America also receded.

The Second Wave – economists come in

All this changed in the 1990s. The rebirth of agency interest launched a second wave. Unlike the first, this time it was big business. In the first wave, L&D had been a marginal activity for most development agencies. But in the 1990s it became a priority area for the World Bank and others: projects proliferated and billions were invested. This L&D boom was partially the result of new ideas in economics and the influence of the economists within the agencies. Economists who looked at the transition from command and State-dominated systems to market economies recognized that legal institutions were essential for markets and supported legal reform. Agencies listened.

Massive investments by the World Bank and other agencies brought academics back into the law and development field. While agency interest stimulated academic work, it did not dominate the second wave of university L&D work the way it had in the 1960s. By the 1990s the overall scene in US law schools had changed substantially. Interdisciplinary fields like Law and Society and Law and Economics themselves were brand new when L&D started. But by the 1990s many US legal academics had learned to employ socio-legal and economic analysis and employ empirical methods. A number of subfields developed around specific issues in the relationship between law and social and economic outcomes: they included law and society, law and economics, critical legal studies, feminist jurisprudence, human rights, and law and the environment. US law schools were better equipped to support research and students more sophisticated: university funds for research became available and students started attending L&D courses. At the same time some law schools in the Global South were increasing their capacity to deal with L&D issues. New links were formed between those looking at L&D in the South and those in the North. All this meant the field could make some progress whether or not it received support from the agencies.

The Third Wave – consolidating gains, meeting challenges, building bridges

As the twenty-first century began, the academic study of relationships between law, society and economy in the Global South was robust. But it faced four challenges. The first was that it had fragmented into many specializations that do not necessarily communicate with one another: law and economics people do not necessarily talk to people concerned with human rights or gender equality and vice versa; critics do not exchange ideas with those they criticize. The second is that the field has moved away from "meta-narratives" and embraced new development theories. These stress the need for local and contextual knowledge but the capacity to produce such knowledge is limited. The third is "hegemony": the field contains asymmetrical North-South linkages in which the scholars and institutions in the North sometimes have more power and influence even though these networks are created to deal with issues in the South. The fourth is relations with the aid agencies that were severed after the first wave and never entirely re-established.

DAVID M. TRUBEK

a)   Fragmentation

The field is fragmented because much of the research is carried on as a subpart of other specialties. Thus "trade and development" and "international investment law and development" are as much part of the well-developed field of international economic law as they are of law and development and "human rights and development" tends to be studied as part of human rights. Similar patterns and centrifugal forces can be seen in areas like financial law and development, women's rights and development, environment and development and so on.

In many cases these new topics were inspired and sometimes supported by advocacy organizations and transnational non-governmental organizations (NGOs) that promoted specific policy goals for the Global South. There now exist organized transnational academic networks that help train scholars and disseminate ideas and information. There are active law-oriented networks in human rights, trade and investment law, women, environment, and other subfields. While these topical specializations enrich our knowledge of the prospects and pitfalls of law in development, they may not communicate with one another and this weakens the effort to fully understand law's overall role in a particular place and time.

There are counteracting forces that help overcome fragmentation. Three stand out. The first is in the teaching of law and development. Courses that look at the whole picture are taught around the world and to one degree or another bring together work and ideas from the separate strands. The second is the Law and Development Review, which publishes articles on a number of topics. The third are efforts in the US and Europe to create and sustain broad-gauged law and development networks.

The most promising forces counteracting fragmentation today are the Law and Development Research Network (LDRN) founded in 2015 by universities in Belgium, the United Kingdom (UK), Netherlands, Germany, Argentina and Finland and the Collaborative Research Network of the Law and Society Association (LSA CRN) founded in 2017. LDRN is the result of the rebirth of Law and Development Studies in Europe. Although European scholars like Max Weber served as an inspiration for early L&D theorizing, and L&D work was done in the UK and other European countries in the twentieth

century, US scholars and US universities tended to hold the lead in that period. But by the second decade of the twenty-first century universities in Europe had taken up the challenge. LDRN arose in Northern Europe but has now incorporated universities from the Global South. LDRN holds regular annual meetings and training workshops for junior scholars. In 2021, it will meet in South Africa.

The LSA CRN is an interdisciplinary group that meets annually as part of the annual Law and Society Association meeting. It brings law and development scholars from many countries together and exposes them to the broader field of socio-legal studies worldwide. It has a broad mandate, welcoming papers related to various theoretical, empirical and interdisciplinary debates – from scholarship focused on Max Weber's work on legal families to the more contemporary accounts of the new developmental State and different conceptions of development as well as the role of institutions and markets in development.

Both LDRN and the LSA CRN have a holistic view of law and development and seek to bring together people from the various strands. Sessions and panels may be organized around specific topics but cross cutting events may be included. The 2019 LDRN conference highlighted the plurality of law and development and ways to deal with it, as well as offering streams on finance, human rights, gender, public law, legal pluralism and practice.

b)   Context

The contextualization challenge arises for three reasons. First, development policy increasingly favors local experimentation, not universal strategies, so effective policies will vary with the local context. Second, legal systems are deeply embedded in national cultures, transplants rarely work as intended if at all, and effective strategies for legal change must take account of local legal culture and conditions. Third, while we can break "development" down into subparts (economic, social, political) these strands come together in specific reforms in specific countries and their interaction can only be understood in that context.

The context challenge means that local capacity is ever more important to the field. Whether research involves scholars in the North or not, the final word and truly usable knowledge must come from those familiar with local conditions in the South. While capacity has grown in some parts of the Global South, it falls short of what is needed. Legal education in many places remains formalistic, underfunded, and focused on training professionals not researching law's role in society and economy. To allow the field to deal with the challenge of context, local institutions in the Global South need to be strengthened, more interdisciplinary and empirical research fostered, and South-South collaboration enhanced so developing countries can learn from one another.

c)   Hegemony

Hegemony is a challenge because of the disparity in resources between North and South. Because Northern Universities have greater resources for training scholars and conducting research in the South, they can exercise disproportionate influence on the definition of issues, the choice of research topics, selection of methodologies, and the orientation of proposed solutions. Students from the South studying in the North can become part of North-led projects and networks and find themselves under the influence of mentors in the North. Unless these relations are managed with care, the result may be to skew the field. Fears expressed by some that the very concept of "development" is a neo-colonial idea and "law and development" an imperialist undertaking reflect concerns of this nature.

The solution must lie in building capacity in the South and ensuring equality of voice to all scholars. There are clusters of L&D expertise in some developing countries that are creating autonomous capacity. For example, the group in Brazil centered at FGV Direito São Paulo and the State University of São Paulo (USP) holds major international law and development conferences frequently and FGV has just created a doctorate in Law and Development. More South-South contacts are developing, in part fostered by groups like LDRN and LSA CRN.

d)   Agencies

Law and development has always aspired to produce "usable knowledge". Founded as handmaiden to development assistance, the field struggled to secure an independent base in the academy. Now that that has been accomplished, there are efforts to reengage with aid agencies. This seems more advanced in Europe where the LDRN has built links to aid agencies in Germany, Belgium, the Netherlands and the UK. If the field is strong enough so that it is not dependent on the agencies, it should be able to find ways to work with them without being captured.

DAVID M. TRUBEK

References

Abel, Richard and David Trubek. *Inventing the Field of Law and Development: The Short, Happy Life of the Yale Program in Law and Modernization* (forthcoming).

Dann, Phillip (2013). *The Law of Development Cooperation: A Comparative Analysis of the World Bank, the EU and Germany.* Cambridge University Press.

De Sousa Santos, Boaventura (1981). "Science and Politics: Doing Research in Rio's Squatter Settlements" in Robin Luckham (ed.), *Law and Social Inquiry: Case Studies of Research.* Scandinavian Institute of African Studies Uppsala and International Legal Center New York.

Jensen, Erik and Thomas Heller (eds) (2003). *Beyond Common Knowledge: Empirical Approaches to the Rule of Law.* Stanford University Press.

Tamahana, Brian (1995). "The Lessons of Law and Development Studies", American Journal of International Law 89, 470.

Trebilcock, Michael (2016). "Between Universalism and Relativism: Reflections on the Evolution of Law and Development Studies", University of Toronto Law Journal 66, 330.

Trubek, David and Marc Galanter (1974). "Scholars in Self-Estrangement: Reflections on the Crisis in Law and Development Studies in the United States", Wisconsin Law Review, 1062–1102.

Trubek, David and Alvaro Santos (2006). "Introduction: The Third Moment in Law and Development Theory and the Emergence of a New Critical Practice" in David Trubek and Alvaro Santos (eds), *The New Law and Economic Development: A Critical Appraisal.* Cambridge University Press.

Trubek, David (2016). "Law and Development: Forty Years after 'Scholars in Self Estrangement'", University of Toronto Law Journal 66(3), 301–329.

3. Actors and Instruments

Development is not a pre-existing ontological category but a contested concept that must be defined anew for every place and time. Defining development is ultimately a political process of making choices about the use of economic, social, cultural or epistemic instruments. To understand this process, it is crucial to know who has voice in it, and how this voice can be raised and made heard. Law plays an important role in assigning voice to actors and in providing instruments through which they act and make their voice heard. Instruments are tools for actors and forms of voice in the political process of development. The institutional law of development governance is the area of law in which the legal configuration of these actors and instruments are described and normative standards of their evaluation and critique can be developed. The institutional law of development governance is hence a central field to critically study, reconstruct and evaluate them. It has become an important field of study and debate in the past years as it connects institutional questions of agency, voice and accountability with those of human rights protection and more particular substantive legal regimes, such as economic or environmental law.

This entry provides a brief overview of institutions as actors and instruments in the international process of development and the institutional law of development governance. Other entries cover specific actors and the domestic level.

Actors

The inter- and transnational development process today includes a great plurality of actors. Since the 1990s, the group of actors has changed from being dominated by Western public institutions to a wide variety of institutions of all shapes and origins (Dann, 2019). Binary distinctions (such as developed vs. developing countries) can serve as a useful starting point but must not be reified as they never capture their object in its entirety.

The distinction between developed and developing countries structures rights and obligations in many international regimes, including development cooperation, international economic law and environmental law. These regimes use different methods of definition. Some have established objective criteria like per capita gross national income, e.g. the World Bank; in others, countries self-designate as developing, e.g. in the General Agreement on Tariffs and Trade (GATTs) generalized system of preferences; and again others use a positive list of countries, e.g. in the climate change regime (Dann, 2013, pp. 203–205).

These categorizations overlap with a second distinction, namely that between donors and recipients in the field of development cooperation. Bilateral public donors are typically rich countries in the Global North like the US, Germany, UK and France, which tend to provide most funding in absolute terms, but rising economies like China, India and Brazil have also emerged as new donors. Multilateral donors include the European Union (EU), development banks like the World Bank and its regional counterparts, as well as UN development agencies.

A third category of actors are standard-promoting collectives. Donor countries are collectively organized in the Development Assistance Committee of the Organization for Economic Cooperative and Development (OECD), which sets standards for foreign aid. Developing countries and recipients are organized in the G77, the UN Conference on Trade and Development (UNCTAD) or the Africa-Caribbean-Pacific Group vis-à-vis the EU, and they dominate the UN General Assembly, at least numerically (Dann, 2013, pp. 209ff).

Besides these public institutions, private actors play a significant role in the political process of development at the international level. Transnational civil society and non-governmental organizations (NGOs) shape public opinion, participate in some international decision-making processes and have an important watchdog and accountability function. Business organizations and multinational enterprises also influence international policy processes, and their investment decisions and internationally protected property rights impact significantly on the policy space of national actors and on the lives of affected populations and individuals. Finally, sub-national entities like cities are increasingly active in global governance of urban development or climate change. As cities are, in principle, mediated by their States, their international role is often more akin to that of NGOs and businesses, but in some instances, they acquire their own para-diplomatic standing, e.g. when they sign loan agreements with the World Bank.

In sum, the international system of actors is characterized by a plurality of public and private actors. The relationship of public actors is formally defined by legal heterarchy, which stands in tension with significant de facto power asymmetries. These power asymmetries also affect the way in which actors can use instruments to shape the political process of development.

Instruments

Instruments that shape and give voice in the process of development are varied but most of them have a legal dimension and should hence be critically analysed by legal scholarship. We distinguish between instruments that directly create rules with developmental impact from those that are shaped by law, such as financing or informational instruments.

A primary instrument is law-making or standard-setting through treaties and second-ary law. Particularly important are multilateral treaties that found international development institutions, like the UN Charter or the Articles of Agreement of the World Bank, or law-making like the World Trade Organization (WTO) Agreements or the Paris Agreement on climate change. In these treaties, States col-lectively define competences, procedures and voice in the development process, and they col-lectively agree on substantive aspects of that process. Bilateral treaties also influence these substantive aspects, especially where they func-tion like standard contracts that effectively mul-tilateralize a regime, as is the case with bilateral investment treaties or foreign aid agreements between international donors and recipients.

Secondary law of international institutions impacts the process of development at the polit-ical and operational level. General Assembly resolutions that establish global objectives like the Sustainable Development Goals influ-ence development discourse, policy and prac-tice. At an operational level, institutional law pre-structures the procedure and content of development projects and bilateral aid agree-ments. A typical example are the World Bank's environmental and social safeguard policies, which evolved incrementally since the 1990s in response to problems in concrete projects.

Safeguards protect specific environmental goods, like natural habitats or the climate, or specific groups like indigenous peoples or resi-dents affected by project-related displacement (Bradlow and Naudé Fourie, 2013). They are incorporated in bilateral funding agreements with recipients and thus establish binding rights and obligations. The older safeguards were replaced in 2017 by a new "Environmental and Social Framework", which resulted from a systematic overhaul and multi-stakeholder law-making process. The evolution of the safe-guards reflects the evolving power balance and shifts in voice among donors, recipients and civil society (Jokubauskaite, 2019; Dann, 2019).

The increasing use of legal instruments has led to a juridification of the development process, which is accompanied by a certain measure of judicialization. Specialized dispute settlement mechanisms have emerged that adjudicate and enforce many of the legal instruments named above. This includes the WTO Appellate Body and investment arbitration based on the ICSID Convention, but also the less promi-nent Inspection Panel of the World Bank and analogous accountability mechanisms at other Multilateral Development Banks (MDBs). The Inspection Panel is tasked to hear complaints of project-affected people that allege a viola-tion of the Bank's safeguards. It has evolved into a quasi-judicial review mechanism and channels the voice of individuals and groups into an institutionalized dispute settlement and feedback mechanism (Naudé Fourie, 2009).

Next to law-making and adjudication there are many instruments that are shaped by law. These instruments include operative activities like financing, information and knowledge governance as well as uses of technology. They have important functions, such as shaping and concretizing norms and understandings of development, providing resources and exper-tise, and impacting the daily lives of people in developing countries and increasingly in the developed world.

Financing is the single most important instru-ment of international development institutions. Donors do not regulate, they finance recipients. Yet, financing creates important economic incentives, and conditionalities can consider-ably limit the sovereignty and policy space of aid-dependent recipients. Financing instru-ments are thus a key locus for the exercise of donor voice and power and for the negotiation of recipient autonomy. Financing instruments fall into two broad categories: project finance and budget support (Dann, 2013, pp. 361ff; Dann, 2019). Project finance involves the transfer of donor funds for a specific investment or capacity-building project, such as building roads or training public officials. Such projects typically come with procedural conditionalities, namely the requirement that recipients use the funds in a specific manner and comply with environmental and social safeguards. Budget support transfers funds that are not earmarked for specific projects but go directly into the recipient budget. This financing instrument is typically reserved to recipients with a satisfactory governance record and often comes with broader conditionalities, such as requirements for economic and institutional reforms. This was the case with controversial structural adjustment conditionalities imposed by the World Bank and the IMF since the 1980s. These conditionalities were typically not included as requirements in the legal agreements, but rather in an informal "letter of development policy", or they are treated as conditions for the conclusion of the financing agreement in the first place (Tan, 2011).

Another set of instruments of development policy that is gaining importance are knowledge instruments and information governance (Dann, 2019; Riegner, 2015). As development institutions increasingly see their comparative advantage over private finance and new donors in the expertise they house, they shift their focus from the transfer of funds to the transfer and governance of knowledge. The World Bank has declared itself to be a "knowledge bank" already in 1998. Since then, the Bank and other donors have invested considerable sums in in-house research and knowledge production, enhanced technical assistance and advisory services and have defined formalized "knowledge products". These include influential reports and indicators, such as the World Development Report, the Doing Business ranking, and the UN Human Development Index. Some of these activities have been controversial due to methodological weaknesses, ideological assumptions and their uncontrolled exercise of epistemic authority. The World Bank's Doing Business ranking, in particular, has drawn much legal criticism (Davis et al., 2012). These controversies show

that knowledge governance may be equally influential as legal regulation and finance but still lacks an adequate legal framework, which remains to be developed (Riegner, 2015). This task is all the more urgent as international actors increasingly use new technologies like big data or biometrics, which creates both opportunities and risks for the development process (Johns, 2017; Riegner, 2016).

PHILIPP DANN AND MICHAEL RIEGNER

References

Bradlow, Daniel D. and Andria Naudé Fourie (2013). "The Operational Policies of the World Bank and the International Finance Corporation", International Organizations Law Review 10(1), 3–80.

Dann, Philipp (2013). *The Law of Development Cooperation: A Comparative Analysis of the World Bank, the EU and Germany*. Cambridge University Press.

Dann, Philipp (2019). "Institutional Law and Development Governance: An Introduction", Law and Development Review 12(2), 537–560.

Davis, Kevin, Angelina Fisher, Benedict Kingsbury, and Sally Engle Merry (2012). *Governance by Indicators: Global Power through Quantification and Rankings*. Oxford University Press.

Johns, Fleur (2017). "Data, Detection, and the Redistribution of the Sensible in International Law", American Journal of International Law 111(1), 57–103.

Jokubauskaite, Giedre (2019). "The World Bank Environmental and Social Framework in a Wider Realm of Public International Law", Leiden Journal of International Law 32(3), 457–463.

Naudé Fourie, Andria (2009). *The World Bank Inspection Panel and Quasi-Judicial Oversight*. Eleven International Publishing.

Riegner, Michael (2015). "The International Institutional Law of Information", International Organizations Law Review 12(1), 50–80.

Riegner, Michael (2016). "Implementing the 'Data Revolution' for the Post-2015 Sustainable Development Goals – Toward a Global Administrative Law of Information" in Laurence Boisson de Chazournes, Kevin Davis, and Frank Fariello (eds), *The World Bank Legal Review: Financing and Implementing the Post-2015 Development Agenda*, World Bank.

Tan, Celine (2011). *Governance through Development: Poverty Reduction Strategies, International Law and the Disciplining of Third World States*. Routledge.

4. Approaches to Law and Development

Law and Development (L&D) as a field of study aims at answering questions on the interactions between law and development (law and/as/in/for development). Traditionally, L&D focuses on the role of the State in development, however, its central role is contested and the unequal power distribution worldwide remains the main challenge. From a State legal perspective, L&D covers a variety of legal areas such as labor law, environmental law, and (public and private) international law (Buchanan and Zumbansen, 2014). Legal scholars do not necessarily connect with L&D scholars because the latter crucially assess the role of legal systems in development, which implies an extra-legal perspective, beyond the scope of positive law. This interdisciplinary nature of L&D complicates its distinction from "development studies". For some, L&D is fragmented and conceptually complex (Van Rooij and Nicholson, 2013), for others it is convergent because it has progressively brought together conceptual approaches dealing with development (Buchanan and Zumbansen, 2014; Lizarazo-Rodríguez, 2017). Over time, L&D approaches have been described as "currents" and/or "waves" (Tan, 2019; David M. Trubek (2016). "Law and Development: Forty Years after 'Scholars in Self-Estrangement'", University of Toronto Law Journal 66(3), 301–329; David Kennedy (2006). "The Rule of Law, Political Choices and Development Common Sense" in David M. Trubek and Alvaro Santos (eds), *The New Law and Economic Development: A Critical Appraisal.* Cambridge University Press). Many authors agree that L&D emerged as a field aiming at assessing legal systems in Asian and African colonies, and then, at implementing the US "rule of law" development cooperation programs oriented towards reforming legal systems to foster economic growth (Trubek, 2016, above). Simultaneously, socio-legal studies aimed at assessing colonial law and its interaction with local law. From a geopolitical perspective, L&D was an American reaction towards colonialism and the Cold War. From a conceptual perspective, L&D approaches result from the Critical Legal Studies movement that inquired into the limits of legal positivism and from the New Legal Realism that empirically inquires how legal systems work in practice (Lizarazo-Rodríguez, 2017). The philosophical/ideological understanding of L&D influences the conceptual approach and the methodological perspective adopted. The conceptual approaches to L&D reflect the tension between liberal and modernizing approaches and critical perspectives, in turn reflecting various paradigms (e.g. modernization school, dependency school, neoliberalism, new institutionalism, etc.). They coincide with the modern and postmodern philosophical approaches to the interactions between law and development. L&D has conceptually interacted with diverse fields (economics, sociology, anthropology, environmental or ecological sciences, criminology etc.), and consequently, applies diverse methods.

Mainstream L&D (hereafter L&D) sought to "modernize" legal systems in developing countries to foster economic prosperity by promoting investment for industrialization that transformed rural collective communities into urban citizens and by implementing an "objective" rule of law. The rule of law aimed at overcoming institutional shortcomings linked to underdevelopment of fragile States, and at promoting global markets by limiting States' role on the economy. L&D methods are labelled as top-down because they replicate the model of developed States via aid and cooperation channels (Humphreys, 2012). The evolution of L&D is linked to the transformation of bilateral into multilateral development cooperation, mainly because Europe advocated the transformation of colonial questions into global issues through the conceptualization of global governance. International Development Law (IDL) or "*Droit International du Développement*" gave rise to multiple international organizations (IOs), mainly from the United Nations (UN), aiming at preventing a Global North-South polarization. Therefore, L&D and IDL focused initially on the regulation of economic relations worldwide and the exploitation of natural resources, which connect with the regulation of environmental protection. International financial institutions (IFIs) became the drivers of development cooperation by fueling financial means to developing countries, under the framework of the Washington Consensus based on neoliberal and New Institutional Economics (NIE) approaches (John Williamson (1990). "What Washington Means by Policy Reform" in John Williamson (ed.), *Latin American Adjustment: How Much Has Happened*. Peterson Institute of International Economics, 1–24; Douglas North (1990). *Institutions, Institutional Change and Economic Performance*. Cambridge University Press). These approaches explain the level of economic performance by institutional quality differences (Christian Bjørnskov, Axel Dreher, and Justina A.V. Fischer (2010). "Formal Institutions and Subjective Well-Being: Revisiting the Cross-Country Evidence", European Journal of Political Economy 26(4), 419–430). Consequently, the rule of law cooperation programs incorporated conditionality aiming at, firstly, increasing private investors' role in development through trade liberalization and, secondly, dismantling the "developmental State" to reduce State control of the economy. That is, the State is only expected to correct market failures, to protect property and to provide justice and security. This provoked a massive privatization of public services worldwide and a shift from public law regulation of development towards private law regulation (see World Bank (1997–1998). *World Development Report* (WDR); Lizarazo-Rodríguez, 2017). Recently, the rule of law cooperation programs were focusing on increasing accountability of State and non-State actors as a condition for governance (WDR, 2017, above).

Within mainstream L&D, several conceptual approaches further emerged: firstly, the Theory on Legal Origins that connects development performance with European colonization (Daniel Oto-Peralías, and Diego Romero-Ávila (2014). "The Distribution of Legal Traditions around the World: A Contribution to the Legal-Origins Theory", The Journal of Law and Economics 57(3), 561–628). Secondly, Law and Finance and Law and Economics that assess (and quantify) economic performance of legal systems and economic (and human) benefits of the rule of law (Bjørnskov et al., 2010, above). The main concern hereby is that by quantifying the institutional quality of States via indicators, the latter appear as "objective criteria" but they might be powerful instruments that can be strategically used at the cost of vulnerable communities (Merry et al., 2015). Thirdly, Global Administrative Law, that assesses the coexistence of multilateral hybrid regulation, and claims for accountability of IOs and public and private transnational actors for their (soft

and hard law) regulatory and funding activities (Benedict Kingsbury, Nico Krisch, and Richard B. Stewart (2013). "The Emergence of Global Administrative Law", Revue internationale de droit économique 27(1), 37–58).

Postmodern approaches to L&D (PL&D) share many research topics with post-development that rejects the assimilation of development with modernity, understood as the "westernization" of societies (Wolfgang Sachs (ed.) (1997). *The Development Dictionary: A Guide to Knowledge as Power*. Orient Blackswan). PL&D is mainly represented by the Third World Approaches to International Law (TWAIL), a geopolitical perspective that critically assesses and resists L&D and the international legal order, considered as an instrument used to preserve post-colonial hegemony, to prevent former empires to be held accountable and to protect individual rights (Antony Anghie (2007). *Imperialism, Sovereignty and the Making of International Law*. Cambridge University Press; Tan, 2019). TWAIL has been influenced by, firstly, the Latin American National Economic Control, with the "Calvo Doctrine" (Carlos Calvo (1868). *Derecho internacional teórico y práctico de Europa y América*. Vol. 2. Durand et Pedone-Lauriel) and the 1902 "Drago Doctrine" (Gathii, 2009). Secondly, by the Dependency Theory that claimed a more equitable international legal order to foster endogenous development (import substitution, exchange controls and land reform). The latter gave rise to the New International Economic Order (NIEO) (Gathii, 2009), associated with the East Asian Developmental State model. The NIEO seeks permanent sovereignty over natural resources as a cornerstone of the right to self-determination (Raúl Prebisch (1964). "Vers une nouvelle politique commerciale en vue du développement économique", Rapport du Secrétaire Général de la Conférence des Nations Unies sur le commerce et le développement. Dunod). African and Asian scholars have joined this approach and pursued the idea that cultural, social and political aspects should remain a policy sphere of States. Currently PL&D claims a fair international legal order, empowerment of social movements through self-governance and self-determination, and South-South cooperation (Twining, 2009; De Feyter, 2011). PL&D rejects the rule of law programs because of their post-colonial features, their top-down methods that neglect local context and their disregard towards second and third generation rights (Van Rooij and Nicholson, 2013; Lizarazo-Rodríguez, 2017; Humphreys, 2012). Moreover, PL&D rejects the quantitative assessment of the institutional quality of legal systems because it excludes non-economic values of development, and affects power relations (Merry et al., 2015). PL&D and TWAIL have contributed to inclusive L&D as follows: firstly, progress towards a fairer international order, such as the integration of human development, the adoption of the Declaration on the Right to Development, the adoption of UN Conventions against discrimination, and torture, and the progressive recognition of group rights to vulnerable communities. Secondly, the recognition of a differentiated treatment to empower developing countries in IOs. Thirdly, the recognition of the common heritage of mankind to reach global redistributive justice. Fourthly, the translation of resistance as an explicit recognition of an autonomous policy space for States in all areas of governance (Gathii, 2009; De Feyter, 2011; Twining, 2009). PL&D has influenced regional movements, e.g. the new Latin American "pluri-national" constitutionalism (Roberto Gargarella (2017). "Latin American Constitutionalism, 1810–2010: The Problem of the 'Engine Room' of the Constitution" in Pedro Fortes et al. (eds), *Law and Policy in Latin America*. Palgrave Macmillan) and the African Transformative constitutionalism (Eric Kibet and Charles Fombad (2017). "Transformative Constitutionalism and the Adjudication of Constitutional Rights in Africa", African Human Rights Law Journal 17(2), 340–366).

Alternative L&D (AL&D), the "Another Development" or development from below, contests the central role of the State in development and argues that L&D needs to incorporate legal pluralism as a way to focus on the needs of local communities (Van Rooij and Nicholson, 2013). Legal pluralism is the coexistence of multiple normative orders, including State law. It is grounded in the American Legal Anthropology (Sally Falk Moore (1973). "Law and Social Change: The Semi-Autonomous Social Field as an Appropriate Subject of Study", Law and Society Review 7(4), 719–746) that was used to assess legal systems in the European colonies, and then, socio-legal approaches became the main conceptual framework to assess the role of plural local legal systems in development. Other concepts used to describe legal pluralism are "rules of conduct" or "social norms" (Baudouin

Dupret (2007). "Legal Pluralism, Plurality of Laws, and Legal Practices: Theories, Critiques, and Praxiological Re-Specification", European Journal of Legal Studies 1(1), 296–318), "living law" (Eugen Ehrlich (1962). *Fundamental Principles of the Sociology of Law*. Transaction Publishers), "legal Development" (Brian Tamanaha (2011). "The Rule of Law and Legal Pluralism in Development", Hague Journal on the Rule of Law 3, 1–17), or "interlegality" (Boaventura de Souza Santos (2002). *Toward a New Legal Common Sense: Law, Globalisation and Emancipation*. Butterworths). AL&D also claims for the empowerment of marginalized communities by valuing formal and informal institutions as an expression of hybrid governance that should guarantee their right to define their own goals and values (De Feyter, 2011). As a socio-legal approach, AL&D uses bottom-up and ethnographic case study methods to understand the local interaction between law and development from below to respond to the failures of the rule of law projects. AL&D rejects "project law" because it reproduces capitalist values and its "top-down" methods are focused on State regulations that neglect local normative orders (Franz von Benda-Beckmann and Keebet von Benda-Beckmann (2014). "Places That Come and Go: A Legal Anthropological Perspective on the Temporalities of Space in Plural Legal Orders" in Irus Braverman et al. (eds), *The Expanding Spaces of Law*. Stanford University Press). AL&D's methodology, however, might lack universal reach as colonization and the rule of law projects did not have uniform global effects, nor did State and non-State norms interact homogenously in all regions. Moreover, AL&D has not been able to demonstrate that the rule of law projects are irrelevant (Van Rooij and Nicholson, 2013; Lizarazo-Rodríguez, 2017).

Nevertheless, AL&D has been influential in shaping the scope of sustainable development that connects economic development with environmental protection, in shifting the focus on developing countries towards a focus on social justice and the empowerment of vulnerable communities and by claiming inclusive and contextualized socio-economic development. UN agencies have progressively incorporated other topics beyond the role of State law for economic development and increasingly focus on populations in extreme poverty (Van Rooij and Nicholson, 2013; Paul Collier (2007). "The Bottom Billion: Why the Poorest Countries are Failing and What Can Be Done About It", Wider Angle (2), 1–3). AL&D has undoubtedly contributed to developing the concepts of transnational law and hybrid governance that capture globalization and the consequent limits of the regulatory capacity of States and IOs to implement the rule of law as a development paradigm. Transnational law succeeds where international law fails in capturing the complexity of world legal systems, shaped by colonialism, multilateral development programs, globalization etc., and conceptualizes their evolution and diffusion into local norms (William Twining (2006). "Diffusion and Globalization Discourse", Harvard International Law Journal 47(2), 507–515).

New paradigm? A multidimensional/multidisciplinary approach to transnational L&D

Transnational law is capturing the glocalization of legal orders further challenged by the UN multidimensional approach to development that goes beyond the State sphere and that has been crystallized by the Sustainable Development Goals (SDGs) agenda. The SDGs focus on eradicating poverty and empowering marginalized groups, by development policies that deal with "prosperity, people, partnership, planet and peace" (Human Development Report, UNDP 2016; Kaltenborn et al., 2020). L&D, PL&D and AL&D research agendas seem to converge with these dimensions, but still diverge in the conceptual/ideological approach and methodology. Mainstream L&D focuses on how to implement the SDGs and acknowledges the "hybrid" (plural) character of institutions (WDR, 2017, above). PL&D contests the SDGs agenda because IOs appropriate AL&D ideas without changing the political economy of IFI interventions. AL&D appears as an important influencer of the SDG setting and focuses on marginalized communities affected by the deterioration of the planet and conflicts. Therefore, the SDGs agenda and the transnationalization of the law might be shaping a new L&D paradigm beyond the categories North/South, developing/developed, Western/Non-Western. Currently, L&D, PL&D and AL&D focus on the following multidimensional topics:

Firstly, the **human rights-based approach to development (HRBAD)** incorporates human rights concerns into development, mainly through two components: the improvement of human rights compliance in partner countries instrumentalized by human rights conditionality, and the promotion of inclusive development cooperation focused on human dignity of marginalized communities, through local ownership and diversity recognition. L&D, PL&D and AL&D address the HRBAD but with a different understanding on what are human rights (Marie-Bénédicte Dembour (2010). "What Are Human Rights? Four Schools of Thought", Human Rights Quarterly 32(1), 1–20). L&D shares ideas with "natural scholars" who consider human rights as given and universal, and this has been the IOs approach. PL&D can be linked to "discourse scholars" who consider human rights as talked about and depend on power relations. PL&D is also linked to "cultural relativism" that uses the discourse of local relevance of human rights to challenge the universal scope of human rights at the cost of local culture (Twining, 2009). Simultaneously, cultural relativism has also been used by authoritarian regimes to restrict civil and political rights to improve socio-economic conditions. Soft AL&D can be identified with the "deliberative scholars" that consider human rights as universal but to-be-agreed-upon, whereas hard AL&D (and PL&D) share ideas with "protest scholars" who claim that human rights are fought for and should focus on marginalized communities. AL&D also claims that access to justice and legal empowerment programs of IOs ("justice for the poor", "justice for all", and "micro-justice") should go beyond State centered remedy mechanisms, or commercial alternative dispute resolution. The main reason is that most claims do not reach the State because of its weak or inexistent presence or because vulnerable people are unaware of their rights (William L.F. Felstiner et al. (1980/1). "The Emergence and Transformation of Disputes: Naming, Blaming, Claiming", Law and Society Review 15(3/4), 631–654; De Feyter, 2011).

Secondly, **sustainable L&D** emerged to address the fact that ecosystems are being irreversibly destroyed by unlimited economic growth (Donella H. Meadows et al. (1972). *Limits to Growth*. New American Library). Mainstream L&D focuses on how IOs implement the environmental rule of law, mainly promoted by the UN Environmental Programme, and the SDGs to protect ecosystems with an anthropocentric perspective through the recognition and enforcement of environmental rights. PL&D criticizes the environmental rule of law because, despite the impressive enactment of hard and soft law, ecosystems dramatically deteriorate and so it argues for a shift from anthropocentrism towards eco-centrism that recognizes the intrinsic value to ecosystems (Joan Martinez-Alier et al. (2016). "Is There a Global Environmental Justice Movement?", The Journal of Peasant Studies 43(3), 731–755). Conceptual approaches such as "Earth Jurisprudence" (Jamie Murray (2014). "Earth Jurisprudence, Wild Law, Emergent Law: The Emerging Field of Ecology and Law", Part 1 and 2, Liverpool Law Review 35(3), 215–231), "Law and Ecology" (Richard O. Brooks and Ross Jones (2017). *Law and Ecology: The Rise of the Ecosystem Regime.* Routledge) or "Community Ecological Governance" (Burns H. Weston and David Bollier (2013). *Green Governance: Ecological Survival, Human Rights, and the Law of the Commons.* Cambridge University Press) shape eco-centrism from a legal and political perspective. AL&D focuses on the active promotion of the interconnection between collective rights, ecosystems protection and legal empowerment of the poor. Self-identified groups such as indigenous or peasant communities, consumers and/or forced displaced populations become the center of the AL&D research agenda and have been progressively protected at the constitutional level, with varied levels of empowerment (Lizarazo-Rodríguez, 2017).

Thirdly, **peace building** is the most recent research topic addressed under the umbrella of L&D, also included into the SDGs. Mainstream L&D has focused on how IOs can secure peace and security through the rule of law projects in fragile States as necessary conditions for institutional legitimacy, economic prosperity and justice (UNDP, 2016, above; WDR, 2017, above; Collier, 2007, above). PL&D and AL&D contest these projects and the role of the International Criminal Court and of the UN Security Council in fighting crimes of war. These approaches claim for local alternative mechanisms to address structural inequality, socio-economic factors and power misbalances that harm marginalized communities, besides the need of addressing accountability, truth and reconciliation (Buchanan and Zumbansen, 2014; Roger Duthie and Paul Seils (eds) (2017). *Justice Mosaics: How Context Shapes Transitional Justice in Fractured Societies.* International Center for Transitional Justice).

LILIANA LIZARAZO-RODRÍGUEZ

References

Buchanan, Ruth and Peer Zumbansen (eds) (2014). *Law in Transition: Human Rights, Development and Transitional Justice.* Hart Publishing.

De Feyter, Koen (2011). "Sites of Rights Resistance", in Koen De Feyter, Stephan Parmentier, Christiane Timmerman, and George Ulrich (eds), *The Local Relevance of Human Rights.* Cambridge University Press.

Gathii, James T. (2009). "War's Legacy in International Investment Law", International Community Law Review 11, 353–386.

Humphreys, Stephen (2012). *Theatre of the Rule of Law: Transnational Legal Intervention in Theory and Practice.* Cambridge University Press.

Kaltenborn, Markus, Markus Krajewski, and Heike Kuhn (eds) (2020). *Sustainable Development Goals and Human Rights.* Springer Open.

Lizarazo-Rodríguez, Liliana (2017). "Mapping Law and Development", Indonesian Journal of International and Comparative Law 4(4), 761–898.

Merry, Sally Engle, Kevin E. Davis, and Benedict Kingsbury (eds) (2015). *The Quiet Power of Indicators: Measuring Governance, Corruption, and the Rule of Law.* Cambridge University Press.

Tan, Celine (2019). "Beyond the 'Moments' of Law and Development: Critical Reflections on Law and Development Scholarship in a Globalized Economy", Law and Development Review 12(2), 285–321.

Twining, William (ed.) (2009). *Human Rights, Southern Voices: Francis Deng, Abdullahi An-Na'im, Yash Ghai and Upendra Baxi.* Cambridge University Press.

Van Rooij, Benjamin and Pip Nicholson (2013). "Inflationary Trends in Law and Development", Duke Journal of Comparative and International Law 24, 297–348.

5. Armed Conflict

Defining 'armed conflict'

Armed conflicts have been an omnipresent feature of human relations and have presented a constant challenge to the international community as a result. However, even though 'armed conflict' is used ubiquitously in the parlance of international humanitarian law (IHL), there is no unanimous definition of this term. Nevertheless, each definition has one common feature: 'armed conflict' must consist of the use of force of certain intensity.

One of the most-used definitions of 'armed conflict' has come from the International Criminal Tribunal for the former Yugoslavia (ICTY) in the Tadić case. In Tadić, the Appeals Chamber stated that 'an armed conflict exists whenever there is a resort to armed force between States or protracted armed violence between governmental authorities and organized armed groups or between such groups within a State' (ICTY, The Prosecutor v. Duško Tadić, IT-94-1, Appeals Chamber, Decision on the Defence Motion for Interlocutory Appeal on Jurisdiction, 2 October 1995, para. 70).

Whatever definition is applied, five facts about armed conflicts are evident. First, armed conflicts result in: mass casualties and the urgent need for medical care to treat serious injuries, economic stagnation and the destruction of state infrastructure, and the forcible transfer and internal displacement of people. Second, armed conflicts are getting more complex. This is seen in the fragmentation of armed groups and the new types of weapons and methods used in increasingly asymmetrical warfare. Third, the causes of armed conflicts are varied and complex, with endemic economic and political conditions serving as the most common catalyst for conflict. Hence, theoretical explanations for these causes must involve the analysis of multiple variables and focus on their interactions. Fourth, the existence of an armed conflict (and therefore the applicability of IHL) is a legal question that should be assessed according to legal principles and the facts of the particular situation, regardless of the reasons and the subjective views of the parties to the conflict (ICTY, The Prosecutor v. Ljube Boškoski and Johan Tarčulovski, IT-04-82-T, Trial Judgement, 10 July 2008, para. 176; International Criminal Tribunal for Rwanda, The Prosecutor v. Jean-Paul Akayesu, ICTR-96-4, Trial Chamber 1, 2 September 1998, para. 603). Declarations of armed conflict by such parties are, therefore, of no importance. Accordingly, the viewpoints of some self-interested Western countries (such as the US and the UK) have been (and should have been) widely criticized since, on particular occasions, they have declared the existence of an armed conflict between them and other parties regardless of this rule (see, e.g., Lachenmann and Wolfrum, 2017). Fifth, parties to a conflict can consist of both States and non-State actors.

Classifying 'armed conflict'

Modern international law divides all armed conflicts into two types: international armed conflict (IAC) and non-international armed conflict (NIAC). However, academics are increasingly emphasizing the need to introduce a new form of armed conflict called 'internationalized' armed conflict, which bridges the concepts of IACs and NIACs.

The most important difference between IAC and NIAC is the more limiting enforcement of IHL on the latter. Still, in the largely decentralized, anarchical system of international law, there is no central authority in charge of classifying conflicts. As a result, this classification is generally determined by States and international bodies, such as the International Committee of the Red Cross (ICRC), on a case-by-case basis, which often depends on the facts on the ground. However, it is evident that many States view NIACs as an internal matter of the State in which the armed conflict is occurring, and, as a consequence, resist any outside interference based on the fundamental principles of State sovereignty and non-intervention. Furthermore, States are reluctant to treat the other parties in a NIAC as juridically equal and instead tend to label them as merely rebels or criminals acting outside the protection of the law. That is why only Common Article 3 and Additional Protocol II to the Geneva Conventions of 1949 are applicable in NIACs (along with customary international law, of course). Nevertheless, IHL imposes certain obligations in NIACs as well, although without conferring any legal status on the non-State armed groups involved.

This different level of application of IHL in IACs and NIACs is difficult to defend on legal, moral, or practical grounds. In any conflict, it is the victims who need to be protected, and for this reason, the nature of the armed conflict is irrelevant. In both types of conflict, the State infrastructure is attacked using the same weapons, affecting armed belligerents and protected civilians alike. Hence, the only relevant criterion when deciding on the application of IHL in armed conflict should be the need to protect victims of conflict. Therefore, there is a slow but visible tendency to mitigate the differences in the application of IHL in IACs and NIACs, mostly by customary international law but also by proposals of some actors. For example, in September 2019 Switzerland proposed to deem the intentional starvation of civilians a war crime in NIAC. Nevertheless, it is doubtful that a single set of new rules will develop in the near future.

1 International armed conflict

According to the 1949 Geneva Conventions (GC), international armed conflicts are:

1. all cases of declared war between two or more States that are party to the GC (there has been, however, none since 1945);
2. all cases of other armed conflict which may arise between two or more States that are party to the GC, even if the state of war is not recognized by one of them; and finally
3. all cases of partial or total occupation of the territory of a State that is a party to the GC, even if the said occupation meets with no armed resistance (GC, common Article 2).

The duration, the level of fatalities, the formal declaration of war or the recognition of the situation is of no relevance to the existence of an IAC. IACs can arise even if a State uses unilateral force against another State, which does not or cannot respond with military means, or even if the attacking State's resort to force is not directed against the armed forces of another State (but on its territory or population) (ICRC, 2015). Any hostile act against another State that has led to the intervention of armed forces constitutes an IAC. The author of this contribution agrees with this for protection reasons. Specifically, less protection would be afforded to persons involved in the conflict if a threshold requirement with respect to 'intensity of violence' were introduced.

2 Non-international armed conflict

While Common Article 3 and Additional Protocol II regulate NIAC, there are some differences in the way in which these conventions do so. Common Article 3 specifies that it applies only to armed conflicts not of an international character occurring in the territory of one of the GC parties, whereas Protocol II establishes certain requirements that must be fulfilled for a NIAC to exist. Hence, there are situations in which only Common Article 3 will apply because the criteria set out in Protocol II will not be fulfilled, and vice versa.

NIACs do not have to take place on the territory of one State. The distinct feature of this type of conflict is not territorial scope, but the kind of actors who take part in hostilities. Hence, under the minimum requirements of Common Article 3, one side to the conflict must be a non-State actor. In addition, there must be a certain level of intensity and organization in order for a NIAC to exist. If not, there is no NIAC but merely 'internal disturbances and tensions'.

Moreover, the Rome Statute of the International Criminal Court provides a new threshold of application: an 'armed conflict' has to be protracted and between governmental authorities and organized armed groups or between such groups (Article 8(2)(f)).

3 Internationalized armed conflict

This type of conflict implies the existence of an external (second) State that becomes militarily involved in a NIAC. The term 'militarily involved' does not mean that this external State has to participate directly in conflict. It means exercising effective control over a military group, such as organizing, coordinating, or planning the military actions; or financing, training, equipping, or providing operational support to that group (ICTY, The Prosecutor v. Duško Tadić, 1997, above, para. 595). This is not, however, the case in dealing with military or paramilitary groups. In these cases, it is not sufficient for a State to financially or militarily assist armed group(s) in order for a conflict to become internationalized but to have overall control over the armed group (ICTY, The Prosecutor v. Duško Tadić, IT-94-1-A, Appeals Chamber, Opinion and Judgement, 15 July 1999, para. 131).

The need for introducing this new type of conflict emerges due to the increasing complexity of armed conflicts occurring in practice, making the current division of armed conflicts insufficient to deal with the reality of existing conflicts on the ground. Yet, some scholars are of the view that almost any situation represents a mix of internal and international features and that the introduction of this new type of conflict would be confusing or misleading. Specific features of this type of conflict, however, lead the author of this contribution to the conclusion that it would be more confusing or misleading to leave such armed conflicts unregulated. The question is not whether the international community should label something that might exist, but something that already exists.

The impact of armed conflicts on society and development

Armed conflict is a development issue since it creates a gap in this regard between those States that have experienced armed conflict and those that have not (Gates et al., 2012). Moreover, armed conflict often leads to forced migration and refugee flows, and it certainly negatively affects education, access to food, life expectancy, GDP per capita rates, and infant mortality rates (Gates et al., 2012).

However, modern armed conflicts differ from the ones fought in the past. Namely, through history, armed conflicts were predominantly fought in open battlefields and between soldiers (who were mainly men). They have, however, drastically changed over time, moving into the lives and homes of ordinary people in a more vicious way than ever before (ICRC, 2017). New actors in conflicts have been introduced, ranging from private military and security companies to multinational corporations. Modern armed conflicts have become longer. The violence generated in one State often spreads through entire regions with long-term consequences. Conflict-related sexual violence is a growing issue. Civilians are becoming the main combatants and primary victims. They represented 63 per cent of recorded war deaths in the 1960s and 74 per cent in the 1980s; these numbers have only increased in the last three decades (Epps, 2013, p. 23). Other emerging

issues are new war crimes and new means of warfare, such as the use of drones, artificial intelligence, and autonomous weapon systems. The phenomena of the foreign fighters, child soldiers, and nuclear weapons demand urgent regulation.

All of this changes the impact that armed conflicts have on society and the consequences they impose on its development, making it more challenging and difficult to effect change. IHL is indeed dynamic, as reflected in the ICRC's recent Commentaries to the Geneva Conventions of 1949 (see, e.g., the 2019 ICRC Challenges Report, that presents some of the new trends and complexities of contemporary armed conflicts and the legal challenges they entail), but it has not yet evolved to fully adapt to these new challenges. At the same time, for it to be useful and to address these new challenges, IHL must adapt to new conflicts. To this end, the more effective use of resources that already exist is paramount, such as the use of the UN Security Council and early warning systems. Among academics and practitioners, there are growing demands to adopt a uniform body of rules for both types of conflict and leave the outdated dichotomy behind, because in the eyes of many, it no longer addresses contemporary conflicts. Nevertheless, it is necessary to remind all actors of IHL's principles in peacetime as well as in conflict. Good governance must include respect for human rights in order for peace to be lasting.

AJLA ŠKRBIĆ

References

Epps, Valerie (2013). 'Civilian Casualties in Modern Warfare: The Death of the Collateral Damage Rule', Georgia Journal of International and Comparative Law 41, Suffolk University Law School Research Paper No. 11-39.

Gates, Scott et al. (2012). 'Development Consequences of Armed Conflict', World Development 40(9), 1713–1722.

ICRC (2015). International Humanitarian Law and the Challenges of Contemporary Armed Conflicts, 32IC/15/11, Report prepared for the 32nd International Conference of the Red Cross and Red Crescent, Geneva, 8–10 December 2015.

ICRC (2017). President Peter Maurer's Statement, 4 April 2017, Retrieved from https://www.icrc.org/en/document/war-cities-what-stake-0, accessed 10 September 2019.

ICRC (n.d.). The reports of the ICRC: Annual reports and Challenges reports. Available at: https://blogs.icrc.org/cross-files/annual-reports/

and https://www.icrc.org/en/document/icrc-report-ihl-and-challenges-contemporary-armed-conflicts accessed 10 September 2020.

Lachenmann, Frauke and Rüdiger Wolfrum (eds) (2017). *The Law of Armed Conflict and the Use of Force*. The Max Planck Encyclopaedia of Public International Law. Thematic Series Volume 2. Oxford University Press.

Mačák, Kubo (2018). *Internationalized Armed Conflicts in International Law*. Oxford University Press.

Sassòli, Marco, Antoine A. Bouvier, and Anne Quintin (1999). *How Does Law Protect in War? Cases, Documents and Teaching Materials on Contemporary Practice in International Humanitarian Law*. International Committee of the Red Cross.

The Geneva Conventions of 12 August 1949: Geneva Convention for the Amelioration of the Condition of the Wounded and Sick in Armed Forces in the Field, Geneva Convention for the Amelioration of the Condition of Wounded, Sick and Shipwrecked Members of Armed Forces at Sea, Geneva Convention relative to the Treatment of Prisoners of War, Geneva Convention relative to the Protection of Civilian Persons in Time of War.

UN General Assembly (1998). Rome Statute of the International Criminal Court, 17 July 1998, entered into force 1 July 2002.

AJLA ŠKRBIĆ

6. Biodiversity

Definition

"Biodiversity" or "Biological Diversity" is defined in the *Dictionary of Sustainability* (Margaret Robertson (2017). *Dictionary of Sustainability*. Routledge, p. 165) as "the variety of genes, species and ecosystems found in a given area". This definition perceives biological diversity at different scales, from the nano-level (gene) to the macro one (ecosystems), and relates living beings with their environment in interdependent relationships. Looking in the Cambridge Dictionary, this definition is widened to "the number and types of plants and animals that exist in a particular area, or the problem of protecting it", thereby introducing the problem of biodiversity loss and destruction requiring protection and conservation. After the Second World War, and particularly in the 1970s and 1980s, nature protection movements began to voice an alarm call for protecting our planet and wildlife from human destruction, thereby fostering the theory of Environmental Justice. The United Nations (UN) institutions and the scientific community backed up these calls with numerous reports on the state of biodiversity, water or air pollution, deforestation, extinction of endangered species etc. New academic disciplines emerged to address these problems, such as "conservation biology" or "sustainable development law". The father of conservation biology, Michael Soulé, explains that it:

> addresses the biology of species, communities and ecosystems that are perturbed, either directly or indirectly, by human activities or agents. Its goal is to provide principles and tools for preserving biological diversity . . . Conservation biology differs from most other biological sciences in one important way: it is often a crisis discipline . . . In crisis disciplines, one must act before knowing all the facts; . . . their pursuit requires intuition as well as information. (Soulé, 1985: p. 727)

A few years later, the UN Conference on Environment and Development (UNCED, or 'Rio Earth Summit', 3–14 June 1992) was held in Brazil, designing worldwide measures to protect biodiversity. Three conventions were opened for signature, including the Convention on Biological Diversity (CBD) where biological diversity is defined as the "the variability among living organisms from all sources including, inter alia, terrestrial, marine and other aquatic ecosystems and the ecological complexes of which they are part; this includes diversity within species, between species and of ecosystems" (Article 2). The CBD designs various conservation strategies: at the genetic diversity scale through in situ and ex situ conservation approaches; at the ecosystem scale through preservation of habitat or protected area plans.

The origin of biodiversity destruction is clearly anthropocentric (Intergovernmental Science-Policy Platform on Biodiversity and Ecosystem Services (IPBES), Global Assessment Report on Biodiversity and Ecosystem Services, 2019; Intergovernmental Panel on Climate Change (IPCC) reports). However, exploitation, extraction and destruction of natural resources such as forests, land, wetlands, fisheries and oceans or freshwater do not affect people and countries in the same way around the globe. On the one hand, developing countries are generally poor in financial and technical/technological resources but rich in biological diversity, with 15 States being called "megadiverse countries" that is to say countries with the majority of Earth's species and high numbers of endemic species (what some have featured as "green gold"). On the other hand, developed countries are generally poor in biological resources (except the USA and Australia) but have the financial and technical means to exploit nature, on their territory or elsewhere, thereby contributing to their economic growth, often without destroying their own territory. From a Law and Development perspective, it should be highlighted that environmental, economic and social impacts of biodiversity exploitation are clearly not equitably nor fairly distributed on the globe, the richest countries benefiting from the largest share of the cake, the poorest suffering from the biggest destruction and pollution (UN Environment Programme (UNEP), "Global Environment Outlook 6", 2019).

Biodiversity cannot be reduced only to natural resources. It also encompasses a cultural and immaterial dimension, inter alia through traditional knowledge (TK) related to genetic resources. TK is based on the accumulation of empirical observations by indigenous and local communities (ILCs) and on interaction with their environment. This includes, for example, knowledge related to agricultural practices, midwifery, ethnobotany and ecological knowledge or traditional medicine. TK is generally crucial for the subsistence of ILCs. It has been demonstrated that biodiversity losses go hand-in-hand with cultural losses, such as the disappearance of local languages. This shows that immaterial aspects of biodiversity – i.e. its related knowledge and information – are inseparably entangled with the physical resources and that they play an essential role in conserving and using biodiversity in a sustainable manner.

The conservation and use of biodiversity cover many different scientific fields (from agronomy, genetics, biology, ethnobotany, to law, economics, anthropology or political sciences). This explains why an interdisciplinary approach is compulsory to mitigate the destruction of our environment and the ongoing sixth mass extinction (IPBES, Global Assessment Report, 2019, above). Up to now, the international regulatory instruments put in place to protect our environment have clearly not enabled to revert the destruction pathway.

International biodiversity law regime complex

Since the beginning of the twentieth century, a complex web of national, regional and international regulatory tools has developed to handle environmental degradation, but has not been governed in a coherent manner. Within the field of international environmental law, specific conventions address biodiversity conservation in two major ways: protecting areas through a "sanctuary approach" (e.g. protected areas) or controlling the exploitation of nature through conservation and sustainable use obligations (e.g. quotas in deforestation or fisheries, sometimes assorted with restoration obligations when a destruction is inevitable). They all regulate the access to the area or to the resources (plant, animal or mineral) and their "sustainable use". There are numerous conventions dealing with biodiversity conservation. Only a few will be mentioned here and three will be briefly explained: the CBD and its Nagoya Protocol on Access to Genetic Resources and Fair and Equitable Sharing of the Benefits Arising from their Utilization, and the International Treaty on Plant Genetic Resources for Food and Agriculture. Other treaties include: The

International Plant Protection Convention; The Convention on Wetlands of International Importance especially as Waterfowl Habitat (Ramsar Convention); The Convention Concerning the Protection of the World's Cultural and Natural Heritage (World Heritage Convention); The Convention on International Trade in Endangered Species of Wild Fauna and Flora (CITES); The Convention on the Conservation of Migratory Species of Wild Animals (CMS or Bonn Convention) and The UN Convention to Combat Desertification in Those Countries Experiencing Serious Drought and/or Desertification, Particularly in Africa (UNCCD). In addition to the latter convention and besides the non-binding Rio Declaration on Environment and Development, Agenda 21 and the Forest Principles, the Rio Earth Summit also resulted in the following two supplementary conventions: the Framework Convention on Climate Change (UNFCCC), and the Convention on Biological Diversity.

The CBD (signed at the Rio Earth Summit on 5 June 1992, entered into force 29 December 1993; 196 contracting parties as of August 2019) has three objectives (Article 1): "the conservation of biological diversity, the sustainable use of its components and the fair and equitable sharing of the benefits arising out of the utilization of genetic resources". The CBD was complemented by two protocols. The Cartagena Protocol on Biosafety to the Convention on Biological Diversity (Cartagena Biosafety Protocol, adopted on 29 January 2000, entered into force on 11 September 2003; 171 contracting parties as of August 2019) is an international treaty governing the transboundary movements of living modified organisms resulting from modern biotechnology. The Nagoya Protocol on Access to Genetic Resources and the Fair and Equitable Sharing of Benefits Arising from their Utilization (ABS) to the Convention on Biological Diversity (Nagoya Protocol, adopted on 29 October 2010 in Nagoya, Japan, entered into force on 12 October 2014; 118 contracting parties as of August 2019) provides a transparent legal framework for the effective implementation of the fair and equitable sharing of benefits objective of the CBD, which contracting parties had difficulties to implement effectively for 20 years.

The CBD has numerous substantive provisions relating to: (in situ and ex situ) measures for the conservation of biodiversity; incentives for the conservation and sustainable use of biodiversity; research and training; public awareness and education; assessing the impacts of projects upon biodiversity; access to and transfer of technology; and the provision of financial resources. Most importantly, it creates a "fair and equitable access and benefit sharing" (ABS) mechanism to control access to genetic resources and compensate the access with monetary and non-monetary benefit sharing obligations. The CBD and its Nagoya Protocol regulate ABS through a contract that includes the prior informed consent from the Contracting Party providing the resources – often a developing country – (CBD, Article 15§5) and, when appropriate, from the ILCs (Nagoya Protocol, Article 6§2). Furthermore, fair and equitable sharing of benefits that arise from the use of genetic resources as well as subsequent applications and commercialization are guaranteed through mutually agreed terms, negotiated between the provider and the user – generally a user from a developed country – (CBD, Article 15§3 and §7; Nagoya Protocol, Article 5§1) (Morgera et al., 2014) in the access contract. However, the effective implementation of these ABS provisions remains thorny and one might question whether this contractual approach to commodifying genetic resources is the best way to efficiently and equitably conserve and use biodiversity.

The International Treaty on Plant Genetic Resources for Food and Agriculture (the FAO Seed Treaty, signed in Rome, Italy on 3 November 2001, entered into force on 29 June 2004; 145 contracting parties as of August 2019) has three objectives to reach sustainable agriculture and food security: the conservation of plant genetic resources for food and agriculture, their sustainable use, and the fair and equitable sharing of the benefits arising out of their use, in harmony with the CBD. The treaty covers all plant genetic resources for food and agriculture, while its Multilateral System of ABS, which functions as a virtual common basket where all stakeholders can access seeds upon standard terms, covers 64 crops and forages listed in its Annex I. The treaty also includes provisions on farmers' rights (Frison, 2018). The Seed Treaty is currently under review to enhance the functioning of its multilateral system.

Critical state of biodiversity at the dawn of 2020: what response from a law and development perspective?

As stated in a previous publication:

> the Convention on Biological Diversity formalized the objectification of biodiversity as mere economic resources, the use out of which benefits should be derived, but also consecrated the market to be the most appropriate regulating instrument for reaching biodiversity conservation and sustainable use objectives. (Frison, 2018)

Marketing nature was presented as progress and development to the Global South. Similar reasoning can be made for the other international biodiversity conventions sketched-out above. By exporting Western (neoliberal capitalist) norms on Nature to the rest of the world, these instruments address biodiversity conservation from an anthropocentric perspective: biodiversity is conserved so that it can be further used by humans today or in the future, not because it deserves, per se, not to be destroyed. They all embody and facilitate the commodification of Nature (Dhandapani, 2015), treating elements of Nature as direct, physical (e.g. agricultural products, mining resources) or indirect, immaterial (ecosystem services, carbon quotas) market resources. By relating biodiversity conservation to economic instruments and purposes (UNEP, Green Economy Report, 2011), these conventions design mechanisms that sustain the (hyper-)appropriation and exploitation of Nature, mainly by the Global North. Scholars have named these processes 'extractivism' (Gudynas, 2018) or "extractive biocolonialism" (Harry, 2011). This concept can be related to a form of "Biopiracy", where industries from the North dispossess the South from their resources and TK.

It is a fact that we are now in the sixth mass extinction (IPBES, Global Assessment Report, 2019, above). This means that the way we govern biodiversity conservation is not effective, notwithstanding the new tools and instruments attempting to internalize the external costs and damages to the environment by our neoliberal global market (Dhandapani, 2015). Consequently, one may call for a radical change in global environmental governance and regulation, moving away from the inequitable consumption and exploitation pathway: "a radical cultural and institutional transformation – a transition to an altogether different world" (Escobar, 2015: p. 453). A change where Nature and human beings would both be equally important subjects of law, what Capra and Mattei call "an ecological legal order" (2015), paving the way for a transition towards resilient and interdependent societies around the globe. Focusing on cooperation rather than competition and on the key role of local communities in governing resources, alternatives are explored both in Western and non-Western societies through the revival of common governance systems (Bollier and Helfrich, 2014; Frison, 2018). "Commoning" biodiversity would allow to re-empower communities in governing their ecosystems in an ecological way, aside from private or State appropriative management (Bollier and Helfrich, 2014). Focusing on a **holistic**, non-anthropocentric environmental ethic, where Nature has an intrinsic value in line with Aldo Leopold's environmental philosophy, would allow communities of human and non-human living beings to play a central role in conserving our ecosystems. "In emphasizing the inter-dependence of all beings, [new transition discourses] bring to the fore one of the crucial imperatives of our time: the need to reconnect with each other and with the non-human world" (Escobar, 2015: p. 454). But to do so, the white Western man would need to look, listen to, learn from and implement other cosmologies from other societies living on our planet (Kothari et al., 2014).

CHRISTINE FRISON

References

Bollier, David and Silke Helfrich (eds) (2014). *The Wealth of the Commons: A World Beyond Market and State*. Levellers Press.

Capra, Fritjof and Mattei, Ugo (2015). *The Ecology of Law: Toward a Legal System in Tune with Nature and Community*. Berrett-Koehler Publishers.

Dhandapani, Selvakumar (2015). "Neo-liberal Capitalistic Policies in Modern Conservation and the Ultimate Commodification of Nature" Journal of Ecosystem and Ecography 5, 167.

Escobar, Arturo (2015). "Degrowth, Postdevelopment, and Transitions: A Preliminary Conversation" Sustainability Science 10(3), 451–462.

Frison, Christine (2018). *Redesigning the Global Seed Commons: Law and Policy for Agrobiodiversity and Food Security*. Routledge.

Gudynas, Eduardo (2018). "3 Extractivisms. Tendencies and Consequences" in Ronaldo Munck, and Raul Delgado Wise (eds), *Reframing Latin American Development*. Routledge.

Harry, Debra (2011). "Biocolonialism and Indigenous knowledge in United Nations discourse" Griffith Law Review 20(3), 702–728.

Kothari, Ashish, Federico Demaria, and Alberto Acosta (2014). "Buen Vivir, Degrowth and Ecological Swaraj: Alternatives to Sustainable Development and the Green Economy" Development 57(3-4), 362–375.

Morgera, Elisa, Elsa Tsioumani, and Matthias Buck (2014). *Unraveling the Nagoya Protocol: A Commentary on the Nagoya Protocol on Access and Benefit-Sharing to the Convention on Biological Diversity*. Martinus Nijhoff Publishers.

Soulé, Michael E (1985). "What is Conservation Biology? A New Synthetic Discipline Addresses the Dynamics and Problems of Perturbed Species, Communities and Ecosystems" Biosciences 35(11), 727–734.

7. Cities

Introduction

Cities are regarded as one of man's greatest inventions as they generate wealth, improve living standards and provide the density, inter-action and networks that promote economic and social growth. The focus on cities has gained momentum as the urban population of the world has grown from 2 percent to nearly 50 percent in the last two centuries. Megacities (that have in excess of 10 million people) illustrate how the world has become urbanized. Whilst in 1975 only four megacities existed, in 2000 there were 18 and by 2019 this number had grown to 33.

It is predicted that much of the future growth will not be in these huge agglomerations but will be in the small- to medium-sized cities around the world. By the year 2030, more than five billion people (six out of every ten human beings) are predicted to live in cities and urban centers. Although the world's cities occupy just 3 percent of the Earth's land, cities are the main source of global economic growth and produc-tivity. At the same time, cities account for most resource consumption and greenhouse gas emissions and cause unprecedented pressure on the environment.

Planning a city

The way in which cities are planned has changed from the first "garden cities" planned in 1898 by Sir Howard Ebenezer in the United Kingdom. They consisted of self-contained communities surrounded by greenbelts with proportionate areas of residences, industry, and agriculture. The primary benefits of a countryside environ-ment and a city environment were created with the vision of avoiding the disadvantages pre-sented by both. This style of building cities is still relevant from an environmental and town planning perspective today. Unfortunately, however, in many parts of the developed world, the legacy of the garden city has devolved into countless automobile-dependent, repetitive garden suburbs. The growth of these numer-ous suburbs is stretching the planet's natural resources to breaking point.

Avoiding the impact on the environment and avoiding sprawl and encroachment on sur-rounding agricultural and environmental areas has resulted in the newer trend of building cities upwards. The modern city of Singapore, with its constellation of high-density new towns all linked together by a circular metro system which surrounds the port city, though different, still bears a resemblance to Howard Ebenezer's polycentric city.

Challenges and problems faced by cities

While cities can be powerhouses of economic growth and development, without proper plan-ning and regulation, they could, among other things, suffer soaring levels of poverty, crime and pollution. Failure to adequately manage cities leads to declining levels of access to ser-vices, congestion of infrastructure networks, slum developments and growing bottlenecks to economic growth.

Challenges facing many cities throughout the world include rapid urbanization, conges-tion, lack of funds to provide basic services and infrastructure, a shortage of adequate housing and rising air pollution. Urban and rural sprawl is rampant in many parts of the world. Sprawl has been created mostly through the modes and character of transportation and has the most noticeable impact on the natural environment as it results in increased energy use and pollu-tion, which in turn impacts on public health, the environment and climate change. Although regarded as "hot spots" of production, con-sumption and waste generation, cities also pos-sess the potential to increase the efficiency and sustainability of society as a whole.

United Nations' Sustainable Development Goal 11 and the New Urban Agenda

The United Nations' 17 Sustainable Development Goals (SDGs) were born at the United Nations Conference on Sustainable Development in Rio de Janeiro in 2012 and were adopted in 2015 for achievement by 2030. The unprecedented urbanization in various parts of the world justified the adoption of Goal 11 of the SDGs. The objective of Goal 11 is to produce a set of universal goals (applicable to all cities irrespective of their size or loca-tion anywhere in the world) to meet the urgent environmental, political and economic chal-lenges facing the world. The creation of more sustainable human settlements with a reduced ecological footprint is of prime importance. This goal is directed at ensuring access to safe and affordable housing, upgrading slum settlements, investing in public transport, creating green public spaces and improving urban planning and management so that it is both participatory and inclusive in cities.

The SDGs are intended to be universal and although all the goals and targets apply to both developed and developing countries alike, when it comes to implementation, different countries focus on different priorities in the quest to balance social, economic and environmental interests and achieve sustainable development. The pursuit is for social and economic goals together with a move towards environmental sustainability with communities that are resilient.

At Habitat 3 the United Nations Conference on Housing and Sustainable Urban Development, held in Quito, Ecuador in 2016, the New Urban Agenda was adopted. This set global standards of achievement in sustainable urban development. The focus is on the way we build, manage, and live in cities and the absolute need for participation by committed partners, relevant stakeholders, urban actors at all levels of government as well as the civil society and the private sector.

The need to develop smart, sustainable and resilient cities

Cities are critical in achieving a sustainable future for the world and efficient urban planning and management laws and practices must of necessity be in place to deal with the challenges brought by urbanization. The ways in which cities develop, and how they cope with various issues, including rapid urbanization, are of great importance not only to the particular city itself but to the well-being of all the world's occupants. The struggle for global sustainability, according to the United Nations, will either be won or lost in cities. For this reason, the United Nations recommends that cities should be compact with a high-density mixed-use and an intensified urban form.

Further, cities and their managers may benefit from implementing the "smart city agenda", which entails improving the quality of life of citizens by strengthening and diversifying the economy while at the same time prioritizing environmental sustainability through the adoption of smart solutions. Technology, economics, culture and politics can help bring about the required change although human scale factors also play an important role in achieving a better quality of life.

The consideration of the effects of the local environment must now become a key component of town planning and environmental quality must become an assumed output of a well-governed modern city. The formidable task of managing growing cities in ways that support and drive economic growth while at the same time reducing pollution and safeguarding health is what matters. Resource efficient cities take up the challenge to achieve greater productivity and innovation with lower costs and reduced environmental impacts but with increased opportunities for consumer choices and sustainable lifestyles.

For cities to survive, non-renewable natural resources have to be limited whilst at the same time waste produced by cities and pollution has to be effectively absorbed by the natural environment. Building urban resilience and improving the sustainability of the urbanization processes so as to protect the environment and mitigate disaster risk and climate change is crucial.

Cities of the future need to do more with less and win support for change by delivering results swiftly. Some of the ways they can do this is by using green technology (such as autonomous buses), by securing the best growth opportunities (while simultaneously protecting the environment), by adding eco-friendly housing to combat shortages and by reducing sprawl areas by connecting them with public transport routes. The main aim for future cities should be to make people happier and healthier, as well as bring people together socially and economically in a way that all citizens may enjoy prosperity.

Criticism of SDGs

The picture projected by the SDGs is attractive but total success is unlikely for all cities. Critics believe that in practice, sustainability appears to be an unstable and often unreliable way of mitigating ecological collapse caused by cities. Some of the criticisms levelled against the SDGs are that they are challenging and difficult to achieve, that not all sub-goals may be attained simultaneously, that they are mere guidelines and are not clearly defined and compliance is not compulsory. While some critics state that the SDG 11 goals should be more integrated, there are others that believe that they are unattainable because they presume that economic growth, environmental protection and social justice can go hand-in-hand. Monitoring the progress towards attaining the SDGs is also regarded and there is a need for globally identified and comparable indicators that all cities may use. Many cities continue preferring the economic goals and ignoring the environmental goals. Blending economic objectives with sustainability considerations is necessary to ensure that sustainable growth is achieved in cities.

Singapore

Singapore, a tiny island city-State which boasts ultra-modern architecture and noticeable economic innovation, has in a short period emerged from being an underdeveloped and poor city-State to become one of the wealthiest in the world. At the same time, it has actually improved its urban environment and for this reason it continues to win favor with both urban planners and environmentalists. Apart from the Planning Act 3 of 1998, all the coordination and planning in Singapore is carefully laid out in two key planning documents. The Concept Plan (monitored by the Urban Redevelopment Authority) sets out the broad planning and introduced the concept of the Ring Plan and the vehicle-free central business district where mobility is achieved by mass transit and not by motor vehicles. In 1971 the first Concept Plan focused on social and economic policies, but by 1991 it took into account new priorities including demographic changes, economic restructuring and environmental considerations. As a result, Singapore is interspersed with high-density residential areas close to light industries and hard-core industrial development is located away from residential areas in a separate area, Jurong.

The success of the Master Plan lies in its transparent implementation and the fact that it sets out detailed development control guidelines that are clear. It regulates how land is developed and used. Singapore's commitment to achieving the aims of the SDG 11 resulted in the 2013 reviewed Master Plan. The focus was to bring jobs closer to home, to make Singapore a green and healthy city connected with strong community interaction and spirit. A National Cycling Plan was introduced as a healthier and greener option in keeping with a "car lite" alternative.

Singapore is seen as a model of what good land-use planning should look like in the twenty-first century as it commenced environmental management policies from its early years. It integrated environmental policies with its economic and social policies and although it pursued a policy of rapid industrialization, it also "cleaned up and greened" its environment. Like many other countries, it has a Land Use Plan 2030 in accordance with SDG 11. Singapore adopts a multi-pronged approach to manage its environmental issues. These are regulatory measures, planning controls, economic incentives and encouragement of public awareness and participation. The effective legal and administrative system deals with the implementation and enforcement of laws relating to land-use planning, pollution, public health and the environment, with planning and the environment being integrated through a dynamic system of urban governance.

Despite Singapore's success some environmental lawyers and planners have correctly lamented the lack of EIA (Environmental Impact Assessment) laws in Singapore whilst other critics complain about the autocratic implementation and governance of environmental controls.

Kigali

A city in a developing continent like Africa that is faced with growing populations that need housing and services is in stark contrast to a city like Singapore. Kigali in Rwanda, Africa, has an urban growth rate estimated to be one of the highest in Sub-Saharan Africa and as such is a city in a developing country, experiencing challenges of rapid urbanization and transformation. Successful and sustainable development of Kigali is being achieved through various initiatives, environmental policies and laws which make Kigali one of the continent's most ambitious and successful urban planning projects. The challenge of urban sprawl in Rwanda is acknowledged and there is a focus on achieving adequate density to optimize the use of urban land, reduce the cost of infrastructure and promote a compact city that is totally spotless and clean.

URMILA SONI (GOVINDJEE)

Conclusion

Universally, there is a school of thought that strongly believes that the future of the planet depends on what happens in and to cities. The slow destruction of the natural world is said to be caused by corporations that ignore the natural world, believe that the universe has boundless resources, and that humans have the freedom to exploit resources of the Earth for their exclusive benefit without regard to the ecological costs of doing so. More and more cities are accepting economic advancement over environmental protection. For this reason, there is a dire need for good urban governance globally and for wider ranging legal frameworks that fully protect nature. The ideal place to implement these will be in cities around the world.

URMILA SONI (GOVINDJEE)

References

Archer, Kevin and Kris Bezdecny (2016). *Handbook of Cities and the Environment*. Edward Elgar.

Aust, Helmut and Anel Du Plessis (2018). "Good Urban Governance as a Global Aspiration: on the Potential and Limits of SDG11" in Duncan French, and Louis Kotzé (eds), *Sustainable Development Goals – Law, Theory and Implementation*, Edward Elgar.

Batchelor, Peter (1969). "The Origin of the Garden City Concept of Urban Form", Journal of the Society of Architectural Historians 28(3), 186.

Howard, Ebenezer (1902). *Garden Cities of To-morrow*. Swan Sonnenschein & Co Ltd.

McKinsey Report (n.d.). How to Make Cities Great. Available at: https://www.mckinsey.com/featured-insights/urbanization/how-to-make-a-city-great accessed 10 September 2020.

Mega, Voula P. (2010). *Sustainable Cities for the Third Millennium: The Odyssey of Urban Excellence*. Springer.

Osborn, Derek, Amy Cutter, and Farooq Ullah (2015). Universal Sustainable Development Goals: Understanding the Transformational Challenge for Developed Countries. Report of a Study by Stakeholder Forum May 2015. Stakeholder Forum.

United Nations (2008). World Urbanization Prospects: The 2007 Revision, Executive Summary. Available at: https://www.electroluxgroup.com/en/wp-content/uploads/sites/2/2010/07/2007WUP_ExecSum_web.pdf.

United Nations (2015). Sustainable Development Goals. Available at: http://www.un.org/sustainabledevelopment/sustainable-development-goals/ accessed 10 September 2020.

United Nations (2017). New Urban Agenda – Habitat III. Available at : habitat3.org/wp-content/uploads/NUA-English.pdf.

United Nations Environmental Programme (2011). Summary Report "Rwanda – from Post-Conflict to Environmentally Sustainable Development" Islands of Wealth in a Sea of Slums. Available at: https://wedocs.unep.org/bitstream/handle/20.500.11822/17460/Rwanda_postconflict_sust_dev.pdf?sequence=1&amp%3BisAllowed= accessed 10 September 2020.

8. Civil Society

Introduction

Prominent among the early writings on civil society is the work of Alexis De Tocqueville who observed that "[w]herever at the head of some new undertaking you see the government in France ... in the United States you will be sure to find an association" (Alexis de Tocqueville (1835). "Democracy in America" in Brian O'Connell (ed.) (1983). *America's Voluntary Spirit: A Book of Readings*. The Foundation Centre, p. 54). Associational life constitutes the primary expression of civil society, which itself predates contemporary forms of Statehood. Civil society associations exist alongside the State, in a variety of forms and in varying relationships to the State, sometimes in confrontation and sometimes in constructive engagement. The non-profit, non-governmental voluntary character of associations of civil society provides the accessibility and flexibility that enable an association to act as a single group, in partnership with other groups and as a network with an even wider spread of organizations, with the freedom and capacity to reorganize when necessary (Harding, 1994). In academic study, the concept of civil society is found in the social science disciplines and is a broad construct for non-State public sphere activity which is inclusive of social movements. The terminology conundrum for this field of study has persisted, leading to the observation that "nobody can even agree on what they should be called . . . It is the unsatisfactory term 'non-governmental' that seems most intent on not going away" (Ian Smillie (1993). "Changing Partners: Northern NGOs, Northern Governments" in Ian Smillie and Henny Helmich (eds), *Non-Governmental Organisations and Governments: Stakeholders for Development*. OECD, pp. 13–43, at 14). This is also the term used in the Economic and Social Council (ECOSOC) resolution regulating consultative status for non-governmental organizations (NGOs) at the UN. In legal terms, however, the term "non-profit" organization is often used to capture the civil society construct in its structural form. Therefore, whether it is the Institute of Directors or some other professional association engaging with the State on a new law on corporations, or a human rights agency challenging a legal provision in court, or a community organization joining issues on State policy or a social movement protesting non-delivery of the social contract, all these organizations, in legal terms, find their home in the non-profit sector. The connectedness of the twin concepts of civil society and non-profit association makes it possible to examine more comprehensively the role of civil society in development. In other words, the understanding of the non-profit sector complements and completes the study of civil society. This commentary on civil society therefore begins with a description of the non-profit sector, followed by a discussion of civil society engagement with the State, capped off by a highlight of ways in which civil society activity has shaped the role of law in development.

The non-profit sector

Given its character as the component of the public sphere that hosts most citizen initiatives, the non-profit sector is at the heart of development activity and is key to generating local participation essential for legal interventions to succeed. The non-profit sector is itself norm-generating as its numerous associations possess codes which members voluntarily adhere to and which in many cases have more binding recognition than State law among the people to whom they apply (see, e.g., the CSO governance initiative *Accountable Now* available at https://accountablenow.org/ (accessed 10 September 2020) – much like the self-regulating trend among multinational companies). Himonga et al. describe how State laws operate as only one of many other sources of law in plural normative contexts (Himonga et al., 2014, pp. 46–47). Indeed, the prevalence of normative orders beyond the State readily confronts any scholar of governance processes in developing societies (Stephens, 2009, p. 134; De Sousa Santos and Carlet, 2010). This is particularly so because social ordering in traditional communities is intertwined with governance structures, property ownership and economic influence – the informal overlapping with the formal, the commercial intersecting with the non-profit.

Non-profit sector organizations are defined by certain characteristics, including the fact that they are constituted by private citizens, self-governing, non-profit-distributing, voluntary and directed at public benefit (Lester Salamon

(1999). *America's Nonprofit Sector: A Primer.* 2nd edition. Foundation Centre, pp. 10–11). Economic, political and sociological theories have put forward explanations for the existence of the non-profit sector. Political theory views the non-profit sector as the outcome of the exercise of the freedom of association which creates the space for people to set up organizations to serve public purposes – a key feature of democracies (Douglas, 1987). In economic theory, the limitations of government provision coupled with the disinclination of markets to cater to narrow population segments in a heterogenous society make it possible and necessary for non-State and non-profit agencies to provide public goods (James, 1990). A mix of economic and political theory asserts that non-profit initiatives foster quicker response to new issues which would otherwise receive delayed State reaction as a result of government bureaucratic requirements (Salamon, 1999, above). Sociological theory views the character of the non-profit sector as one that predisposes it to serve as a buffer zone between the State and its citizens, in one role, mitigating socio-political tension and in other roles, contributing to policy-making, providing services and serving as an inermediary between the government and the people (Seibel and Anheier, 1990).

In a mutually influencing relationship, the law shapes the operating environment for the non-profit sector, while non-profit sector organizations of civil society contribute to the development of the law. Key channels through which domestic law shapes the work of civil society include registration provisions, donor-deductible incentives and the overarching constitutional guarantee of freedom of association, described as "permissible purposes of association" (Salamon and Toepler, 2000, p. 2). Others include employment laws, access to information laws, administrative justice laws and broad tax provisions.

Civil society engagement with the State

Civil society is constituted by the associational life of citizens and residents who interact with the State in the public sphere in various ways that empower citizens and supplement the role of the State. In discharging their mandate to the constituencies they represent, civil society associations and organizations often serve as information channels and bridges for extending the reach of the State to target recipient communities in the delivery of development programmes. Complementary State-civil society cooperation such as this results in mutual capacity-building between the two entities. This constructive relationship is also a feature of Global North State-civil society relations and is, to varying degrees, found in North-South engagement. However, Government suspicion of foreign-funded civil society organizations in North-South relations often leads to the imposition of tighter legal requirements (see 16(2) (2014) International Journal of Not-for-Profit Law, themed issue on Civil Society in Africa). When necessary, the same civil society formation or a segment of it serves as a countervailing force to the formidable power of the State. As Paul and Dias observe of associations of civil society, "some are small and rooted in tradition; some simply provide organizational forms for mutual self-help, savings or construction of desired community facilities; some have evolved into vehicles of protest; some are in overt opposition to governments of the day" (James C.N. Paul and Clarence J. Dias (1992). "Alternative Development: A Legal Prospectus" in Anthony Carty (ed.), *Law and Development.* Dartmouth Publishing Company, pp. 303–331 at 304).

The diversity and complementarity of associations of civil society mean that a non-profit organization may be registered with the aim of engaging in civic-advocacy campaigns to press government for the provision of housing, education etc., while another mobilizes private citizens to raise funds to build low-cost housing, set up schools or other kinds of learning centres (Douglas, 1987, p. 51; De Feyter, 2001, pp. 223–224). This is illustrated in the activities of the Nigeria-based Social and Economic Rights Action Project (SERAP), which, at various times, took the Nigerian government to the Economic Community of West African States (ECOWAS) Court of Justice seeking an order compelling the government to deliver on its constitutional and international law obligations to provide accessible basic education for all citizens (see SERAP v. Nigeria ECW/CCJ/JUD/07/10; see also SERAP and Another v. Nigeria (Communication No. 155/96) (2001) ACHPR 34 in respect of human rights violations in Ogoniland). On the other hand, the organization LEAP Africa partners with public schools (as well as private schools) to provide training in leadership, life skills and innovation for senior high school students in Lagos. LEAP stands for leadership, effectiveness, accountability and professionalism.

As Paul and Dias maintain, collective action is essential for the creation of the leverage needed by people to engage the State and the further removed from the State people are, the more they need to be connected to support groups in order to claim basic resources from the State (Paul and Dias, 1992, above, pp. 318, 325). It is through group representation that critical issues are channelled into the deliberations of planning bodies and other government agencies for the development of long-term interventions for alternative development (Paul and Dias, 1992, above, p. 322). In this way, existing and emerging civil society formations, be they formal or informal, structured or ad hoc, constitute a system of institutions that feed into governance processes.

Often civil society groups that lack access to resources for engaging government strengthen their position by organizing en masse, taking on the character of social movements. For example, the 2019 student protests in Hong Kong against the Extradition bill gradually gained momentum, as its numbers expanded to include a broad range of citizens. Similar developments across Africa in the mid-late 2010s signalled the emergence of a stand-by social movement apparatus, aided by access to enhanced information technology and social media platforms. Zimbabwe's resilient civil society for instance, was galvanized into action in 2016 by an online video in which an activist clergyman lamented his difficulty in fending for his children, criticizing the Zimbabwean government for failure to deliver on the social contract. This led to a social media movement called "This Flag", which generated an unrest that ultimately resulted in the end of Robert Mugabe's almost four-decade rule in 2017. In Uganda, popular musician Bobi Wine, who defeated a candidate from the ruling party to win a seat in parliament in 2017, suffered State persecution as a result, including unlawful arrest and detention. The massive show of solidarity via social media by youths in Uganda and Kenya contributed to his release. In Nigeria, Jones Abiri, a journalist who was unlawfully detained in 2016 for two years on charges of treasonable felony, was freed only when activists shifted their campaign for his release from official petitions to social media, amassing a huge following. In South Africa, the 2015 to 2017 student protests against the high cost of access to tertiary education and the crippling financial burden on young graduates secured the government's attention, resulting in the reallocation of more funds to student financial aid. The campaigns #ThisFlag, #FreeBobiWine, #FreeJonesAbiri, #FeesMustFall and #EndSARS have become iconic of the changing character and demographic of social movements in Africa, featuring a younger, technologically connected population, who are poised to flag issues of civil liberties and social justice at the swipe of a screen.

Civil society, law and development

Not only do associations of civil society use legal provisions in their work, they also contribute to law and policy reform. The South African example shows how an assortment of community-based organizations drove the 2004 financial sector campaign to open up financial services to the unbanked; how the Women on Farms Project organization succeeded in securing an extensive audit of working conditions on farms in the mid-to-late 2000s; how StreetNet contributed informal economy representations to the International Labour Organization (ILO) fora on decent work and migrant work in the 2000s (Ordor, 2014).

Civil society vibrancy in a geopolitical territory at any given point in time ensures that law and policy provisions receive careful scrutiny and that issues that affect fundamental rights are brought to the centre stage of governance processes. The case of the landless rural workers movement in Brazil presents a useful example of how civil society engagement with the State can contribute to the development of the law. The landless rural workers movement in Brazil (Movimento dos Sem Terra – MST) employed a variety of political, legal and judicial strategies in their extended campaign for socio-economic rights. Political strategies employed by MST include collective occupation of rural spaces, marches, hunger strikes, vigils and public demonstration in large cities (De Sousa Santos and Carlet, 2010, pp. 67–68). The MST faced the formidable opposition of property owners and government agencies who were more intent on criminalizing their activities than on engaging the people. However, their lawyers innovatively constructed arguments which sought to invoke Brazil's constitutional and statutory principles to consider the social purposes of law, the fundamental human rights of families involved in land occupation in relation to pure property rights, and the connection between private property rights, social solidarity and responsibility for a dignified existence. That being so, land occupation by rural workers who find themselves homeless is primarily an expression of need rather than an exercise in trespass, and mobilizing a grassroots movement to seek land ownership reform should not be interpreted as a crime against property owners, but as the expression of a collective right of citizenship (De Sousa Santos and Carlet, 2010, pp. 77–78).

Thus, from this example, the organization of vulnerable groups into social movements, employing political strategies triggered off judicial responses by way of lawsuits brought against MST leadership. This in turn called into play legal arguments urging alternative interpretations of the law such as the promotion of human rights over property rights. Of particular relevance was the social function provision of Article 5 of the Brazilian Constitution which predicated constitutional protection of land ownership on its productive use and the fulfilment of its social function, and which simultaneously serves as a means of proving possessory occupation (De Sousa Santos and Carlet, 2010, pp. 68–69).

As Santos and Carlet observe, the MST's sustained engagement with the justice system tempered the landless peoples' distrust of the law and its hegemonic institutions and to a large extent "led the judiciary to abandon its individualistic and privatistic conceptions of law and property and to open itself up to a broader conception of the rule of law, according to which social and collective rights may be effectively realized" (De Sousa Santos and Carlet, 2010, p. 76).

Conclusion

Civil society, by its very nature, performs an undergirding role in the governance and development of any society. Given their character as citizen-led, representative of diversity, associational rather than institutional, civil society formations present flexible, dynamic, tailored responses and interventions which contribute both to the implementation and the development of the law. Civil society partnership and collaboration with other sectors hold great value for advancing progress in all fields of human engagement, including decent work, corporate responsibility, community development and human rights generally. Ultimately,

the intersectionality of civil society with all aspects of human endeavour uncovers or creates complementary, supplemental and alternative development pathways which are most likely to be compatible with Sustainable Development Goals.

ADA ORDOR

References

De Feyter, Koen (2001). *World Development Law: Sharing Responsibility for Development.* Intersentia.

De Sousa Santos, Boaventura and Flavia Carlet (2010). "The Movement of Landless Rural Workers in Brazil and Their Struggles for Access to Law and Justice" in Yash Ghai and Jill Cottrell (eds), *Marginalized Communities and Access to Justice.* Routledge.

Douglas, James (1987). "Political Theories of Nonprofit Organisations" in Walter Powell (ed.), *The Nonprofit Sector: A Research Handbook.* Yale University Press.

Harding, David (1994). *From Global to Local: Issues and Challenges Facing NGOs.* Avocado Series 94. Olive.

Himonga, Chuma, Thandabantu Nhlapo, IP Maithufi, Sindiso Mnisi-Weeks, Lesala Mofokeng, and Dial Ndima (2014). *African Customary Law in South Africa: Post-Apartheid and Living Law Perspectives.* Oxford University Press.

James, Estelle (1990). "Economic Theories of the Nonprofit Sector: A Comparative Perspective" in Helmut K. Anheier and Wolfgang Seibel (eds), *The Third Sector: Comparative Studies of Nonprofit Organisations.* De Gruyter.

Ordor, Ada (2014). "Exploring Civil Society Partnerships in Enforcing Decent Work in South Africa" in Deirdre McCann, Sangheon Lee, Patrick Belser, Colin Fenwick, John Howe, and Malte Luebker (eds), *Creative Labour Regulation: Indeterminacy and Protection in an Uncertain World.* Palgrave Macmillan/ILO.

Salamon, Lester and Stephan Toepler (2000). The Influence of the Legal Environment on the Development of the Nonprofit Sector. Johns Hopkins University Institute for Policy Studies, Centre for Civil Society Studies Working Paper Series No 17.

Seibel, Wolfgang and Helmut K. Anheier (1990). "Sociological and Political Science Approaches to the Third Sector" in Helmut K. Anheier and Wolfgang Seibel (eds), *The Third Sector: Comparative Studies of Nonprofit Organisations.* De Gruyter.

Stephens, Matthew (2009). "The Commission on Legal Empowerment of the Poor: An Opportunity Missed", Hague Journal on the Rule of Law 1(1), 132–155.

Yakubu, Nagu and Chikaonda, Gloria, social media consultants.

9. Climate

Climate and the law

There is huge amount of scientific evidence to explain climate change, and that its scale is global (Synthesis Report (SYR) of the IPCC Fifth Assessment Report (AR5), 2014). Greenhouse gas emissions affect the atmosphere at large, without boundaries, rendering the issue global in nature. In that context, climate change has been labelled as a 'super wicked problem': it is a social and cultural problem difficult to solve as opinions on how to find solutions diverge and contradict each other, the economic burden is large, and there are complex interdependencies, some of which will be analysed later (Lazarus, 2009). In regulatory terms, it means that a multi-level governance approach has been advanced to tackle the climate crisis (Jänicke, 2017). Globally, neither a top-down nor a bottom-up approach has been preferred to climate regulation. Interactions between actors at all levels happen in the shaping of climate regulation, representing different interests and coming with different powers. This includes international organizations, States, sub-State entities, transnational companies, non-governmental organizations and civil societies.

At the international level, the climate change regime is led by the United Nations Climate Regime, now with the Paris Agreement at its core. This Agreement contains a series of obligations and creates a structure within which States must act. It includes the 'intended nationally determined contributions' (INDCs), where States declare their targets towards climate mitigation and adaptation. It is therefore up to each individual country to decide how much they are willing to commit to (Bodansky et al., 2017).

Moreover, the impacts of climate change are so far-reaching that other legal regimes are affected and must adapt and respond to climate change. This is well reflected in the development of climate litigation, where a variety of laws – from domestic private law, constitutional law, public international law – are invoked to condemn private and public actions for not respecting climate change policies.

This contribution will look into various aspects of the climate problem, unpacking some interdependencies between climate change and economic issues, climate change and justice, climate change in particularly affected territories, and how climate change is financed.

Climate and the economy

First, no climate change action will be effective if it ignores the intricacies between climate change and the economy. Indeed, the development of a carbon-based economy since the nineteenth century is now deeply entrenched, making climate mitigation and adaptation harder. Malm explains how intricate the relationships between the current economic model and carbon emissions are, climate change being the 'unintended by-product' of the 'fossil economy' (Malm, 2013).

Moreover, depending on when countries have industrialized and how, their economies have had different impacts on the climate. Older economies based on fossil fuels such as the UK have contributed to greenhouse gas emissions far longer than newer economies. To reflect this, and the fact that countries do not have the same levels of economic development, the creation of obligations on a basis of 'common but differentiated responsibilities' arose to tackle that issue under the United Nations Climate Regime. Differentiation was necessary to reach global consensus.

Globalization has also had impacts on global climate regulation, as trade and global competition in goods has increased greenhouse gas emissions, as exemplified with the commerce through air transport. Trade and investment regimes clash with climate change regulation, as the former can – if interpreted in certain ways – justify to constrain or limit the latter (Gehring et al., 2012). This is especially relevant since climate regulation entails multiple market-based approaches. Within the climate change regime, carbon trading schemes have been created, using the 'cap and trade' principle, whereby companies can sell and buy emission allowances to others to stay within the cap set in law.

The existence itself of market mechanisms for climate change – such as emissions trading schemes – can be questioned, as Sandel did in his book, *What Money Can't Buy* (2013). The creation of a monetary value of our planet's resources should be assessed on moral and ethical grounds, and not only on economic grounds: should everything – including the climate – be monetarized?

Climate and justice

Concepts of fairness and equity exist within the current United Nations Climate Regime. Present and future generations are mentioned, creating an intra- and intergenerational need for further protection. However, these mentions in the legal framework may not be enough to reach climate justice. The climate justice movement emphasizes the need to understand climate change policies in an integrated manner. Indeed, it is pushing towards better recognition of the potential negative impacts of climate change on existing human rights, and it also wants to further tackle the fight against climate change together with broader inequalities. Climate change and poverty should be tackled together, linking human rights and development in the climate context. Climate change has not only a poverty perspective, but also a gender perspective, and a minorities perspective. Tackling inequalities is part and parcel of the climate justice movement. However, legal protection for climate harms is not always compatible with legal protection of human rights. In this context, some linkages between the climate change and the human rights frameworks must be found at the substantive level (Humphreys, 2010).

Moreover, moral thresholds must be discussed in the context of climate justice. The creation of inequities in how global actors act towards climate change are manifold. The way climate justice is conceived has impacts on the interpretation of human rights and moral thresholds in the context of climate change. It has been said that, at the very least, the obligation not to violate basic human rights should mean that governments – especially the most economically developed – should create regimes for mitigating climate change (Humphreys, 2010).

The case of the protection of indigenous peoples through climate justice shows the inadequacies that can exist in climate policies. Indeed, indigenous peoples are at the centre of the fight against climate change, and if not taken into consideration, climate laws and policies can have negative impacts on indigenous peoples. Often the territories where climate change actions must be taken include

indigenous lands (Tsosie, 2007). Failing to take that into account can have devastating impacts for those communities, hence the need to understand climate change and human rights together. The REDD+ framework is trying to achieve this (Tehan et al., 2017).

It is important to note that not everyone is of the opinion that the most effective way to tackle the climate crisis is by contextualizing it and using a rights-based approach to climate change. Famously, Posner and Weisbach (*Climate Change Justice*, Princeton University Press, 2010) have argued for a clear separation between climate law and justice, suggesting that principles of justice should be left out of climate action, and rather focusing on a narrow understanding of climate action. However, such views arguably misunderstand the integrated nature of the climate crisis. For many scholars and activists alike, climate action cannot be separated from its social context, and therefore climate law is bound to interact with other areas of law, and in particular human rights law.

Climate and territories

Specific territories pose a series of interesting questions about the shape and form of climate regulation and action. Forests and small islands in particular will be discussed.

Forests

Forests are carbon sinks and in grave danger of deforestation. Moreover, forests often host local communities and indigenous peoples. In order to protect them, traditional mechanisms may fall short, as they are under the national control of specific States. Indeed, they embody the tensions between the concept of sovereignty and global concern. On the one hand, States have permanent sovereignty over their natural resources, and on the other hand, they need to respect broader frameworks of international environmental and climate change law.

Forests had been left out of the global framework until both the United Nations and the European Union started to develop the REDD+ programme and the FLEGT Action Plan. They are trying in various ways to combat deforestation and illegal logging, without infringing on State sovereignty. They are part of broader development policies and experiment with transnational interactions linking different actors at different stages in the process of policy-making. Concepts such as 'free, prior and informed consent', indigenous property claims and 'benefit-sharing' are part and parcel of those frameworks, linking democratic empowerment and economic development with climate awareness and protection of local communities and indigenous peoples (Tehan et al., 2017). The question whether this is successful is still unresolved.

Small island States

Small island States also have a set of specific issues, among others rising sea levels due to global warming, and undue natural catastrophes such as hurricanes. This particular context creates problems in agriculture, when saltwater invades crops, reef erosion and changes in sources of fish, but also people who cannot stay in their homes become climate migrants. The United Nations Climate Regime contains certain mechanisms to address some of these concerns, such as loss and damages, liability concerns and compensation mechanisms (Maxine Burkett, 'Rehabilitation: A Proposal for a Climate Compensation Mechanism for Small Island States', Santa Clara Journal of International Law 13(1) (2015)). However, the United Nations Climate Regime is not enough, especially for climate migrants. They fall outside the technical definition of the UN Refugee Convention, yet are in dire need of protection. Numbers as high as 200 million climate migrants by 2050 are expected, according to the International Organization for Migration. One of the ways to mitigate forced migration due to climate change is by creating adequate adaptation strategies in each country affected, but that cannot necessarily be achieved depending on the economic strength of each country. An expansion of the definition of a refugee to include climate migrants, as well as specific immigration policies for climate migrants in countries less affected, have been proposed.

Climate finance

Climate finance plays a central role in climate mitigation and adaptation. Various institutions and mechanisms have been developed within the climate framework to push States towards implementing measures mitigating and adapting to climate change. They take different forms, but overall always promote some form of transfer of resources from developed to developing economies (Thompson, 2016). For that, the Global Environment Facility exists, alongside different multilateral development banks, the World Bank, specific treaty mechanisms within REDD and the Clean Development Mechanism, as well as the Green Climate Fund. This means the picture is quite complex and navigating the world of climate finance is quite opaque. Coordination between those financial institutions and within them is hard, and often actions do not have the intended effects. The governance of climate finance is therefore a sticky point in the climate regime, and many disagreements in the design of climate finance exist, especially between donor countries and developing countries. Moreover, there is a mix between public and private financing, with different expectations and behaviours towards regulation. Each body that awards money in some form (aid, investment, loan, etc.) puts a set of conditions that can vary and thus one country receiving funds for climate change mitigation or adaptation can end up with having to comply with contradictory regulations. As Thompson said, 'political and legal progress on North-South finance is key to forging an effective regime for climate change' (Thompson, 2016, p. 160).

JUSTINE BENDEL

References

Bodansky, Daniel, Jutta Brunnée, and Lavanya Rajamani (2017). *International Climate Change Law*. Oxford University Press.

Edenhofer, Ottmar, Johannes Wallacher, Hermann Lotze-Campen, Michael Reder, Brigitte Knopf, and Johannes Müller (eds) (2012). *Climate Change, Justice and Sustainability: Linking Climate and Development Policy*. Springer.

Gehring, Markus W., Marie-Claire Cordonier Segger, and Jarrod Hepburn (2012). 'Climate Change and International Trade and Investment Law' in Rosemary Rayfuse and Shirley V. Scott (eds), *International Law in the Era of Climate Change*, Edward Elgar.

Humphreys, Stephen (ed.) (2010). *Human Rights and Climate Change*. Cambridge University Press.

Jänicke, Martin (2017). 'The Multi-level System of Global Climate Governance – The Model and Its Current State', Environmental Policy and Governance 27, 108–121.

Lazarus, Richard (2009). 'Super Wicked Problems and Climate Change: Restraining the Present to Liberate the Future', Cornell Law Review 94, 1153–1234.

Malm, Andreas (2013). 'The Origins of Fossil

Capital: From Water to Steam in the British Cotton Industry', Historical Materialism 21(1), 15–68.

Tehan, Maureen F., Lee C. Godden, Margaret A. Young, and Kirsty A. Gover (eds) (2017). *The Impact of Climate Change Mitigation on Indigenous and Forest Communities. International, National and Local Law Perspectives on REDD+*. Cambridge University Press.

Thompson, Alexander (2016). 'The Global Regime for Climate Finance: Political and Legal Challenges' in Kevin R. Gray, Richard Tarasofsky, and Cinnamon Carlarne (eds), *The Oxford Handbook of International Climate Change Law*, Oxford University Press.

Tsosie, Rebecca (2007). 'Indigenous People and Environmental Justice: The Impact of Climate Change', University of Colorado Law Review 78, 1625.

JUSTINE BENDEL

10. Common but Differentiated Responsibility

The expression 'common but differentiated responsibility' (hereinafter referred to as CBDR) connotes that in common concerns pertaining to the entire human kind, the obligations and treatment of States should be guided by recognition of their differential circumstances. CBDR has been expressed in the form of an equation (Rajamani, 2006) as follows:

CBDR = Capacity + Contribution
(Historical + current + future) =
Differential Treatment in favour of
Developing Countries + Leadership of
Industrial Countries

Based on first explicit enunciation of the concept of CBDR (Rio Declaration on Environment and Development, 1992, Principle 7), the equation broadly captures the constitutive elements of CBDR as well as offers an insight into the rationale behind the same. It is nevertheless essential to add many qualifications and nuances to this broad and useful insight, keeping in mind the rationale behind the concept, its implications and its gradual evolution.

Differentiation in responsibilities is not something new in multilateral agreements (Stone, 2004). The nature, form, extent, strength and centrality of differentiation normatively incorporated in international environmental law, however, is what makes the concept an integral part of the same. Despite being normatively embedded in international environmental law, the emergence and further metamorphosis of the concept of CBDR has been strongly influenced by the international development discourse. International development discourse is in turn influenced by historical developments and international political and economic relations. The persistent interface of environmental and development discourses, especially the way the broader notion of sustainable development, which takes within its fold economic, social and environmental aspect, has ensured that CBDR persists as a dynamic rather than a static concept. Numerous techniques of differentiation and debates around the same also resulted in

the concept assuming dynamic connotation. Initially developing through three distinct phases ranging from 1972–1992, 1992–2002, 2002–2012 (Rajamani, 2012) the current form that CBDR assumes is different from what had gradually emerged through the process of historical development of the notion through the three phases.

CBDR originated as an effort to infuse the notion of substantive equality into the basic tenet of international law, i.e. sovereign equality of all States. The discourse on the New International Economic Order (NIEO) offered the context for initial conceptualization of CBDR, which found its first expression in the Stockholm Conference convened by the United Nations (UN) in 1972. The Declaration of the UN Conference on the Human Environment, 1972 identified underdevelopment as a cause of environmental problems in developing countries and industrialization as the cause in developed countries (Preamble, paragraph 4). It also recognized that the "standards" which may be "valid" for "most advanced countries" may be "inappropriate or impose unwarranted cost" on "developing countries" (Principle 23). Recognizing the limited capacity of developing countries to address the same, it recognized the need for cooperation to raise resources for developing countries (Preamble paragraph 7). These considerations witnessed fruition in a legally binding instrument, the Montreal Protocol on Substances that Deplete the Ozone Layer in 1987. Unlike the UN Declaration of 1972, the Montreal Protocol differentiated on twin accounts, i.e. level of development as well as level of consumption of controlled substances, whereby it brought together developmental and environmental considerations. In terms of obligations, differences pertained with respect to countries identified in terms of delayed compliance in order to enable them to meet their domestic needs (Article 5(1)), selection of different base years (Article 5(1) as amended) and obligations imposed on developed country parties to "facilitate access to technology" (Article 5(2)), as well as to facilitate the provision for financial assistance to developing countries (Article 5(3)). The first phase of development of the concept culminated in explicit incorporation of the expression CBDR in the Rio Declaration on Environment and Development, 1992 (Principle 7), which was in tune with the development discourse at the time. The concept also formally reinforced the inter-linkage between environment and sustainable development.

This approach towards CBDR structured along the developing/developed country axis further strengthened between 1992–2002, primarily due to the explicit recognition of developed countries' contributions to global environmental degradation and their enhanced capacities to address the issue. This phase was also marked by a move towards greater recognition of territorial differentiation through the recognition of more specific situations of countries apart from just the two categories of developed and developing countries. Other differentially placed territories that found recognition in the UN Framework Convention on Climate Change 1992 (UNFCCC) were small island countries, countries with low-lying coastal areas, countries with arid and semi-arid areas, forested areas and areas liable to forest, decay, countries with areas prone to natural disasters, countries with areas liable to drought and desertification, countries with areas of high urban atmospheric pollution, countries with areas with fragile ecosystems, including mountainous ecosystems, countries whose economies are highly dependent on income generated from the production, processing and export, and/or on consumption of fossil fuels, landlocked and transit countries and least developed countries (Articles 4(8), 4(9), 5). Differentiation in this phase not only pertained to taking cognisance of territorial features but it also moved beyond differentiation in implementation apparent in the first phase, to differentiation in core obligations under the law. The Kyoto Protocol to the UNFCCC (1998) imposes obligations to limit greenhouse gas emissions only on countries included in Annex 1 to the protocol, which consists of developed countries. UNFCCC enhances the strength of positive commitment of developed States towards the developing ones. It mandates developed countries to "take all practicable steps to promote, facilitate and finance, as appropriate, the transfer of, or access to, environmentally sound technologies and know-how to other Parties" (Article 4(5)). Technology transfer related to climate change has remained an area of concern given the norms pertaining to Trade-Related Aspects of Intellectual Property Rights (TRIPS) (Cullet, 2016). Moreover, the legitimacy of differentiation is reinforced by making the implementation of commitments by developing countries linked to the effective implementation of commitments by developed countries (UNFCCC, Article 4(7); Convention on Biological Diversity (1992), Article 20(4); Stockholm Convention (2001), Article 13(4); Montreal Convention (1987), Article 5(5)). All this together constituted a high watermark of differentiation, which subsequently emerged as a bone of contention. The turn of the Millennium did not witness any concrete change in this conceptualization of CBDR since even the Millennium Development Goals could not strike a distinct chord given that the obligations under the Kyoto Protocol extended until 2012 (Kyoto Protocol, Article 3).

Not only the absence of obligations on developing countries with respect to emissions came to be challenged, but also the treatment of developing countries as a homogenous category. Differences among developing countries, some of them being fast growing economies, came to be highlighted as problematic with respect to the protection of the environment. Normatively, the challenge in turn came to be directed at the principle of CBDR. The decisions taken by the Conference of Parties (UNFCCC, Article 7) especially at the end of the first decade of the new millennium and the beginning of the second one reiterate the principle of CBDR, but with qualifications (Copenhagen Accord (2009); Cancun Agreement (2011)). In fact, the Cancun Agreement expresses the principle in conjunction with respective capabilities making it common but differentiated responsibilities and respective capabilities (CBDRRC). Qualifications to CBDR under these agreements are recognized by requiring the obligations of transfer of technology to be guided by a "country-driven approach and be based on national circumstances and priorities" (Copenhagen Accord) and by generally providing the long-term cooperation be carried out taking into "consideration different circumstances of parties" (Cancun Agreement). The latest global effort at taking the next step in addressing the climate change issue now presents a compromise between the developed and developing countries whereby the principle stands incorporated in the Paris Agreement (December 2015) but only to the extent that provides the Agreement to be implemented "to reflect equity and the principle of common but differentiated responsibilities and respective capabilities, in the light of different national circumstances" (Article 2(2)). The Paris Agreement reflected the general trend that had already been formally established under the Sustainable Development Goals (SDGs) adopted in September 2015, which envisage commitments pertaining to the environment to be undertaken by all the States (targets and indicators under SDG 13) rather than focusing only on certain countries as it existed in the Kyoto Protocol. Apart from general differentiation in terms of different national circumstances, the Paris Agreement does recognize differentials between developed and developing countries in general and identifies distinct situation of least developed countries, small island nation States and economies most affected by the impact of response measures (Articles 4(6), 4(15)). Though the differentiation largely remains along the developed and developing countries axis, it is mediated through "different circumstances of parties" therein. Moreover, unlike the Kyoto Protocol, the Paris Agreement does not limit the commitment of reduction in greenhouse gases only to developed countries, but imposes a general obligation on "each party" to pursue mitigation measures (Article 4(2)). These mitigation measures are to be based on self-determination (Article 4(2)) but at the same time require parties to make ambitious and progressive commitments beyond the current nationally determined contributions (Article 4(3)). Developed countries are expected to continue to take the lead in mitigation efforts, while developing countries are expected to enhance their efforts over time (Article 4(4)). Self-differentiation in the Paris Agreement represents a pragmatic choice securing flexibility, broader participation and privileging sovereign autonomy rather than determining commitments on the basis of "responsibilities for environmental harm" (Rajamani, 2016).

Differentiation within the Paris Agreement spans not only mitigation efforts but also provisions pertaining to transparency, finance and adaptations. Differentiation developed in the UNFCCC regarding the obligations of the developed country parties to provide financial resources to developing country parties is sustained in the Paris Agreement (Article 9). Developed countries are also required to take the lead in mobilizing climate finance and enhance the same progressively (Article 9). Further binding obligations are imposed on developed country parties to provide information on financial, technology transfer and capacity-building support provided to developing country parties (Articles 9, 10, 11). Developing countries are also offered flexibility with regard to implementation of the transparency provisions under the agreement to be operationalized through the transparency framework (Article 13). Provisions pertaining to adaptation take a further step in differentiation by not only recognizing the peculiar position of developing countries with respect to adaptation efforts but also framing the need for adaptation efforts to be particularly sensitive to the needs of vulnerable groups within developing countries (Article 7).

Considered applicable in the world order, which is otherwise largely guided by the notion of formal equality, the principle of CBDR as developed under the Kyoto Protocol has been criticized as privileging fast growing economies despite the transboundary harm that they may cause and thus compromising on the primary concern of international environmental law, i.e. climate change (Weisslitz, 2002). On account of absence of reciprocity, it is argued that differential treatment offers weak norms (Boyle, 1995) which in turn adversely affect the goal of sustainable development. The narrative of CBDR has witnessed many shifts and its current stage merely represents the victory of pragmatism over addressing historical and current wrongs in a way that is to a large extent oblivious of structural inequalities and environmental degradation that prevails in the world. Stone argues that it is not wise to use goals like environmental goal to accomplish global wealth redistribution (Stone, 2004), howsoever just the latter may be. It is also suggested that greater distinction in terms of developed, rapidly developing, developing and least developed may be useful in order to operationalize CBDR (Boyte, 2010). Rajamani opines that the Paris Agreement with "rigorous goals, extensive obligations and rigorous oversight", containing "nuanced differentiation" demonstrates "remarkable political will" and believes that the latter (if not the regime created by the Paris Agreement) has the potential to overcome climate challenge (Rajamani, 2016). On the other hand, Philippe Cullet attacks the differentiation embodied in the Paris Agreement as "differentiation based on individual preferences and the self-interest of countries" rather than individual differentiation based on "internationally agreed framework" and suggests that "in the future, differential treatment should be based on a social and environmental assessment"

(Cullet, 2016) especially in a world marred by deep structural inequalities.

AMITA PUNJ

References

Boyle, A. (1995). "Comments on the Paper by Diana Ponce-Nava" in Lang, Winfried (ed.), *Sustainable Development and International Law*, Graham and Trotman, pp. 137–140.

Boyle, Rachael (2010). "Common but Differentiated Responsibilities: Adjusting the 'Developing'/'Developed' Dichotomy in International Environmental Law", New Zealand Journal of Environmental Law 14, 63–101.

Cullet, Philippe (2016). "Differential Treatment in Environmental Law: Addressing Critiques and Conceptualising the Next Steps", Transnational Environmental Law 5(2), 305–328.

Honkonen, Tuula (2009). *The Common but Differentiated Responsibility Principle in Multilateral Environmental Agreements: Regulatory and Policy Aspects.* Wolters Kluwer.

Rajamani, Lavanya (2006). *Differential Treatment in International Environmental Law*. Oxford University Press.

Rajamani, Lavanya (2012). "The Changing Fortunes of Differential Treatment in the Evolution of International Environmental Law", International Affairs 88(3), 605–623.

Rajamani, Lavanya (2016). "Ambition and Differentiation in the 2015 Paris Agreement: Interpretative Possibilities and Underlying Politics", International and Comparative Law Quarterly 65, 493–514.

Stone, Christopher D. (2004). "Common but Differentiated Responsibilities in International Law", American Journal of International Law 98(2), 276–301.

Voigt, Christina and Felipe Ferreira (2016). "Dynamic Differentiation: The Principles of CBDR-RC, Progression and Highest Possible Ambition in the Paris Agreement", Transnational Environmental Law 5(2), 285–303.

Weisslitz, Michael (2002). "Rethinking the Equitable Principle of Common but Differentiated Responsibility: Differential Versus Absolute Norms of Compliance and Contribution in the Global Climate Change Context", Colorado Journal of International Environmental Law and Policy 13(2), 473–509.

11. Common Heritage of Mankind

General characteristics

The common heritage of mankind (or CHM) establishes that some spaces – such as the seabed lying beyond national jurisdiction and outer space – belong to all humanity and that their resources must be available for everyone's use and benefit, taking into account future generations and the needs of developing countries (Taylor, 2011). The innovation of the CHM concept is to presuppose a third kind of regime different from both of the traditional concepts of sovereignty and freedom (Scovazzi, 2010). Arvid Pardo, the Maltese representative to the UN, is widely credited with introducing this principle in the international scene as a way to prevent mineral resources of the deep seabed being monopolized by industrialized States with a consequent "tragedy of the commons". Subsequently, the G-77 States championed this idea as a manner to change the international economic order in their favor (Charter of Economic Rights and Duties of States, 1974, Article 29). The CHM principle is unambiguously affirmed by the UN Convention on the Law of the Sea while its presence in space law is more ambiguous. Article 11(5) of the Moon Treaty refers to it explicitly, but that agreement has attracted only five ratifications.

Broadly speaking, the CHM principle has five normative elements:

1. **Non-appropriation.** States and persons cannot unilaterally appropriate a zone or a resource designated as CHM. Mankind is indicated as the owner of these resources: this notion of mankind spans further than the current international community and embraces future generations (Wolfrum, 1983, p. 318). This does not mean that States play no role in the exploration and exploitation of those resources. However, whatever role States may play they do so as the representative agents of all mankind (Joyner, 1986, p. 191).

2. **A regime of common management of the resources at issue.** The principle demands that the economic exploitation of common resources be administered by an international institution granting exploration and exploitation rights (Feichtner, 2019, p. 607). In the Law of the Sea, this role is played by the International Seabed Authority set up by Article 137 of United Nations Convention on the Law of the Sea (UNCLOS). Under UNCLOS, for States parties and for their nationals, exploration and exploitation of the Area are possible only through a contract concluded with the Authority (UNCLOS, Article 153).

3. **The sharing of benefits.** This aspect of CHM is rooted in the New International Economic Order (NIEO) movement and reflects the "uncontroversial idea of the need to promote the development of developing countries" (Tladi, 2015, p. 126). Article 150(d) UNCLOS and Article 13 of its third Annex set the obligation by contractors to carry out payments to the Authority in respect of exploration and exploitation. No such obligation is in place for activities in outer space.

4. **Peaceful purposes.** Any area governed by the CHM principle can be used only for peaceful purposes (UNCLOS, Article 141). This notion is not defined by UNCLOS, however further guidance may be derived from analogous provisions of the Antarctic Treaty and of the Moon Treaty that provide some illustrations of what is not considered to be a peaceful purpose (Guntrip, 2003).

5. **The need to manage natural resources in a sustainable way so that they can be transmitted to future generations** (Kiss, 1985, p. 424). CHM includes elements of intergenerational equity (Tanaka, 2008, p. 131), implying the obligation to explore and exploit resources in a sustainable manner. Article 145 UNCLOS obliges the International Seabed Authority to ensure effective protection for the marine environment from harmful effects resulting from activities in the Area. The Regulations of the Authority incorporate important standards of environmental law such as the precautionary approach and the obligation to conduct environmental impact assessments.

CHM in the Law of the Sea

The Area, which is "the seabed and ocean floor and subsoil thereof beyond national jurisdiction", is governed by a complex legal regime based on UNCLOS, the 1994 Agreement Relating to the Implementation of Part XI of UNCLOS, and the rules approved by the International Seabed Authority. This regime recognizes the Area and its resources as the "common heritage of mankind" (UNCLOS, Article 136). Whereas the Area as a whole is defined as CHM, the disciplines of Part XI UNCLOS concern the exploration and exploitation of "all solid, liquid or gaseous mineral resources in situ in the Area at or beneath the seabed, including polymetallic nodules" (UNCLOS, Article 133).

Extractive activities in the Area are allowed, but "for the benefit of mankind as a whole" (UNCLOS, Article 140) and taking particular account of the interests and needs of developing States. In addition, they must be "carried out with reasonable regard for other activities and the marine environment" (UNCLOS, Article 147). For these purposes, the International Seabed Authority is given prescriptive and executive competences to regulate deep sea mining activities. A contract with the Authority is necessary for any extractive activity in the Area and incorporates the rules adopted by that international organization (Standard Clauses for Exploration Contract, section 13). Other UNCLOS provisions provide important guarantees of stability for contractors. Article 153(6) states that contracts shall provide for "security of tenure" and Article 19(2) of Annex III stipulates that such contracts may be revised only with the parties' consent. The only explicit exception is in Article 18 of Annex III, whereby the Authority can suspend or terminate the rights of a contractor where there are "serious, persistent and wilful violations of the fundamentals terms of the contract". The same article enables the Authority to impose monetary penalties proportionate to the seriousness of violations.

Mining activities may be carried out by States parties themselves as well as by public or private enterprises sponsored by their State of nationality or of control. Thus, the existing legal framework foresees a triangular relationship involving: (1) the contractor which prospects, explores, and exploits minerals located in the Area, (2) the State sponsoring it, and (3) the Authority. Sponsoring States have a responsibility to ensure the contractor's compliance with UNCLOS and the instruments based thereupon (see UNCLOS, Annex III, Article 4(4)). Governing this activity through contractual arrangements alone does not fulfil the requirements set by UNCLOS (Responsibilities and Obligations of States Sponsoring Persons and Entities with respect to Activities in the Area, 2011, para. 223): sponsoring States are required to adopt and enforce reasonably appropriate legislation and regulations.

The deep sea miner as well holds obligations that are attributed directly to it by UNCLOS and its related agreements. Indeed, under Article 21 of Annex III UNCLOS, contracts between the seabed miner and the Authority "shall be governed by the terms of the contract, the rules, regulations and procedures of the Authority, Part XI and other rules of international law not incompatible with this Convention". In the same vein, Article 33(5) of the Authority's Regulations on prospecting and exploration for polymetallic sulphides in the Area imposes directly on each contractor the duty to "take necessary measures to prevent, reduce and control pollution and other hazards to the marine environment arising from its activities in the Area as far as reasonably possible, applying a precautionary approach and best environmental practices".

The sharing of benefits derived from mining is still in the process of negotiation at the International Seabed Authority. Initial UNCLOS provisions on payments to the Authority and on compulsory technology transfers in favor of developing States proved unsatisfactory to the industrialized State parties. This led to the conclusion in 1994 of the "Agreement relating to the implementation of Part XI of the United Nations Convention on the Law of the Sea of 10 December 1982" (or Implementing Agreement) which made the CHM more compatible with private economic activity (Feichtner, 2019, p. 623). For example, under section 5 of the agreement's Annex, "developing States wishing to obtain deep seabed mining technology, shall seek to obtain such technology on fair and reasonable commercial terms and conditions on the open market, or through joint-venture arrangements".

Besides, the Implementing Agreement affirms that the payment system should be "royalty-based or consist in a combination between royalties and royalty system or a combination of a royalty and profit-sharing system" while "the rates of payments under the system shall be within the range of those prevailing in respect of land-based mining of the same or similar minerals in order to avoid giving deep seabed miners an artificial competitive advantage or imposing on them a competitive disadvantage" (Implementing Agreement, Annex, section 8). The most recent Draft Regulations on Exploitation of Mineral Resources in the Area do not specify the applicable royalty rate, which is since 2014 the object of negotiations at the General Council of the International Seabed Authority. Nevertheless, the draft regulations provide for a value-based royalty based on the value of their metal components (Draft Exploitation Regulations, appendix IV).

CHM and marine genetic resources beyond national jurisdiction: a principle in retreat?

It is unclear whether the CHM principle extends to marine genetic resources (or MGRs) in waters beyond national jurisdiction. The 2007 UN Informal Consultative Process on Oceans and the Law of the Sea documents disagreements about the legal regime for marine genetic resources. Some States insisted that all resources in the Area, including marine genetic resources, are the resort of the CHM principle (Scovazzi, 2013, p. 120). This view is seemingly supported by Article 136 of UNCLOS, whose wording refers to the Area itself as well as its resources as being the object of the CHM principle. Other States argued that these resources are subject to the customary regime of freedom of the high seas (Tanaka, 2008, p. 132). Their position is backed by the limited definition of resources in Article 133 UNCLOS and by the fact that under Article 137(2) UNCLOS only the rights over the **resources** of the Area are vested in mankind as a whole. Consequently, the Authority's power to act on behalf of humanity is explicitly related to those resources. This said, Part XI of UNCLOS contains other provisions, such as Article 145 on the protection of the Area's environment, that are not predicated exclusively on the resources of the Area. It can be concluded that certain components of the CHM principle apply to both mineral and genetic resources while its common management regime applies to the former and not to the latter.

The question of applicability of CHM to MGRs has become particularly cogent during the ongoing negotiations for an Agreement on Marine Biodiversity in Areas beyond National Jurisdiction. In practice, whereas references to the CHM principle were absent in the draft from May 2019, that principle made it back to the revised draft of November 2019. CHM appears in brackets in draft Article 5, on general principles, indicating a lack of convergence of views on that point. Even so, the draft does incorporate certain features of CHM. Draft Article 9 stipulates that "utilization of marine genetic resources of areas beyond national jurisdiction shall be for the benefit of mankind as a whole" and "for peaceful purposes". At the same time, Article 10 refers to the functions of a treaty secretariat set up by the parties to monitor the utilization of MGRs from areas beyond national jurisdiction. However, draft Article 10 does not make a choice between two differing alternatives on the powers of that secretariat: to make in situ access to marine genetic resources subject to notification by the secretariat or to entrust to States the regulation of access through licenses. Finally, draft Article 11(3)(a) shows that the negotiating States cannot agree on whether monetary benefits shall or may be shared.

In the end, the CHM principle's clearest formulation, aimed at activities in the Area, is still incomplete pending the approval of complete regulations for deep sea mining. Furthermore, it is unlikely that the CHM in its entirety will ground the legal regime for MGRs beyond national jurisdiction. Nonetheless, certain elements thereof are being incorporated in the Draft Agreement on the conservation and sustainable use of marine biological diversity of areas beyond national jurisdiction.

ALBERTO PECORARO

References

Feichtner, Isabel (2019). "Sharing the Riches of the Sea: The Redistributive and Fiscal Dimension of Deep Seabed Exploitation", European Journal of International Law 30(2), 601–633.

Guntrip, Edward (2003). "The Common Heritage of Mankind: An Adequate Regime for Managing the Deep Seabed?", Melbourne Journal of International Law 4(2), 376–405.

Joyner, Christopher C. (1986). "Legal Implications of the Concept of Common Heritage of Mankind", The International and Comparative Law Quarterly 35(1), 190–199.

Kiss, Alexandre (1985). "The Common Heritage of Mankind: Utopia or Reality?", International

Journal: Canada's Journal of Global Policy Analysis 40(3), 423–441.

Scovazzi, Tullio (2010). "The Seabed beyond the Limits of National Jurisdiction: General and Institutional Aspects" in Alex G. Oude Elferink and Erik J. Molenaar (eds), *The International Legal Regime of Areas beyond National Jurisdiction: Current and Future Developments*. Nova et Vetera Iuris Gentium Series, Volume 26, Martinus Nijhoff Publishers.

Scovazzi, Tullio (2013). "Open Questions on the Exploitation of Genetic Resources in Areas beyond National Jurisdiction", Proceedings of the Annual Meeting of the American Society of International Law 107, 119–122.

Tanaka, Yoshifumi (2008). "Reflections on the Conservation and Sustainable Use of Genetic Resources in the Deep Seabed beyond the Limits of National Jurisdiction", Ocean Development and International Law 39(2), 129–149.

Taylor, P. (2011). "Common Heritage of Mankind Principle" in Klaus Bosselmann, Daniel S. Fogel, and J.B. Ruhl (eds), *The Encyclopaedia of Sustainability*. Volume 3: The Law and Politics of Sustainability. Berkshire Publishing Group.

Tladi, Dire (2015). "The Common Heritage of Mankind and the Proposed Treaty on Biodiversity in Areas beyond National Jurisdiction: The Choice between Pragmatism and Sustainability", Yearbook of International Environmental Law 25(1), 113–132.

Wolfrum, Rüdiger (1983). "The Principle of the Common Heritage of Mankind", Zeitschrift für ausländisches öffentliches Recht und Völkerrecht 43, 312–337.

12. Comparative Law

Law and Development is an area of scholarship that – in a very broad sense – explores the relationship between legal systems and socio-economic progress (Lee, 2017). Under this label, it is possible to find a wide variety of studies that could be clustered in two main groups (Mota Prado, 2010). In this sense, some researchers focus on "Law in development" (where the rule of law and certain legal institutions are conceived as tools that serve to achieve development-related goals), while others focus on "Law as development" (where the rule of law and certain legal institutions imply the idea of development in themselves). Within these categories there are different viewpoints about what is understood by "law" and by "development".

The Law and Development movement can be linked with Comparative Law, since both studies present – at least – one basic aspect in common: both compare different legal systems and analyze legal transplants and receptions among them. Of course, the first has a particular concern on development issues while the second may take into account several other matters.

This leads to a first fundamental question. Is Comparative Law the main discipline and Law and Development just one of its branches, or is it Law and Development the main discipline and Comparative Law just one of its methods? In fact, it is widely discussed if Comparative Law is a subject (i.e., one of the several branches of law with a specific object and method of study), or if it is only a method (i.e., to examine the several objects of study that different branches of law may have). It could be thought that Comparative Law is not a topic, but a method. Or even, that it is barely a perspective on law. Having said this, it can be argued that Comparative Law is an intellectual activity with law as its object and comparison as its process (K. Zweigert and H. Kötz (1998). *An Introduction to Comparative Law*. Oxford University Press).

Whatever epistemological status may be recognized for Comparative Law, there are some fundamental issues to understand its theory and practice that – as it will be noticed – should be as well considered in Law and Development. For example, what is the meaning of "comparison" and "law" and what kind of methods and purposes are involved on these fields.

It is clear that comparative work is not the obsessive compilation and transcription of statutes and decisions from several legal systems. To "compare" is firstly to understand and describe certain phenomena and secondly to establish a system of similarities and differences between them in relation to some qualities (Reimann and Zimmerman, 2006). Therefore, the duty of comparison is not only about classifying different phenomena, but also qualifying them. While Comparative Law is centered on comparing different legal systems in response to multiple aims, Law and Development not only compares the law but also the development of different communities.

As it is also evident, there are multiple concepts and conceptions about what is law. While some positions define law – in a strict sense – as a system of regulations formally adopted by public authorities, other positions define it – in a broad sense – by including different types of principles, institutions and practices that can even be informally settled in society. Both in Comparative Law and in Law and Development the broad notion of law is generally used. Certainly, in order to understand how legal systems work, it is essential – in both fields – to start from the letter of the law and then to go beyond it. Nevertheless, while Comparative Law has particular interest on legal traditions and cultures in general, Law and Development pays special attention to the different legal frameworks, regulations and institutions that are related to the adoption, implementation and enforcement of law (Lee, 2017).

Furthermore, several controversies arise in regard to the methods to be employed on these fields. It seems convenient to present here a brief selection under a set of schematic dichotomies (Samuel, 2014).

Holistic vs. individualistic paradigm. The first model believes that groups have a global existence of their own and a dynamic that is different from that of a mere sum of individual components. On the contrary, the second model assumes that there are only individual entities such that the groups' existence and dynamics can be only explained by the sum of their elements. This ontological argument delineates – in a very general scale – the possible objects and results of a comparative investigation.

Regarding Law and Development, this matter raises different perspectives with regard to the kind of factors that may promote or restrain development. For example, does development depend on individual or collective actions?

Macro vs. micro approach. The first approach is interested in a comparison that embraces entire legal systems or traditions. In contrast, the second narrower view focuses on a comparison of specific topics or areas in law. Even though the different scope of both approaches is clear, it must be observed that it is not possible to carry out an analysis at a micro comparative level without having in mind some notions that belong to the macro comparative one, and vice versa. In the case of Law and Development, this matter would allow to identify the kind of amplitude and deepness that legal changes should count with, in order to achieve development. Thus, does development depend on global or local reforms? This opens up another avenue: Should changes be radical or progressive in order to achieve effective outcomes?

External vs. internal perspective. On one side, the comparatist could remain like an observer that intends to describe the rules and principles of the legal systems under comparison from an external point of view. On the other side, the comparatist could assume the role of a participant that attempts to apprehend the rules and principles of the different legal systems from an internal point of view. From this perspective, it is important to be capable of approaching the foreign law's cosmovision without prioritizing one's own view. In Law and Development, this turns into a relevant advice as it usually leans to evaluate law from North to South and from West to East.

Functionalism vs. alternative methods. As far as the method of investigation is concerned, the functionalist proposal is the most important in Comparative Law. This method does not focus on the formal rules and structures of the law, but on the concrete manner in which the law effectively provides answers to real-life situations. Functionalists struggle to exhibit how legal systems really work and which of them offer the best answers according to the effects that they produce. Nevertheless, there are also other alternatives to be considered. On the one side, the structuralist method points that legal systems are not an amorphous body of rules and principles, but that its design responds to a determined order based on certain properties and relationships of their components. On the other side, the hermeneutic method points that legal systems cannot be understood by a simple textual interpretation, but it becomes essential to dive into the mentality and culture that surround it. This is also a crucial discussion for Law and Development, given that if it is about boosting legal reforms that promote socio-economic progress, then it must be taken into account how norms work as well as how they are structured and experienced by each community.

Analytical vs. genealogical orientation. The first compares different legal systems to find differences and similarities, no matter if there is any contact or influence that binds them. Instead, the second sets that same comparison but in order to find a common ancestor and establish a filial relationship between the legal systems considered. In the case of Law and Development, it may seem that their studies are just related to the analytical field. However, as they generally suggest that "developing countries" should follow the recipes of "developed countries", they are logically also related to the genealogical field.

Synchronic vs. diachronic exploration. The first focuses on contemporary legal systems and proposes to adopt a timeless point of view for their examination. In contrast, the second delves into successive legal systems and proposes to explore them with a historical perspective. Regarding Law and Development it seems that its studies are usually centered on contemporary legal systems. However, it is common ground that in this subject it is not enough to contemplate just a "picture" without watching the complete "film" in order to provide a proper analysis of reality.

Similarity vs. difference presumption. Some comparatists assume that there are similarities between different legal systems – according to the sort of problems and solutions that they regulate – and consider that the end of comparison is to demonstrate that there is certain homogeneity. Others assume that there are differences among those various legal systems and consider that the end of comparison is to rescue certain heterogeneity. In the case of Law and Development, it seems that the strong inequality between legal systems among different countries is assumed, but at the same time, it recognizes some possibilities of relative equality.

Natural vs. cultural framework. This fundamental matter is related to the key question as to whether natural and social phenomena are dominated by identical or different laws. In the case of Comparative Law, the first position is associated with the idea of progress as the dissolution of diversities between different legal systems and the achievement of one superior standard that is above all the ones that have been provided by each of them. Instead, the second is merged with a perspective that rejects such idea of progress while it does not promote the suppression of differences but suggests recording those existing between various legal systems in order to comprehend their particularities against any imposition of uniformity. With regard to Law and Development, a dose of "naturalism" emerges when it is intended to adapt the law of "developing countries" to the shape of "developed countries". However, legal operators are being gradually more conscious about the necessity of incorporating a dose of "culturalism" in their analysis.

Enquiry vs. authority spirit. The first attitude considers that knowledge is a matter of rigorous examination of empirical evidence that involves observation, induction, hypothesis and falsification. In contrast, the second one considers that knowledge is a matter of authority requiring the study of some authoritative texts or figures. In some way, when Law and Development is intended to boost legal reforms from one country to another, instead of making recipes based on the different local realities, it seems that the spirit of authority is assumed more than the spirit of enquiry.

Comparative Law serves as a tool for legal knowledge, as a mean to interpret and reform a legal system and as a mechanism to harmonize and unify various legal systems. In contrast, Law and Development is circumscribed to the study of legal reforms that promote socio-economic progress and even global justice goals. Moreover, it is generally oriented towards a particular direction, i.e.: promoting law of "developed countries" in "developing countries" as a way of reaching their kind of development.

However, paradoxically, with that unique direction it would turn into a Non-Comparative Law, as it would not have an interest in comparing and sharing different legal experiences, but on transplanting legal systems from one to another without considering a similar reception in the reverse path (Kroncke, 2012).

In the end, whatever might be the relationship between Law and Development and Comparative Law, it seems certain that the first one can contribute to the second one's construction. In fact, comparative work can help to clarify some core concepts for Law and Development, i.e. "law" (positivist or realist notion?), "rule of law" (formal or substantive contents?), "democracy" (procedural rules or substantial values?), liberties (negative or positive sense?), "human rights" (universalist or relativist perspective?), "Justice" (commutative or distributive concern?), and "development" (economic growth or non-economic values?).

In the end, it also serves to answer a fundamental question: Does law matter for Development? In this sense, comparative work seems to show that some legal reforms are necessary, but definitely not enough to achieve socio-economic progress (Davis and Trebilcock, 2008).

DIEGO A. DOLABJIAN

References

Cao, Lan (2016). *Culture in Law and Development: Nurturing Positive Change*. Oxford University Press.

Davis, Kevin E. and Michael J. Trebilcock (2008). "The Relationship between Law and Development: Optimists versus Skeptics", American Journal of Comparative Law 56(4).

De Moerloose, Stéphanie (2017). "Law and Development as a Field of Study: Connecting Law with Development", Law and Development Review 10(2), 179–186.

Kroncke, Jedidiah J. (2012). "Law and Development as Anti-Comparative Law", Vanderbilt Journal of Transnational Law 45.

Lee, Yong-Shik (2017). "General Theory of Law and Development", Cornell International Law Journal 50(3).

Legrand, Pierre (2011). *Le droit comparé*. Presses Universitaires de France.

Mota Prado, Mariana (2010). "What is Law and Development?", Revista Argentina de Teoría Jurídica 11(1). Spanish version available: "¿Qué es 'Derecho y desarrollo'?".

Reimann, Mathias and Reinhard Zimmerman (eds) (2006). *The Oxford Handbook of Comparative Law*, Oxford University Press.

Samuel, Geoffrey (2014). *An Introduction to Comparative Law Theory and Method*. Hart Publishing.

Trebilcock, Michael J. and Mariana Mota Prado (2014). *Advanced Introduction to Law and Development*. Edward Elgar. Spanish version available: (2017) Derecho y desarrollo. Guía fundamental para entender por qué el desarrollo social y económico depende de instituciones de calidad. Siglo XXI.

13.　Corruption

Corruption is the abuse of public office – either as a politician or bureaucrat – for private gain. We generally conceive of corruption involving illegal actions such as bribe taking and embezzlement, the pilfering of State coffers. Yet in more advanced economies, in particular, legal actions such as accepting vast campaign contributions and the revolving door between public service and industry are deemed by some as also detrimental acts that weaken governance. Over half the world's population lives in a country where the illegal form is pervasive, as reported by Transparency International, and few countries exist without concerns about the more diffuse, legal forms.

Harm of corruption

Under the efficient corruption hypothesis, many economists previously viewed corruption as simply a transaction cost or even a beneficial phenomenon because it enabled business to get deals done by circumventing burdensome regulation. Yet few now believe corruption is efficient, given it would incentivize public officials to invent more bureaucratic roadblocks to solicit more bribes. Also, many governmental regulations are to protect lives, improve citizens' health, and sustainably maintain environmental resources, so circumventing these regulations negates their benefits. Furthermore, corruption undermines governance, the rule of law, and the economy. As Tim Harford has explained, why bother getting an education if you do not have the money to pay the bribes to gain admission, why bother starting a business if you do not have the money to bribe those to get registered or to win contracts (Harford (2005). *The Undercover Economist*. Oxford University Press)? Corruption destroys citizens' autonomy by destroying any semblance of a level playing field. Finally, research has demonstrated that corruption not only reduces economic growth but also increases inequality.

Not all corrupt acts generate equal harm. For example, Andrei Shleifer and Robert Vishny (1993) have argued that some harm can be mitigated if the corruption is organized in a disciplined manner from the top-down – e.g., where businesses are only asked for one bribe and the proceeds are distributed among the bureaucratic hierarchy instead of bureaucrats at every level of hierarchy demanding to be paid off individually. Further, relatively less harm occurs from corruption when those being asked to pay a bribe are reasonably assured that the public officials will hold up their end of the "bargain".

Theories of corruption

There are numerous competing theories of corruption that either attempt to explain the causes of corruption and/or emphasize how to reduce it.

Poverty trap theory

One such approach argues that corruption is the cause of poverty – e.g., reformers must first generate sustained and robust economic growth before corruption can be meaningfully addressed. This poverty trap theory suggests that, by definition, there are too few valuable resources that developing country citizens are competing for – e.g., access to a doctor (commonly there is roughly one doctor for every 200–300 citizens in a developed country, but only one doctor for every 10,000 citizens in numerous developing countries). For those with money, this scarcity suggests they will buy access through bribes. Some call this framework a "modernization" approach. Yet not only might some 1950s modernization theorists agree with it, but so would many others, such as Ha-Joon Chang (2009), whose approach to development is a combination of State encouraged industrialization along with import limitation and export promotion in line with how Japan and South Korea developed economically.

History may be on the side of a poverty trap vision of corruption, in that countries have usually made substantial progress on corruption only after generating a middle class – i.e., only one country classified by the World Bank as a "low-income economy" ($1,025 or less gross national income (GNI) per capita) has an encouraging Transparency International Corruption Perceptions Index (CPI) score above 50 – Rwanda. The United Nations Sustainable Development Goals, as articulated in the 2030 Agenda for Sustainable Development, de-emphasize the centrality of reducing corruption as being one of the main drivers of development: of the 17 goals and 169 targets, only one target addresses corruption. Yet, it is likely that poverty causes corruption and also that corruption causes poverty. As importantly, one can view the theory as taking a defeatist perspective in regard to corruption until middle-income status is attained.

Equilibrium of social expectations

Another way of conceptualizing corruption is as an equilibrium of social choices, as articulated by Susan Rose-Ackerman and most recently by Ray Fisman and Miriam Golden (2017). If corruption is widespread, it is against any one individual's interest not to pay or accept a bribe, yet if corruption is very low, the risks of engaging in corruption are not worth it. Those taking bribes are unlikely to desire to change the system given they are benefiting from it. This suggests that movement to reduce systematic corruption will come from those paying bribes, a supply side take on reform. This behavioral approach also emphasizes that those who participate in corruption in a country rife with it are not morally inferior to others – e.g., citizens will pay bribes to get the services they are entitled to because they need those services. Such citizens probably detest the high-corruption environment they find their country in, yet they do not know how to change the norms.

Thinking of social expectations and established norms as equilibriums is important, yet other considerations cannot be excluded from this perspective. For example, a leading advocate of this theory, Ray Fisman, and a colleague, Edward Miguel, wrote a paper on parking tickets received by diplomats to the United Nations from different countries (Fisman and Miguel (2009), *Economic Gangsters*. Princeton University Press). While they were protected by diplomatic immunity up until 2002 for parking violations, diplomats from countries with low levels of corruption did not accumulate unpaid parking tickets, while those from countries with high levels of corruption accumulated scores of unpaid tickets. Once New York City was given authority to take the diplomatic license plates of those who did not pay tickets, there was a dramatic reduction in unpaid fines.

Strong, enlightened leadership

Another perspective on why corruption is so prevalent is the lack of strong, enlightened political leaders. The perspective of former Finance Minister of Nigeria, Ngozi Okonjo-Iweala (2018), is that simply a desire from the top to reduce corruption is encouraging but not enough; such desire needs to be paired with capable, effective leadership that makes tough decisions and builds coalitions with public officials and the public. While in developing countries with weak institutions, if political leadership is against corruption reform, very little can be accomplished.

Like the poverty trap theory for developing countries, strong, enlightened leaders historically are correlated with progress in reducing corruption – e.g., Lew Kuan Yew in Singapore, Park Chung-hee in South Korea, and Antanas Mockus in Bogotá. Tellingly, while the theory that democracy would be better at reducing corruption as compared to dictatorship is compelling in the abstract – democratic politicians have the people to answer to – in practice there is no such clear link. Voters generally do not vote out corrupt officials.

What makes this theory enticing – its perspective that what developing countries require are capable, honest politicians – also highlights the two challenges of such a theory: (1) how to increase the odds that good leaders ascend to power, and (2) coming up with practical policy reform to reduce corruption in spite of political leadership being against reform (all theories stumble in this regard when faced with corrupt leaders).

There are meaningful differences between disparate accounts of corruption, yet policy solutions to corruption can be consistent with all theories, at least some of the time. While not necessarily suggesting that the leadership theory is the best explanation of why corruption is rampant in the majority of countries around the world, the theory provides a clear way to classify policy responses – i.e., policy levers to use when a dedicated, effective leader is in power, and ideas to address corruption when the president is against reform. While some of the later tools can be used by reformist leaders, most tools only work well with honest leaders – e.g., national biometric identifications have been shown to reduce corruption when those implementing programs are clean, yet in the hands of corrupt public officials no benefits occur because the use of the cards can either be discontinued or evaded.

Ideas to reduce corruption when capable leaders desire reform

Years of experimentation have enabled anti-corruption reformers to develop a robust set of policies for a capable, reformist leader to implement. The list is long and consists of several obvious moves, such as removing tainted public officials and prosecuting corrupt bureaucrats. Numerous institutions should be established or reinvigorated, including an anti-corruption taskforce, an office of auditor general, and an ombudsperson office. They should have the ability to investigate not just all governmental accounts but the finances of politicians, public servants, and parastatal offices, and they should publicize their efforts to the public. Reformist leaders should have their countries join the Extractive Industries Transparency Initiative, implement the provisions of the OECD Convention against Bribery and the UN Convention against Corruption, and support the proposed International Anti-Corruption Court. While such international legal efforts cannot sufficiently motivate corrupt leaders, they can provide modest support and guidance to countries desiring to build reform momentum.

While needless regulation and tariffs should be simplified or reduced and the media should be privatized, other laws should be strengthened, including protections and financial incentives for whistle-blowers, expansive freedom of information laws, robust legal protections for journalists, asset disclosure laws requiring all high-level bureaucrats, politicians, and judges to publicly disclose their assets each year, and life appointments for senior judges with dedicated escrow accounts to fund their salaries to further insulate them.

There are a few more unorthodox ideas such as Paul Romer's charter cities, creating special zones of good governance, which builds off of earlier proposals to export bureaucrats from countries with good governance to those without it (P. Romer (2010), *Technologies, Rules, and Progress: The Case for Charter Cities*. Center for Global Development). Also, there are some under-acknowledged tensions among policy suggestions – e.g., Robert Rotberg (2017) suggests that permitting and licensing should be brought online in order to reduce bureaucratic discretion, while Mariana Mota Prado, Michael J. Trebilcock and others have promoted the idea of institutional bypasses, giving multiple bureaucracies the ability to issue permits and licenses to create competition and prevent the creation of a bottleneck for bureaucrats to exploit (Prado and Trebilcock (2019), *Institutional Bypasses*. Cambridge University Press).

Ideas to reduce corruption when leaders are resistant to reform

If political leaders will not spearhead rule of law and anti-corruption reform, which is all too often the case, the task rests either with citizens, civil society organizations, or international actors. Unfortunately, there are a limited number of tools to address corruption when the political leadership want to continue to benefit from their corrupt ways.

One proposal aims at altering the entire social norm of corruption at once. The idea is to offer substantial performance-based financial incentive bonuses (10 to 20 times official salaries) at the end of every year to all high-level politicians and bureaucrats on one condition – that corruption decreases from the prior year as measured by one or more of the main measures of corruption, such as Transparency International's CPI index. The premise relies on aligning financial incentives with public officials' actions (unlike simply raising their salaries, which has proven to be ineffective) in combination with a big push to dramatically and quickly change social expectations. It would further enable those in charge to use the tool of legal enforcement to instigate change and enable everyone to publicly view the public officials' progress.

Novel educational and information campaigns have shown promise against corrupt, local public officials. One idea that has proven effective to reduce embezzlement of school funds is to post the amount of central government funds that are allocated to a school on its front doors and in local media (of course, this requires some cooperation from the central government in order to obtain the figures). Another similar, proven idea, by Abhijit Banerjee and others, is to simply send all eligible recipients of a social welfare program information about what they are entitled to on a postcard (Banerjee et al. (2018), "Tangible Information and Citizen Empowerment",

Journal of Political Economy 126(2), 451–491). Whether such innovative ideas can be applied to central government figures also largely remains to be seen.

Ideas to change national politicians' motivations concentrate around foreign aid proposals. One idea is to not distribute foreign aid to developing countries unless wealthy, domestic elites match the funds from their own pockets. Such "foreign aid challenge commitments" would get those who donate committed to applying pressure on politicians and bureaucrats to reduce corruption because any pilfered funds would include the elites' own contributions. Another such option is "macro aid". It takes the premise of micro aid – joint liability – and applies it to groups of aid-recipient countries instead of individuals. If any country within a macro aid group fraudulently managed their foreign aid, no one in the group would be given aid in the future in an effort not only to encourage reform but to stop facilitating graft. Finally, Ngozi Okonjo-Iweala has urged international actors to "strengthen the hands of those on the front line" by providing fellowships abroad that would provide recipients "breathing space away from their adversaries" (Okonjo-Iweala, 2018, p. 132).

MARTIN SKLADANY

References

Chang, Ha-Joon (2009). *Bad Samaritans: The Myth of Free Trade and the Secret History of Capitalism*, reprint edition. Bloomsbury Press.

Fisman, Ray and Miriam A. Golden (2017). *Corruption: What Everyone Needs to Know*. Oxford University Press.

Lambsdorff, Johann Graf (2008). *The Institutional Economics of Corruption and Reform: Theory, Evidence and Policy*. Cambridge University Press.

Li, Shaomin (2019). *Bribery and Corruption in Weak Institutional Environments: Connecting the Dots from a Comparative Perspective*. Cambridge University Press.

Mungiu-Pippidi, Alina (2015). *The Quest for Good Governance: How Societies Develop Control of Corruption*. Cambridge University Press.

Okonjo-Iweala, Ngozi (2018). *Fighting Corruption Is Dangerous: The Story Behind the Headlines*. The MIT Press.

Rose-Ackerman, Susan and Bonnie J. Palifka (2016). *Corruption and Government: Causes, Consequences, and Reform*. 2nd edition. Cambridge University Press.

Rotberg, Robert I. (2017). *The Corruption Cure: How Citizens and Leaders Can Combat Graft*. Princeton University Press.

Shleifer, Andrei and Robert W. Vishny (1993). "Corruption", *Quarterly Journal of Economics* 108(3), 599–617.

Skladany, Martin (2009). "Buying Our Way Out of Corruption: Performance-Based Incentive Bonuses for Developing Country Politicians and Bureaucrats", *Yale Human Rights and Development Law Journal* 12(1), 160–204.

14. Courts

What role, if any, can courts play in advancing development? This is the overarching focus of this entry, which is divided into three sections. In the first one, I explain the inevitable complexity of the issue, which is due, mainly, to the contested nature of the concept of development. In the second section, I briefly discuss an additional challenge to the enterprise, namely the difficulty of establishing clear-cut causal relationships between courts' work and development outcomes. I then discuss what, in my view, those interested in the issue may do when trying to address the complexities explained. In the final section, I give some illustrative examples of the kind of approach I recommended as useful in section 2.

Conceptual complexity

Answering the opening question of this entry would be hard enough if development were not a contested concept, i.e. an idea on which there is a reasonable measure of disagreement about what it means (John Rawls (1971). *A Theory of Justice*. Oxford University Press). But this is, of course, not the case. The concept of development is a highly contested one, at a similar level, perhaps, to the concept of justice, and certainly more contested, in my view, than the concepts of human rights, democracy, and the rule of law, which are all also significantly contested.

The answer to the opening question of this entry will therefore vary, and likely significantly, depending on the conception of development one has in mind. Let me illustrate the point with some examples. Take, first, development in one of its most popular senses, i.e. one that focuses on the economic aspects of development (call it 'economic development'). Even here, of course, there is a lot of disagreement on what economic development means. But let us adopt a very simple and narrow definition to avoid further complexity at this stage. Let us define economic development as gross domestic product (GDP) growth. Can courts play a role in advancing development defined in that narrow way? There is a long lineage of literature that studies that question. The most popular hypothesis within that literature is that economic growth can be furthered or hindered depending on whether the legal system of the country in question provides strong protection for private property and effectively enforces commercial contracts. Courts are seen as relevant as they can serve as tools not only to enforce property and contracts, but also feature as a credible threat to prevent breaches in the first place.

Let us take now a broader conception of development, i.e. one that goes beyond economic aspects and includes the well-being of individuals as part of development (call it 'social' or 'human development'). Assessing courts' potential role becomes now much more complex and contested. For some, the focus ought still to be on the role of judges as enforcers of property and contracts, as this is what, in that view, guarantees well-being, albeit indirectly, i.e. through economic development creating the wealth on which well-being depends. The view depends on the further assumption that once wealth is increased it will eventually benefit everyone and not only those who manage to accumulate it in the first place (the so-called 'trickle-down' effect). But others will view human development as necessarily linked to direct State provision of goods, e.g. health, education, housing etc., that constitute components of well-being. In this view, courts' potential role in advancing (or hindering) development changes significantly. Beyond, or even contrary to the protection of private property and contracts, it focuses on courts' ability to implement redistributive policies, often via the enforcement of social and economic rights.

Another available route is to adopt an even broader conception of human development, i.e. one that views the existence of an independent and impartial judiciary as a constitutive element of development, i.e. as part and parcel of development and not simply an instrument to achieve development defined in one of the narrower ways mentioned above. Under this conception, the very existence of a judiciary that can resolve societal disputes in a manner that is legitimate, independent, fair and accessible to the population is one of the hallmarks of a developed society, irrespective of the actual impact that judicial decisions can have on the economy, redistribution etc. As Amartya Sen persuasively put it, '[w]e cannot very well say that the development process has gone beautifully even though people are being arbitrarily hanged, criminals go free while law-abiding citizens end up in jail, and so on ... Development has a strong association of meanings that makes a basic level of legality and judicial attainment a constitutive part of it' (Sen, 2000, pp. 9–10).

Causation

The brief and necessarily simplified discussion of section 1 is sufficient to demonstrate how complex it is even to determine the meaning of the question whether courts can play a role in advancing development. The other main difficulty of the enterprise is of an empirical nature. Even if there were consensus on the meaning of development, or if we simply stipulated what we meant by development in order to assess courts' potential role, the task of establishing causal relationships between development and the work of the judiciary would still be fraught with problems. Apart from the well-known challenges of collection of reliable data, there is also the extremely complex issue of confounding explanatory variables, i.e. how can we be sure that a certain outcome is solely or even partly attributable to the activity of courts rather than the upshot of other more complex social, economic and political processes?

These challenges were well summarized in an insightful paper by two leading experts discussing the broader question of law and development. To adapt their conclusions to our narrower focus on courts, we could divide the project into the following three difficult questions: (1) do courts matter? (causation); (2) can courts be reformed to play a positive role? (legal reform), and (3) is it possible to identify what exactly needs to be reformed for courts to matter? (specific policies) (Davis and Trebilcock, 2008).

But such difficulties should not demotivate those interested in pursuing the issue of courts and development. It should simply caution against the temptation to find clear and simple answers and, worse, universal recipes to be transplanted into countries, as has unfortunately happened only too often under international programmes of legal reform or rule of law promotion in which '[h]ordes of Western consultants descend on transitional societies with Western legal models in their briefcases' (Carothers, 2006, p. 11).

More fruitful initiatives – both from an academic and practical perspective – are possible so long as the challenges above are taken seriously, which point towards more nuanced and contextual, empirically based analyses of the work of courts in specific countries and on specific aspects of development, rather than on the elusive idea of development as a single all-encompassing goal that courts can help to advance following ready-made and simple universal recipes.

Some examples of such more illuminating efforts have appeared in the literature in the past couple of decades but are still few and far between (e.g., Carothers, 2006; Sikkink, 2011; Epp, 2009; Yamin and Gloppen, 2011; Gauri and Brinks, 2010; Gargarella et al., 2006). In the final section of this entry we will describe some of them.

Examples

Let us start with the perhaps more classic example of the potential role of courts to help advance development in the narrow conception of economic growth. The usual assumption, as already mentioned, is that protection of property and enforcement of contracts, which effective courts can help to ensure, will have a positive effect in the economy through the encouragement of investment and economic activity (Douglas North (1990). *Institutions, Institutional Change, and Economic Performance*. Cambridge University Press; World Bank (2005). *A Better Investment Climate for Everyone: World Development Report 2005*. World Bank). The assumption is certainly plausible, but it needs to be tested to see if it really holds on the ground in specific countries. The assumption may fail on any of the three, layered components described above. We may well find that there is no necessary strong relationship between the existence of independent and effective courts and economic growth, as some claim China may be a good example (Carothers, 2006). Or we may find that, despite attempts of reforms through legislative change and institutional reforms, it is not easy to change the actual behaviour of judges or parties, especially the government (failed attempts of judicial reform in Argentina and Russia are perhaps good examples, see Carothers, 2006). Finally, one may come to the conclusion that the reforms themselves were not well targeted as it is difficult, if not impossible, to identify what reforms are needed in the first place. Carothers' analysis is rather insightful here:

> Law is also a normative system that resides in the minds of the citizens of a society. As rule-

of-law providers seek to affect the rule of law in a country, it is not clear if they should focus on institution building or instead try to intervene in ways that would affect how citizens understand, use, and value law. (Carothers, 2006, p. 20)

The empirical literature on the relationship between courts and economic development is far from supportive of the positive nexus. Some even claim that the direction of causality is the opposite to the popular hypothesis, i.e. that it is only once countries achieve a higher level of economic development that strengthening of courts takes place (Daniel M. Klerman (2007). 'Legal Infrastructure, Judicial Independence, and Economic Development', Pacific McGeorge Global Business and Development Law Journal 19, 427–434).

Another interesting area where more empirical research has grown in the past couple of decades is on the potential role of courts in advancing social development, i.e. development in the broader sense mentioned earlier of improvements in the well-being of the population. The issue has become particularly salient with the growing recognition of rights to health, education, housing, food and water ('social rights') in international and domestic law, in particular constitutions. The hypothesis, similarly to the courts-economic development one yet more direct, is that independent courts are willing and capable of enforcing those rights against recalcitrant governments who fail to abide by their legal, often constitutional duties. The empirical findings are not conclusive and, in some areas, such as health, raise important concerns about both the willingness and capacity of courts to play a positive role (Yamin and Gloppen, 2011; Ferraz, 2020). As regards capacity, there is consistent evidence showing that persistent access to justice barriers diminish significantly the potential of courts to advance social development through litigation as the most disadvantaged will rarely manage to take their grievances to the courts in the first place (Epp, 1998; Ferraz, 2020) and also that, when they do, governments are often neither willing nor able to implement judicial decisions (Gauri and Brinks, 2010).

As a final example, let us look at the issue of police brutality. Yet again, the hypothesis is that well-resourced and staffed, independent courts, should be willing and capable of holding police officers to account when they abuse their powers and, as a consequence, this should

lead to a decrease in such behaviour through the disincentivizing effects of legal sanctions. Here the available empirical research seems to allow for more positive conclusions. According to Kathryn Sikkink's important study of human rights prosecutions in Latin America, for instance, countries where 'prosecutions have taken place are less repressive than countries without prosecutions' (2011, p. 27). An equally positive relationship between litigation and decrease in police abuse has been found by Charles Epp in America (2009). Yet, as he has also emphasized in his previous seminal study of 'rights revolutions' (Epp, 1998), some favourable conditions which are not easily obtainable should be present for litigation to become an available and effective tool of social advancement, in particular a strong and well-resourced constituency in civil society willing and capable to channel their grievances through the judiciary.

Conclusion

This necessarily cursory treatment of a huge and complex topic is nonetheless sufficient, I hope, to highlight three crucial points about the relationship between courts and development. Firstly, the contested nature and significant breadth of the concept of development makes it impossible (not to say meaningless) to attempt to draw useful universal conclusions about the potential role of courts in advancing development. Secondly, more nuanced and useful conclusions are still possible and worthwhile so long as a more contextual, specific and empirically grounded approach is adopted. Finally, most studies that have adopted this strategy have highlighted important obstacles on the way of the optimistic hypothesis that courts can play a significant role in advancing development.

OCTÁVIO LUIZ MOTTA FERRAZ

References

Carothers, Thomas (ed.) (2006). *Promoting the Rule of Law Abroad: In Search of Knowledge*. Carnegie.

Davis, Kevin E. and Michael J. Trebilcock (2008). 'The Relationship between Law and Development: Optimists versus Skeptics', American Journal of Comparative Law 56(4), 895–946.

Epp, Charles R. (1998). *After the Rights Revolution: Lawyers, Activists and Supreme Court in Comparative Perspective*. University of Chicago Press.

Epp, Charles R. (2009). *Making Rights Real.* University of Chicago Press.

Ferraz, Octávio Luiz Motta (2020). *Health as a Human Right. The Politics and Judicialisation of Health in Brazil.* Cambridge University Press.

Gargarella, Roberto, Pilar Domingo, and Theunis Roux (2006). *Courts and Social Transformation in New Democracies: An Institutional Voice for the Poor?* Ashgate.

Gauri, Varun and Daniel M. Brinks (2010). *Courting Social Justice: Judicial Enforcement of Social and Economic Rights in the Developing World.* Cambridge University Press.

Sen, Amartya (2000). 'What is the Role of Legal and Judicial Reform in the Development Process?', World Bank.

Sikkink, Kathryn (2011). *The Justice Cascade.* W.W. Norton & Company.

Yamin, Alicia Ely and Siri Gloppen (2011). *Litigating Health Rights: Can Courts Bring More Justice to Health?* Harvard University Press.

15.   Cultural Heritage

In international law, cultural heritage encompasses a wide conceptual area. Traditionally, and for many still mainly, it was intended to refer to tangible cultural heritage, both movable (works of art, such as paintings, sculptures etc.) and immovable (monuments, archaeological sites, etc.). The definition now also includes intangible cultural heritage (oral traditions, food culture, rituals etc.) and natural heritage (to the extent it exists in symbiosis with humans and is affected and incorporated in both tangible and intangible cultural heritage).

Cultural heritage of course existed before and beyond its conceptualization as a distinct area of regulation and enforcement in international law. Nation States have used their cultural heritage as a way to affirm or construct a national identity; they have devised national laws to protect it and promote it; they have criminalized the trafficking or destruction of it; they have edited it and embellished it, selecting what qualifies as 'cultural heritage' for the purpose of protection.

Internationally, the appropriation of cultural heritage of the 'colonial other' was a considerable element of the colonial and/or imperial experience, ever since the conquest of Greece by Rome, famously commented by the poet Horace *Graecia capta ferum victorem cepit* (captured Greece has conquered its savage captor). More recently, the colonial experience included the encounter with the cultural heritage of colonial subjects. The experience passed through several stages:

The first stage of discovery, where no professionalization of the figure of the explorer had yet happened. For example, in the Near East, we have the figure of Sir Austen Layard, British diplomat and traveller who also excavated Nimrud and Nineveh.

Following this stage, European museums expanded their collections with their colonial finds. These collections still constitute a considerable percentage of the cultural heritage preserved in museums in Paris, London, Berlin and Turin. These objects can then become the pawns in a tug-of-war battle between colonies or source countries and former colonial powers, as is the case for the Benin Bronzes or the Parthenon Marbles in the British Museum.

From the beginning, the discovery and appropriation of cultural heritage accompanied the discovery and appropriation of economic resources. In the second phase, the romantic figure of the traveller/discoverer was replaced by the professional figure of the archaeologist (and of the anthropologist, for non-tangible cultural heritage).

The third phase consisted in the anti-colonial movement of liberation, as much a movement to recover sovereignty over natural resources as one of recovering sovereignty over cultural heritage, and this process of recovery was a return to the past as well as an invention of the past. Symbolic in this context is the reconstruction of Babylon initiated by Saddam Hussein in 1978, which was as much about constructing an Iraqi national identity and situating it in an ancient past, as it was about excavating and preserving the archaeological site.

The decolonization movement is the moment in which, internationally, cultural resources (to be taken at will) become cultural 'heritage', a piece in the puzzle of creation of the sovereign nation States. At the same time, this is the moment when the distinction between civilized and uncivilized peoples is abandoned in favour of the one between developed and developing countries, and cultural heritage, not vulnerable anymore to imperial appropriation, is now vulnerable to destruction resulting from economic development and to illegal trafficking (with the destination countries almost seamlessly mapping onto the old colonial powers).

In this context, it is important to remember that a considerable amount of archaeological work is 'salvage work', that is, the excavation and recording of archaeological sites prior to managed destruction (in the context of a development project such as the construction of a dam). This means that destruction of cultural heritage is a consequence that is at times 'factored in' the projected economic development. Archaeology as a practice is already 'managed destruction'. The excavation of a site, following and recording its stratigraphy (i.e., the chronological development) results in the progressive destruction of the different layers in order to arrive either at the oldest layer, which will then either be preserved or eventually destroyed either by nature or by economic development.

The 'creation' of cultural heritage as a distinct concept, including a distinct legal concept, was co-adjuvated by the institution of specific international bodies, and dedicated international treaties, for the protection and promotion of cultural heritage. These include the 1972 UNESCO Convention concerning the Protection of the World Cultural and Natural Heritage, the 1970 UNESCO Convention on the Means of Prohibiting and Preventing the Illicit Import, Export and Transfer of Ownership of Cultural Property, the 1995 UNIDROIT Convention on Stolen or Illegally Exported Cultural Objects, the 2016 World Customs Organization Council Resolution on the Role of Customs in Preventing Illicit Trafficking of Cultural Objects and at the European level, the 2017 Council of Europe Convention on Offences relating to Cultural Property. Additionally, international trade rules allow for exceptions under Article XX GATT for the protection of natural treasures and similar exceptions clauses are included in the new generation international investment agreements. The wanton destruction of cultural heritage in Mali has been declared a war crime by the International Criminal Court. The United Nations Security Council has issued resolutions on the destruction of cultural property in situations of conflict and on the link between the trade in cultural objects and terrorism.

Finally, and importantly, cultural heritage and culture have been included, for the first time, in the work of the United Nations on sustainable development through its 2015 Sustainable Development Goals. Target 4.11 of Sustainable Development Goal 11 recites: 'Strengthen efforts to protect and safeguard the world's cultural and natural heritage' and UNESCO has been actively involved in working towards this target, including through its Sustainable Tourism Programme.

From a legal perspective, a preoccupation with the vulnerability of cultural heritage to criminal activities is understandable. Movable tangible heritage is very vulnerable to trafficking, especially in situations of civil disturbances or war. Following the 2003 invasion of Iraq, the traffic of cultural objects was second in volume only to the trade in oil products. The criminalization of trafficking is common in municipal laws and coordinated internationally with varying degrees of effectiveness, as it encounters numerous problems in the somewhat ambiguous relationship with the international art market and the world of auction houses, galleries and museums, that do not always conduct the proper due diligence for the traceability of the artefacts in their collections.

Internationally, the criminalization of trafficking is the object of the 1970 UNESCO Convention and other relevant instruments of international private law, but is also recognized in international trade law, and trafficking of cultural goods is explicitly mentioned in the EU-Algeria and EU-Iraq Partnership Cooperation Agreements. More work needs to be done on fighting trafficking of cultural objects, especially in conflict zones, where the criminal traffic not only affects the cultural heritage of the country, but constitutes a source of income for the warring parties and can exacerbate and lengthen the conflict. Online platforms have become a considerable source for trafficked objects, or objects with an unclear provenance.

While academics and policy-makers sometimes consider the potential consequences for cultural heritage of trade and investment activities, the effect of economic development on the illicit trade of cultural and artistic artefacts is mostly ignored and little understood outside the field of experts. Conversely, experts and practitioners in art trafficking and art crime tend to focus on adverse events such as wars and civil strife and not on the vulnerability of cultural objects to legal economic development. When foreign investors enter into concession contracts for the development of pipelines, roads and other infrastructure, with or without the further protection of an international investment agreement, they set in motion events that will inevitably result in increased vulnerability for the cultural artefacts that might be exposed by the excavation and construction work. The objects thus found might be stolen, or sold, and enter the international illicit market of cultural artefacts.

The orthodox view of international economic law scholars and practitioners is that the protection of cultural (and natural) heritage might conflict with economic development, trade and foreign investment. Such seminal investment arbitrations as Santa Elena v. Costa Rica and Parkerings v. Lithuania evidenced the potential for investors to use investment treaties to challenge governmental measures and legislation adopted to protect cultural (and natural) heritage – although the latter ultimately resulted in an award that took due account of the status of the Vilnius City Centre as a UNESCO World Heritage site.

However, cultural heritage has a more complex relationship with development and with public policy than the potential for conflicts. One can identify three major forms of value-creating potential for cultural heritage:

1. Domestic economic value (revenue from tourism);
2. International economic value (foreign investment revenue);
3. Political value (soft power).

The first and the second strands of revenue are more conventionally connected with trade and investment policies and are evident, for example, in the incorporation of cultural heritage sites in Belt and Road Initiative (BRI) projects to improve the connectivity of major tourist sites in Asia. The BRI, and especially its twenty-first century Maritime Silk Road, is being seen as a driver for infrastructural development to sustain, promote and expand the tourism industry. This development has the potential to increase the gross domestic product of the countries involved but also to attract foreign investment (from China as well as from other countries) for the creation of the necessary infrastructure, from airports, rail and road to connections, to hotels, restaurants and entertainment facilities, around sites of cultural or natural significance, from temples, historic cities and archaeological remains to beaches and mountain resorts.

The third strand, political value, is a less investigated aspect of cultural heritage. Specialists in international economic law and economics often ignore and minimize the political aspects of economic development unless it takes the form of 'political risk', which needs to be mitigated via the introduction of specific protections in investment treaties and contracts. There is in general less attention paid by specialists to the synergic aspects of political strategies and economic policies, i.e. to the role performed by politics in the promotion of economic development and international investment, to the exclusion of those political strategies that have a direct effect on international investment and development, such as the conclusion on investment treaties, which are the political/legal arm of international investment. So there is not enough attention being paid to the political use of cultural heritage, or the role played by cultural heritage in fostering economic development, or being a driver

of economic development (for example, in 'cultural heritage tourism').

At the international and institutional level, an agreed marker of a country's commitment to its cultural heritage is the inclusion of sites of cultural, archaeological and architectural significance in the World Heritage List maintained by the UNESCO as part of the implementation of the 1972 World Heritage Convention. China has recently joined Italy for a number of World Heritage sites with a total of 55. Italy, the country with currently the highest number of listed sites, ratified the Convention in 1978, and listed its first site in 1982. China ratified the Convention in 1985 and listed its first six sites in 1987. It currently has 60 more tentative sites awaiting approval (Italy has 41) so it is slated to become the first country for number of World Heritage sites in the near future. It is therefore quite evident that China is pursuing a sustained policy of promotion of its cultural heritage, or at least, a selective view of the cultural heritage worth preserving and promoting.

To draw some conclusions on the concept of cultural heritage in international law, cultural heritage as a resource is both fragile and resilient. Fragile because it is vulnerable to destruction, both as a tangible and intangible artefact (for example, the effects of globalization on local cultural traditions). Resilient because, to the extent that the culture that produced it is still viable, it can sometimes be re-created. On the other hand, ancient cultural artefacts are irreplaceable, which confers on them the symbolic value that makes them vulnerable and valuable.

The fragility and vulnerability of cultural heritage makes it both valuable in economic terms and irreplaceable in monetary terms, rendering it difficult to fit into the framework of international law and its compensatory model of remedies.

Contrary to the perception that cultural heritage needs protection against illegal activities (including destruction in times of conflict and trafficking at any time), one of the greatest threats to cultural heritage is unregulated economic development. This affects both tangible heritage and intangible heritage, eminently vulnerable to the flattening effects of globalization.

In the specific case of the interaction between economic development and protection of cultural heritage as conceptualized in international law, the clauses for protection of cultural heritage in trade and investment instruments are seldom used as defences, but they have a 'signalling function' and can, for example, restrict the legitimate expectations of the investors re regulatory environment.

ALESSANDRA ASTERITI

References

Blake, Janet (2015). *International Cultural Heritage Law*. Oxford University Press.

Francioni, Francesco (ed.) (2008). *The 1972 World Heritage Convention: A Commentary*. Oxford University Press.

Francioni, Francesco and James Gordley (2013). *Enforcing International Cultural Heritage Law*. Oxford University Press.

Lixinski, Lucas (2013). *Intangible Cultural Heritage in International Law*. Oxford University Press.

Lostal, Marina (2017). *International Cultural Heritage Law in Armed Conflict*. Cambridge University Press.

Mackenzie, Simon, Neil Brodie, Donna Yates, and Christos Tsirogiannis (2020). *Trafficking Culture*, Routledge.

Nafziger, James A.R. and Robert Kirkwood Paterson (eds) (2014). *Handbook on the Law of Cultural Heritage and International Trade*. Edward Elgar.

Nafziger, James and Tullio Scovazzi (eds) (2008). *The Cultural Heritage of Mankind*. Hague Academy of International Law.

Vadi, Valentina (2014). *Cultural Heritage in International Investment Law and Arbitration*. Cambridge University Press.

Vadi, Valentina and Hildegard Schneider (eds) (2014). *Art, Cultural Heritage and the Market Ethical and Legal Issues*. Springer.

16.   Decent Work

Philosophical background

John Rawls focused on the notion of "meaningful work" in his *Theory of Justice* (1971) and emphasized that the content of work was essential and one of the fundamental "primary goods". Richard Arneson (1987) defined "meaningful work" as "work that is interesting, that calls for intelligence and initiative, and that is attached to a job that gives the worker considerable freedom to decide how the work is to be done and a democratic say over the character of the work process and the policies pursued by the employing enterprise". These philosophical notions have gradually taken root in international law, with a clear correlation between such notions and the alleviation of poverty becoming apparent.

The United Nations and International Labour Organization

Full and productive employment and decent work are the primary goals of both the United Nations Organization (the UN) and the International Labour Organization (the ILO). Both organizations acknowledge that the improvement of the conditions of work and decent work are central to the elimination of poverty. Decent and productive work can be achieved through improved work conditions of freedom, equity and human dignity.

The UN aims to promote higher standards of living, full employment, and conditions of economic and social progress and development (Charter of the United Nations 1945, Article 55). This is aptly captured in the Universal Declaration of Human Rights, 1948 (UDHR) which provides:

- Everyone has the right to work, to free choice of employment, to just and favourable conditions of work and to protection against unemployment;
- Everyone, without any discrimination, has the right to equal pay for equal work;
- Everyone who works has the right to just and favourable remuneration ensuring for himself and his family an existence

worthy of human dignity, and supplemented if necessary by other means of social protection;
- Everyone has the right to form and to join trade unions for the protection of his interests.

The ILO was established in 1919 to foster a lasting peace built upon social justice, recognizing that the prevalent inhuman working conditions were a real threat to international peace. Accordingly, the primary goal of the ILO is the achievement of decent and productive work in conditions of freedom, equity and human dignity. The ILO's major objective is to eliminate poverty through finding decent work and improving the lives of workers and their families.

In line with the UDHR emphasis on just and favourable working conditions, the preamble to the Constitution of the ILO provides that unjust labour conditions, hardship and privation create a potential threat to world peace and harmony (Constitution of the International Labour Organization, 1919). In order to eliminate that threat, the preamble acknowledges that an improvement of those conditions is urgently required (Constitution of the International Labour Organization, 1919). Amongst other things, the preamble highlights the need for the:

- regulation of the hours of work;
- prevention of unemployment, the provision of an adequate living wage;
- protection of the worker against sickness, disease and injury arising out of his employment;
- provision for old age and injury;
- recognition of the principle of equal remuneration for work of equal value; recognition of the principle of freedom of association.

The Declaration of Philadelphia, 1944, reaffirmed the ILO's fundamental principle that "labour is not a commodity" and committed the ILO to the promotion of programmes that attempt to achieve "full employment and the raising of standards of living ... (and) the employment of workers in the occupations in which they can have the satisfaction of giving the fullest measure of their skill and attainments and make their greatest contribution to the common well-being". For Deranty and

MacMillan (2012), the ILO has a conception of work that goes beyond the terms and conditions of employment and entails reference to the actual activity of work and the quality of work, although this dimension of the concept of "work" has remained underdeveloped.

The ILO's Declaration on Fundamental Principles and Rights at Work, 1998, reaffirmed various core principles and rights which have been incorporated in the ILO's Decent Work Agenda, adopted in 1999. This maintains the ILO's primary focus of regulating the exchange of labour to improve the terms and conditions of the employment relationship. The ILO remains focused on making work "decent" by striving to ensure just terms and conditions of work. To give content to this, it proposes that decent work can be achieved through four strategic pillars or cardinal objectives. These are:

1. fostering employment and creation of jobs of quality;
2. respect of the rights of workers through acknowledging freedom of association and the right to collective bargaining, elimination of forced labour, abolition of child labour and elimination of discrimination in employment;
3. the provision and improvement of social protection and social security; and
4. strengthening social dialogue and supporting tripartite consultation, negotiation and agreements between workers, employers and society.

The ILO's understanding of decent work has remained fairly consistent over time. For example, a 2006 report focused on Realizing Decent Work in Asia defined decent work as involving a decent job that "respects and confers the dignity of work, promotes a sense of self-worth and is central to family stability" (ILO (2006). *Realizing Decent Work in Asia*. Fourteenth Asian Regional Meeting, Busan, Republic of Korea, available at https://www.ilo.org/public/english/standards/relm/rgmeet/14asrm/dgrealizing.pdf accessed 15 September 2020). In particular, the dimensions of decent work that were identified in the report include:

- maintaining the traditional link between work and employment;
- creation of a decent quantity of jobs through the process of economic growth;
- safe jobs, not involving excessive hours;

- permission for workers to organize and express their interests collectively;
- most importantly, payment of a wage that does not leave workers and their dependants below the poverty line.

The ILO Declaration on Social Justice for a Fair Globalization, adopted by the ILO at its 97th Session in Geneva, on 10 June 2008, stressed that the four cardinal pillars of decent work are "inseparable, interrelated and mutually supportive" and that a holistic and integrated approach is a useful means of achieving all of them.

Challenges in promoting decent work in developing countries

The goal of promoting decent work in developing countries faces major challenges, especially in Africa. The rise of informal employment, which is mainly based on the informal economy comprising self-employed, micro and small enterprises, has resulted in a category of employees whose productivity is low and weakened by lack of or inadequate social protection. In ECA/RSFD/2019/1 (a paper prepared by the Economic Commission for Africa with inputs from the International Labour Organization and the United Nations Entity for Gender Equality and Empowerment of Women) it was noted that Africa has the highest rate of informal employment in the world, constituting 8.5 per cent of total employment. The informal economy in Africa in 2018 accounted for around 79 per cent of women employment, compared to around 68 per cent of men employment. With informal employment characterized by working under hazardous conditions and absence of social protection it means that a large number of women are vulnerable since they may not be covered in the event of injuries at work and also during times of economic recession. This may result in the increase of poverty. In order to address this challenge, there is a need to extend to informal employment the coverage of social protection, which tends to be largely limited to formal employment.

Another challenge in developing countries relates to outdated legislation which has been lagging behind when it comes to employees working in the informal sector. For example, domestic workers tend to be left out in some pieces of legislation relating to social security. For instance, in South Africa domestic workers were excluded from the Compensation for Occupational Injuries and Diseases Act 130 of 1993 (COIDA), which compensates employees or their survivors for work-related injuries, illnesses or death. It was only in 2019 that COIDA was declared unconstitutional for excluding domestic workers from its coverage. This emphasizes the importance of ensuring that legislation relating to social security should be extended to informal employment.

It is also important to note that efforts to extend social protection can only be successful if there is effective enforcement. In many developing countries, labour inspectorates play a big role in the enforcement of employment legislation to ensure that employees work under safe conditions. However, in some developing countries there is an acute shortage of labour inspectors due to budgetary constraints. This weakness of the enforcement mechanism hampers the efforts to promote decent work, particularly in informal employment.

One of the pillars of the Decent Work Agenda is social dialogue. For social dialogue to be effective, there must be meaningful engagement relating to advocacy and policy formulation amongst the stakeholders, which include the trade unions, employers' organizations and the government. In some developing countries there is also limited capacity of trade unions and employers' organizations to engage in advocacy, dialogue and policy formulation.

Analysis

Authors have distilled the four strategic objectives of the decent work agenda as follows: the promotion of rights at work; the generation of opportunities for decent employment and income from work through macroeconomic policy, which promotes full employment; social protection; and social dialogue. In essence, it is clear that decent work is not merely about numerical creation of jobs but also about the improved quality of employment. It signifies a significant departure from the traditional focus on job satisfaction to quality employment based on social justice.

The notion of decent work is based on the understanding that work that respects the rights and human dignity of a worker is an integral component of quality employment that will stimulate social progress and development and also contribute towards the elimination of poverty. It is also an acknowledgment that

dignity at the workplace, including just and decent working conditions, are at the heart of quality employment (Bolton, 2007).

Deranty and MacMillan (2012) have delineated three areas in which, they argue, a richer account of the content of work could be helpful to complement the ILO campaign for decent work, namely the level of individual capacities; the level of the working collective; and the level of the political culture of work. They have also questioned the situation where individuals knowingly agree to perform arduous work (work which is "anything but decent", as they put it), in situations where there is no discrimination, where contracts have been signed without undue influence, and where workers remain in this type of working arrangement of their own accord, with reasonable working hours and access to social protection.

Extending the concept of "decent work"?

Christophe Dejours' (2006) "psychodynamics of work" has integrated elements from ergonomics, psychology and psychoanalysis, philosophy and sociology in proposing an overall approach to work, providing key signposts for identifying work that is decent. At the individual level, the crucial element is the encounter of a subject with the difficulty of fulfilling a task. In addition, the central role played by the work collective in terms of the actual productivity of work activity and in respect of the experience of work for individuals is also highlighted. Finally, it is argued by Dejours that work is so impactful upon individual subjective identity, that its significance transcends the development and well-being of individuals and affects collective, social and political life. Deranty and MacMillan (2012) have suggested that decent work should include an educational and cultural dimension, which would aim to alert authorities and the general public to the central importance of work relations in democratic life.

From the perspective of the ILO, decent work remains the foundation for achieving the 2030 Agenda for Sustainable Development. A set of broader underpinnings of the notion of decent work is reflected in the 2030 Agenda, demonstrating the importance of achieving "decent work" in its various dimensions, and includes the following:

- No poverty: decent work for all, including social protection, is viewed as the main route out of poverty for individuals, communities and countries;

- Zero hunger: decent work in sustainable agriculture and food value chains is seen as crucial to achieving this;
- Good health and well-being: healthy workers and decent and safe working conditions increase the productive capacity of the workforce;
- Quality education: education, while an outcome in itself, is viewed as a means to obtain a decent job. According to Sustainable Development Goal 4, quality education is critical to the creation of sustainable development. It improves the quality of life. Over 265 million children are currently out of school and 22 per cent of them are of primary school age. Even those children who are attending school are lacking basic skills in reading and mathematics. Poor quality education is caused in some instances by lack of adequately trained teachers and poor condition of schools, particularly in rural areas. To address these concerns, there is a need for investment in educational scholarships, teacher training workshops, building of schools and improvement of water and electricity access to schools;
- Gender equality: closing gender gaps in employment, ensuring decent work for all women and equal pay for work of equal value is key to achieving gender equality; Sustainable Development Goal 5 aims at providing women with equal access to educational facilities, health care and decent work in order to enhance the development of sustainable economies. Implementing legal frameworks which will eliminate gender-based pay disparities and ensuring equal pay for work of equal value regardless of gender is very important. Harmful practices like sexual harassment, which tend to predominantly affect women, will have to be dealt with decisively and eliminated at the workplace;
- Clean water and sanitation: investments in water and sanitation can create paid and decent jobs and contribute to sustainable development. Sustainable Development Goal 6 seeks to ensure access to clean water for all and that there is sufficient fresh water. Water scarcity, poor water quality and inadequate sanitation nega-

tively impact food security, livelihood choices and educational opportunities for poor families. There is a risk of reduced access to fresh water by 2050, and at least one in four people is likely to live in a country affected by chronic or recurring shortages of fresh water. There must be an increased investment in management of freshwater, ecosystems and sanitation facilities on a local level in several developing countries in Sub-Saharan Africa, Central Asia, Southern Asia, Eastern Asia and South-Eastern Asia;

- Affordable and clean energy: international guidelines for a just transition towards environmentally sustainable economies and societies for all are based on the principles of decent work;
- Industry, innovation and infrastructure: industrial development is crucial to the world of work, and decent work is seen as fundamental to making such development inclusive, innovative and socially sustainable;
- Reduced inequalities: decent work, with its emphasis on a fair income, security in the workplace and social protection for individuals and families, is a direct means to reduce inequalities in income, wealth and economic influence;
- Sustainable cities and communities: the creation of decent work opportunities is fundamental to sustainable urban development and a decent work agenda for urbanization is understood to make cities more productive, inclusive and sustainable;
- Responsible consumption and production: decent work for all, in particular green jobs, is expected to contribute to making development environmentally sustainable;
- Climate action: climate change action requires active involvement from the world of work and should benefit from the application of the decent work agenda. Sustainable Development Goal 13 acknowledges that climate change is a global challenge. It has a disruptive effect on the national economies. It requires solutions to be coordinated at the international level to help developing countries move towards a low-carbon economy. In 2016 the Paris Agreement was concluded wherein all countries agreed to strive

to limit global temperature rise to well below 2 degrees centigrade. As of April 2018, 175 countries had ratified the Paris Agreement and ten developing countries had submitted their first iteration of their national adaptation plans for responding to climate change;

- Life below water: decent work for all, including fair remuneration and working conditions to the world's seafarers and fishers, is a foundation for conserving marine resources and reducing overfishing. Oceans and seas are vital conduits for trade and transportation. They must be carefully managed since they play a critical role in sustainable development. Due to the important role of the oceans and the seas it is important that those who work in that arena are protected from abusive and exploitative working conditions. To achieve this, the ILO Work in Fishing Convention No. 188 sets out binding requirements to address the main issues concerning work on-board fishing vessels including occupational safety and health and medical care at sea, rest periods, written working agreements and social protection;

- Life on land: ensuring that protecting the terrestrial environment is integrated into poverty-reducing national and local development strategies requires a focus on decent work for all land workers;

- Peace, justice and strong institutions: effective and inclusive institutions that promote decent work for all, based on respect for international labour standards and shaped through social dialogue are fundamental to just and peaceful societies and participative decision-making. The threats of international homicide, violence against children, human trafficking and sexual violence are some of the challenges that must be addressed in order to promote peaceful and inclusive societies for sustainable development. Approximately 28.5 per cent of primary school age children who are out of school live in conflict-ridden areas. These problems are exacerbated by the absence of the rule of law in some countries due to corruption in State institutions. This results in monies that could be used for development being lost through corruption. There must be an effort to reduce all forms of violence and eliminate all forms of abuse, exploitation and torture of children. There must be a concerted effort to reduce corruption and bribery in all forms through development of effective, accountable and transparent measures at all national levels. This will restore the rule of law, which is important for sustainable development.

AVINASH GOVINDJEE AND
THANDO QOTOYI

References

Arnesen, Richard J. (1987). "Meaningful Work and Market Socialism", Ethics 97(3), 517–545.

Bolton, Sharon C. (2007). *Dimensions of Dignity at Work*. Butterworth-Heinemann.

Dejours, Christophe (2006). "Subjectivity, Work and Action", Critical Horizons 7(1), 45–62.

Deranty, Jean-Philippe and Craig MacMillan (2012). "The ILO's Decent Work Initiative: Suggestions for an Extension of the Notion of 'Decent Work'", Journal of Social Philosophy 43(4), 386–405.

Gross, James A. (2010). *A Shameful Business: The Case for Human Rights at the American Workplace*. Cornell University Press.

International Labour Organization (1999). Decent Work: Report of the Director-General-International Labour Conference (87th Session). International Labour Office.

International Labour Organization (2008). ILO Declaration on Social Justice for a Fair Globalization.

MacNaughton, Gillian and Diane F. Frey (2016). "Decent Work, Human Rights and the Sustainable Development Goals", Georgetown Journal of International Law 47, 607–663.

Rawls, John (1971). *A Theory of Justice*. Harvard University Press.

United Nations General Assembly (1948). Universal Declaration of Human Rights.

17. Democracy

Origins of democracy

The *idea* and *value* of democracy is better understood than the *concept* of democracy. This is because while the *idea* of democracy renders itself to an intuitive understanding, there is no singular meaning or unique set of attributes the presence of which could ascribe the polity as democratic. Democracy is everywhere approved, though its true meaning is almost nowhere understood.

While ancient City States of Greece are credited for the idea of democracy, similar understandings have existed elsewhere as well, including in ancient India and Rome (Sen, 1999). The term democracy emerged from 'demokratia', *demos* referring to common people, and *Kratia* or *Kratos* signifying '*rule by*' or '*to rule*'. Literally translated, democracy implied 'rule by the people' or 'rule by the citizens'. In this way, democracy was distinguished from aristocracy (rule of few) and monarchy (rule of one). Ancient Greeks practised what is referred to as direct democracy, where an assembly of all citizens directly participated in framing of laws and policy, while officeholders were selected by lots (Dahl, 1998). That said, ancient understanding of democracy was far from inclusive, as women, slaves and *metoikos* (resident aliens) were not considered citizens and not included within the democratic process.

Yet democracy's near-universal appeal is only of recent origin. For long, democracy was condemned and, in some cases, outrightly rejected. As democracy's claim rested on rule of numbers, and not on any other virtue, from Plato and Aristotle through Kant and Hegel, democracy was understood as incompatible with good rule. This was especially true of the early nineteenth century, where fear of class rule was associated with mob rule and disorder. On the whole it was considered to be – (a) *unreasonable* for its failure to adequately utilize existing capacities, and (b) *unfair* for its failure to sufficiently reward existing merits (Levin, 1992).

Those times have long changed, and even though democracy is not universally practised, it is considered a universal value – a solution to all socio-political-economic ills. Modern understandings of democracy have adopted *kratos* (rule) of *demos* (people) as the starting point. A widely accepted understanding of democracy is found in the Vienna Declaration and Programme of Action (1993), which provides 'Democracy is based on the freely expressed will of the people to determine their own political, economic, social and cultural systems and their full participation in all aspects of their lives.' Thus, democracy is considered to be a system of governance *of*, *for* and *by* the people. Nowadays, States label themselves as democratic, irrespective of the particular political arrangement they adopt. Its appeal stems from *first*, its acknowledgment that all people are free and equal; *second*, recognition of the ability of people to know what is best for them; and *third*, its focus on preventing abuse of power of State. The last is of particular value. Concentration of power in the hands of few would eventually corrupt their working. Democracy prevents such a situation by spreading the power among all, in the process empowering them to take decisions for themselves. Only through such empowerment could public welfare be realized.

I   Ideals and institutions of democracy

Democracy, on a rudimentary level, could thus be considered as an institution for arranging political power through self-rule by a politically constituted social group. This understanding, however, marked the initial limits of unanimity as regards understanding of democracy. Over the years, scholars have attempted to further this understanding, and their efforts could broadly be classified into two frames of reference – normative attempts, which includes ascertaining appropriate *ideals*, the presence of which would render a polity as democratic, and empirical attempts, which focuses on ascertaining *empirically observable attributes/elements* (institutions) common among polities that refer to themselves as democratic. Combining the two, democracy could be understood as incorporating both, political ideals (autonomy, liberty, equality, fraternity, self-governance, civic mindedness, etc.) and institutions (inclusive suffrage, free and fair elections, right to run for office, guaranteeing legal entitlements, protection of free and fair expression, associational autonomy, alternative information protected by law, etc.) designed to realize them (Sen, 1999).

Expanding on the above, democracy could be said to comprise of the following (Dahl, 1998; Held, 2006):

1. Individuals' (citizens) interests are affected by decisions of the collective;
2. every individual is of equal worth;
3. every individual is endowed with the capability to ascertain what is good or bad for themselves and the collective;
4. public debates and deliberations involving meaningful expression of interests and preferences by all, individually and/or collectively (i.e. through political parties) are likely to produce better decisions over the long run;
5. in the event the above is unable to render a common outcome, final decisions could be arrived at by means of voting by participating individuals through the application of the one-person-one vote principle.

Further engagement with the idea of democracy leads to additional queries; for instance, if democracy is rule by the people, it would necessitate an enquiry into who 'the people' are and 'why democracy at all?', i.e. what is the justification for having a political setup of the nature of democracy. The first query is an obvious outcome of the understanding of democracy, i.e. democracy is rule of people. People can be understood from everyone to very few acting either individually or as a sub-unit within the larger collective. Similarly, 'rule' could imply everyone participating actively in governance to few *rulers* merely acting in the interests of the ruled. As a consequence, the concept of democracy is often qualified – liberal, guided, direct, deliberative, participatory, representative, etc. (Held, 2006).

Addressing the second, Sen argues that the value of democracy lies in its fivefold contribution to political lives – *firstly*, by enabling political rights and freedoms it positively contributes to human life and well-being of individuals as social beings. *Secondly*, it empowers people to express and garner support for their claims and opinions as regards political issues within a larger collective; *thirdly*, by promoting associational interactions, it gets diverse groups to participate; *fourthly*, democratic processes keep the government responsible and accountable, and, *finally*, democratic practices help both the individual and society to conceptualize and better articulate their needs, values, priorities and duties, through public discussions, and exchange of information, views and analyses (Sen, 1999).

II Democracy and development

While there is broad acceptance of the proposition that democracy and human development are intrinsically linked, the dynamics of their linkage raise complex and dialectical concerns. Two in particular stand out: *one*, whether democracy and development are conflicting (mutually limiting) or complementary (mutually reinforcing) notions; and *two*, in the event of the latter, whether democracy is a *precondition* for human development or a *product* of a level or form of development (Barsh, 1992). The conflict perspective argues that democracy impedes development by waylaying tough policy choices required for development but that carry the potential to induce disruptions and dislocations in social and economic life. Compatibility viewpoint, on the other hand, suggests that democracy facilitates development by disciplining crucial drivers of development including the markets, trade and investment processes. It does so by stressing efficiency, addressing inequalities and managing inevitable conflicts within a rule of law framework, and in the process securing sustainability of development.

In response to the second concern, scholars have attempted to empirically ascertain existence and direction of a demonstrable correlation between democracy and development. However, studies in this regard, though suggestive, remain inconclusive. So, while both a negative and positive correlation have been found, there are those who remain agnostic of any such correlation. On the extreme, empirical comparative attempts to establish causal relations between the two have been outrightly rejected for being unpersuasive on account of poor data and suspect methodology (Bardhan, 1999). Normatively, though, democracy, development and human rights form a crucial trio in the contemporary political, sociological and ideological language of legitimacy. Failure of States to proclaim a commitment to these notions places their national and international legitimacy at risk. Attainment of these values and degree thereof, on the other hand, remain contingent on the underlying social, cultural and structural values, realities and conditions prevalent in the societies, with each polity generating varying institutional arrangements to accommodate different trade-offs among the three (Sen, 1999).

III   Challenges to democracy: democracy on the retreat

In the decades post the Cold War, it had seemed that democracy and modernization had won the epic battle against communism and authoritarianism. However contemporary times has put that hubris to the test. Recent studies have expressed concerns over the decline of democracy across the globe marked by growing disenchantment with and declining trust in political elites, democratic process and institutions.

A key driver of this democratic erosion is partisan polarization. In the past, high levels of homogeneity of the polity had been identified as an important factor for the success of democracy. Homogeneity fostered a sense of collective identity, which was considered crucial for sustenance of citizen self-government. The past is strewn with instances where loss of collective solidarity, and perceived threats to established national identities, have unravelled existing democratic systems and institutions (Issacharoff, 2018). In recent times too, such unravelling has occurred when democracies have been called upon to accommodate and sustain pluralistic polity within the existing democratic framework. Such accommodation often involves redistribution of power, representation and resources. Failure to do so is likely to reduce the quality of democracy, while attempts of inclusion are likely to result in a backlash fuelled by xenophobia and economic insecurity.

Politics of national identity and fear of 'other' have also helped construct new narratives about democracy that see any questioning of the existing political establishment (leaders, parties and their policies) as an attack on the institution of democracy itself. The brooding sense of alienation and marginalization, carefully cultivated among the polity by leaders engaging in identity politics, have fuelled rejection of any pluralist account of democracy. Politics no longer remains an arena for fair contestation among different ideas, instead it is recast as a permanent and vicious confrontation among sections of polity (Issacharoff, 2018). The result is an illiberal democracy, which is characterized by parliamentary supermajority translating into total control by the ruling party. These democracies promise efficiency and collective

purposes stemming from nationalistic pride, to be achieved through centralization of authority. Yet such directions deconsolidate democracy by decimating liberal norms including individual liberties, tolerance, due process, independence of judiciary, free press, transparency, civil society, etc. (Mounk, 2018).

On the other end of the spectrum, the ability of democracy to accommodate diffuse interests may contribute to the rise of what Fukuyama calls 'vetocracy', where 'special interests can veto measures harmful to themselves, making collective action for the common good exceedingly difficult to achieve' (Fukuyama, 2016). There remains the ever-present concern of such deliberations being hijacked by sectional interests by overwhelming a passive majority. The consequence is poor governance resulting in the rise of the three Cs – clientelism, cronyism and corruption – which may prove fatal for democracy (Issacharoff, 2018).

An unfortunate outcome of increasing sophistication of elections is the role played by corporate lobbying in political decision-making both at the national and international level. Though plurality of concerns emanating from the society and the need to mainstream them are often advanced as the rationale for lobbying, corporate lobbyists are concerned only with advancing interests of their clients who overwhelmingly are business interests. By attempting to influence policy decisions by influencing politicians, lobbyists supplant general public interests. The consequence is a post-democratic State, i.e. a State which though seemingly democratic, is in practice a managed democracy, where the policies of the State are a result of private and non-transparent interaction between the elected representatives and lobbyists (Paul-Erik, 2013).

Globalization by forcing integration and interdependence of economies has also fuelled economic insecurity and democratic deficit. On the one hand, it has contributed to States experiencing complex economic and political challenges, while on the other, it has significantly reduced the ability of States to adequately address them. Ease of global movements of resources (capital, goods, labour, money) and significant power wielded by transnational corporations have threatened the very concept of the welfare State, exacerbating social and economic insecurities (Fuchs and Klingemann, 2019). A stretched State is then forced to choose between international economic integration, national sovereignty and democratic legitimacy. Its inability to find an appropriate balance may further fracture the society and weaken democratic institutions by hastening the socio-economic exclusion of the less privileged. Failure to correct such a situation in the long run may threaten the very legitimacy of a democratic setup as a solution to the concerns of the masses.

IV Conclusion

Democracy is both a political system and political aspiration. Yet its meaning and roles remain a matter of hard contestation. As a concept it contains many conceptions and means different things to different people. On the one hand, democracy, both ideals and outcomes, are considered to be valuable and desirable for its ability to attain just, efficient, and stable ends in a society. On the other hand, lived experiences militate against the intrinsic worth doctrine as a justification for democracy, as most common forms of political engagement often degenerate into a power struggle, and as a result stultify and corrupt the polity. In recent decades, while even stable democracies have been severely tested by wide-ranging challenges, such as widening inequalities, the rise of ultranationalism and lack of bipartisan cooperation, their continuing failure to meaningfully address these issues has remained a major cause of concern. This seeming crisis in democracy has, on the one hand, intensified anxieties with performance of democracy, while on the other, enhanced the attractiveness of alternatives such as the Chinese model of 'democratic centralism' or the Singaporean model of 'soft developmental' authoritarianism. Unless future understandings of democracy are able to respond, both nor-matively and institutionally, to its discontents, including the perception and reality of increasing inequalities and disempowerment, democracy runs the risk of losing both its legitimacy and appeal.

DANIEL MATHEW

References

Bardhan, Pranab (1999). 'Democracy and Development: A Complex Relationship', available at: https://eml.berkeley.edu/~webfac/bardhan/papers/BardhanDemoc.pdf.

Barsh, Russel Lawrence (1992). 'Democratization and Development', Human Rights Quarterly (14), 120.

Dahl, Robert A. (1998). *On Democracy*. 2nd edition. Yale University.

Fuchs, Dieter and Hans-Dieter Klingemann (2019). 'Globalization, Populism and Legitimacy in Contemporary Democracy' in Ursula van Beek (ed.), *Democracy under Threat: Crisis of Legitimacy*. Palgrave Macmillan.

Fukuyama, Francis (2016). 'America: The Failed State', *Prospect*, 30, available at: https://www.prospectmagazine.co.uk/magazine/america-the-failed-state-donald-trump accessed 25 September 2020.

Held, David (2006). *Models of Democracy*. 3rd edition. Polity Press.

Issacharoff, Samuel (2018). 'Democracy's Deficits', The University of Chicago Law Review 2(85), 485.

Paul-Erik, Korvela (2013). 'Postdemocracy and the End of History', Economic and Political Studies 1(1), 136.

Levin, Michael (1992). *The Spectre of Democracy: The Rise of Modern Democracy as Seen By Its Critics*. Palgrave Macmillan.

Mounk, Yascha (2018). *The People vs. Democracy*. Harvard University Press.

Sen, Amartya (1999). 'Democracy as a Universal Value', Journal of Democracy 3(10).

18.   Duty to Cooperate

Defining the term 'duty to cooperate' requires clarifying if the duty is legally recognized and its content. The verb 'to cooperate' is generally defined as 'to work together for a particular purpose, or to be helpful by doing what someone asks you to do' (Cambridge Dictionary). Thus, cooperation can entail either the coordination of efforts, or the provision of assistance. Depending on the area concerned, the legal recognition and content of the duty to cooperate may vary widely.

A mere ability to cooperate in general international law

An ability to cooperate

Traditionally, international law is described as the legal system governing the coexistence of independent sovereign States (Lotus case). State sovereignty is a twofold principle, expressing itself through negative and positive effects. Firstly, it implies that States abstain from various actions in order to respect the equal sovereignty of other States (as expressed in the non-interference principle, or the prohibition of the use of force). However international law goes further and also aims to coordinate States' efforts in the 'achievement of common aims' (Lotus case). Here, sovereignty finds a positive form of expression in allowing States to cooperate (notably to adopt treaties defining their respective obligations or creating institutions).

Sovereignty confers upon States an ability to cooperate, but a legally framed one. Indeed, when States choose to cooperate, they have to do so 'in good faith' (Nuclear test case, 1974, para. 46). This means that they have to negotiate in good faith (with the aim of attaining agreement) and also implement and interpret the agreement in good faith (in accordance with the spirit of the norm) (Kolb, 2000).

A general, but 'soft' duty to cooperate

The UN Charter defines 'international cooperation in solving international problems of an economic, social, cultural, or humanitarian character, [. . .]' as one of the purposes of the Organization (Article 1 §3). Moreover, Articles 55 and 56 create an obligation for all Member States to cooperate with the Organization in the achievement of economic and social development, in order to promote solutions to international economic, social, health, and related problems; and universal respect of human rights. States also have a duty to cooperate among themselves in order to achieve these purposes (UNGA Declaration on Principles of International Law concerning friendly relations and cooperation among States in accordance with the Charter of the United Nations, Resolution 2625, Annex, §1), but this duty remains only a 'soft' one (i.e. not legally binding).

As a preliminary conclusion, international law provides States with the ability to use certain legal means to cooperate and encourages them to do so. In practice, the growing importance of global issues has led States to use their ability to cooperate more and more and to progressively create a proper duty to cooperate in some areas of international law.

The emergence of a legal duty to cooperate in some specific areas

A vague and soft duty to cooperate for development

In the 1970s, decolonized States advocated strongly for the establishment of a new and more equitable international economic order (hereinafter NIEO). As a consequence, the UNGA called for the development of an international economic cooperation based on equity (UNGA Resolution 2626) and adopted in 1974 a declaration (UNGA Resolution 3201) and a programme of action (UNGA Resolution 3202) on the establishment of a NIEO. The declaration defines the principles governing the NIEO (§4) and calls for a broader cooperation among States for the benefits of developing countries (notably through the extension of assistance and the use of economic preferential and non-reciprocal treatment). The programme of action makes a similar call and identifies more specific actions to these ends. In parallel, the 1974 Charter of Economic Rights and Duties of States (UNGA Resolution 3281) defined the obligations of States in the establishment of the NIEO and asked them to cooperate, taking into account specific interests of developing countries. Finally, the Declaration on the Right to Development adopted in 1986 (UNGA Resolution 41/128) affirms the States' duty to cooperate 'in ensuring development and eliminating obstacles to development' (Article 3 §3). However, it uses vague terms, leaving States with a wide margin of discretion on adequate measures to be taken. In conclusion, all the instruments on NIEO call for a broader cooperation between States, based on equity (requiring provision of assistance to the benefit of developing countries). However, because of their recommendatory nature or the wording used, the duty to cooperate for development remains 'soft' in its nature and vague in its content.

A precise but soft duty to cooperate in the realization of human rights

Several of the above-mentioned instruments (UN Charter, Articles 1 §3, 55 and 56; NIEO resolutions) also call for cooperation in the realization of human rights. More importantly, three of the human rights conventions contain a general provision providing that States parties shall undertake to take measures to implement the convention, individually and through international assistance and cooperation (International Covenant on Economic Social and Cultural Rights (hereinafter ICESCR), Article 2; Convention on the Rights of the Child (hereinafter CRC), Article 4; Convention on the Rights of Persons with Disabilities (hereinafter CRPD), Article 4). Based on preparatory works, some authors (Philip Alston and Gerard Quinn (1987). 'The Nature and Scope of States Parties' Obligations under the International Covenant on Economic, Social and Cultural Rights', Human Rights Quarterly, (9), 156–229) have contested that a provision such as Article 2 of ICESCR create a general duty to cooperate, while others, using interpretations given by the ESCR Committee (General Comment 3, 1990), argued in favour of the existence of such a general duty (Sepulveda, 2006). However, if general comments of the Committee are authoritative interpretations of the treaty, they do not bind parties. Thus, in my opinion, States have only a 'soft' and programmatic duty to cooperate in the implementation of these conventions. Because of the vague wording used, the same conclusion may be reached for additional provisions promoting cooperation on specific matters (CRC, Articles 24 §4 and 28 §3; ICESCR, Articles 11 and 15 §4). The only exception to be mentioned is Article 32 of CRPD, which provides that parties 'will undertake' appropriate cooperative measures to support national implementation of the Convention.

The content of States' duty to cooperate is nevertheless precise. Article 32 of CRPD specifies some of the appropriate measures to be taken (inclusion of persons with disabilities in international cooperation programmes, capacity-building and exchange of scientific knowledge, technical and economic assistance). Similarly, interpretations given by the ESCR Committee allow us to identify respective duties of both developed and developing States that are parties to the ICESCR. The former shall abstain from and prevent activities that could have a negative impact abroad, and also provide technical and economic assistance, while the latter shall identify their needs and actively seek assistance (Sepulveda, 2006). General comments and concluding observations of the CRC Committee identify similar obligations for parties to the CRC (Wouter Vandenhole (2009). 'Economic, Social and Cultural Rights in the CRC: Is there a Legal Obligation to Cooperate internationally for Development?', International Journal of Children's Rights (17), 23–63).

A duty to cooperate in international environmental law

A soft general duty to cooperate

In international environmental law, the duty to cooperate takes different forms depending on its 'raison d'être', which could be 'a spirit of global partnership' or 'a transboundary context' (Dupuy and Viñuales, 2018). This distinction is useful because only the latter form of the duty is of a customary nature (see below). However, in my opinion, the former represents a general duty and a further distinction may be made depending on whether cooperation aims to preserve the environment or to assist developing countries. Both aspects have been promoted in the main recommandatory instruments (Stockholm Declaration, Rio Declaration, Agenda 21) and in multilateral environmental agreements. Nevertheless, these conventions use a soft language. They affirm the duty to cooperate in the preservation of the environment using terms like 'should' (UN Convention to Combat Desertification, Article 12), 'as far as possible' (UN Convention on Biological Diversity, Article 5); or they leave measures to be taken at States' discretion

(Convention on the Conservation of Migratory Species of Wild Animals, Article II), or to be defined in accordance with national priorities and capabilities (Ozone Convention, Article 2.2; UN Framework Convention on Climate Change, Article 4). The same conclusion may be reached for equity-based duties to cooperate, as these agreements merely provide that States parties should cooperate in order to promote financial and technical assistance toward developing countries. To conclude, the legal nature of the instruments or their wording prevents them from creating more than a 'soft' and general duty to cooperate in a spirit of global partnership.

A customary duty to cooperate in the prevention of transboundary damage
States have a customary duty to cooperate in order to prevent transboundary environmental damages in the context of shared natural resources (Pulp Mills case), and more broadly for every activity that could have a significant adverse impact in a transboundary context (Costa Rica/Nicaragua case, 2015, para. 104). This is a procedural obligation linked to the States' obligation of due diligence (Nuclear advisory opinion; Iron Rhine case; Pulp Mills case), requiring them to prevent or at least mitigate transboundary environmental damages. When there is a potential risk of transboundary damage, the State of origin shall conduct an environmental impact assessment (EIA), and when, and only when, the EIA confirmed this risk, they have a duty to cooperate in order to identify appropriate preventive measures (Costa Rica/ Nicaragua Case, para. 104). The duty takes the form of a complex of three procedural customary duties (see below) (Owen McIntyre (2011). 'The World Court's Ongoing Contribution to International Water Law: The Pulp Mills Case between Argentina and Uruguay". Water Alternatives 4(2), 124–144), also stated in several international instruments (e.g. Rio declaration, OECD principles on transboundary pollution, Espoo Convention, Convention on long-range transboundary air pollution).

Firstly, the State of origin shall give prior notification to potentially affected States of the potential transboundary harmful activity (Costa Rica/Nicaragua case) including all technical information (data and their analyses) and should not take any decision on the activity within a period of six months (Project of article on transboundary damages, Article 8). Some

celerity is required in the specific case of imminent risks (notification shall be made without delay). This is a customary obligation (Corfu case), also stated in several conventions (e.g. Convention on the Law of the Sea, Convention on the prevention of marine pollution by dumping of wastes and other matter, Convention on early notification of a nuclear accident).

Secondly, the duty to cooperate implies a constant exchange of information during the implementation of the activity (through bilateral or multilateral channels) and in a timely manner, in order to allow for consultations on appropriate preventive measures (Project of article on transboundary damages, Article 12).

Finally, before and during the implementation of the activity, the State of origin shall consult 'in good faith' potentially affected States (Costa Rica/Nicaragua case, para. 104). This means that States shall not go through a mere formal process of negotiations (North Sea continental shelf case, para. 85). They shall take into consideration adverse proposals or interests, but this does not imply a right of veto or of co-decision to potentially affected States (Lac Lanoux case).

A duty to cooperate within spaces beyond national jurisdiction

States parties to the Antarctic Treaty have a duty to cooperate, but in a limited spectrum: to ensure the freedom of scientific investigations in Antarctica (Article 2). Parties shall cooperate with international organizations (by establishing working relations) and with each other (through exchange of: information regarding plans for scientific programmes; of scientific personnel; and of scientific observations and results – Article 3). The treaty on outer space defines a similar, but broader duty (Article 1). The exploration and the use of outer space shall be guided by the principle of cooperation (Articles III and IX), which supposes prior consultation before proceeding with activities that could potentially cause harmful interference with activities of other States undergoing peaceful exploration and use of outer space.

Similarly, the Convention on the Law of the Sea affirms the States' duty to cooperate in order to prevent and minimize marine pollution (Articles 198–200), which is now recognized as a customary obligation (Mox case, para. 82). More broadly, the duty to cooperate represents one of the main features of the legal regime applying to the high sea and the deep seabed. In the high seas, States have to cooperate for the prevention and repression of some illicit activities (Articles 100, 108 and 109), but more importantly in the conservation and management of marine biological resources (Articles 63–66 and 117–118). Even if the customary nature of this last duty is contested (Ndiaye and Wolfrum, 2007) and treaty provisions remain vague, some authors consider that it requires States to become members and participate in the activities of regional fisheries organizations (Rayfuse, 2005). Finally, the entire legal regime on the deep seabed (called the 'Area') is rooted in the objective of cooperation. The Convention creates a specific institution (the Authority) in charge of managing resources of the Area, that are recognized as the common heritage of humankind and whose benefits shall be equitably shared between States. Parties shall also cooperate among them and with the Authority in order to promote the transfer of technology and the exchange of scientific knowledge with developing countries.

Concluding remarks

The duty to cooperate illustrates the ongoing evolution of international law; the shift from an independent to a cooperative sovereignty (Wolfgang Freidman (1964). *The Changing Structure of International Law*. Stevens & Sons; Franz Perez (2000). *Cooperative Sovereignty: From Independence to Interdependence in the Structure of International Environmental Law*. Kluwer Law International), and from an international society to an international community. In the words of R. Wolfrum, this duty 'balances the principle of sovereignty of States and thus ensures that community interests are taken into account vis-à-vis individualistic State interests' (sep. op., Mox case, last paragraph). Its scope in international law goes further than the most salient areas identified here and it also applies in dispute settlement (Wolfrum, 2015, §38), the repression of genocide (Orna Ben-Naftali and Miri Sharon (2007). 'What the ICJ Did Not Say about the Duty to Punish Genocide', Journal of International Criminal Justice (5), 859–874), and might even find applications in cybersecurity (Akiko Takano (2018). 'Due Diligence Obligations and Transboundary Environmental Harm: Cybersecurity Applications', Laws 7(4), 1–12).

As shown, while the duty to cooperate is of growing importance in international law, it is of variable intensity. In a broad perspective, when the duty to cooperate is based on equity and expresses itself through the provision of assistance to developing countries (for development, or in the implementation of human rights) it has a 'soft' legal value. When the duty tends to preserve States' interests (related to potential damages or spaces beyond jurisdiction), it benefits from a greater legal recognition. Thus, we shall not conclude too quickly on the transformation of international law. Indeed, even if cooperation is widely promoted, community interests are only properly taken into account and genuinely recognized when they coincide with individual State interests.

JULIEN DELLAUX

References

Arts, Karin and Atabongawung Tamo (2016). 'The Right to Development in International Law: New Momentum Thirty Years Down the Line?', Netherland International Law Review (63), 221–249.

Dupuy, Pierre-Marie and Jorge E. Viñuales (2015). *International Environmental Law*. Cambridge University Press.

Kolb, Robert (2000). *Le principe de bonne foi en droit international public: contribution à l'étude des principes généraux de droit*. Presses Universitaires de France.

Ndiaye, Tafsir Malick and Rüdger Wolfrum (2007). *Law of the Sea, Environmental Law and Settlement of Disputes*. Martinus Nijhoff Publishers.

Rayfuse, Rosemary (2005). 'To Our Children's Children's Children: From Promoting to Achieving Compliance in High Seas Fisheries', The International Journal of Marine and Coastal Law (20), 509–532.

Rothwell, Donald R. and Tim Stephens (2010). *The International Law of the Sea*. Hart Publishing.

Salomon, Margot E. (2007). *Global Responsibility for Human Rights: World Poverty and the Development of International Law*. Oxford University Press.

Peel, Jacqueline and Philippe Sands (2012). *Principles of International Environmental Law*. Cambridge University Press.

Sepulveda, Magdalena (2006). 'Obligations of International Assistance and Cooperation in an Optional Protocol to the International Covenant on Economic, Social and Cultural Rights', Netherland Quarterly of Human Rights 2(24), 271–303.

Wolfrum, Rüdiger (2015). 'Cooperation' in *Max Planck Encyclopaedia of Public International Law*, Oxford University Press.

19. Education

Introduction

The right to education is one of the most complex in human rights law and is a core component of the sustainable development agenda, with Sustainable Development Goal 4 (SDG 4) aiming to achieve "inclusive and equitable quality education and promote life-long learning opportunities for all" by 2030. The right has been classified as an economic right, a civil and political right, and a social and cultural right. According to the Committee on Social, Economic and Cultural Rights (CESCR), it is all of these, because it is central to the full realization of all rights. Education is therefore an empowerment right and enhances all rights and freedoms. Its violation, however, compounds other rights' violations and perpetuates poverty.

Since enshrined in the Universal Declaration of Human Rights (UDHR) 1948, there has been considerable progress worldwide in promoting access to education, especially at primary level. However, according to the May 2019 United Nations (UN) Economic and Social Council Report of the Secretary General, which records progress towards the achievement of the SDGs, "262 million children and youth aged 6 to 17 were still out of school in 2017" and over 50 per cent of children "are not meeting minimum proficiency standards in reading and mathematics". Plus, many developing countries lack the basic facilities for effective learning. Quality of education remains a challenge. Thus, it is clear that "(r)efocused efforts are needed to improve learning outcomes for the full life cycle, especially for . . . marginalized people in vulnerable settings". This is a worrying outlook. Given the disparities in the distribution of educational opportunities and education's importance, sustained international attention is urgent.

Developmental purpose of education

The empowering purpose of education and its link to human development is most obvious in the CESCR's General Comment 13, 1999. Education is described as "a human right in itself and an indispensable means of realizing other human rights". Education is the "primary vehicle" by which marginalized people "can lift themselves out of poverty" and participate fully.

Similarly, Article 1(4) of the UN's World Declaration on Education for All, 1990, recognizes that basic education underpins "life-long learning and human development". The link to sustainable development is clear in the Education for All: Meeting our Collective Commitments: The Dakar Framework for Action 2000, where education is described as critical to the attainment of sustainable development and peace, stability and effective global economic participation.

As an empowerment right, education serves multiple purposes: it enables the full development of human personality and the enjoyment of other rights; it liberates people; it capacitates participation; it is essential for socio-economic development; and it promotes global understanding.

The right to education in international and domestic law

The right to education is widely recognized in international human rights law and in many domestic constitutions.

Education rights are expressly included in the following instruments: the UDHR 1948; the Convention on the Elimination of All Forms of Racial Discrimination (ICERD) 1966; the Covenant on Economic, Social and Cultural Rights (ICESCR) 1966; the Convention on the Elimination of All Forms of Discrimination against Women (CEDAW) 1979; and the Convention on the Rights of the Child (CRC) 1989.

Many international instruments protect education rights for specific groups, for example: the Convention on the Rights of Persons with Disabilities, 2006; the Convention on the Protection of the Rights of All Migrant Workers and Members of their Families, 1990; the Convention Relating to the Status of Refugees, 1951; and the Declaration on the Rights of Indigenous People, 2007.

In regional law, the right to education is protected inter alia in the African Charter on Human and Peoples' Rights, 1981; the European Convention for the Protection of Human Rights and Fundamental Freedoms, 1953; the American Declaration of the Rights and Duties of Man, 1948; and the Revised Arab Charter on Human Rights 2004.

Numerous UN Declarations and UNESCO normative instruments address the right to education. These include: the UNESCO Convention against Discrimination in Education, 1960; the Convention on Technical and Vocational Education, 1989; the World Declaration on Education for All, 1990; the Dakar Framework for Action, 2000; and the Education 2030: Incheon Declaration and Framework for Action for the Implementation of SDG 4, 2015.

The central provisions protecting the right to education in international human rights law are the ICESCR's Articles 13 and 14 and the CRC's Articles 28 and 29, building on the ICESCR obligations. The two most important obligations, namely providing everyone with free compulsory primary education and access to education without discrimination, are also part of customary international law. The following State obligations are imposed: primary education shall be compulsory and available freely to all; if not secured at ratification, States parties must develop a plan to provide such education within two years, to be implemented within a reasonable period after ratification; secondary education shall be made generally available and accessible; while higher education shall be made equally accessible to all, based on capacity.

Despite the importance of economic, social and cultural rights (ESCR) in the human rights framework, it is difficult to determine whether a State party has satisfied its treaty obligations. Like most ESCRs, the right to education is subject to progressive realization. This gives States the flexibility to achieve full realization of ESCR over time through all appropriate means, with reference to the maximum extent of available resources, and individual State disparities. However, progressive realization does not entitle States to strip the right of meaningful content, nor deliberately halt or retrogress on progress. Instead, States must move expeditiously and effectively towards full realization. Moreover, if States are to meet the SDG 4 targets, they must allocate the maximum of their available resources to free, quality, public education for all.

At domestic level, the primary obligation to implement the right to education rests with the State, which must make education available and accessible and ensure equal educational opportunities. The State's obligations include both positive and negative dimensions. The positive obligation encompasses the social aspect of the right to receive an education. The negative obligation means that individuals must be free to choose between State-based and private education. The State must follow a policy of non-interference in private matters, but ensure that private schools conform to minimum standards.

In General Comment 13 the CESCR sets out the three levels of State obligations, namely to respect, protect and fulfil. To respect requires the State to avoid measures that obstruct the enjoyment of the right to education. To protect is to ensure that third parties do not interfere with the right to education. To fulfil requires taking positive measures to facilitate education.

Common to all levels of education are the 4-A requirements. These are availability, accessibility, adaptability and acceptability. Availability requires "functioning educational institutions and programmes" in sufficient quantity. Adaptability means that education must be flexible to adapt to changing needs. Acceptability entails that the substance of education must be relevant, of good quality, and culturally appropriate. Accessibility means that educational institutions must be physically and economically accessible to everyone, without discrimination.

The content of the right to education

The right to education can be interpreted both widely and narrowly. The wider context refers to the entire educative process. In international human rights law, however, education is interpreted narrowly to include quality formal instruction imparted at various levels.

The vague normative content of the right to education has attracted criticism. Critiques include: the right is vague conceptually; the absolute right is confined to primary education; insufficient attention is given to other levels of education; schools are assumed to be the appropriate vehicle for the delivery of education; and there is an over-emphasis on access to education, not quality education.

In response, the CESCR has identified the minimum core content of each right that a State cannot diminish "under the pretext of permitted reasonable differences". The minimum core is the State's obligation to ensure the satisfaction of minimum essential levels of each ESCR.

Where a State fails to meet its obligations because of a lack of available resources, it must demonstrate that it has, as a priority, used all available resources to implement the minimum core of the right.

The minimum core for education encompasses five core obligations:

- Ensuring access to public educational institutions and programmes on a non-discriminatory basis;
- Ensuring that education conforms to the ICESCR Article 13(1) objectives;
- Providing free and compulsory primary education for all;
- Adopting and implementing a national educational strategy providing for secondary, higher and fundamental education;
- Ensuring free choice of education without interference, conforming to "minimum educational standards".

Although education is an ongoing lifelong process, international human rights law prioritizes the right to primary and basic education. The term "basic education" has its origins in the 1990 World Declaration, which shifted education strategies from primary education towards basic education. Article 1 describes basic education as a guarantee for everyone "to benefit from educational opportunities designed to meet their basic learning needs". These include learning tools and content required to develop full capacities. Thus, a basic education is one capable of satisfying the individual's basic learning needs, identified by the objectives of education. The standard, however, is a flexible one, because needs vary according to capacities and context.

In General Comments 11 and 13, the CESCR clarifies that whilst primary and basic education are not synonymous, they are interconnected, with primary education treated as the core constituent of basic education. Primary education is linked to the delivery of compulsory and free primary schooling, while basic education refers to an education with substantive content.

Article 13(2)(b) of the ICESCR provides that secondary education, although not compulsory, shall be made generally available and accessible in its different forms, including technical and vocational secondary education. This is to be achieved by the progressive introduction of free education, aiming at better accessibility for all.

Technical and vocational education and training straddles the rights to education and to work. It includes formal and informal learning about "aspects of the educational process involving . . . technologies and related sciences, and the acquisition of practical skills . . . and knowledge relating to occupations. . .".

The ICESCR provides that higher education "shall be made equally accessible to all, on the basis of capacity, by every appropriate means, and in particular by the progressive introduction of free education". Capacity is assessed by reference to expertise and experience. Higher education includes all types of education provided by universities, colleges, etc. It is intended for students having completed a secondary education, and whose objective is the acquisition of a title, certificate or diploma. These programmes are specialized and prepare students for professional occupations.

Monitoring and enforcement of the right to education

The CESCR oversees State parties' implementation of ESCR. The Optional Protocol to the ICESCR creates complaint mechanisms and capacitates the CESCR to investigate grave violations. Similarly, the Committee on the Rights of the Child has oversight over the CRC obligations. The UN's Special Rapporteur on the Right to Education is an independent expert responsible for gathering information on the implementation of the right to education. The Rapporteur conducts country visits, receives individual complaints and identifies measures for enhancing the right.

Regional human rights bodies are also responsible for monitoring their Member States' implementation of regional human rights treaties.

SDG 4 – quality education

Building on the Millennium Development Goals (MDGs), the UN adopted the SDGs in 2015 as shared global goals for development. SDG 4, which aims to ensure inclusive and equitable quality education and improve lifelong learning opportunities for all by 2030, is broader than its MDG predecessors. SDG 4 encompasses the multidimensional aspects of education and focuses on quality of education and enhancing effective learning. In addition, countries have expressed commitment to the

Incheon Declaration, affirming their support to SDG 4 and the 2030 Agenda. The adoption of the Education 2030 Framework for Action followed. The Framework provides implementation guidance. The term SDG 4-Education 2030 encompasses both SDG 4 and the education-related targets in the other SDGs. SDG 4, itself, has ten associated targets which are universally applicable.

SDG 4-Education 2030 is aligned with the international right to education. It seeks to ensure the full enjoyment of human rights, especially education, as fundamental to achieving sustainable development. Although not legally binding, SDG 4 sets clear State commitments to align domestic law with the right to education. This provides an opportunity to introduce reforms and ensure that State practice adapts. The OHCHR has confirmed that all SDGs must be implemented by States in a manner consistent with their international law obligations and the political goals set by SDG 4 should be seen as a means of implementing that right. Thus, the Special Rapporteur has explained in her 2019 Report to the UN Human Rights Council that: "[t]he fact that States commit both politically and legally to education does not mean that measures taken to comply with the realization of either are mutually exclusive. Rather, these commitments aggregate . . . each other, requiring States to ensure that efforts taken to achieve SDG 4-Education 2030 . . . are human rights compliant".

JOANNA BOTHA

References

Beiter, Klaus Dieter (2005). *The Protection of the Right to Education by International Law: Including a Systematic Analysis of Article 13 of the International Covenant on Economic, Social and Cultural Rights*. Brill.

CESCR (1990). General Comment No. 3: The Nature of States Parties' Obligations: Article 2(1). CESCR.

CESCR (1999). General Comment No. 11: Plans of Action for Primary Education: Article 14. CESCR.

CESCR (1999). General Comment No. 13: The Right to Education: Article 13. CESCR.

CESCR (2017). General Comment No. 24: State Obligations under the ICESCR in the Context of Business Activities. CESCR.

Coomans, Fons (1995). "Clarifying the Core Elements of the Right to Education" in Fons Coomans and Godefridus J.H. Hoof (eds), *The Right to Complain about Economic, Social and Cultural Rights*. SIM special.

Kalantry, Sital, Jocelyn Getgen Kestenbaum, and Arrigg Koh Stephen (2017). "Enhancing Enforcement of Economic, Social, and Cultural Rights Using Indicators: A Focus on the Right to Education in the ICESCR" in Manisuli Ssenyongo (ed.), *Economic, Social and Cultural Rights*. Routledge.

McCowan, Tristan (2010). "Reframing the Universal Right to Education", Comparative Education 4(46), 509.

UNESCO and the Right to Education Initiative (2019). *Right to Education Handbook*. UNESCO.

UNHRC (2019). Report of the Special Rapporteur on the right to education: The Implementation of the Right to Education and Sustainable Development Goal 4 in the Context of the Growth of Private Actors in Education. A/HRC/41/37 para. 6.

20.   Enabling International Environment

Introduction

The enabling international environment (EIE) refers generally to the international conditions that facilitate and support sustainable development policies. Domestic strategies to progress sustainable development objectives and meet social and economic needs of communities cannot be implemented successfully in a globalized world without an international economic environment that enables countries to do so. This environment would include international economic rules and policies, such as in the arena of trade, finance and investment, that are systematically coherent and conducive to sustainable development, as well as institutions of international law and global economic governance that are participatory, equitable, non-discriminatory and inclusive of all nations and communities.

The importance attached to this enabling international environment is reflected in State commitments to the creation of such an environment in successive international agreements on sustainable development, including the recent United Nations (UN) 2030 Agenda for Sustainable Development, and the Monterrey Consensus and Addis Ababa Action Agenda (AAAA) for Financing for Development.

But the concept of an enabling international environment also has a longer contested history in international law and the policy and practice of international development cooperation. The EIE notion is rooted in post-colonial demands for a just and equitable international economic order and in continuing calls for strengthening and advancing the voice and representation of developing countries in international economic law and policy-making processes. It is also a concept that reflects a technicization of a political project of transformative restructuring at the global economic level but one that continues to serve as a useful countervailing narrative to those that view development as primarily a domestic concern of individual States.

Beyond operational realities of development policy-making, the notion of an enabling environment therefore engages wider debates on economic justice, global redistribution and economic sovereignty of States and communities in the Global South. It invites conversations about the nature and impact of international economic law (IEL) on development and the relationship between States, communities and transnational capital and the role of international law and global economic policy-making in structuring the engagement between these different actors.

From the NIEO to an enabling international environment

Contemporary articulations of the need for creating an enabling international environment for sustainable development can be traced back to the decolonization period. The calls by newly independent States for a reclamation of national sovereignty over natural resources and a transformation of the international economic order to accommodate their specific needs and development trajectories began soon after formal independence from their colonizers. For post-colonial States, economic independence came hand-in-hand with political self-determination and concerted efforts were made by these States collectively to reorient the imperial system of international economic relations that privileged multinational capital from the colonial metropolitan centres. Post-colonial States sought to reclaim control over domestic economic policies and engagement with the economic exterior.

From the Bandung Conference in 1955, which represented the first collective attempt by non-European States to reframe the tenets of the imperial geopolitical and legal international order, to the landmark UN General Assembly resolutions on 'Permanent Sovereignty over Natural Resources' (UNGA 1803, 1962) and the 'Declaration on the Establishment of a New International Economic Order' (UNGA, 3201, 1974), developing countries have consistently sought to place issues of economic concern firmly within the realm of the UN where they have greater voice and representation. Importantly, developing countries have continually resisted the conceptual and operational separation of 'political' and 'economic' spheres within the international law and institutions of global governance, arguing that issues of trade, finance and investment cannot be segmented and dealt with in silos without considering the broader systemic constraints of the asymmetrical global economy into which they have been inserted (Faundez, 2017).

Located within this broader historical legacy, one can view the EIE concept as part of the ongoing struggles of Third World States to position the UN as the appropriate forum for international economic law-making and development cooperation in the face of attempts by former imperial powers and industrialized countries to shift the conceptual and operational debates to institutions they control, notably the International Monetary Fund (IMF), the World Bank and the Organization for Economic Cooperation and Development (OECD). Even as the period of neoliberal economic globalization took hold after the collapse of the Bretton Woods system in the late 1970s and the Third World debt crisis of the 1980s, developing countries have continued to steer demands for an equitable international economic order through the UN and its agencies, including through the Declaration on the Right to Development 1986 and more recent resolutions on international financial system and development, sovereign debt restructuring, international trade and development and illicit financial flows.

The notion of an enabling international environment remains a means through which countries of the Global South have continued to push the development agenda within the broader international fora for international economic law-making and development cooperation policy-making. It reflects the assertions of developing countries that the responsibility in overcoming sustainable development gaps lies less with the restructuring of domestic economies, à la Bank and Fund-led structural adjustment programmes (SAPs), and more with reconstituting their terms of engagement with a highly inequitable international economic order and correcting the maldistribution of resources resulting from these asymmetries.

Creating an enabling international environment

All contemporary agreements referring to an enabling international environment place primary responsibility on States to deliver national and international development objectives but call for a conducive external economic architecture to complement and support policies. For example, when discussing the means of implementation for the Sustainable Development Goals (SDGs), the UN 2030 Agenda reiterates that while the onus for delivering economic and social development remain the domain of nation States, 'national development efforts need to be supported by an enabling international economic environment' (UN, 2015a, para. 63). The concept of the EIE also pivots around the notion of a global partnership on development cooperation, such as the AAA outcome document starting with a 'strong political commitment to address the challenge of financing and creating an enabling environment at all levels for sustainable development in the spirit of *global partnership and solidarity*' (UN, 2015a, para. 1, emphasis added).

At the heart of contemporary commitments to establish an enabling international environment for sustainable development is a call to reorient the international legal, policy and regulatory landscape to support sustainable development objectives, including poverty reduction, economic growth, reduced inequalities, climate change adaptation and mitigation and access to health, education and other essential public services. This is premised on three intersecting concerns: (1) international support for policies and programmes at the national level to deliver sustainable development objectives, notably adequate financing on appropriate, equitable and reasonable terms; (2) removal of external impediments that preclude countries from taking action to meet sustainable development objectives, including the mobilization of domestic resources for sustainable development; and (3) systemic coherence to ensure coordination, coherence and consistency of the international monetary, financial and trading systems so that the rules and institutions of international economic law, regulation and governance do not undermine the former objectives.

Towards these ends, there have been several key demands that have featured consistently in calls by developing countries, civil society groups and the international organizations for an EIE.

First, international public finance is seen as a central plank of an EIE, including commitments to sustaining and increasing volumes of official development assistance (ODA), harmonizing ODA policies and practices and eliminating practices of 'tied aid' (UN, 2015b, paras 50–58).

Second, addressing debt and debt vulnerabilities and the instability of transnational financial flows is also seen as crucial to creating an EIE for sustainable development, notably supporting developing countries to attain long-term debt sustainability through coordinated policies on debt financing, debt relief and restructuring and debt management as well as strengthening international mechanisms for financial crises prevention, mitigation and resolution and regulating the volatility of cross-border capital flows (Akyüz, 2010).

Third, an EIE includes reforming the multilateral trade and transnational investment regime to remove built-in asymmetries in international trade and investment law that place constraints on development pathways of developing countries and to strengthen compliance with rules and policies which enable the use of trade and investment as 'an engine' for sustainable development (UN, 2015b). Here, commitments to recognize and implement special and differentiated treatment provisions and affirm the right of developing countries to take advantage of flexibilities accorded within the trade regime, notably within the World Trade Organization (WTO) and bilateral and regional free trade agreements (FTAs), are seen as important ways of harnessing trade flows for sustainable development yet ensuring that trade and investment rules do not constrain the policy space of developing countries to pursue domestic development strategies and regulate in the public interest (UN, 2015b, paras 79–91). Equally important is the reform of the rules and practices of international investment law which currently privilege the protection of foreign investors over the autonomy of developing countries to make policies and enact regulations in the public interest.

Fourth, and perhaps most importantly, reform of international law and institutions of global economic governance are seen as crucial to plugging the regulatory gaps in the international economic architecture that do not facilitate an EIE for sustainable development. Successive agreements on international development have reiterated calls for broadening and strengthening the voice, representation and participation of developing countries in international economic law-making, policy decision-making and norm-setting. This includes reforming asymmetrical governance structures in formal institutions such as the IMF and the World Bank but also including more developing countries into transgovernmental networks such as the Basel Committee on Banking Supervision and other standard-setting regulatory bodies. The greater inclusion of developing countries within the decision-making structures of international economic law and governance is seen as fundamental to creating an environment supportive of domestic development strategies and also to ensure greater systemic coherence across all areas of trade, finance and investment as well as the consistency of these 'economic' areas with States' commitments under human rights and environmental regimes.

Contested meanings and structural transformations

The concept of an enabling environment for development reflects the historical and contemporary economic and geopolitical conflicts that underlie the institutions of international law and global economic governance. Within contemporary articulations of the concept of an enabling international environment, we can see the legacy of a more ambitious transformative project of structural change aimed at fundamentally reversing the iniquities of the colonial era. However, it is also clear that the concept of an EIE is increasingly articulated in more instrumentalist language than the previous normative calls for a just and equitable international economic order. This enables it to be utilized as a technocratic tool for challenging the narratives of the Washington Consensus model of deregulation, liberalization and privatization without the politically charged narratives that animated earlier demands.

At the same time, it is this very absence of political content that correspondingly renders the concept of EIE vulnerable to alternative interpretations, including by donor/creditor-controlled institutions, such as the IMF, World Bank and the OECD, whose prescribed paths to the attainment of sustainable development conflict with the more transformative aspirations of developing countries and communities, and can undermine more progressive calls for a structural transformation of the global economy.

These tensions are evident in the framing of an EIE within the different international texts for development cooperation, particularly its absence in corresponding documents and agreements promulgated through the Bretton Woods institutions and the OECD, such as the OECD's Paris Agreement on Aid Effectiveness and the landmark policy document,

'From Billions to Trillions: Transforming Development Finance' that sets out the IMF and multilateral development banks' vision for a post-2015 financing architecture (World Bank et al., 2015). Here, an enabling environment is confined to the domestic sphere where the onus is on developing countries to create enabling regulatory and policy climates conducive to foreign investments and international trade and finance. Where the international environment is referred to within these articulations of development cooperation, it is focused on countries' compliance with the rules established by the international economic legal order, even where such rules remain iniquitous or restrictive of the aforementioned domestic policy space.

These normative contests between different visions of the relationship between international law and development can and do have significant impacts on the trajectories of domestic sustainable development policies today. This history needs to be appreciated to understand the salience of the concept of an enabling international environment, its pivotal role in shaping sustainable development outcomes, and its relevance to the international economic legal order that hinders or enables these outcomes.

CELINE TAN

References

Akyüz, Yilmaz (2010). 'Multilateral Disciplines and the Question of Policy Space' in Julio Faundez and Celine Tan (eds), *International Law, Economic Globalization & Developing Countries*, Edward Elgar.

Faundez, Julio (2017). 'Between Bandung and Doha: International Economic Law and Developing Countries' in Luis Eslava, Michael Fakhri, and Vasuki Nesiah (eds), *Bandung, Global History, and International Law: Critical Pasts and Pending Futures*. Cambridge University Press.

Girvan, Norman and Ana Luiza Cortez (2014). 'The Enabling International Environment' in José Antonio Alonso, Giovanni Andrea Cornia, and Rob Vos (eds), *Alternative Development Strategies for the Post-2015 Era*. UNDP and Bloomsbury.

Linarelli, John, Margot Salomon, and M. Sornarajah (2018). *The Misery of International Law: Confrontations with Injustice in the Global Economy*. Oxford University Press.

Mohamadieh, Kinda (2019). 'Challenges of Investment Treaties on Policy Areas of Concern to Developing Countries', South Centre Investment Policy Brief 17.

Tan, Celine (2017). 'Development' in Krista Nadakuvaren-Schaffer and Thomas Cottier (eds), *Encyclopedia of International Economic Law*. Edward Elgar.

UN (2015a). 'Transforming Our World: 2030 Agenda for Sustainable Development', UN General Assembly Resolution 70/1.

UN (2015b). 'Addis Ababa Action Agenda of the Third International Conference on Financing for Development', The final text of the outcome document adopted at the Third International Conference on Financing for Development (Addis Ababa, Ethiopia, 13–16 July 2015) and endorsed by the General Assembly in its Resolution 69/313 of 27 July 2015.

UN (2019). The Least Development Countries Report 2019: The Present and Future of External Development Finance: Old Dependence, New Challenges. UNCTAD.

World Bank et al. (2015). 'From Billions to Trillions: Transforming Development Finance: Post-2015 Financing for Development: Multilateral Development Finance', Development Committee Discussion Note Prepared jointly by African Development Bank, Asian Development Bank, European Bank for Reconstruction and Development, European Investment Bank, Inter-American Development Bank, International Monetary Fund and World Bank Group, 2 April 2015.

21. Energy

When we talk about energy and sustainable development, we must address its economic, political, social and environmental aspects. The economic development and governance of any country in the world are closely related to energy security, understood as the uninterrupted availability of energy sources at an affordable price. In addition, energy consumption is an unavoidable condition of social welfare to the extent that it meets the needs of transportation, lighting, cooking, heating, among others. Finally, the environmental impacts of energy production, transport and consumption must be addressed. Energy law and policy aims to ensure that societies meet their energy targets whether that is about the provision of increased energy security and/or economic benefits, and/or environmental goals.

Currently, the energy sector is facing global changes at the political and technological level that suppose different challenges for central countries and peripheral countries, given the structural asymmetries existing in the world economic system. Some of these changes have been incorporated into international legal instruments, which have an increasingly strong influence on the energy law and policies at the national level. The purpose of this entry is to analyse the ongoing transformations of the global energy sector and how they particularly affect peripheral countries. Before that, we will begin with a historical review of the oil age, especially its main actors.

The oil age

The transition from coal to oil enabled not only a demographic explosion, but also the expansion of capitalism due to the lowering of the transport costs and the increase in labour productivity. Oil control also favours market concentration and the law had to intervene early to avoid monopolies at the beginning of the oil industry: in 1911 the US Supreme Court forced Standard Oil to divide into several independent companies when the company had become a threat to the national economy.

If during the First World War oil became a strategic resource and a matter of security for the great world powers, after the Second World War the US became a net energy importer and the "centre of gravity" of international energy policy was moved to the Middle East. Until at least the 1960s, the control of international supply and prices remained in the hands of the "Seven Sisters" cartel, which was composed of Shell, British Petroleum, Texaco, Gulf Oil, Exxon, Mobil Oil and Chevron (the last three were detachments of Standard Oil).

The 1973 oil crisis, following the embargo promoted by the Organization of Petroleum Exporting Countries (OPEC), determined that central countries needed to seek new suppliers beyond the Middle East and, at the same time, diversify energy sources through innovation, investment in infrastructure and the promotion of energy efficiency.

The Iranian revolution marked the beginning of the second oil crisis in 1979, which effects lasted until the early 1980s when OPEC's main producer, Saudi Arabia, decided to stall the price. Since then, the world oil market has undergone a metamorphosis that led to privatizations of State oil companies, mega mergers between private companies and financialization through the purchase and sale of futures in the New York and London stock exchanges.

The financial oil market bubble peaked at $147 a barrel in mid-2008, which coincided with the biggest global economic crisis since 1929, and then fell sharply. It was then when a new stage in the global energy system was opened.

The global energy system today

The changes that are shaping the energy sector globally can be grouped into two interrelated dimensions: technological changes and political changes. The first dimension is associated with the shale revolution, falling costs of renewable technologies and the expansion of liquefied natural gas (LNG) trade. The second dimension is related to the return of the US as an energy power, the rise of China as a main consumer of energy, but also as a leader in innovation in renewable technologies and the limits imposed by the commitments linked to the fight against climate change.

Due to its finite nature, from the 1950s until a few years ago, there was a debate about when the peak of oil production would happen. However, recent innovations in hydrocarbon extraction techniques from unconventional reservoirs have alienated the fear of scarcity.

The basis of the shale revolution consisted of two significant technological innovations: horizontal drilling and hydraulic fracturing (fracking). These innovations were possible because of the US federal government's activism since the 1970s, which introduced tax incentives and funded research with the aim of achieving energy independence. The shale revolution has allowed the US to significantly increase the production of oil and natural gas during the 2010s and, consequently, reduce its imports and contribute to excess supply in world markets and to lower prices. In contrast, OPEC together with other producing countries such as Russia have decided to impose cuts in their production in order to sustain the price and, therefore, their income. Thus, market financialization has ceased to be the main cause of volatility, but prices are the result of the geopolitical dispute: they are pushed down by the increase in US shale production and pushed up by production cuts from OPEC + non-OPEC countries.

A paradigm shift is under way: from an era of scarcity to an era of fossil fuel abundance. In this context, the focus has been redirected to the effects of fossil fuel use on global warming and the notions of peak oil demand and energy transition emerge strongly.

The concept of peak demand refers to different forecasts in which oil demand could peak in the coming decades, although demand is unlikely to fall sharply when it reaches its peak. An energy transition is a structural change in the system of provision and use of energy, which occurs as a consequence of technological and economic transformations, but which is also the product of political decisions in the long term. Under the influence of global climate change, energy transition implies that the current domain of fossil fuels will be transferred to renewable energies. According to the International Energy Agency, the energy sector accounts for two-thirds of total greenhouse gas (GHG) emissions and 80 per cent of CO_2, so any effort to reduce emissions and mitigate climate change must include the energy sector.

Among the international agreements that impact the energy sector, two stand out. First, the Paris Agreement concluded in 2015, which was signed by virtually every country in the world to reduce GHG emissions in order to limit the average global temperature rise below 2 degrees Celsius and as close as possible to 1.5 degrees Celsius, thus avoiding the severe impacts of climate change. Given the impossibility of reaching a consensus on a single universal emission mitigation formula, it was agreed that each country would decide its own objectives for the period 2020–2030. Each country must submit its nationally determined contributions (NDC), which consists of a climate plan that aims at reducing its GHG emissions, taking into account its domestic circumstances and capacities. In general, the energy sector plays an important role in each NDC due to its high contribution in GHG emissions at national level. However, the intention of US President Donald Trump to leave the Paris Agreement has left a blanket of uncertainty about the effectiveness of the global fight against climate change, given that it is the country with the highest GHG emissions per capita.

In second place, the 17 Sustainable Development Goals (SDGs) of the 2030 Agenda for Sustainable Development (2030 Agenda) were adopted at the United Nations level in September 2015 and entered into force in 2016. They contain a specific energy objective (SDG 7), which aims at ensuring access to affordable, reliable, sustainable and modern energy for all by 2030. This means, firstly, guaranteeing universal access to electricity, which contributes to an emerging discussion on energy access as a human right. Secondly, this objective aims at fighting against climate change by doubling the rate of improvement in energy efficiency and increasing the share of renewable energies in the global energy mix. Another target is to increase international cooperation to facilitate access to clean energy research and technology, including renewable sources, energy efficiency and advanced and less polluting fossil fuel technologies, as well as to promote investment in energy infrastructure and clean technologies.

China has a leading position in innovation and manufacture of renewable energy technologies. It competes with US and European companies in the clean energy race. In this framework, electric vehicles and heat pumps are expanding the deployment of renewable energy in transport, industry and buildings, besides innovations in digitalization and energy storage. It is expected that renewable energies will transform geopolitics in the future because, unlike fossil resources, they are available anywhere in the world. They can also be implemented at almost any scale and facilitate decentralized forms of energy production and consumption, which could have a democratizing effect on the energy system.

IGNACIO SABBATELLA

Meanwhile, natural gas is seen as a cleaner option among fossil fuels. It produces around half the CO_2 emissions of coal when burned to generate power and it is the ideal complement to renewables as it can be a lower carbon, cost-effective back-up to the variability of wind, solar and hydropower generation. In this transition scenario, the global gas market is evolving rapidly due to the US shale revolution, but also the LNG revolution. LNG is a natural gas cooled to the point that it condenses to liquid and represents an alternative to the transportation of natural gas by gas pipelines. As part of the decarbonization transition, the role of LNG is forecast to grow not only for power supply, but also in new markets such as fuel for the haulage and maritime sectors. The technology of LNG, in addition to new significant resources such as US shale, is gradually turning natural gas into a global commodity. Also, flexible LNG solutions can be more viable than a gas pipeline scheme because they do not require political arrangements.

Challenges for peripheral countries

For peripheral countries, energy is a crucial problem, as well as an opportunity. Many of their inhabitants do not have access to electricity and non-polluting or modern cooking appliances. In other cases, they face monetary restrictions to access energy services, which is called energy poverty. On the other hand, energy is also an opportunity because it allows the development of industrial chains linked to the exploitation of renewable and non-renewable energy resources.

Under the scenario described above, peripheral countries face a series of challenges. First of all, both importing countries and oil exporting countries must adapt their national budgets to market fluctuations. Price volatility is here to stay, at least until there is a clear winner in the contest between US shale and the OPEC + non-OPEC countries. Regarding the opportunities of the global scenario, the greater availability of natural gas in the world market is favouring the replacement of coal-based electricity generation in many countries and thus contributing to both environmental sustainability and energy security.

Second, the climate agenda adds pressure on the petrol-States since they have to diversify their economies for a world in which they can no longer depend indefinitely on oil revenues as their main source of income. On the other hand, the voluntary emission reduction mechanism established in the Paris Agreement leads to retaking the principle of common but differentiated responsibilities. In all international fora, the central countries have prevented the recognition of their historical responsibilities for environmental pollution from becoming a legal obligation to provide financing and technologies to developing countries. In that sense, the term climate justice has been coined to establish a principle of equity when designing and implementing climate policies. For this, it is necessary that peripheral countries agree on common positions in international fora in order to demand from the central countries a greater commitment and also determine the way and speed in which they will adopt measures to mitigate emissions, in this case diversification towards cleaner energy matrices. While the greater debt of the central countries is environmental, connected to the emission of GHGs, the greater debt of the peripheral countries is social and has to do with energy access to the population. For that reason, peripheral countries should have SDG 7 as a priority and, in that sense, they should demand international assistance in order to establish universal access to electricity as a human right.

Third, innovations in renewable energies lead to an old discussion about the technological dependence of peripheral countries. In that sense, it is important to note the interest of core economies and global governance organizations to promote a massive transfer of green technology to non-central regions, especially after the 2008 financial crisis, with the objective of relaunching capitalist accumulation. Actually, the development of renewable energy sources may be an opportunity for peripheral countries to develop endogenous technological capacities from the initial stage of a new leading sector.

Finally, the complex global energy landscape for peripheral countries requires a new energy law and policy in which national planning should be strengthened, with the support of regional blocs. There are too many challenges to be left in the hands of the market.

IGNACIO SABBATELLA

References

Boersma, Tim and Akos Losz (2018). "The New International Political Economy of Natural

Gas" in Andreas Goldthau, Michael F. Keating, and Caroline Kuzemko (eds), *Handbook of the International Political Economy of Energy and Natural Resources*. Edward Elgar.

Dale, Spencer and Bassam Fattouh (2018). *Peak Oil Demand and Long-Run Oil Prices*. The Oxford Institute for Energy Studies. Available at: https://www.bp.com/content/dam/bp/en/corporate/pdf/energy-economics/bp-peak-oil-demand-and-long-run-oil-prices.pdf.

Global Commission on the Geopolitics of Energy Transformation (2019). *A New World: The Geopolitics of the Energy Transformation*. International Renewable Energy Agency.

Goldthau, Andreas, Kirsten Westphal, Morgan Bazilian, and Mike Bradshaw (2019). "How the Energy Transition Will Reshape Geopolitics", Nature (2)569, 29–31.

Heffron, Raphael J. and Kim Talus (2016). "The Development of Energy Law in the 21st Century: A Paradigm Shift?", Journal of World Energy Law and Business 3(9), 189–202.

Hurtado, Diego and Pablo Souza (2018). "Geoeconomic Uses of Global Warming: The 'Green' Technological Revolution and the Role of the Semi-Periphery", Journal of World-Systems Research 1(24), 123–150.

Sabbatella, Ignacio and Thauan Santos (2019). "The IPE of Regional Energy Integration in South America" in Ernesto Vivares (ed.), *The Routledge Handbook to Global Political Economy*. Routledge.

Sovacool, Benjamin K. and Ishani Mukherjee (2011). "Conceptualizing and Measuring Energy Security: A Synthesized Approach", Energy 8(36), 5343–5355.

Van de Graaf, Thijs, Benjamin K. Sovacool, Arunabha Ghosh, Florian Kern, and Michael T. Klare (eds) (2016). *The Palgrave Handbook of the International Political Economy of Energy*. Palgrave.

Yergin, Daniel (2006). "Ensuring Energy Security", Foreign Affairs 2(85), 69–82.

22. Extraterritorial Human Rights Obligations

Scholars, human rights bodies and tribunals have labelled State obligations beyond their borders most often as extraterritorial obligations but also as external obligations, transborder obligations, third State obligations or international obligations. All these terms attempt to cover the specific nature of human rights obligations that reach beyond a State's territory. The foundation for the differentiation between territorial and extraterritorial human rights obligations is a belief that we are dealing with another type of obligation or at least obligations that are triggered in a different manner. What is at play is a tension between States' pursuit for universal observance of human rights and the realistic or conceivable State compliance with their human rights obligations outside their territory. The idea being that it would simply be impracticable to argue that States have obligations towards everyone, everywhere. Some limitation on States' obligations towards individuals outside their borders appears warranted.

Many scholars and human rights bodies start – at least implicitly – from this point when examining human rights obligations of States beyond their borders. Consequently, extraterritorial obligations of States are used under an 'exceptionality doctrine' developed by human rights courts and bodies, spurred on in particular by the European Court of Human Rights (ECtHR). This doctrine implies that human rights obligations are grounded in a State's territory and can only exist outside of that territory in exceptional circumstances. Such doctrine has been developed through case law on extraterritorial obligations in the field of civil and political rights, in particular in contexts of foreign military occupation or interventions. The key issue in the case law centred around jurisdiction or the attribution of (extraterritorial) obligations to a (foreign) State. The developed jurisdictional tests used by human rights courts, in particular the ECtHR, implicate (effective) control over territory or persons. Yet many extraterritorial issues such as transboundary environmental harm, international (harmful) economic policies or transnational surveillance are actually committed outside the limited scenarios that fall under effective control over territory or persons. The relevance of extraterritorial obligations in responding to such negative consequences of a globalized, interdependent world, as well as the above indicated restricted application by human rights bodies, triggered an intense academic debate about the suitable principles for the attribution of obligations (jurisdiction) and responsibility beyond a State's territory. Such debates focus to a lesser extent on instances involving negative obligations in which a clear link exists between the individual and the State. Most scholarly attention has been paid to the existence of positive human rights obligations – that is, whether a State should act (absent a prior link between the individual and the State).

Although it is clear that States should not harm human rights abroad, it is still unclear when a State needs to act in order to protect or fulfil human rights beyond its borders. States can directly or indirectly interfere with, or violate, the rights of an individual, making the link between a duty-bearer and the individual too remote or non-existent to generate obligations for that duty-bearer. Absent a direct or prior link with the individual, human rights bodies and scholars still struggle to find suitable principles for the attribution of extraterritorial obligations. Furthermore, even if we can attribute obligations it is unclear how issues of shared responsibility between different actors (including non-State actors) would play out. Such and other debates remain unresolved to a great extent but have culminated around the adoption of the Maastricht Principles on Extraterritorial Obligations of States in the area of Economic, Social and Cultural Rights (ETO principles). These ETO principles were adopted by a group of scholars and human rights experts in 2011. The principles, born out of frustration with the limited recognition and applicability of ETOs to economic, social and cultural (ESC) rights, reflect the state-of-the-art but certainly also extend beyond it. States' human rights obligations are clearly recognized to extend beyond borders. In particular UN human rights bodies, such as the Committee on ESC rights, have favourably received the principles and used them in drafting their general comments.

The tension between what can be expected of States and their existing human rights obligations is again noticeable in the ETO principles.

According to the ETO Principles, extraterritorial obligations are:

1. obligations relating to the acts and omissions of a State, within or beyond its territory, that have effects on the enjoyment of human rights outside of that State's territory (ETO Principle 8(a)); and
2. obligations of a global character that are set out in the Charter of the United Nations and human rights instruments to take action, separately, and jointly through international cooperation, to realize human rights universally (ETO Principle 8(b)).

Principle 8(a) accommodates extraterritorial obligations stricto sensu; it recognizes a link between the act or omission of the State and the effect (the harmful outcome). Principle 8(b) does not require such a prior link and represents so-called "global obligations" that refer to States' positive obligations to take action, separately, and jointly through international cooperation, to fulfil socio-economic rights. Yet, in an attempt to accommodate or reconcile the desire to ensure State implementation and compliance with extraterritorial obligations to respect, protect and fulfil, scholars have not only argued for different types of ETOs but also proposed a sequencing of obligations as well as a differentiation according to duty-bearers. One can find notions of primary, secondary or complementary duty-bearers as well as simultaneous, parallel, concurrent and subsidiary human rights obligations. Scholars have stressed that the extraterritorial obligation to respect and protect are simultaneous or concurrent obligations that exist independently of the acts or omissions of the domestic State. They are understood as obligations that complement the obligations of the domestic State to ensure the enjoyment of human rights. The State's extraterritorial obligation to fulfil, however, is believed to be of a subsidiary nature. In an attempt to limit the attribution of the obligation to fulfil, it is argued to trigger these types of obligations by determining either the capacity (resources) of the domestic State or the foreign State. Others again found that positive obligations to ensure rights extraterritorially only exist when a State exercises control over territory (including extraterritorial control over territory). According to the ETO principles, in particular Principle 9 (jurisdiction), States' extraterritorial obligations are triggered in:

1. situations over which it exercises authority or effective control, whether or not such control is exercised in accordance with international law;
2. situations over which a State's acts or omissions bring about foreseeable effects on the enjoyment of economic, social and cultural rights, whether within or outside its territory;
3. situations in which the State, acting separately or jointly, . . . is in a position to exercise decisive influence or to take measures to realize economic, social, and cultural rights extraterritorially, in accordance with international law.

Such allocation of extraterritorial obligations between States through various concepts based on facticity ("control", "influence", "in a position to assist or regulate"; "take measures" . . .) remains contested (see below). What is clear is that all have been conjured up with a concern for the realistic compliance of States in mind. They are based on the various degrees of power or capacity of a State to affect the enjoyment of an individual's human rights. The reasoning – albeit often implicit – being that it would simply not be realistic to attribute wide-ranging (positive) obligations in instances beyond, for example, control over territory, influence or being in a position to assist or regulate.

The use and acceptance of the different concepts indicated above depends very much on one's starting point when discussing human rights obligations of States beyond their borders. Importantly, scholars have challenged the exceptionality of the extraterritorial application of human rights treaties and the subsequent distinctiveness of extraterritorial human rights obligations. The idea of universal and effective recognition and observance of fundamental human rights does not include any sort of territorial limitation. Based on this idea of universality, States should strive to respect, protect and fulfil human rights everywhere. Moreover, globalization, as in an increasing interdependence of States, stands in contrast with a grounding of human rights protection on the basis of territory. Human rights law needs to adapt and be synched with reality in order for it to be effective in addressing contemporary human rights issues. Leaving aside the discussion on the potential of ETOs to deal with the negative consequences of globalization, the idea is we need to step away from the use of territory as a starting point for the attribution of obligations. One should and could simply use "human rights obligations". Besides, in practice, the distinction between extraterritorial and territorial obligations is arguably not so easily made (e.g. cases involving extraordinary rendition or non-refoulement). When rejecting the inherent distinctiveness of extraterritorial human rights obligations, one can also reject subsequent differentiations between primary and secondary duty-bearers or complementary versus subsidiary obligations. In other words, a rejection of so-called latent (extraterritorial) human rights obligations that need to be triggered by some sort of jurisdictional or attributional test constructed on the factual capacity of a State to secure its obligations. Scholars have argued that the assessment of whether or not a State is able or unable to implement its obligations under a given treaty should take place at the merits stage, i.e. in determining the responsibility of the State for a violation of human rights law. As such States always carry their obligations with them and should attempt to fulfil them within the limits of international law.

The doctrine of "exceptionality" for the extraterritorial application of a human rights treaty naturally presupposes a restricted interpretation of the attribution of obligations. Scholars in turn have suggested incremental changes and novel interpretations of jurisdiction in order to move forward while coping with the limited interpretation or exceptionality paradigm of human rights bodies and courts. The grounding of obligations on actual capacity happened in an attempt to demonstrate that extraterritorial obligations do not impose a disproportionate burden on States. Indeed, the "legal fictions" in the ICESCR and other treaties are considerable. Yet, human rights law is replete with legal fictions (even at the domestic level). The fear of imposing unrealistic or utopian obligations on States should, however, not be dispelled at the level of attribution of obligations but rather when determining a State's responsibility for a violation of a human right. Stating a State has extraterritorial human rights obligations is legally very different from stating it has an extraterritorial responsibility. To determine the latter intricate rules of responsibility based – inter alia – on capacity are needed. Hence a future research agenda appears where scholars should liberate themselves from only discussing jurisdiction and start analysing the content, and applicability, of the rules of responsibility in transnational contexts.

ARNE VANDENBOGAERDE

References

Den Heijer, Maarten (2013). "Shared Responsibility before the European Court of Human Rights", Netherlands International Law Review 3(60), 411–440.

De Schutter, Olivier et al. (2012). "Commentary to the Maastricht Principles on Extraterritorial Obligations of States in the Area of Economic, Social and Cultural Rights", Human Rights Quarterly 4(34), 1084–1169.

Gibney, Mark (2013). "On Terminology: Extraterritorial Obligations" in Malcolm Langford et al. (eds), Global Justice, State Duties: The Extraterritorial Scope of Economic, Social, and Cultural Rights in International Law. Cambridge University Press.

Khalfan, Ashfaq (2013). "Division of Responsibility amongst States" in Malcolm Langford et al. (eds), Global Justice, State Duties: The Extraterritorial Scope of Economic, Social, and Cultural Rights in International Law. Cambridge University Press.

Salomon, Margot (2007). Global Responsibility for Human Rights: World Poverty and the Development of International Law. Oxford University Press.

Vandenbogaerde, Arne (2015). "Jurisdiction Revisited: Attributing Extraterritorial State Obligations under the International Covenant on Economic, Social and Cultural Rights", Human Rights and International Legal Discourse 1(9), 6–34.

Vandenhole, Wouter (ed.) (2015). Challenging Territoriality in Human Rights Law: Building Blocks for a Plural and Diverse Duty-Bearer Regime. Routledge.

Vandenhole, Wouter and Wolfgang Benedek (2013). "Extraterritorial Human Rights Obligations and the North-South Divide" in Malcolm Langford et al. (eds), Global Justice, State Duties: The Extraterritorial Scope of Economic, Social, and Cultural Rights in International Law. Cambridge University Press.

Vandenhole, Wouter, Gamze Erdem Türkelli, and Rachel Hammonds (2014). "Reconceptualizing Human Rights Duty-Bearers" in Anja Mihr and Mark Gibney (eds), The SAGE Handbook of Human Rights. SAGE Publications.

Wilde, Ralphe (2018). "Socio-economic Rights, Extraterritorially" in Eyal Benvenisti and George Nolte (eds), Community Obligations in Contemporary International Law. Oxford University Press.

23. Financing for Development

Introduction

This entry approaches financing for development as a field of two interconnecting realms of activity. The first is the main monetary, financial, trade and investment activities that constitute the macroeconomic flows of international public and private finance, and the complex patchwork of institutions, instruments and frameworks that make up its governance architecture. Such flows provide finance for development, as well as impact on development. The second is the United Nations (UN) initiative on financing for development (FfD). FfD is a series of UN-supported international conferences and related activities that focus on how development might be better financed, and how the wider macroeconomic field of financial activity that shapes this could be better governed. The former, broader macroeconomic field provides the structural policy context that shapes much of the debate and activities within the latter FfD field. The following section traces the main kinds of macroeconomic international financial activities that influence the financing of development, along with high-level features of their governance architecture that pose particular challenges for developing countries. The third section focuses on the FfD initiative, highlights aspects that distinguish it from other UN-led international conferences, briefly examines one aspect of its policy agenda and speculates on its impact. In light of knowledge from more recent initiatives on sustainable development and climate change, this entry concludes with a reflection on how FfD may effectively contribute to debates on the financing of sustainable development in the near future.

The structural context of financing for development

The main macroeconomic activities that shape how development is financed and also impact on development consist of several interrelated kinds of financial activity. At the international level, these include finance from long-recognized areas such as trade and foreign direct investment; international development cooperation (including Official Development Assistance (ODA) and other official flows (OOF) such as grants and other finance from the World Bank and other development finance institutions and loans from the International Monetary Fund (IMF)); international remittances from workers abroad, as well as initiatives on international tax cooperation, tax avoidance/evasion and illicit financial flows (including capital flight and repatriation). At the national level, activities such as the management of sovereign debt and maintenance of national reserves; the management of foreign exchange markets; the role of sovereign wealth funds and national development banks and, of course, taxation emerge more to the fore. In recent years, new areas of finance that either explicitly aim at a "development impact" or influence development more broadly have also come under the ambit of international development finance. These include activities from institutional investors (also known as the shadow banking system); activities in fintech, insurance, pension fund and asset management (portfolio management by private equity firms and hedge funds), along with philanthropic finance and blends of many of these via initiatives focused on "impact investing" or "innovative finance".

From this overview, it is clear that the governance architecture of this international financial landscape is marked by three key features – first, a deep heterogeneity of regulatory institutions, instruments, actors and agendas, operating via a range of governance sites and levels; secondly, a complexity – sometimes to the point of incoherence – in the interrelationships between these governance frameworks, and finally, a strong disparity in States' representation and participation in the institutions of global economic decision-making. For developing countries, this governance architecture poses distinct challenges. These include the legacy of control by the major developed countries of existing formal institutions such as the IMF and World Bank, whose capital-laden voting structures give richer countries extra leverage (José Antonio Ocampo (2017). *Resetting the International Monetary (Non) System.* Oxford University Press). This exclusion of developing countries from the major financial regulatory bodies is not adequately addressed by the emergence of largely ad hoc, informal institutional arrangements such as the G7/8 and G-20. These, as well as many of the less institutionalized groups, particularly those grounded in non-binding bylaws, charters, and accords such as the Financial Stability Board, continue to be led by the major developed countries (Chris Brummer (2015). *Soft Law and the Global Financial System: Rule making in the Twenty-first Century*. Cambridge University Press).

Furthermore, globalization has fundamentally altered the landscape for financing for development in ways that militate against global financial stability and the creation of systemic conditions and pathways for the financing of development, in particular for lower-income countries. For example, the significance of capital flows now far exceeds those of trade to the global economy (Buckley and Arner, 2012). This rise in capital mobility almost inevitably leads to a push for ever greater exchange rate flexibility, which can be better managed by countries with more developed financial markets and stronger policy-making institutions (lower-income countries remain reluctant to relax capital controls since it is not certain that foreign capital will flow into appropriate sectors and uses) (Barry Eichengreen (2019). *Globalizing Capital: A History of the International Monetary System*. Princeton University Press).

With capital markets now much more thoroughly integrated, periodic financial crises of a national (e.g. Mexico 1994), regional (e.g. the Asian financial crisis of 1997 affecting South Korea, Thailand, Malaysia, Indonesia, Singapore, and the Philippines), and international nature (e.g. the international financial crisis that snowballed from the collapse of the giant US investment bank Lehman Brothers in 2008) have clearly revealed several flaws in the governance architecture for international finance. Though dedicated international initiatives now exist to address particular challenges faced by developing countries (e.g. the IMF's Heavily Indebted Poor Countries Initiative and Multilateral Debt Relief Initiative, and the World Bank-IMF Debt Sustainability Framework for low-income countries), arguably the prevailing technocratic approach to debt management by the international financial institutions (e.g. IMF Debt Sustainability Analysis approach) elides from the view that systemic and structural factors perpetuate a crisis-prone international finance system, in which

developing countries are particularly vulnerable. An understanding of this wider context is helpful in order to trace the debates and contribution of the UN-supported FfD initiative and critically analyse its merits and potential.

The international Financing for Development (FfD) initiative

The international FfD initiative is the only multilateral setting where the international community can discuss the broad concept of "financing for development" in a comprehensive way (Lesage et al., 2010). FfD is a series of international conferences and summits consisting of Monterrey (2002), Doha (2008) and Addis Ababa (2015), with the latter strongly focused on the UN Sustainable Development Goals (SDGs) (an international conference in New York (2009) that focused on the international response to the 2008 economic crisis may also be included, though will not be discussed here). Follow-up on the FfD within the United Nations is coordinated and supported by the Financing for Development Office (FfDO), established in 2003 within the Department of Economic and Social Affairs of the United Nations Secretariat.

Inaugurated in Monterrey (2002) (which more than 50 Heads of State and Government and over 200 ministers of foreign affairs, trade, development and finance attended), the FfD initiative was prompted by several developments. At the macroeconomic level, some developing countries were suffering the effects of two decades of a markets-focused model of development based on neoliberal orthodoxy tied to the policies of the Washington Consensus. Furthermore, there had been a decline in international levels of ODA, and the volatility, unevenness and lack of productive investment deriving from the huge increase in international financial flows, described in the section above, caused concern that progress on the recently internationally agreed Millennium Development Goals (2000) may be compromised.

The Monterrey conference was different to previous international initiatives on development finance. First, FfD was intended to take a "beyond-UN" approach to the subject of financing for development and directly engage with key international financial institutions such as the World Bank and the IMF. Secondly, it sought to involve the UN in a more direct role in international economic affairs (Caliari, 2016). Though the UN Charter (Articles 1.5 and 55) gives the UN a role in international economic cooperation, this had been side-lined over several decades. Thirdly, it was a quadripartite exchange between governments of States, and representatives of civil society, the business sector, and the major international institutions, a departure from previous UN international conferences held in the 1990s. Fourthly, it shifted focus on development finance from its historic preoccupation with ODA, to consideration of wider systemic issues such as debt, the nature of foreign direct investment, and the roles of various development finance institutions. Finally, it shone a light on problematic areas of global economic governance, such as the participation and decision-making roles of developing country States in the major international finance organizations and proclaimed again a role for the UN and the General Assembly (with universal membership) "as fundamental to the promotion of international cooperation for development and to a global economic system that works for all" (UN, 2002).

The unanimous adoption of the Monterrey Consensus captured a vision and framework for financing development for the twenty-first century (Subedi, 2002), one that rhetorically committed to the goal of eradicating poverty, achieving sustained economic growth and promoting sustainable development while "advance(ing) to a fully inclusive and equitable global economic system" (UN, 2002). The Consensus addressed in detail a range of challenges at the macro-institutional governance level as well as specific issues relating to productive foreign direct investment, international trade, the management of sovereign debt and international cooperation on taxation.

However, the deeper impacts of the Consensus might best be described as ambiguous. Ffrench-Davis viewed it as "a substantive step forward in the international development agenda", and welcomed its attention to previously ignored issues such as the productivity of financial investment, attention to financial crises, the fair management of unsustainable debt and the necessity of cooperation on international taxation to address tax evasion and money-laundering (Ffrench-Davis, 2009). In contrast, Soderberg viewed Monterrey as an effort to manage the negative effects of globalization, embrace a market-led model of development underpinned by governance and institutions and practices in service of that aim, and depoliticize the power of transnational capital "by portraying their role as equal partners with civil society and States of the South but also (by) represent(ing) their growing role in the development agenda as some sort of natural occurrence" (Soderberg, 2005).

Two follow-up conferences have taken place after Monterrey: Doha (2008) (with official representatives from over 170 countries and 40 Heads of State attending, from which the Doha Declaration on FfD was produced), and Addis Ababa (2015) (with 24 Heads of State and representatives of 174 countries attending, from which the Addis Ababa Action Agenda (AAAA) was produced (UN, 2015)). Report of the Third International Conference on Financing for Development, Addis Ababa, Ethiopia, 13–16 July 2015, A/CONF.227/20). Given the link between the Addis conference and preparations for the post-2015 agenda Summit and the UN's SDGs – whose scope was far broader and more detailed than the Millennium Development Goals – the stakes at Addis were considerably higher (Caliari, 2016). A key question was whether the FfD initiative, with its attention to problematic issues within the international economic system that hampered both the financing and outcomes of development, would become inexorably bound up with the Means of Implementation of the SDGs, or could continue a life beyond the SDGs. While Caliari, perhaps optimistically, clearly identifies a distinction between the AAAA and the wider FfD initiative, it remains to be seen whether the FfD initiative can hold a dedicated space for a distinctive UN voice in international economic affairs.

Initial signs urge caution. On the important area of international cooperation to address tax evasion and illicit financial flows, for example, a generic call within the Monterrey Consensus (2002) to strengthen international tax cooperation had evolved in Doha (2008) to a commitment to make tax systems "pro-poor" (para. 16). However, in the AAAA (2015), this became a mere commitment to increase the number of sessions of the Committee of Experts on International Cooperation in Tax Matters (a subsidiary body of the Economic and Social Council) from once to twice per year, with a duration of four working days each. Normatively, this was a watering-down of a proposal, supported by several representatives from States from the Global South, to upgrade that Committee to an intergovernmental tax body under the auspices of the UN, one with the mandate and resources to ensure that all countries could participate in the setting of international tax norms (UN, 2015, above). From a governance perspective, it leaves the Organization for Economic Cooperation and Development (OECD) (an international organization whose membership is from predominantly Northern capital-exporting States) as the main governance site where initiatives to improve international tax policy is addressed (such as the OECD's base erosion and profit shifting (BEPS) initiative). Though valuable, the latter is recognized as not principally geared to developing country concerns (Civil Society Forum, 2015; AU/ECA, 2012).

The field and concept of financing for development

With more recent information now available on the grave threats to the ability of our natural environment to sustainably support life, it is clear that the current model of neoliberal, capitalist, growth-oriented development not only generates periodic economic crises of a global nature along with great inequality and concentration of wealth, but it also consumes an unsustainable share of the Earth's natural resources and has dramatic consequences for our climate. An uncritical adoption of the "sustainable" moniker to the prevailing model of development and its financing arguably masks the more fundamental question of whether it is possible to reconcile this model with caring for and protecting the environment and achieving social equity. It remains to be seen how the main governance institutions of international public and private finance respond to the challenge of ensuring sustainability. In this context, it remains all the more necessary for the FfD – as the only international institutional space where developing country members have, superficially at least, an equitable voice to debate interna-

tional financing for development – to sharpen its critique and develop proposals that address effective reform and oversight of the institutions that govern international finance.

SIOBHÁN AIREY

References

AU/ECA (2012). Illicit Financial Flows, Report of the High-Level Panel on Illicit Financial Flows from Africa (the Mbeiki Report). Commissioned by the AU/ECA Conference of Ministers of Finance, Planning and Economic Development.

Buckley, Ross P. and Douglas W. Arner (2011). *From Crisis to Crisis The Global Financial System and Regulatory Failure*. Wolters Kluwer.

Caliari, Aldo (2016). "Guest Editorial: The Monterrey Consensus, 14 Years Later", Development (59), 5–7.

Civil Society Forum (2015). Declaration from the Addis Ababa Civil Society Forum on Financing for Development, 12 July 2015. Available at https://csoforffd.org/2015/07/14/addis-ababa-cso-ffd-forum-declaration/ accessed 10 September 2020.

Ffrench-Davis, Ricardo (2009). "The Global Crisis, Speculative Capital and Innovative Financing for Development", CEPAL Review 97, 57–74.

Lesage, Dries, David McNair, and Mattias Vermeiren (2010). "From Monterrey to Doha: Taxation and Financing for Development", Development Policy Review 2(28), 155–172.

Soderberg, Susanne (2005). "Recasting Neoliberal Dominance in the Global South? A Critique of the Monterrey Consensus", Alternatives: Global, Local, Political 3(30), 325.

Subedi, Surya (2002). "The International Conference on Financing for Development, Monterrey, Mexico, 18–22 March 2002", International Law Forum du droit international (4), 52.

UN (2002). Report of the International Conference on Financing for Development, Monterrey, Mexico, 18–22 March 2002, A/CONF.198/11.

UN (2008). Doha Declaration on Financing for Development: outcome document of the Follow-up International Conference on Financing for Development to Review the Implementation of the Monterrey Consensus, Doha, Qatar, 29 November–2 December 2008, A/CONF.212/L.1/Rev.1.

24. Future Generations

The term "generation" usually describes the set of people in a society that is born and lives around the same period of time. For 30 years, the legal status of future generations has been the subject of an intense doctrinal debate. The following sections will analyse it, as well as its recognition in positive law.

The necessity to protect future generations

The risks faced by future generations

Human lifestyle has always had an impact on the environment. The use of fire for hunting by Australian Aboriginals or of agriculture's slash-and-burn techniques by local communities around the world has shaped local environments. Nevertheless, impacts have been greater as technology has improved, and mankind is nowadays causing long-term and global changes such as climate change, loss of biodiversity, ozone depletion, and pollution from plastic, from the use of persistent organic pollutants or from nuclear wastes. While this jeopardizes interests of future generations, short-term thinking in politics has prevented States from adopting effective measures (Collins, 2007).

The reasons to protect the interests of future generations

Moral considerations

Moral concerns about future generations are widely shared historically and globally (Collins, 2007). Recognition of their rights can morally be enriched on modern human rights, utilitarianist or contractualist doctrines, socio-evolutionist arguments or simply on the no-harm principle. Nevertheless, such recognition faces deep theoretical difficulties and objections. A first set of counter-arguments is ontological and contests the possibility of future generations' rights entitlement, based on the non-existence argument (Ruth Macklin (1981). "Can Future Generations Correctly Be Said to Have Rights?" in Ernest Partridge (ed.), *Responsibilities to Future Generations*. Prometheus Books, pp. 151–156; Richard De George (1981). "The Environment, Rights,

and Future Generations" in Ernest Partridge (ed.), *Responsibilities to Future Generations*. Prometheus Books, pp. 157–166), or on the non-identity problem (Derek Parfit (1987). *Reasons and Persons*, Clarendon Press). The second set of arguments is epistemological. Firstly, it can be argued that recognition shall be limited in its extent because of our inability to identify preferences of distant generations (Martin Golding (1981). "Obligations to Future Generations" in Ernest Partridge (ed.), *Responsibilities to Future Generations*. Prometheus Books, pp. 61–72; Alexander Gillespie (2014). *International Environmental Law, Policy and Ethics*, Oxford University Press). But several authors argue that this should not prevent us from trying (e.g. Catherine Redgwell (1999). *Intergenerational Trusts and Environmental Protection*, Juris Publishing) and that we may be able to identify at least some of their needs linked to critical natural resources (Kristian Skagen Ekeli (2007). "Green Constitutionalism: The Constitutional Protection of Future Generations", Ratio Juris 3(20), 378–401). Secondly, our ability to weigh needs and thus rights of succeeding generations remains questionable. In this respect, several and contradictory solutions have been suggested based on approaches such as egalitarianism, prioritarism, Rawlian's "just saving" part, or a discounting rate.

Intergenerational equity theory

In 1989, E.B. Weiss made a pioneer contribution in the definition of a consistent intergenerational equity theory. The Earth is conceived as a "trust passed to us by our ancestors for our benefits, but also to be passed on to our descendant for their use" (Weiss, 1992). Each generation holds rights (to use the environment), but also bears obligations (to protect the environment). Allocation of rights and duties is governed by a set of three principles of conservation (of diversity, quality, and access to Earth's natural and cultural resources), and four criteria (Weiss, 1989): equitable repartition (of rights and burdens), value neutrality (on future generations' preferences), clearness (foreseeability in their application), and wide acceptance (in different social systems). While this theoretical framework overcomes above-mentioned difficulties such as the non-existence and the non-identity problems (in defining collective generational rights: Weiss, 1992) and the preference's indeterminacy (using the value neutrality criterion), several aspects remain criticized in doctrine (for an overview: Beckerman, Wilfred (2006). "The impossibility of a Theory of Intergenerational Justice", in Joerg Chet Tremmel, *Handbook of Intergenerational Justice*, Edward Elgar Publishing, 53–71; Collins, 2007; Anstee-Wedderburn, 2014), and no consensus exists on any theory for future generations.

Legal recognition of the rights of future generations

International recognition

Declarative instruments
Every major environmental declaration refers to future generations' interests or intergenerational principle (Stockholm Declaration, 1972, preamble, principles 1 and 2), generally anchoring them within the sustainable development principle, according to which needs of present generations shall be fulfilled without jeopardizing those of future generations (Rio Declaration on Environment and Development, 1992, principle 3; Rio Principles for Forests, 1992, principle 2 (b); Johannesburg Declaration on Sustainable Development, 2002, §37; Rio +20 Declaration: The Future We Want, 2012, §86). Two instruments directly deal with future generations' interests, and affirm the correlative responsibility of present generations to preserve them (UNGA, Resolution 35/8 on Historical Responsibility of States for the Preservation of Nature for Present and Future Generations, adopted on 30 October 1980, §1; UNESCO, Declaration on the Responsibilities of Present Generations towards Future Generations (1997), Article 1). Such interests and responsibility are also mentioned in the Millennium Development Goals and succeeding Sustainable Development Goals (UNGA, Resolution 55/2, §2 and 6; UNGA, Resolution 70/1, preamble and §18). Despite the fact that we observe a growing concern for needs and interests of future generations in international declarations, none of these texts recognizes rights for future generations. The only text following an approach similar to E.B. Weiss's theory (but on a limited scope) is the UNESCO Universal Declaration on Cultural Diversity that calls for recognition of cultural diversity as the common heritage of humanity (Article 1).

Conventions
Concerns about interests of future generations were initially mentioned in preamble provisions (first in the 1946 Convention for the Regulation of Whaling and then in some environmental agreements: Convention on the Conservation of Migratory Species and Wild Animals; Convention on International Trade in Endangered Species of Wild Fauna and Flora). Greater legal recognition came along with the link made between the States' duties to protect and the benefits for future generations. This was first stated in the UNESCO World Heritage Convention (Article 4) and then more systematically within the three Rio conventions. Two of these last conventions go beyond by taking into account needs and interests of future generations in the definition of "sustainable use" (Convention on Biological Diversity, Article 2), and in a principle governing parties' implementation of the Convention (UN Framework Convention on Climate Change, Article 3§1, Paris Agreement, preamble).

Jurisprudence
The International Court of Justice (ICJ) shows some reticence in referring to future generations. It firstly did in its advisory opinion on the legality of threat or use of nuclear weapons in order to define the "environment" (para. 29) and risks of nuclear weapons (paras 35–36). In the Gabcikovo-Nagymaros case, the Court noted that new norms and standards have been developed in international environmental law because of growing awareness of the risks for present and future generations (para. 140) but did not explicitly base its decision on any intergenerational equity considerations. Some judges have supported more progressive positions. In 1993, Judge Weeramantry, in his dissenting opinion on the Nuclear Weapon case, affirmed that the rights of future generations "have woven themselves into international law through major treaties, through juristic opinion and through general principles of law recognized by civilized nations" (p. 233). In several separate opinions, Judge Cançado Trindade has given special attention to the intergenerational equity principle, considering it as a general principle of international environmental law (Pulp Mills case, Sep. op., para. 220) and affirming that the Court should have used it for interpretation (Whaling case, Sep. op.) and in order to define monitoring obligations (Pulp Mills, Sep. op., para. 124).

Regional instruments
At the regional level, rights of future generations benefit from a better recognition.

The European Union's duty towards future generations is explicitly recognized (Charter of Fundamental Rights, §6) and their rights are taken into account through the sustainable development principle (Collins, 2007). Conversely, whereas the European Court of Human Rights sometimes mentions international provisions about future generations (Tatar c. Romania case), it does not directly use them in its *ratio decidendi* or recognize any right to them. The Inter-American Court of Human Rights has been more progressive. In the Mayana (Sumo) Awas Tingni Community v. Nicaragua case, the Court affirmed the collective right of a community on its land because of their special relationship with this land, considering that it represents a material and cultural element that they ought to enjoy "to preserve their cultural legacy and transmit it to future generations" (para. 149).

National recognition

Since 1990, intergenerational equity and needs of future generations explicitly became included in various legislative and executive acts (Brazilian Laws No.12.305; No. 9.985/ 2000; No. 12.187) where they are often linked to the purpose of these acts (through the concept of sustainability: New Zealand Resource Management Act 1991, s. 5; Australian Environment Protection and Biodiversity Conservation Act, s. 3A; French Environment Code, Article L.110-1 II; Canadian National Marine Conservation Areas Act, s. 4§3). Interests of future generations have also been enriched in constitutional provisions. Some of them only recall that choices made to fulfil present needs shall not jeopardize those of future generations (Charter for the Environment, which is part of the French Constitution), or the government's duty to preserve the environment for present and future generations (Brazilian Constitution, Article 225). But various constitutions go further and recognize the right for present and future generations to a healthy environment (Bolivian Constitution, Article 7; Norwegian Constitution, Article 110 b; Japanese Constitution, Articles 11 and 97; South African Constitution, Article 24). While national courts have faced some difficulties to effectively protect such rights (Hollis, 2010; Ekeli, 2007), they managed in some cases to deduce from them practical consequences such as the government's responsibility in ensur-ing access to healthy water by constructing a sewage system (High Court of Kenya, Mr Peter Waweru v. Republic of Kenya, 2006, para. 48); some environmental impact assessments' requirements (Land and Environment Court of New South Wales, Gray v. The Minister of Planning and Others, 2006, para. 126); or a limit of annual mineral excavation (Supreme Court of India, Goa Foundation v. Union of India & Others, 2013, para. 71).

Ways to protect the rights of future generations

Commissioner, ombudsman, guardian for future generations

Calls for the appointment of a person representing the interest of the environment (Christopher Stone (1972). *Should Trees Have Standing?: Toward Legal Rights for Natural Objects*, Southern California Law Review (45), 450–501) or future generations (Weiss, 1989) have been heard for a long time (Brundtland Report, 1987, §84, Agenda 21, paras 38–45). Several States created a commission, a council or a commissioner, who shall, in fulfilling its mandate, promote the interests of future generations and intergenerational equity (New Zealand, Finland, Canada, Germany, Hungary, Malta. Some existed only for few years: in France, Israel, and Australia). Nevertheless, these institutions lack power to effectively protect future generations' rights because they only have advisory and consultative functions, and cannot stand for future generations in judicial processes. On the road to Rio+20, a nongovernmental organization (NGO) proposed to create a High Commissioner for Future Generations (within the UN system) in charge of formulating advice, investigating, advocating for future generations, and defining their legal rights. Even if this was discussed, the final declaration adopted only asked the Secretary General to present a report on future generations (§86). In the near future, this proposition is unlikely to succeed because even if the Secretary General recommended the appointment of a High Commissioner he limited its mandate to advisory functions (UNSG (2013). Intergenerational solidarity and the Needs of Future Generations, UN Doc. A/68/322, §§ 53–58) and this point is absent from the agenda of the High-level Political Forum.

Standing for future generations

Even if no existing institutions can stand for future generations, young living generations could work as a proxy. The 1993 decision of the Supreme Court of the Philippines gave some hope in this context. Based on Article II of the Philippines Constitution, the Court recognized standing to a group of children to represent themselves but also generations to come. In a recent case, the Colombian Supreme Court ruled in a similar way on this aspect and concluded to the State's responsibility for insufficient action to reduce deforestation (Colombian Supreme Court of Justice, sentencia 4360-2018, 5 April 2018). Nevertheless, national courts around the world remain reluctant to recognize such standing to children. The question has been raised in the 2013 Urgenda case in the Netherlands, where a NGO sued the government for insufficient action to prevent climate change. Whereas The Hague Court of Appeals made a reference to the interest of future generations (2018, para. 8), it decided not to consider the question of Urgenda's ability to act on behalf of future generations (para. 37). In December 2018, four French NGOs initiated a similar action where they notably referred to interests of future generations (Administrative Tribunal of Paris, "L'affaire du siècle", Complementary memoir, 2019), but there is little indication that the French tribunal will decide differently from The Hague Court in this respect. Finally in January 2020, the US ninth Circuit Court of Appeal ruled that the plaintiffs (21 children) lacked standing in the so-called Juliana v. United States case (United States Court of Appeals for the ninth circuit, January 17, 2020, Case n° 18-36082).

Concluding remarks

Even if intergenerational equity has long been discussed in doctrine, the concept did not reach a binding status under international law. Future generations' interests are mainly enshrined in preambles or declarative instruments. While it could be argued (and some judges do) that this principle and rights of future generations are part of general international law, the ICJ has never drawn conclusions to support this interpretation. Similarly, arguing that intergenerational equity is a part of the sustainable development principle would not be useful

because the legal status and implications of the latter also remain unclear. It seems unlikely to see future generations become right holders under international law in the near future. Nevertheless, the principle of intergenerational equity will probably gain legal recognition and produces its effects as a meta-principle (like sustainable development) that allows in a flexible way the articulation of other rights, norms and principles. Effective protection of the rights of future generations will mainly depend on the extent of their recognition in national legal systems, the ability of people or organizations to stand for them and the will of courts to give to these rights some content.

JULIEN DELLAUX

References

Agius, Emmanuel and Busuttil, Salvino (eds) (2013). *Future Generations and International Law*. Earthscan.

Anstee-Wedderburn, Jane (2014). "Giving a Voice to Future Generations: Intergenerational Equity, Representatives of Generations to Come, and the Challenge of Planetary Rights", Australian Journal of Environmental Law 1(1), 37–70.

Collins, Lynda Margaret (2007). "Revisiting the Doctrine of Intergenerational Equity in Global Environmental Governance", The Dalhousie Law Journal (30), 79–140.

Ekeli, Kristian Skagen (2007). "Green Constitutionalism: The Constitutional Protection of Future Generations", Ratio Juris 3(20), 378–401.

Farber, Daniel A. (2003). "From Here to Eternity: Environmental Law and Future Generations", University of Illinois Law Review, 289–335.

Hollis, Sacha (2010). "Old Solutions to New Problems: Providing for Intergenerational Equity in National Institutions", New Zealand Journal of Environmental Law (14), 25–61.

Tremmel, Joerg Chet (ed.) (2006). *Handbook of Intergenerational Justice*. Edward Elgar.

Vibhute, K.I. (1998). "Environment, Present and Future Generations: Inter-Generational Equity, Justice and Responsibility", Indian Journal of International Law 1(38), 65–73.

Weiss, Edith Brown (1989). *In Fairness to Future Generations: International Law, Common Patrimony and Intergenerational Equity*. Transnational Publishing.

Weiss, Edith Brown (1992). "In Fairness to Future Generations and Sustainable Development", American University Journal of International Law and Policy (8), 19–26.

25.   Gender Equality

Introduction

Gender equality and the empowerment of women and girls are key priorities for the law and development agenda, with gender equality featuring prominently in both the United Nations' 2030 Agenda for Sustainable Development and international human rights law.

Gender equality is important for two main reasons. Firstly, it matters intrinsically. Womanhood must be valued for its own sake, as it is core to life, and women and girls must be entitled to live as they choose, expand their opportunities, and be free from discrimination and violence. Secondly, addressing the needs of women and girls is valuable instrumentally and is integral for the achievement of "security, development, and economic stability" (Sen, 1999; World Bank, 2012). The empowerment of women and the promotion of gender equality also underlie the acceleration of sustainable development and the achievement of Agenda 2030, with discrimination against women having "a multiplier effect across all other development areas".

However, despite significant progress towards gender equality, discrimination and violence against women and girls (including harmful cultural and religious practices) remain pervasive, especially in the Global South. Gender also impacts disproportionately on poverty and socio-economic disparities. Discriminatory gender laws perpetuate poverty for women and obstruct their access to resources. Many women are also not given equal protection under the law, influencing the subordination of women. Even where women have attained formal equality, structural inequalities restrict women from participating fully.

For this reason, the UN's 2030 Agenda acknowledges the imperative of implementing both a human rights-based approach and a development agenda to achieve gender equality. A symbiotic framework enables transformative gender equality and the elimination of gender-based discrimination and violence.

The meaning of "gender equality"

Gender equality interventions play an important role in the struggle for equality for women and are aimed at enhancing women's rights and participation. The term "gender equality", however, is a complex and contested one. There is little consensus about what gender equality means, specifically in relation to: structural inequality and hierarchical power relations; the LGBTQI+ movement, multiple genders and the perception of gender as a binary system; and the complaint that the gender narrative is based on gender myths and "essentialisms". The latter is said to postulate a "hierarchical and oppositional relationship" between men and women and paradoxically depicts women as both inferior subjects and as persons deserving of development because of their intrinsic characteristics, including being hardworking and nurturing (Cornwall and Rivas, 2015).

These contestations are valid. From a definitional perspective, however, "gender" is traditionally defined as the behavioural, cultural, and social characteristics, attributes, norms and expectations that are linked to womanhood or manhood. "Gender equality" refers to the way in which these aspects determine how men and women interact and the resulting power differences between them (World Bank, 2012). According to the Committee on the Elimination of Discrimination against Women (CEDAW), gender equality entails "that all human beings, regardless of sex, are free to develop their personal abilities, pursue their professional careers and make choices without the limitations set by stereotypes, rigid gender roles and prejudices" (CEDAW, GR No. 28, 2010). Thus, gender equality entails the equal promotion of rights and opportunities for men and women, specifically advancing women's economic participation, decision-making, freedom from violence, political empowerment and gendered citizenship.

Additionally, a full understanding of gender equality is incomplete without an appreciation of women's multidimensional societal roles, the contexts in which women live, and the causes of gender inequality. Women's lives are shaped by various social, cultural, familial, economic, political and religious demands, responsibilities and domains. These roles are complicated by mechanisms of oppression which stereotype women and subordinate them. The promotion of transformative gender equality must be cognisant of gender stereotypes and women's lived reality and also reflect women's intersectional roles.

Substantive gender equality

Both the UN's 2030 Agenda, through the various Sustainable Development Goals (SDGs), and international human rights law, envisage the achievement of formal and substantive equality for women.

The traditional notion of equality is formal equality. This requires that likes be treated alike, regardless of race, gender or other equivalent attributes. Formal equality is crucially important for women, as it enables equality before the law. In many countries, however, women are not treated equally to men, especially where pluralistic customary or religious legal systems apply. Consequently, many women are denied equal rights and are discriminated against by the laws of marriage, property and succession (Fredman, 2018). Additionally, whilst formal equality is the first step towards true gender equality, it can entrench disadvantage.

The problem is that even when women are treated equally before the law, women usually lag behind men, particularly in social and economic respects. This is caused inter alia by structural gender inequalities; the historical exclusion of women from employment, property and capital; mechanisms of gender oppression; and power structures within families and gender stereotypes. It is only through the promotion of substantive equality that gender inequality is addressed. Substantive equality is usually explained with reference to equality of outcome and equality of opportunity, but Fredman's four-dimensional approach to substantive equality is best suited to overcoming gender inequality (Fredman, 2011; 2018). These dimensions are: (a) distributive equality, requiring redistributive mechanisms, such as affirmative action measures, redressing disadvantage and cognisant of intersectional inequality; (b) the recognition dimension, requiring steps to redress the prejudice, humiliation, stereotypes and violence experienced by women; (c) the participative dimension, facilitating the participation of women in society and emphasizing individual agency; and (d) the transformative dimension, aimed at breaking down the barriers creating structural inequality. All four dimensions must be addressed simultaneously to achieve substantive transformative equality

and when designing policy or legal interventions. This approach is gaining traction and components thereof are included in both international human rights law and in the UN's SDG agenda.

SDG 5: Achieve gender equality and empower all women and girls

The 2030 Agenda is a global framework for advancing sustainable development and comprises 17 SDGs and 169 targets aimed at "quantifying shared global development", measured by way of "indicators".

The SDGs have better potential to achieve their vision of development than their predecessors, the Millennium Development Goals (MDGs). Compared to the limited focus of the MDGs, the SDGs are more nuanced and are based on a commitment to the realization of human rights and the achievement of development. They also acknowledge the connections between inequality, marginalization and poverty and embody a more substantive appreciation of development. The comprehensive focus on women's empowerment and the elimination of gender inequality in the SDGs is also a vast improvement on the MDGs, as these did not deal with gender equality in the non-gender specific goals (Esquivel and Sweetman, 2016).

Gender equality is positioned as an independent SDG in SDG 5. Gender perspectives are also included in the targets of other SDGs (see, SDG 1 and SDG 4). Specifically, the Agenda recognizes that women must receive "equal access to quality education, economic resources and political participation", plus "equal opportunities with men and boys for employment, leadership and decision-making at all levels". The Agenda proclaims that it aims to "promote gender equality and the empowerment of women and girls" and achieve "a world in which every woman and girl enjoys full gender equality and all legal, social and economic barriers to their empowerment have been removed".

Goal 5 comprises nine specific targets, including the elimination of all forms of gender-based discrimination, gender-based violence and harmful practices (e.g. female genital mutilation), and promoting access to reproductive health. Many targets encompass aspects of substantive equality. For example, Target 5.A embraces distributive equality by requiring reforms giving women equal rights to economic resources. The impact of this target, however, is undermined by the rider "in accordance with national laws". Another example is Target 5.5, which promotes the participative dimension of substantive equality and requires "women's full and effective participation . . . at all levels of decision-making. . .".

However, despite the amplified commitment to gender equality as both a developmental goal and a human right, discriminatory laws remain extant and women continue to suffer excessive discrimination and violence on a global level (UN, 2019). Women still perform "a disproportionate share of unpaid domestic work", do not enjoy full access to health rights, and experience lack of autonomy. Women are also amongst the poorest people in the world, with poverty a direct cause of gendered discrimination. The UN's 2019 report thus acknowledges that the achievement of gender equality "will require bold and sustainable actions that address the structural impediments . . . of discrimination against women", plus laws and policies advancing gender equality, backed by adequate resources and "stronger accountability" measures.

Gender equality in international human rights law

Commencing in 1948, the Universal Declaration of Human Rights (UDHR) proclaimed the equal entitlement of women and men to human rights "without distinction of any kind" on various grounds, including sex. The Declaration was drafted in gender neutral terms, avoiding the term "all men" and instead using "all human beings" and "everyone" to demonstrate that it protected men and women.

Both the International Covenant on Social and Political Rights (ICCPR) and the International Covenant on Economic, Social and Cultural Rights (ICESCR) in their common Article 3 prohibit discrimination based on inter alia "sex". Article 2(1) and Article 2(2) of the ICCPR and ICESCR, respectively, provide that each State party guarantee that the Covenant rights be exercised without discrimination on various grounds, including sex, birth or other status. These obligations require States to respect, protect and fulfil women's human rights on the basis of equality and non-discrimination. In short, States must: (a) refrain from State conduct that results in the denial of women's equal enjoyment of their human

rights; (b) protect women from discrimination by private actors; and (c) take proactive steps to ensure that women and men enjoy equal rights both in law and in practice (CESCR, General Comment (GC) No. 16 on The Equal Right of Men and Women to the Enjoyment of all Economic, Social and Cultural Rights, 11 August 2005; Human Rights Committee, GC No. 28 on Article 3 Equality of rights between men and women, 29 March 2000; CESCR GC No. 20 on Non-discrimination in Economic, Social and Cultural Rights, 2 July 2009). Article 26 of the ICCPR also creates a freestanding right to equality and provides that everyone is equal before the law and entitled to its equal protection.

In 1967 the UN adopted the Declaration on the Elimination of Discrimination against Women. It provides that discrimination against women offends human dignity and demands of States to abolish existing laws and practices which are discriminatory against women, and to establish adequate legal protection for equal rights of women. This led to a proposal for a legally binding treaty protecting women's rights.

The result was the Convention on the Elimination of All Forms of Discrimination against Women, 1979 (CEDAW). Described as the International Bill of Rights for Women, its preamble acknowledges that notwithstanding other international human rights instruments, women do not enjoy equal rights with men and that "extensive discrimination against women" prevails. CEDAW is comprehensive and sets out State obligations to eliminate unfair discrimination on the basis of gender and to achieve substantive equality for women. It entrenches women's civil and political rights (e.g. the right to vote) and women's economic, social and cultural rights (e.g. the right to education). It requires States parties to take all appropriate measures, including legislation, to ensure the full development of women. In addition to the general unfair discrimination provision in Article 1, CEDAW also adds substantive anti-discrimination provisions, such as Article 5, providing that States should strive to eliminate social, cultural and traditional patterns perpetuating harmful gender stereotypes.

Many international instruments also prohibit discrimination against women and girls belonging to specific groups, for example: the Convention on the Rights of Persons with Disabilities (CRPD), 2006; the International

Convention on the Protection of the Rights of All Migrant Workers and Members of Their Families (ICRMW), 1990; and the Convention on the Rights of the Child (CRC), 1989.

On a regional level, gender equality is protected inter alia in the African Charter, 1981; the Maputo Protocol, 2005; the European Convention on Human Rights (ECHR), 1953; and the Inter-American Convention on the Prevention, Punishment and Eradication of Violence against Women (CBdP), 1994.

Numerous UN Declarations also address gender equality through international commitments. Activism promoting women's rights was particularly prevalent from 1975 to 1995, with the convening of four UN World Conferences on Women (Mexico City in 1980, Copenhagen in 1985, Nairobi in 1990 and Beijing in 1995). These resulted in a Platform for Action to promote gender equality and to hold States accountable for discrimination and violence targeting women. The Beijing Platform for Action is particularly significant as it articulated women's rights as human rights and included strategic objectives to eliminate discrimination against women and achieve gender equality. Other notable global commitments proclaiming gender equality include the Rio Conference on Environment and Development (1992), the Vienna Conference on Human Rights (1993), the Cairo Conference on Population and Development (1994), the Copenhagen World Summit for Social Development (1995) and the Istanbul Conference on Human Settlements (1996).

Conclusion

The eradication of gender inequality requires an inclusive and holistic approach (Arts, 2017), with an appreciation of meaning and causes. Not only must substantive equality be positioned at the forefront of the gender equality agenda, but, in addition, a synergy between the human rights-based and developmental frameworks must be attained to achieve transformed gender equality (Alston and Robinson, 2005). A balance is needed to ensure that an unnecessary burden is not placed on women, making them work for development, instead of making development work for gender equality and the empowerment of women (Cornwall and Rivas, 2015).

JOANNA BOTHA, WITH THE INPUT OF
GLANCINA MOKONE

References

Alston, Philip and Mary Robinson (2005). "The Challenges of Ensuring the Mutuality of Human Rights and Development Endeavours", in Philip Alston and Mary Robinson (eds), *Human Rights and Development: Towards Mutual Reinforcement*, Oxford University Press.

Arts, Karin (2017). "Inclusive Sustainable Development: A Human Rights Perspective", Current Opinion in Environmental Sustainability (24), 58–62.

Cornwall, Andrea and Althea-Maria Rivas (2015). "From 'Gender Equality' and 'Women's Empowerment' to Global Justice: Reclaiming a Transformative Agenda for Gender and Development", Third World Quarterly 2(36), 396.

Esquivel, Valeria and Caroline Sweetman (2016). "Gender and the Sustainable Development Goals", Gender and Development 1(24), 1–8.

Fredman, Sandra (2011). *Discrimination Law*. Oxford University Press.

Fredman, Sandra (2018). "Working Together: Human Rights, the Sustainable Development Goals and Gender Equality". Available at: https://ssrn.com/abstract=3295693 accessed 10 September 2020.

Sen, Amartya (1999). *Development as Freedom*. Oxford University Press.

UN (2019). Department of Economic and Social Affairs "The SDG Report" 2019. Available at: https://unstats.un.org/sdgs/report/2019/ accessed 10 September 2020.

UNHRC (2014). *Women's Rights are Human Rights*. United Nations Publications.

World Bank (2012). *World Development Report 2012: Gender Equality and Development*. Available at: https://openknowledge.worldbank.org/handle/10986/4391 accessed 10 September 2020.

26. Global Governance

Global governance commonly refers to a phenomenon of governance arrangements encompassing our globe, increasingly so from the downfall of the bi-polar world order. It denotes a sum of collective efforts of global, national, and local actors to address consequences of increasing interdependence and to pursue global order based on specific goals and values. The definition provided by the UN Commission on Global Governance in 1995 is a standard reference among scholars. It famously described governance as 'a sum of the many ways individuals and institutions, public and private, manage their common affairs'. Because of broad, dynamic, and complex processes of interactive decision-making involved in managing common affairs on the global level, the report pointed out that 'there is no single model or form of global governance, nor is there a single structure or set of structures' (Commission on Global Governance (1995). Our global neighbourhood: The report of the Commission on Global Governance. Oxford University Press). Global governance scholars focus on decreasing effectiveness of State interventions in the face of exponential effects of global challenges and crises; increase in number and influence of international and regional organizations; rising importance of private actors and empowerment of individuals within international system; increasing multiplicity of levels and actors involved in decision-making and implementation across different sectors of global politics; complex nature of relationships and interactions between them; and criticisms based on concerns for democratization and legitimacy of these mechanisms and interactions.

Global governance also serves as an analytical framework to better understand and explain contemporary political developments and socio-economic transformations. As such, it has become a dominant tool of social scientists studying world politics. Weiss (2000) famously referred to global governance as a 'heuristic device to capture and describe the confusing and seemingly ever-accelerating transformation of the international system'. In a recent attempt, Domínguez and Velazquez Flores (2018) conceive global governance as 'a framework of analysis or intellectual device to study the complexity of global processes involving multiple actors that interact at different levels of interest aggregation'.

Global governance has become one of the defining elements of international law's context. The centrality of global governance to debates about how our world should be governed necessitates cross-fertilization between debates on the future of global governance and that of international law. International law has represented an idea of progress in world political thought. It is oftentimes seen as 'an inherent progressive value for humankind, along the Kantian mantra that internationalism signifies a desirable move towards a superior State of social development' (Orford et al. 2016). Similarly, some maximalist conceptions of global governance see it as a way and means of realizing an ideal of an orderly and just world. Global governance also helps to realize the progress of international law. The potential of global governance for internal improvement of international law is underlined in Klabbers' recent statement of international law where he sees international law as part of a broader pattern of global governance. International law needs to accept this reality and update its tools to adapt to the changing world. Embracing global governance, in its turn, helps international law to maintain its relevance in global order and helps it to continue (re)producing meaningful and useful discourse and praxis on the conduct of international politics (Klabbers, 2017).

Development is a major global governance goal. Global governance has relied on sectoral approaches to questions of global economic governance, global security governance, global environmental governance, or global governance for development. The latter's importance is gradually increasing. The United Nations development agenda is one of the main drivers of this transformation. UN action on development includes milestones like the 1986 Declaration on Right to Development, Millennium Development Goals launched at Millennium Summit in 2000, or Sustainable Development Goals (SDGs) as announced in the 2030 Agenda for Sustainable Development. The status of the United Nations, which pursues social progress of world countries, as a centre-piece of global governance architecture reinforces the link between global governance and development. Development also has a transcendental character as success of governance efforts in the fields of security, economy, or environment largely depends on capacity of world countries to effectively accomplish these objectives. Achievement of global governance goals for development necessitates special attention to the needs and capacity of developing countries. Solidarity with developing countries has been a constant feature in world politics since the 1940s.

Global governance is ubiquitous and ambiguous. However, the imprecise and undetermined nature of the term demonstrates that, despite its sceptics, global governance has become a fundamental phenomenon in world politics. As such, multiplicity, complexity and ambiguity are inherently part of it. This multiplicity can be addressed by emphasizing three perspectives on global governance. These perspectives are transformationalist, managerial and critical perspectives.

Transformationalist perspectives on global governance

For transformationalists, global governance holds the potential to carry humankind into an orderly future. It fights disorder caused by human behaviour by changing the behaviour of the latter, both on individual and collective levels. Global governance denotes the belief that humankind must re-evaluate the ways it conducts business in order to adapt to changing circumstances. Political and economic tools we use for international cooperation were largely the product of certain historical and socio-political circumstances; they are nowadays inadequate to deal with challenges facing the world community. Our world is transformed by events which have been unfolding since the end of the Second World War. The slow yet gradual emergence of global constitutionalism around the UN system, consolidation of human rights as the main politico-legal framework, the establishment of liberal economic order as the dominant system for world economic affairs, or ongoing formation of global civil society are signs of deep transformations of world politics. The world is also facing great environmental challenges. For scholars like James Rosenau, one of the most eminent representatives of this perspective, these developments lead to transformation of the world wherein the nature of authority is fundamentally changing, rendering traditional distinctions between international and domestic meaningless (Bevir, 2007). Global governance presents itself as the most adequate framework to deal with and accompany these transformations. For Castells (2008), the globalization has already transformed the world: the emergence of global civil society and of ad hoc forms of global governance are direct consequences of this transformation. While dissolving nation States into a global government is not possible nor desirable, leaving the current atomistic structure of the international system as it is is also counter-productive. In this constellation, global governance appears the most relevant framework for mitigating frictions between the passing vestiges of the Westphalian system and the necessities of the unfolding new world, and for consolidating the accomplishments of the long-running transformation of world politics. Embracing global governance is desirable for upgrading our political philosophy.

The famous 1995 report of the UN Commission on Global Governance was clearly transformationalist in terms of definition, scope, and the courses of action it contained. It proclaimed a 'new world' which needed 'a new vision that can galvanize people everywhere to achieve higher levels of co-operation in areas of common concern and shared destiny'. Some of its unorthodox recommendations included introducing global taxation, establishing an economic security council, rendering the ICJ's verdicts binding, or expanding the authority of the Secretary General. The Agenda 2030 announced 'a supremely ambitious and transformational vision' in order to 'shift the world on to a sustainable and resilient path'. It identified 17 goals with the purpose of achieving sustainable development in its three dimensions – economic, social and environmental. The transformationalist approach thus sees global governance as an excellent opportunity to reconsider our conceptions of national and global governance to better reflect change. Two important consequences as well as goals of this transformation for the international system must be singled out: on the one hand, global governance permits to add nature into the traditional equation between State and individual; on the other hand, it erects global justice as one of the main goals of the international system.

Managerial approach to global governance

For Klabbers, who used the term with respect to international organizations, the managerial approach presupposes two things: first, that institutionalized cooperation between independent States will contribute to the solution of common problems and second, that increased cooperation through international organizations will lead to a better world. Much of the debate around global governance adopts the same logic: States are increasingly ineffective to deal with global challenges; hence they need to promote new forms of inter-State and beyond the State cooperation in order to manage the consequences of globalization and to improve the world. For Castells (2008), the 'increasing inability of nation States to confront and manage the processes of globalization of the issues that are [the] object of their governance leads to ad hoc forms of global governance'.

The functionalist definition of global governance stands as 'collective efforts to identify, understand, or address worldwide problems and processes that went beyond the capacities of individual states' (Domínguez and Velazquez Flores, 2018). The function of global governance is to enable States and other actors of the international system to manage the consequences of globalization and international interdependence. The main difference of the managerial approach from the transformationalist approach appears in two ways. First, relying on States as the main promoters and enforcers of global governance while at the same time requiring from them to address questions of legitimacy and democratization (i.e. the need to enlarge the scope of their partnerships, to adopt inclusive understanding of stakeholders, to institute environmental issues as global policy-making domains and further democratize and globalize their decision-making procedures). Second, adopting specific and sectoral goals which remain modest compared to the mission of reconfiguring the world political system: the main objective of global governance is not reconfiguring conventional political and socio-economic structures of world politics, it is rather improving and bettering the day-to-day governance of the world relying on global regulatory regimes. As such, the managerial approach seems to claim primacy among different approaches to global governance today. This shift from transformationalist to managerial perspective is clearly evident in a change of language in the UN vision toward global governance.

The Committee for Development's report on 'Global governance and global rules for development in the post-2015 Era' adopts a distinctly managerial approach. The report restates intergovernmental cooperation at the centre of the global partnership for development. It states that 'intergovernmental cooperation has a vital role to play in the achievement of global development goals, in terms not only of the resources and technical assistance it can provide but also in the areas of policy decision-making and norm-setting. Global governance encompasses the totality of institutions, policies, norms, procedures, and initiatives through which States and their citizens try to bring more predictability, stability, and order to their responses to transnational challenges. Effective global governance can only be achieved with effective international cooperation' (Committee for Development Policy, 2014). The Agenda 2030 relies on the managerial approach to launch a global partnership for achieving the SDGs. Firstly, it identifies the main challenges preventing humankind from achieving sustainable development. It then specifies 17 goals and 169 targets covering different sectors of economic, social and environmental development in order to overcome those challenges. It announces a global partnership bringing together governments, the private sector, civil society, the UN systems and other actors and stakeholders to mobilize all available resources to achieve SDGs.

The managerial approach is also conducive to the expansion of global governance. It advances the demand for more global governance to increase the efficiency of global efforts for development. The Committee for Development put forward two conditions for effectively tackling development challenges in the post-2015 era. It called for reappraisal of the role of governments in global governance, especially that of developing countries. At the same time, it articulated a need for strengthening global governance rules in order to manage increasing interdependence among countries efficiently. More specifically, it expected the United Nations to strengthen its position in global governance in order to spearhead global efforts to promote sustainable development. The ambitious scope of SDGs can also be partly explained by the feeling that fulfilment of MDGs still left an unfinished business.

IKBOLJON QORABOYEV

Esty's elaborate definition of global governance summarizes well different aspects of this global governance bargain, which is built on the premises of continuing to see States as main enablers of global governance while at the same time asking them to adopt an inclusive and innovative stance to governance. For Esty:

> supranational governance as any number of policy-making processes and institutions that help to manage international interdependence, including (1) negotiation by nation States leading to a treaty; (2) dispute settlement within an international organization; (3) rule-making by international bodies in support of treaty implementation; (4) development of government-backed codes of conduct, guidelines, and norms; (5) prenegotiation agenda-setting and issue analysis in support of treaty-making; (5) [SIC] technical standard setting to facilitate trade; (6) networking and policy coordination by regulators; (7) structured public private efforts at norm creation; (8) informal workshops at which policymakers, NGOs, business leaders, and academics exchange ideas; and (8) private sector policymaking activities. (Esty, 2005 [footnotes omitted])

Critical accounts of global governance

Critical perspectives stem from various schools of thought in International Relations and international law. Two elements characterize International Relations scholars' stance on global governance. First, they question universal origins and the universal language of global governance. Second, they adopt a sceptical stance towards goals of global governance as well as motivations of actors promoting it. For some scholars, global governance's universal language masks the hegemonical position of the United States across different spectrums of international and global governance. For Ikenberry (2014), the 'system of global governance emerged after the World War II as an American order-building project'. For him, current global governance is a strange mix of Westphalian and liberal internationalist projects and as such follows both hierarchical and democratic logics at the same time. It is American leadership which provides management of tensions between these two contradictory logics. Thus, global governance is 'management of liberal internationalism'. Great power origins of global governance can also be read in parallel to geopolitical considerations behind development discourse. Development scholars denote that contemporary develop-

ment theory originated from US Government backed social inquiries to promote development models along capitalist lines among newly decolonized countries, which constituted the developing world after the Second World War. Hence, development practices in global governance is a way of perpetuating and reinforcing the gap between developed and developing worlds.

Critical scholars also focus on the legitimacy deficit of global governance. For them, the global governance bargain is less legitimate than that associated with government. These criticisms single out major deficiencies of current global governance arrangements and highlight the need to reform them. For Wilkinson, these deficiencies may appear as absence of long-term efficiency of some governance innovations, lack of truly equitable and participatory mechanisms, or inadequate care for environmental, justice and human rights concerns of world community (Bevir, 2007). For international lawyers, global governance raises substantial challenges. Uncertainty about the nature of actors participating in global governance, ambiguity around the basis of authority for global governance, or lack of accountability of global governance actors are among the most pressing ones. Contemporary discourses on multipolarity, democratizing the world order, and globalizing International Relations bring additional criticisms towards global governance. Their main concern is who exercises authority to define the frame and scope of global governance and who does it benefit most, rather than why we need global governance (the transformationalist argument) or how we should design it (the managerial approach).

IKBOLJON QORABOYEV

References

Bevir, Mark (ed.) (2007). *Encyclopaedia of Governance* (Volumes 1 and 2). SAGE.

Castells, Manuel (2008). 'The New Public Sphere: Global Civil Society, Communication Networks, and Global Governance', The Annals of the American Academy of Political and Social Science 1(616), 78–93.

Committee for Development Policy (2014). *Global Governance and Global Rules for Development in the Post-2015 Era*. United Nations.

Domínguez, Roberto and Rafael Velazquez Flores (2018). *Global Governance*. Oxford Research Encyclopaedia of International Studies.

Esty, Daniel C. (2005). 'Good Governance at the

Supranational Scale: Globalizing Administrative Law', Yale Law Journal (115), 1490–1562.

Ikenberry, John (2014). 'The Quest for Global Governance', Current History 759(113), 16–18.

Klabbers, Jan (2017). *International Law*. 2nd Edition. Cambridge University Press.

Ocampo, José A. (ed.) (2016). *Global Governance and Development*. Oxford University Press.

Orford, Anne, Florian Hoffmann, and Martin Clark (eds) (2016). *The Oxford Handbook of the Theory of International Law*. Oxford University Press.

Weiss, T. G. (2000). 'Governance, good governance and global governance: conceptual and actual challenges', Third World Quarterly, 21(5), 795–814.

27. Good Governance

Emergence

The concept of good governance burst onto the development scene at the beginning of the 1990s and quickly entrenched itself as an essential part of development thinking. According to the World Bank's website, in 2019 the Governance Practice section will deliver 24 projects, totalling $1.8 billion, and 128 advisory and analytical services. A further $3.6 billion has already been committed to governance projects in 2020. Moreover, according to the same source, 40 per cent of all World Bank actions in development policy financing are governance related.

The emergence of good governance as a development concept was driven, at least in the early years, by the World Bank. In a 1989 report focusing on the long-term perspectives of growth on the African continent, the World Bank announced that 'a crisis of governance' was responsible for much of Africa's development problems (World Bank 1989. Sub-Saharan Africa: From Crisis to Sustainable Growth: A Long-term Perspective Study, available at http://documents.worldbank.org/curated/en/498241468742846138/pdf/multi-0page.pdf accessed 2 October 2019, p. 60). In addition to calling for a "drastic" overhaul of public administration and the enforcement of the rule of law, the report pronounced on the need for political renewal (World Bank, 1989, p. 192). A governance task force was quickly established and in 1991, the World Bank published a discussion paper entitled "Managing Development – the Governance Dimension". From here, good governance went mainstream. By 1998, the then UN Secretary General, Kofi Annan, could declare in his annual report that, "good governance is perhaps the single most important factor in eradicating poverty and promoting development" (United Nations 1998. Annual Report of the Secretary-General on the Work of the Organization). Today, the OECD website continues to proclaim that "good governance at all levels is fundamental to economic growth, political stability, and security".

As has been widely noted, the emergence of good governance as a policy tool coincided with a need for the international financial institutions to repurpose themselves following the much-noted failures of the Washington Consensus. However, it owes much as well to shifts in economic thinking. At the beginning of the 1990s, development economists began to focus on the importance of institutions and on the long-term "rules of the game" as a necessary requirement for economic growth (Douglass North (1990). *Institutions, Institutional Change and Economic Performance.* Cambridge University Press). This "intellectual resurrection" of the State (Grindle, 2012, p. 263) was given additional support by the recognition of the role of State action in the economic wunderkinds in East Asia, the so-called East Asian Tigers. At the same time, the end of the Cold War prompted reflection on conditionalities within development. Support no longer needed to be structured by membership in a political bloc, opening the door for internally directed political conditionality (Doornbos, 2001, p. 97).

Defining good governance

It has become commonplace to highlight the lack of conceptual clarity of "good governance" and each development actor has their own understanding of it. While "governance" commonly denotes the act of governing, "good governance" introduces a judgment about the quality of governance. In 1992, the World Bank pronounced that "Good governance is synonymous with sound development management" (World Bank 1992. Governance and Development, available at http://documents.worldbank.org/curated/en/604951468739447676/Governance-and-development accessed 25 September 2020, p. 1). Yet by the time of its World Development Report on governance and the law in 2017, no definition of good governance is offered. Instead, good governance – still seen as vital to the processes of development – appears to be both a process and a goal. As process, good governance takes a primarily pragmatic approach to governance. This is visible in the World Bank's "Three principle for rethinking governance for development". Governance is good where it focuses on the function of institutions not their form; reflects on power asymmetries instead of institutional capacity; and concentrates on the role of law rather than the rule of law (World Bank, 2017, p. 29). As a goal, good governance entails "progress toward achieving security, growth and equity" (World Bank, 2017, p. 29).

The United Nations Development Programme (UNDP), on the other hand, views good governance as a collection of seven core principles. These are: participation; equity, non-discrimination and inclusiveness; gender equality; rules-based; transparency; and accountability and responsiveness (UNDP, 2011, p. 279). These principles are presented by the UNDP as "congruent with" basic human rights principles as laid down in the core UN human rights declarations and treaties. This relationship between good governance principles and human rights is presented here as intuitive rather than as a hunch requiring interrogation.

These two positions – the World Bank and the UNDP – represent the two poles of good governance thinking within development: the first is more technocratic, focusing on effective and efficient public management and accountability; the second has a stronger political element. Put differently, while financial institutions tend to view good governance as a means to development, UN agencies and many donor agencies see good governance equally as an end of development. Gisselquist notes that the UN uses the terms "good governance" and "democratic governance" interchangeably (Gisselquist, 2012, p. 10). This split partly reflects the limitations on certain institutions as regards their freedom to intervene in the political affairs of States, but also stems from a predominance of New Institutional Economics thinking, whereby institutions are important for allowing economic actors to flourish.

This distinction in how good governance is defined is not reflected in the characterization of its relationship to development. The elements of good governance are not seen solely as a good thing in themselves but because they are essential for the promotion of development – however defined. That is, good governance "became a defining quality of development and a necessary condition for it" (Grindle, 2012, p. 268). This is true independent of whether one understands good governance as a technocratic or as a political intervention. The 2002 Human Development Report, for example, had as its core message that human development was predicated upon effective governance (UNDP 2002. Human Development Report: Deepening Democracy in a Fragmented World, Oxford University Press, p. vi). In more recent years,

good governance is more commonly part of a list of elements that governments need to ensure if X (insert your goal) is to be achieved. In the 2030 Agenda for Sustainable Development, for example, good governance is listed alongside equality, rule of law, and the creation of transparent, effective and accountable institutions as essential for peace and security, which in turn is given as essential for the realization of sustainable development (UN, 2015, para. 35). This move further blurs the definition of good governance; if equality, the rule of law and the creation of effective institutions are separate from good governance, what then is good governance? This conceptual blurring continues in the relationship of the term to corruption, another star of development discourse. From the beginning, good governance and corruption have been used in the same sentence simply as each other's antithesis (Polzer, 2001): good governance is the opposite of a corrupt institution or society. This "elasticity" of the concept has entailed that the 2002 World Development Report provided 116 different ways in which developing countries should pay attention to good governance elements (Grindle, 2012, p. 269).

Measuring good governance

If good governance was to be accepted as essential to development, it was going to be necessary to provide evidence of this relationship. To this end, the World Bank created a unit dedicated to the measurement of good governance. In 1999, in a seminal paper entitled 'Governance matters', Kaufmann, Kray and Zoido-Lobatón laid out an empirical connection between six categories of governance and economic growth in a large cross-country study. They concluded that there was a "strong positive association between each of the six aggregate governance indicators and three development outcomes: per capita incomes, infant mortality and adult literacy" (Kaufmann et al., 1999, p. 12). Moreover, they concluded that this association was a causal one. For example, the governance indicators of rule of law and graft appear to have a clear correlation to reduced infant mortality outcomes; and a one-standard-deviation increase in governance across the indicators led to a 15–25 per cent point improvement in adult literacy.

Nowadays, measuring governance is a massive sector within the development business.

There is a raft of global indicators that claim to measure good governance, from the Actionable Governance Indicators, led by the World Bank, to the World Bank's Doing Business Indicators, which provide a measure of governance in relation to the ease of doing business at a country level. These indicators are complemented by indicators by private actors, the best known perhaps being the corruption measure built by Transparency International. These indicators have in common that they focus on stability, most frequently understood as strong and functioning institutions, democratic governance, including citizen voice and participation, and a minimal State.

Critics

> In its brief life, [good governance] has . . . muddied the waters of thinking about the development process, confounding causes and consequences, ends and means, necessity and desirability. (Grindle, 2012, p. 1)

Criticisms of the concept of good governance can be split into three distinct lines. The first set of criticisms focuses on the lack of conceptual clarity of good governance. At its worse, this sees the concept become little more than a placeholder for things that the user of the term sees as good. This very vagueness is of course an important part of the concept's success. Yet it also means that different actors place different governance demands on the same institutions. Moreover, in the thinner characterization of good governance, the term is stripped of its political nature and becomes a technocratic tool of market intervention.

The second type of critique concerns the empirical claims made for good governance. While almost everyone within the development field now accepts that there is some connection between well-run institutions and a well-functioning society capable of providing services, such as health care, education and so on, a fundamental question remains over the causal nature of the relationship. Do good institutions lead to development or are they an outcome of development? Moreover, even if the relationship is indeed a causal one, we are no closer to understanding why some institutions function well and others do not, i.e. what it is that makes them "good", nor how to transform a poorly functioning institution into a good one. This lack of understanding of how good governance

works has not stopped it from becoming the most important form of conditionality in development assistance (Doornbos, 2001).

The third line of criticism concerns the governance effects of the concept. Good governance as it is used within development activities forms part of a long pattern of interventionism and disciplining of States of the Global South by States and institutions of the North. As such, good governance can be seen as representing a contemporary form of the civilizing narrative, which identifies moral and practical failings in certain countries and locates the answers, both technical and moral, in others. Moreover, the focus on good governance – as with the rule of law and corruption – serves to shift the responsibility for continuing poverty onto institutions in developing countries (Goodwin, 2017, p. 495).

Future

Despite it being 30 years since the emergence of good governance, we seem to be no further forward in agreeing what the concept entails, nor in understanding how governance works in relationship to development. As a result, the term has largely disappeared from more recent academic literature on development. Instead, we see a shift in language towards institutions (e.g. Michael J. Trebilcock and Mariana Mota Prado (2011). *What Makes Poor Countries Poor? Institutional Dimensions of Development*. Edward Elgar). However, in the policy realm, good governance fulfils an important function for many development actors – acceptability, conditionality, justification, discipline – and, as such, it is a term that is likely to be very difficult for them to resist.

Morag Goodwin

References

Doornbos, Martin (2001). "'Good Governance': The Rise and Decline of a Policy Metaphor?", Journal of Development Studies 6(37), 93–108.

Gisselquist, Rachel M. (2012). Good Governance as a Concept, and Why This Matters for Development Policy. WIDER Working Paper No. 2012/30.

Goodwin, Morag (2017). "The Poverty of Numbers: Reflections on the Legitimacy of Global Development Indicators", International Journal of Law in Context 4(13), 485–497.

Grindle, Merilee (2012). "Good Governance: The Inflation of an Idea" in Bishwapriya Sanyal, Lawrence J. Vale, and Christina D. Rosan (eds), *Planning Ideas That Matter: Livability, Territoriality, Governance and Reflective Practice.* The MIT Press.

Kaufmann, Daniel, Aart Kray, and Pablo Zoido-Lobatón (1999). Governance Matters. Policy Research Working Paper 2196. Available at: http://web.worldbank.org/archive/website00818/WEB/PDF/GOVMAT-9.PDF.

Polzer, Tara (2001). Corruption: Deconstructing the World Bank Discourse. London School of Economics Destin Working Paper No. 01-18.

UNDP (2011). *Towards Human Resilience: Sustaining MDG Progress in an Age of Economic Uncertainty.* UNDP.

United Nations (2015). *Transforming our World: The 2030 Agenda for Sustainable Development.* General Assembly Resolution 70/1, 21 October 2015, A/RES/70/1.

Weiss, Thomas G. (2000). "Governance, Good Governance and Global Governance: Conceptual and Actual Challenges", Third World Quarterly (21), 795–796.

World Bank (2017). *The World Development Report: Governance and the Law.* World Bank.

28. Growth and De-growth

Growth

In mainstream development literature, the assumption of economic growth is central to development. Initially, development was understood as economic development and was equated with economic growth. Development was seen as a linear process of economic progress and modernization, mimicking the industrialization process of the Global North. The economics of growth relies on some major growth paradigms. It typically focuses on finance, technology (transfer), institutions and market size as aspects of the growth process, and thinks of growth in terms of stages (Aghion and Howitt, 2009).

Gradually, while economic growth remained important, broader meaning was given to development, to include environmentally sustainable and social dimensions. In the late 1980s, the Brundtland Commission introduced an ecological dimension to development, emphasizing limits to growth. The UN Development Programme's (UNDP) Human Development Reports from the early 1990s added a social dimension. In addition to economic growth, human well-being (as reflected in longevity, education and income) became a yardstick for development as well.

In the 2030 Agenda, economic growth (referred to as prosperity), social development and ecological sustainability go hand-in-hand. The language of inclusive and sustainable development illustrates more generally an incorporation of the social and ecological dimension in thinking about development. It is thus acknowledged that development is more than economic development: social and ecological aspects matter too. The 2030 Agenda mentions, moreover, peace and partnership: both are needed for sustainable development.

The relative weight of economic growth in development

Commonly, sustainable development is explained in terms of a triple bottom-line (the three Ps of profit, planet and people), suggesting that it is about balancing economic growth with environmental and social considerations. This approach can be called the weak definition of sustainability. In this weak definition, economic growth is taken for granted. For example, the Sustainable Development Goal (SDG) 8 mentions the promotion of sustainable and inclusive economic growth. In other words, economic development and poverty alleviation are based on orthodox economics, and therefore on assumptions of (the need for) never ending economic growth: "growth is an axiomatic necessity" (Kallis et al., 2012, p. 172).

Strong definitions of sustainable development have challenged the reductionist tendency to equate the notion of sustainable development with "environmentally friendly economic growth" (Kerschner, 2010, p. 549). For proponents of these strong definitions, sustainable development means the prevalence of the environmental dimension over the economic one. The prioritization of the environmental (planet) pillar over the economic (profit) one, requires a radical departure from assumptions of economic growth, including zero-growth or even de-growth, as argued in ecological economics.

De-growth

Strong definitions of sustainable development suggest that no-growth is to replace economic growth as the new normal (Martínez-Alier et al., 2010). Given the "limited ecological space" circumscribed by the planet's carrying capacity, "managing without growth" becomes the challenge (Kallis et al., 2012, p. 172).

There are several strands in ecological economics which hold divergent positions on the need for de-growth (commonly referred to as negative growth), zero-growth or selective growth: Steady-state Economics, the New Economics of Prosperity and De-growth. None of them see de-growth as a permanent feature, nor as a global requirement: rather, it is "the path of transition" toward ecologically sustainable development (Kallis et al., 2012, p. 173). Nonetheless, de-growth will lead to "a dramatic restructuring of the State and a reconfiguration of work" (Kallis et al., 2012, p. 174).

The de-growth literature seems to target primarily advanced economies in the North. In Kerschner's analysis, economic de-growth is "the rich North's path towards a globally equitable" zero-growth economy (Kerschner, 2010, p. 544). The reason is twofold. From an environmental perspective, Northern economies have meanwhile transgressed sustainable levels as determined by planetary boundaries, and need to shrink therefore: "rich industrialized countries have evidently surpassed sustainable limits already, and de-growth is therefore essential" (Kerschner, 2010, p. 549). From a social and distributional perspective, the North needs to downsize in order to allow the South to grow without further transgressing sustainable levels globally. Arguably, the North-South dichotomy is in need of further refinement. In fact, the 2015 Paris Agreement on Climate Change has moved beyond the North-South dichotomy and speaks of nationally determined contributions that apply to all countries.

De-growth scholars have not confined themselves to making a (daunting) analysis of the current growth paradigm and its destructive and untenable environmental impact; they have also come up with an alternative, that is how "prosperous de-growth" can be realized. At the core is the idea of (re-)distribution. An important starting point of prosperous de-growth is provided by happiness economics, which submits that "a more equal distribution of income and investment in public services that make a difference in the quality of life, can have greater welfare effects than generalized growth" (Kallis et al., 2012, p. 174). Prosperous de-growth also seeks to ensure full employment in a de-growth scenario through work-sharing, unpaid work and a basic income (Kallis et al., 2012, p. 176). Inevitably, de-growth implies a strong State, given the level of intervention that is required, for example in imposing social and ecological caps (Kallis et al., 2012, p. 176).

Growth agnosticism

Van den Bergh has coined the notion of "agrowth", that is "deliberate agnosticism about growth", as a third way between what he sees as progrowth and antigrowth positions (Van den Bergh, 2015, p. 16). In his view, society should be indifferent to GDP growth and move away from growth fetishism (because of GDP information failure), and seek to better realize human welfare (Van den Bergh, 2017).

Raworth's Doughnut Economics is agnostic about growth too. She proposes "an economy that promotes human prosperity whether GDP is going up, down, or holding steady" (Raworth, 2017, p. 245). Raworth identifies three main shifts in focus in Doughnut Economics: towards more attention for goods and services provided outside the monetary economy; towards changes in the level of wealth; and towards the distribution of economic benefits. Key is the subservience of the economic objective to the ecological and social one: "The economy's over-arching aim is no longer economic growth in and of itself, but rather to bring humanity into the safe and just space – inside the doughnut – and to promote increasing human well-being there" (Raworth, 2017, p. 8).

Conclusion

For centuries, economic growth has been at the centre of development. Whereas the dominant development paradigm continues to focus on growth, de-growth scholarship has emphasized that endless economic growth of the North is untenable on ecological and social grounds. Other scholarship has suggested growth agnosticism: this implies an indifference to economic growth, and a prioritization of human welfare within planetary boundaries. At a minimum, this heterodox scholarship challenges the idea of economic growth as a goal in and of itself.

WOUTER VANDENHOLE

References

Aghion, Philippe and Steven N. Durlauf (eds) (2005). *Handbook of Economic Growth*. Vol. 1. Elsevier.

Aghion, Philippe and Steven N. Durlauf (eds) (2014). *Handbook of Economic Growth*. Vol. 2. Elsevier.

Aghion, Philippe and Peter W. Howitt (2009). *The Economics of Growth*. The MIT Press.

Kallis, Giorgos, Christian Kerschner, and Joan Martinez-Alier (2012). "The Economics of Degrowth", Ecological Economics (84), 172–180.

Kerschner, Christian (2010). "Economic De-growth vs. Steady-State Economy", Journal of Cleaner Production 6(18), 544–551.

Martínez-Alier, Joan, Unai Pascual, Franck-Dominique Vivien, and Edwin Zaccai (2010). "Sustainable De-growth: Mapping The Context, Criticisms and Future Prospects of an Emergent Paradigm", Ecological Economics 9(69), 1741–1747.

Raworth, Kate (2017). *Doughnut Economics. Seven Ways to Think Like a Twenty-first-Century Economist*. Random House Business Books.

Van den Bergh, Jeroen C.J.M. (2015). *Green "Agrowth" as a Third Option: Removing the GCP-growth Constraint on Human Progress*. WWWFor Europe.

Van den Bergh, Jeroen C.J.M. (2017). "A Third Option for Climate Policy within Potential Limits to Growth", Nature Climate Change 2(7), 107–112.

29. Health

The World Health Organization (WHO) defines health as "a State of complete physical, mental and social well-being and not merely the absence of disease or infirmity". This is the most-referenced and read definition of health. However, scholars have called for a reconceptualization of the word "health" to promote a normative definition that will be functional and operational. Health as a concept is admittedly multi-faceted. It includes mental fitness, emotional stability, physical strength, sexual capability, and fertility. All these components and dimensions of health are necessary for a person to enjoy optimal wholeness at every point in time. Health is also a fundamental human right indispensable for the exercise of other human rights, for instance, the right to life and human dignity. Consequently, every human being is entitled to the enjoyment of the highest attainable standard of health conducive to living a life of dignity (CESCR, GC 14). However, the theoretical framework of health, its conceptualization, and the legal protection of individuals' entitlement to enjoy being wholesome in respect of their health, is a multi-disciplinary discourse.

Scholars like Meikirch advocate a definitional paradigm shift based on the determinants of health. From this perspective, Meikirch defines health as a State of well-being emergent from conducive interactions in relation to individuals' potential, life's demands, and social and environmental determinants (Bircher and Kuruvilla, 2014, p. 368). Meikirch's health model considers health based on different determinants including individual determinants, social determinants, and environmental determinants. According to this model, health is "when individuals use their biologically given and personally acquired potentials to manage the demands of life in a way that promotes well-being" (Bircher and Kuruvilla, 2014, p. 368). Health can, therefore, be considered as the result of a maximized State of optimal well-being that seeks to maximize an individual's potential. Health entails a lifelong process of focus on the enhancement of an individual's physical, intellectual, emotional, social, spiritual, and environmental well-being.

Classification of health

The right to health is "an inclusive right extending not only to timely and appropriate health care but also to the underlying determinants of health, such as access to safe and potable water and adequate sanitation, an adequate supply of safe food, nutrition and housing, healthy occupational and environmental conditions, and access to health-related education and information" (OHCHR, 2000 para.11).

Health is classified as a human right and various international instruments focus on the realization of health, provision of access to health care services to individuals, and protection of health care rights. Access to health care services is a *sine qua non* to ensure that everyone enjoys good health and access to health care services. "Health" in the context of the UN and WHO can only be given appropriate and adequate legal protection where there is unrestricted access to health care services. As Huls puts it "access to health is an often-overlooked aspect of the right to health. Without practical access, the right to health becomes an empty promise" (Huls, 2004, p. 20).

The international efforts towards the protection of health and ensuring that there is adequate access to health care rights are duplicated at the continental, regional, and national levels. For women and female adolescents, health includes sexual health and reproductive health. Under the WHO framework on the protection of women's Sexual and Reproductive Health Rights (SRHR), sexual health includes prevention of domestic violence and sexual abuse, family planning and safe abortion care services. Sexual and reproductive health is a major aspect of women's health and the international community continues to address women's SRHR concerns through the international human rights legal framework. The rights to education, information, housing, and social security are relevant to the health of adolescents and youth, as these rights are social determinants that may positively or negatively affect the realization of good health. Human rights encompass both freedoms and entitlements. In this context, health rights and freedoms include the right to control one's health and body and to be free from interference. Health rights entitlements include the right to a system of health protection that gives everyone an equal opportunity to enjoy the highest attainable level of health.

International protection of health as a human right

The international recognition of health as a human right establishes a legal and global platform for the protection and implementation of access to health care services. The legal platform makes providing acceptable access to affordable health care services in addition to safe and potable water, sanitation, food, housing, health-related information and education, and gender equality the duty and primary obligation of the State. In 1966, the international community again strengthened the recognition of health as a human right through the International Covenant on Economic, Social and Cultural Rights (ICESCR). State parties to international instruments on health rights are saddled with the responsibility to allocate available resources to progressively realize health rights-related goals while there are international human rights mechanisms, such as the Universal Periodic Review, or the Committee on Economic, Social and Cultural Rights, which review these goals. A key SRHR entitlement is women's right to access safe abortion care services and post-abortion care services in such circumstances they choose in order to terminate a pregnancy.

UN and health rights

The human rights advocacy approach to the realization of women's sexual and reproductive health serves as a platform for the promotion and implementation of human rights under the International Bill of Rights. The Universal Declaration of Human Rights (UDHR), 1948 provides an internationally accepted human rights standard for all nations. The UDHR provides for the protection of the right to life; the right to liberty and security of person; the right to be free from torture or any cruel, inhuman or degrading treatment or punishment; the right to marry at full age; the right to a standard of living adequate for health and well-being of everyone and their family members; and the right to participate freely in the cultural life of the community and to enjoy or share in scientific advancement and its benefits. The provisions of the UDHR identify and protect related components of an individual's right to a standard of living adequate for health and well-being. These rights are also reiterated in the International Covenant on Civil and Political Rights (ICCPR), 1966, and the ICESCR also provides for the protection of the right to health.

The ICESCR is the most authoritative conceptualization of the protection of the right to health under the international legal framework. The ICESCR provides explicitly for the protection of everyone's enjoyment of the highest attainable standard of physical and mental health. The Covenant also provides for the right of everyone to marry, and the right to enjoy the benefits of scientific progress and its applications. Under the Covenant, the right to health includes SRHR and States parties are required to take steps necessary for the realization of reduction of the stillbirth-rate, infant mortality and the healthy development of a child. Notably, under the International Bill of Rights, that is, the UDHR, ICCPR, and ICESCR, women's rights to enjoy and control their SRHR are interconnected and linked to the enjoyment of civil, political, economic and social-cultural rights. For women, SRHR is an integral part of the right to health and a significant component of enjoying the right to health.

In 1981, the UN also addressed issues relating to women's health rights and freedoms, such as the right of women to be free from discrimination in the field of health care and access to health care services through a focused Convention and health-related issues such as family planning. Under the Convention on the Elimination of All Forms of Discrimination against Women (CEDAW), a State is required to ensure to women health care services needed during pregnancy, confinement and the post-natal period as well as adequate nutrition during pregnancy and lactation. This Convention also addresses some customs and traditions that affect women's enjoyment of human rights such as local and traditional rules relating to women's sexual and reproductive rights. For example, female genital mutilation (FGM), forced marriage and non-autonomous control over reproductive rights are related customs and customary practices that affect (African) women's enjoyment of SRHR. Expectedly, the concept of the right to health in its broad terms includes women's SRHR under the ICESCR. Clearly, there is a comprehensive and universal approach to the protection of women's SRHR, which includes access to safe abortion as well as post-abortion care under the International Bill of Rights, particularly under the ICESCR.

The International Conference of People and Development (ICPD), 1994, introduced a paradigm shift in the advocacy for women's rights. The ICPD Programme of Action acknowledges that protecting and fulfilling reproductive rights' obligations rest on the recognition of the fundamental right of all couples and individuals to decide freely and responsibly the number, spacing, and timing of their children and to have adequate information about their reproductive health. This Programme of Action defines the reproductive health right to include sexual health, thus all couples and individuals may have the right to decide freely and responsibly the number and spacing of their children and to have the information, education and means to do so.

The ICPD Programme of Action projected the international community's commitment to women's rights generally, with emphasis on reproductive health, family planning, health and mortality. Other international efforts toward the protection and fulfilment of women's SRHR include Declarations and Programmes of Action. Another international effort on the protection of health is the Beijing Declaration. This Declaration recognizes that for every woman to enjoy the right to health, it is necessary that women participate in all areas of public and private life. Women are also to have control over matters relating to their sexuality, including sexual and reproductive health throughout the whole life cycle. In 2001, the UN Declaration of Commitment on HIV/AIDS made undertakings towards enacting, strengthening or enforcing legislation and regulations and putting in place measures to eliminate all forms of discrimination against vulnerable groups and people at risk, especially women and young people.

In recent times, the Millennium Development Goals focused on universal access to sexual and reproductive health services in line with the agenda of the UN to ensure the protection of human rights for sustainable development. Women's SRHR has also been integrated into the Sustainable Development Goals, while the Family Planning 2020 (FP2020) initiative highlights access to contraception.

Continental protection of health rights

At the continental level, the African Charter on Human and Peoples' Rights, 1982 (Banjul Charter) restates the provisions of the International Bill of Rights on human rights. In addition, Member States are required to guarantee the elimination of discrimination against women and ensure the protection of women's rights stipulated in international declarations and conventions. The Protocol to the African Charter on Human and Peoples' Rights on the Rights of Women in Africa, 2003 (African Women's Protocol), otherwise known as the Maputo Protocol, also guarantees comprehensive women's rights. The African Women's Protocol defines a woman's right to self-protection to include the right to be informed on one's health status and the health status of one's partner, particularly if affected with sexually transmitted infections, including HIV/AIDS, and the right to have family planning education. The African Women's Protocol recognizes the SRHR of women in Africa explicitly.

The first Maputo Plan (MPoA 2007–2015) was set to achieve the domestication and protection of SRHR in Africa by 2020. The SRHR protected in the context of the African Women's Protocol includes women's right to control their fertility; the right to decide whether to have children and the number of children and the spacing of children; the right to choose any method of contraception; and the right to self-protection and to be protected against sexually transmitted infections, including HIV/AIDS. In addition to the MPoA 2007 – 2015, the Sexual and Reproductive Health and Rights Continental Policy Framework was adopted in 2005 and endorsed by African Heads of State and Government in 2006. This Policy was explicitly drafted to provide a harmonization model for the national, sub-regional and continental efforts to promote "reproductive health" and "reproductive rights" in Africa.

In Europe, the Charter of Fundamental Rights of the European Union provides that everyone has the right of access to preventive health care based on the conditions established by national laws and practices. Also, everyone has the right to benefit from medical treatment (Charter of Fundamental Rights of the European Union (2000/C 364/01), Article 35). This Charter provides a broad base legal framework for the protection of health rights within the European Union. In Asia, there is an ongoing effort towards having a regional instrument for the protection of human rights after the Final Declaration of the Regional Meeting for Asia of the World Conference on Human

Rights known as the Bangkok Declaration, 1993. The 1993 Declaration contains the aspirations and commitments of the Asian region. In the Declaration, the Region reaffirmed its commitment to the principles contained in the Charter of the United Nations and the UDHR as well as the full realization of all human rights throughout the world.

More recently, Southeast Asia, through ASEAN, made a definite advancement in 2012 when Member States adopted the ASEAN Human Rights Declaration (AHRD). The ASEAN effort is commendable as its dedication established a reference point for further advancement. Articles 28 and 29 of the ASEAN Human Rights Declaration focus on access to health care and the protection of health rights. The articles make provision for the protection of South Asian citizens' rights to medical care and social services. Specifically, the Declaration provides that "every person has the right to the enjoyment of the highest attainable standard of physical, mental, and reproductive health, to basic and affordable health care service, and to have access to medical facilities".

Conclusion

The question, what is health, still exists more than half a century after the Second World War and the international community is concerned with health issues, interventions, debates on the promotion and funding of health programmes. This concern keeps reoccurring with significant implications for health policy formulation, defining individuals' health rights and the protection of health rights components. One fact is undeniable; the lack of a concise definition of health practically affects the accessibility and affordability of health care services globally.

AVINASH GOVINDJEE AND MAYOWA AJIGBOYE

References

African Union Commission (2006). Sexual and Reproductive Health and Rights Continental Policy Framework. Available at: https://au.int/sites/default/files/documents/30921-doc-srhr_english_0.pdf.

Bircher, Johannes and Shyama Kuruvilla (2014). "Defining Health by Addressing Individual, Social, and Environmental Determinants: New Opportunities for Health Care and Public Health", Journal of Public Health Policy 3(35), 363–386.

Huls, Natalie (2004). "Access to Health", Human Rights and Human Welfare. Available at: https://www.du.edu/korbel/hrhw/researchdigest/health/access.pdf.

Office of the High Commissioner for Human Rights (OHCHR) (ed.) (2000). CESCR General Comment No. 14: The Right to the Highest Attainable Standard of Health (Art. 12). Available at: https://www.refworld.org/pdfid/4538838d0.pdf.

Preamble to the Constitution of the World Health Organization as adopted by the International Health Conference, New York, 19–22 June 1946; signed on 22 July 1946 by the representatives of 61 States (Official Records of the World Health Organization, no. 2, p. 100) and entered into force on 7 April 1948.

30. Human Rights

This contribution explains what human rights are and what their foundations may be. It introduces the main instruments and mechanisms of human rights law, and explores some themes at the intersection of human rights and development, in particular human rights relativism, context-specificity and human rights-based approaches to development.

What are human rights?

Human rights are often defined as a set of fundamental rights held by every individual on the basis of his or her humanity. In a classic liberal reading of human rights, key elements include that (1) the power of a ruler is not unlimited; (2) subjects have a sphere of autonomy; (3) there exist procedural mechanisms to limit the arbitrariness of the ruler; (4) the ruled have rights that enable them to participate in decision-making; (5) the authority has not only powers but also some obligations; and (6) all rights and freedoms are granted equally to all persons (Osiatýnski, 2009, pp. 1–2).

This classic idea of human rights has been superseded in at least four important ways. First, beyond a shield against State interference, human rights are seen as a sword to claim State action. Second, beyond civil and political rights, the area of economic, social and cultural rights has been included. Third, the nation State oriented approach has been expanded to one in which questions of global injustice are addressed, which requires that other actors than the territorial State are included as duty-bearers, such as foreign States, international organizations or business enterprises. And fourth, on the rights-holders side, in addition to individual rights, collective rights (group rights) have been added, most clearly with regard to indigenous peoples.

The first two developments are reflected in the categorization of human rights into three categories or generations: civil and political rights; economic, social and cultural rights; and solidarity rights. Civil and political rights include the right to life, the prohibition of torture, the right to a fair trial, the right to respect for private and family life, and freedoms or liberties (of assembly, association, religion, . . .). The category of economic, social and cultural rights includes the right to work and fair working conditions, health, education, social security and an adequate standard of living among others. The right to development, the right to a healthy environment and the right to peace belong to the category of solidarity rights. There is no watertight division between the different categories. The categorization is politically and legally relevant. Typically, the human rights nature of civil and political rights is taken for granted, whereas it remains highly contentious for solidarity rights. Legally, while civil and political rights are generally well protected, economic, social and cultural rights tend to be seen as more programmatic. Civil and political rights must be realized immediately, whereas the realization of economic, social and cultural rights is made subject to the availability of resources. Also, a different typology of obligations has been used for these two categories. With regard to civil and political rights, a distinction is made between negative and positive obligations (i.e. obligations to abstain and obligations to take action). A tripartite typology of obligations relating to economic, social and cultural rights has been introduced, with obligations to respect (abstention), to protect (against third parties) and to fulfil. The obligation to fulfil can be further dissected into sub-obligations to facilitate, to promote and to provide. Other conceptual developments too have helped to improve the legal understanding of economic, social and cultural rights and to consider them more on a par with civil and political rights, such as the presumption that retrogressive measures are not permitted and the identification of minimum core obligations. For some, minimum core obligations must be realized immediately and their non-observance cannot be justified. For others, minimum core obligations impose a higher threshold for justification in case of non-observance (Vandenhole, 2003).

The third development, in which the exclusively territorial application of human rights treaties is challenged, is a more recent development. Traditionally, it was assumed that human rights obligations only applied to the territory of the State party concerned. States may affect human rights beyond their borders though. Their policies, for example to provide agricultural subsidies to their farmers, may lead to export at dumping prices with harmful effects on human rights elsewhere. Through participation in peace operations, they may interfere with the right to life and the right to liberty, among other rights, on the territory of other States (see entries in this volume on Extraterritorial Human Rights Obligations, International Solidarity, and Duty to Cooperate). A debate is also emerging on other duty-bearers than the State. In particular, it has been proposed to extend human rights obligations to non-State actors such as companies as well as to international financial institutions, amongst others (Kinley, 2009).

The fourth development has to do with the question who are the rights-holders of human rights. The most prominent extension to collective rights has so far happened with regard to indigenous peoples (see entry in this volume on Indigenous Peoples).

Foundations of human rights

A number of ideal-typical schools of thought may be identified on the foundations of human rights as well as on their universality, realization, legal codification and emancipatory potential: the natural school, the deliberative school, the protest school and the discourse school. The natural school sees human rights as a given; they are "based on 'nature', a shortcut which can stand for God, the Universe, reason, or another transcendental source" (Dembour, 2010, p. 3). Traditionally, this was the dominant school. Deliberative scholars consider human rights as politically agreed upon values. The protest school sees human rights as claims against injustice, which need to be fought for. The discourse school sees human rights as "talked about": it accepts that human rights discourse is a powerful political language (Dembour, 2010).

Proponents of a distinctive Third World approach to human rights tend to identify more with the protest school. Baxi, for example, has argued that human rights arise from resistance against injustice. Those who suffer are therefore the real authors of human rights (Baxi, 2002).

Human rights law: instruments and mechanisms

Legally, the foundational global human rights document is the Universal Declaration of Human Rights (UDHR), adopted by the United Nations (UN) General Assembly in 1948 in the aftermath of the atrocities committed during the Second World War.

Over the past 70 years, nine core human rights treaties have been adopted within the framework of the UN. There are two general human rights treaties, which legally codify the UDHR, both adopted in 1966: the International Covenant on Civil and Political Rights, and the International Covenant on Economic, Social and Cultural Rights. Together with the UDHR, they form the International Bill of Rights. Two of the other early core human rights treaties deal with racial and gender discrimination: the International Convention on the Elimination of All Forms of Racial Discrimination (1965), and the Convention on the Elimination of All Forms of Discrimination against Women (1979). There are also two thematic treaties, on torture and on enforced disappearance: the Convention against Torture and Other Cruel, Inhuman or Degrading Treatment or Punishment (1984) and the International Convention for the Protection of All Persons from Enforced Disappearance (2006). The other core human rights treaties focus on particular groups: children (Convention on the Rights of the Child, 1989), migrant workers (International Convention on the Protection of the Rights of All Migrant Workers and Members of Their Families, 1990), and persons with disabilities (Convention on the Rights of Persons with Disabilities, 2006).

For each treaty, a specific monitoring body ("Committee") has been established. The Committees have three monitoring procedures available: the reporting procedure, whereby States parties report on average every five years on the implementation of the treaty; the complaints procedure, allowing individuals or States to complain about violations of their human rights; and the inquiry procedure, which is initiated by a Committee in order to examine grave or systematic violations. Only the reporting procedure is mandatory for States parties. The Committees offer authoritative interpretations in general comments or general recommendations (available: General Comments, see http://www.ohchr.org/EN/HRBodies/Pages/TBGeneralComments.aspx, accessed 6 September 2020). These general comments or general recommendations help to understand particular issues and to interpret particular rights.

The Human Rights Council is the main political body dealing with human rights within the

United Nations. The Human Rights Council assesses States' human rights performance through the Universal Periodic Review. The Council is assisted by an Advisory Committee and by special procedures (for a full list of special procedures: http://spinternet.ohchr.org/_ Layouts/SpecialProceduresInternet/ViewAll CountryMandates.aspx?Type=TM accessed 6 September 2020). The latter are thematic or country-specific.

There exist three regional systems of human rights protection: the African Union, the Organization of American States and the Council of Europe. Each has its own human rights treaties and monitoring bodies. In addition, there are also regional instruments such as the ASEAN Human Rights Declaration and the Arab Charter on Human Rights.

Human rights and development

There is a longstanding debate on the universality of human rights. Whereas it is often proclaimed that human rights are universal, that universalism has been under attack. The cultural relativist or particularist critique of human rights has emphasized Asian or African values, amongst others, and proposed a new global ethic based on human duties and responsibilities instead. Others have argued that human rights are Western and liberal, part of the imperialist enterprise, and at best offering an anti-hegemonic (that is challenging the status quo) but not a counter-hegemonic (that is an alternative) ideology for radical transformation (Shivji, 1995).

Moving away from the abstract and ideological discussions, some authors have emphasized the context-specificity of human rights realization. Levitt and Merry look at local uses of human rights (of women) in terms of vernacularization, that is the "process of appropriation and local adoption" of international human rights (Levitt and Merry, 2009, p. 446). What they are interested in is how human rights are received and adapted in local contexts. In his localization of human rights, De Feyter takes context-specificity one step further, by focusing primarily on standard setting. He wants to take:

the human rights needs as formulated by local people (in response to the impact of economic globalization on their lives) as the starting point both for the further interpretation and elaboration of

human rights norms, and for the development of human rights action, at all levels ranging from the domestic to the global. (De Feyter, 2007, p. 68)

Human rights-based approaches to development (HRBAD) are about mainstreaming human rights into development. The UN common understanding revolves around three pillars: that all UN development cooperation must further the realization of human rights; that it needs to be guided by human rights standards and principles; and that it is in particular about the capacity development of duty-bearers to meet their obligations and of rights-holders to claim their rights. In other words, it reflects a vision of development as well as a process to development. Central principles of most HRBADs can be summarized in the acronym PANEN, that is, participation, accountability, non-discrimination, empowerment, and normativity. Notwithstanding more empirical work on HRBADs since the mid-2000s, HRBADs remain poorly understood and implemented, and assessments of achievements and success have shown mixed results. Recent scholarship that explicitly factors in power (Andreassen and Crawford, 2013) and change (Gready and Vandenhole, 2014) has helped to better understand HRBADs.

WOUTER VANDENHOLE

References

Andreassen, Bard A. and Gordon Crawford (eds) (2013). Human Rights, Power and Civic Action. Comparative Analyses of Struggles for Rights in Developing Countries. Routledge.

Baxi, Upendra (2002). The Future of Human Rights. Oxford University Press.

De Feyter, Koen (2007). "Localising Human Rights" in Wolfgang Benedek, Koen De Feyter, and Fabrizio Marrella (eds), Economic Globalisation and Human Rights. Cambridge University Press.

Dembour, Marie-Bénédicte (2010). "What Are Human Rights? Four Schools of Thought", Human Rights Quarterly 1(32), 1–20.

Gready, Paul and Wouter Vandenhole (2014). Human Rights and Development in the New Millennium: Towards a Theory of Change. Routledge.

Kinley, David (2009). Civilising Globalisation: Human Rights and the Global Economy. Cambridge University Press.

Levitt, Peggy and Sally Merry (2009). "Vernacularization on the Ground: Local Uses of Global Women's Rights in Peru, China, India and the United States", Global Networks 4(9), 441–461.

Osiatýnski, Wiktor (2009). *Human Rights and Their Limits*. Cambridge University Press.

Shivji, Issa G. (1995). "The Rule of Law and Ujamaa in the Ideological Formation of Tanzania", Social and Legal Studies 2(4), 147–174.

Vandenhole, Wouter (2003). "Completing the UN Complaint Mechanisms for Human Rights Violations Step by Step: Towards a Complaints Procedure to the International Covenant on Economic, Social and Cultural Rights", Netherlands Quarterly of Human Rights 3(21), 423–462.

WOUTER VANDENHOLE

31. Humanitarian Crisis

Definition and concepts

A humanitarian crisis (also sometimes referred to as a humanitarian emergency or humanitarian disaster) can be defined as one or more events entailing a critical, exceptional threat to human life or well-being on a large scale, particularly where this affects a population rendered vulnerable by pre-existing factors such as poverty or inequality (European Commission – DG ECHO, 2016). The concept of humanitarian crisis thus covers situations where danger to a human population reaches a certain gravity and scale, with the cause, onset and duration of the threat (or its manifestation) being generally left rather open.

While "humanitarian crisis", "disaster", and other related terms are sometimes used interchangeably, a disaster is defined in the field of disaster risk reduction (DRR) as "a serious disruption of the functioning of a community or a society at any scale" caused by exposure of a vulnerable population to hazardous events which exceed their coping capacity and cause loss (United Nations Office for Disaster Risk Reduction / United Nations General Assembly, 2016, p. 13). Such a disruption may be among the events triggering or compounding a broader situation of humanitarian crisis, although the majority of humanitarian crises cannot be ascribed to one cause, but result from the "interaction between natural hazards, armed conflict and human vulnerability" (UN Office for the Coordination of Humanitarian Affairs (UN OCHA), 2019, p. 12). However, even crises primarily related to natural hazards engage human responsibility, given the often socially and economically determined distribution of vulnerability and coping capacity. Inequalities between countries are also reflected in the impact of disasters, as people exposed to natural hazards in the poorest countries are seven times more likely to be killed (UN OCHA, 2019, p. 13). Aside from the social aspect of disaster impact, human agency is also increasingly implicated in causation. It has been argued that anthropogenic climate change is affecting the prevalence of natural hazards to the extent that the distinction between human-made and natural hazards is losing relevance (Stephens, 2016, pp. 169–172).

Disasters are often classified according to the nature of the hazards involved or their onset and duration. However, the distinction between humanitarian crises that involve armed conflict and those that do not is considered to be key in terms of context analysis and response. This categorization is also legally relevant, as international legal instruments relating to disasters tend to exclude armed conflicts from their scope in order to maintain a distinction from situations governed by international humanitarian law (Bartolini, 2018). In the field of humanitarian action, the concept of "complex emergency" – i.e. a humanitarian crisis in the context of a breakdown in authority caused by conflict – is often used to distinguish humanitarian crises involving conflict from others. Such emergencies may include a combination of hazards and causes of vulnerability and are particularly characterized by their political nature, their impact on all facets of society, and the need for a large-scale and complex response at various levels (IASC, 1994, paras 6–8).

Relevant international legal frameworks

As far as they entail armed conflict, humanitarian crises are regulated by international humanitarian law (IHL) – a field of public international law constituted primarily by widely ratified treaties (e.g. the 1949 Geneva Conventions and their Additional Protocols) and a well-developed body of customary rules. IHL seeks to mitigate the humanitarian impact of conflict, especially on vulnerable people such as civilians, prisoners or the wounded, including by setting out a framework for humanitarian assistance.

Humanitarian crises connected to natural hazards are generally governed by international disaster law (IDL), which broadly covers issues related to DRR, disaster relief and longer-term recovery and rehabilitation. Although the corpus of treaties in this area is less systematic and comprehensive than in IHL, IDL has seen rapid development over the past 20 years, particularly through key soft law instruments such as the Guidelines for the Domestic Facilitation and Regulation of International Disaster Relief and Initial Recovery Assistance (IDRL Guidelines), the Draft Articles on the Protection of Persons in Disasters, and the Sendai Framework for Disaster Risk

Reduction. These instruments have met with wide acceptance and recognition, and many of their provisions are rooted in principles of international human rights law (IHRL) and international environmental law, particularly in the field of DRR (Zorzi Giustiniani, 2018).

Whether or not armed conflict is present, IHRL continues to protect people in humanitarian crises, although its application may be modified where a rule of IHL applies as *lex specialis* or limited where a State has made a valid derogation from human rights treaty obligations in an emergency situation. In times of humanitarian crisis, a State retains obligations to respect the rights of affected persons (e.g. by refraining from forced evictions or from limiting freedom of movement unnecessarily), as well as protect them from violations (e.g. by providing information about risks, or enforcing the law against private actors carrying out forced evictions). International and regional human rights mechanisms and soft law initiatives have provided a forum for further elaboration and interpretation of IHRL obligations relating to disaster preparedness, response and recovery (McDermott et al., 2017, pp. 558–562).

Finally, as humanitarian crises often entail mass displacement, international refugee law and international norms on internal displacement (such as the Guiding Principles on Internal Displacement and the African Union Convention for the Protection and Assistance of Internally Displaced Persons in Africa) also apply, giving more specific content to IHRL in this regard. In the broader migration field, the Global Compact for Safe, Orderly and Regular Migration also integrates commitments to reduce drivers of forced migration through DRR, as well as to develop solutions for people forced into cross-border migration by slow-onset disasters, such as those caused by climate change.

Connection to development

Many of the risks and vulnerabilities contributing to humanitarian crises can be linked back to failures of or a lack of sustainability in development processes – for example, high levels of poverty, or the increasing prevalence of natural hazards linked to human impact on the environment. Furthermore, longer-term recovery will necessarily involve a developmental perspective and may be an opportunity to reduce future risks. The relationship of development to other areas of activity aimed at preventing or responding to humanitarian crises, such as DRR and humanitarian action, is therefore highly relevant. On a normative level, links between DRR and sustainable development have mainly arisen with regard to disaster prevention, international cooperation, and the human rights dimension of protection of persons (Karimova, 2016).

Both the Sendai Framework for Disaster Risk Reduction and the Sustainable Development Goals, as key agenda-setting instruments in their respective fields for the period until 2030, reflect these links. The Sendai Framework stresses a primary responsibility on States to reduce disaster risks, including through inter-State cooperation and particularly vis-à-vis developing countries. It also incorporates elements common to a rights-based approach to development, in particular by adopting the protection of human rights (including the right to development) as an aim of disaster risk management, as well as emphasizing principles such as participation and inclusion, non-discrimination and equality, and empowerment of rights-holders (Principle 19 (a)–(d)). The Sustainable Development Goals, for their part, include an objective to reduce human impacts and economic losses caused by disasters (with a focus on poor or vulnerable people), including through adoption of integrated plans for climate change mitigation/adaptation and disaster resilience, implementation of holistic disaster risk management, and assistance to least developed countries for resilient buildings (Sustainable Development Goal 11, Targets 11.5, 11.B and 11.C). Overall, these connections between DRR and sustainable development reflect a common aim of reducing vulnerability to disasters, and thereby the occurrence or impact of humanitarian crises.

In humanitarian crises involving armed conflict, IHL sets out a number of rules which, when respected, can at least minimally safeguard sustainable development. These rules include limitations on weapons and tactics of war, and rules protecting civilian infrastructure and the natural environment. With regard to IHL's regulation of humanitarian assistance, however, the response to protracted conflicts or complex emergencies may activate tensions between IHL-based humanitarian assistance, founded on the principles of neutrality, impartiality and independence, and rights-based interventions which can be perceived as more political (Churruca-Muguruza, 2018, pp. 12–13).

Conclusion: humanitarian crises – a challenge for development, humanitarian action and disaster risk reduction

In response to a global context of increasingly protracted and complex humanitarian crises, which provide fertile ground for a vicious cycle of recurring disasters and spiralling vulnerability, there are increasing calls for greater interconnection between development, humanitarian action and DRR. Addressing human vulnerability, a key element of disasters and humanitarian crises, is an objective which these fields share, and numerous coordination models and strategies exist. However, there is in practice an overstretching of the humanitarian sector, often in substitution of development and DRR activities, which reflects that the root causes of crises are being insufficiently addressed through longer-term approaches (Churruca-Muguruza, 2018, pp. 10–15). As put by Churruca-Muguruza, "the main challenge lies in how to respond to the demands of developing countries, which seek support to create resilient national and local capacities to sustainably end the underlying conditions that create humanitarian crises" (Churruca-Muguruza, 2018, p. 13). While existing normative frameworks cannot in themselves remedy this state of affairs, they do play a role in shaping the strategies and operating space of the growing range of actors operating in humanitarian crisis situations, whether in the humanitarian, development or DRR fields. From a legal perspective, a deeper understanding of the growing links between IHL, IHRL, IDL and development, as well as their divergences, may serve to better underpin the interrelationship of humanitarian action, development and DRR that is needed to address humanitarian crises in a durable way.

DEBORAH CASALIN

References

Bartolini, Giulio (2018). "A Taxonomy of Disasters in International Law" in Flavia Zorzi Giustiniani et al. (eds), *Routledge Handbook of Human Rights and Disasters*. Routledge.

Churruca-Muguruza, Cristina (2018). "The Changing Context of Humanitarian Action: Key Challenges and Issues" in Hans-Joachim Heintze and Pierre Thielbörger (eds), *International Humanitarian Action*. Springer.

European Commission – DG ECHO (2016). "Humanitarian Protection: Improving Protection Outcomes to Reduce Risks for People in Humanitarian Crises", European Commission: Brussels.

Inter-Agency Standing Committee (1994). Definition of Complex Emergencies, Working Group XVIth Meeting. Available at: https://interagencystanding-committee.org/content/definition-complex-emergency accessed 10 September 2020.

Karimova, Tahmina (2016). "Sustainable Development and Disasters" in Susan C. Breau, and Katja L.H. Samuel (eds), *Research Handbook on Disasters and International Law*. Edward Elgar.

McDermott, Ronan et al. (2017). "International Law Applicable to Urban Conflict and Disaster", Disaster Prevention and Management 5(26), 553–564.

Stephens, Tim (2016). "Disasters, International Environmental Law and the Anthropocene" in Susan C. Breau, and Katja L.H. Samuel (eds), *Research Handbook on Disasters and International Law*. Edward Elgar.

UN OCHA (2019). *Global Humanitarian Overview*. United Nations: New York.

United Nations Office for Disaster Risk Reduction / United Nations General Assembly (2016). Report of the open-ended intergovernmental expert working group on indicators and terminology relating to disaster risk reduction. UN Doc. A/71/644.

Zorzi Giustiniani, Flavia (2018). "Something Old, Something New: Disaster Risk Reduction in International Law", QIL – Questions of International Law, 49, 7–27.

32. Hunger

The term hunger defies any comprehensive definition. Neither the feeling of hunger, peculiar and variable requirements of each human body nor the bodily manifestations or implications can be fully captured on account of the heterogeneity prevailing in all aspects. Definitions per se adopt a set of criteria as the comprehensive basis for identification to the exclusion of all others and the discourse on hunger is no exception to the same. However, the dire need to address the prevalence of hunger in the world and for monitoring the progress in this regard necessitate that a certain broad understanding of the condition be developed. Thus, a definition of hunger may be an evil on account of homogenization and exclusion, but is nevertheless necessary. Furthermore, any conceptualization of hunger happens within the spectrum of related or rather intertwined notions like undernourishment, food deprivation, food insecurity etc. With these caveats, this entry on hunger delves into prevailing discourse on hunger, entailing varied ways in which it is sought to be defined and measured, international developments pertaining to its identification, and efforts at combating the same and the debate thereto.

Three broad ways of understanding hunger have been based on three distinct but related criteria:

1. Dietary intake;
2. Individual experience of hunger;
3. Anthropometry.

These three ways of conceptualizing hunger relate to three different aspects of bodily need for food, namely, dietary energy/food requirement and intake; the individual feeling of hunger, and bodily measurements as an indicator of nutritional status. Three broad measurement techniques are adopted for identifying hunger while conceptualizing it in terms of dietary intake. These are the Food and Agriculture Organization (FAO) method, the individual dietary survey method, and the household income and expenditure survey.

The FAO, a specialized agency of the United Nations Organization, established with the purpose of eliminating hunger and improving nutrition, measures undernourishment by comparing usual food consumption expressed in terms of dietary energy (Kilo calories) with certain energy requirement norms (Naiken, 2003). The FAO method measures the per capita dietary energy consumption from the daily dietary energy supply (DES) per capita for a country (Cunningham, 2005). Dietary energy supply is derived from food balance sheets which indicate the adequacy of food supply in a country in relation to nutritional requirement (FAO, "Food balance sheets", available at http://www.fao.org/economic/ess/fbs/en/ accessed 6 September 2020). As this assessment is based on mean energy consumption rather than how energy consumption is distributed within the population, and food acquired by a household rather than food intake by individuals, it is likely to overstate or understate undernourishment (Cunningham, 2005). Individual dietary surveys, on the other hand, measure actual food intake of individuals by asking the respondents to recall what they ate in the past 24 hours and then compare the same with the dietary energy requirement to determine the proportion of population with deficient energy intakes. The third method by which dietary intake is measured is through household income and expenditure surveys, which examine measures like household food energy deficiency, dietary diversity and percentage of household expenditure on food. Since the unit surveyed is the household, intra-household disparities in food consumption may remain hidden.

Dietary intake methods primarily reveal the gap between the dietary requirement and intake by measuring dietary intake through different techniques and thus view hunger as a phenomenon of mismatch between dietary requirements and consumption. However, it is the qualitative method of measuring hunger that reveals individual experience of hunger in context-specific manner and thus moves away from the broad homogenization prevailing in other quantitative methods for measuring hunger. Finally, anthropometry measures food deprivation at the cellular level by taking into account bodily measurements like body mass index, low birth weight etc. as indicators of hunger.

The question that arises out of the brief survey of methods for measuring hunger is whether what is being measured is hunger, food deprivation, undernourishment or food insecurity. These terms are related but distinct as is also evident from the discourse on hunger and food security at the international level. The first target of Sustainable Development Goal 2 is to end hunger by 2030 and ensure access by all people to safe, nutritious and sufficient food all year round. Thus, apart from the technical/scientific ways of understanding hunger, one way to understand the same is in terms of lack of access to food, i.e. food insecurity, where food insecurity may be understood as *genus* while hunger being a *specie* within the former. These notions constitute a spectrum where hunger/severe hunger lies at one end and food security would lie at the other end of the spectrum. Whereas food insecurity includes varied levels of lack or uncertain availability of food or existing or foreseeable uncertain ability to acquire food, hunger is generally limited to involuntary *lack* of access to food. However, overlapping of the two phenomena occurs, as the term lack is envisioned as absence of physical, social and economic access to safe, nutritious or sufficient food which may be extended to take into account food preference. Thus, understanding hunger as part of this spectrum ensures a broader, dynamic and contextual view of the phenomenon rather than treating the condition of hunger as an autonomous realm unconnected to anything beyond itself. Such an understanding not only focuses on the fact of hunger but also on the processes that contribute to its existence, duration, magnitude and intensity. The same also situates hunger at the interface of various discourses pertaining to human rights, sustainable development, international economic order, poverty, prevailing national and international institutional structures etc. Understanding hunger in terms of food insecurity also stands much more in tune with the 2030 Agenda for Sustainable Development, which recognizes all the Sustainable Development Goals as constituting an integrated, indivisible and interconnected whole.

The notion of food security as including physical, social, economic, cultural, health and climatic dimensions determining the stable intake and utilization of nutritious and safe food that meets dietary needs and food preferences for an active and healthy life emerged historically within the international arena through various international efforts in this direction. Each effort added to the already prevailing understanding of food security. Some of the major landmarks in this regard are the Report of the World Food Conference, 1974; Director General's Report on World Food Security: A Reappraisal of the Concepts and Approaches, 1982 (FAO); Poverty and Hunger: Issues and Options for Food Security in Developing Countries, 1986 (World Bank); Human Development Report, 1994 (UNDP); Rome Declaration on World Food Security, 1996, along with World Food Summit Plan of Action, 1996; The State of Food Security, 2001 (FAO); and The State of Food Security and Nutrition in the World, 2018 (FAO). Conversely, food insecurity is also understood as a condition where people lack secure access to safe, nutritious and sufficient food for growth and development and an active, healthy life. Food insecurity may be chronic, seasonal or transitory and may be caused by the unavailability of food, insufficient purchasing power or the inappropriate distribution or inadequate use of food at the household level (FAO, "The State of Food Security in the World", 2001). In other words the understanding of food insecurity is the lack of food security in all its dimensions, i.e. availability, access, utilization and stability. Most of these reports also refer to, or to a limited extent engage with, the notion of hunger. Especially the FAO in its reports has been using the term hunger as being synonymous with chronic undernourishment since 2013, with the notion of "uncomfortable or painful physical sensation caused by insufficient consumption of dietary energy" added to the former elaboration in its 2018 report, whereas food insecurity, as mentioned earlier, is considered in all its four dimensions, i.e. availability, access, utilization and stability. This fortifies the relationship between hunger and food insecurity developed earlier in this entry, but limits the understanding of the former to a particular condition/status devoid of the processes contributing to the same and thus its connection with other aspects of our existence, which the FAO includes only in its notion of food insecurity. Only in its 2012 report the FAO defined the term "hidden hunger" as referring to "vitamin and mineral deficiencies or micronutrient deficiencies. Micronutrient deficiencies can compromise growth, immune function, cognitive development and reproductive and work capacity. Somebody who suffers from hidden hunger is malnourished, but may not sense hunger."

International efforts at addressing hunger also buttress the integral connection between food insecurity and hunger. Especially Principle

3 of the "five Rome Principles for Sustainable Global Food Security" proclaimed in the Declaration of the World Summit on Food Security, 2009, which calls for a "comprehensive twin track approach to food security" consisting of "direct action to immediately tackle hunger for the most vulnerable" and medium- and long-term sustainable agriculture, food security, nutrition and rural development to eliminate root causes of hunger and poverty, including through the progressive realization of the right to adequate food". Hunger, in all its forms and manifestations, can be eliminated comprehensively only by ensuring food security. This integrated approach towards addressing hunger is also visible in the human right to adequate food (Article 11.1), including freedom from hunger (Article 11.2) embodied in the International Covenant on Economic, Social and Cultural Rights, 1966. The integral relationship of hunger with *genus* of food insecurity is also demonstrated in the way in which the core content of the right to adequate food is envisaged as encompassing both its availability and accessibility. The former focuses on availability of sufficient quality and quantity of food to satisfy dietary needs of individuals, free from adverse substances and acceptable within a given culture, whereas the latter encompasses sustainable economic and physical access to food without interference with the enjoyment of other human rights (Committee on Economic, Social and Cultural Rights, General Comment No. 12, para. 8). While emanating primarily in the domain of economic, social and cultural rights, the deep connection that hunger has with other rights including civil and political rights has been well established through the seminal work of Amartya Sen titled *Poverty and Famines: An Essay on Entitlement and Deprivation*, which unquestionably demonstrates the irrelevance of understanding hunger merely as a condition unconnected with the system and structures around.

Despite efforts at understanding hunger and food insecurity and proclamation of the right to adequate food and freedom from hunger as a human right, all with the purpose to eliminate hunger and ensure food security, the prevalence of hunger in the world indicates the prevalence of deep-rooted structural causes of hunger. The High Level Task Force on the Global Food Security Crisis in its Updated Comprehensive Plan of Action identified increasing inequalities in access to and control over productive resources, under investment in agriculture, inconsistent attention to markets for food and trading systems, and lack of support for safety nets as the primary structural factors for food insecurity (para. 4). The question that therefore arises is to what extent the existing human rights regime which seeks to secure freedom from hunger and food insecurity trumps other prevailing structures like the international trade regime, shrinking policy space for countries within the globalized world, and existing distribution of, and legal rights of ownership over, productive resources in case the two conflict with each other in the context of increasing hunger. The continued existence, magnitude and intensity of hunger prevailing in the world then depends on inter alia the will to revisit existing structural causes of hunger, which may require us to re-imagine and reconstitute the building blocks of our organization as human society.

AMITA PUNJ

References

Alston, Philip and Katarina Tomasevski (eds) (1984). *The Right to Food*. Martinus Nijhoff.

Bernstein, Henry, Ben Crow, Maureen Mackintosh, and Charlotte Martin (eds) (2013). *The Food Question: Profits versus People*. Earthscan.

Chadwick, Anna (2017). "World Hunger, the 'Global' Food Crisis and (International) Law", Manchester Journal of International Economic Law 14(1), art. 4.

Cunningham, Louise (2005). *Assessing the Contribution of Aquaculture to Food Security: A Survey of Methodologies, FAO*. Available at http://www.fao.org/3/y5898e/y5898e00.htm accessed 10 September 2020.

De Schutter, Olivier and Kaitlin Y. Cordes (eds) (2011). *Accounting for Hunger: The Right to Food in the Era of Globalisation*. Hart Publishing.

Dreze, Jean, Amartya Sen, and Athar Hussain (eds) (1995). *The Political Economy of Hunger: Selected Essays*. Clarendon Press.

Naiken, Loganadan (2003). Keynote Paper: FAO Methodology for Estimating the Prevalence of Undernourishment. Available at http://www.fao.org/3/Y4249E/y4249e06.htm accessed 10 September 2020.

Nyeleni Declaration of the Forum for Food Security (2007). Available at http://nyeleni.org/IMG/pdf/DeclNyeleni-en accessed 10 September 2020.

Sen, Amartya (1981). *Poverty and Famines: An Essay on Entitlement and Deprivation*. Oxford University Press.

Ziegler, Jean et al. (2011). *The Fight for the Right to Food*. Palgrave Macmillan.

33. Imperialism

Since the late nineteenth century, imperialism has come to refer to the extension and maintenance of a State's power and influence over other States through trade, diplomacy, as well as military, economic and/or cultural dominance. The earliest systematic analyses of modern imperialism were written at the beginning of the twentieth century by critics rather than proponents of the policy. During the second half of the twentieth century the terms colonization and imperialism came to be used interchangeably. Attempts to generate solidarity between newly independent nation States as well as those struggling for national independence may provide a partial explanation. Over the course of the 1990s, "modernization" came to replace "capitalism" and "development" as a central preoccupation of scholarship on the Global South. This interest in modernization has also been accompanied by a focus on governance, law and rights.

The etymology of the word, imperialism, includes the following terms: enperial (Anglo-Norman and Middle French) and imperiālis (Latin). Both terms connote that which is worthy of or befitting an emperor as well as that relating to or belonging to the Roman Empire of Antiquity. Prior to the late nineteenth century, the word referred to an emperor or a supreme ruler's system of government. Given its associations with the Roman Empire, the word could be used in a pejorative sense when alluding to the persecution of early Christians. It could also be used in a commendatory sense when alluding to the territorial expanse of the Roman Empire and the institutions associated with it. During the 1870s, imperialism was increasingly used by British Prime Minister Benjamin Disraeli, his supporters, and his opponents to refer to empire building as a principle of statecraft. Extending and maintaining political dominion or control over dependent territories – whether or not formally annexed – was advocated in order to protect national trade and investment interests in foreign territories. Imperialism was soon adopted as State policy by other competing States – France, the United States, Germany, Italy, Russia, the Ottoman Empire and Japan.

English economist John Atkinson Hobson's book, *Imperialism: A Study of the History, Politics and Economics of the Colonial Powers in Europe and America*, published in 1902, is widely considered to be an important influence on twentieth-century thinkers and leaders across political spectra. Hobson claimed that empire in antiquity had been understood in terms of a federation of States under a hegemony coinciding with the "known world". Hence, the conception of several, competing empires was completely modern. Positioning himself as a national reformer, Hobson distinguished between colonization and imperialism on the grounds that unlike colonization, imperialism perverted the political institutions, economies and social structures of nation States. Since emigrating colonists frequently held full rights of citizenship in their countries of origin, or succeeded in establishing local institutions of self-governance similar to those of their home countries, colonization was an expansion of nationality. Modern imperialism, however, required governance with methods antithetical to the principles that the ruling nation valued for itself. This, Hobson argued, was not due to "greed of tyranny" on the part of the imperial State, but due to starkly different climatic and natural conditions in the annexed territories and protectorates, as well as the presence of subject peoples who were unassimilable. Moreover, imperialism as State policy benefited only those economic sectors and classes associated with militarization and the administration of dependent and annexed territories. The concentration of power in their hands not only undermined the national political institutions of the imperial State, it also undermined the internationalism promised by free trade. The preparation and education of dependent and annexed territories for self-governance, "the civilizing mission", was revealed to be an ideological justification for the use of public funds to serve the private interests of financial capitalists, industrialists supplying imperial militaries, as well as members of the liberal professions – civil servants and missionaries – who gained employment as a consequence of imperial expansion. Thus, Hobson argued, imperialism could not provide a solution to the social question of the time – widespread poverty and unemployment within the imperial powers.

Hobson's analysis was enormously influential for proponents of working class and national independence movements in different parts of the world. It is, however, unclear whether Hobson regarded subject peoples as unwilling to assimilate due to their own sense of identity, or incapable of assimilation due to essential difference.

Lenin drew on Hobson's analysis in his influential 1917 pamphlet titled *Imperialism: The Highest Stage of Capitalism*. According to Lenin, this use of "bourgeois scholarship" enabled evasion of tsarist censorship, while simultaneously revealing his leftist critics to be self-interested parties benefiting from the imperialist policies of their respective States. Drawing on Hobson's analysis, Lenin argued that imperialism is the form taken by capitalism at an advanced stage of its development. At this stage, some of capitalism's fundamental characteristics are transformed into their opposite. Capitalist free competition is displaced by capitalist monopoly. Lenin charged imperialism with the devastation of the First World War, the co-optation of the international proletariat through the creation of a labour elite that enjoyed "petit-bourgeois" conditions of life, and "economic parasitism" over annexed territories. Therefore, the destruction of capitalism as imperialism was both necessary and inevitable.

Across the political spectrum, Hannah Arendt also drew on Hobson's analysis in her examination of the relationship between modern anti-Semitism, imperialism, and Nazi and Soviet totalitarianisms. Asserting a sharp distinction between nationalism and totalitarianism, Hannah Arendt argued that unlike nationalism, the latter was a direct consequence of the importation of imperial ruling practices back into the metropole. These practices were characterized by the institutionalization of racial hierarchies and rule by the distant and impersonal bureaucracy of a superior race. According to Arendt, "Race was the emergency explanation of human beings whom no European or civilized man could understand and whose humanity so frightened and humiliated the immigrants that they no longer cared to belong to the same species" (Arendt, 1973, p. 185). While drawing on Hobson's analysis of imperialism as a perversion of the nation State, Arendt soundly refuted Hobson's claims that Jewish bankers and financiers had possessed the power to manipulate European statesmen and foreign policy for their own gain during this period. She also highlighted the fact that since Social Darwinism provided ideological

justification for race and class rule, it could be used in support of as well as against racial discrimination.

In the second half of the twentieth century, the terms "colonialism" and "imperialism" came to be used interchangeably. A possible explanation of this phenomenon is that it began with attempts to generate solidarity between newly independent nation States as well as those struggling for national independence in South-East Asia and Africa. The emergence during this period of the Non-Aligned Movement of nation States that did not want to ally themselves with either Cold War superpower lends credence to this partial explanation.

During the 1950s and 1960s a number of scholars who were actively involved in the national independence movements in North Africa wrote about the violence of colonial rule and the brutality with which demands for independence were being suppressed. The works of Franz Fanon and Albert Memmi are significant for their analyses of the dehumanization brought about by French rule in terms of race, class, gender, sexuality and religious identity. Drawing on Hegel's analysis of the dialectic between lordship and bondage, and their own experiences of French rule, these scholars examined the ways in which the processes of colonial rule created the colonizer and the colonized. They were concerned with the political, economic, and psychological processes by which the racial hierarchies instituted by colonial policies were internalized by colonizer and colonized. In Fanon's words: "It is in white terms that one perceives one's fellows" (Fanon, 1952, p. 138).

In the 1970s, drawing on Marxist critiques of imperialism, a body of scholarship emerged, examining underdevelopment in the Global South. Dependency theory, as it has come to be termed, posited that the expansion of capitalism through colonization and imperialism resulted in the systematic impoverishment and underdevelopment of colonial possessions for the benefit of colonial and imperial States and societies. Hence, despite political independence, former colonies remained peripheral and dependent on their former rulers, who now formed the core of the new international system created after the Second World War. Immanuel Wallerstein's analysis of capitalist expansion as a framework for studying world history, and Samir Amin's work on the underdevelopment of the African continent, are widely regarded as important contributions to this body of literature.

During the 1980s scholarly attention turned to an examination of culture, knowledge production, and imperialism. This shift may in part be explained by the collapse of the Soviet Union and a de-legitimation of positions and critiques deemed Marxist. Drawing on Foucault's method of discourse analysis, literary theorist Edward Said argued that European and American scholars studying the East rely on many of the same exotic tropes used in eighteenth- and nineteenth-century British and French novels to represent the East. Terming them "Orientalism", Said argued that these fantastic representations of the East were instrumental in legitimating the "civilizing mission", and remain important in contemporary justifications of Western dominance. Anthropologists such as Lila Abu-Lughod have drawn on Said's critique to argue that gender and human rights movements in non-Western countries facilitate neo-imperialism by reproducing Orientalist discourse.

During the 1990s, the term "modernization" came to replace "capitalism" and "development" as a central preoccupation of scholarship that identifies itself as post-colonial. In part this shift may be explained by the significance accorded to Edward Said's work, which regarded earlier critiques of capitalism and development as partaking of Orientalist reductionism and essentialism. In part, the shift may also be explained by the de-legitimation of many left-leaning, secular post-colonial States as intolerant and authoritarian. Drawing on Foucault's analysis of power and the modern State, political scientists such as Timothy Mitchell have determined that the political, economic, and social changes instituted in annexed and Mandate territories continued after national independence to be instantiations of the discipline and governmentality associated with modernity.

This interest in the modernization of former colonies and Mandate territories has also been accompanied by a focus on governance and legal systems. Mahmood Mamdani has argued that internecine conflicts in post-colonial African states must be understood not as the clash of primordial identities, but as a consequence of legal hierarchies established by colonial States. A sphere of customary law was demarcated by the colonial State, in which the authority of compliant local leaders over their own communities was absolute and violently maintained with the sanction of the colonial State. In his examination of the Mandate System established by the League of Nations, Antony Anghie (2005) has argued that the history of Western colonization continues to shape existing international legal frameworks and institutions. For Anghie, this raises the question of how to construct international law that is responsive to the needs and aspirations of peoples in post-colonial nation States.

While supporting the goal of fostering solidarity between former colonies, dependencies, and protectorates, the collapse of the distinction between colonization and imperialism has resulted in the conflation of very different historical experiences and forms of violence. Subsumed under the term, "colonization", the experiences of the Banda under French rule in what is today the Central African Republic, for example, can thus be equated with the experiences of Sunni-Muslim Arab peasants in French Mandate Lebanon. The designation of colonization and imperialism as Western and European makes the recognition of non-Western and post-colonial nation States' use of colonial and imperial policies difficult. This in turn facilitates the representation of opposition to these policies as "militancy" and "terrorism" and legitimates its brutal repression in the name of national unity. Lastly, dismissing human rights movements as Orientalist delegitimates local activists' recourse to such reform on the grounds that their attempts further Western neo-imperialism. Given the long history of Western States and international institutions attaching political and economic strings to development and humanitarian aid, suspicion of proffered aid is not only justified, but necessary. However, denouncing all human rights movements as Orientalist forecloses a potential basis for building global coalitions across national, racial, religious and class divides. It also renders the efforts of local activists – who are often drawn from the ranks of marginal groups – further susceptible to charges of cultural inauthenticity and national betrayal.

NADIA LATIF

References

Abu-Lughod, Lila (2013). *Do Muslim Women Need Saving*. Harvard University Press.

Amin, Samir (1977). *Imperialism and Unequal Development*. Monthly Review Press.

Anghie, Antony (2005). *Imperialism, Sovereignty and the Making of International Law*. Cambridge University Press.

Arendt, Hannah (1973). *The Origins of Totalitarianism*. Houghton Mifflin Harcourt Publishing.

Fanon, Frantz (1952). *Black Skin White Masks*. Grove Press.

Mamdani, Mahmood (1996). *Citizen and Subject: Contemporary Africa and the Legacy of Late Colonialism*. Princeton University Press.

Memmi, Albert (1965). *The Colonizer and the Colonized*. Beacon Press.

Mitchell, Timothy (1988). *Colonizing Egypt*. Cambridge University Press.

Said, Edward (1978). *Orientalism*. Routledge.

Wallerstein, Immanuel (1979). *The Capitalist World-Economy*. Cambridge University Press.

NADIA LATIF

34. Indigenous Peoples

"Indigenous Peoples" is used today to refer to communities found in several countries around the world with a set of distinctive characteristics rooted in tradition that set them apart from members of dominant societies. In some contexts, "aboriginals", "first peoples", and "first nations" or "natives" are used to capture the same reality. Etymologically, "indigenous", used broadly, carries the idea of original or authentic belonging to a geographic space. According to the Cambridge Dictionary, it refers to things or persons "naturally existing in a place or country rather than arriving from another place". A people, on the other hand, remains a loosely defined notion under international law: it refers to a community sharing historical, ethnic, religious, social and/or cultural attributes that warrant recognition in the form of self-determination.

Contemporary discourses on indigeneity are framed within a global movement pushing for recognition and protection of individual and collective rights of indigenous communities by States where they live. In view of the diversity of participant communities within the global indigenous rights movement, indigenous identity has eluded strict definitions. The global framework on indigenous peoples' rights builds on centuries of domestic legal and political struggles for survival and redress for patterns of discrimination and victimization by dominant societies across the history of their encounters. However, since the 1970s, the United Nations has been a focal battleground for recognition of indigenous rights. One of the most quoted attempts at a definition of indigenous peoples is found in the 1970s–1980s UN Study of the problem of discrimination against indigenous populations conducted by, and commonly named after, Special Rapporteur José Martinez Cobo. According to the conclusions of his five volume report published in 1987:

> Indigenous communities, peoples and nations are those which, having a historical continuity with pre-invasion and pre-colonial societies that developed on their territories, consider themselves distinct from other sectors of the societies now prevailing in those territories, or parts of them.

They form at present non-dominant sectors of society and are determined to preserve, develop and transmit to future generations their ancestral territories, and their ethnic identity, as the basis of their continued existence as peoples, in accordance with their own cultural patterns, social institutions and legal systems. (E/CN.4/Sub.2/1986/7/Add.4, para. 379)

The Martinez Cobo report was compiled based on information gathered from 37 countries and the Special Rapporteur acknowledged that his study did not cover all geographic landscapes of discriminatory practices against indigenous communities (E/CN.4/Sub.2/1986/7/Add.1, para.156). During and after Martinez Cobo's studies, the establishment of global platforms and advocacy networks on indigenous rights contributed to the internationalization of the underlying movement. A United Nations Working Group on Indigenous Populations (UNWGIP) was established by the United Nations' Economic and Social Council (ECOSOC) Resolution 1982/34 of 7 May 1982, tasked with developing "standards concerning the rights of indigenous populations, taking account of both the similarities and the differences in the situations and aspirations of indigenous populations throughout the world". As recounted by the first Chairman of the UNWGIP (Eide, 2006), it adopted an unprecedented open-door policy – for a rather State-centric institution – towards participation of indigenous peoples' representatives in, among others, its yearly sessions in Geneva. The UNWGIP remained active until it was abolished under the 2006/2007 reforms introduced by the creation of the Human Rights Council. Nearly three decades after the establishment of the UNWGIP, ECOSOC Resolution 2000/22 of 28 July 2000 created a Permanent Forum on Indigenous Issues (PFII) to act as its advisory body on matters of concern to indigenous peoples. To date, the PFII remains an important space where indigenous peoples from around the world engage in dialogue with governmental delegates on matters of concern to them, mainly during yearly sessions held at the Headquarters of the United Nations in New York. Furthermore, since 2001, three successively appointed Special Rapporteurs on the Rights of Indigenous Peoples have produced general or country-specific studies documenting issues of concern to individuals and communities covered by their mandate. The Human Rights

Council also established an Expert Mechanism on the Rights of Indigenous Peoples in 2007 tasked with providing the Council with expertise on the subject-matter. Finally, the adoption of a United Nations Declaration on the Rights of Indigenous Peoples (UNDRIP) in 2007 concluded a long and often contentious negotiation process initiated with the establishment of the UNWGIP in 1982 and, more formally, the production of a first draft of the declaration in 1993.

From a movement initially focused on the predicament of, among others, descendants of pre-Colombian societies, the Aborigines of Australia or the Maoris of New Zealand, indigenous rights came to embrace numerous other communities from Asia, Africa, Europe and the Pacific. The PFII sessions have welcomed participants from such diverse communities as the Navajo and other Native/first peoples/ Nations of the Americas, the Inuit of the Arctic circle, the Sami of Scandinavia and Russia, the Maori of New Zealand, the Aboriginals and Torres Strait Islanders of Australia, the Batwa/Pygmies and hunter-gatherer communities of Central and East Africa, the Maasai and other pastoralists of East Africa, the San and Khoekhoe of Southern Africa, the Ainu people of Japan, the Adivasi/ Scheduled Tribes of India, the Igorot of the Philippines to name a few. According to several sources, including the United Nations, "[t]here are an estimated 370 million indigenous people in the world, living across 90 countries. They make up less than 5 per cent of the world's population, but account for 15 per cent of the poorest. They speak an overwhelming majority of the world's estimated 7,000 languages and represent 5,000 different cultures" (United Nations, "We Need Indigenous Communities for a Better World", available at https://www.un.org/en/observances/indigenous-day/background accessed 25 September 2020). Interestingly, records show that these estimate figures on the world's indigenous population have repeatedly been quoted in various studies, including the United Nations, for more than 16 years; suggesting that they are merely indicative (UNGA, Agenda item 114: Programme of Activities of the International Decade of the World's Indigenous People, UN Doc. A/C.3/58/SR.21, 3 November 2003, para. 3). UNESCO currently proposes the figure of "at least 370–500 million, indigenous peoples" in the world (UNESCO, "Indigenous Peoples and UNESCO", available at http://www.unesco.org/new/en/indigenous-peoples/ accessed 25 September 2020).

Participation of diverse groups in the global indigenous rights movement, including communities whose claims to historical continuity and prior occupancy of ancestral land are, at times, disputed has required a readjustment of identification criteria for indigenous peoples. Indigenous rights advocates have increasingly shifted their focus from essentialized narratives over first occupancy of lands to situational characteristics of marginality (Ndahinda, 2011, p. 24; Summers, 2013, p. 10). To remain inclusive, the issue of a comprehensive definition, frequently raised during the protracted negotiation process of the UNDRIP, was deliberately disregarded. Instead, the long-serving chairperson of the UNWGIP, Erica-Irene Daes, listed a set of factors "which may be present, to a greater or lesser degree, in different regions and in different national and local contexts" used by actors involved to understand the concept "indigenous", namely:

1. "Priority in time, with respect to the occupation and use of a specific territory";
2. The voluntary perpetuation of cultural distinctiveness, which may include the aspects of language, social organization, religion and spiritual values, modes of production, laws and institutions;
3. Self-identification, as well as recognition by other groups, or by State authorities, as a distinct collectivity; and
4. An experience of subjugation, marginalization, dispossession, exclusion or discrimination, whether or not these conditions persist (E/CN.4/Sub.2/AC.4/1996/2, para. 69).

UNDRIP lists a catalogue of individual and collective Rights of Indigenous Peoples. Those rights are intricately connected to a recognition of indigenous peoples' entitlement to self-determination, a right entailing the ability to "freely determine their political status and freely pursue their economic, social and cultural development" (Article 3). It encompasses the right to "autonomy or self-government" (Article 4) and "to maintain and strengthen their distinct political, legal, economic, social and cultural institutions, while retaining their right to participate fully, if they so choose, in the political, economic, social and cultural life of the State" (Article 5). It is often asserted that self-determination in this context is, in principle, a right to be exercised within the boundaries of a State (internal self-determination) but whether this right also carries the possibility of remedial secession for violations of indigenous peoples' rights (external self-determination) is still debated (Summers, 2013, p. 55). States are further required to seek free, prior and informed consent of indigenous peoples "before adopting and implementing legislative or administrative measures that may affect them" (Article 19), including those directed at dispossession of indigenous peoples' lands or territories (Article 10).

The development of the United Nations' indigenous rights legal framework capitalized on the standard-setting work of the International Labour Organization (ILO), which has formally been involved in the field since the 1950s, with the adoption of ILO Convention 107 of 1957, criticized for adopting an assimilationist approach to indigenous rights and eventually replaced by ILO Convention 169 of 1989 on Indigenous and Tribal Peoples. As reflected in the very title of the treaty, ILO Convention 169 establishes a distinction between "indigenous" and "tribal" peoples. Indigenous is used to refer to descendants of inhabitants of lands and territories that were subsequently conquered or colonized by newcomers. They possess and aspire to preserve distinctive social, economic, cultural and political institutions that differentiate them from members of dominant settler societies. Tribal peoples, on the other hand, refers to populations not necessarily claiming to be the original inhabitants of lands and territories they currently occupy, but who, like indigenous peoples, possess distinctive social, cultural and economic attributes that they intend to perpetuate for future generations. It should be noted that this ILO dichotomy has increasingly disappeared from international current narratives on indigeneity whereby references to indigenous peoples, claims, or rights generally capture both categories of peoples. Whether codified in a soft law instrument such as UNDRIP or in the binding, albeit under-ratified ILO Convention 169, indigenous rights have gained global recognition. They are reaffirmed in numerous international documents, including the United Nations' Sustainable Development Goals.

The global indigenous rights movement has given visibility and a voice to communities whose marginality had kept them in the shadows for ages. In different corners of the globe, indigenous peoples use the developing international standards and global solidarity as negotiation tools in their struggle for survival, redress and empowerment. The vote by 144 UN Member States in favour of UNDRIP in 2007 suggested a strong and growing support for indigenous rights. However, in many inherently multi-ethnic countries across Africa and Asia whose Statehood was shaped through European colonization, demands for recognition and protection of territorial rights on the basis of prior occupancy are still widely resisted on grounds that all local communities are indigenous. These critiques of indigenousness are shared by some anthropological scholarship that denounces essentialist and romanticized views on indigenous peoples and the correlation between this socio-legal category and yesterday's notion of "primitive societies" (Kuper, 2005). Negotiation of the indigenous identity and indigenous rights is therefore still an ongoing process.

FELIX MUKWIZA NDAHINDA

References

Anaya, S. James (2004). *Indigenous Peoples in International Law*. Oxford University Press.

Eide, Asbjørn (2006). "Rights of Indigenous Peoples – Achievements in International Law during the Last Quarter of a Century", Netherlands Yearbook of International Law 37, 155–212.

Hohmann, Jessie and Marc Weller (eds) (2018). *The UN Declaration on the Rights of Indigenous Peoples: A Commentary*. Oxford University Press.

Kingsbury, Benedict (1998). "'Indigenous Peoples' in International Law: A Constructivist Approach to the Asian Controversy", American Journal of International Law 92, 414–457.

Kiwanuka, Richard N. (1988). "The Meaning of 'People' in the African Charter on Human and Peoples' Rights", American Journal of International Law 82(1), 80–101.

Kuper, Adam (2005). *The Reinvention of Primitive Society: Transformations of a Myth*. Routledge.

Ndahinda, Felix Mukwiza (2011). *Indigenousness in Africa: A Contested Legal Framework for Empowerment of Marginalised Communities*. Asser Press.

Niezen, Ronald (2003). *The Origin of Indigenism: Human Rights and the Politics of Identity*. University of California Press.

Summers, James (2013). *Peoples and International Law*. 2nd revised edition. Brill.

Xanthaki, Alexandra (2007). *Indigenous Rights and United Nations Standards: Self-Determination, Culture and Land*. Cambridge University Press.

35. Industry and Infrastructure

In development parlance, industry and infrastructure have become indistinguishable with foreign investment in two areas: primary industries for natural resource development and the construction and operation of asset infrastructure.

Physical asset infrastructure consists of building assets and contracting services for transport (roads, ports, bridges and so on), power, water, telecommunications, health and sanitation. The natural resource industry concerns the development, financing, operation and maintenance of oil, gas, mineral and agricultural resources. This phenomenon is especially the case in developing countries as they tend to be rich in natural resources, lack infrastructure facilities and face informational, technological, financial, labour and structural barriers that impede their ability to climb up the ladder into secondary manufacturing and tertiary service industries.

One view is that these barriers keep developing countries locked into a perpetual dependency role: (deliberately) tied to the economies of the Global North and its thirst for the raw materials of construction and modern technology. The so-called 'peripheral' economies end up serving the raw material interests of the Global North whilst forfeiting their own development. In parallel, the Global South's increasing demand for capital, reliable energy supply and modern infrastructure systems make it dependent on the capital, skills and technology from the Global North required to develop natural resource and infrastructure projects. The State becomes enterprise led and collectively with private companies can use power and leverage to cut and self-regulate around the social, human rights and environmental impacts of natural resource and infrastructure development within the legal, regulatory and contractual frameworks underpinning a project.

Nonetheless, classical economic theory presents foreign direct investment into industrialization and infrastructure as fundamental for development: providing engines along a linear path of economic development, progress and modernity in the host country.

Investors are presumed to provide local employment, technology, taxes for the national budget and new or upgraded infrastructure facilities which will benefit the entire economy. In practice however, power asymmetries, corruption, unequal wealth distribution and institutional behaviours result in differing access to these benefits. For instance, feeder roads, rail links and port infrastructure built for an extractive project are typically not public private 'shared' infrastructure, as the investor will have exclusive property rights over the rights of way as negotiated within an underlying investment agreement. Yet, traditional neoliberal economics has largely avoided complex issues around how access to industry, infrastructure and thus economic development will be affected by asymmetries in power, trade, negotiation capacity, colonial histories and the presence of historically disadvantaged communities in a host country.

Assumptions around the inherent value of industry and infrastructure are part of a larger economic paradigm called the Washington Consensus (the Consensus). Coined by the English economist John Williamson in the 1980s, the Consensus refers to a set of free market economic values which are aimed at incentivizing foreign investment into developing countries through decreased State intervention, tax reform, financial liberalization and the primacy of investor property rights. When translated into infrastructure and industry, certain legal and policy aspects of these values stand out for their privatizing and inequitable effects, discussed below.

First, that minimal State intervention and, concretely, the rising tide of the competitive market economy will unlock vast reserves of wealth. For developing countries this translates as releasing the wealth locked within vast land and water resources. The assumption runs that the increased State gross domestic product generated from these investments will trickle down, lifting standards of living and ending poverty for all. Perhaps the most extreme method for unlocking value was rooted in the belief that construction of infrastructure and associated delivery of public services would be most efficiently achieved through an outright sale by the State to the private sector of long-term contracts for the production and supply of power and infrastructure. This is commonly known as privatization and involves the reassigning of property rights and economic functions to the private sector through legal means. In developing countries and especially those with contexts of weak State capacity, elite capture and corruption, privatization practices have been met with resistance due to the resulting high costs of power and water which are ultimately placed on the shoulders of communities least able to accommodate them. Examples are seen in the waves of power and water privatizations in Latin America and Sub-Saharan Africa from the 1980s onwards.

A version of privatization or 'creeping privatization' can be seen in modern public private partnerships (PPPs). A group of deep-pocketed companies will, in collaboration with a host State, set up a separate privately owned limited liability (Company X) in which the government will be a minority shareholder. The sole purpose of Company X will be to develop, construct and operate, for instance, a 60-year hydropower project that will produce electricity to be sold by Company X to the government electricity board at a cost determined within a private power purchase agreement. Whilst this structure does not result in the outright sale of assets, the commercial reality is that under the shareholder agreement, the government will have agreed to limited rights and control (or in most cases, no control) over project governance, pricing and operation in its minority shareholder capacity. The State will contractually relinquish important sovereign immunity rights by doing business like a private person through its shareholding in Company X, and will contractually submit to private dispute resolution.

The second aspect of the Consensus that stands out for industry and infrastructure concerns the creation and registration of private property rights and their essentiality for the development of natural resource industries and infrastructure. Legal devices were designed to provide protective and aggressive mechanisms for recognizing and implementing investor property rights. For instance, State laws that permit the creation of private property, land expropriation and foreign investment and thus create a legal framework for the negotiation of a complex, long-term exclusive contractual licence to a multinational company to explore and exploit land. Other legal 'rules of the game' derive from rules of company law, contract, secured transactions that create a system

whereby the creditors' complex financial and security instruments are made legally valid, binding and enforceable. This gives foreign investment into industry and infrastructure projects in developing countries a predictable, secure and superior legal quality. So, rules of security can legally prevent Company X from creating any other security that would rank in priority over the foreign creditors (a 'negative' negative pledge clause) and insolvency rules will cloth creditors with reorder enforcement and repayment rights in the event of Company X's insolvency. This creates a type of universal ring fence around these legal structures so that they can be enforced against the world and all other interests, even public ones. Through these mechanisms and others, domestic financial markets are opened up to international capital flows for natural resource and infrastructure projects.

Against this background, modern, large oil, gas, mineral and infrastructure development projects involving the State, companies, commercial lenders, domestic, regional and international development financial institutions and export credit agencies have become a core mechanism for delivering Consensus policies and, also, engaging the private sector into the sustainable development agenda. Yet, the social, developmental and vulnerability impacts of the underlying legal devices that frame natural resource and infrastructure projects have long escaped analysis.

This is largely because nearly all of the legal work behind these projects takes place behind the closed doors of private lawyers and through the technicalities of private commercial law: in the shadows of international law. There are also structural and ideological forces that have locked out conversations around the role of private law and institutional behaviours. Orthodox approaches to international law and international economic law in particular have also supported Consensus policies and the economic power of capital-exporting countries. This has been facilitated through the creation of bilateral investment instruments that back the view that foreign investment stimulates the flow of capital, technology and economic development to developing countries. Moreover, international economic law's traditional allegiance to the national State means that, structurally, it has struggled to cope with the many sites of global economic governance and commercial reality.

KINNARI BHATT

Private multinational companies are still a relatively new phenomenon in international law and are not formally recognized and regulated as legal entities capable of bearing binding rights and duties, despite their enormous economic and political power. Likewise, due to their private mandates the lending activities of international and regional financial institutions have largely escaped formal international legal regulation even though they are comprised of States. Yet, companies and financial institutions play a significant role in mobilizing the capital needed to further the economic and sustainable development agenda. However, little legal analysis has drawn attention to the private actors, contractual instruments, policies and institutional behaviours that uphold modern natural resource and infrastructural development projects, how they are implemented, the surrounding power dynamics and incentives and their impacts on communities and vulnerability.

Exceptions do exist, emanating from critical and frequently marginalized fields of interdisciplinary legal scholarship. These include approaches to international economic law that focus on the increasing global plurality of legal orders and the business and human rights movement flowing from the United Nations Guiding Principles on Business and Human Rights. These principles have successfully articulated a soft law responsibility on companies to respect human rights, not to infringe on the rights of others and to do no harm through their operations. Valuable contributions have also been made within strands of development economics that focus on inequality and human development and also within socio-legal studies, anthropology and Third World approaches to law. The latter movement enables a historical line to be traced between the practices of modern development banks and colonial/imperial policies for power and control. The repeated references to the 'productive potential' of land within development bank finance environmental and social safeguarding policies arguably echo a colonial mindset around the superior value of cultivated land. This was routinely used to support colonial power and indigenous expropriation for more 'effective' and 'productive' intensive land use and later, national 'development' plans. Another illustration can be seen in the creation, in 1948, of the UK government's development finance institution, the Colonial Development Corporation,

which continues today under the more politically correct name of the Commonwealth Development Corporation (CDC) Group Plc.

Civil society has also questioned the uniform belief in the benefit of industry and infrastructure as a panacea for economic development, evidencing how it can fuel inequities. Non-governmental organizations (NGOs) have long protested against the international regime of investment codes designed to liberalize capital movement, encourage foreign direct investment and protect multinational companies without taking account of how investment can erode human rights and environmental impacts. This asymmetrical power relationship, in which rights are granted to investors, can be enforced against the State and do not impose obligations on investors, has resulted in the cautious emergence of a new generation of investment agreements in which investors are increasingly expected to consider human rights issues within their operations. Some NGOs such as Amnesty International have examined the long arm reach of underlying negotiated contractual, financial and taxation frameworks of specific natural resource and infrastructure projects on the development of local laws and the rights of communities.

In this context, new questions are finally being asked. How has the law, its legal frameworks and institutions furthered classic development policy and in so doing impacted on issues of poverty and vulnerability in the context of industry and infrastructure? How, in this context, do power relations, institutional behaviours and incentives affect outcomes for communities facing these projects? Who actually benefits from industry and infrastructure and does everyone have access to infrastructure?

There is evidence that development policy around industry and infrastructure has switched on to debates about the real contribution of public private infrastructure projects to sustainable development and poverty eradication. The realization that whilst trickle-down theory may work it does so in unequal ways, can perhaps be seen in the creation of a 'people first PPP' centre within the United Nations and a related set of guiding principles. Under this model, people, not the private sector, are the main beneficiaries. PPP projects are used to promote access to food, water, energy and transport through projects that are equitable, sustainable and work for all. Suggested policy includes the construction of small-scale 'people

KINNARI BHATT

to people' projects for small- and medium-sized enterprises and projects that 'do good' for the environment, alongside a large cross-border natural resource or infrastructure project. It is not clear if, and how, this will happen in practice. Meanwhile, failure to interrogate the technical context of how the contractual and financial mechanisms, institutional behaviours and incentives that mobilize industry and infrastructure in developing countries will continue to impact upon rights, human development and access could make people first PPPs an episode in window dressing.

KINNARI BHATT

References

Bhatt, Kinnari I. (2020). *Concessionaires, Financiers and Communities: Implementing Indigenous Peoples' Rights to Land in Transnational Development Projects*. Cambridge University Press.

Calderón, César and Luis Servén (2010). 'Infrastructure and Economic Development in Sub-Saharan Africa', Journal of African Economies 19(1), 13–87.

Estrin, Saul and Adeline Pelletier (2018). 'Privatization in Developing Countries: What Are the Lessons of Recent Experience?', The World Bank Research Observer 33(1), 65–102.

Meyersfeld, Bonita (2017). 'Empty Promises and the Myth of Mining: Does Mining Lead to Pro-Poor Development', Business and Human Rights Journal 2, 31–53.

Pistor, Katharina (2019). *The Code of Capital, How Law Creates Wealth and Inequality*. Princeton University Press.

Sarfaty, Galit A. (2012). *Values in Translation: Human Rights and the Culture of the World Bank*. Stanford University Press.

Sassen, Saskia (2014). *Expulsions: Brutality and Complexity in the Global Economy*. Harvard University Press.

Sonarajah, Muthucumaraswamy (2009). *The International Law on Foreign Investment*. Cambridge University Press.

Tan, Celine (2019). 'Beyond the "Moments" of Law and Development: Critical Reflections on Law and Development Scholarship in a Globalised Economy', Law and Development Review 12(2), 285–321.

World Bank (1994). *World Development Report 1994: Infrastructure for Development*. Oxford University Press.

36. Inequality

Introduction

Inequality is one of the prime challenges facing humanity today. As a phenomenon, it is connected to other phenomena such as poverty, vulnerability and insecurity, and the prevalence of considerable inequality both globally and within societies is a significant impediment to the achievement of goals such as poverty reduction and sustainable development. While the Millennium Development Goals of 2000 addressed some aspects of inequality, the 2030 Agenda for Sustainable Development, adopted by the UN Member States in 2015, makes the reduction of inequality a key developmental goal. Reduction of inequality within and among countries is put forward as one of the 17 Sustainable Development Goals (SDGs) and inclusiveness and the principle of leaving no one behind underlies the whole SDG agenda.

Definitions

There is no single settled understanding of inequality. In terms of definitions, a distinction can be made between inequity (injustice) and inequality. In contrast to inequity, of which the determination requires a value judgment, inequality generally refers to unequal situations that can be empirically observed and measured. In practice, inequality is evaluated by comparing a particular aspect of a person/unit with the same characteristic of another person/unit. Generally, what is striven for is equitable distribution, but different views exist on what such distribution is.

Where scholars differ, as well, is in their answer to the question "equality of what" (Sen, 1992). The different dimensions of inequality form key research topics in several different academic fields, including economics, sociology and law. Traditionally, attention has been given to economic inequality, which often is evaluated by comparing income or wealth, or more generally living standards or the distribution of resources. Research has, however, clearly shown that the relationship between economic growth and inequality is not straightforward. The realization that economic growth in fact can result in greater inequality has resulted in a refocus of the development agenda towards themes such as poverty reduction, but also to a more general acknowledgment that development cannot be equated with economic growth alone. The concept of human development introduced by the UNDP in 1990 shifted the focus in development to factors advancing human well-being, such as education and health. Subsequently, the concept of inclusive growth entered the development thinking. Through such approaches, focus in addressing growth was shifted to the equitable share of the benefits of economic growth with a view to increasing the capabilities and opportunities of individuals in a more equal manner.

Today, the understanding of inequality is perhaps more multi-faceted than ever, and many different dimensions of inequality are recognized. Beside the inequality of outcomes (that is, the achieved levels of particular goods or assets, such as education, nutrition, health and income), different forms of inequality of opportunity are acknowledged to give attention to factors beyond the control of individuals (disadvantageous circumstances) that significantly affect outcomes. The opportunities outlook on inequality has an intellectual pedigree in the capability approach by Sen and Nussbaum, which emphasizes a person's freedom to achieve a life of his or her choosing. The capability approach defines a person's capability to live a good life in terms of central functionings, such as being healthy, that a person has access to and that make it possible to choose a life of one's choosing. A central element of the theory is the attention given to "contingent circumstances", such as disability, age and contextual factors (Sen, 1999, pp. 70–71), and the "capability failures that are the result of discrimination or marginalization" (Nussbaum, 2011, p. 19).

In terms of different types of inequalities, social inequality generally refers to the uneven access to various societal goods and services, such as adequate housing and education. When looking at education inequality, one pays attention to the differences across and within countries regarding, for example, the average years of schooling and the quality of education. In terms of inequalities in health status and health care, different aspects of inequalities in health and in the distribution of health determinants are examined. Gender inequality, again, refers to the different and disadvantageous opportunities availed to individuals on the basis of their sex or gender. Gender inequality takes many different forms and affects not only women.

The various forms of inequality are often strongly interrelated. For example, gender inequality is often connected to other forms of inequality, such as inequalities in health and education. People may also experience compound discrimination and inequality based on individuals' different social and other identity markers, such as race, gender and sexuality. This is emphasized in the intersectionality theory (Crenshaw, 1989), which underlines that inequalities tend to interact with other inequalities, resulting in situations where some persons experience cumulative disadvantage and discrimination. Significantly, many forms of inequality correlate with inferior possibilities to participate and lower actual levels of participation in public decision-making (participation inequality). This link between inequality and the lack of societal power and influence entails particular challenges for addressing inequality.

"Inequality between whom?" is another central question to address when studying inequality. Besides inequality within countries, the rate of global inequality remains significant both in terms of outcome and opportunities. With global interdependence and globalization intensifying, it is becoming more and more clear that a key determinant of, for example, a person's living conditions is his or her place of birth. In the current global political and economic architecture, there are significant drivers of global inequality. Global inequalities arise from a variety of factors, including historical reasons, such as conflicts and colonialization, as well as geopolitics, environmental degradation and the architecture of international trade and financial systems, but also the different levels of inequality that exist within nations. As a result of global inequality, individuals in some countries are left behind and are not able to enjoy the benefits of development in its different forms on an equal basis.

Inequality, law and development

Law is often considered a powerful tool to address inequalities. Legal equality is seen to require that the State embraces its legislative, executive and judicial functions towards its subjects in an equal manner regardless of factors such as wealth, gender or ethnicity. In international human rights law, the principle of equal protection of the law demands that States refrain from sustaining or creating discrimination against certain groups of people. In practice, legal strategies are not always neutral and may as such also give rise to and maintain inequalities and unequal power structures. This is in particular the case where laws and courts function as instruments of domination or direct discrimination against certain groups of individuals. Despite the progress made in some countries, both direct and indirect discrimination based on law continues to be a significant problem in many parts of the world for groups such as ethnic minorities, women, people living with HIV and sexual minorities.

Eradication of discriminatory laws and policies as well as the adoption of appropriate legislation to ensure equal opportunity and to reduce inequalities is endorsed as one of the central goals of the SDGs. This is striven for through the promotion of the principles of rule of law, equal access to justice and respect for human rights at the national and international levels (SDGs 10, 16 and Preamble). Rule of law is a concept that builds on principles such as even application of laws and neutral, equal enforcement and non-arbitrary application of justice. The principle that all are equal before the law lies at the heart of rule of law, which means that everyone is entitled to equal protection of the law without discrimination of any kind (Universal Declaration of Human Rights, Article 7). The related principle of equal access to justice stands for the right of everyone, including the disadvantaged and marginalized groups, to effective, impartial, fair, accountable and non-discriminatory services and mechanisms, either formal or informal, for solving disputes and to challenge abuses of power. Effective access to justice is increasingly recognized as an essential element in the fight against inequality; unequal access to justice is often both a cause and a consequence of poverty, disadvantage and lacking access to rights.

Sometimes mechanisms for access to justice are formally there, but people may not have access to them in practice due to lack of access to other rights and capabilities. Measures to address equal access to justice should therefore go hand-in-hand with measures to address, inter alia, illiteracy, poverty and lack of identity documents. A further prerequisite for the equal access to justice is that accessible and reliable information on the rights and on the tools to

MIKAELA HEIKKILÄ AND MAIJA MUSTANIEMI-LAAKSO

access them is available and that individuals and groups are empowered to use such tools through, for example, access to quality legal aid. Legal services and processes should also be accessible, affordable, adaptable and acceptable as regards standards of standing and costs for litigation, amongst others. Different forms of legal empowerment that seek to contribute to the use of law via formal and informal legal systems so that it strengthens and empowers the disadvantaged are often seen as essential in this regard. In terms of outcomes, equal access to justice means that the legal system produces just and effective remedies. In a wider sense, access to justice is sometimes seen to include access or capability for effective and meaningful participation in the processes of creating law.

Another way law is instrumentalized to produce equality is through the idea of substantive equality that works for the abolition of constructions that sustain discrimination and inequity. While the suspension of discriminatory laws and the institution of pro-equality laws work to treat different groups of individuals the same in the form of formal equality, substantive equality has as its goal the equity of outcomes, which may require treating individuals or groups of individuals differently. Such an approach builds on the idea that the mere prohibition of discrimination or calling someone equal are not sufficient guarantees to equality, asserting that a more contextual approach is needed to address different types of disadvantage and systemic discrimination. In this way, substantive equality builds on the idea of equality of opportunity and attaches attention to what actually needs to be done for individuals to be able to access their rights on an equal basis with others effectively. A focus on the actual capabilities and possibilities of individuals to access their rights both legitimizes and requires affirmative positive action in the form of, for example, reasonable accommodation in the case of disability for equality to be realized. Besides such a redistributive dimension, substantive equality is seen to include a dimension of recognition that seeks to address violence, stereotypes and prejudice experienced by the disadvantaged and the marginalized; a dimension enabling participation, as well as a transformative dimension for the structural accommodation of difference (Fredman, 2016). A related term of equal benefit of the law refers to the obligation of States to eradicate hurdles for equal access to rights and legal protection.

The principles of non-discrimination and substantive equality are at the heart of the human rights-based approaches to development, which emphasize the abolition of root causes for non-realization of human rights in the form of gaps in the laws and policies affecting the actual opportunities that individuals have to enjoy their rights. Similarly, different approaches to vulnerability both within human rights law and beyond attach attention to the societal structures that both mitigate and sustain disadvantage and marginalization, and call upon the State to act responsibly for such vulnerabilities to be addressed through State action. While human rights form the essence of many such approaches, the limitations of the rights project in addressing inequality are also recognized. It is held, for example, that legal rights can only be effective in tackling inequality where they are coined with measures to address power relations within and among societies (Moyn, 2018).

At the global level, international legal structures remain relatively toothless in tackling unequal power imbalances. Several calls to address inequalities arising from the architecture of the global community have been made over the years. For example, the 1980s saw the adoption of the UNGA Declaration on the Right to Development, entrenched in a movement initiated by the Global South in the 1970s as a claim for a new fairer international economic order for equality of opportunity for development as a prerogative both of nations and of individuals. Lately, social protection has been globally advanced as a central tool for reducing inequality and poverty, based on the idea that everyone should have a decent income level and access to basic social services. Despite advances in reducing the equality gap in, for example, basic living standards, equality of opportunity remains out of reach for a large part of the world's population. With new inequalities arising from climate change as well as the developments in education and technology, the world is faced with new challenges to address systemic inequality and the opportunity gaps in benefiting from development (UNDP, 2019).

MIKAELA HEIKKILÄ AND MAIJA MUSTANIEMI-LAAKSO

References

Christiansen, Christian Olaf and Steven L.B. Jensen (eds) (2019). *Histories of Global Inequality: New Perspectives.* Palgrave Macmillan.

Crenshaw, Kimberle (1989). "Demarginalizing the Intersection of Race and Sex", University of Chicago Legal Forum, 139–167.

Fredman, Sandra (2016). "Emerging from the Shadows: Substantive Equality and Article 14 of the European Convention on Human Rights", Human Rights Law Review 16(2), 273–301.

Linarelli, John, Margot E. Salomon, and Muthucumaraswamy Sornarajah (2018). *The Misery of International Law: Confrontations with Injustice in the Global Economy.* Oxford University Press.

Moyn, Samuel (2018). *Not Enough: Human Rights in an Unequal World.* Harvard University Press.

Nussbaum, Martha C. (2011). *Creating Capabilities: The Human Development Approach.* Harvard University Press.

Nyamu-Musembi, Celestine (2016). "Legal Rights as Instruments for Challenging Inequality", World Social Science Report: Challenging Inequalities, Pathways to a Just World, 225–228.

Salomon, Margot E. (2011). "Why Should It Matter that Others Have More? Poverty, Inequality, and the Potential of International Human Rights Law", Review of International Studies 37, 2137–2155.

Sen, Amartya (1992). *Inequality Reexamined.* Clarendon Press.

Sen, Amartya (1999). *Development as Freedom.* Anchor Books.

UNDP (2019). *Human Development Report 2019.* UNDP.

37. Intellectual Property Rights

As an integral discipline in international economic law, intellectual property rights (IPRs), broadly conceptualized, are State-granted, mostly time-limited rights that protect creative and innovative intellectual works of natural or legal persons. Three main categories of IPRs are (1) Copyright and Related Rights, (2) Industrial Property, and (3) Sui Generis Rights. Copyright and Related Rights apply to literary works (such as novels, plays and poems), artistic works (such as drawings, paintings, photographs and sculptures), films, musical compositions, performances, phonograms and broadcasts. Industrial Property is a compound term for Patents, Industrial Designs, Trademarks and Geographical Indications (GIs). Patents are granted for inventions, which could be either products or processes. Industrial designs are granted for the aesthetic or ornamental features of products including lines, patterns, shapes or surfaces. Trademarks are granted for distinctive signs or features that distinguish goods or services. Akin to Trademarks, albeit centred on provenance, GIs are granted for products that have distinctive qualities, reputation or characteristics, attributable to their geographic origins. Sui Generis rights, literally 'of its own kind', are unique types of IPRs, such as Plant Breeders Rights, granted for new varieties of plants and Database Rights, granted for database compilations. The aforementioned categorizations are non-exhaustive as IPRs' subject-matters continuously proliferate.

In line with Article 27.2 of the Universal Declaration of Human Rights, which provides for the 'right to the protection of the moral and material interests resulting from any scientific, literary or artistic production', holders of these IPRs have exclusive rights to their creations and inventions. Theories proffered for IPRs include (1) Reward for Labour (John Locke), (2) Personality (Georg Wilhelm Friedrich Hegel), and (3) Utilitarian (Jeremy Bentham). The Reward for Labour theory emphasizes the efforts exerted to create the intellectual works or the 'sweat of the brow'

as the core justification for IPRs. However, Locke never mentioned IPRs. The Personality theory posits that IPRs protect creators' and inventors' dignity, reputation and personhood because intellectual works are extensions of their personalities. Unlike Locke, Hegel briefly mentioned IPRs. The Utilitarian theory asserts that IPRs incentivize investment in creativity and innovation, providing the 'greatest good for the greatest number'. Each of these theories is contentious, with marked asymmetries in their relevance to the disparate categories and subsidiary categories of IPRs.

Beyond the theories, 'development' is often presented as the underlying objective or principle for introducing IPRs at the international, regional and national levels. For example, at the international level, Article 8 of the Agreement on Trade-Related Aspects of Intellectual Property Rights (TRIPS) provides for World Trade Organization (WTO) members to introduce IPRs systems that promote socio-economic and technological development. This flexibility permits WTO members to introduce imaginative TRIPS-compliant IPRs systems tailored to their national needs and realities or public policy priorities. The application of the flexibility could either increase or reduce the rights conferred in TRIPS. However, in certain circumstances, as will be discussed below, Global South WTO members have been constrained through bilateral agreements or economic partnership agreements, from introducing such suitable IPRs systems. Indeed, the design and introduction of IPRs systems at all levels reveal the role of powerful actors, concerted interests and relentless pressures.

The international intellectual property rights landscape

The variety of overlapping international treaties for IPRs reflects its wide-ranging categories and subsidiary categories. Three of the treaties that form the foundation of the current international IPRs architecture were adopted in the late nineteenth century. The Paris Convention for the Protection of Industrial Property (Paris Convention) that covers Patents, Trademarks and Industrial Designs was adopted in 1883. The Berne Convention for the Protection of Literary and Artistic Work (Berne Convention), relevant to literary and artistic works, was adopted in 1886. The Madrid System for the International Registration of Marks that provides the first international IPRs filing service for trademarks was adopted in 1891. The adoption of these treaties was driven by the lack of international legal protection for creators and inventors. While piecemeal systems covered the disparate categories and subsidiary categories of IPRs at national levels in the Global North, no international systems set standards or ensured enforcement. For example, the central driving force behind the United Kingdom's push for an international copyright system was to protect British authors' and publishers' interests in foreign jurisdictions. Despite enacting the earliest copyright law, the Statute of Anne in 1710 and its subsequent revisions, the laws were only enforceable in the United Kingdom, its colonies and dominions, while piracy exacerbated in foreign jurisdictions.

Although the Berne Convention, Paris Convention and Madrid Convention were introduced inter alia to stall piracy, one shared shortcoming of these treaties through the Global North lens is the lack of effective enforcement and dispute settlement mechanisms. By the middle of the twentieth century, upon independence, former colonies and dominions joined their colonial administrators in the international organizations established to administer the IPRs treaties. Initially, the United International Bureaux for the Protection of Intellectual Property was established in 1893 to administer the Paris Convention and the Berne Convention. Subsequently, the World Intellectual Property Organization (WIPO) was established in 1967 to promote IPRs around the world. Consequently, with minimal contributions to framing the contents and contours of the international treaties and institutions, most Global South countries introduced IPRs systems, either through colonial affiliations or post-colonial international organization membership. Here, IPRs are a quintessential example of what Boaventura de Sousa Santos refers to as 'globalized localism' – that is, the successful globalization of a particular local phenomenon.

To address the enforcement and dispute settlement challenges of the WIPO administered treaties, Global North countries, led by the United States, the European Community and Japan, employed forum-shifting techniques to introduce IPRs in the General Agreement on Tariffs and Trade (GATT) during the Uruguay Round of Multilateral Trade Negotiations (1986–1994). According to John Braithwaite

and Peter Drahos, forum-shifting encompasses three kinds of strategies: moving an agenda from one organization to another, abandoning an organization, and pursuing the same agenda in more than one organization. The United States, European Community and Japan, primarily influenced and instructed by private sector actors, succeeded in moving the IPRs agenda from WIPO to the WTO by linking IPRs to trade in the WTO, which accelerated Global South countries' acceptance of the WTO 'package deal', despite their initial resistance. During the Uruguay Round of Multilateral Trade Negotiations, Global South countries led by India and Brazil, who asserted that the WIPO remain the focal IPRs institution, were stifled through pressure and threats of United States' trade sanctions under Section 301 of the United States Trade Act 1974 and the Generalized System of Preferences.

The adoption of the Agreement Establishing the WTO in 1994 proved successful as over 100 countries interested in participating in the multilateral trading system signed up. As part of the binding package deal (or single undertaking), TRIPS, set out in Annex 1C of the Agreement Establishing the WTO, introduced high minimum IPRs standards with specified deadlines. Marking a watershed in the international IPRs landscape, TRIPS combines the disparate categories and subsidiary categories of IPRs in a single agreement (Part II, Articles 9–40), but mandates members to implement substantial parts of existing treaties such as the Paris Convention and Berne Convention. Unlike the weak enforcement mechanisms in the Paris Convention and Berne Convention, TRIPS is linked to the WTO's Dispute Settlement System (DSS) set out in Annex 2 of the Agreement Establishing the WTO (which is currently in crisis due to the United States' foreign policy – one outcome of the DSS collapse would be nonexistent international enforcement for IPRs). For the most part, Global North countries only had to make minor changes to their IPRs laws and frameworks, which is unsurprising as TRIPS was mainly modelled on the United States and European laws. Conversely, Global South countries had to make comprehensive, multi-faceted IPRs revisions. For example, although IPRs for plant varieties was broadly alien to Global South countries pre-TRIPS, many of these countries introduced compliant systems to fulfil obligations under Article 27.3(b) TRIPS.

Tensions, contestations and discontents in intellectual property rights

The historical trajectories of IPRs uncover countries' fluctuating standpoints. In the early phases of designing and introducing IPRs, countries with interests to protect pushed for stronger IPRs in their spheres of influence (for example, the United Kingdom's push for copyrights) – at the national levels, in colonies and dominions, and subsequently, through bilateral and international agreements. During the Uruguay Round of Multilateral Trade Negotiations, there was a sharp divide between Global North and Global South standpoints. The former pushed for stronger IPRs, the latter resisted. Nonetheless, a nuanced historical examination of IPRs reveals that the divide between the Global North and Global South is not so neatly cut. In other words, the Global North or Global South standpoints are not always homogenous. The core rationale for the differing standpoints on IPRs is the underlying interests promoted. These include private sector interests/instructions, socio-economic interests/realities, technological capabilities and external pressures.

Indeed, many of the Global North countries who currently push for stronger IPRs systems openly endorsed copying and reverse engineering to provide access to essential technologies and knowledge as well as to promote national industrial capacity, generate employment and grow their economies. William Fisher points out that until the middle of the nineteenth century, piracy was a norm in the United States. In contrast, Susan Sell finds that by the late twentieth century, driven by technological advancements and private sector actors including Hewlett-Packard, IBM, Pfizer, Monsanto and Warner Bros, the United States had become one of the most active proponents for strengthened IPRs. However, the United States is not an active proponent for strengthening all IPRs' categories and subsidiary categories. For example, with GIs, where the United States is less competitive, it pushes for weaker national and international protection systems. It argues that the Trademark system adequately protects products originating from specific geographic origins and a distinct GI system is unnecessary. On the other hand, with Europe's smorgasbord of rich traditional products, its countries are active proponents of strengthened GIs. The differences in Global North standpoints on IPRs, especially the United States and Europe, tend to be challenging to resolve. Despite Europe's push for strengthened GIs, the United States has maintained its Trademark system. Attempts to introduce stronger systems through bilateral/regional agreements, such as the United States–European Union Transatlantic Trade and Investment Partnership, were unsuccessful.

Interestingly, there are certain categories and subsidiary categories of IPRs on which some countries in the Global North and South have shared perspectives. One example would be GIs, which sees shared opinions between the European Union and many Global South countries. Global South countries, such as those in Africa and Asia, like Europe, have a rich array of traditional products. At the Doha Development Round (DDR) launched in 2001 to address Global South concerns around the implementation of WTO Agreements – including TRIPS – the European Union alongside Global South countries like Kenya, Sri Lanka and Thailand proposed strengthening GI provisions in TRIPS. Other IPRs issues that the Global South WTO members tabled at the DDR with potential for socio-economic development include access to medicines, disclosure of genetic materials for patent applications, traditional knowledge/traditional cultural expressions alongside the review of the IPRs for plant varieties (TRIPS, Article 27.3(b)) and the general review of the Agreement (TRIPS, Article 71.1). WTO members approved a firm decision on access to medicines in August 2003, allowing compulsory licences to produce, export and import pharmaceutical products. However, the other IPRs issues tabled remained unresolved with the breakdown of negotiations in 2008, thanks to the Global North and Global South impasse.

With the breakdown of multilateral negotiations, WTO members resort to bilateral agreements. It has become apparent that Global North actors, especially the United States and European Union, through such bilateral agreements, tend to pressure Global South countries to design and introduce specific IPRs provisions, which go beyond the TRIPS minimum standards. These are referred to as the 'TRIPS-plus' provisions. A topical example relates to Article 27.3(b) TRIPS. The United States and European Union pressured Global South countries such as Ecuador, Jordan, Morocco, Nicaragua and Tunisia, through bilateral trade agreements or economic partnership agreements, to introduce the Plant Breeders' Rights system set out under the 1991 Act of the International Convention for the Protection of New Varieties of Plants (UPOV). The Plant Breeders' Rights system is a TRIPS-plus provision because unlike the Paris Convention and Berne Convention expressly mentioned in TRIPS, TRIPS neither mentions UPOV nor obligates WTO members to introduce its Plant Breeders' Rights system. Despite the pressures, Global South countries ambitiously underscore the 'development' objective of IPRs in both multilateral and bilateral negotiations. Indeed, while the Global South joined the complex international IPRs scene much later than their Global North counterparts, one of the Global South's seminal contributions to TRIPS was Article 8, which promotes the introduction of IPRs for social, economic and technological development. This position stems from the recognition that development needs at the national levels differ; there are no 'one-size-fits-all' IPRs systems suited to all realities. Global South WTO members have significant policy space to delineate and design IPRs systems consistent with their needs and realities. Therefore, the flexibilities in TRIPS should be respected, not invaded.

TITILAYO ADEBOLA

References

Braithwaite, John and Peter Drahos (2000). *Global Business Regulation*. Cambridge University Press.

Correa, Carlos M. (2000). *Intellectual Property Rights, the WTO and Developing Countries: The TRIPS Agreement and Policy Options*. Zed Books.

Deere, Carolyn (2009). *The Implementation Game: The TRIPS Agreement and the Global Politics of Intellectual Property Reform in Developing Countries*. Oxford University Press.

Dutfield, Graham and Uma Suthersanen (2007). *Global Intellectual Property Law*. Edward Elgar.

International Centre for Trade and Sustainable Development (2005). *UNCTAD-ICTSD Project on IPRs and Sustainable Development: Resource Book on TRIPS and Development*. Cambridge University Press.

Oguamanam, Chidi (2013). *Intellectual Property in Global Governance: A Development Question*. Routledge.

Okediji, Ruth L. (2003). 'The International Relations of Intellectual Property: Narratives of Developing Country Participation in the Global Intellectual Property System', Singapore Journal of International and Comparative Law 7, 315–385.

Sell, Susan K. (2003). *Private Power, Public Law: The Globalisation of Intellectual Property Rights*. Cambridge University Press.

Sherman, Brad and Lionel Bentley (1999). *The Making of Modern Intellectual Property Law*. Cambridge University Press.

Watal, Jayashree (2001). *Intellectual Property Rights in the WTO and Developing Countries*. Oxford University Press.

38. International Commodity Agreements

International commodity agreements (ICAs) were an important way that national governments organized international trade from the 1930s until the 1980s. ICAs' general purpose was to moderate global commodity price fluctuation. These multilateral intergovernmental agreements and their respective organizations first became popular in the 1960s. They were an important site where the Third World met the First and Second Worlds in the spirit of dialogue, debate, and decision-making. ICAs featured in development plans as a way to ensure that national economies that depended on commodity exports benefited from a stable and remunerative global market. Often such plans included using the influx of capital from commodity exports to diversify the economy and kick-start an industrial sector.

The intellectual and institutional history of ICAs remains understudied today. This is unfortunate since they have been key institutions where ideas about trade, development and global life were constructed and debated. While the WTO Agreement on Agriculture focuses on tariffs and subsidies, ICAs were primarily about market stability and supply management. Since the food crisis of 2007 and global financial crisis of 2008, policy-makers in different fora sometimes mention ICAs as a possible solution in light of erratic commodity prices. More importantly, because international trade's institutional landscape is currently in flux, it is worth reimagining ICAs for the future.

The life and death of ICAs

With the global collapse of commodity prices in 1980–1982 and the ensuing global economic recession, many people lost faith in ICAs' ability to stabilize prices. The demise of the International Tin Agreement and the bankruptcy of the International Tin Council along with its stabilization fund in 1985 made ICAs even less politically and intellectually popular. Today, the Organization of the Petroleum Exporting Countries remains as one of the few commodity organizations that regulate supply.

The first ICAs were negotiated in the interwar years. They gained some attention within the League of Nations, and in the 1930s there were a small number of systemic studies of ICAs (and potential ICAs). In the final years of the Second World War, systemic ICA studies started to sprout. The discussion was about more than the technical aspects of supply management and price control. This was an active field of study where scholars from different disciplines debated with each other about the relationship amongst international law, international trade and economic development.

The 1970s and early 1980s marked the high-point of ICA studies in terms of vigor and quantity. Some legal scholars considered the ICAs and their respective implementing agencies as forming a particular sort of international institution with legal personality, quasi-judicial functions, and norm-generating capabilities. By this time, many ICAs had a wide variety of goals and functions. Agreements included objectives such as market access and supply reliability, diversification and industrialization, and increased consumption. Some made explicit provision for alleviating domestic economic hardships such as the prevention of unemployment or under-employment. Those that did not have these explicit purposes still took domestic development concerns very seriously and allowed for special and differential treatment for developing countries. It has been difficult to gauge the general success of ICAs in light of the unique context of each commodity and the different mechanisms used by different agreements. International buffer-stock schemes involved the creation of an international agency to buy and maintain surpluses or an international system to coordinate nationally held stocks. Trade quota schemes involved establishing permissible price ranges where producing countries were allotted quotas in times of surplus while consuming countries were allotted quotas in times of shortage. Purchase contract schemes regulated long-term agreements between producers and consumers that set the price and quantities of trade. It has also been difficult to determine if individual ICAs succeeded or failed because agreements' objectives (beyond price stabilization) were ambiguous. Those that failed by any measure were usually not well funded or did not have enough members to achieve any objective.

Institutional politics

What made many ICAs legally and politically notable was the fact that each agreement was accompanied by a permanent organization. Each organization was uniquely designed to reflect and manage the particular political economy of each commodity in light of changing conditions. Often, voting power was allocated according to a formula reflecting import and export volume. As a result, each commodity organization was defined by a complex matrix of alliances that held together tensions amongst exporting/importing, developing/developed, and small/large countries.

Starting in the 1950s, a mix of Third World leaders, transnational agriculturalists, Keynesian economists, and dependency theorists succeeded in ensuring that ICAs and price stabilization remained an important feature of trade law and policy until the 1980s. Commodity prices have always been notoriously capricious and all these actors came together at a time when Europe needed to be reconstructed, newly independent countries in Asia and Africa needed to rebuild their post-colonial economies, and life in Latin America continued to be at the mercy of exporting primary commodities to international markets. ICAs were a key aspect of agricultural policy in the Global North and South and were thought to complement domestic supply management schemes. Amongst ICA supporters, an important debate was over how to enmesh ICAs within a broader landscape of international institutions and how to distribute power amongst the multitude of global interests.

For example, after the Second World War, the Food and Agriculture Organization (FAO) under the leadership of John Boyd Orr called for the creation of agricultural ICAs under its purview. Orr put forward an outline to the world's governments proposing that they work together to create a World Food Board whose purpose would be to rationally organize world food production and distribution through these ICAs in order to eliminate hunger. This vision included a comprehensive system made up of buffer stocks, surplus-disposal mechanisms, and provisions for relief operations. US and British diplomats reacted against this idea because they wanted to focus more on freer trade and less on food security; they succeeded in ensuring that global ICA discussions were held instead under the auspices of International Trade Organization negotiations.

There are also some instances of trying to embed ICAs within the General Agreement for Tariffs and Trade (GATT). For example, the International Dairy Arrangement, a Western-friendly ICA, was successfully negotiated as part of the GATT Tokyo Round (1973–1979) and would later be renewed and incorporated into the WTO (1995–1998).

During the 1970s, Third World governments and international civil servants succeeded in establishing a global consensus that the United Nations Conference on Trade and Development (UNCTAD) would be the best place to negotiate global commodity policy and house most ICAs. The Third World plan was to gain and hold as much power as possible in the natural resource sector. The reasoning behind this plan was that this sector was where the stakes were the highest: most of these countries had a comparative advantage in natural resource markets and most Third World people derived their livelihood specifically from agriculture, pastoralism and hunting.

The relationship between UNCTAD and ICAs was complicated by the fact that most ICAs and their respective secretariats had their own institutional histories predating UNCTAD. Some export-dependent Third World countries had significant power within certain ICAs and were reluctant to diffuse their influence by rolling ICAs into UNCTAD. It was therefore always a matter of political negotiation within the Third World as to what it meant for ICAs to be part of UNCTAD.

As such, ICAs were also a place where people put forward competing Third World projects. Some (such as Raúl Prebisch) focused more on describing and addressing global inequality of wealth in terms of national economic outputs. This way of thinking imagined the landscape of international trade institutions to consist of a mix of domestic and international institutions. This was a popular idea in the late 1960s and during this time most ICAs were loosely held together by UNCTAD through general principles. Whereas others (such as Celso Furtado) preferred to frame patterns of global wealth distribution and development as the product of the lasting impact of imperial and colonial structures. This approach imagined a more singular global economy and wanted to empower one multilateral institution (namely

MICHAEL FAKHRI

UNCTAD) to rectify global power imbalances and manage the world's commodities.

This global, anti-imperial perspective would be articulated in international instruments such as the UN General Assembly's 1974 New International Economic Order (NIEO). This included creating the Integrated Programme for Commodities and the Common Fund for Commodities. The UNCTAD Secretariat positioned the Integrated Programme for Commodities and Common Fund as an all-or-nothing component of NIEO, thereby raising the stakes behind ICAs and interlinking the fate of the commodity policy with NIEO doctrines. Because this agenda demanded a global redistribution of wealth from rich to poor countries, most people from the First World treated NIEO (and its commodity policies) as a radical threat from the Third World.

By the early 1980s, those from the North and South who had not given up entirely on ICAs as an idea, started to look to the GATT, rather than UNCTAD, as the institutional milieu for ICAs. There was also a shift from discussing ICAs in terms of debating over the economic mechanism that was the most appropriate to regulate prices to suggesting that commodity organizations should focus on administrative functions such as research, consultation and international cooperation – which is the status of most ICAs today.

Reimagining ICAs

One cannot understand the contemporary history of trade law, development policy and international institutions without appreciating ICAs. These agreements were not just part of economic development plans but were also part of food security debates. What is untested is whether a trade agreement that brings together all parties with a significant interest in a particular commodity can create a regime that principally addresses food security concerns (meeting right to food obligations and Sustainable Development Goals).

There is some historical precedent in the 1967 International Wheat Arrangement (aka International Grains Arrangement). What is remarkable about this treaty was that it was made up of a Wheat Trade Convention and (the first ever) Food Aid Convention. Because of the latter, it was understood at the time to be a clear benefit for developing countries since it created a scheme to distinguish food aid from dumping.

The key to reimagining ICAs as food security agreements is not to start with their historic function of stabilizing prices since their track record on this front is controversial and remains unclear. Moreover, missing from ICA practice was any sense of how different communities live within very particular ecological relationships. Even today we still have a long way to go to better understand how the international governance of natural resources operates within such a plurality of biomes.

What makes ICAs promising then is their form and diverse institutional design. Doctrinally, ICAs are exempt from GATT (Article XX(h)) and can therefore still theoretically operate as legitimate exceptions to WTO law. We can therefore start with the fact that each commodity has its own particular geography, ecology and political economy. And each commodity is uniquely situated in the global economy. It is easy to imagine a future in which certain key commodities are governed by an ICA that reflects and responds to each particular complexity. A wheat agreement, for instance, should not be the same as a rice agreement. ICAs were always renegotiated every five years (on average) giving policy-makers the ability to be nimble and creative in ways that we do not see today. As ecological changes precipitate, this sort of flexibility will only become more necessary.

It is also easy to imagine how different ICAs would be informed by different development theories, met with different anti-imperial tactics, and serve the most vulnerable communities. Correspondingly, each commodity organization would grant procedural standing and allocate voting power in their own way reflecting the political struggles and compromises necessary to come to an agreement. And much like today, all this would be done while we continually advance our understanding of how different economies around the world are always inherently interconnected when it comes to natural resources and ecological conditions.

MICHAEL FAKHRI

References

Brown, Christopher P. (1980). *The Political and Social Economy of Commodity Control*. Macmillan Press.

Chimni, B.S. (1987). *International Commodity Agreements: A Legal Study*. Croom Helm.

Chrispeels, Erik (ed.) (2002). *International Commodity Organisations in Transition*. Cameron May.

Ernst, Ervin (1982). *International Commodity Agreements: The System of Controlling the International Commodity Market*. Martinus Nijhoff.

Fakhri, Michael (2014). *Sugar and the Making of International Trade Law*. Cambridge University Press.

Fakhri, Michael (2019). "A History of Food Security and Agriculture in International Trade Law, 1945–2015" in Akbar Rasulov and John Haskell (eds), *International Economic Law: New Voices, New Perspectives*. Springer.

Gilbert, Christopher L. (2007). "International Commodity Agreements" in James D. Gaisford, and William A. Kerr (eds), *Handbook on International Trade Policy*. Edward Elgar.

Khan, Kabir-ur-Rahman (1982). *The Law and Organisation of International Commodity Agreements*. Martinus Nijhoff.

Maizels, Alfred (1999). *Commodities in Crisis: The Commodity Crisis of the 1980s and the Political Economy of International Commodity Prices*. Clarendon Press.

North-South Institute (1978). *Commodity Trade: Test Case for a New Economic Order*. North-South Institute.

39. International Financial Regulation and Sustainable Finance

Introduction

Conventional accounts of International Financial Regulation (IFR), originated from the 1944 Bretton Woods conference, describe the transnational institutional architecture that engages in agenda-setting, standard-setting, implementation, supervision and enforcement of financial law, regulation and standards, towards ensuring an orderly and stable international financial system, and lately, containing systemic risk. The historical and continuing contestation of IFR by States, social movements and academics, has elicited more critical accounts that problematize the objectives, institutional architecture and outputs of the regulatory system, and of the concept of finance itself, thus resulting in the concept of 'sustainable finance'. Consequently, critical IFR research has focused on how IFR can be adapted to realize and secure 'sustainable finance'.

Conceptualizing 'finance' and 'sustainable finance'

Mainstream neoclassical economics describes finance as the inter-temporal monetary exchange between parties holding surplus money and parties requiring additional purchasing power, thereby creating debt and credit. Relatedly, financial markets are the abstract mechanisms that price financial assets and allocate or determine their flow into productive areas of the global economy. Comprehensive accounts reject the conceptual separation of the financial from the real economy, recognizing international financial markets and flows as not merely apolitical, neutral and abstract mechanisms of demand and supply, but rather powerful intervenors in social life. International finance constitutes and performs the inequitable relationships between ostensibly equally sovereign developed and developing States, conditions the juridical relationship between the debtor State and its citizens, and constrains the capacity of the State to realize human and economic development and protect its citizens' fundamental rights.

Indeed, these competing conceptions of finance are central to developing economies' historical contestation of the dominant regulatory paradigms undergirding IFR: financial market liberalization and deregulation, privatization, trade liberalization, capital account liberalization, and related policies. Despite constituting the global political economy of inequality, IFR is legitimated as neutral and apolitical, and not amenable to fundamental restructuring, especially after recurrent international financial crises that have widened the global inequality gap. Nevertheless, continuous contestation has established the concept of 'sustainable finance', which, while recognizing the constitutive power of finance in exploiting debt vulnerability and patterning social life according to its (financial) imperatives, integrates environmental, social and governance considerations into investment decisions, for the lasting benefit of global society.

Pluralist conception of international financial regulators

Hard law: public and private international law

Since 1944, the normative framework of IFR has become increasingly pluralistic, decentred, and multi-polar, consisting of both hard and soft law. The first tier of IFR is 'hard law', which consists of State-constituted treaty organizations, including the International Monetary Fund (IMF) and the World Bank. The IMF was originally mandated to promote international monetary cooperation, international trade, maintain exchange stability and orderly exchange arrangements, and a multilateral system of payments. The World Bank, on the other hand, was mandated to finance economic development projects in developing countries, and promote, as part of its financing conditionalities, specific institutional, policy and regulatory reforms within the member countries in need of financing. Anghie (2005) argues that the analytical frameworks governing traditional scholarship in these treaty organizations have obscured the central role of imperialism and colonialism in shaping IFR, and establishing it as a continuation of the dual mandate of civilizing developing States, while exploiting them economically. The 'civilizing mission' is encapsulated in the expansion of the Bretton Woods institutions' (hereinafter BWI) mandate to include economic development and human rights protections, which have ideologically legitimated the BWIs' management of Third World economies in the interests of (mostly Western) transnational finance, through capital account liberalization and financial market deregulation. Economically dominant States established the juridical and institutional foundations of these BWIs on the basis of a false dichotomy between the 'economic' and the 'political', thereby establishing control of these international regulatory institutions on the basis of GDP metrics and economic power. This undermined democratic participation, and sovereign equality of developing States. This set the basis for the continued contestation of these institutions by the Third World States, social movements and academia.

Private International Law (PIL), or *Lex Mercatoria*, also provides foundational legal norms that play a constitutive and regulatory role in international finance. PIL refers to the previously autonomous body of legal norms and procedures that evolved from the customs and practices of medieval merchants, and which sought to govern the transnational spaces of commerce that were not covered by increasingly differentiated national commercial laws, but have now been largely codified in national laws. PIL is currently developed and enforced by international arbitral bodies. Since the arbitral decision in Abaclat and Others v. Argentine Republic, which conceptualized foreign holders of sovereign bonds as foreign investors under bilateral investment treaties and the International Centre for Settlement of Investment Disputes (ICSID) Convention, the corpus of the international treaty law of foreign investments can be considered as part of IFR.

Soft law

The second tier of IFR consists of State-to-State contact groups that have also originated 'soft law' regulations, that is, non-legally binding financial regulatory standards that have nevertheless achieved the compliance efficacy of legally binding hard law. At the apex of the soft law pyramid is the G20, a Heads of State contact group that achieves political consensus and sets the regulatory reform agenda. The main State-State contact groups that implement the G20's agenda include: the Basel Committee on Banking Supervision (BCBS), whose capital adequacy standards are considered the most influential transnational banking regulatory standards, and the Financial Stability Board (FSB), the central technical regulatory authority tasked with coordinating regulatory efforts among all the other international regulators and standard setters. The Bank for International Settlements (BIS) also convenes six other standard setters, alongside the BCBS.

Since 1944, soft law financial regulatory standards have been preferred by the dominant rule-making and agenda-setting Western States, due to their flexibility, in terms of the efficacy of originating and promulgating new standards, the need to maintain the Western-centric, undemocratic constitution of the standard setters, and rejection of additional legal duties on States and market actors. For example, UNCTAD's 2012 'Principles on Promoting Responsible Sovereign Lending and Borrowing', while crucial to promoting sustainable international finance and addressing global inequality, have been relegated to non-binding soft law.

Despite their democratic deficit, soft law standards have achieved high compliance levels due to their enforcement mechanisms. First, BWIs include compliance with soft law standards, e.g. capital account liberalization and Basel III, as part of their loan conditionalities with borrower States. Second, large economic blocs such as the European Union have translated these soft law standards into hard law, such as the Basel III-inspired Capital Requirements Directive (CRD), which then binds EU Member States and even Third Countries as hard law. Third, the financial markets compel State compliance with these standards, as investors refrain from channelling their funds to jurisdictions with financial markets deemed risky due to sub-standard regulatory frameworks. Market enforcement is demonstrated especially where States rush to implement transnational financial standards (such as Basel III Accord) before issuing foreign-denominated sovereign bonds in the international markets. The force of these soft law standards and fora, whose fitness for purpose were challenged by the 2008 financial crisis, has provided a powerful argument for their institutional reform, to provide for democratic participation and inclusion, especially of developing economies that bore the brunt of the ensuing economic recession.

JEREMMY OKONJO

Financial markets as regulators

The third tier of transnational financial regulation represents a significant shift in the normative character of regulatory power, from State to non-State private actors, especially financial market actors. Transnational Financial Associations (TFAs) play an important constitutive and regulatory role in global finance. They concentrate and coordinate the power and interests of finance towards: creating and extending the domain of financial markets into social life; originating self-regulatory standards for financial institutions; lobbying transnational and national regulators to adopt market-friendly financial regulations; and engaging in private-public partnerships with transnational regulators in the formulation, implementation and enforcement of financial regulations. For example, the International Swaps and Derivatives Association (ISDA) contractual documentation relating to close-out netting and other provisions of derivatives contracts have been adopted by the FSB in its various International Financial Regulatory Standards (IFRS), including its Effective Resolution Regimes and Policies. ISDA's contractual interpretations are also deemed legally authoritative by national courts in contractual disputes. Similarly, the Institute of International Finance (IIF) and the Group of 30 (G30) have also been instrumental in lobbying the BCBS to adopt market-centric self-regulatory mechanisms in Basel II. Both derivatives contracts, governed by ISDA, and Basel II played significant roles in the 2008 crisis.

In addition to TFAs, other financial market intermediaries also play regulatory roles. Credit Rating Agencies (CRAs) employ deeply political and subjective risk calculation methodologies in undertaking their normative and performative roles of curating profitable and non-profitable financial investments, and thereby ordering the flow of global capital. The regulatory role of CRAs in global markets was entrenched by the BCBS under Basel II, which pegged calculation of risk weights on external credit ratings. Their central role in precipitating the 2008 crisis has led to tighter regulation of CRAs, even though this regulatory reform has not addressed the fundamentals of risk calculation. The role of transnational private actors in originating IFRs with significant negative impacts on States and their citizens underscores the legitimacy and democratic deficits of these regulators.

Ideas and technological practices as regulators

The 2008 global financial crisis was heralded as a constitutional moment for deconstructing and rebuilding the transnational financial regulatory architecture. Yet, more than a decade later, despite the lingering economic and social crises triggered by the subsequent economic recession, the post-crisis reforms have failed to radically restructure the global financial order, while the legitimacy of the discredited economic, legal and technological regulatory ideas and practices have been rehabilitated.

This failure of financial regulatory reform demonstrates the resilience and reproduction of the market-centred perspectives on economic organization, and specifically, financial market regulation, enabled by the continuous evolution of regulatory hegemony from structural and economic, to material and ideological power of dominant State and non-State actors. The emergence and growth of financial technologies (including credit-rating and scoring technologies, blockchain, digital finance, and Artificial Intelligence) represents the latest iteration of free market economic organization, as economic, legal and technological ideas are embedded and entangled in ostensibly efficient, neutral and apolitical technologies and practices that then constitute financial markets in the digital age.

The under-appreciation of the ideological and performative role of ideas and technological practices in establishing and sustaining particular modes of economic organization, especially in the Global South, has obscured their regulatory role in international finance. Perspectives from ideology-critique and legal materiality have enabled a conceptualization and appreciation of the nature of legal, economic, and technological ideas, practices and technologies (embedded within the ideational infrastructure of norm entrepreneurs and technological innovators) as disciplinary discourses and practices that order the policies and priorities of sovereign States. This conceptualization of international financial regulators is key to successful contestation and fundamental reform of IFR by States, citizens and communities that have suffered the brunt of economic and social inequality caused by the structure of global financial markets.

JEREMMY OKONJO

Conclusion: securing sustainable finance in IFR

The post-2008 transnational financial regulatory reform promised fundamental changes to international finance and its regulatory structure, but failed to deliver, owing to various reasons, including the structural power of hegemonic actors in the global economy, increasing materiality of the dominant perspectives, e.g. in technological arrangements, increased cohesiveness of a transnational financial elite served well by the status quo, and the resilience and reproduction of the ideational infrastructure of the status quo. Consequently, fundamental aspects of the international financial market structure, e.g. market failure, economic externalities, public goods and social equity, have been side-lined in the reform project as incidental rather than central issues to be dealt with in the post-crisis reform programme, in favour of piecemeal reforms geared towards macro-prudential regulation.

Successful contestation and reform of the IFR to secure sustainable finance is a continuous project that calls for the deconstruction of its ideational infrastructure, and the mainstreaming of alternative praxis by States and communities that have been negatively impacted by the nature and structure of international finance. This requires a comprehensive conceptualization of the continuously evolving, pluralist modalities of transnational financial regulation.

JEREMMY OKONJO

References

Anghie, Antony (2005). *Imperialism, Sovereignty, and the Making of International Law*. Cambridge University Press.

Cutler, A. Claire (2003). *Private Power and Global Authority: Transnational Merchant Law in the Global Political Economy*. Cambridge University Press.

Eslava, Luis and Sundhya Pahuja (2011). 'Between Resistance and Reform: TWAIL and the Universality of International Law', Trade, Law and Development 3, 103–130.

Ho, Daniel E. (2002). 'Compliance and International Soft Law: Why Do Countries Implement the Basle Accord?', Journal of International Economic Law 5(3), 647–688.

Kern, Alexander (2006). *Global Governance of Financial Systems: The International Regulation of Systemic Risk*. Oxford University Press.

McKeen-Edwards, Heather and Tony Porter (2013). *Transnational Financial Associations and the Governance of Global Finance: Assembling Wealth and Power*. Routledge.

Okonjo, Jeremmy Odhiambo (2018). *Expert Ideas and Technological Practices as Financial Market Regulators: The Ideological and Performative Reproduction of Regulatory Neoliberalism*. PhD Thesis, University of Kent.

Pahuja, Sundhya (2011). *Decolonising International Law: Development, Economic Growth, and the Politics of Universality*. Cambridge University Press.

Tan, Celine (2014). 'Reframing the Debate: The Debt Relief Initiative and New Normative Values in the Governance of Third World Debt', International Journal of Law in Context 10(2), 249–272.

40. International Law

Enhancing economic growth, eradicating poverty, implementing human rights and improving the living conditions for people are some key concerns for developing countries. International law has increasingly become a tool for them to meet their development objectives. International law is a set of rules that governs international relations between countries in an array of areas from human rights, humanitarian and criminal law to the Law of the Sea, environmental and economic law, to name a few. Such rules are mainly found in international agreements between States (treaties; perhaps the most renowned example being the United Nations Charter), customary international law (consisting of both State practice and States' belief to have carried out the practice as a legal obligation), general principles of law recognized by States, judgments rendered by international court and tribunals, and doctrinal scholarship.

The most prominent sources of international law, treaties and customary international law, are the fruit of international negotiations or decisions made by States. Herein lies a difficulty of this discipline: its entire existence is dependent on States' willingness to cooperate with and abide by the rules they have created. What is more, there is no "international judge" capable of sanctioning, against their will, governments that do not respect their international obligations. The International Court of Justice (ICJ) in The Hague resolves disputes only between governments who have consented to this. The International Criminal Court (ICC), another tribunal based in The Hague, prosecutes grave international crimes committed by individuals, but only in States who are parties to the Rome Statute (its constitutive treaty) and who refer such crimes committed by their nationals or on their territory to the ICC. The ICC's Prosecutor may start a preliminary examination *proprio motu* but only in States that have consented to this. The only exception that does not require States' consent is that the ICC may intervene in a country if the United Nations Security Council has requested it to do so, but this process may be hindered by the veto, which will be discussed later.

The necessity of consent reflects the broader principle of State sovereignty, a defining feature of international law. In theory, this sovereignty is equally attributed to all States regardless of the size of their territory or their military, political or economic power. In reality, however, such inequalities between countries are undeniable and thus certain economically, politically, militarily or territorially dominant States play a greater role and enjoy more privileges than certain developing countries in the international legal framework.

This sovereign inequality can be seen through at least three examples: the funding of international organizations, procedural prerogatives in international organizations and the Responsibility to Protect doctrine. All examples concern international organizations, which have become predominant fora wherein international legal rules related to development have been crafted, adopted and promoted. An international organization is an association of States constituted by a treaty, made up of organs and having an international legal personality distinct from that of its Member States. It is therefore an actor in the international legal system bearing responsibility for breaching its international obligations and capable of concluding treaties. It may also produce resolutions, policies or significant non-binding documents (referred to as "soft law"), which may bear significance in international development. The most renowned example of an international organization is the United Nations, a complex system comprised of a number of institutions such as funds (such as the United Nations Population Fund), programmes (such as the United Nations Development Programme) and specialized agencies (such as the World Health Organization – WHO, the United Nations Educational, Scientific and Cultural Organization – UNICEF, or the World Bank). Through resolutions, the United Nations adopted eight Millennium Development Goals (MDGs) in the year 2000, followed by 17 Sustainable Development Goals adopted in 2015 for the year 2030 – both with a principal objective of eradicating poverty.

A first example of sovereign inequality concerns the funding of international organizations. The United Nations system is predominantly funded by assessed contributions of its Member States, which are yearly obligatory payments owed due to membership and largely based on per capita income. It has been noted that countries who pay more may have, in the past, exercised greater de facto influence in that organization. For instance, the United States of America (USA) contributes 22 per cent to the United Nations' regular budget – the maximum that any country is authorized to pay – and contributes generously to the budgets of specialized agencies as well (despite the Trump Administration's funding decrease in 2017). Thus, when the Palestinian Liberation Organization (PLO) requested membership to the WHO in 1989, the USA, due to its foreign policy stance in the Israeli-Palestinian conflict, threatened to cut the WHO's funding should the request be accepted. This explains why, to this day, the PLO is not a member of the WHO. Similarly, in 2011, the USA cut 240 million US dollars of funding from UNESCO (approximately 22 per cent of UNESCO's budget) when the latter accepted the State of Palestine as a Member State of the Organization, plunging it into a financial crisis. Such influence in international institutions may only be enjoyed by more economically powerful States.

A second example of sovereign inequality concerns procedural prerogatives in international organizations. The United Nations Security Council, one of the six principal organs of the United Nations, is composed of five permanent members – the USA, France, China, Russia and the United Kingdom (the "P5") – and ten non-permanent members elected for two-year terms, and is responsible for the maintenance of international peace and security. Article 27(3) of the United Nations Charter empowers the five permanent members, who were allies and victors of the Second World War, to block any Security Council resolution on non-procedural matters, regardless of its support by the other Member States of the Council or by the Organization at large. Although originally believed to be a mechanism that would prevent the breakout of another war, the veto may be a means for members of the P5 to safeguard their national interests at the expense of international peace and security and, particularly, the prosecution of grave international crimes (as mentioned earlier, the veto may block the Council from referring alleged international crimes to the ICC, as Russia and China did with regard to Syria in 2014). Elsewhere, at the World Bank, which provides financial and technical assistance to developing countries around the world, each Member State has one vote for each share of the Bank's capital stock held by the Member. The USA remains the largest shareholder and also the only one with veto power over changes in the Bank's structure.

A third example of sovereign inequality concerns a fairly recent practice in international law named the Responsibility to Protect doctrine or "R2P". At the 2005 United Nations World Summit, Member States agreed that all States have a responsibility to protect all populations from grave international crimes such as genocide, war crimes, ethnic cleansing and crimes against humanity and therefore, gave the United Nations Security Council the power to allow the use of force as a last resort in any country no longer upholding its responsibilities. While, in theory, any State may intervene in any other State in such circumstances, practice has only recorded economically powerful States intervening in other States (a prominent example is the military intervention of the North Atlantic Treaty Organization – an alliance between European and North American countries – in Libya in 2011, to implement Security Council Resolution 1973). This is because the former States have the means to intervene in the latter. Despite the welcomed emphasis that the R2P doctrine places on every State's responsibility towards the international community to uphold human rights and promote peace in their territories, and the commendable progress made to obstruct grave international crimes, the practice has been criticized for violating State sovereignty and for being abused as a pretext for intervening countries to impose a regime change. Further, the required approval of the Security Council implies problems in inequality related to the veto, examined above.

The inequality of nations therefore visibly seeps into the practice of international law, making it an arguably challenging tool for developing countries to achieve their socioeconomic objectives. This inequality may be better understood by examining international law's origins. Traditionally, international law is said to have been born in 1648 with the Peace of Westphalia, which was a series of peace treaties considered to have marked the end of the European wars on religion and, specifically, the Thirty Years' War. Conversely, many Asian and African states only achieved independence from their European colonial rulers mainly between 1945 and the 1960s. It became increasingly desirable to enhance the economic growth, alleviate poverty and improve the living conditions of the people in these newly decolonized nations, through free trade policies and international organizations such as the United Nations and the World Bank. The latter institutions sought to provide technical assistance to public administrations of decolonized countries in order to enhance their economic development. Yet, developing societies were envisaged to be modelled after developed societies in the Western world, applying international legal norms that had been fashioned by this region of the world centuries prior. This historical background sets the scene to understand some potential challenges in enhancing a developing State to its optimum while preserving its own traditions, culture and identity.

Regardless, developing countries have certainly managed to safeguard their interests on the international stage, mainly through significant international treaties. For instance, at the World Trade Organization (WTO), which regulates international trade between countries, many trade agreements contain provisions allowing for "special and differential treatment", catered particularly towards developing countries. The 2015 Paris Agreement within the United Nations Framework Convention on Climate Change (UNFCCC) states, amongst other things, that developed countries are to take the lead in mobilizing climate finances, and emphasizes capacity-building in the developing world in order to improve climate change resilience. The 1982 United Nations Convention on the Law of the Sea (UNCLOS) guarantees that the seabed, ocean floor and subsoil thereof (referred to as "the Area") are the common heritage of mankind, as opposed to being subject to any one State's national jurisdiction, which is also favourable to developing nations. More generally, international law has served developing countries in many ways, giving them the means to define their territorial and maritime boundaries and guaranteeing rights to their populations, including the right to self-determination which buttressed many decolonized countries' quest to independence.

As long as there are States, there will be inequality between them. Centuries of history propelling certain States ahead of others, from a development perspective, cannot be reversed, nor can the consequences be altered. Accordingly, such inequalities will always be at the forefront of how States deal with each other on the international stage. However, developing countries may continue to further enhance their international legal expertise and negotiation prowess in order to defend their interests and make decisions that are conducive to their economic development in all areas of international law, within and outside of international organizations.

YUSRA SUEDI

References

Chimni, B.S. (2006). "Third World Approaches to international Law: Manifesto", International Community Law Review 8, 3–27.

Chowdhury, Subrata Roy, Paul J.I.M. de Waart, and Erik M.G. Denters (1992). *The Right to Development in International Law*. Martinus Nijhoff Publishers.

De Serpa Soares, Miguel (2015). "Room for Growth: The Contribution of International Law to Development", Chinese Journal of International Law 14, 1–13.

Klabbers, Jan (2009). *An Introduction to International Institutional Law*. 2nd edition. Cambridge University Press.

Kwakwa, Edward (1987). "Emerging International Development Law and Traditional International Law – Congruence or Cleavage?", Georgia Journal of International and Comparative Law 17, 431–455.

Mahiou, Ahmed (2015). *International Law of Development*. Oxford Public International Law. Oxford University Press.

Shaw, Malcolm (2008). *International Law*. 6th edition. Cambridge University Press.

Sinclair, Guy Fiti (2020). "Forging Modern States with Imperfect Tools: United Nations Technical Assistance for Public Administration in Decolonized States", Humanity Journal (forthcoming).

Tamanaha, Brian Z. (1995). "The Lessons of Law-and-Development Studies", American Journal of International Law 89, 470–486.

41. International Solidarity

Introduction

The topic on which I focus in this brief Encyclopaedia entry, "International Solidarity", calls upon all of us to grapple systematically, if briefly, with the meaning and valency of this principle that grounds various international measures and initiatives, including the Sustainable Development Goals or SDGs. The chapter is thus organized into five sections, this introduction included. In the first section, I discuss the question of the definition of international solidarity. The second section is devoted to a consideration of the normative status of the principle of international solidarity. In the third section, a case is briefly made for moving beyond State-centrism in the conception and understanding of international solidarity. The fourth section briefly considers international solidarity as a Janus-faced concept. The fifth concludes the chapter with some brief remarks.

Defining "international solidarity"

According to Danio Campanelli's compelling work on this topic, ideas about the "pivotal importance of mutual help among individuals as well as among States" have been with us for a very long time, including in African, Buddhist, European and Islamic thought (Campanelli, 2011, p. 2; Khomba, 2011, p. 128). The Western political notion of solidarity was firmed up in modern times in the 1790 French Revolution's concept of fraternité, which elevated solidarity to the level of a fundamental (political) right in that country (Carozza and Crema, 2014, p. 3). In 1793, the French National Assembly passed legislation compelling solidarity from the State to every citizen in need of help, firming up its politico-legal quality in the domestic order of that country. It was, however, Immanuel Kant's work that solidified the presence of the idea of international solidarity as a moral obligation in Western political thought, with his argument that as the human community shares the surface of the same Earth, all individuals must support each other. It bears emphasis here that in Kant's conception, international

solidarity was not an act of charity but one of obligation (Campanelli, 2011, p. 2).

Yet, while the principle of solidarity has been referred to (either explicitly or implicitly) in an increasing number of UN Resolutions and even in some treaties (e.g., the Convention to Combat Desertification, 1994, 1954 UNTS 3, Article 3), until the relatively recent work of the mandate of the UN Independent Expert on Human Rights and International Solidarity, international relations and law and the corresponding academic literature, had – with a few exceptions – been slow to offer a tight and authoritative definition of international solidarity (Campanelli, 2011, p. 2; MacDonald, 1996, p. 259; Wolfrum, 2009, p. 8).

Writing for the then UN Sub-Commission on Human Rights, Rui Baltazar Dos Santos Alves had defined international solidarity in 2004 as implying "a communion of responsibilities and interest between individuals, groups, nations and States" (Rui Baltazar Dos Santos Alves (2004). Human Rights and International Solidarity. Working Paper, UN Doc. E/CN.4/Sub.2/2004/43, para. 22). Dos Santos Alves' definition basically aligns with the trend that is discernible in the definitional discourses and the praxis of the three persons who have so far held the post of the UN Independent Expert on Human Rights and International Solidarity since that mandate was established in 2005 (all of whom have applied that principle to various issues and themes, including the Sustainable Development Goals (SDGs), climate change, and migration). The first Independent Expert, Rudi Mohammed Rizki, defined international solidarity as:

> the union of interests, purpose and actions among States and social cohesion between them, based on the interdependence of States and other actors to preserve the order and very survival of international society, and to achieve common goals that require international cooperation and collective action (A/HRC/15/32, 2010, para. 57)

Rizki's immediate successor, Virginia Dandan, produced a Draft UN Declaration of Human Rights and International Solidarity that stated that international solidarity is the expression of a spirit of unity among individuals, peoples, States and international organizations, encompassing the union of interests, purposes and actions and the recognition of different needs and rights to achieve common goals (Draft UN Declaration on the Right to International Solidarity, Annex to UN Doc A/HRC/35/35, 2017). That draft instrument also identified the components of international solidarity as preventive solidarity (through which stakeholders act to proactively address shared challenges), reactive solidarity (collective action to respond to situations of crisis, and international cooperation. The current Independent Expert has adopted the very similar and excellent definitions that were offered by his predecessors-in-office.

On the normative status of the principle of international solidarity

There is now fairly widespread explicit and implicit agreement that, at the very least, there is now a moral obligation on definable actors in our world to act in solidarity toward each other (Boisson de Chazournes, 2010, pp. 94–95; Puvmanasinghe, 2013, p. 186). The still controversial question is whether the international solidarity obligation is of a legal character.

In the context of general international law, Carozza and Crema were not that far off the mark when they declared – paraphrasing Dos Santos Alves – that "the place of solidarity in international law remains uncertain" (2014, p. 7). Yet, even they themselves recognize that many of the key scholars who have reflected on the issue, as well as the independent experts charged by the UN to study and report to that global body on the topic, have concluded that at the very least, solidarity is a principle of international law. Carozza and Crema also suggest, correctly in my view, that State practice supports this position (2014, pp. 14–15). Even while arguing that "it would be hardly sustainable that solidarity is today a fully acknowledged legal principle governing international law", Campanelli still more or less agrees, noting the "influence exercised by solidarity in various domains of international law, with different degrees of intensity". He goes even further to offer a concrete example of the explicit manifestation in hard international law of the international solidarity obligation (Convention to Combat Desertification, 1994, 1954 UNTS 3, Article 3) (Campanelli, 2011, pp. 3, 5). Puvamanasinghe argues convincingly, in my view, that (at least in the human rights sphere) one of the three aspects of the international solidarity obligation that are identified in the Draft UN Declaration of Human

Rights and International Solidarity – the international cooperation obligation – is of constitutional (and therefore legal) status; having been enshrined in Articles 55 and 56 of the UN Charter (2013, p. 182).

The official position of the UN Independent Expert on Human Rights and International Solidarity on this question was restated in his October 2018 Report to the UN General Assembly (UN Doc. A/73/45710, 2018, para. 7). It is that "international solidarity is a foundational principle underpinning contemporary international law and is based on respect for and protection and fulfilment of human rights and fundamental freedoms for all individuals, without distinction or discrimination". This position echoes the conclusion reached by his immediate predecessor, Virginia Dandan, discussed in her July 2017 Report to the UN General Assembly (A/72/171, 2017).

The Draft UN Declaration of Human Rights and International Solidarity frames international solidarity as a "right of peoples and individuals" (Article 4, para. 1). While this instrument has not yet been adopted, it represents the official position of the relevant mandate holders and is thus of persuasive authority. However, some scholarly and diplomatic opposition to the notion of a right to international solidarity continues to exist (Carozza and Crema, 2014, pp. 14–15, 19).

In the specific global refuge protection context, there is no doubt that the solidarity principle imposes – at the very least – a soft international legal obligation on UN Member States. Thus, Türk and Garlick (2016) stand on firm ground when they point to 1970 UN Declaration of Friendly Relations as an important interpretive tool in international law that allows us to read several treaties as containing an international obligation to cooperate in the social, political and economic spheres (A/RES/25/2625, 1970). And if international cooperation is one aspect of international solidarity (especially under the Draft Declaration), then this logic is applicable to at least one dimension of the latter. As Türk and Garlick correctly observe, the formally non-binding "Preamble" of the 1951 UN Convention on the Status of Refugees implies a duty among States to cooperate (Türk and Garlick, 2016, p. 659). What is more, the Executive Committee of the UN High Commissioner's Program (EXCOM) has repeatedly referred to the role of international cooperation, as an essential principle that States should adhere to. Its "Conclusions" can be properly characterized as soft international law. Several (formally non-binding) UN General Assembly Resolutions also reinforce this conclusion (Türk and Garlick, 2016, p. 660). Perhaps even more importantly, Türk and Garlick are also correct to argue that the pledge by all UN Member States in Articles 55 and 56 of the UN Charter to "take joint and separate action in cooperation", in order to achieve such human rights goals as global refugee protection, imposes a hard "legal obligation for States to cooperate with each other . . ." (2016, p. 660). Regional hard law international solidarity obligations also exist in relation to each of Africa, and the European Union (OAU Convention Governing the Specific Aspects of Refugee Problems in Africa, 1969, 1001 UNTS 45, Article 2; Treaty on the Functioning of the European Union, Article 80). In addition, several soft international law instruments explicitly provide for similar obligations, including the 1967 UN Declaration on Territorial Asylum and a number of EXCOM Conclusions (2545 UNTS 189, Article 2(2)). A similar regional soft international law obligation exists in relation to the Americas (Cartegena Declaration on Refugees of 1984; follow-up Declarations and Plans of Action, AS/Ser.L/V/II.6, doc 10, re 1, 190–193).

Somewhat similar arguments can also be made regarding the ways in which the SDGs, non-binding as they are, still impose soft international law obligations that are deeply grounded in the solidarity principle.

Beyond State-centrism

Whatever the normative status of the principle and/or right to international solidarity, its orientation and valence are better understood in a non-State-centric way. Puvamanasinghe has correctly observed that international solidarity "manifests itself through the daily actions of a range of stakeholders, including States, civil society, global social movements, corporate social initiatives and people of goodwill" (2013, p. 188). The concept and praxis of international solidarity is, therefore, not simply a State-to-State affair, but can and does in fact encompass other forms of solidarity across international borders.

International solidarity as a Janus-faced concept

As much as the expression of international solidarity is capable of being directed at the achievement of the "good", it is just as susceptible to being deployed toward the advancement of the "bad". There is obviously a world of difference between the kind of international solidarity expressed by the NGOs who rescue drowning asylum-seekers in the Mediterranean Sea, and that shown by the European Union (EU) toward the Libyan Coast Guard toward the facilitation of their efforts to intercept and return asylum-seekers to Libya, a place where these asylum-seekers are without doubt routinely killed, tortured and even enslaved (Eugenio Cusumano and James Pattison (2018). "The Non-Governmental Provision of Search and Rescue in the Mediterranean and the Abdication of State Responsibility", Cambridge Review of International Affairs 31, 53–75). Thus, as Melber has correctly observed in the broader migration context, all too often enthusiasm for the expression of international solidarity:

> leaves unanswered [questions about] who practices solidarity with whom and for which purpose . . . We therefore should be careful when somewhat naïvely assuming that solidarity by definition means something "good". (Melber, 2016, p. 1)

Thus, the key question that must always be asked is international solidarity for what ends and for whose benefit? It is for these reasons that the Independent Expert on Human Rights and International Solidarity has more recently begun to use the more politically aware and less naïve expression "human rights-based international solidarity", instead of the bare concept of "international solidarity" (A/HRC/38/40, 2018, para. 5).

Conclusion

For the international solidarity principle to serve humanity better, nothing more than the augmentation of the solidarity of the (re)imagination is required. First, we need to do more than we have already done to continually re-imagine the world as the world, and not merely as Europe (Ibrahim Awad and Usha Natarajan (Summer 2018). "Migration Myths and the

Global South", Cairo Review of Global Affairs, 3). And given Deborah Cowen's reminder to us that infrastructure (in our case the infrastructure of international solidarity) can "both connect and contain", we also need to re-imagine international solidarity itself and how to harness the progressive side of its duality while containing its negative possibilities (Deborah Cowen (25 January 2017). "Infrastructures of Empire and Resistance". Available at http://www.versobooks.com/blogs/3067-infrastructures-of-empire-and-resistance, accessed 7 September 2020, p. 5).

OBIORA CHINEDU OKAFOR

References

Boisson de Chazournes, Laurence (2010). "Responsibility to Protect: Reflecting Solidarity" in Rüdiger Wolfrum et al. (ed.), *Solidarity: A Structural Principle of International Law*. Springer.

Campanelli, Danio (2011). "Principle of Solidarity", *Max Planck Encyclopaedia of Public International Law*. Oxford University Press.

Carozza, Paolo G. and Luigi Crema (2014). *On Solidarity in International Law*. Caritas in Veritate Foundation.

French Constitutional Court, M. Cédric H. et autre (délit d'aide à l'entrée, à la circulation ou au séjour irréguliers d'un étranger), 2018-717/718 QPC, 6 July 2018. Available at: https://www.conseil-constitutionnel.fr/decision/2018/2018717_718QPC.htm accessed 10 September 2020.

Khomba, James K. (2011). "The African Ubuntu Philosophy" in James K. Khomba, *Redesigning the Balanced Scorecard Model: An African Perspective.* University of Pretoria.

MacDonald, Ronald St. J (1996). "Solidarity in the Practice and Discourse of Public International Law", Pace International Law Review 8, 259–302.

Melber, Henning (2016). "International Solidarity as an Emerging Norm in the United Nations". Available at: http://www.hammarskjoldinquiry.info/pdf/ham_105_Melber_speech_Berlin_010916.pdf.

Puvimanasinghe, Shyami (2013). *"International Solidarity in an Interdependent World". Realizing the Right to Development.* United Nations.

Türk, Volker and Madeline Garlick (2016). "From Burdens and Responsibilities to Opportunities: The Comprehensive Refugee Response Framework and a Global Compact on Refugees", International Journal of Refugee Law 28, 656–678.

Wolfrum, Rüdiger (2009). "Solidarity among States: An Emerging Structural Principle of International Law", Indian Journal of International Law 49, 8–20.

42. International Trade Law

Introduction

In contrast with other fields of international law, international trade law seems to be comparatively resistant to theoretical abstractions, methodological disagreements and historical controversies. Its close links with economics and political science have shaped the dominant understandings of the role of law and lawyers in global governance of international trade. In general terms, international trade law has habitually been defined in two different ways. There is a more general meaning that derives from the abstract notion of international economic law. Specifically, international trade law is conceived as a subject or branch of international economic law that establishes rules and institutions for governing international trade. This broad concept has been rarely employed in the field. Instead, the conventional understanding identifies international trade law essentially with the law of the World Trade Organization (WTO).

The consensus around the narrow definition of international trade law led lawyers to embrace a relatively stable framework of economic, political and development ideas and practices underlying WTO law. Consequently, the field has devoted itself continuously to increase its technical specialization and normative formalization around the areas covered under the WTO agreements, particularly trade in goods and services, intellectual property rights and investments and trade regionalism. This apparent consensus hides, nonetheless, disagreements, which often come up to the surface throughout debates about how international trade law is (or ought to be) made, interpreted and applied. Putting it differently, the unspoken argumentative frames that structure the understanding of the nature and purpose of international trade law tend not to be openly discussed but serve as a way to solve concrete problems. Since they are found (implicitly or explicitly) entangled in law-making and interpretation, it is possible to organize intellectually their analyses around the domains of institutions and jurisprudence. This articulation is merely heuristic, since each domain shapes and, at the same time, is shaped by the other.

Jurisprudential debates about international trade law

Two jurisprudential views have shaped the ways in which international trade law has been thought and practised since the Second World War. The instrumentalist view has dominated the field since the 1980s, while the formalist view has continuously gained influence as the technocratization and legalization of WTO law has progressed.

WTO law as instrument of international trade

This view conceives of international trade law as an instrument of international trade. Its main preoccupation rests on questions about WTO law as a reflection of the world trading system. This line of thinking has produced two compelling ways of approaching WTO law.

An 'external' perspective portrays international trade law as the expression of economic relations. For instance, some have conceived WTO law as the institutionalization of either the value of interdependence embedded in the constitutional economic order, or the harmonious policies shared by the international society, or the needs and effects of economic and social forces. By contrast, an 'internal' perspective tends to portray international trade law as an element of diplomatic and expert processes of decision-making. For example, some have understood WTO law as authoritative processes of aggregating preferences of politically relevant (state or non-state) actors. Consequently, this instrumentalist view often relies on economics and political science to identify and analyse the exogenous social and economic forces that are understood to determine the form and substance of WTO law.

The instrumentalist view suffers from some limitations. In its attempt to avoid moral or formal abstraction, it seeks to align international trade law with social facts. The external perspective seeks to evidence the concreteness of WTO law by showing its function in a globally interdependent economy, whereas the internal perspective aims to demonstrate that the WTO law's empirical force rests on material power. Both perspectives tend to take the existing distribution of economic and political power for granted. The consequence is to reduce the normative force of international trade law to its utility to those in a position of institutional power. The more critical one becomes of the world trading system, the less useful the instrumentalist approach will seem to be for those whose values, policies, preferences or effects it initially committed to advance. Thus, WTO law may lose its normative and binding character and becomes a mere sociological description or a policy instrument in the service of powerful actors.

WTO law as norms of international trade

The formalist view conceives international trade law as norms with binding force. WTO law is understood as a 'normative order' that not only responds to the interests and preferences of member states but also imposes a code of conduct upon them. In other words, the world trading system is assessed from the standpoint of the normativity of WTO law. This line of thinking has also produced two persuasive ways of approaching WTO law.

An 'external' perspective conceptualizes international trade law as a body of special norms empowered by some superior notion of legitimacy and substantive justice to command states' behaviour. For instance, some have described WTO law as grounded in an 'international economic constitution' or, perhaps, in a given set of values and needs of a hypothesized world trading system. Conversely, an 'internal' perspective conceives international trade law as a set of special norms ultimately created by state consent. For instance, WTO law is understood pursuant to its legal sources. Some mainly focus on the texts of the WTO agreements, while others also include the (disputed) list of subsidiary sources that follows from the combined interpretation of Articles 3.2 and 7 of the Dispute Settlement Understanding.

The formalist view also suffers from blind spots and inconsistencies. The central problem lies in its tendency to overemphasize the formal authority of international trade law while neglecting the economic and political aspects of the world trading system. The external perspective – that seeks to demonstrate the binding force of WTO law from 'beyond' sovereignty – is subject to controversies, since it is often unable to explain the legitimacy or correctness of the chosen outside criteria (e.g. whose justice, whose policy, or whose values and needs?). The internal perspective – that aims to evidence binding force on sovereignty – tends to blur the distinction between sources of power and authority: if a state could always withdraw from whatever it had consented to, WTO law would not be really binding.

These shortcomings have been expressed in ongoing controversies over the legal sources of WTO law. The emergence of new trade regimes (e.g. regional trade agreements and dispute settlement mechanisms) and novel forms of law (e.g. soft law, transnational law) created by state and non-state actors, international organizations, and transnational networks, gave rise to debates about normative hierarchy. Specifically, the preoccupation with the relationship of WTO law to other areas of international law (e.g. environmental, labour, and human rights) and international economic law (e.g. domestic and regional trade, development) illustrates the destabilizing effects of normative fragmentation.

Thus, to avoid becoming an instrument of economic power, this view seeks to defend the normativity of WTO law without referring to the facts of the world trading system. However, neither the external nor the internal perspective seems to offer a compelling justification for why WTO law would be binding. The consequence is to make the formalist view vulnerable to the critique of subjecting international trade law to normative indeterminacy, abstract considerations, or unrealistic conclusions.

Institutional debates about international trade law

Institutional debates have produced different ways of understanding the role of international legal institutions in the world trading system. They tend to focus particularly on the nature and function of the WTO in global trade governance. The field has been overwhelmingly dominated by the free market view since the 1980s, whereas alternative views are varied but much less influential.

WTO as free market

This view conceives the WTO as 'the' international legal institution for governing the world trading system. It draws inspiration primarily from neoclassical economics, which nurtures a strong normative preference for 'free' and 'fair' markets as the ultimate form of wealth creation. Markets, not politics or governments, are regarded as the decisive model of economic governance by which everyone can achieve harmonious prosperity and freedom.

RAFAEL LIMA SAKR

Particularly, the economic growth of developing countries can be attained by accessing capital and technological resources via global private markets.

At the most fundamental level, the world trading system is understood (at least aspirationally) as a single global free and fair market, whose efficiency and fairness must be continuously promoted by an international guardian – the WTO – and protected from state intervention. At the institutional level, the WTO is itself reconceived as a marketplace, where member states bargain for commitments to reduce trade-distorting barriers. For instance, it can help WTO members to negotiate trade policies for economic and social prosperity while agreeing on efficient solutions to the global challenges specified in the United Nations' 2030 Agenda for Sustainable Development. At the legal level, the WTO serves as the guarantor of trade law and commitments against the state arbitrariness. For example, WTO law can contribute to making the world economy more sustainable and resilient by ensuring that WTO members' trade measures operate to reduce market and government failures that may lead to environmental and social degradation and poverty rather than to promote unfair competition.

The ultimate purposes of the WTO are, therefore, to serve as a venue for exchanging mutually beneficial concessions, and also to promote welfare-enhancing economic growth and sustainable development through the realization of a single global market.

WTO as trade order

There is a wide range of critiques and alternatives to the free market view of the WTO drawing from economics itself and other disciplines. Their degree of criticism and influence vary considerably depending on the context. At present, an attempt to recover and renovate the view of the WTO as a liberal-welfarist trade order seems to have gained traction in the field. This understanding conceptualizes the WTO as 'one' of the international law institutions mandated to govern the world trading system. Its core ideas rest on liberal-free trade and welfarist-interventionist theories that embrace a normative preference for a publicly governed open economy as the primary model for sustainable development and prosperity. Governments and markets are regarded as

co-responsible for managing the economy and providing social protection.

At the core, the world trading system is understood (at least aspirationally) as part of the wider global economic and social system, which is constituted and managed by a constellation of transnational norms and institutions (e.g. the United Nations specialized agencies, such as the United Nations Conference for Trade and Development, the World Intellectual Property Organization, and the United Nations Environment Program) with the goal of promoting full employment, prosperity for all, sustainable development and environmental protection.

Institutionally, the post-war understanding of the General Agreement on Tariffs and Trade (GATT) as a venue for pursuing a collective project of international economic order is revived. The GATT was not created as, and the WTO should not be conceived as, a marketplace. Rather, the WTO is (or should return to be) a public interest regime for promoting fair and sustainable international trade by governing the interface among different economies. It operates accordingly as a forum for WTO members to coordinate their trade-related policies. It may also assist them in achieving their Sustainable Development Goals. From a legal viewpoint, the WTO should function as a legal order under which individual and collective policies are implemented and assessed. For instance, WTO law ensures policy space for members to adopt measures concerning environmental protection and social-economic inequality that may also restrict trade, to the extent that these measures are in compliance with WTO rules.

Therefore, the WTO's aims are to serve as a space where States can (jointly or individually) discover and adopt (liberal or welfare) policies and measures on trade and trade-related affairs that allow the realization of sustainable development while managing their potential negative impacts on other economies.

International trade law today: alliances, clashes and assaults

International trade law is a field of expert knowledge and practice. It is about making competent use of legal expertise to persuade target audiences such as politicians and diplomats, officials and courts, lawyers and experts about the correctness (i.e. legality, lawfulness, legitimacy, fairness, efficiency, etc.) of a particular view of the law and governance of international trade. Putting it differently, what is accepted as a definition of international trade law has more to do with what counts as a persuasive argument in a given context rather than the transcendental validity of any particular attempt at description.

Two features are central to the persuasiveness of a definition. First, it must be acknowledgeable as a valid and legitimate 'legal' explanation, and not, for instance, as a convincing 'philosophical', 'sociological' or 'economic' explanation. Yet, it is a process of consensus-building within the field that determines the intra-disciplinary correctness of a legal definition at any given time and place. Second, the persuasiveness of a legal definition depends primarily on two factors: its own recognition as intellectually sound and practically relevant in the wider domain of global trade governance; and the specific influence of the legal field, and to some extent international law itself, over a particular venue of trade decision-making.

Since the Second World War, many schools of thought and forms of thinking have sought to define international trade law. Much of the debate has been about its nature and function. The dominant position in jurisprudential discussions has swung between formalism and instrumentalism. From the post-war until the early 1980s, formalist conceptions of international trade law prevailed in most academic settings worldwide, while instrumentalist definitions were favoured in the GATT context. From the 1980s onwards, instrumentalism has been predominant in academic communities, while both views seem to have been influential in and over WTO governance. By contrast, the institutional debates have experienced a clearer transition from an understanding of the GATT/WTO as collective trade order to the GATT/WTO as marketplace for trade preference. The latter prevailed in the post-war period, while the former has been widely dominant since the 1980s.

Those jurisprudential and institutional views have clashed, juxtaposed or combined, producing periods of consensus and dissensus: from formalist definitions of the 1950s–1970s conceiving international trade law as a liberal-welfarist trade order undergirded by international norms and organizations; to instrumentalist definitions of the 1970s–1990s as a free trade regime centred on the GATT/WTO; to eclectic definitions

of the 1990s–2010s as a global free market governed by the WTO. It is clear that those understandings have not remained static nor have the debates been at the forefront of the profession either. They have been continuously (re-) articulated in the background in reaction to new challenges. Lawyers have constantly reworked the notion of international trade law as a strategy to ensure its relevance as a legitimate and valid mode of trade governance. The ability to offer novel or renewed solutions to problems by redefining itself – and, in turn, its normative and disciplinary boundaries – has become a central feature of the field.

At present, the most influential definitions of international trade law are centred on WTO law, whose jurisprudential justifications draw eclectically from instrumentalism and formalism. Such variations rely on the disciplinary outcome of political and intellectual compromises. WTO law is 'international trade law' not only because of its legal body of rules and institutions regulating individual or collective behaviour of States but also because it aspires to be the legal expression of what constitutes the world trading system.

However, assaults on this disciplinary common sense have gradually grown since the wake of the 2008 global financial crisis, having been intensified with the populist backlash against globalization, elites and experts. These attempts to destabilize the consensus on free trade have allowed alternative views – such as the liberal-welfarist understanding of the WTO as part of a wider trade order – to (re-)emerge. The success of this or other contenders in gaining traction inside or outside the field is yet highly uncertain.

RAFAEL LIMA SAKR

References

Bethlehem, Daniel et al. (eds) (2009). *The Oxford Handbook of International Trade Law*. Oxford University Press.

Fabri, Hélène Ruiz (2012). 'Chapter 16 – Regulating Trade, Investment and Money' in James Crawford and Martti Koskenniemi (eds), *The Cambridge Companion to International Law*. Cambridge University Press.

Hoekman, Bernard and Michael Kostecki (2013). *The Political Economy of the World Trading System*. Oxford University Press.

Jackson, John H. (1997). *The World Trading System: Law and Policy of International Economic Relations*. MIT Press.

Lang, Andrew (2011). *World Trade Law after Neoliberalism: Reimagining the Global Economic Order*. Oxford University Press.

Orford, Anne (2016). 'Theorizing Free Trade' in Anne Orford, Florian Hoffman, and Martin Clark (eds), *The Oxford Handbook of the Theory of International Law*. Oxford University Press.

Pauwelyn, Joost, Andrew T. Guzman, and Jennifer A. Hillman (2016). *International Trade Law*. Wolters Kluwer.

Rodrik, Dani (2018). *Straight Talk on Trade: Ideas for a Sane World Economy*. Princeton University Press.

Trebilcock, Michael J., Robert Howse, and Antonia Eliason (2012). *The Regulation of International Trade*. Routledge.

WTO and UNDP (2019). *Making Globalization More Inclusive: Lessons from Experience With Adjustment Policies*. Available at https://www.wto.org/english/res_e/booksp_e/makingglobalinc_e.pdf.

43. Investor

The term 'investor' can be defined by taking stock from international investment protection agreements and from the corresponding investment arbitration case law. Notwithstanding some broad and sometimes tautological definitions found in some treaties, some specific criteria are generally used to identify an investor, thereby making the latter more comprehensible and operational. As such, the investor, which can indeed be a natural or a legal person, must have the nationality of one of the signatory States parties to the investment agreement, and its economic activity must be imperatively defined as an investment. These are the two main criteria used to define an investor. Its corporate social behavior can also act as an alternative parameter.

The investor must be a national of one of the State parties to an international investment agreement

Firstly, the investor must be a national of one of the State parties to an investment agreement. The criteria to define the investor's nationality vary from agreement to agreement. Traditionally in public international law, private companies' nationality is determined as per their State of incorporation while the nationality of natural persons is determined by the criterion of effectiveness, that is, the State with which they have the most intrinsic social links. Of course, at a national level, all States are sovereign to fix their rules of nationality. In international investment law, the rule of incorporation is still considered by many investment agreements. Other criteria are, however, also applied: these are the company's seat and the company's control. Some agreements qualify more rigorously the incorporation criterion by imposing substantial economic activities in the State of incorporation; others highlight that the investor's effective business administration must be located in the State of incorporation. In such cases, the investment agreements do not apply to the so-called shell companies, which are a means to avoid *treaty shopping*. In this vein, some investment agreements contain a denial of benefits clause which specifies that the treaty does not apply to investors, absent a substantial activity in the State of incorporation. It is also possible to legally provide for a mixed criteria method to define an investor's nationality. This is, for instance, the case of the bilateral investment protection treaty between Ethiopia and Sweden: the treaty uses simultaneously the criteria of incorporation, of seat and of control. This is in line with the practice of international investment law. Indeed, if a company's center of control is located in a State which is not the one of incorporation, the company can be still considered as a national of the State of control. Undeniably, this has important consequences, namely in the arbitration procedure: in international investment law, a company cannot sue its home State before an international arbitral tribunal; the arbitral procedure always opposes a State to an investor from another State. However, if this same company is controlled by the shareholders of a third State, it can – by the mechanism of the control criterion – be considered as an investor of that State. This is, for instance, provided for by Article 25(2) of the Washington Convention which instituted the International Centre for the Settlement of Investment Disputes (ICSID). Foreign control, which is examined by the arbitral tribunal on a case-by-case basis, can thus be a factor to determine an investor's nationality in specific cases. A company cannot, however, transfer its control to foreigners or to a foreign entity after the advent of a dispute with the host State. In such a case, this practice would be potentially tantamount to a nationality manipulation in bad faith. It must also be recalled that a company can have a double nationality without this being a legal impediment to its qualification as an investor and to its legal protection by an investment treaty unless provided for otherwise by the latter.

Having fulfilled the above criteria, the investor is also expected to make an investment.

The investor must make an investment in its host State

Given that the investor must be a source of 'investments', the latter must correspondingly be defined. Investment is sometimes defined following a double test approach, especially in ICSID arbitration cases. Firstly, the definition must be looked for in the applicable investment agreement. At this point, the elements to identify an investment can be laconic and/or tautological in the sense that the agreement might simply mention that an investment is any investment done on the territory of the other party. While some agreements broadly State that an investment can be any asset or any property, others are more specific in their description. This is, for example, the case of two bilateral investment protection agreements signed by Morocco, namely with The Democratic Republic of Congo, on one hand, and with Nigeria, on the other, both of which state that the investment must be an enterprise established and operated in good faith by the investor together with a contribution in capital, a certain duration, the existence of a risk, an expectation of profits and interestingly, a contribution to the sustainable development of the host State.

These indicators, which tentatively enable better understanding of what an investment is for these signatory States, are in part derived from the arbitral case law – specifically from one landmark Salini v. Morocco case – according to which an activity must have a contribution, a duration, a certain level of risk and must contribute to the host State's development to qualify as an investment. The last criterion has been the object of much debate between arbitral tribunals and within the legal doctrine. It has been duly considered by some arbitral tribunals and systematically rejected by others. Both these categories of tribunals, however, have a non-technical understanding of development, let alone a designed methodology to calculate how a given activity contributes to a State's development. The concept of development is as such never defined but yet used to identify an investment. The Moroccan agreements take one further step by stating that an investment must contribute to sustainable development without, however, providing clear guidelines or criteria. In practice, perusing the latter will be incumbent upon the arbitrators who are not necessarily (sustainable) development experts. Alternatively, it would be recommended that the domestic investment law of the host State makes provision for the parameters of (local) sustainable development, following a bottom-up approach. This would provide clearer information to potential investors while reducing the margin of appreciation of future arbitral tribunals. Providing for sustainable development as a criterion of investment means that the legal protection of the foreign investor by the investment agreement will potentially depend on available evidence of its contribution to the host States' sustainable development. The criteria chosen to define the latter might accordingly force some investors out of the investment agreements' protective umbrella.

This background of sustainable development also lurks behind the landscape of the investor's protection under the aspect of its diligence in terms of corporate social responsibility.

Alternatively, the investor must show corporate social responsibility diligence

The United Nations 2030 Agenda for Sustainable Development (United Nations General Assembly (2015), A/RES/70/1), with its Sustainable Development Goals (SDGs), state that the protection of the environment (for instance, SDGs 13, 14 and 15), of human rights (for instance paras 7, 8, 10, 20, 29, 35 and SDG 4), the fight against corruption (SDG 16) or decent working conditions (SDG 8) are components of sustainable development. These components also constitute the core of corporate social responsibility. Therefore, an investor showing corporate social responsibility diligence would, in a way, set its activities on the tracks of sustainable development. Some recent investment agreements have established such corporate social responsibility duties for investors. The Brazilian investment treaty model is but an example. If these duties are not always binding, they at least set a code of behavior expected from international investors. It is worth recalling that investors' claims have already been declared inadmissible because of practices of corruption even absent a codified international obligation in this sense (World Duty Free v. Kenya) or that, more recently, an investor has been condemned by an international arbitral tribunal in a counterclaim procedure for the violation of its host State's environmental laws (Burlington v. Ecuador). It is commonly admitted that investors do not have an automatic and a systematic right to protection by applicable investment agreements. Their corporate social responsibility diligence acts as one of the yardsticks of their legal protection and even though not, as such, an element of the definition of 'investor', it does establish a minimum standard of expected corporate social behavior.

NITISH MONEBHURRUN

References

De Nanteuil, Arnaud (2017). *Droit international de l'investissement*. Pedone.

Dubin, Laurence, Pierre Bodeau-Livinec, Jean-Louis Iten, and Vincent Tomkiewicz (2017). *L'entreprise multinationale et le droit international*. Pedone.

Lim, Chin Leng, Jean Ho, and Martin Paparinskis (2018). *International Investment Law and Arbitration. Commentary, Awards and other Materials*. Cambridge University Press.

Miles, Kate (2013). *The Origins of International Investment Law. Empire, Environment and the Safeguarding of Capital*. Cambridge University Press.

Monebhurrun, Nitish (2012). 'The Political Use of the Economic Development Criterion in Defining Investments in International Investment Arbitration', Journal of International Arbitration 29(5), 567–580.

Monebhurrun, Nitish (2016). *La fonction du développement dans le droit international des investissements*. L'Harmattan.

Monebhurrun, Nitish (2017). 'The (mis)use of Development in International Investment Law: Understanding the Jurist's limits to Work with Development Issues', Law and Development Review 10(2), 451–476.

Monebhurrun, Nitish (2017). 'Mapping the Duties of Private Companies in International Investment Law', Brazilian Journal of International Law 14(2), 50–72.

44. Law and Development Experts

Today, law is increasingly seen as central to development. Although there are about as many histories of law and development as there are laws and developments, let me situate the genesis of this recent trend in the rise of a particular way of understanding markets and economic exchange. In the 1980s and 1990s, and influenced by the emergence of New Institutional Economics in the academy of the North Atlantic, development economists came to appreciate (again) how the global economy was embedded in and enabled by institutional arrangements – or "governance". This shift eroded the disciplinary hegemony of economics in development (at least a little bit), and the silos between economic, political, social and legal development thought. At a practical level, legal reform returned to fashion, as States in the Global South had to pay attention to the legal fads and ideas of development policy-makers when shaping their own legal systems.

So, now that "institutions rule", does this mean that lawyers are taking up their rightful place at the heart of development policy, jostling alongside economists for power? The answer, it appears, is: "it's hard to say, but probably not".

First, "it's hard to say". The above question is not just empirically difficult to answer – it is also obscured for structural reasons. Irrespective of the number of lawyers working in development, it is unclear whether they are doing "law and development" (whatever that is), who else might be doing it, and where those other people might be. In one of the few extant studies of law and development experts, Simion and Taylor (Kristina Simion and Veronica Taylor (2015). 'Professionalizing Rule of Law: Issues and Directions', Folke Bernadotte Academy, p. 12) remark that

> today's [law and development] agenda appears all-inclusive[,] to include topics as diverse as customary or non-State justice, gender equality, economic development, antiterrorism measures, anti-corruption strategies, alternative dispute resolution, access to justice, conflict prevention and human rights monitoring.

As a result of the hard-to-define boundaries of law and development, its

> practitioners are as diverse. Many are practising lawyers, court personnel or are legally educated; some are military personnel; others are non-lawyers with particular technical skills or development experience. The work often requires teams of professionals such as sociologists, political scientists, anthropologists and country specialists. (pp. 12–13)

Note that Simion and Taylor not only remark on the diversity of topics and people. They also show how the professional *status* of law and development people is unclear, moving between "practitioners", "professionals", and experts with "technical" skills and knowledge. Similarly, and as I have argued elsewhere, the distinction between law and development "experts" and "practitioners" – thinkers and doers – is hard to sustain in light of the diversity and fragmentation of the field. Indeed, training programs and hiring practices now routinely disavow core technical content, instead emphasizing disciplinary and topical eclecticism, along with contextual and interpersonal competencies (Deval Desai (2014). "In Search of 'Hire' Knowledge: Donor Hiring Practices and the Organization of the Rule of Law Field" in David Marshall (ed.), *The International Rule of Law Movement: A Crisis of Legitimacy and the Way Forward.* Harvard University Press; Deval Desai (2018). "Ignorance/Power: Rule of Law Reform and the Administrative Law of Global Governance" in Moshe Hirsch and Andres Lang (eds), *Research Handbook on the Sociology of International Law.* Edward Elgar).

So, what can we say about law and development experts as a category? Many studies approach this puzzle by narrowing the field of enquiry, focusing on specific geographic regions, international institutions, normative or ideological commitments, epistemic or disciplinary communities, or types of law and development intervention (see Dezalay and Garth, 2002; Santos, 2006; Humphreys, 2010). Others (e.g. Grasten, 2016) work through particular case studies, in particular to draw out *how* law and development expertise works, while bracketing the extent or scope of those claims. But on the whole, we only have – and can only have – a patchwork sense of the nature and scope of law and development experts.

Turning to "probably not". Whoever and wherever law and development experts are, it appears that they are not hegemonic actors in the operations of development. Even as they ever more boldly proclaim law's importance to the development enterprise, law and development experts shy away from their own expertise. They are beset by self-doubt, so much so that, following Carothers, they ask whether they are even part of a coherent "field[,] if one considers a requirement for such a designation to include a well-grounded rationale, a clear understanding of the essential problem, a proven analytic method, and an understanding of results achieved" (Carothers, 2006, p. 28).

Now, this sort of self-doubt could in fact be an alternative route to hegemony. Self-doubt could be no more than a series of one-off or bad-faith proclamations by people who secretly believe that they know what they are doing. Or it could be a strategic effort by experts to inject just enough ambiguity into the meaning of "law and development" to maintain wriggle room to pursue their own interests or needs in the future. Or it might even be productive of an expert affect that is disenchanted and cynical, and all the more casuistically effective for it. Common to these explanations is the assumption that law and development experts will assert their authority at some future moment of policy-making or implementation, and that self-doubt is a ploy in the furtherance of that eventual assertion. In these explanations, law and development experts are powerful (whether or not they are hegemonic). They continue to give shape to development's technical, modernizing and/or imperial claims.

In recent years, however, other scholars, myself included (Desai and Woolcock, 2015), have argued that this self-doubt is increasingly baked into the very structure and implementation of law and development projects and programs – and needs to be taken seriously on its face. In these projects and programs, experts take as their starting point that "doing" law and development entails tackling "wicked" and complex problems that by their very definition cannot be framed by a "well-grounded rationale, a clear understanding of the essential problem", or any of the other components of a "field" that Carothers articulated.

And so we might understand why today's law and development "agenda" seems so wide-ranging, and its experts appear so diverse and fragmented: the complexity of doing law and development work means that there is no shared core around which law and development experts might cohere. Yet, in spite of this self-doubt, diversity and fragmentation (or perhaps because of them), law and development experts have produced numerous sociological markers of their own coherence. These include journals (such as the Law and Development Review and the Hague Journal on the Rule of Law), degree courses (including a multi-institution PhD program, EDOLAD), professional networks (such as the globe-spanning Law and Development Research Network), training programs, specialist consultancies and annual conferences.

This strange combination of mainstreamed self-denial and vehicles for professional reproduction – embraced and enacted amongst a highly fragmented and indefinable group of people – does not reflect a group of experts asserting their authority and seeking hegemonic power within the operations of development, as, say, economists have done. Rather, it raises two questions that need to be theorized and answered if we are to understand who law and development experts are and what they do – both of which scholars are only beginning to address.

The first question is sociological: what sort of expertise is reflected by this strange mixture of expert denial and (re)production? Take the following example, from a two-day UN workshop to develop global indicators for the rule of law. These indicators were intended to measure the future success of the Sustainable Development Goals. The nearly two-dozen "rule of law" experts populating the room kept remarking on the futility – even absurdity – of developing meaningful global indicators for the rule of law. For them, the rule of law was too multi-faceted, too political, too essentially contested to be captured in indicator form. And after a coffee break, they sat down and got to work, haggling out the details of just such an indicator. As I have recounted elsewhere (Desai and Schomerus, 2018), this tension between self-denial and ongoing professional work was constitutive of the role of the law and development experts in the room. The tension produced a weak or thin form of expertise, which was ultimately reconfigurable and able to adapt to the future complexities of indicator implementation – for example, by developing "provisional" or placeholder indicators to be "piloted" and adapted to local contexts, rather than authoritative indicators to be implemented.

DEVAL DESAI

Importantly, this form of expertise, while adaptable, is also hard to hold to account. How, for example, can a law and development expert be accountable for a "pilot" indicator, given that it was always destined to have some degree of failure built into it? This gets to the heart of the practical legitimacy of the contemporary law and development enterprise.

The second question is political: what are the real-world effects of this sort of expertise? While the literature on law and development has little to say on this, there are some hints from a broader literature on transnational law and governance, which is beginning to detail the operations of this sort of expertise in domains such as trade law, humanitarian law and the laws of war. This literature puts forward the basic proposition that this sort of expertise keeps legal arrangements open-ended, flexible and amenable to ongoing intervention. In the context of law and development, we might thus understand its experts to be producing the relationship between law and society (or politics, or the economy) as a provisional and unstable practice rather than a social fact – thereby continually raising and never resolving issues of distribution, representation and, ultimately, legitimation.

So, even if law and development experts are neither clearly a type of thing nor clearly the most important thing when it comes to development, they remain worthy of study – often for the ways in which they purport, to themselves and others, to be non-hegemonic, fragmented, and elusive.

DEVAL DESAI

References

Carothers, Thomas (2006). "The Problem of Knowledge" in Thomas Carothers (ed.), *Promoting the Rule of Law Abroad: In Search of Knowledge.* Carnegie Endowment for International Peace.

Desai, Deval and Mareike Schomerus (2018). "'There Was A Third Man . . .': Tales from a Global Policy Consultation on Indicators for the Sustainable Development Goals", Development and Change 49(1), 1–27.

Desai, Deval and Michael Woolcock (2015). "Experimental Justice Reform: Lessons from the World Bank and Beyond", Annual Review of Law and Social Science 11(1), 155–174.

Dezalay, Yves and Bryant Garth (2002). *The Internationalization of Palace Wars: Lawyers, Economists, and the Contest to Transform Latin American States.* University of Chicago Press.

Grasten, Maj (2016). "Whose Legality? Rule of Law Missions and the Case of Kosovo" in Nicholas Rajkovic, Tanja Aalberts, and Thomas Gammeltoft-Hansen (eds), *The Power of Legality: Practices of International Law and Their Politics.* Cambridge University Press.

Humphreys, Stephen (2010). *Theatre of the Rule of Law: Transnational Legal Intervention in Theory and Practice.* Cambridge University Press.

Mosse, David (2004). "Is Good Policy Unimplementable? Reflections on the Ethnography of Aid Policy and Practice", Development and Change 35(4), 639–671.

Santos, Alvaro (2006). "The World Bank's Uses of the 'Rule of Law' Promise in Economic Development" in David M. Trubek and Alvaro Santos (eds), *The New Law and Economic Development.* Cambridge University Press.

Tamanaha, Brian (2011). "The Primacy of Society and the Failures of Law and Development", Cornell International Law Journal 44, 209–247.

Trubek, David M. (2016). "Law and Development: Forty Years after 'Scholars in Self-Estrangement'", University of Toronto Law Journal 66, 301–329.

45. Law, Finance and Development

Development has had an ever-evolving definition and there has been no common ground how it is to be achieved or financed, either in economics or law.

The United Nations Declaration on the Right to Development, adopted by the UN General Assembly in 1986, establishes that the right to development is an inalienable human right and puts people at the centre of the development process, in which all human rights and fundamental freedoms can be fully realized. In this way, the 1986 Declaration recognizes a comprehensive definition of development, encompassing its economic, social, cultural and political dimensions and the fair distribution of benefits resulting therefrom. Nevertheless, the Declaration does not specify the pathway to development.

Different theories have been suggested since the first half of the twentieth century on how development can be achieved. Just after the 1930 Great Depression, a Keynesian theory of development became dominant. Keynes proposed, inter alia, that State intervention was the key to promoting full employment, price stability and economic growth. Law was one of the main instruments used by governments to adopt the Keynesian model. In the beginning of the second half of the twentieth century, the industrialization theories were developed. These theories were based on the process of capitalization and economic growth, based on instruments of industrialization, investments, savings and aid. These theories also promoted structural change, with the need for countries to transform their structures from agriculture to industrial activity. In 2018, Stephen and some other scholars argued that underdevelopment was a consequence of the established economic order with an industrialized centre and a periphery based on agriculture. In this sense, law has had to play a key role as an instrument to construct development as one of the main ways by which governments implemented industrialization policies as well as capitalization.

Dependency theories arose in reaction to industrialization theories, to explain that resources flow from a periphery of poor and underdeveloped countries to a core of developed and rich States. According to dependency theories, a certain degree of protectionism in trade should be allowed to follow a self-sustaining development path based on the economic features of each country. In this model, the main way to implement protectionist trade measures is by legislation and again law plays an important role.

Neoliberal theories emerged in the 1980s and 1990s and preached minimum intervention from the State in the economy. These theories were also termed the Washington Consensus on behalf of the policies proposed by the World Bank and the IMF, which promoted privatization policies and minimum State intervention in the economy. According to Paul Krugman, as a further development in the 1990s, these theories recognized the pivotal function of institutions, including international legal institutions such as the World Trade Organization. Both domestic law and international law play an important role by shaping deregulation and privatization, from multilateral orientation to national implementation.

In all these approaches, the emphasis is predominantly on economic growth. By presenting the dilemma of Maytree, in *Development as Freedom* (Oxford University Press, 1999), Amartya Sen points to the fact that just as wealth does not lead the path to eternity, wealth does not lead the path to development. In other words, development cannot be based on economic growth alone. Development cannot be measured using national GDP alone. Sen suggests that development is a path to guaranteeing freedoms at the same time that guaranteeing freedoms is a path to development. By freedoms, Sen wants to affirm, inter alia, the right to access food, water and basic sanitation, housing, welfare, health, work, culture and education, which are the pathway to development. Back in 2011, Celine Tan remarked that reduction of inequalities leads to development and that can only be achieved by a combination of economic, social and environmental policies, developed together. Again, law might be one of the best instruments to achieve this type of holistic development.

In the end of the twentieth and beginning of the twenty-first centuries, the UN came up with a model of development, based on the 1987 Brundtland Report and officially enshrined first in Agenda 21 of the 1992 UN Conference on Environment and Development, later in the Millennium Development Goals (UN Summit, 2000) and, in 2015, in the 17 Sustainable Development Goals (SDGs, Agenda 2030). In this new model of development, just as the tri-dimensional meaning came up in the 1987 Brundtland Report (protection of the environment combined with social and economic development), the expression 'sustainable' became ubiquitous. 'Sustainable development' now encompasses core issues such as, inter alia, reduction of poverty, gender inclusion and climate change mitigation. Law was also called to make promotion of this new model of development, but, most of the time, in a soft way (soft law – a law that educates and influences; as opposed to hard law, which is mandatory legislation).

Ever since, sustainable development has been built around a global governance structure. The term 'governance' comprises State and inter-State bodies as well as private institutions, formal or non-formal ones, non-governmental organizations and sets of rules and standards that identify some specific areas of knowledge. In this way, Andreia Vieira highlighted, in 2017, that this governance structure presupposes a plurality of actors, rules, institutions, intentions and actions.

In this context of global governance, contemporary international law has been consolidated – as well as 'welfarist international law' – a law that aims at creating a Welfare International Community, based on common interests, a concept developed by Emmanuelle Jouanet in 2012. This new face of international law is regarded as concomitant with the phenomena of multi-faced regulation, networks and world governance, along with a polycentric and negotiated public international regulation.

In 2015, the same year that the UN adopted the 2030 Agenda and its 17 SDGs, the Third UN Conference on Financing for Development came up with a very influential document: the Addis Ababa Action Agenda (hereinafter, the AAAA), whose main task is to further strengthen the framework to finance sustainable development and means of implementation for the 2030 Agenda. The AAAA sets a global framework for financing development post-2015 and, for such, pinpoints seven action areas: (1) domestic public resources; (2) domestic and international private business and finance; (3) international development cooperation; (4) international trade as an engine for development; (5) debt and debt sustainability; (6) addressing systemic issues; and (7) science, technology, innovation and capacity-building.

Although the AAAA might seem like a very positive market-oriented document, it confirms the main economic points of view on sustainable development for developing and emerging countries and it does not differ from the Un Conference on Trade and Development (UNCTAD) Agenda. In 2016, the UNCTAD launched an Investment Facilitation Action Package as a way of suggesting that investments could be used as instruments to achieve the SDGs. Both the AAAA and the UNCTAD Agenda share a commitment to respect all human rights, including the right to development, setting the goal to promote inclusive societies and advance towards an equitable global economic system, while preserving the planet for future generations.

Just as highlighted in the AAAA and in the UNCTAD Agenda, financing development might be domestically implemented by setting nationally appropriate spending targets for quality investments in essential public services for all, including health, education, energy, water and sanitation, which are consistent with national sustainable development strategies. Moreover, the AAAA also suggests that there should be a commitment to enhancing revenue administration through modernized, progressive tax systems and more efficient tax collection, as well as improving the fairness, transparency, efficiency and effectiveness of domestic tax systems, including policies to integrate the informal sector into the formal economy. At the same time, countries should enforce law to combat tax evasion and corruption, assuming that tax incentives can be an appropriate policy to promote sustainability, such as environmental taxes. Domestic policies should also concentrate on promoting inclusive and sustainable industrialization, as the AAAA points out, in order to address challenges such as jobs creation, efficient resources consumption and energy efficiency, pollution and climate change, as well as innovation, knowledge sharing and social inclusion.

From the 2030 Agenda, the AAAA, the UNCTAD's work and other documents that came out in the twenty-first century, there is evidence of a global call for the private sector to engage in the development process, by investing in areas that are critical to sustainable development, as well as shifting to more sustainable consumption and production patterns. In this way, sustainable consumption becomes an instrument to finance development. When concerns come to inefficient fossil fuel subsidies that encourage wasteful consumption, domestic policies should propose removing market distortions by working on tax systems as well as supporting sub-national authorities to promote sustainable development practices, as pointed out by Andreia Vieira and other scholars in 2017. As such, cooperation is needed to promote public and private investment in energy infrastructure and clean energy technologies including carbon capture and storage technologies. The AAAA highlights that the share of renewable energy should be increased and the global rate of energy efficiency and conservation should be doubled, aiming at universal access to affordable, reliable, modern and sustainable energy services for all.

Recognizing the diversity of the private sector, ranging from micro-enterprises to cooperatives and multinationals, a good policy would consider private business activity, investment and innovation as major drivers of productivity, inclusive economic growth and job creation. However, in many developing countries, investments are concentrated in few sectors and often bypass regions most in need, and international capital flows might be short-term oriented. All these distortions could be remedied by the right public policies towards sustainable foreign direct investment (FDI), taking into account international investment agreements and codes of multinational enterprises.

Liberalization and promotion of FDI represented the majority of national investment policies according to both the AAAA and the UNCTAD Agenda. As such, liberalization of FDI comprehends attraction and facilitation of FDI, which should be allowed under the principle of public interest and within a careful consideration to certain sensible sectors, which vary from country to country. In many countries, liberalization of FDI has to obey general rules enshrined in the Constitution of the country itself; in others, a more open market is allowed. In general, restrictions for FDI inflows have been limited or abolished for most industries, and, in many developing countries, privatization policies have been pursued mainly in telecommunications, energy and water services. Yet, privatization of water services, according

to Andreia Vieira (2016), has not proven to be the best way to make inclusive water and sanitation policy. In most countries, including those that have adopted liberalization policies, public water and sanitation services remain the best option to achieve sustainable development in this sector. In this respect, the promotion of sustainable FDI needs to envisage adequate public policies that are able to create a culture of compliance with social and environmental norms as devised, for instance, by soft law instruments such as the Global Compact, the UN Guiding Principles on Business and Human Rights, the OECD Guidelines on Multinational Enterprises and hard law commitments such as the ILO Labour Standards and the ILO Conventions. As such, liberalization policies towards FDI should be constructed bearing in mind a sustainable development for the country and, therefore, previous regulation should require compliance with sustainable development characteristics. A study developed by Karl Sauvant and Howard Mann, in 2017, points towards an indicative list of good FDI sustainability characteristics that should be included in the promotion and facilitation of FDI, mainly for developing and least developed countries, and compliance with the documents mentioned above is one of the elements in this list.

Nonetheless, public and private investments have equal importance in financing infrastructure. Public policies should pay attention to the work of development banks, development finance institutions and public private partnerships, which combine concessional public finance with non-concessional private finance and expertise from the public and private sector. Moreover, there should be incentives for international and domestic development banks to promote finance for Micro, Small and Medium Enterprises (MSMEs), including industrial transformation through the creation of credit lines and technical assistance for MSMEs, recognizing that MSMEs create the majority of jobs in many countries but often lack access to finance. In this respect, just as suggested both by the AAAA and the UNCTAD Agenda, national governments should adopt policies towards strengthening positive spill overs from FDI, such as know-how and technology, in order to establish linkages with domestic suppliers and encourage integration of local enterprises, mainly MSMEs in developing countries, into regional and global value chains.

Actions related to South-South cooperation

for development should not substitute, but instead complement North-South cooperation. In this way, multilateral development banks and other international development banks should give priority to financing sustainable development and providing know-how to developing countries. As suggested by the AAAA, multilateral development banks can provide countercyclical lending, which includes concessional terms to complement national resources for financial and economic shocks, natural disasters and pandemics. In order to have access to available funds and enhance public and private contributions to initiatives such as the Global Environment Facility, it would be necessary to support infrastructure policies in developing countries, such as maritime logistics and other sectors that allow transfer of technology and job creation, since such features would be a necessary outcome for policies related to facilitation of sustainable investments.

In this sense, multilateral arrangements and integration processes could play an important role in providing a cooperation scenario for financing development. The World Trade Organization and its liberalization policies have not just worked on improving market access for goods and services but also on inclusion programmes, such as the Aid for Trade program, which promotes inclusive trade via direct investments for developing and least developed countries. Regional integration, such as the European Union and the Mercosur, amongst new ones, such as the Transpacific Partnership and the Regional Comprehensive Economic Partnership, have also paved the regional way for investing in the development of their member countries, including investments in transport, energy, water and sanitation for all. At the same time, new informal arrangements, such as the BRICS, have established a new forum to bridge the infrastructure gap. This led to new initiatives for financing and promotion of development, such as the New Development Bank of the BRICS, with a focus on projects of infrastructure and energy.

Last, but not the least, promotion of peaceful and inclusive societies would take into account alternative methods of dispute settlement, such as mediation, ever since features related to financing development are at stake. Peaceful solutions are usually more sustainable since they are composed by the parties to the dispute and take into account side effects of the dispute settlement. Also, combating corruption is a way of promoting peaceful solutions and, at the same time, a way of financing development, since public revenue or biased support to private projects drive away efficiency and public resources that could be invested in the real promotion of sustainable development.

ANDREIA COSTA VIEIRA

References

Jouannet, Emanuelle (2012). *The Liberal-Welfarist Law of Nations: A History of International Law*. Cambridge University Press.

Krugman, Paul R., Maurice Obstfeld, and Marc J. Melitz (2014). *International Economics: Theory and Policy*. 10th edition. Pearson.

Sarkar, Prabirjit and Ajit Singh (2010). 'Law, Finance and Development: Further Analyses of Longitudinal Data', Cambridge Journal of Economics 2(34), 325–346.

Sauvant, Karl P. and Howard Mann (2017). *Towards an Indicative List of FDI Sustainability Characteristics*. ICTSD and WEF.

Stephen, Frank H. (2018). *Law and Development: An Institutional Critique*. Edward Elgar Publishing.

Tan, Celine (2011). *Governance through Development: Poverty Reduction Strategies, International Law and the Disciplining of Third World States*. Routledge.

United Nations (2015). Addis Ababa Action Agenda of the Third International Conference on Financing for Development.

Vieira, Andreia C. (2016). International Law, 'Governance and Trade of Water Services' in Photini Parzatzis and Maria Gavouneli (eds), *Reconceptualising the Rule of Law in Global Governance, Resources, Investment and Trade*. Hart Publishing.

Vieira, Andreia C. (org.) (2017). *International Economic Law and the Environment: Promoting Sustainable Development on Local, Regional, National and Global Contexts*. Leopoldianum.

Vieira, Andreia C. (2019). *Inclusive Trade through the lenses of the WTO Aid for Trade Programme*, RDCI. Thomson Reuters.

46. Law of Foreign Investment

Law of foreign investment comprises norms and rules enshrined in international investment treaties, national investment laws as well as jurisprudence of investor-State tribunals interpreting and applying such provisions. An historic impetus for the emergence and consolidation of this field of law came with the end of the Second World War, when the newly independent developing countries asserted their right to overhaul the rules of international law created before their admission to the family of nations. Prior to that, assets of foreign investors had been protected through a combination of customary international law, bilateral agreements, concession contracts and, most importantly, political and military pressure. Since asserting economic independence inevitably entailed the nationalization of hitherto foreign-owned assets, an overwhelming majority of developing States opposed customary international rules arguing that the latter no longer suited the new economic and political reality. The primary bone of contention was the rule mandating that any expropriation or nationalization of foreign-owned investments are accompanied by a prompt, adequate and effective compensation. Faced with a difficulty to convince developing States to endorse customary international law on the protection of foreign property, capital-exporting States resorted to bilateral investment protection and promotion agreements. These agreements were designed to ensure that foreign investments would at all times be protected against expropriation and nationalization as well as other forms of host government interference.

Many of the contemporary investment treaties owe their origins to the so-called Abs-Shawcross agreement, named after a German banker Herman Abs and a British lawyer and diplomat, Lord Shawcross. The Abs-Shawcross Draft Convention on Investments Abroad was conceived and drawn up in 1959 as a unified 'system of joint measures' designed 'to resuscitate, on a reciprocal basis, the principle of inviolability of private property and other private rights'. Although it has never been formally adopted, the draft convention became a blueprint for a rapidly growing number of investment treaties between developed and developing countries. The Abs-Shawcross Convention has also considerably informed the content of national laws on investment protection which developing States were encouraged to adopt in the 1980–1990s as part of a wider move towards liberalization of domestic investment regimes. The content of national investment laws considerably overlaps with investment treaties in that they provide for a range of investor rights and guarantees, including the guarantee against uncompensated expropriation and access to independent investor-State dispute settlement.

Conceptual issues underpinning the relationship between foreign investment law and development can be grouped into a number of key themes. At the core of one such theme are the questions pertaining to substantive and procedural investment protection rules. Are these rules development-friendly? To shield foreign investors from political and other vicissitudes when investing in developing States investment treaties offer substantive and procedural guarantees that are largely unparalleled in other areas of international law. These guarantees can be categorized as three key pillars of foreign investment law. First, under traditional investment treaties investors can enjoy broad and far-reaching substantive rights vis-à-vis host governments, such as the guarantee of fair and equitable treatment, compensation for expropriation, non-discrimination and sanctity of contract. These guarantees go beyond what investors would enjoy under the national laws of developed economies. Second, in a manner unseen in other areas of international law, such as World Trade Organization (WTO) law and international human rights, investment treaties enable investors to bypass national courts and to claim monetary redress in cases where the host State fails to comply with the prescribed standards of protection. Third, arbitral awards rendered in investor-State arbitration cases are readily enforceable in most jurisdictions and can be executed even against the will of a respondent State. Supported by its own bespoke dispute settlement mechanism (investor-State dispute settlement or investment arbitration) the contemporary law of foreign investment both reaffirms and goes beyond the historically contested rules on investment protection. Similar wide-reaching investor rights and guarantees can be found in national investment laws.

Recent studies suggest that developing States did not appreciate the content and implications of investment treaties and national investment laws at the time of their adoption. Profound concerns have been voiced about the large sums awarded to claimant investors, the high cost of the arbitration process and the budgetary implications of these losses for developing countries. To comply with the arbitral awards, respondent States could be forced to divert the already limited funds from important socio-economic objectives, such as investment in infrastructure, education and health. Even in cases where the final award is in favour of the respondent State, the latter would have to bear significant amounts in legal expenses and the costs of the arbitral proceedings. The amounts claimed by investors at times exceed the foreign exchange reserves of a respondent State. As developing countries tend to bear the brunt of investment arbitration awards, the question inevitably arises as to whether development could achieve through the imposition of crippling financial sanctions on host States. Despite the purported importance of development to its core mission, contemporary law on foreign investment protection does not concern itself with the weak and disadvantaged, and is yet to replace its focus on economic growth with the pursuit of human development. Development concerns are currently far from being fully operationalized in investment treaty law and arbitration.

One of the principal justifications for granting foreign investors extensive legal privileges is that by doing so developing countries would signal about a good investment climate, thus attracting more investments and reducing the cost of capital needed for economic growth. International and national laws on foreign investment were thus conceived as a grand bargain whereby developing States would promise to protect foreign investment in return for the prospect of more investment. Yet the link between investment treaties, investment flows and economic growth has also been contested in a number of recent econometric studies. A number of qualitative and quantitative studies tend to concur in that investment treaties are unlikely to have a significant effect on the majority of foreign investment decisions. Some obvious examples casting doubt on the importance of investment treaties for attracting foreign direct investment and fostering development can also be found in the patterns of investment treaty-making. For instance, Brazil, which has enjoyed a large influx of foreign investment despite having historically refrained from ratifying any bilateral investment treaties. Conversely, the signing and ratification of numerous investment treaties between African states and developed economies has not entailed a tangible increase in investment flows and economic growth.

Another key theme in a debate about foreign investment law and development relates to the impact of foreign investment activities on the socio-economic conditions in host States. Do the norms comprising the contemporary foreign investment law provide sufficient room for host States to pursue public policy objectives, including policies fostering sustainable development? Do they provide safeguards and incentives for foreign investors to not only create economic growth but also to do so in an environmentally and socially friendly manner? Even if it could be proven that investment treaties lead to more foreign investment leading to higher growth, concerns have been raised about the negative impact investors may have on societal welfare, especially once resource depletion, environmental degradation and other externalities are taken into account. Historically, investment treaties have unequivocally prioritized investment protection over any other competing policy considerations. Similarly, national investment laws tend to refer to general economic development objectives, such as economic growth, industrial development, skill transfer; however, only a very small number of such laws contain express provisions on protection of environment, plant life, animal life, climate change and sustainable development. There is a growing acknowledgment that the rules constituting a global investment regime need to be reformed to maximize the positive contribution investment can make and to avoid negative impacts on the host communities and the environment. The contemporary investment law is essentially asymmetrical in its nature as it grants foreign investors extensive rights without imposing corresponding responsibilities.

Even prior to the proliferation of investor-State disputes where investors successfully challenged regulatory measures adopted by host States, experts forewarned that, in a drive to attract foreign investment, developing States may be prone to de-valuing various public policy objectives. The need to promote economic growth, including through facilitation and protection of foreign investment, may stall regulatory innovation and at times encourage States to lower their regulatory standards. Fears that foreign investment protections, especially under investment treaties, might discourage legitimate regulatory measures in the public interest – often referred to as regulatory chill – have led to revisions in the recent drafting templates which now feature exceptions and carve-out to safeguard the host State's rights to regulate. Such revisions are prominent in the model treaties of major developed economies such as the United States and Canada. Despite these changes, criticisms continue to be voiced that a more significant overhaul of both substantive and procedural aspects of the international investment regime is needed. The very process of investment treaty reform has so far been largely driven by the growing dissatisfaction by developed States with being drawn into investment disputes in a respondent capacity. There is an ongoing debate, among both scholars and policy-makers, about the legitimacy of international investment law and the need to address its current deficits of transparency, consistency and accountability. A growing number of voices advocate for replacing or supplementing the contemporary investment protection regime with a policy framework that focuses on investment facilitation.

Finally, a growing area of legal discourse straddling investment law and development studies concerns the making and change of international investment norms. Were the views and concerns of developing countries taken into account when international investment law was conceived? Does the investment regime sufficiently enable developing countries to make a tangible input in the process of formation, reform and application of investment rules? A growing body of empirical scholarship reveals the lack of meaningful participation of developing countries in international investment law-making. Historically, developing States have had very limited input into the drafting and negotiation of investment treaty norms. Critics have also highlighted limited opportunities for developing States to participate in the ongoing reform and recalibration of investment treaties and investor-State dispute settlement mechanisms. To this one can add a low number of arbitrators from developing countries that could influence the formation of investment jurisprudence by being appointed to panels and partaking in shaping investment jurisprudence. Developing States are disadvantaged by lack of bargaining power to negotiate treaties that better serve their interests, as well as lack of economic and institutional capacity to navigate the increasingly complex landscape of investment treaty law and investment arbitration practice. Arbitrators tend to disregard these inequalities and consider them irrelevant for the outcome of concrete investor-State cases. Even the inclusion of express references to development objectives in investment treaties has proven to be ineffective: there are multiple instances of arbitral tribunals dismissing the relevance of such references in their interpretation of various core provisions.

The workings of international investment law have generated a backlash in both developed and developing States. While the erstwhile advocates of investment treaties, such as the United States and Canada, have been revising and reforming their models, a number of developing States manifested their dissatisfaction with the regime through a decision to disengage. For instance, in 2007 Bolivia submitted a notice of its denunciation of the ICSID Convention, and Venezuela followed the suit in 2012. Some developed countries, including South Africa and Indonesia, have embarked on a substantive revision of their investment policy frameworks. Although developing States by and large continue to remain rule-takers rather than rule-makers, a new generation of investment treaty models is also emerging, as exemplified by the international investment agreement between Nigeria and Morocco and the Investment Agreement for the COMESA Common Investment Area. These treaties feature provisions that seek to reconcile the need to attract foreign investment with the pursuit of developmental objectives. The extent to which the newly emerging drafting patterns from the Global North would reflect the interests of the Global South is still open to question. A different normative and institutional framework is needed to help redress the existing power asymmetries and to enable the emergence of investment treaties reflecting the needs and preferences of developing States to a greater extent than they do now.

MAVLUDA SATTOROVA

References

Bonnitcha, Jonathan, Lauge N. Skovgaard Poulsen, and Michael Waibel (2017). *The Political Economy of the Investment Treaty Regime*. Oxford University Press.

Gallus, Nick (2005). 'The Influence of the Host State's Level of Development on International Investment Treaty Standards of Protection', Journal of World Investment Trade 6, 711–730.

John, Taylor St (2017). *The Rise of Investor-State Arbitration: Politics, Law, and Unintended Consequences*. Oxford University Press.

Miles, Kate (2013). *The Origins of International Investment Law: Empire, Environment and the Safeguarding of Capital*. Cambridge University Press.

Monebhurrun, Nitish (2017). 'Novelty in International Investment Law: The Brazilian Agreement on Cooperation and Facilitation of Investments as a Different International Investment Agreement Model', Journal of International Dispute Settlement 8, 79–100.

Montt, Santiago (2009). *State Liability in Investment Treaty Arbitration: Global Constitutional and Administrative Law in the BIT Generation*. Hart Publishing.

Salacuse, Jeswald W. (2007). 'The Treatification of International Investment Law', Law and Business Review of the Americas 13, 155–166.

Schill, Stephan W., Christian J. Tams, and Rainer Hofmann (eds) (2015). *International Investment Law and Development: Bridging the Gap*. Edward Elgar.

Schneiderman, David (2008). *Constitutionalizing Economic Globalization: Investment Rules and Democracy's Promise*. Cambridge University Press.

Yackee, Jason W. (2010). 'Do Bilateral Investment Treaties Promote Foreign Direct Investment? Some Hints from Alternative Evidence', Virginia Journal of International Law 51, 397–442.

47. Law, Race and Development

Propositionally, development, law and race are quite straightforward concepts. Law, which is an objective and neutral mechanism, allows us to prevent and/or punish racial discrimination, but also provides a framework enabling development. But a critical examination of the nexus between the three also uncovers how they co-constitute each other, sometimes in negative ways. This entry – an exploration of the epicentre of law, race and development – requires a working definition of 'race'. Historically, there have been divergent definitions; one definition sees race as a significant biological phenomenon, i.e. that racial identities with biological origins have moral/character implications and meanings. This has been largely dismissed. It is now accepted that there is no scientific merit in categorizing humans according to race. Race has also been defined as a cultural phenomenon; in this characterization, 'race' and 'ethnicity' are considered synonymous concepts. This categorization is problematic, as it makes the fluidity of culture coterminous with the immutability of skin colour. Race is increasingly more acceptably defined as a socially constructed phenomenon. This means that society, including law and knowledge producers, give moral and social meaning to perceived racial classifications, and those meanings crystallize but also evolve over time. Another definition of 'race' is predicated on social constructionism. Here, race is considered, mainly in liberal scholarship and policy-making, as something we can refuse to see – what Bonilla Silva calls 'colour-blind race'. Osagie Obasogie explains social constructionism thus: 'economic, and political forces create the meanings that come to attach to various bodies ... law can be seen as an instrumental "glue" in congealing the meanings that adhere to racialized bodies, making the ideological fit seem natural so as to go unquestioned' (Osagie K. Obasogie (2015). 'The Constitution of Identity' in Austin Sarat and Patricia Ewick (eds), *The Handbook of Law and Society*. John Wiley and Sons, p. 345). It is also important to note, that in popular and academic discourse, the divergent meanings and contexts of race are often conflated or interchanged.

To understand the interaction between law, race and development, we must first understand the economic imperatives behind the social construction of race. These created and continue to maintain racialized narratives and attendant hegemonic hierarchies which the Sustainable Development Goals do not account for. Not only is a global historical analysis of the evolution of the relationship between the three concepts required, but also an appreciation of the different domestic contexts of this epicentre in the past and in the present. I will conclude this entry with suggestions for thinking differently about the relationship between race, law and development.

A short history of academic race-thinking

During the enlightenment, racial classifications became part of socio-legal perceptions and, consciously or subconsciously, still remain in our jurisprudence, in international Global North-South relations, and domestic legislations. It is often suggested that Carl Linnaeus's 1735 *Systema Naturae* was key to 'inventing race'. The proposition is, until the advent of scientific classifications of humans by race, 'race' as a concept carried no moral or character meaning, and therefore no legal meaning. Thus, race told us nothing about a person other than what colour their skin was. The effect of various, mostly European, academics theorizing about race as key to creating a hierarchy of humanity, was to effect epistemic violence on people thus racialized as non-white – an academic non-recognition of personhood. Therefore, the further removed a person racialized thus was from the top of the racial hierarchy, the further removed they were from the physical and material benefits of personhood. These ideas were articulated in the writing of many enlightenment academics. Their scholarship still remains mainstream and have influenced legal histories and legal presents. For example: Johann Friedrich Blumenbach, Immanuel Kant, John Locke, David Hume, Georg Wilhelm Friedrich Hegel, to name a few. John Locke, for instance, argued that a property right was created in the land of the Other, if that Other was not using their land in a manner recognized in Europe (it is also interesting to note that Locke was also an original shareholder in the Royal African Company, a company which was chartered in 1672 and which monopolized English participation in the slave trade). These legal arguments gave foundation and legitimation for the appropriation of resources and labour of the racialized Other. Subsequently, this race-thinking has become fundamental to the current legalized structure of the world, and power disparities marked by racial inequalities.

Law, race-thinking and geopolitics

The race-thinking, which is embedded in intellectual foundations, led Charles Mills to suggest in his book, *The Racial Contract*, that the world is predicated, not on a social contract, but on a racial contract. This is a global political system which permits White populations to dominate by economic means, inter alia, racialized Other populations. Within the racial contract, a moral ideal upheld in the Global North may legitimately be violated when engaging with racially othered populations (for example, while Locke was vehemently against slavery, he had no qualms about supporting and benefiting from it when it involved Africans being abducted to the Americas). Or as Theo Goldberg argues in *The Racial State*, socially constructed race is essential to all aspects of the formation and maintenance of the modern nation State, its borders and its composition. The racial State excludes racialized Others in order to construct homogeneity, and internally maintains, through various legal means and invented histories, a racially hierarchized polity. These disparities put in motion by race-thinking are – often unthinkingly, often by law – kept in place. Law has embedded, deep within it, a particular vision of humanity, a vision from which the majority of the world, due to being racialized and gendered as Other, are in various degrees, excluded. Law, by nature, in its quest for social order, replicates and revalidates itself, as it maintains a particular conceptualization of the world. Those racialized as the centre of humanity have had that centredness made invisible and thus the effect of racialization is often invisible – sometimes referred to as White Privilege. Nevertheless, no matter what it has been called, 'enlightenment', 'civilization', 'progress', 'social evolution', 'economic growth', 'modernization', 'development', racial hierarchizations have always had at their core economic imperatives, either in creating financial and power dominance in the Global North or in maintaining said dominance.

Evolution of economic imperatives

Both the practice of slavery and the period of empire were both predicated upon a demarcation of the world into hierarchized and racialized binaries such as 'Christian and heathen', or 'civilized and uncivilized'. Both slavery and colonialism were justified, in whole or in part, as missions to 'improve' those enslaved, or those whose territories were appropriated, using legal tools of legitimization and justification. Both were founded, however, on hegemonic and economic imperatives, and so continued for as long as it was profitable to do so. Laws were drafted to ensure ease of processes. However, when slavery and formal colonization ended, the economic dominance achieved by controlling the body and land of the Other were maintained by the facilitation of neo-colonization. Neo-colonization describes a situation where a formerly colonized State still has its economics and politics directed by forces from outside of it. Often, this is exemplified by very prescriptive relationships between said State and international financial bodies such as the World Bank and the International Monetary Fund, or State donor bodies such as the UK Department For International Development (DFID) or the US Agency for International Development (USAID). These relationships are also described by the broader concept of 'coloniality'. Coloniality explains the permanence of patterns of power established by race-thinking, supported by law, maintained by economic imperatives. This is observable in power relations (demarcated by race, upheld by law) in cultural production, global labour and resource differentials, as well as power disparities in knowledge production.

Post-colonial law (or the continuing complicity of law)

That law has been used to create and maintain the global racial order and direct the economic imperatives of our geopolitics, is evidenced by the use of slave codes to regulate and maintain the practice of slavery, and also the concept of *terra nullius*, which legitimized the seizure and ownership of the land of the racialized Other. This complicity lives on in the dominance of Euro-American law, as Darian-Smith identifies it, which formally and institutionally provided the continuing means for colonial/settler governments to oppress and control indigenous

FOLUKE ADEBISI

peoples and land. Thus, the law has long been entangled with racializing and marginalizing Othered populations. This effected not only epistemicides of laws – killing legal knowledges of the Other – but also physical death, either by forceful and immediate destruction of indigenous populations or by, in creating an unequal global economic system, placing on them conditions of life guaranteed to slowly destroy. For example, the British government in 1833, with the passing of Emancipation Act, which abolished slavery, also authorized the payment of compensation of £47 million to slave-owners. In doing so, slaveholders lost nothing by ending the practice of slavery, but were able, in many cases, to establish the foundation of an affluent life for themselves and their descendants, all on the labour of enslaved people. Another example is the mismanagement and control that led to the Great Bengal Famine of 1943–1944 in India, resulting in the deaths of two million people out of a population of around 60 million. Amartya Sen's famine analyses illustrate how British colonial administrative mismanagement of events leading up to famine, reflected ideologies of who is considered to be entitled to resources. Ideologies already examined in this section.

Thus, 'sustainable development' of racialized populations cannot be divorced from the material dispossession of the Other from the category 'human', the material effects thereof and the continuing complicity of law in this process. Taking these as a background, future discussions of development from the perspective of the underdeveloped (who have been strategically underdeveloped), and not the developed, may yield alternatives to implementing sustainable development within a geopolitical structure underpinned by race-thinking. Justice may mean, at the very least, acknowledging the harm done, or thinking of ways to repair the harm and ensuring that it is not revisited.

Complexity of racialized otherness

It is important to appreciate the variation of identities within the signifier 'racialized Other', as explained through concepts such as intersectionality and subalternity, for example. 'Intersectionality' is a term that explains how oppressions can combine. In a racialized, gendered, classist, heteronormative, geopoliticized, ableist global economy, a person may suffer quite a specific combination of disadvantages (NB: 'disadvantages' not 'iden-

tities'!). Subalternity, alternatively, describes how the 'subaltern' is placed at the bottom of the global social, political and economic order. The subaltern has no access to hegemonic power, illustrated by our failure to 'hear' the subaltern, even when the subaltern 'speaks'. Studying the situation of the racially Othered, is often dependent on understanding the complexity of their socially constructed identity and where they stand within the global order. Thus, it is worthy of note that most higher education degrees in development are placed in the Global North and study the 'problems' of the Global South. Therefore, we make world problems regional, and consequently racialized problems. How then do we achieve 'sustainable developmental goals', when to insist on development as a right suggests that we ahistorically prescribe the means by which development is to be fulfilled and therefore, revisit epistemic and physical violence on populations already Othered and subjected to the unequal global economic order with specific combination of disadvantages? How can the subaltern speak when we are not listening?

Where do we go from here? Decolonizing development

Decolonization can be defined very categorically as the undoing of colonization and all its forms or 'the bureaucratic, cultural, linguistic and psychological divesting of colonial power' (Linda Tuhiwai Smith (2013). *Decolonizing Methodologies: Research and Indigenous Peoples*. Zed Books Ltd., pp. 97–98). This includes reversing the poverty, ecological degradation, dispossession, criminalization of being, etc. that have resulted from morphing forms of colonization. Therefore, decolonization requires more than cosmetic change but necessitates altering the terms upon which we have geopolitical conversations. Rutazibwa (2018) suggests three strategies for decolonizing development: ontology, epistemology and normativity. She argues that by fragmenting the problems of what we call 'international development' from other geopolitical factors, we create a false mythology about our world and who benefits from the global political legal order. Consequently, the racial inequalities and hierarchies in law, race and development will continue to be reproduced if not disrupted. Whose voices do we hear at the intersection of law, race and development? In the final legal

FOLUKE ADEBISI

analysis, in our understanding of law, race and development, can the subaltern speak? Only if we are ready to listen to her.

FOLUKE ADEBISI

References

Crenshaw, Kimberle (1991). 'Mapping the Margins: Intersectionality, Identity Politics, and Violence against Women of Color', Stanford Law Review 43(6), 1241–1299.

Eze, Emmanuel Chukwudi (1997). 'The Color of Reason: The Idea of 'Race' in Kant's Anthropology' in Emmanuel Chukwudi Eze (ed.), *Postcolonial African Philosophy: A Critical Reader*. John Wiley and Sons Ltd.

Goldberg, David Theo (2002). *The Racial State*. Blackwell Publishing.

Hannaford, Ivan (1996). *Race: The History of an Idea in the West*. Woodrow Wilson Center Press.

McCarthy, Thomas (2009). *Race, Empire, and the Idea of Human Development*. Cambridge University Press.

Mills, Charles W. (1997). *The Racial Contract*. Cornell University Press.

Rutazibwa, Olivia U. (2018). 'On Babies and Bathwater: Decolonizing International Development Studies' in Sara de Jong, Rosalba Icaza, and Olivia U. Rutazibwa, *Decolonization and Feminisms in Global Teaching and Learning*. Routledge.

Saini, Angela (2019). *Superior: The Return of Race Science*. Beacon Press.

Spivak, Gayatri Chakravorty (1988). *Can the Subaltern Speak? Reflections on the History of an Idea*. Columbia University Press.

White, Sarah (2002). 'Thinking Race, Thinking Development', Third World Quarterly 23(3), 407–419.

48. Legal Pluralism

Providing a unique definition of legal pluralism is a hard task for several reasons. First, as the concept indicates, there is a plurality of phenomena to highlight. Homogenizing this essential diversity by looking for a common denominator is quite a contradiction. However, this inconvenience may not be unsurmountable if we consider that a definition is useful for theoretical and epistemological approaches. Second, characterizing something as "legal" requires having an ontological idea of what law is. Although there have been many philosophical debates, there are diverse positions on what law is and what it is not (for example, is natural law law? Are local customs law? Is Brazilian favelas' normativity law?). Third, and related to the second one, since there is no consensus on what law is, it is not easy to delimitate where the legal field ends and where the pure social non-legal one begins (as law is a social phenomenon, the distinction is very fuzzy). Law is only one among multiple social control mechanisms. Moreover, the idea of legal pluralism implies recognizing more senses of legal realities than just States' rules. As a result, it is not easy to include and exclude prescriptions that determine conducts in social groups without destroying the plural essence. An interesting criterion to trace a frontier is the one that proposes that, in the context of social imagination and world symbolizing (Geertz, 1983), law has to do with a communicative system that moves around the binary code of legal and illegal (Teubner, 1991–1992). In this way, law allows or forbids. In addition, in order to see if an act is allowed, mandatory or forbidden, the concept of sanction is important.

With the above-mentioned obstacles in mind, defining "legal pluralism" is a challenge that can be attempted by promising no certainty and a lot of contests. The concept demands sensibility to notice its own incompleteness. Perhaps the best way to show what it is, might be starting by describing its opposite: legal monism. This concept implies that there is only one law, the one made by the State. Positive rules are the main source of rights. The legal system is equal to the State. Custom is relevant when recognized by positive rules. The State legal system is the only valid one in one territory at a certain time, it must be known by and applied to every citizen. The legal system is grounded on the idea of ruling for one nation conceived as a homogeneous group of population that inhabits a national space and every citizen is equal in rights and duties to the others. Mainly, this conception comes from the Nation States of Modernity. Legal monism has faced many troubles in practice even though it has been a very useful category for theoretical studies. So far, in reality, it seems not to exist since for different reasons people behave according to more than one kind of motivations that can be considered "law".

When more than one legal system is valid in one State's territory and influence (or should influence) individuals at the same time, we are in the presence of legal pluralism. It is an intersection of legal rules that classify human actions in legal or illegal categories and that are interpenetrated in people's minds in order to guide their actions.

An important idea to remark is that law is not only State-made law. However, it is still almost impossible to find definitions of legal pluralism that do not mention the State legal system. As a consequence, we can say that the binary of State law and non-State law seems to be essential in thinking about this concept.

Another idea to emphasize is that non-State legal systems can coincide, complement or contradict the State one. In the first and the second cases, they prescribe the same action but there is coincidence only if both of them provide the same reasons to act according to law. Determining which normativity is ruling a person's action is very hard since it depends on the motivation of the individual; it is an internal rather than an external aspect. It is complementary when the non-State legal system provides more reasons than the State one to act in a certain way (for example, by giving more severe sanctions in case of violation) or when it fills a gap without conflicting with State law (for example, by sanctioning conduct that has no sanction in State rules but that are still duties). The most interesting case is the one of contradiction between different legal systems since it may imply legal insecurity and social chaos and conflicts (for example, about the case of early sexual relations with a child in the Wichi indigenous community in Argentina, see the documentaries "El etnógrafo" produced by Fortunato Films, 2012 and "Wichi: pueblos distantes" produced by Encuentro, 2009. The indigenous community customs might have allowed this conduct but in the State's law it was a crime).

Nowadays we think of legal pluralism at least in two ways according to whether the concept is applied to former colonized or to non-colonized societies. The first way (which Merry (1988) denominates "classical legal pluralism") has to do with colonialization processes in which there is a colonial legal system that is imposed on the colonized people. A clear example is indigenous people that had rules and institutions which were not taken into account by the occidental legal system. However, they did not stop existing. This way of legal pluralism implies an important challenge for contemporary democratic political organizations since they depend on the principles of representation and people empowerment. Recognizing the pre-existence of indigenous peoples or national groups by the State, requires allowing them to keep the also pre-existent cultures and rules (which are dynamic and can change through time). Two issues should then be noted. The first one has to do with the matter of who can decide which non-State's legal systems are allowed and the second one implies determining if the allowed non-State's legal systems can rule any content or if the State can limit this faculty.

The first issue highlights the way of recognizing their pre-existence and their validity. Usually, the State legal system rules that other kinds of law are also in force in a territory and for some communities. This implies a hierarchical organization between legal systems. It is up to the colonial legal system to decide whether or not to recognize other legal systems. Plurality exists but depends on one central power source.

The second issue is that when the already recognized indigenous rules and institutions are contradictory to the State's legal system, a decision must be made: whether or not to allow certain actions (such as corporal punishments, for example) and to renounce a bit on the recognition of these diverse legal systems as it requires imposing certain contents; or to allow them and create distinctions within the population (for example, some individuals could receive corporal punishments while others not; some can solve their conflicts according to their religions and customs and others not; some would be judged by indigenous courts while others by regular courts, etc.). The first alternative has the problem of considering colonial law as the one that can determine to what extent indigenous legal systems can or cannot be valid, which seems to be not very plural. The second alternative has the inconvenience of establishing criteria to create groups of citizens and to distribute rights and duties differently among them. In political theory, the status of "citizen" implies certain equality in order to claim for rights and have duties. So, creating distinctions between social groups requires building an argumentation that is legitimate and not arbitrary.

The second way of considering legal pluralism (which Merry calls the "new" one) has to do with a wider conception of subgroups' social control mechanisms. Instead of focusing on the relation between the colonizers and the colonized, it emphasizes the interactions between dominant groups and subordinated groups and between subgroups themselves in a determined State. This kind of approach to legal pluralism would be useful as a cohesion factor in diverse societies but also could be a tool for perpetuating the domination relationship. Nevertheless, not every legal pluralism implies domination structures. A conception of plurality as inter-discursivity, as different world symbolisms and providing meanings is also possible. According to these notions, plurality would come from different kinds of institutionalization of what is or not allowed, mandatory or forbidden. For example, in this way, intra-family rules, corporate rules, neighbourhood rules, immigrant groups rules, among other cases, are legal systems. This idea shows that there are many social orders that provide reasons for actions. However, it still cannot trace a frontier between law and other social control systems. If every social control system is law, then, it makes no sense to talk about law or legal pluralism. As De Sousa Santos (1987) says, if law is everywhere, it is nowhere.

A subtype of this kind of legal pluralism is the one of subgroups that have developed as a consequence of inequalities and are a result of industrialization processes and concentration of wealth as, for example, in the case of Brazilian favelas. In these places, the State is absent and the inhabitants develop their own rules for building streets, having services, urbanization codes, access and circulation allowance, etc. that have different and more flexible formalities and sometimes very contradictory parameters compared with the so-called "asphalt law" (State law).

HELGA MARÍA LELL

Another special case that is beginning to appear as a political topic is the State law recognition of legal consequences to acts that have not been celebrated according to it but to other kinds of social systems (that are non-State legal systems). For example, if a marriage is celebrated according to a religious ceremony, it should not be considered as performed in a civil way. However, there are cases in which courts have recognized some civil effects in these cases in order to award a divorce and living support (for example, see High Court of England and Wales, Akhter v. Khan, 2018). An act is considered as analogous to another in order to have formal legal consequences. These kinds of cases emerge in an ever more global world of intercultural contact and migration waves. On one hand, the main advantages are that this, sometimes, might help to integrate populations and show how law develops according to social context. On the other hand, the risk is that it might lead to legal insecurity and inequalities between citizens since they are exceptions to general rules and, also, these answers have come from courts in order to solve particular cases but still do not provide general criteria.

So far, we can conclude that a definition of legal pluralism is challenging and probably always incomplete. However, there are some relevant ideas that can lead a discussion and that provide common characteristics to get different phenomena together. Postmodern legal theory cannot lack a reflection on how legal pluralism is present in societies. This task implies a deep compromise to dialogue with other disciplines in order to understand the linguistic, anthropological, psychological, political, sociological and economic aspects, among others, that are involved in legal pluralism.

HELGA MARÍA LELL

References

De Sousa Santos, Boaventura (1987). "Law: A Map of Misreading: Toward a Postmodern Concept of Law", Journal of Law and Society 14(3), 279–302.

Galanter, Marc (1981). "Justice in Many Rooms: Courts, Private Ordering, and Indigenous Law", Journal of Legal Pluralism 13(19), 1–47.

Geertz, Clifford (1983). *Local Knowledge: Further Essays in Interpretive Anthropology*. Basic Books.

Griffiths, John (1986). "What is Legal Pluralism", Journal of Legal Pluralism 18(24), 1–55.

Kleinhans, Martha-Marie and Roderick Macdonald (1997). "What is a *Critical* Legal Pluralism", Canadian Journal of Law and Society 12(2), 25–46.

Merry, Sally Engle (1988). "Legal pluralism", Law and Society Review 22(5), 869–896.

Pospisil, Leopold (1971). *Anthropology of Law: A Comparative Theory*. Harper & Row.

Schiff Berman, Paul (2007). "Global Legal Pluralism", Southern California Law Review 80, 1155–1238.

Tamanaha, Brian (2000). "A Non-Essentialist Version of Legal Pluralism", Journal of Law and Society 27(2), 296–321.

Teubner, Gunther (1991–1992). "The Two Faces of Janus: Rethinking Legal Pluralism", Cardozo Law Review 13, 1443–1462.

49. Life below Water

Introduction

Covering more than two-thirds of the globe, the oceans have always had a major indirect impact on humankind by influencing weather patterns and events on land. By contrast, their direct impact has long been much smaller. Indeed, until half a millennium ago, the oceans only dominated the lives of coastal and insular communities as well as small polities based in the main trading ports located at strategic locations. The relationship between the oceans and humankind changed radically and irrevocably when European States started venturing onto the seas, initially to build global trade networks relying on the freedom of navigation and, later, to increase and intensify the exploitation of the ocean resources thanks to the innovations that those networks generated. As a result, there is hardly anybody today who is not affected in his or her daily life by the state of the oceans and the wide range of human activities taking place within their vast expanses.

Sustainable Development Goal (SDG) 14 within the 2030 Agenda for Sustainable Development

In view of the impact that the oceans have on humankind today, one would have expected ocean-related issues to have a prominent place in the 2030 Agenda for Sustainable Development (UN General Assembly, Resolution 70/1 of 25 September 2015), after they were absent from the UN Millennium Declaration (UN General Assembly, Resolution 55/2 of 8 September 2000) and were given their own section in the outcome document of the UN Conference on Sustainable Development entitled 'The future we want' (UN General Assembly, Resolution 66/288 of 27 July 2012). Instead, the three paragraphs of the Agenda describing the Heads of State and Government's vision only mention the 'oceans and seas' as part of the natural resources the use of which ought to be sustainable (para. 9). As far as they are concerned, the three paragraphs describing our world today contain only one sentence pointing to the serious impacts of climate change on 'coastal areas and low-lying coastal countries' (para. 14).

Likewise, the 21 paragraphs in the Declaration describing the new Agenda merely refer to sustainable fisheries, the need to support 'fishers in developing countries' and the commitment to 'adopt policies which increase ... sustainable ... fisheries development' (paras 24 and 27). Finally, indicator 2.3 involves inter alia doubling by 2030 the incomes of small-scale fishers. This limited focus on the oceans must be interpreted taking into account that '[t]he Sustainable Development Goals and targets are integrated and indivisible' (para. 55), although that fact is not reflected by the overall level of integration in the Agenda, which is 'far lower than justified from a science perspective and far lower than discussed in the ... preparation process' (Nilsson and Costanza, 2015, p. 9). From an integrative perspective, ocean-related policies and activities can contribute to SDGs other than SDG 14 – which is to 'conserve and sustainably use the oceans, seas and marine resources for sustainable development' – such as ending poverty (SDG 1), ending hunger (SDG 2), achieving gender equality (SDG 5), promoting full and productive employment (SDG 8) and fostering innovation (SDG 9). At the same time, a contribution to SDG 14 will be made by SDGs such as SDG 10 (reduce inequality within and among countries), SDG 13 (take urgent action to combat climate change and its impacts) and SDG 16 (promote peaceful and inclusive societies for sustainable development, provide access to justice for all and build effective, accountable and inclusive institutions at all levels).

SDG 14 within the ocean governance framework

Natural environment bias

An integrative approach to the SDGs is essential in the light of the fact that the scope of SDG 14 is narrower than the wide range of factors and interests that the ocean governance framework tries to reconcile under the umbrella of the 1982 UN Convention on the Law of the Sea (UNCLOS). Indeed, the majority of the SDG 14 targets (i.e. Target 14.1, Target 14.2, Target 14.3, Target 14.4 and Target 14.5) aim at addressing issues directly related to the natural environment. This bias towards the natural environment is confirmed by the fact that, when the Agenda refers explicitly to the UNCLOS, it is only with regard to '[e]nhanc[ing] the conservation and sustainable use of oceans and their resources' (means of implementation 14.c). As a result, the targets do not adequately reflect the concern expressed during the SDG negotiations that, unless human rights agreements are duly taken into account, local communities, indigenous groups and vulnerable individuals could be unjustifiably harmed in the process of trying to reach them (Ntona and Morgera, 2018, p. 215).

Limited focus on inequalities

By contrast, SDG 14 largely skirts around other developmental challenges embedded in the international economic order (IEO) and already highlighted half a century ago in the 1974 Declaration on the Establishment of a New International Economic Order. It is true that it acknowledges some structural inequalities that scar the IEO when it allows itself to drift beyond its focus on the natural environment, while remaining, however, locked inside a narrow living-resources paradigm. However, the Agenda contributes little to addressing those issues. Target 14.6 requires

> prohibit[ing] certain forms of fisheries subsidies which contribute to overcapacity and overfishing, eliminat[ing] subsidies that contribute to illegal, unreported and unregulated fishing and refrain[ing] from introducing new such subsidies recognizing that appropriate and effective special and differential treatment for developing and least developed countries should be an integral part of the World Trade Organization fisheries subsidies negotiations.

In this regard, Target 16.8 calls for '[b]roaden[ing] and strengthen[ing] the participation of developing countries in the institutions of global governance'. However, neither targets provide any concrete guidance on how the legal, political and economic context within which those negotiations take place will be changed in such a way that so-called 'developing and least developed countries' are able to ensure that they receive 'appropriate and effective special and differential treatment'. As far as it is concerned, Target 14.7 entails 'increas[ing] the economic benefits to small island developing States and least developed countries from the sustainable use of marine resources, including through sustainable management of fisheries, aquaculture and tourism'. It does not give guidance on what those economic benefits should be and whether the standard means to measure their increase are still fit for

purpose. As a result, the Food and Agriculture Organization of the United Nations will continue to express the value of sustainable fisheries as a percentage of a State's GDP, despite the need to move beyond the latter if one is to reach SDG 10 and give greater attention to factors such as subjective well-being, economic insecurity as well as social capital, sustainability and trust. Likewise, means of implementation (MoI) 14.b is problematical because it consists in '[p]rovid[ing] access for small-scale artisanal fishers to marine resources and markets' while, in the case of too many of those fishers, that access was taken away in the past and is actually a right that ought to be restored rather than a favour to be expected. It is often the same past injustices that, after robbing coastal communities of their knowledge and culture, provide a basis for the call for increased scientific knowledge, greater research capacity and the transfer of marine technology (MoI 14.a) with, incidentally, little assurance that these steps will produce outcomes adapted to the variety of cultural and natural conditions within which small-scale artisanal fishers operate.

Lack of attention to integrity and participation

The transformative potential of SDG 14 is weakened further by the fact that it does not tackle what are perhaps the two most crucial ocean governance issues relating to sustainable development. The first issue relates to the ability of coastal States to protect the integrity of their maritime zones and the resources over which they have sovereign rights. As one would expect because the sovereign equality of States is a fundamental tenet of international law, the UNCLOS treats all States equally when it comes to their rights and duties relating to their maritime zones and resources. However, there are striking inequalities, which often find their roots in the IEO, with regard to the human, financial and technical capacity of States to ensure that their rights are not infringed and that their duties are fulfilled. As a result, the ocean stakeholders who are the most in need of the steps taken to reach SDG 14 run in too many cases the risk of not being those who benefit from them.

The second issue relates to the ability of both coastal and landlocked States to participate on an equitable basis in the whole range of human activities at sea. SDG 14 ignores the fact that, for reasons often similar to those that explain the integrity challenges, many States do not have the human, financial and technical capacity required for their economies to absorb a fair share of the wealth generated directly or indirectly by activities such as shipping and deep sea fishing. This goes a long way towards explaining why, for instance, no African state is among the 29 entities who have until now contracted with the International Seabed Authority.

Marine spatial planning as implementing process

Marine spatial planning (MSP) offers an opportunity for integrating SDG 14 within the broader ocean governance framework. MSP can be defined as 'a public process of analyzing and allocating the spatial and temporal distribution of human activities in marine areas to achieve ecological, economic, and social objectives that are usually specified through a political process' (Ehler and Douvere, 2009, p. 18). It is the latter that will determine in each case whether and to which extent MSP succeeds in integrating SDG 14. MSP has undoubtedly the potential to do so because it 'brings many of the marine governance instruments together in a holistic manner and integrates different governance mechanisms related to the use of marine space within different sectors and agencies' (Soininen and Hassan, 2015, p. 5). However, 'effective MSP implementation requires the development of societal confidence in the spatial planning venture (ranging from the conviction that MSP will not result in the elimination of economic sea-based activities to the protection of the marine environment)' (Zervaki, 2016, p. 36). In other words, the various stakeholders need to be able to trust that MSP will produce outcomes that strike a fair balance between conflicting interests. Ultimately, that trust may well depend on the capacity of the political process to both capitalize on the inclusion into the 2030 Agenda of SDG 14 and, in the light of the latter's background and limitations, not allow it to play an overwhelming role in the search for widely acceptable compromises.

Conclusion

Life below water is vital to humankind's survival, but it constitutes only one aspect of the central role that the oceans have played in the cultural, economic and political processes that led us to where we find ourselves today and that we need to interrogate if we are to overcome the social threats that are likely to destroy us quicker than the impending changes in our natural environment. To do so requires approaching SDG 14 as part of the whole 2030 Agenda and within the context of the wider ocean governance framework. It also requires striving towards SDG 14 with due regard to the other factors that ought to influence the decision-making processes in order to arrive at decisions as widely acceptable as possible.

PATRICK H.G. VRANCKEN

References

Ehler, Charles and Fanny Douvere (2009). *Marine Spatial Planning: A Step-by-step Approach toward Ecosystem-based Management*. UNESCO.

French, Duncan and Kotzé, Louis J. (2018). *Sustainable Development Goals: Law, Theory and Implementation*. Edward Elgar.

Nilsson, Måns and Robert Costanza (2015). 'Overall Framework for the Sustainable Development Goals' in ICSU and ISSC. *Review of the Sustainable Development Goals: The Science Perspective*. ICSU.

Nordquist, Myron H., John Norton Moore, and Ronan Long (eds) (2018). *The Marine Environment and United Nations Sustainable Development Goal 14*. Brill.

Ntona, Mara and Elisa Morgera (2018). 'Connecting SDG 14 with the other Sustainable Development Goals through Marine Spatial Planning', *Marine Policy* 93, 214–222.

Recuero Virto, Laura (2018). 'A Preliminary Assessment of the Indicators for Sustainable Development Goal (SDG) 14 "Conserve and sustainably use the oceans, seas and marine resources for sustainable development"', *Marine Policy* 98, 47–57.

Soininen, Niko and Daud Hassan (2015). 'Marine Spatial Planning as an Instrument of Sustainable Ocean Governance' in Daud Hassan, Tuomas Kuokkanen, and Niko Soininen (eds), *Transboundary Marine Spatial Planning and International Law*. Routledge.

Stiglitz, Joseph E., Jean-Paul Fitoussi, and Martine Durand (2018). *Beyond GDP – Measuring What Counts for Economic and Social Performance*. OECD.

Wade, Robert Hunter (2003). 'What Strategies Are Viable for Developing Countries Today? The World Trade Organization and the Shrinking of "Development Space"', *Review of International Political Economy* 10(4), 621–644.

Zervaki, Antonia (2016). 'The Legalization of Maritime Spatial Planning in the European Union and Its Implications for Maritime Governance', *Ocean Yearbook* 30(1), 32–52.

50. Local Authorities

Local authority can be defined as the exercise of legitimated public or impersonal power over a given space by institutions or actors which enjoy recognition from subject communities, and which is not based solely on the use of coercive force. The exercise of local authority may comprise combinations of different formal, informal, State, and non-State actors and institutions and involve stakeholders across local, national and global scales. With this, there are two main approaches to understanding and conceptualizing local authority discussed below: a State centred, and society centred approach. Since the late 1980s, a large number of countries throughout the Global South have undergone political restructuring with decentralization, devolution, and local government reforms as influenced by the dominant 'good governance' paradigm of the World Bank and major donors. This has changed systems of local authority and urban governance in cities in the Global South, which continue to be challenged and changed by uneven forces of democratization, domestic economic growth, globalization and, not least, by the ever-increasing populations of most, if not all, Global South cities. Thereby, urban development has increased pressure on local government institutions to deliver services and exercise local authority. At the same time, a mass of non-governmental organization (NGO) and community-based initiatives have endeavoured to offset the challenges of absent basic services. Besides social and political change, these forces have demanded a rethink of conceptual and theoretical approaches and a realization of the heterogeneity of forms of urban governance, local authority and power relations in cities in the Global South.

State centred: The conventional or normative approach to 'local authority' is State centrist, because the term is used synonymously with various institutions of formalized local government, State institutions, the power structures of municipalities, departments and agencies, and statutory institutions, defined as the judiciary, executive, and legislative branches of central government. Similarly, the 'local' in local authority is typically taken to mean public officials positioned in close proximity to the communities they exercise authority over. From this perspective, establishing local authority entails central government demarcating political-administrative boundaries, establishing bureaucracies, and defining legal-rational jurisdictions. Related, the institutionalization of local authority concerns regularizing patterns of interaction between different State institutions and society with the aim of governing and managing social and political life and creating viable social contracts of obligations and privileges between the State and citizenry. The corollary is that 'local authority' carries out a range of important State functions from public service delivery and provision of numerous utilities, to the running of schools, and provision of law and order. The bestowing of rights to subjects to access these services establishes a citizenry and rights subjects, which, in return, pay taxes etc. and recognize the authority of the respective politico-legal institution and governing rules. Operationalizing local authority therefore demands establishing relations of recognition across State and society. Typically, however, the process also produces uneven topographies of power across cities because the resources and interests of central government, ministries, departments and municipalities are unevenly spread between and within the jurisdictions of State institutions and onto different population groups. The State centred perspective is based on an orthodox approach to local authority taking as a point of departure the idea of a unifying and homogenous State apparatus. This understanding has its roots in the perceived trajectory of Western cities and nation States. Thereby, the approach tends to frame Global South cities through a developmentalist lens as different, uncoordinated, or even insignificant compared to their Western counterparts. Related, the State-centrist approach to local authority interprets unfulfilled policy and law objectives in terms of weak State capacity. The corollary is that increasing the efficiency of statutory institutions with political-administrative, technical and managerial improvements is seen as key to solving challenges of governance and local authority. This means any political and power relational contests between and within different State and societal stakeholders tend to be smoothed over with an understanding that reforms will establish compliance and consensus. State-centrist understandings also tend to position formal and informal institutions as mutually exclusive and contentious, with local authority, as a function of statutory institutions, assigned positive traits of rationality and ability. In contrast, non-statutory and informal power relations are characterized as the formal State's ineffective or disorganized counterpart in need of improvement with better and more effective policies and laws. Hence, statutory and formal institutions are assigned with the legitimacy to regulate society and exercise local authority and successful governance is equated with effective government. Urban space and activities that are not formally regulated or are outside the control of government local authority and the 'rule of law' are thus framed teleologically as underproductive. In brief, State-centrist approaches to local authority point our attention to formal political systems, formalized institutions, and political decision-making processes and reforms assumed as based in rational thinking. There is widespread critique of State-centrist thinking related to local authority. Still, it remains a cornerstone of much of developmentalist reform, planning, policy and law.

Society centred: In opposing the above, a newer and critical approach to local authority focuses on subaltern dynamics, local (grassroots) political agency, and actual social realities and power dimensions. The emphasis is on complexity, hybridity, unevenness, fluidity and heterogeneity. This approach rejects the assumption of a central State power, and can take a point of departure in opposing and changing power relations between different formal and informal actors and institutions, which both enable and restrict the ability of different stakeholders to exercise local authority. Common critique points of the State centred approach are its basis in a false dichotomy between formal and informal social and political organization, and it missing the inventiveness and agency of ordinary people who contribute to the production of non-State forms of local authority. Thus, the view recognizes that governance and local authority may not be produced by statutory institutions, but established through ordinary people's everyday activities, interactions and entanglements with other powers as well. One key difference between the two main approaches is the former often alludes to an ideal or idealized end-result of how social and political life should be structured and concentrates on reaching an envisaged (developmentalist) end-goal through a series of governance reforms. Meanwhile, the latter focuses on the open-ended and messy socio-political process through which different State and non-State actors may gain and lose authority. Thereby, less attention is given to the mechanics of improving formal governance: the holding of regular elections, the administration of the welfare State, the paying of taxes, and the bureaucracy and management of government institutions, in favour of focusing on what such changes mean in terms of power and agency in society. Thus, an important dimension is not only to understand the institutionalization of formal local authority towards specific objectives, but to unravel configurations of 'actually existing authority' as combinations of different actors contesting and reaching consensus, though processes of formalization and informalization, and as influenced by local, national and global developmental agendas. The approach seeks to understand how the everyday process of living in a city shapes the ability of some actors to exercise local authority while others cannot, and how local power dynamics impact on different social categories of status around, for example, age, gender, race, ethnicity, class, and religion. This points to how the actual organization and exercise of local and public authority in different parts of cities in the Global South debunks the dominant myth of urban development and governance, habitually explained by adducing modernist theory and developmentalist thinking with assumptions of teleological unfolding that supposedly mirrors Western 'progress'. There is an increased realization both of the limited reach of formal institutions of local (State) authority, as well as the existence of many other types of local authority that shape peoples' lives, provide essential services to urban residents, and establish social contracts. Hence, State-of-the-art scholarship on local authorities in cities in the Global South typically concentrates on the governance perspectives and governmentality processes around who delivers what, what people need, and what they sometimes get. This provides new understandings of emerging power relations, authority and agency at the edge of statutory institutions. Related, local subjectivities and understandings of 'rights' which differ from State logics may also emerge as alternative non-State local authorities provide people with what they need to gain support. In turn, emerging local authorities recognize the claims and demands of urban residents as valid and as something to which they are entitled. Thus, the

PAUL STACEY

ability to live safely in a city and enjoy access to necessary resources may be more dependent on productive relations with non-State actors and alternative local authorities than formal relations with public officials and local government authorities. Accordingly, political spaces are produced and defined by 'alternative' authorities which may or may not cooperate with formal institutions of 'local authority'. Of particular relevance is therefore to understand cities and local authority in their own right and from emic perspectives of lived lives and from what actually is, rather than from theoretical and conceptual standpoints and expectations developed in the context of the Global North. The aim of such emic perspectives is to establish knowledge that much of the fabric of Global South urban life is in fact 'invisible' to urban planners and convincingly defies conventional urban development thinking.

The multiplicity of urban local authorities: Recent scholarship on urban local authority points out its unevenness and fluidity. Establishing local authority, whether by statutory or non-statutory instances, involves efforts to establish and legitimate control over space, land and people. In the process, understandings of identity and belonging, relations of recognition, rights to property and citizenship, access to representation, influence over decision-making, and jurisdictions are carved out. Thus, exercising local authority involves the everyday hammering out of formal and informal social contracts and relations of privileges and obligations, and relates to the production of social difference, space, inclusion and exclusion. In practice, processes of informalization and formalization towards establishing local authority may shift from interdependence to contention. A key objective of local authority, however, is to influence the way rulings and rules are made and followed by ordinary people in the spaces they live in, to increase legitimacy, and shape the social and political functioning and fabric of the given polity. Understanding, conceptualizing and analysing 'local authorities' in Global South cities therefore demands a realization of the multiplicity of forms that local authority can take. To exemplify, the forms that local authority take in Global South cities can be influenced by a range of forces derived from different, overlapping norms, sets of rules and legal standards. These may be complementary or contentious and include histories of laws and policies, colonial, traditional and customary institutional and structural legacies, influence from rural and domestic political and social economies, cultural tropes such as religion, and currents of developmental thinking around good governance, democratization, and neoliberalism. Hence, local authority can be shaped by legal pluralism and urban areas can experience a plethora of stakeholders that claim authority on the basis of different and changing registers and strategies of legitimacy. Governments may lack political incentives, resources, or staying power, and alternative authorities may step in to deliver goods and shape local social, political, cultural and moral codes on the basis of other legitimizing strategies. Despite increased attention in recent years, the realms and nuances of urban governance and urban local authority in the Global South remain understudied, particularly from the perspectives of the urban poor, marginalized and vulnerable. In especially marginalized urban areas such as slums and informal settlements, the governance of service delivery and operations of local authority can comprise hybrids of statutory and non-statutory actors and institutions. Stakeholders can include hometown organizations, faith based and religious organizations, charities, NGOs, individual entrepreneurs and businesses, political parties, parliamentarians, youth groups, community leaders and elders. The diversity of potential urban authorities demands that conceptualizations allow for the inclusion of non-State and non-statutory powers and consider who actually governs and exercises influence in areas where the reach of the formal State is limited. Furthermore, conceptualizations should consider that State institutions are not the only makers and endorsers of rights and claims to property and citizenship.

PAUL STACEY

References

Banerjee-Guha, Swapna (2010). *Accumulation by Dispossession: Transformative Cities in the New Global Order*. SAGE Publications.

Davis, Mike (2006). *Planet of Slums*. Verso.

De Boeck, Filip and Marie-Françoise Plissart (2004). *Kinshasa: Tales of the Invisible City*. Leuven University Press.

Falola, Toyin and Bisola Falola (2017). *The African Metropolis: Struggles over Urban Space, Citizenship, and Rights to the City*. Routledge.

Ferguson, James (1999). *Expectations of Modernity: Myths and Meanings of Urban Life on the Zambian Copperbelt*. University of California Press.

Lund, Christian (2008). *Local Politics and the Dynamics of Property in Africa.* Cambridge University Press.

Myers, Garth Andrew (2011). *African Cities: Alternative Visions of Urban Theory and Practice.* Zed Books.

Roy, Ananya (2003). *City Requiem, Calcutta: Gender and the Politics of Poverty.* University of Minnesota Press.

Simone, AbdouMaliq (2004). *For the City Yet to Come: Changing African Life in Four Cities.* Duke University Press.

Stacey, Paul (2019). *State of Slum: Precarity and Informal Governance at the Margins in Accra.* Zed Books.

PAUL STACEY

51. Migration

Migration is one of the most relevant issues in the worldwide scenario of the twenty-first century. In a very well-known work dated 1993, Castles and Miller introduced the expression the "age of migration" to highlight how, on the one hand, migration "has gained increasing political salience over the past decades" in the United States, in Europe but also in new immigration destinations such as Dubai. On the other hand, they tried to emphasize, also, how migration is reshaping our societies.

However, migration had remained as an uncontested domestic matter during the whole twentieth century; the arrival to the sphere of "high politics" is quite recent), even when scholars mainly agree that people have been always on the move, taking into account for example that the entire world was populated through mobility of people.

In this framework, two related breaking points are worth noticing: capitalism and migration controls. On the one hand, capitalism and migration are pointed out as inseparable processes (Zolberg, 1989; Sayad, 2010; Mezzadra, 2005). From a political philosophical insight, such an accumulation of people in the cities was going to create a problem both for the space in terms of circulation and for the "bodies", people, that were going to be reshaped to the new fashion of capitalism production.

The beginning of early industrialization in Europe moved masses of people from the countryside to the new-born cities. In this manner, Polish, Italians and even Algerians, among many others, almost literally built Europe at the end of the nineteenth century. At the very beginning, the organization was made through bilateral agreements or national laws that established, for instance, that Polish workers should leave the country each December. This whole process founded another modern product: the nation State. Although these new entities were in formation after Westphalia (1648), mobility did not represent a challenge at those times. In fact, the very idea of "illegality" to refer to the situation of an unauthorized mobility would appear later. In the words of Hollifield (2004, p. 890), "World War I marked a crucial turning point in the history of migration

and international relations". Particularly in the post First World War context, States that were being born at the same time encounter a powerful, organizing and excluding principle: nationality. In this manner, a foreign presence with intentions to remain in the territory (situation that started occurring after the First World War) posits a challenge on these new entities that were being built on the basis of the fictional idea of homogeneity. This is how migration control appeared: the passport, for instance, is created in the aftermath of the First World War. In South America, two countries of immigration such as Argentina and Brazil passed regulations to remove foreigners. In conclusion, human mobility was not an issue for States until the beginning of the twentieth century.

Worldwide economic development and its influence on migrations were going to have an impact also in the academic field. The insight in terms of economy, remittances, the "costs and benefits" of migration, etc. was and still is quite strong. The *laissez faire* view also gave rise to a certain understanding of migrants as isolated individuals, workers above all, that seek to maximize their benefits also by migrating. Pursuant to this understanding, migration is supposed to be a voluntary action whose responsibilities will fall, thus, on migrants.

Interestingly, another consequence of this influence can be noticed in the role of States. For many years, theoretical developments on migration paid little attention to the role of States in migration; as Saskia Sassen notes, the State remains as a backdrop, probably as a result of the limited place that liberal theories thought for States in general. In the words of Giuraudon and Joppke (2000), there has been a "peculiar divide between the study of migration flows and the study of State policies that seek to solicit, channel or contain these flows"; in particular, Massey (1999) suggests that few had attempted to describe in theoretical terms the behaviour of the State.

A more historical, social and even critical view appeared only during the 1990s (Zolberg, 1989). The political approach that brought the State back to the spotlight appeared only in the last years.

The final emergence of the State was understood as a "crucial role" it has to play (Arango, 2003) and among the factors (1. factors resulting from the social dynamics of the migration process; 2. factors related to globalization, transnationalism and North-South relations, among them politics regarding human rights; 3. domestic factors that belong to political systems (Castles, 2006)), that make and unmake migrations States have an outstanding place.

Somehow, this new attention to the State provokes a sort of overreaction that blurs the social dimensions of migration. Some scholars were going to say that national states were acting in such a way (by inhibiting, encouraging, impelling or forcing movement of people) that international migration is dominated by state policies that "nothing is so determinant of the volume of flows and types of wanted migrations as politics of admission" (Arango, 2003). One of the most quoted perspectives around the State is going to be provided by James Hollifield and his idea of the "emerging migration State": "the migration State is almost by definition a liberal State inasmuch as it creates a legal and regulatory environment in which migrants can pursue individual strategies of accumulation" (Hollifield, 2004, p. 901). Interestingly, neither the views that overemphasize the role of States nor the analysis that reduce such players to a minimal entity will provide a critical perspective about their role.

One of the most critical ideas was introduced by Sayad (2010) whereby his well-known postulate suggests "to think about immigration is to think the State" and "the State thinks itself by thinking immigration". Pursuant to this idea we become aware of (1) how migration challenges three main pillars of modern States: population, borders and (particularly by unwanted immigration) sovereignty, and (2) on the other hand, that an analysis that does not include the State shall provide an inaccurate perspective about migration. Moreover, Sayad holds that it is not possible to think of immigration separately from emigration, as far as they are part of the same process. In this manner, this perspective allows to challenge also other categories such as refugees, asylum-seekers, migrant workers, etc.: in the end, they all were created by entities; in the end, it is people on the move.

The reincorporation of the State into the migrations' field encountered another trend that was also related to human mobility: international human rights. Also a product of Modernity, the first appearance of these rights in the worldwide scope occurred after millions of displaced persons became *pariah* and *superfluous: We, the refugees.* The situation, dramatically described by H. Arendt as a perplexity of human rights, also shows the profound relation between human rights and movement. Precisely, human rights were "created", in theory, to recognize rights for people that (1) did not enjoy rights in the place where they belong by nationality, (2) so flew their country, but (3) are not welcomed anywhere. Human rights become a sort of portable rights for, as Arendt has noted, those that have nothing more to fall back upon than their life.

However, the relation between human rights and migrations is far from being that simple. International human rights present some blanks at the time of protecting migrants. Public international law in general and, particularly, the international human rights law (IHRL) provide few guidelines as to the way in which the migration policy of a State must be applied with respect to persons who are not their nationals. The core of the IHRL is the principle of equality and non-discrimination, a principle that was actually recognized as having a *ius cogens* character. Main covenants in human rights start by establishing that all the rights should be enjoyable for "all persons" without discrimination on the bases of "national origin". The reference to "legality" is included only for residence within a State but not for other rights.

Even so, migrant persons seem not to be covered by those provisions: at the international level, it is recognized that States enjoy an important margin of appreciation. The starting point in many documents on human rights is the power of the State to establish its own migration policy and to decide who and under which conditions may become a national. In the words of the Inter-American Court of Human Rights (IACtHR), although "the regular situation of a person in a State is not a prerequisite for that State to respect and ensure the principle of equality and non-discrimination ... this does not mean that they [States] cannot take any action against migrants who do not comply with national laws ... when taking the corresponding measures, States should respect human rights and ensure their exercise and enjoyment to all persons who are in their territory, without any discrimination ..." (IACtHR 2003. Condición Jurídica y Derechos de los Migrantes Indocumentados, Advisory Opinion OC-18/03, 17 September 2003. Series A No. 18, paras 118–119). Summing up, there is no human right to migrate or to enter into a State and the international legal background ended subordinating several rights to the condition of legality: the whole convention for migrant workers and their families is organized around legality. Legality is, in this manner, elevated from the right to residence and circulation (section 12, International Covenant on Civil and Political Rights) to an organizing principle to access all rights.

Against this background, recently some Latin American States have recognized the human right to migrate in their domestic laws, an experience without precedent in other countries throughout the world. In 2004, the first milestone of an ambitious project on migrations came into force in Argentina, which is an immigration country since the nineteenth century and still the main destination in South America: Federal Law 25,871. On the basis of a National Constitution that recognizes equal rights for "all inhabitants", this law brought two new and outstanding aspects: (1) the recognition in respect to migrants and foreigners of a right to migrate, together with other rights regardless of their administrative situation that even exceed the standards set forth at international level. For example, the right to vote in local elections was recognized by law; (2) the conferral of powers to the Judicial Branch to control the behaviour of the Immigration Board or to take certain decisions in migration control: e.g. the detention of foreign persons for migratory reasons should be authorized by the judiciary.

Other Latin American States have followed this trend by recognizing the human right to migrate (Uruguay and Ecuador in 2008; Bolivia in 2013) or key human rights for migrants regardless of their administrative situation (Mexico in 2013; Ecuador and Brazil in 2017). Even so, the implementation of these laws experienced great challenges. For instance, Argentinean law did not open borders. To the contrary, it established that the Immigration Board may exclude people by denying admission or cancelling residency based on a number of reasons, ranging from criminal grounds to more generic provisions such as non-compliance "with the requirements set forth in the law". In doing so, the law itself embodied a tension between conflicting provisions: the right to migrate and the State's sovereign power to determine who to admit and who to expulse. Particularly in the last years, Latin America is experiencing a context where countries throughout the region are tightening immigration controls, so the new

restrictions in Argentina such as Decree 70/2017 are not an exception.

The international scenario that arose from the 2001 terrorist attacks, the huge worldwide economical and financial breakdown from 2008 and the consequences of humanitarian crises in many countries in the last years (from Afghanistan and Syria to Central America and Venezuela) have installed a sensation of continued migration "crisis". However, insofar as a crisis is something exceptional, its continuity only speaks of the States' incapacity to deal with contemporary human mobility and to recognize their global responsibility on migration from, sometimes, devastated countries. Not even the Global Compact for Migration, a covenant adopted in 2018 under the scope of the United Nations, has taken more than baby steps to face a massive phenomenon. Despite the influence of a *human rights approach* in this agreement, the tension between States' sovereign and rights for humans fleeing because their life, security or future is at risk was not solved. People are not going to stop moving because more fences and controls are established. On the contrary, legal or physical barriers force migrants to seek another path, commonly most risky and increasing vulnerability. The only asset they usually carry with them is their humanity, their lives. After the untold consequences of millions of people, refugees, wandering throughout the world is that the international community agreed on recognizing rights anchored in the human being. As far as the current situation with migrants and refugees remains the same, maybe there is not enough awareness that we are attending a phenomena that might be referred to in the future as the twenty-first century genocide.

LILA GARCÍA

References

Arango, Joaquin (2003). "La explicación teórica de las migraciones: luz y sombra", Migración y Desarrollo. Available at: http://awww.redalyc.org/articulo.oa?id=66000102 accessed 10 September 2020.

Castles, Stephen (2006). "Factores que hacen y deshacen las políticas migratorias" in Alejandro Portes and Josh DeWind (eds), *Repensando las migraciones: Nuevas perspectivas teóricas y empíricas*. Porrúa.

Castles, S. and Miller, M. (1993). *The Age of Migration: International Population Movements in the Modern World*. Macmillan.

Guiraudon, Virginie and Christian Joppke (2001). "Controlling a New Migration World" in Virginie Giuraudon and Christian Joppke (eds), *Controlling a New Migration World*. Routledge.

Hollifield, James F. (2004). "The Emerging Migration State", International Migration Review 38(3), 885–912.

Massey, Douglas S. (1999). "International Migration at the Dawn of the Twenty-first Century: the Role of State", Population and Development Review 25, 303–322.

Mezzadra, Sandro (2005). *Derecho de fuga.* *Migraciones, ciudadanía y globalización.* Tinta Limón.

Orrenius, Pia, Philip Martin, and James Hollifield (1994). *Controlling Immigration: A Global Perspective.* Stanford University Press.

Sayad, Abdelmalek (2010). *La doble ausencia. De las ilusiones del emigrado a los padecimientos del inmigrado.* Anthropos, originally published 1999.

Zolberg, Aristide (1989). "The Next Waves: Migration Theory for a Changing World", International Migration Review 3(23), 403–429.

LILA GARCÍA

52. Mother Earth

Mother Earth

(also Earth Mother or Mother Nature)

Planet Earth and nature might be approached as a subject or as an object. Often the postures that sustain the first are eco-centric paradigms and advocate the unity of all its elements, in contrast with anthropocentric and Western understandings that assert a duality through a clear differentiation between the human and the human society from the flora, fauna and nature (Schillmoller and Pelizzon, 2013). Referring to Mother Earth commonly implies a biocentric stance and is the personification of what could be termed as nature, fertility and the sources of life.

Many cults and beliefs have developed and named their particular representations of Mother Earth, with attributes and characteristics that are far from being universal. Myths, deifications, legends and cosmologies, among others, relate and describe the origins, meanings, reasons or purposes of Mother Earth. For instance, it is related to the Greek primary goddess *Gaia* (also *Gaea*), termed Terra in the Roman myth, which arose from Chaos and is the embodiment of Earth in whose numerous offspring accounts the sky Uranus and the mountains Ourea. Another example comes from the South American Andean beliefs, particularly the Aymara and Quechua peoples, with the term *Pachamama* (*Pacha Mama* or *Mama Pacha*). This indigenous word is translated with certain inaccuracies as Mother Earth since the meaning of *Pacha* encompasses not only the abundance for being the source of food but also the cosmos, the order of the universe, time, space and movement (Albó, 1988). Human beings form part of Pachamama, making the society – nature duality non-existent. Communities, not individuals, interact in nature, comprising a community as all living and non-living elements, material and spiritual that exist in a local environment that particularizes them. There is no sense of domination of the environment, but of retribution and correspondence for the fruits and products received: *Pachamama* cares or punishes, gives life or illness, then for humans to be protected, it must be preserved and fed (Gudynas, 2014).

The Gaia Hypothesis of Margulis and Lovelock, which was developed mainly by the latter, considers the Earth 'a self-regulating system made up from the totality of organisms, the surface rocks, the ocean and the atmosphere tightly coupled as an evolving system. The theory sees this system as having a goal – the regulation of surface conditions so as always to be as favourable for contemporary life as possible' (Lovelock, 2010, p. 166). Human predatory intervention affects Gaia's self-regulation, producing ecological and climatic alterations that will eliminate the cause of the disturbance.

In *The Tragedy of the Commons*, Hardin accounted that although the world is finite, humanity mistakenly believes that its consumption is infinite, which imposes temperance on the free use of the commons through education, 'a fundamental extension in morality' and legal coercion to avoid ruin to all (Hardin, 1968, p. 1243). Boff understands that it is one thing to refer to it as land since it can be bought, sold, exploited economically and researched scientifically; nevertheless, quite another to name it Mother Earth because a mother has dignity and is a subject of rights that cannot be exploited, bought, or sold, but cared for, loved and venerated (Boff, 2010, pp. 141–142).

The dreadful consequences of environmental changes, rooted in pollution and overexploitation of nature, are commencing to encourage law-makers to grant legal protection to planet Earth. While a human-centered legal approach claims such a safeguard for the sake of human beings (for instance, the right to a healthy environment), the Earth-centered perspective pursues the recognition of rights to nature itself and regardless of their usefulness to people.

In this sense, Earth Jurisprudence (Berry, 2000) aims at human governance based on the welfare of the Earth as a whole. Wild Law (Cullinan, 2011) comprises the implementation of Earth Jurisprudence to maintain Earth's integrity and functioning. Earth Law argues the possibility to defend in court the ecosystems' rights to exist, thrive and evolve. According to Thomas Berry, '[e]very component of the Earth community has three rights: the right to be, the right to habitat, and the right to fulfill its role in the ever-renewing processes of the Earth community' (Berry, 2011, p. 229). Those rights should not be construed as opposed to human rights and the satisfaction of their vital needs (Zaffaroni, 2011).

The 2008 Constitution of Ecuador was the

first to recognize rights of nature, stating the respect to its existence, maintenance, restoration and regeneration of its life cycles, structure, functions and evolutionary processes (Articles 71–72). The Ecuadorian constitution bestows to all persons, communities, peoples and nations the possibility to claim the enforcement of these rights and, at the same time, gives them the right to benefit from the environment and natural resources that allow them good living (Articles 71 and 74).

The first successful case in favor of defending Pachamama's rights in Ecuador happened on 30 March 2011, when the Loja Provincial Court of Justice granted a constitutional injunction in favor of the Vilcabamba River and against the Loja Provincial Government. The widening of the Vilcabamba-Quinara road was intended at the cost of environmental damage due to the severe movement and deposit of rocks and excavation materials. The Court protected the rights of nature and suspended works until the Government objectively demonstrates that nature will not be affected. The Court dismissed the argument of a collision of the rights of Pachamama and the concerned population that the Loja Government raised, as the road widening can be done if no damage is caused. However, the Court held that even if there were such a conflict of rights, rights of nature would prevail.

On 21 December 2010 Bolivia enacted Law 71 on the Rights of Mother Earth, which comprises Mother Earth in its Articles 3 and 5 as a collective subject of public interest and a dynamic living system formed by the indivisible community of all life systems and living beings, interrelated, interdependent and complementary, that share a common destiny. In an enumeration not limited to other rights, Article 7 recognizes Mother Earth's rights to life, diversity of life, to water, to clean air, to balance, to restoration, and to a life free of contamination.

The World People's Conference on Climate Change and the Rights of Nature convened in Cochabamba, Bolivia, and proclaimed on 22 April 2010 the Universal Declaration of the Rights of Mother Earth. Article 1 defines Mother Earth as a 'living being ... unique, indivisible, self-regulating community of inter-related beings that sustains, contains and reproduces all beings'. Article 2 recognizes to Mother Earth inherent and inalienable rights: (a) to life and to exist; (b) to be respected; (c) to regenerate its bio-capacity and to continue its vital cycles

and processes free from human disruptions; (d) to maintain its identity and integrity as a distinct, self-regulating and interrelated being; (e) to water as a source of life; (f) to clean air; (g) to integral health; (h) to be free from contamination, pollution and toxic or radioactive waste; (i) to not have its genetic structure modified or disrupted in a manner that threatens its integrity or vital and healthy functioning; and (j) to full and prompt restoration for violation of its rights by human activities.

The civil society organized around the world International Rights of Nature Tribunals, which acknowledges rights to nature. These Tribunals are non-binding and were convened in Quito, Ecuador (2014), in Lima, Peru (2014), in Paris, France (2015), in Bonn, Germany (2017), and in Santiago de Chile (2019).

The rights of Mother Earth remain contested in most countries and international law continues to protect the environment for the sake of human interests. Even though the United Nations (UN) General Assembly unanimously adopted in 2009 a resolution designating the 22 April of each year as the International Mother Earth Day (A/63/L.69), there is still no official international recognition of her rights. In this context, the 1972 UN Stockholm Declaration seeks 'the preservation and enhancement of the human environment ... for it is essential to his well-being and to the enjoyment of basic rights'. The 1992 Rio Declaration on Environment and Development proclaims that 'human beings are at the centre of concerns for sustainable development' (principle 1), which is coupled with environmental protection (principle 4). The parties of the 1994 UN Convention to Combat Desertification in Those Countries Experiencing Serious Drought and/or Desertification declare in the preamble their determination 'to take appropriate action in combating desertification and mitigating the effects of drought for the benefit of present and future generations'. The first principle of the 1992 UN Framework Convention on Climate Change states that 'the Parties should protect the climate system for the benefit of present and future generation of humankind' (Article 3), which also guides the 1997 Kyoto Protocol. The 2000 Millennium Development Goals set the seventh goal to 'ensure environmental sustainability' to reverse the loss of environmental resources, improve access to safe drinking water and improve the lives of slum dwellers, among others. The common vision (I.1) of the 2012 Declaration of the UN Conference on Sustainable Development or Rio+20 to ensure 'the promotion of an economically, socially and environmentally sustainable future for our planet and for present and future generations'. The preamble of the UN General Assembly Resolution Transforming our world: the 2030 Agenda for Sustainable Development refers 'to protect the planet ... so that it can support the needs of the present and future generations'.

LEONARDO VILLAFUERTE PHILIPPSBORN

References

Albó, Xavier (1988). *Raíces de América: El mundo aymara*. UNESCO.

Berry, Thomas (2000). *The Great Work: Our Way into the Future*. Bell Tower.

Berry, Thomas (2011). 'Rights of the Earth: We Need a New Legal Framework Which Recognizes the Rights of All Living Beings' in Peter Burdon (ed.), *Exploring Wild Law: The Philosophy of Earth Jurisprudence*. Wakefield Press.

Boff, Leonardo (2010). 'Panel Derechos de la Madre Tierra' in *Conferencia Mundial de los Pueblos sobre el Cambio Climático y los Derechos de la Madre Tierra. Discursos y Documentos Seleccionados. Tiquipaya, Cochabamba, 20 al 22 de abril 2010* (pp. 141–145). Estado Plurinacional de Bolivia – Ministerio de Relaciones Exteriores.

Cullinan, Cormac (2011). *Wild law: A manifesto for Earth justice* (2nd ed). Chelsea Green Pub.

Gudynas, Eduardo (2014). *Derechos de La Naturaleza y Políticas Ambientales*. Tinta Limón.

Hardin, Garrett (1968). 'The Tragedy of the Commons', Science 162(3859), 1243–1248.

Lovelock, James (2010). *A Final Warning*. Penguin Books Ltd.

Schillmoller, Anne Louise and Alessandro Pelizzon (2013). 'Mapping the Terrain of Earth Jurisprudence: Landscape, Thresholds and Horizons', Environmental and Earth Law Journal 3(1), 1–32.

Zaffaroni, Eugenio Raúl (2011). *La Pachamama y El Humano*. Ediciones Madres de Plaza de Mayo.

53. Multilateral Development Banks

Multilateral development banks (MDBs) are specialized international organizations (IOs) that fund development projects and programs, primarily in the Global South. But they cannot be understood without reference to the wider geopolitical context, in which they were created and evolved over time. To capture the interaction between law and context, we begin by sketching the post-war environment in which the pillars of the international economic order were erected (I). The World Bank (the Bank), as the oldest MDB and a blueprint for the institutional design and standards of younger MDBs, will then serve as a prime example as we go on to address the effects of decolonization, the Cold War, and the new focus on poverty eradication and governance. This also entails challenges against the Bank which have increased its legal accountability (II/III). A further section will reflect on the pluralization through new actors and more recent *informal* modes of governance (IV). Finally, we offer three key take-aways from the historical contextualization provided (V).

I   The international economic order after the Second World War

The emergence of MDBs was closely linked to the international economic order in the aftermath of the Second World War. At the time, reconstruction of war-torn countries, not least in Europe, required multilateral investment cooperation. For this reason, the allied forces convened an international conference in Bretton Woods (US) in July 1944 to design key pillars of the post-war financial and economic architecture – now known as the International Monetary Fund (IMF) and the International Bank for Reconstruction and Development (IBRD). The goal was to establish an institutionalized economic framework, which would address the severe financial and economic consequences of the war, and create a regulatory environment, in which the international economic conditions could be monitored, influenced, and shaped proactively through multilateral channels. Constituting this new institutional framework, the IMF was tasked to provide international monetary cooperation, currency exchange stability, and emergency funds (IMF Charter, Article I), while the IBRD should assist in the reconstruction and development of its Member States (IBRD Charter, Article I(i)).

The institutional design and intellectual matrix of the IBRD reflected the economic and political interests and preferences of Western powers, particularly of the United States. It was ensured through three key institutional features laid down in the founding treaty. First, voting power in the Bank was not based on the principle of one state, one vote, but weighted according to the financial support to the base capital of the Bank. This ensured that the US and its wealthy Western allies could dominate the decision-making of the Bank. Second, the non-political mandate translated the liberal idea of a (supposed) separation of economic and political aspects into the law of the Bank and secured the ideological orientation toward (Western) liberal capitalist economic policy. Finally, an obligation to focus funding on particular projects excluded larger, non-specific funding (Sundhya Pahuja (2011). *Decolonizing International Law.* Cambridge University Press; Dann, 2013).

II   Decolonization, regionalization of MDBs, and the creation of the International Development Association

During the 1950s, the financially prudent business model of the IBRD quickly gained the trust of both the public and private sector and resulted in a large-scale and broad membership portfolio. By the time the Inter-American Development Bank (IADB) was founded in 1959, institutional imagination was heavily influenced by the IBRD model, providing the ground for its lasting influence on other MDBs (Devesh Kapur, John P. Lewis and Richard C. Webb (1997). *The World Bank: Its First Half-century.* Brookings Institution Press).

The unfolding decolonization process then exerted pressure on the existing institutional framework on various fronts, in particular the demand for funding by newly independent States. In response and within a relatively short time period, the African Development Bank (AfDB) in 1964, the Asian Development Bank (ADB) in 1966, the Caribbean Development Bank (CDB) in 1969, and the Islamic

Development Bank (IsDB) in 1975 were founded. Beyond the mere need for funding, regional MDBs were also established to create an institutional power balance to predominately Western authority at the IBRD. However, even newer MDBs like the IADB and the ADB were dependent on significant shareholding by Northern donor countries, and particularly the US, which ensured their influence even inside the new institutions (Suzuki, 2008).

At the same time, newly independent States further demanded a Special UN Fund for Economic Development (SUNFED) to support their economic needs. The creation of the International Development Association (IDA) in 1960 was a compromise, mitigating strong resistance of some donor countries. IDA was not created as a separate agency as originally demanded by countries of the Global South, but as the concessional lending arm of the already existing IBRD. While the modalities of re-financing the Bank (through cyclical replenishments by Member States instead of issuing bonds on capital markets and collecting interest rates from borrowers) and lending (in the form of grants or loans well below the market rate offered by the IBRD) were new, IDA's institutional and legal framework adopted the operational and institutional modalities already in place at the IBRD. Despite regionalization and institutional pluralization, the World Bank – now consisting of the IBRD and IDA – maintained its influential position (Dann, 2019).

Political and financial factors contributed to the World Bank's status of *primus inter pares* in the MDB landscape. On the one hand, the Bank's financial resources further expanded and remained unmatched through more diversified borrowing on capital markets beyond the US and the strong backing by Western States. On the other hand, the Western powers had a clear political interest in a well-funded World Bank that supported poorer countries, which were seen to be in constant danger of succumbing to the communist lure of the Cold War if their economic situation further deteriorated. This also prompted a shift from reconstruction to development, described as the Bank's 'discovery of poverty' (Arturo Escobar (2012). *Encountering Development: The Making and Unmaking of the Third World*. Princeton University Press), which had an immense impact on its institutional identity and legal framework. Until today, the goal to 'end extreme poverty by 2030' in line with the UN's 2030 Agenda for Sustainable Development continues to serve as an enduring and sufficiently malleable justification for the Bank's development activities.

III The evolution of the mandate and its problems

While reconstruction included (re-)building cities, highways and dams, the so-called 'poor' or 'underdeveloped' were now considered to lack a whole lot more – be it food, health, or education. At Bretton Woods, the vague notion of development was more a terminological afterthought to the more self-explanatory mandate of reconstruction. Now, 'development' began to serve both as an instrumental legal concept and as the Bank's self-given *raison d'être* in times of shifting geopolitical landscapes. This turn from infrastructure financing to combating poverty was driven in particular by the new president McNamara and resulted in a more far-reaching and intrusive approach as part of the support offered to borrowing countries. It also set in motion an ever-expanding understanding and rethinking of the concept of development. While it was initially equated exclusively with measurable economic growth, the re-interpretation allowed the Bank to usurp broader competences but also brought about legal problems.

Beginning in the 1980s, the Bank began offering program assistance (sector and budget support), known as structural adjustment programs, which not only financed concrete projects but directly aimed at the borrower's domestic regulatory space. This already stretched the legal framework of the founding treaty provisions that required 'special purpose' for each project. Furthermore, the consistent failure to achieve the desired results led in the 1990s to a turn to 'governance', assuming that underlying systemic and governmental failures were causal for the success or failure of any development project. This, however, ran counter to the World Bank's Charter, which explicitly provides for the Bank's non-political mandate (IBRD Charter, Article V Sec. 10; IDA Charter, Article V Sec. 6) and mirrors the institution's self-understanding from early on as a purely technocratic bank serving as a specialized agent for its principals, i.e. the Member States. In a legal opinion from 1990, the Bank's General Counsel, Ibrahim Shihata, defended this broadening of the Bank's engagement by offering a distinction between political and economic considerations – only the latter would have 'direct and obvious economic results' and thus permit funding by the Bank. Irrespective of whether this argument holds due to the underlying political assumptions naturally inherent in almost any economic consideration, however, a broader engagement could also be justified by reference to the term's substantive evolution (Sinclair, 2017; Dann, 2013).

At the same time, external pressure by civil society mounted against the Bank (Rajagopal, 2003). It was triggered by its structural adjustment lending and by its financing of projects with massively adverse impacts on people's lives. Resistance against the Narmada dam project in Gujarat (India), which displaced more than 100,000 people, in particular, is seen as the tipping point. Embedded in a wider civil society discourse and activism addressing the Bank's lack of accountability, protests against the project pressured the Bank to introduce more rigorous environmental and social policies applicable to its projects. This led to the creation of a new internal accountability framework. The Bank created the Inspection Panel (IPN) in 1993, which provides an internal, independent remedy to counterbalance MDBs' far-reaching functional immunity from legal process in front of national courts (Naudé Fourie, 2009). In 2017–2018, the Board of Directors authorized a review of the IPN which resulted in clarifications regarding the Bank's accountability in cases of Bank-executed trust funds and co-financing scenarios, while also formalizing the IPN's advisory role in its mandate and allowing for earlier disclosure of IPN investigation reports. Until today, all other MDBs have created similar mechanisms like the IPN or are in the process of establishing them. Despite the improvement they offer, the impact and competences of these quasi-judicial fora should not be overestimated because of their limited fact-finding and advisory function vis-à-vis the management and the Board of Directors. However, recently introduced access to information policies with the default rule of public disclosure have further strengthened the accountability mechanisms due to an increase of transparently accessible internal documentation needed to challenge the Bank's activities.

IV   Pluralization through new actors and informal modes of governance

In the past years, two new MDBs were founded, the New Development Bank (NDB) in 2014 and the Asian Infrastructure Investment Bank (AIIB) in 2015. This is the institutional manifestation of the increasing economic and geopolitical weight of the BRICS, but also stems from the unwillingness of the West to open the World Bank to more influence from these States. These new banks for the first time have former borrowing States and emerging economies as their biggest shareholders (Dann, 2019). While the AIIB includes many non-regional members from the Global North, they both exclude the US. In a way, this means that a genuinely more pluralistic environment has formed. However, both the AIIB and the NDB are elements of a bigger geopolitical strategy in which the BRICS, and particularly China, seek to establish a complimentary framework of foreign policy and development aid, which entails more funding options but also new dependencies for borrowing countries of the Global South. In the case of the AIIB, the return to a focus on hard infrastructure instead of social investments might also signal a more hands-off approach compared to the World Bank. At the same time, the institutional design and best practices of the new actors only differ slightly from older MDBs. In this regard, the World Bank has thus not surrendered its influence.

The motivation behind what has been described as a wider trend of 'counter-institutionalization' (Michael Zürn (2018). *A Theory of Global Governance: Authority, Legitimacy, and Contestation.* Oxford University Press) in global governance is in the case of MDBs inherently linked to the question of institutional governance and control. Ever since the founding of the IBRD and unlike at other IOs, MDB Member States are not treated as equals in the decision-making processes of these institutions. Rather, weighted voting according to the individual capital contributions and shareholdings of the members define the procedures in the hierarchically highest bodies, i.e. the Board of Governors and the Board of Directors. Even at institutions with comprehensive membership of countries from the South and North, this has established a clear dominance of the donors vis-à-vis the borrowers. Accumulated frustration with the ambivalent results of an extensive 'voice reform' introduced at the World Bank in 2010 is therefore likely to have contributed to creating new institutions with veto powers held by countries other than the US (as is the case for the World Bank, IADB, and European Bank for Reconstruction and Development (EBRD)) or Japan (in the case of the ADB).

Besides increasing institutional plurality, MDBs have in the past years opted for ever more *informal* modes of governance, from standard setting to the production of indicators. Governance tools, like the 'Doing Business Indicators' by the World Bank Group or the ADB's annual 'Key Indicators for Asia and the Pacific', are part of a highly effective yet opaque global regulatory framework in which MDBs are part of a diverse range of public, private, and hybrid actors. Not constituting black-letter law, these indicators diffuse the policy ideas developed within the epistemological space of the banks in order to nudge actors and regulate the international economic sphere. These kinds of instruments build upon a broader evolution of MDBs in which a focus is put on the extensive collection and interpretation of economic information and data, transforming development banks into knowledge banks that evaluate and propose solutions in line with their own scientific models and their inherent biases (Riegner, 2015). Data, for instance, constitutes one of three key pillars of work the World Bank has identified to contribute to the Sustainable Development Goals (SDGs) and the 2030 Agenda for Sustainable Development (besides finance and implementation) (Frank Fariello, Laurence Boisson de Chazournes and Kevin E. Davis (eds) (2016). 'Financing and Implementing the Post-2015 Development Agenda: The Role of Law and Justice Systems', The World Bank Legal Review 7). It will be interesting to observe whether the AIIB and NDB will also broaden the scope of their engagement once they have the institutional capacity to do so. Besides infrastructure investments, the AIIB's mandate already provides for less clearly defined investments in 'other productive sectors' (AIIB Charter, Article 1 Sec. 1).

V Three key take-aways

Three observations stand out. First, MDBs reflect how global order evolves – be it after the Second World War, during the era of decolonization, after the fall of the iron curtain or most recently through the increasing economic and political weight of the BRICS. Second, MDBs have become key pillars of the international financial and economic order. The standards, rules and solutions they promote have significant regulatory effect vis-à-vis borrowing countries and the individuals on the ground. Third, MDBs' mandates evolve over time – from reconstruction, to development, to (informal) governance. At the same time, institutional law mechanisms like weighted voting helped fend off challenges to the existing power structures, which long favored the Western members. Notably, these institutional features were readily adopted by new actors like the AIIB and NDB with the mere change that now other States sit in the driver's seat of these institutions.

PHILIPP DANN AND THOMAS DOLLMAIER

References

Bradlow, Daniel D. and David Hunter (eds) (2010). *International Financial Institutions and International Law*. Wolters Kluwer.

Dann, Philipp (2013). *Law of Development Cooperation*. Cambridge University Press.

Dann, Philipp (2019). 'Institutional Law and Development Governance', Law and Development Review 12(2), 537–560.

Lichtenstein, Natalie (2018). *A Comparative Guide to the Asian Infrastructure Investment Bank*. Oxford University Press.

Naudé Fourie, Andria (2009). *The World Bank Inspection Panel and Quasi-Judicial Oversight*. Eleven International Publishing.

Rajagopal, Balakrishna (2003). *International Law from Below*. Cambridge University Press.

Riegner, Michael (2015). 'Towards an International Institutional Law of Information', International Organizations Law Review 12(1), 50–80.

Sinclair, Guy Fiti (2017). *To Reform the World: The Legal Powers of International Organizations and the Making of Modern States*. Oxford University Press.

Suzuki, Eizuke (2008). 'Regional Development Banks' in Rüdiger Wolfrum (ed.), *Max Planck Encyclopaedia of International Law*. Oxford University Press.

Xu, Jiajun (2016). *Beyond US Hegemony in International Development: The Contest for Influence at the World Bank*. Cambridge University Press.

54. Multistakeholderism

Background

Multistakeholderism is an umbrella term, broadly used to denote a preference for including multiple interested parties or stakeholders in a process, project or policy. One particularly illuminating definition suggested by Raymond and Denardis is of multistakeholderism "as two or more classes of actors engaged in a common governance enterprise concerning issues they regard as public in nature, and characterized by polyarchic authority relations constituted by procedural rules" (Raymond and Denardis, 2015, p. 573). Multistakeholderism allows, at a minimum, various interested parties to participate, share preferences, experiences and expertise in public policy-making.

At the global level, multistakeholderism emerged with the promise of a panacea to governance problems and gaps in traditional global governance mechanisms. This shift from purely State-based interaction models to governance permeating above and beyond the State coincided with the end of the Cold War and the shift from a bi-polar global political system into one that favoured, at least on the surface, multilateralism. Of course, the emergence of new policy areas that tested and exposed inadequacies in the ability of the State to govern led to a search for requisite technical and capacity-related competences both at the domestic and the international level. There was thus a turn to the involvement of intergovernmental organizations, non-governmental actors and the private sector, in various areas of common concern or interest. Multistakeholderism was thus presented as the future of multilateralism, which was traditionally statist (Martens, 2007).

Multistakeholderism and governance gaps

The impetus behind the multistakeholder model was one of creating complementarity, or a type of "horizontal subsidiarity" as Reinicke termed it, between traditional State-led governance models and the new type of models incorporating the public and the private under one roof. In the absence of world government, multistakeholderism was proposed as the designated filler for governance gaps. The various iterations of the multistakeholder governance model seek to address regulatory gaps, expertise gaps, information gaps, resource gaps and implementation gaps. In this respect, Gleckman distinguishes three categories of "multistakeholder governance groups": policy-oriented (such as the Kimberley Process Certification Scheme for managing so-called blood diamonds or the World Commission on Dams), product and process-oriented (such as the International Standardization Organization or the Better Cotton Initiative), and project-oriented (such as public private partnerships (PPPs) at the national level) (Gleckman, 2018). Multistakeholderism may inform law-making in all three categories but as Benedek notes, the contributions and the influence of non-State stakeholders are more readily visible when it comes to international law-making in its softer forms in policy and product or process-oriented settings (Benedek, 2011). Legally speaking, agreements adopted by multistakeholder coalitions are non-binding in nature, based on voluntary commitments. Compliance with the voluntary agreements often relies on reporting and/or certification, sometimes accompanied by external audits. The premise is to create a compliance pull among peers based on jointly agreed action, targets or principles. Whether such compliance pull is achieved through multistakeholderism remains a question as research points to mixed results in terms of compliance and effectiveness.

Many multistakeholder mechanisms purport to address multiple governance gaps at the same time. For instance, the rapid advance of information and communication technologies (ICT), particularly the Internet of Things, created a strong impetus for multistakeholder approaches towards the regulation of this policy area that defied traditional territorial constraints by definition. Private actors that were already involved in the advent and dissemination of the new technological advancement were considered better-positioned to make policies, given their more complex understanding of the public policy questions and their access to technological know-how. Of course, different facets of internet governance are handled by different mechanisms and States are incorporated into the process in so far as they coordinate internationally, regulate and enforce standards domestically.

Various multistakeholder mechanisms,

including the Global Fund to Fight AIDS, Tuberculosis and Malaria (The Global Fund) or the Global Alliance for Vaccines and Immunisation (Gavi) have addressed global health issues, such as transmittable diseases (HIV/AIDS, malaria, tuberculosis) and immunization. These mechanisms sought, first and foremost, to fill expertise, resource and implementation gaps. For instance, Gavi was launched at the World Economic Forum (WEF) in 2000 with a 750 million USD pledge from the Bill and Melinda Gates Foundation, incorporating UN agencies such as the World Health Organization (WHO) and UNICEF, the World Bank, the private sector and civil society. The Gates Foundation is likewise a key player in the Global Fund, having contributed over 2.2 billion USD since 2002 (The Global Fund Website, "Bill & Melinda Gates Foundation", available at https://www.theglobalfund.org/en/private-ngo-partners/resource-mobilization/bill-melinda-gates-foundation/ accessed 12 September 2020).

Multistakeholderism in the governance of sustainable development

The 1992 UN Conference on Environment and Development that took place in Rio de Janeiro led to the adoption of Agenda 21 on sustainable development alongside two environmental conventions, namely the UN Framework Convention on Climate Change (UNFCCC) and the Convention on Biological Diversity. Concentrating on the socio-economic aspects of sustainable use of environmental resources, Agenda 21 noted that governments had the responsibility of integrating environment and development in policy-making "in partnership with the private sector and local authorities, and in collaboration with national, regional and international organizations, including in particular UNEP, UNDP and the World Bank" (UN Conference on Environment and Development, 1992, para. 8.2). In addition, Agenda 21 espoused a clear multistakeholder perspective by highlighting the particular roles of the so-called "major groups", which included women, children, youth, indigenous peoples and communities, non-governmental organizations (NGOs), local authorities, workers and trade unions, business and industry, scientific and technological community, and farmers (Ibid, Section III). The motivation behind an expressly multistakeholder-based vision was

linked to the contention that "[o]ne of the fundamental prerequisites for the achievement of sustainable development is broad public participation in decision-making" and that the ability to ensure such participation rested on the access to information on issues in the domain of environment and development (Ibid, para. 23.2). The overall goal was to create a partnership between different stakeholders on sustainable development that would drive more effective efforts at the local, national, regional and global levels.

The Millennium Development Goals (MDGs) formalized the role given to partnerships, and hence multistakeholderism in sustainable development, by calling for the development of a Global Partnership for Development with targets that were linked to the development of "an open, predictable, rule-based, non-discriminatory trading and economic system", addressing the needs of least developed countries (LDCs), small island developing States (SIDSs) and landlocked developing countries, lasting solutions to the problems of high-indebtedness, access to "affordable essential drugs in the developing world – in collaboration with pharmaceutical companies", and collaboration with the private sector in the dissemination of benefits of ICT advancements (MDG 8). Accompanying the MDGs was the launch of the UN Global Compact, which set voluntary principles focusing on corporate sustainability under the headings of human rights, labour, environment and anti-corruption.

Ten years after the Rio Earth Summit, the Johannesburg World Summit on Sustainable Development (2002), dubbed Rio+10, culminated in the Johannesburg Declaration, which recognized a role for partnerships in meeting needs linked to access to basic human needs such as clean water, sanitation, shelter, health care, food, energy, in protecting biodiversity, in regional cooperation, as well as in increasing participation of different stakeholders in global policy-making and implementation. The Johannesburg Summit also prepared the stage for so-called Type II outcomes, the precursor to today's multistakeholder partnerships (MSPs). These Type II outcomes would be distinct from the intergovernmentally negotiated Type I outcomes of the summit and based on voluntary commitments of like-minded stakeholders to be mutually decided and implemented.

Multistakeholderism is incorporated into

the 2030 Agenda for Sustainable Development in various ways. The document calls on the private sector, civil society and philanthropic organizations to assist in the deployment of financial resources for the achievement of the 2030 targets, as well as for the mobilization of knowledge, expertise and technology. The Addis Ababa Action Agenda on Financing for Development also puts an accent on mobilizing private and public financial resources for sustainable development, including from the businesses, civil society and philanthropy sources.

In terms of the implementation of the 2030 Agenda, multistakeholderism is institutionalized through Sustainable Development Goal (SDG) 17, which calls for "[s]trengthening the means of implementation and revitalize the global partnership for sustainable development". Two of the targets defined by SDG 17 are specifically on MSPs in the context of systemic issues linked to partnerships. According to the SDGs, MSPs are mechanisms to "mobilize and share knowledge, expertise, technology and financial resources, to support the achievement of the sustainable development goals in all countries, in particular developing countries" (Target 17.16). This reference highlights the perceived role of multistakeholder approaches particularly in filling expertise/know-how, information, resource and implementation gaps linked to sustainable development. This unbridled confidence in the necessity of multistakeholder approaches in tackling governance issues linked to sustainable development is all the more visible in Target 17.17, which calls for the "encourage[ment] and promot[ion of] effective public, public private and civil society partnerships, building on the experience and resourcing strategies of partnerships".

Benefits and caveats

Multistakeholderism may offer certain benefits over solely State-based models. These may include a broader participation base in making public policies of global relevance. In addition, multistakeholder mechanisms may offer better fitness for purpose and targeted interventions in issue areas that require technical know-how and expertise. From a resource allocation perspective, multistakeholderism may offer a more rapid response to urgent problems such as disasters, dedicated resources from multiple channels with a longer-term perspective in an issue area that is not systematically funded,

and a certain degree of respite from dependence on State-level political agendas in the way resources are allocated. Deploying its strengths, multistakeholderism may create various opportunities at the global stage. Multistakeholder approaches may facilitate the setting of issue-based global agendas, mobilization of financial resources, pooling of dedicated know-how and expertise and the development of capacity. In fact, the move to multistakeholderism over intergovernmental arrangements in the sustainable development domain, particularly in the 2002 Johannesburg Summit, was traced to the desire to bypass what was considered the arduous and not always fruitful process of intergovernmental negotiations, to facilitate financial commitments to specific issue areas and to mobilize implementation capacity faster.

The benefits offered by multistakeholderism are tempered by the inherent weaknesses linked to participation, legitimacy and accountability. The broader participation base offered by multistakeholderism is limited by the selectivity of participants in the various multistakeholder governance mechanisms. Many of the same "usual suspects" may be involved in various multistakeholder mechanisms in a given issue area, raising questions about how representative the purported broad participation actually is. With respect to multistakeholder mechanisms engaged in the delivery of services such as education or health care that are considered public goods, it is unclear to what extent the populations that are the supposed main beneficiaries are involved in the design and implementation of programmes and policies. Legitimacy of multistakeholderism, particularly with respect to making public policy or decisions on resource allocation to public goods and services, is another concern. Multistakeholder initiatives and mechanisms often rely on the participation of private actors such as multinational corporations or philanthropic donors when making and implementing policy and decisions. Whether the public policy choices made by private actors are or can be legitimate is an open question. It has been suggested that low input legitimacy, such as lack of representativeness in policy or decision-making, can be compensated by a strong output legitimacy, that is the effectiveness of the problem-solving capacity of a given mechanism (Bäckstrand, 2006).

Multistakeholderism also presents a number of accountability challenges. Firstly, there are clear democratic accountability deficits in making and implementing global, regional or national public policy by engaging non-public actors, who are not subject to democratic scrutiny the way that governments routinely are. One particular concern is the corporate capture of the sustainable development agenda, which may enhance the structural influence of corporations in setting the rules of the game. Coupled with the fact that corporations and their activities are routinely protected by hard law at the international arena but their impacts on rights-holders often only subject to voluntary guidelines, the partnership model of multistakeholderism may in fact exacerbate the power imbalances at the global level (McKeon, 2017). Secondly, there are accountability questions linked to how financial resources, which often include public financial resources, are allocated. In fact, prioritization of certain policy concerns over others in allocating dedicated resources without public scrutiny may give rise to selectivity and possible fragmentation in the implementation of public policy goals, including those linked to sustainable development (Martens, 2007). Thirdly, the accountability of a given multistakeholder mechanism or partnership vis-à-vis its beneficiaries remains unregulated or at best, regulated ad hoc.

Even before the advent of multistakeholder-based Type II Outcomes at Johannesburg, concerns around the abdication of government duties by outsourcing, undue corporate influence, greenwashing, risk of diverting existing official development assistance (ODA) sources, and lack of accountability and transparency were voiced by various participants (La Viña, Hoff and De Rose (2003). "The Outcomes of Johannesburg: Assessing the World Summit on Sustainable Development", SAIS Review, 23(1), 53–70). In fact, ahead of Johannesburg, the World Summit on Sustainable Development (WSSD) Secretariat had prepared guidelines and principles for partnerships. Various principles such as the harmonization of objectives in line with Agenda 21 and the MDGs, complementarity with intergovernmentally agreed outcomes, the integration of the three dimensions (economic, social and environmental) of sustainable development in partnership programmes sought to overcome possible fragmentation of agendas. The principles of mutual respect and shared responsibility of partners based on voluntary commitments and active engagement with local communities sought to achieve a broad and representative participation base.

In addition, various guidelines on performance such as clearly defined objectives, measurable and time-bound targets, tangible results, identified funding sources, international impact and added value were proposed. Finally, principles linked to accountability such as transparency, good faith implementation, equal accountability among all partners were proposed as a panacea to concerns around misuse of resources and capture of public agendas by private actors. Ultimately, however, these guidelines were not explicitly incorporated into the outcome documents of the Johannesburg Summit by negotiating parties. Nearly two decades after the Johannesburg Summit, concerns linked to harmonization of sustainable development agendas, representative participation, effective performance and accountability remain. Research has uncovered issues linked to effectiveness, accountability and legitimacy and sought to improve the performance of multistakeholderism at the global level by proposing models of performance and engagement. What may be equally important, particularly as the 2030 Agenda and the accompanying SDGs have carved a formal role for multistakeholderism in achieving sustainable development, is to also question whether this model of global governance can adopt the requisite architecture in terms of representativeness, accountability and effectiveness to merit being championed.

GAMZE ERDEM TÜRKELLİ

References

Abbott, Kenneth W. (2012). "Engaging the Public and the Private in Global Sustainability Governance", International Affairs 88(3), 543–564.

Bäckstrand, Karin (2006). "Multi-Stakeholder Partnerships for Sustainable Development: Rethinking Legitimacy, Accountability and Effectiveness", European Environment 16(5), 290–306.

Beisheim, Marianne and Andrea Liese (eds) (2014). *Transnational Partnerships: Effectively Providing for Sustainable Development?* Palgrave Macmillan.

Benedek, Wolfgang (2011). "Multi-Stakeholderism in the Development of International Law" in Ulrich Fastenrach et al. (eds), *From Bilateralism to Community Interest: Essays in Honour of Judge Bruno Simma*. Oxford University Press.

Gleckman, Harris (2018). *Multistakeholder Governance and Democracy: A Global Challenge*. Routledge.

Martens, Jens (2007). *Multistakeholder Partnerships: Future Models of Multilateralism*. Occasional Paper.

McKeon, Nora (2017). "Are Equity and Sustainability a Likely Outcome When Foxes and Chickens Share the Same Coop? Critiquing the Concept of Multistakeholder Governance of Food Security", Globalizations 14(3), 379–398.

Pattberg, Philipp and Oscar Widerberg (2016). "Transnational Multistakeholder Partnerships for Sustainable Development: Conditions for Success", Ambio 45(1), 42–51.

Raymond, Mark and Laura DeNardis (2015). "Multistakeholderism: Anatomy of an Inchoate Global Institution", International Theory 7, 572–616.

Reinicke, Wolfgang H. (1998). *Global Public Policy: Governing without Government?* Brookings Institution Press.

55. National Policy Space

National policy space refers to the capacity of countries to set and implement domestic strategies to support sustainable development, including poverty reduction, economic growth, access to essential public services, climate change adaptation and mitigation and environmental protection. It encapsulates two key ideas: (1) countries should have the scope, flexibility and authority to design and implement national social and economic policies appropriate to their circumstances; and (2) countries retain the right to regulate and impose restrictions on social and economic activities in the public interest. International law and institutions of global economic governance and development cooperation are seen as central to the question of policy space, either as providing an enabling international environment that is supportive of national policy space or constituting a framework which circumscribes this policy space.

Situating national policy space within international law and governance

The first explicit recognition of the concept of policy space and its iteration in a multilateral document can be found in the outcome document of the 11th session of the United Nations Conference on Trade and Development (UNCTAD), known as the São Paulo Consensus in 2004. Defining policy space as 'the scope for domestic policies, especially in the areas of trade, investment and industrial policies', the agreement recognized the importance for developing countries to strike an appropriate balance between the benefits of international legal commitments and integration into the global market and the constraints such undertakings may have on national capacity to formulate and implement country-specific national development strategies (UNCTAD, 2004, para. 8).

The term policy space is now widely used in international agreements on development cooperation, most notably in the UN's 2030 Agenda for Sustainable Development and the Addis Ababa Action Agenda (AAAA) for Financing for Development, both of which commit to respecting 'each country's policy space and leadership to implement policies for poverty eradication and sustainable development, while remaining consistent with relevant international rules and commitments' (UN, 2015a, para. 63 and UN, 2015b, para. 9). Consistent with the language in the São Paulo Consensus, these documents also reiterate the primacy of national policies and development strategies in social and economic development processes and the importance of an enabling international environment to support domestically driven policies.

Despite this contemporary iteration, however, the concept of policy space can be traced back to a longer lineage in international law. It is rooted in key principles underpinning the post-war, post-colonial international legal order, including the principles of self-determination, sovereign equality of States, and non-interference in the internal affairs of sovereign States. The concept of policy space also gives recognition to the principle of special and differential treatment for developing countries within international law, especially international economic law, on account of the historical legacies and contemporary circumstances of their inclusion into the global economy. Asserting national policy autonomy is seen as a corollary to exercising national sovereignty over natural resources and affirming States' and communities' collective right to development, cognisant of the special circumstances of developing countries and their commitments under international law (see South Centre, 2006; UNCTAD, 2004).

In many ways, the notion of policy space, flexibility and recognition of national ownership over the development agenda reflects the continuing battles in international law and institutions of global governance over the scope, content and form of social and economic organization in countries in the Global South. It also reflects the contestation between developing countries over the appropriate international fora to govern international economic relations, with developing countries asserting the UN (where they have greater voice and representation) as the space for negotiations over global economic affairs while industrialized countries have consistently shifted economic issues to institutions they control, such as the International Monetary Fund (IMF), the World Bank and the Organization for Economic Cooperation and Development (OECD).

Accordingly, it is instructive that the term does not feature in the major development texts emanating from these institutions. Instead, the preferred terminology is one of 'country ownership' over national development strategies. The OECD Paris Declaration on Aid Effectiveness, for one, does not contain any references to the concept of policy space but instead uses the term 'ownership' to refer to country leadership and implementation of national development strategies in the context of the harmonization, alignment and accountability of aid practices. Within this framework of understanding, policy space is less about prioritizing national autonomy over broader structural social and economic planning but rather about mapping national strategies (where they exist) onto technical processes of public expenditure management and donor reporting mechanisms and supporting capacities of aid-recipient countries to do so. For example, when approaching the question of aid conditionality, the concerns are less about the impact of conditionalities on national policy space but on how and when such conditions should be drawn from national development plans and how to align them with donor requirements (see OECD, 2005, paras 14–16).

Globalization, international economic law and the curtailment of policy space

Contestations over the usage of the term aside, it is clear that changes in the legal, regulatory and policy landscape of the global economy have resulted in significant constraints on countries to design and implement policies that respond to their domestic circumstances to meet sustainable development objectives. Domestic space for designing and implementing appropriate strategies for sustainable development have been increasingly curtailed by: (a) the rapid integration of countries into global economy through unilateral policies (whether imposed or voluntary) that render countries susceptible to external market conditions and weakening the effects of national instruments; and (b) the design of international economic law and regulatory norms that 'diminish sovereign control over national policy instruments' (Akyüz, 2010).

These two sources of external constraints over countries' policy-making overlap and reinforce each other primarily because of the tentacular reach of international economic law (IEL) and the policies of global economic governance institutions, including international financial institutions (IFIs) in the past three decades. The surge to prominence of IEL over the past few decades has resulted in the proliferation of rules, institutions and jurisprudence and also in its heightened influence over domestic policy-making and national regulation. In terms of its relationship to national policy space, one can argue that contemporary IEL has become both *expansive* and *intimate*. *Expansive* in that the regulatory coverage of international economic rules extend to a broad range of economic and non-economic activities within the territorial jurisdiction of States. IEL is also *intimate* in coverage in that these regulatory intrusions seek to reorganize fundamental aspects of the domestic social, economic and political constitution.

For example, the regulatory scope of international trade law is no longer confined to border controls on imports and exports of goods and services but includes regulation on a vast array of internal policies called non-tariff barriers (NTBs) or 'behind the border' issues, including agricultural and industrial subsidies, intellectual property rights, competition policy and government procurement. The ability of national governments to deploy policy instruments, such as tariffs, quotas, subsidies, and controls over the entry and exit of foreign investment and financial flows have been significantly restricted by binding commitments under the World Trade Organization (WTO), free trade agreements (FTAs) and international investment agreements (IIAs).

In other words, international trade and investment can constrain the ability of governments to adopt policy instruments to support national development strategies, including utilizing tariffs and subsidies to protect and promote domestic economic sectors. The principle of national treatment which prohibits host States from treating foreign investors or imported goods differently from local investors or locally produced goods can also restrict government measures to incentivize and protect industries which are at early stages of development known as 'infant industries'. There have also been concerns over the expansive interpretation of treaty standards by investment arbitral tribunals and the large sums of damages involved is leading to a 'regulatory chill' in host States, where governments are reluctant to support social or economic development or respond to environmental problems for fear of litigation under investment treaties.

All these constraints have arisen primarily because the development of international rules and policies of global economic governance in the post-war period have not been neutral, often reflecting the interests and priorities of industrialized countries which have traditionally controlled the normative and operational agendas in these institutions and law-making platforms (see Akyüz, 2010; Faundez, 2010). Specifically, we have seen a concerted focus in international economic law-making in the realm of trade, investment and finance to deepen economic integration through policies of liberalization, deregulation and privatization and less on developing mutually conducive, multilaterally negotiated rules to effectively manage cross-border trade, finance and investment and resolve disputes arising from trading partners. More recently, we have also seen how powerful States can and do exert geopolitical and economic influence over institutions of global governance to extract greater concessions or, worse, refuse to be bound by commitments under previously agreed terms, leading, for example, to a question mark over the future of multilateral trade agreements.

Finance, regulatory gaps and resource conditionality

The loss of policy space from IEL asymmetries is compounded by the regulatory gaps in the international financial architecture and the policies of the IFIs which have enormous influence over social and economic programming in developing countries. Unlike in international trade or investment where we have seen greater legal consolidation, international financial governance since the collapse of the Bretton Woods system of fixed exchange rates in the late 1970s has moved away from the central supranational structure of financial governance established in the immediate post-war period. It is now a system characterized by decentralization and fragmentation, reliant on transgovernmental networks and non-binding 'soft law' rather than international legal obligations. At the same time, the deregulation and liberalization of financial sectors have resulted in the integration of domestic financial markets with the international financial system, heightening the risk for global financial contagion.

Economists have argued that deepening financial integration without corresponding effective international financial coordination results not only in instability for developing countries with less robust domestic regulatory and policy mechanisms, it can also constrain the policy space of countries in terms of their capacity to utilize financing for national development and undertake measures to prevent or respond to financial crises if they occur (see Akyüz, 2010). For example, reliance on international financial markets for sovereign financing has meant that domestic financial systems are much more vulnerable to decisions and policy-making undertaken in financial centres located in industrialized countries and have little capacity to supervise the policies of these countries due to lack of effective international rules or supervision of these major financial centres.

Where financial crises prevention fails, there are also few rules on how to mitigate or resolve such crises and the attendant socio-economic effects on developing countries. The absence of a comprehensive sovereign debt workout mechanism, for instance, means that resolution of sovereign debt crises is often protracted and uncertain and leads to large-scale, so-called 'bailouts' by institutions of public finance, notably the International Monetary Fund (IMF) and World Bank. This, in turn, leads to another significant constraint on national policy space, which is the imposition of conditionalities attached to public financing extended to indebted countries by the IMF, World Bank and other multilateral development banks. Originally designed to safeguard multilateral public resources, conditionalities today serve more as instruments for inducing fiscal, monetary and structural economic policy reforms in recipient countries. These conditionalities have been criticized as being 'one-size fits-all', imposing generic policy prescriptions which pay little heed to the specific circumstances of individual countries subject to them and which follow a general pattern of fiscal and monetary austerity and the promotion of the aforementioned deregulation, liberalization and privatization policies that seek to integrate domestic economies with the external international economic order without consideration for their domestic development trajectories (see Tan, 2016).

The breadth and depth of international policy and regulatory encroachment into States in the globalized economy today is very significant and the extensive nature of their reach fundamentally reorders national policy space. The lack of control over national policy instruments means that governments do not have the tools available to them to respond to domestic circumstances when they arise or at least, not without incurring a high cost for doing so. However, recognition of the importance of safeguarding or even reclaiming this policy space has increasingly surfaced within international economic law-making and development policy-making fora as discussed above. There are also tentative steps in some arenas, such as the international investment regime, to recalibrate some of the substantive provisions and take into account the policy space for development action in arbitral tribunals and new substantive commitments. It remains to be seen, however, whether these new articulations of policy space will lead to a revision of the existing rules of IEL and global economic governance or are merely marginal revisions to a broader structural asymmetry.

CELINE TAN

References

Akyüz, Yilmaz (2010). 'Multilateral Disciplines and the Question of Policy Space' in Faundez, Julio and Celine Tan (eds), *International Law, Economic Globalization and Developing Countries*. Edward Elgar.

Faundez, Julio (2010). 'International Economic Law and Development: Before and After Neoliberalism' in Julio Faundez and Celine Tan (eds), *International Law, Economic Globalization and Developing Countries*. Edward Elgar.

O'Donoghue, Aoife and Ntina Tzouvala (2016). 'TTIP: The Rise of Mega-Market Trade Agreements and Its Potential Implications for the Global South', Trade, Law and Development 8(2), 181–209.

OECD (2005). *Paris Declaration on Aid Effectiveness*. OECD.

South Centre (2006). Operationalizing the Concept of Policy Space in the UNCATD XI Mid-Term Review Context. South Centre Analytical Note SC/GGDP/AN/GEG/1, May 2006.

Tan, Celine (2016). 'Shifting Sands: Interrogating the Problematic Relationship between International Public Finance and International Financial Regulation' in Marc Bungenberg, Christoph Herrmann, Markus Krajewski, and Jörg Philipp Terhechte (eds), *European Yearbook of International Economic Law* 17, 343–375.

UN (2015a). *Transforming Our World: 2030 Agenda for Sustainable Development*. UN General Assembly Resolution 70/1, 21 October 2015.

UN (2015b). Addis Ababa Action Agenda of the Third International Conference on Financing for Development. General Assembly Resolution 69/313 of 27 July 2015.

UNCTAD (2004). São Paulo Consensus, UNCTAD XI, TD/410, 25 June 2004.

UNCTAD (2019). *The Least Development Countries Report 2019: The Present and Future of External Development Finance: Old Dependence, New Challenges*. UNCTAD.

56. Natural Resources

To describe nature as a "natural resource" presupposes a certain episteme and ontology: the very term "natural resources" is not neutral, but already has assumptions about law and development intrinsically bound up in it. "Natural resources" are commonly defined as "materials or substance of a place which can be used to sustain life or for economic exploitation" or as "material from nature having potential economic value or providing for the sustenance of life" (Schrijver, 2010, p. 2) or as "materials and processes that exist in nature and that are considered of actual or potential use or value to humans" (Morgera and Kulovesi, 2016, x). The World Trade Report on Trade in Natural Resources defines them as, "stocks of materials that exist in the natural environment that are both scarce and economically useful in production or consumption, either in their raw State or after a minimal amount of processing" (World Trade Organization, *World Trade Report 2010: Trade in Natural Resources*). To understand nature as a "resource", thus already presumes an epistemological frame in which nature is subject to human appropriation and a normative frame in which such appropriation is seen as both necessary and desirable. In this conceptualization, "nature has clearly been stripped of her creative powers; she had turned into a container for raw materials waiting to be transformed into inputs for commodity production" (Shiva, 2010, p. 228).

"Nature resources" must therefore, as resource geographers have shown, be understood as irreducibly social and "inherently political" (Bakker and Bridge, 2008, p. 219). The category of "natural resources" reflects the ways in which the non-human world is considered useful or of value to humans as well as "competing claims over access to, control over, and definitions of nature" by different actors (ibid). Understandings of law and development are intimately tied up with the relations of knowledge and control that determine how a "radically heterogenous world of nature is ordered, fractured and delivered up to the economy" (ibid). As Ileana Porras has shown, nature became visible to the European law of nations only once it was articulated "as a material thing subject to appropriation, reducible to property, and capable of entering into the stream of commerce" (Ileana Porras (2014). "Appropriating Nature: Commerce, Property and the Commodification of Nature in the Law of Nations", Leiden Journal of International Law 27, 641: 642). Law, also, plays a critical background role in "the way in which the conceptual transformation of nature ... into 'resources' is institutionalised" (Pahuja, 2012, p. 398). Thus, the very category of "natural resources" is already produced by international law and underpinned by specific normative assumptions about the desirability and type of "development".

The United Nations Environment Programme Global Resources Outlook 2019 documents that natural resource use has tripled since the 1970s and continues to grow, and moreover that current patterns of resource use have negative impacts on both environmental and human health and that benefits of resource extraction are distributed in vastly unequal ways, across and within countries. Therefore, it is urgently necessary to rethink practices of resource extraction and management, and the role international law plays in the governance of natural resources by unravelling the destructive ways in which understandings of international law, development and natural resources have become intertwined.

International legal discourses on natural resources have been framed by concerns about finitude and scarcity and preoccupied with the fact that the occurrence of natural resources is unequally located around the globe (Bothe, 2005). This has raised acute questions of distribution, both "horizontally" between contemporaneous actors and inter-temporally between present and future actors, that scholars and lawyers have sought to address through ethical or justice frameworks as well as utilitarian managerial frameworks. The formal international legal principles applicable to different natural resources depends on the jurisdiction they are subject to. Principles of "equitable share" are applied to shared natural resources that cross the boundaries delineating territorial States. In relation to resources in areas beyond national jurisdiction – fisheries in the high seas, the minerals of the deep seabed and outer space – the "first come, first served" approach, grounded in the principle of the right of appropriation, has gradually been moderated. For the former, duties are imposed to adopt some "conservation measures" to allow for the long-term harvesting "at levels which can produce the maximum sustainable yield, as qualified by relevant environmental and economic factors" (United Nations Convention on the Law of the Sea, Article 119, para. 1(a)). The latter were recognized as part of the "common heritage of mankind", a principle that allows for extraction and exploitation but also imposes some distributional obligations. Although technological challenges placed deep sea mining proposals on hold for a period, there is now a rush towards large-scale exploration and potential future mining of the deep sea bed (Isabel Feichtner and Surabhi Ranganathan (2019). "International Law and Economic Exploitation in the Global Commons: Introduction", The European Journal of International Law 30, 541). Similarly, outer space now appears as the new frontier for mineral exploitation, with proposals for extra-terrestrial mining of asteroids and the moon. Legal reforms in some jurisdictions that recognize the private property rights over minerals mined in space are facilitative and enabling for such developments.

The general position taken in discussions on natural resources is that "international law assigns the exclusive right to use a resource to the State where the resource is situated" and that decisions about its governance as well as "the intertemporal distribution of use is left to the unfettered discretion of that State" (Bothe, 2005, p. 378). Yet, historically and in ongoing ways, international law has shaped the domestic governance of natural resources in ways that have encouraged extraction. The processes of resource extraction were central to colonialism and, as Tendayi Achiume highlights, these legacies continue to structure the present so that "[t]he contemporary political economy of global extractivism cannot properly be understood without reference to its colonial origins" (Achiume, 2019, para. 22). Colonial extraction of precious metals – often dependent upon the violent coercion of Indigenous and slave labour – turned Latin America into the "region of open veins". In Africa the process of colonization – affirmed by the Berlin Conference of 1884–1885 – extracted natural resource wealth from the continent, alongside the dispossession, environmental destruction and exploitation of labour (ibid: para. 23). Under the Mandate System of the League of Nations, resources in non-European territories were characterized by colonial administrators as belonging not just

to the peoples of those territories but also the "international community". This history, and ongoing patterns of unequal accumulation and impoverishment, means that "[e]xtractivsim, both now and in the past, stands at the centre of . . . dependency and inequality" (ibid: para. 8). The structural allocation of wealth and power in the global economy is directly related to the regulation of natural resources and how the benefits and harms of resource extraction are distributed.

More generally, ideas about nature, and especially about its control, extraction and productive use, have shaped key international legal concepts and underpin notions of sovereignty, jurisdiction, territory, human rights, property and more (Usha Natarajan and Kishan Khoday (2014). "Locating Nature: Making and Unmaking International Law", Leiden Journal of International Law 27, 573). Practices and techniques of natural resource governance were, both in the colonies and the "metropole", central to the actualization of State territorial sovereignty and the rise of the administrative State (see Nancy Peluso and Peter Vandergeest (2001). "Genealogies of the Political Forest and Customary Rights in Indonesia, Malaysia, and Thailand", The Journal of Asian Studies 60, 761). Around the end of the nineteenth century, concurrent with the "the growth and 'modernization' of national economies", the contours of contemporary forms of State-centric resource regulation emerged which brought together the science of natural resource management together with administrative capacities of the State started to emerge (Bakker and Bridge, 2008, p. 220). In the post-war period, there were attempts to broaden these techniques of scientific resource management from the national to the international domain, driven in part by concern about the war's drain on resources but also fears that growing demands for decolonization would reduce South-North resource flows. One of the functions of the Food and Agriculture Organization of the United Nations (FAO) established in 1945 was "the conservation of natural resources and the adoption of improved methods of agricultural production" (Constitution of the Food and Agriculture Organization of the United Nations (1945), Article 1.2(c)). The 1949 United Nations Scientific Conference on the Conservation and Utilization of Resources brought technical experts from around the global together to discuss possibilities of continuous development and widespread application of the techniques of scientific conservation and utilization to manage resources and resource scarcity globally. This endeavour was described as key to "point four" of Truman's 1949 inaugural address where he inaugurated the modern logic of development and committed to a "bold new program for making the benefits of our scientific advances and industrial progress available for the improvement and growth of underdeveloped areas".

Given that colonial relations structured patterns of resource extraction and that such extraction of natural resources has been imagined as key to development, it is not surprising that newly decolonized States saw control over natural resources as critical for both political economic self-determination as well as modernization and development. Third World States used international law to make demands for permanent sovereignty over natural resources (PSNR) as part of a broader claim to political and economic self-determination (Schrijver, 1997). The demand of PSNR sought to "leverage a State's resource endowment to bring about greater economic equality" often through the nationalization of resource interests (Pahuja, 2012, p. 403). In 1962 the General Assembly affirmed the right of peoples and nations to permanent sovereignty over natural resources and that this right must be "exercised in the interest of their national development and of the well-being of the people of the State concerned" (GA Resolution 1803 (XVII), para 1). This call for PSNR was subsequently a central element of demands for a New International Economic Order. However, these claims were "deflected by the principles of compensation", which operated to normalize the private ownership of natural resources in international law and made these doctrinally controversial questions subject to the jurisdiction of the international law concerned with protecting the rights of foreign investors (Pahuja, 2012, p. 403).

From the 1970s onwards, the nascent field of international environmental law also imposed limits on the right of nation States to exploit resources within their territory, especially where such exploitation was seen to impact on matters of global "common concern", such as the conservation of biodiversity. Principles of sustainable development highlight the need for the "sustainable use of natural resources and the Earth and the protection of the environment on which nature and human life as well as social and economic development depend" (International Law Association (2002). "Declaration of Principles of International Law Relating to Sustainable Development", preambular para. 13). More recently, the 2030 Agenda for Sustainable Development highlighted that "social and economic development depends on the sustainable management of our planet's natural resources" (General Assembly Resolution 70/1, para. 33).

Yet these imperatives for the sustainable management of resources continuously confront economic imperatives for increased extraction, driven by a globalized market economy with a ravenous demand for raw materials. The global trade regime has been structured in ways that promote the extraction and global circulation of natural resources. The 1947 General Agreement on Tariffs and Trade opens with the preambular recognition that "relations in the field of trade and economic endeavour should be conducted with a view . . . developing the full use of the resources of the world and expanding the production and exchange of goods". When the World Trade Organization (WTO) was founded in 1995, the agreement establishing it included a similar provision, however moderated slightly to suggest that trade relations should be conducted so as to "allo[w] for the optimal use of the world's resources in accordance with the objective of sustainable development, seeking both to protect and preserve the environment and to enhance the means for doing" (Marrakesh Agreement Establishing the World Trade Organization (2005), preambular para. 1). More recently, the WTO has expressed concerns about "resource nationalism" and how restrictions placed on the export of natural resources can undermine the functioning of the world economy by constraining access to raw materials, and has argued for rules to support open markets and the removal of "distortions" in order promote free trade in natural resources. Critics have highlighted how the macroeconomic reforms required by structural adjustment programmes (SAPs) imposed by the World Bank and the International Monetary Fund as part of loan conditionalities had a clear impact on the over-exploitation of the natural resources of countries in the Global South as well as the regulatory framework for their governance (see David Reed (2013). *Structural Adjustment, the Environment and Sustainable Development*. Earthscan).

Whilst natural resource extraction was

historically understood as key to development, in the past few decades there has been an increased focus on how natural resource extraction can pose threats to development. The term "Dutch disease" was first coined by The Economist in 1977 to describe how the manufacturing industry in the Netherlands declined after the discovery and exploitation of gas in the North Sea. Later, Richard Auty developed the term "resource curse" to describe the strong tendency by resource rich countries to waste their resource advantage due to over-optimistic assessments as well as the failure to implement economic and governance policies to ensure direct revenues from resource extraction into productive social investments. In the past two decades, a specific idea of "natural resource governance" has emerged, promoted by international financial institutions as well as certain non-governmental organizations (NGOs) and think-tanks, on the assumption that the "economic future" of heavily impoverished resource rich countries depends on whether the opportunity presented by resource extraction is "seized or missed". The Natural Resource Governance Initiative published their Natural Resource Charter in 2010 in order to provide "policy options and practical advice" on the best ways to manage natural resource wealth. Concurrently there has been the rise of multistakeholder, private governance initiatives such as the Extractive Industry Transparency Initiative (EITI), the Forest Stewardship Council and the Kimberly Process to promote the "good" governance of specific resources.

Human rights principles increasingly inform frameworks for the effective and sustainable management of natural resources (Gilbert, 2018). Human rights-based approaches to the management, use and protection of natural resources seek to remedy the fact that "structural inequities in access to natural resources often lead to the violation of the fundamental rights of specific populations" (ibid: p. 8). Scholars have also emphasized the need for an international legal principle of "fair and equitable benefit sharing" that could assist in ensuring a fairer distribution of the harms and benefits of resource extraction. Yet, most radical perhaps is the assertion by Indigenous peoples of their collective right to self-determination over their natural resources, including the right to freely dispose of those resources (Declaration on the Rights of Indigenous Peoples, GA Resolution 61/295, Article 26). Similarly, the right to sovereignty over natural resources, and thus the right to freely dispose of their wealth and resources, is being reclaimed as a right of "peoples", not of States.

Indigenous peoples, peasants and other local communities are at the frontlines globally resisting the exploitation of natural resources. Such land and environment defenders face intensive violence, threats, intimidation and often death, protecting territories from resource extraction. In such mobilizations against extractivism the tight knot that has characterized the relationship between international law, development and natural resources is disentangled. In the present moment it is particularly urgent to cultivate alternative understanding of the relationship between law and the natural world and to learn from diverse ontologies and epistemologies that have been marginalized by the international legal, economic and political order. Indigenous jurists highlight how Indigenous laws, culture and knowledge systems establish a "relational beingness with the natural world" and "authoriz[e] a relational obligation to care for country" (see Irene Watson (2018). "Aboriginal Relationships to the Natural World: Colonial 'Protection' of Human Rights and the Environment", Journal of Human Rights and the Environment 9, 119). Such articulations of different relationships between law and the natural world and provide vital resources for rethinking and reimagining the destructive triad between international law, development and natural resources.

JULIA DEHM

References

Achiume, Tendayi (2019). *Global Extractivism and Racial Inequality: Report of the Special Rapporteur on Contemporary Forms of Racism, Racial Discrimination, Xenophobia and Related Intolerance*. United Nations.

Bakker, Karen and Gavin Bridge (2008). "Regulating Resource Use" in Kevin R. Cox, Murray Low, and Jennifer Robinson (eds), *The SAGE Handbook of Political Geography*. SAGE.

Bothe, Michael (2005). *Environment, Development, Resources: Collected Courses of the Hague Academy of International Law*. Vol. 318. Brill.

Gilbert, Jérémie (2018). *Human Rights and Natural Resources: An Appraisal*. Oxford University Press.

Merino-Blanco, Elena and Jona Razzaque (2011). *Globalisation and Natural Resources Law: Challenges, Key Issues and Perspectives*. Edward Elgar.

Morgera, Elisa and Kati Kulovesi (eds) (2016). *Research Handbook on International Law and Natural Resources*. Edward Elgar.

Pahuja, Sundhya (2012). "Conserving the World's Resources" in James Crawford and Martti Koskenniemi (eds), *The Cambridge Companion to International Law*. Cambridge University Press.

Schrijver, Nico (1997). *Sovereignty over Natural Resources: Balancing Rights and Duties.* Cambridge University Press.

Schrijver, Nico (2010). *Development without Destruction: The UN and Global Resource Management.* Indiana University Press.

Shiva, Vandana (2010). "Resources" in Wolfgang Sachs (ed.), *The Development Dictionary: A Guide to Knowledge as Power.* 2nd Edition, Zed Books.

57. Official Development Assistance

Introduction

Official Development Assistance (ODA, also known as "development aid") is a concept that holds unique potency within law and development because of its chameleon-like ability to influence and connect diverse yet central debates and issues on the purpose, nature and governance of development. Though strictly speaking, ODA refers to a particular kind of concessional development finance, debates within ODA range from the technical (e.g. what constitutes aid for trade, conditionality, or technical assistance), to the programmatic (e.g. what constitutes effective aid and how can ODA best "blend" with other kinds of development finance), to the politically sensitive (e.g. how to finance the UN Sustainable Development Goals (SDGs), support international responses to pandemics such as COVID-19, and respond to the many people seeking asylum or migrating to the European Union (EU) via flimsy boats across a treacherous Mediterranean Sea). This entry approaches ODA as a powerful instrument through which the purpose of development, the role and responsibilities of different actors (in particular, Northern and Southern States) therein, and the governance of development (who makes decisions and how these are implemented) can be revealed in ways that reveal the hidden politics and role of law in that project. The following sections examine the contemporary definition of ODA, locating it within historical debates on North-South financial flows; discuss two areas of contention – the tying of ODA and the attachment by donors of conditions on ODA; and review the current approach to the assessment of ODA flows and its effectiveness. The aim here is to demonstrate the partiality of the current approach to ODA, and its contemporary significance as a key, if overlooked, instrument of international governance via development finance.

The official definition of ODA and international targets

ODA has been officially defined and is monitored by the Organisation for Economic Co-operation and Development's (OECD) Development Assistance Committee (DAC), making the OECD the predominant international authority on donor ODA policy, as well as the main source of information on the amounts, sources and types of ODA given. The purpose, official and concessional aspects of this kind of finance are key to the OECD's definition of ODA. ODA is "those flows to countries and territories on the DAC list of ODA recipients and to multilateral institutions which are (i) provided by official agencies, including state and local governments, or by their executive agencies; and (ii) each transaction of which: a) is administered with the promotion of the economic development and welfare of developing countries as its main objective; and b) is concessional in character". At the time of writing, all DAC members (including EU institutions), along with 20 non-DAC countries, 46 multilateral organizations and 26 philanthropic (private) donors report data amenable to DAC ODA analysis. In some cases, donors have adopted this definition into national legislative frameworks (e.g. Canada), with many more directly referring to the OECD DAC definition in their domestic ODA policy frameworks. In 1970, the UN General Assembly adopted a Resolution that exhorted economically advanced countries to progressively increase their ODA to developing countries to reach a minimum net amount of 0.7 per cent of their gross national product by the middle of that decade. By 2015, just six countries (United Kingdom, Netherlands, Denmark, Luxembourg, Norway and Sweden) had met this target, with the OECD average never yet exceeding 0.4 per cent.

The OECD's contemporary distinction and separate treatment of ODA from other North-South financial flows belies historic debates since the early 1960s to the mid-1970s on how development should be financed within the UN, a then-fledgling United Nations Conference on Trade and Development (UNCTAD) and the OECD. Within the UN, the designation of 1960s as an international "Decade for Development" began with the controversial Resolution 1522 (XV) of 15th December 1960 that specified a target for the increase of the flow of "international assistance and capital for development" to "approximately 1 per cent of the combined national incomes of the economically advanced countries". Between the first two UNCTAD international conferences in 1964 and 1968, the First Ministerial Meeting of the Group of 77 produced the Charter of Algiers (1967) that included several demands and proposals on financing development that remain relevant to debates on ODA today. For example, the 1 per cent target was to be met by 1968, all aid was to be untied, and the then-prominent support of a private sector-led model of development by donors and lenders was condemned. The Charter's demands targeted both public *and* private international capital flows, illustrating that the G77 clearly understood ODA as structurally embedded within a wider, problematic field of international finance for development for which effective remedies would need to go far beyond the mere reaching of a target on a level of resource transfer as aid from North to South.

The tying of aid, conditionality and technical assistance

Untied ODA refers to loans or grants which are freely and fully available to finance procurement from substantially all aid-recipient countries and from OECD countries. Tied aid refers to aid provided on the condition that the aid-recipient use the lender's own resources, for example where a grant or a soft loan for a capital project is made with the condition that equipment or services are purchased from the donor country only. Tied aid occurs most frequently in a bilateral context, and poses obvious, often hidden costs and constraints on procurement options for aid-recipient States that can have longer-term direct and indirect negative development impacts. Though evidence to support donors' perceptions that tied aid promotes trade and economic opportunity is scarce, there continues to be marked reluctance amongst certain influential donors to untie their aid.

The tying of ODA remains permissible within the current OECD DAC definition of ODA, despite a DAC Recommendation to untie aid to least developed countries (LDCs). Adopted in 2001 and revised in 2014 and in 2018, this Recommendation states that the "intentions" of DAC Members are to "untie their ODA to the LDCs and HIPCs [Highly Indebted Poor Countries] to the greatest extent possible". The scope of this hortatory Recommendation is further limited by several restrictions, including a derogation clause that permits DAC Members to "take measures inconsistent with the terms of this Recommendation" in exceptional circumstances "where they believe it to be justified on the basis of overriding, non-trade-related, development interests" (OECD (2020). DAC Recommendation on Untying Official Development Assistance, OECD/LEGAL/5015). No clarification is offered on what might reach this exceptional circumstance threshold and there is no oversight mechanism outlined for this clause.

Though La Chimia (2013) notes that the Recommendation has had deep resonance within the international community, if one traces the international legal instruments referred to in the Recommendation, one can see that it is really a palimpsest on liberalized public procurement markets. Though the Recommendation's stated aim is to capture the *benefits* of open procurement markets for LDCs HIPCs, Other Low-Income Countries (OLICs) and International Development Association (IDA)-only countries, the legal and other governance instruments identified in support of this are focused solely on the *promotion* of an unfettered markets-centred approach to the public procurement policies of aid-recipient States. Notably, any reference to national, regional or international human rights standards in the approach to the marketization of public goods and services is absent. Similarly, recognition that a public procurement regime may prioritize distributional principles and other social objectives over the promotion of business competition and markets (Calleja, 2016) is also lacking. Carbone's research on the politics of untying aid includes a revealing quote from a DAC official that "the main priority for the DAC is effective competition and getting the best price for aid tenders: contracts must be awarded to the cheapest bidder, regardless of its long-term development impact" (Carbone, 2014). Thus, at the heart of this DAC Recommendation, lies an inherent tension between a poverty reduction approach to public procurement and a neoliberal, markets-maximization one, each with a different view of the donor, the aid-recipient State, and of law and regulation.

Conditionality is the requirement on aid-recipient States to implement certain prescribed policy and legislative reforms as a condition of receiving aid. Initially introduced by the International Monetary Fund (IMF) as a requirement of countries to reduce their fiscal and current account deficits in order to receive a loan, since the 1980s this practice has also been adopted by the World Bank via the promotion of an "enabling environment" by aid-recipient States via the promotion of privatization and public sector reforms. This practice has been de facto adopted by some donors, who require aid-recipient States to be "on track" with IMF and/or World Bank Programmes as a condition of receiving their ODA. Tan (2011) conceptualizes the application of conditionality as a *doctrine*, in order to distinguish between the application of conditionality as due diligence in order to minimize the risk of debt default or a departure from agreed financing objectives, and the far greater scope and much more intrusive exercise designed to discipline the recipient State via the pursuit of domestic legal, regulatory and policy reforms established by the financier.

In recent years, the promotion of an enabling environment for private sector development has emerged as a prominent policy priority within donors' ODA. This term more narrowly refers to policy, legal, institutional, and regulatory conditions that govern business activities, but can include other factors such as labour supply and infrastructure, along with macro-institutional factors that affect business such as trade facilitation and investment rules. An estimated US$9.9 billion in 2015 was spent on this area via loans, equity and grants, with "technical cooperation" used to deliver 17 per cent of enabling environment ODA, a larger proportion than average for ODA activities (Caio, 2018). While in-depth research on the relationship between conditionality practices, donor policy objectives on the promotion of an enabling environment and aid-recipient country need remains to be undertaken, what is important here is the recognition of the unique role of ODA as an instrument of both financial support and leverage over aid-recipient State domestic law, policy and institutions.

Assessing the transparency and effectiveness of ODA – measurement by numbers

How ODA is spent, and how effective it is in promoting development, has attracted much popular and scholarly attention. On the former, two dedicated initiatives on the transparency of donor ODA exist. The International Aid Transparency Initiative (IATI) was launched by donors at the Third High Level Forum on Aid Effectiveness in Accra, Ghana in 2008. This is a list of rules and guidance (the IATI "Standard") for donors and other development actors on a common approach to the content and format of data on the organization's annual development spend and the activities funded. A related initiative is the NGO-led Publish What You Fund Index, first released in 2011. It aims at capturing aid transparency, a commitment reiterated by donors over several international conferences in the early 2000s. Forty-seven donors are now included in the Index.

On the effectiveness of aid, two initiatives exist, with both approaching "effectiveness" mainly from a technical, programmatic (better aid management practices) over a substantive (whether aid reduces poverty and inequality) standpoint. By far, the more prominent is the international Aid Effectiveness agenda, consisting of five core principles developed over four "High Level" international events held in Rome (2003), Paris (2005), Accra (2008) and Busan (2011). The principles include ownership (where developing countries set their own strategies for poverty reduction, improve their institutions and tackle corruption); alignment (where donor countries align behind these objectives and use local systems); harmonization (where donor countries coordinate, simplify procedures and share information to avoid duplication), results (where developing countries and donors focus on development results and aim to measure these) and mutual accountability (where donors and developing countries are accountable for development results). Arising from the Busan (2011) conference, the Global Partnership for Effective Development Cooperation evolved, a multi-stakeholder initiative that aims to track progress with implementing four of the principles, via ten indicators.

Other initiatives include the Quality of ODA (QuODA) by the think-tank Centre for Global Development (CGD) that analyses donors' performance on 31 indicators of aid "quality" to which donors have made commitments. These include maximizing efficiency, fostering institutions, reducing burden and transparency and learning. Related to this is the Commitment to Development Index by CGD and the Brookings Institution. This ranks 27 bilateral donors on the extent to which their policies (including aid, finance, investment, technology) benefit people in poorer countries.

SIOBHÁN AIREY

From a law and development perspective, the predominant reliance on numbers, data, indicators and indexes to capture, analyse and monitor accountability for ODA, and its impacts, has three deeper governance effects. First, and most importantly, by operating to generic data gathering and analytical templates that rely mainly on numerical data, these principles and guidelines reinforce a top-down, donor-led approach to ODA decision-making and programme implementation, away from marginalized people and communities on whose behalf ODA is rhetorically rationalized. Similarly, these numbers-heavy monitoring mechanisms hide from view and implicitly legitimize the differentiated agency accorded to donors over that of aid-recipient States that is already institutionalized within the ODA relationship. Secondly, by foregrounding numerical assessments of ODA financial flows, attention is directed away from the political and structural context of wider capital and resource flows between North and South, and the legal and governance institutions that legitimize them. Thirdly, the framing of aid and development inherent in these initiatives compounds the historical aporia intrinsic to the OECD's definition of ODA, and its approach to donor policies on ODA via its Recommendations and other good practice guidelines. The enduring effects of colonialism and imperialism to contemporary relations between the Global North and South remain hidden. As we have seen earlier in this entry, this ahistorical, narrowly conceived approach to ODA contrasts strongly with the position taken by G77 States in the Charter of Algiers.

ODA, the move to private finance and the UN SDGs

These issues continue to emerge in recent developments on ODA within the OECD. The adoption of a revised definition of ODA introduced in 2018 that now records the "grant equivalent" of concessional loans as "ODA flows" has introduced several anomalies that remain yet to be addressed (Scott, 2019). The promotion of a new concept of Total Official Support for Sustainable Development (TOSSD), framed as a complement to ODA by the DAC, reflects a deeper policy shift within the DAC whereby donor ODA may increasingly engage with private financial sources and actors on investments in aid-recipient States, without recourse to the direct involvement by the latter.

In relation to financing the UN SDGs, while ODA remains a key, if small, source of development finance, arguably its significance now lies far more in its flexibility to engage with private actors and financing instruments through a "Blended Finance" modality. This flexibility, allied to the centrality of ODA's role to the pursuit of institutional reform in aid-recipient States along a markets-led development model, makes ODA a powerful, if hidden, instrument of donor-led global governance.

SIOBHÁN AIREY

References

Caio, Cecilia (2018). "The Enabling Environment for Private Sector Development – Donor Spending and Links to other Catalytic Uses of Aid", Development Initiatives Discussion Paper. Available at https://devinit.org/wp-content/uploads/2018/03/the-enabling-environment-for-private-sector-development_discussion-paper.pdf.

Calleja, Antoinette (2016). *Unleashing Social Justice through EU Public Procurement*. Routledge.

Carbone, Maurizio (2014). "Much Ado About Nothing? The European Union and the Global Politics of Untying Aid", Contemporary Politics 20, 103–117.

Chiba, Daina and Tobias Heinrich (2019). "Colonial Legacy and Foreign Aid: Decomposing the Colonial Bias", International Interactions 45(3), 474–499.

Führer, Helmut (1996). *The Story of Official Development Assistance – A History of the Development Assistance Committee and the Development Co-operation Directorate in Dates, Names and Figures*. OECD.

La Chimia, Annamaria (2013). *Tied Aid and Development Aid Procurement in the Framework of EU and WTO Law*: The Imperative for Change. Hart Publishing.

OECD DAC. Recommendation on Terms and Conditions of Aid, OECD/LEGAL/5006, Adopted on 28 February 1978.

Ruckert, Arne (2008). "Making Neo-Gramscian Sense of the Development Assistance Committee: Towards an Inclusive Neoliberal World Development Order" in Rianne Mahon and Stephanie McBride (eds), *The OECD in Transnational Governance*. UBC Press.

Scott, Simon (2019). A Note on Current Problems with ODA as a Statistical Measure. Brookings Institution. Available at: https://www.brookings.edu/blog/future-development/2019/09/26/a-note-on-current-problems-with-oda-as-a-statistical-measure/ accessed 10 September 2020.

Tan, Celine (2011). *Governance through Development: Poverty Reduction Strategies, International Law and the Disciplining of Third World States*. Routledge.

58. Parliaments

'Development' is not only an economic or a technical concept but also and primarily a political process. What 'development' should mean for each polity has to be debated in a constant political battle over distribution and values. Parliaments are central protagonists in such debates. They are important links between societal mobilization (through political parties, civil society organizations and social movements) and the State's apparatus and fora for political debate. Their legislative action is needed to shape the structures in which the economy operates, set up welfare schemes or create social rights with a more comprehensive reach. Hence, parliaments matter profoundly – as engine room and public stage.

And yet, legal academia widely ignores parliaments and legislatures, when it comes to questions of social justice, inequality and agents of change. Legal and Law and Development scholarship focuses mostly on courts and rights or on executives. This scholarly attention surely is connected to a rise in complexity that favours technocracy, a shift to international relations and global governance that favours the role of executives and also to media's focus on individual personalities, not collectives like a parliament.

So then: What is the relevance of parliaments in 'law and development'? How is this entry justified here? Two reasons are particularly important: One is a political economy perspective on the law of the political process. We point to the connection between the legal regimes of the political process and its substantive (economic, ecologic, social, etc.) outcome. The other reason is based on a critical understanding of 'development': We think it is important to highlight the role of parliaments and the law of the political process more generally to advance and support a pluralistic, political and democratic understanding of development, countering the long dominant but problematic technocratic managerial understanding.

We look at parliaments and their role from three different angles: parliaments in domestic realm, parliaments in foreign policy and parliaments as objects of external aid.

Parliaments as domestic fora and agents of change

Parliaments are central protagonists in the domestic realm in different functions and stages. What 'development' should mean for India or Brazil, Angola or Cambodia is a question that every society has to decide anew many times and in many varieties. Societies have to decide how to balance or sequence competing interests, whether it is achieving economic growth, industrialization, fair distribution, ecological sustainability or other values. Most constitutions allow for different ends and require concretization – and it is up to the political organs to make such decisions.

Parliaments are potentially best placed to do so, because they are supposed to be mirrors of society, reflecting and representing the diverse groups and interests that exist in a given society, giving their different political visions a platform to compete. This view, however, assumes a set of preconditions that allow for a democratic, pluralistic process: the rights to assemble freely and to speak out, the ability to form organizations and political parties to synthesize interests, the right to free and fair elections. All of these preconditions are, of course, embedded in a political, non-legal logic – but they are also framed in law (Issacharoff et al., 2012). Law and Development scholarship should investigate how legal-political regimes impact substantive outcomes, where political processes get (legally) screwed towards certain interests and goals. Some pressing questions for future research may be: How is the organization of elections connected to the advancement of landowning interests and against workers? Do laws allow for the formation of new parties or rather block it? Does the legal framework ensure that political parties are open and autocratic takeovers are avoided? (VRU / WCL Special issue (1), 2014)

Pluralistic debate and informed decision-making are also a question of parliamentary procedure. Opposition rights, voting procedures or rules on defection shape whether parliaments can be open places of pluralistic debate or become rubber stamps for governmental action. Equally important is the relation between parliament and the executive and hence a separation of powers analysis. Many constitutional orders have seen a (re)centralization of power in executives over the past decades. Again, political dynamics play a major role here, as well as the basic constitutional configuration as a parliamentary or presidential or even authoritarian system.

What is important in all of these rather organizational questions is to see their impact on the substantive outcomes. The organization of the political process is not indifferent to the distribution of resources. Here, Legal and Law and Development scholarship should connect with empirical studies which analyse the effects of certain political and constitutional arrangements. Such scholarship cannot replace the necessarily normative analysis of what preferences a society might have – but there are studies that examine the effect of a given system on inequality and it would be the task of legal scholarship to better understand the connections.

There is, for example, the vivid debate whether democracy – whether parliamentary or presidential – enhances or complicates the more equal distribution of wealth. Against the original assumption (especially in Western scholarship) that democracy reduces inequality, recent scholarship shows a much more complex picture (Beramendi and Anderson, 2008; Scheve and Stasavage, 2017). On one hand, it has been shown that democracies can be captured by the owning class, which then uses democratic instruments to shield itself. The change to democracy de jure is countered by de facto defence of privileged socio-economic status. Also, the so-called 'director's law' observes that democratization strengthens the middle class, not the poor and hence hardly reduces inequality. On the other hand, it has been established that there is a positive effect on tax revenues; their share of GDP rises in democracies – and on secondary school enrolment and transformation of economy away from agricultural sector. Other studies underline that 'democracy' can only have a more just impact if elections are embedded in a larger context of free political process (Collier, 2010). More concretely, there are also studies about which type of democratic systems better combats inequality. Some, for example, see 'compelling advantages of parliamentary systems' in that they produce significantly more growth, less inflation and ultimately reduce inequality (McManus and Ozkin, 2018). Presidential systems, on the other hand, are considered more prone to deadlock and executive overreach.

The central task for Law and Development scholars would be to understand the connections – between the legal and constitutional configuration of the political process and its material outcomes. It is, one could say, a political economy perspective on the law of democracy and the political process.

Parliaments as agents of international (development) policy

In international affairs, executives typically have a prerogative. Ministers and bureaucrats negotiate with other States, represent the nation, lead foreign policy. But parliaments play important roles here too – in particular when it comes to shaping international development policy based on their budgetary powers and veto power over international treaties. These parliamentary roles differ considerably between donor and recipient countries.

Parliaments in donor countries have considerable influence over development policy in terms of budget allocation, policy content and sometimes legislation. Again, the configurations vary between presidential and parliamentary systems. In the US, foreign policy is *a priori* the competence of a strong presidential executive, but US Congress has successfully used its power of the purse to steer foreign aid policies and has enacted relatively detailed legislation regarding which countries, projects and multilateral institutions can receive funding. Congress has also been an important conduit for transnational civil society to influence international development policy, e.g. in favour of environmental sustainability (Daugirdas, 2013). Within the EU, a similar dynamic between the Commission and Parliament has led to detailed legislation on development policy. National parliamentary systems display different degrees of parliamentarization. While the UK House of Commons has enacted specific legislation on development policy, the German Bundestag leaves most policy and allocation decisions to the competent ministries but supervises their activities through parliamentary committees (Dann, 2013).

Besides development policy, parliaments have a say in many areas affecting the interests of developing countries, such as trade, investment or climate change. To the extent that they must ratify international agreements, parliaments gain some leverage over these policy areas and can potentially bring in developmental concerns. Whether this happens largely depends on the political orientation of parliamentary majorities, civil society pressure and voters' preferences, among other factors.

Parliaments in the Global South are often in an inverse position compared to their Northern counterparts. They cannot use the power of the purse as effectively and rather tend to be bypassed by executive cooperation in foreign policy matters. Their political and constitutional role differs between constitutional systems but a common problem seems to be the primacy of governments in foreign policy, which includes development cooperation and finance. Also, representation of Southern countries in international financial institutions (IFI) or other multilateral agencies is dominated by executives with little influence of legislatures in general.

Legislatures come into play where aid agreements qualify as international treaties that require parliamentary ratification. They can also perform supervisory functions and channel civil society mobilization for or against particular programmes and projects, if the political system is responsive to such mobilization. Internationally, there have been attempts at strengthening the monitoring and accountability role of African parliaments in the New Partnership for Africa's Development, and the EU and African Caribbean Pacific (ACP)-countries have established a Joint Parliamentary Assembly on New Partnership for Africa's Development (NEPAD). Overall, however, we know relatively little about the extent to which parliaments shape relations to international financial institutions or bilateral donors. Here lies a major research agenda and potential for democratization of law and development. A similar gap in research exists with regard to the influence of parliaments on global development policy, and vice versa, e.g. in respect of the Sustainable Development Goals (SDG)- or Aid-effectiveness-Agendas.

Parliaments as objects of external democracy promotion

Since the 1990s, the external promotion of democracy and of legislatures in particular has become an important, though increasingly contested, field. The Iraq war and its aftermath led to increasing scepticism about the motives behind such support, often driven by Western agencies. But also the lacklustre economic performance and internal turbulences of Western democracies have sowed doubts about the economic benefits of democracy. The promotion of free and fair political processes nonetheless remains a central pillar of a more value-based development policy that goes beyond growth and economics (Carothers, 2015; Faust and Leininger, 2014).

Parliaments / legislative assemblies are particularly important partners and targets of such programs. International donor agencies have supported parliaments in streamlining their internal processes or improving budgetary and supervisory functions. Given that parliaments are political institutions, it is particularly difficult to draw the line between neutral capacity-building and intervention into internal affairs and partisan politics. Hence, Germany, for instance, prefers to leave cooperation with political parties (rather than parliaments as institutions) to German political foundations instead of governmental agencies.

External promotion of parliamentary democracy is ultimately a highly complex task that requires strong local counterparts and multidimensional approaches that include the societal foundations of strong parliamentarism. Civil society organizations and transnational advocacy networks thus also play a role in mobilizing constituencies, political parties and parliamentarians for or against particular causes, which ultimately strengthens democratic feedback mechanisms beyond capacity-building.

Legal research can focus on the role that legal factors (parliamentary, party, election, campaign finance law) play in the functionality of parliaments, and what contribution can external assistance make to improve these laws. It should inquire how the comparison of the law of democracy can inform responsible democracy promotion efforts – or what normative values should guide external promotion of parliamentary democracy. Which legal rules are required for donors in this regard? How are principles of non-intervention, impartiality and ownership to be understood in support to parliaments?

PHILIPP DANN AND MICHAEL RIEGNER

References

Beramendi, Pablo and Christopher J. Anderson (2008). *Democracy, Inequality, and Representation in Comparative Perspective*. Russel SAGE Foundation.
Carothers, Thomas (2015). 'Democracy Aid at 25', Journal of Democracy 26, 59–73.

Collier, Paul (2010). *War, Guns, and Votes*. Perennial.

Dann, Philipp (2013). *The Law of Development Cooperation*, Cambridge University Press.

Daugirdas, Kristina (2013). 'Congress Underestimated: The Case of the World Bank', American Journal of International Law 107(3), 517–562.

Faust, Jörg and Julia Leininger (2014). *Supporting Democracy Abroad: An Assessment of Leading Powers*. Freedom House.

Issacharoff, Samuel, Pamela S. Karlan, and Richard H. Pildes (2012). *The Law of Democracy: Legal Structure of the Political Process*. Foundation Press.

McManus, Richard and Gulcin Ozkan (2018). 'Who Does Better for the Economy? Presidents vs. Parliamentary Systems', Public Choice 176(3), 361–387.

Scheve, Kenneth and David Stasavage (2017). 'Wealth Inequality and Democracy', Annual Review of Political Science 20, 451–468.

VRU / World Comparative Law (2014). Special Issue on Social Rights, e.g. Coutinho, Targeting within Universalism: The 'Bolsa Familia' Program and the Social Assistance Field in Brazil. VRU / WCL 47, 43–61.

PHILIPP DANN AND MICHAEL RIEGNER

59. Peace, Justice and Strong Institutions

Introduction

The significance of peace has been accepted in international fora for several decades. The Preamble of the United Nations (UN) Charter, 1945, opens with Member States expressing their determination "to save succeeding generations from the scourge of war". Furthermore, one of the listed purposes of the Organization is to maintain international peace and security. Almost 40 years later, the UN General Assembly adopted Resolution 39/11 proclaiming "the right of peoples to peace", carrying on the trend of framing peace as an antithesis of war and as a "primary international prerequisite for development". The 2016 Declaration on the Right to Peace transitioned towards a more positive conception of peace, whilst recognizing the mutual interlink and reinforcement among peace, the protection and promotion of human rights and development.

Peace is positioned as a critical component within the Sustainable Development Goals (SDG) framework. This position recognizes that in the absence of peace, sustainable development is a pipe dream; similarly, peace and security will be at risk without sustainable development. Some regions experience peace and security, while others are subject to seemingly endless cycles of conflict and violence, which manifest as threats of international homicide, violence against children, human trafficking and sexual violence. The 2030 Agenda for Sustainable Development acknowledges that this is by no means inevitable and must be addressed.

Goal 16 specifically "recognises the need to build peaceful, just and inclusive societies that provide equal access to justice". These societies must also be based on respect for human rights, effective rule of law, good governance at the different levels with effective, accountable and inclusive institutions. Goal 16 has 12 targets that are complemented by 23 indicators. A challenge within the goal is identified that could lead to the SDGs falling short of their promise not to leave anyone behind. This contribution includes a focus on sexual violence by peacekeepers while deployed on peacekeeping missions. Following a brief context of the SDGs, Goal 16 and the role of peacekeepers, this contribution endeavours to conclude with possible legislative recommendations to support the achievement of Goal 16.

Context of SDG 16

The standard definition of sustainable development, judging by its widespread use and frequency of citation, stems from the 1987 Brundtland Commission's report. This definition, which focuses on intergenerational equity, defines sustainable development as "development that meets the needs of the present without compromising the ability of future generations to meet their own needs". Since then, numerous alternative definitions have been proffered by scholars and practitioners – a discussion which falls beyond the scope of this contribution. Evidently, an immutable definition remains elusive. This elusiveness, however, serves a purpose because the human societies and natural ecosystems which this development should serve are complex and heterogeneous. Hence, the versatility of the concept of sustainable development allows it to remain an evolving idea that can be adapted to fit different challenges and contexts across space and time.

At the dawn of the new millennium, the UN General Assembly adopted the Millennium Declaration from which the eight Millennium Development Goals (MDGs) were derived. The MDGs heralded world leaders' commitment at the start of a new millennium to combat poverty, hunger, disease, illiteracy, environmental degradation and discrimination against women by 2015. The MDGs provided the world with an overarching development framework with concerted efforts at global, regional, national and local levels.

In 2011, the World Bank centred its World Development Report on conflict, security and development. The report underlined the negative impact of persistent conflict on a country and region's development prospects. The vulnerability of societies when their institutions are unable to protect their citizens from abuse or provide equitable access to justice and economic opportunity was highlighted. Eleven years after the MDGs were launched, no conflict-affected State with low-income levels had achieved a single MDG. These conclusions accord with the final MDGs report in 2015, which found that despite the significant achievements made, fragile and conflict-affected States usually had the highest poverty rates. These States also achieved significantly less MDG related progress than other developing countries. The harrowing conclusion drawn was that conflicts remain the biggest threat to development.

The close of 2015 saw the conclusion of the MDGs. Striving to reflect the lessons learned, the UN General Assembly adopted 17 SDGs and 169 associated targets included in the 2030 Agenda for Sustainable Development. This post-2015 agenda signified the transition from an "exclusive focus on development" as was the MDGs approach, "to factors that are integrally related to development". The 2030 Agenda recognizes extreme poverty in its varied forms and dimensions as the "greatest global challenge and an indispensable requirement for sustainable development". World leaders, therefore, committed through these integrated, indivisible goals and targets to achieve sustainable development in a manner that balances its three dimensions – economic, social and environmental.

One facet of this universal blueprint for sustainable development is the recognition of the role that violence, conflict and insecurity play in inhibiting development. The vision envisages a world free of fear and violence and specifically resolves to build peaceful, just and inclusive societies. Goal 16, which is phrased in identical language, is the decisive outcome of the international community's acknowledgment that peace is fundamental to development. This approach no longer couches peace as an abstract concept that is merely aspirational but identifies measurable targets and indicators. The 12 targets of SDG 16 mainly aim to measure direct violence, drivers of violence, governance and justice. These targets speak to the key aspects of negative peace, which is defined as "the absence of violence or the fear of violence" and certain aspects of positive peace, which is defined as "the attitudes, institutions and structures that create and sustain peaceful societies". The distinction between negative and positive peace provides an opportunity to appreciate the interconnection amongst the SDGs and their respective targets. Negative peace is related to four targets – 16.1, 16.2, 5.2 and 5.3, which all address an eradication of a form of violence. While positive peace can be linked to goals 1,

3, 4 and 5, which are broadly aimed at the creation of an optimum environment for human potential to flourish. Having set out the context from which Goal 16 emanates, the discussion turns to peacekeepers' role in conflict and the unintended consequence of their presence. This matters because the failure of a peacekeeping operation's mandate impacts on a host State's progress in achieving the targets of Goal 16.

Enter peacekeepers: a solution with an unintended consequence

UN peacekeeping operations have for decades provided essential security and support to millions of people and fragile institutions emerging from conflict. Although not expressly provided for in the Charter, peacekeeping is one of the main tools used by the UN to achieve the first listed purpose of maintenance of international peace and security. Its foundational principle is that the impartial presence of multinational troops on the ground can ease tensions and allow negotiated solutions in conflict situations. The unique mandate of peacekeepers involves inter alia the protection of civilians alongside the protection and promotion of human rights and building the rule of law and security institutions. Through this role, peacekeepers are directly involved in the lives of the local populations hosting the UN peacekeeping operation. However, over the past three decades, reports of sexual exploitation and abuse (SEA) by peacekeepers while on a mission have emerged with predictable regularity.

The UN Secretary General's Bulletin "Special measures for protection from sexual exploitation and sexual abuse" (United Nations Secretariat, 2003) defines the scope of SEA in the following manner, sexual exploitation is "any actual or attempted abuse of a position of vulnerability, differential power or trust, for sexual purposes", such as, "profiting monetarily, socially or politically from the sexual exploitation of another". Examples of such conduct includes "transactional sex, solicitation of transactional sex and exploitative relationships". Sexual abuse is the "actual or threatened physical intrusion of a sexual nature, whether by force or under equal or coercive conditions". Examples of such conduct include sexual assault, rape and any sexual activity with a minor (a person under the age of 18). Whilst the aforementioned conduct may also constitute a crime at the international and domestic level, peacekeepers who perpetrate this conduct do so with apparent impunity. This impunity for their actions is rooted in the perception of immunity from prosecution for crimes committed while on deployment. This approach has been justified because in numerous cases it has been the norm.

The arrival of peacekeepers into a conflict or post-conflict setting increases the power differentials between the vulnerable local community and these personnel. These settings are often characterized by collapsed economies, weak judicial systems, corrupt and ineffective law enforcement agencies, and weak or non-existent rule of law. Women and children are particularly vulnerable to SEA by peacekeepers, who use their access to humanitarian aid and services intended to benefit local populations as tools of exploitation.

The UN Security Council in Resolution 2272 recognizes that SEA committed by peacekeepers undermines both the implementation of peacekeeping mandates and the credibility of UN peacekeeping operations. SEA committed by peacekeepers impedes the achievement of SDG 16 as a whole, and specifically Target 16.2, which relates to ending abuse, exploitation, trafficking and all forms of violence and trafficking against children. Sexual violence in its varied forms threatens the physical security of individuals, their families and communities at large. Thus, whole communities may live in fear of violence perpetrated by personnel deployed to protect and promote their human rights, which is the antithesis of the vision envisaged in the 2030 Agenda.

Furthermore, a local population's perceived legitimacy of a peacekeeping operation is subverted by sexual violence committed by peacekeepers. A host population may be reluctant to cooperate with peacekeepers in the fulfilment of their mandate. Consequently, peacekeepers' conduct undermines the creation and sustenance of peaceful societies.

Way forward

The 2030 Agenda acknowledges the role national parliaments play through the enactment of legislation as a means to ensure accountability for the effective implementation of the SDGs. The enactment of legislation is an important step in addressing the specific impediment to peace and thus, sustainable development that SEA committed by peacekeepers' causes. Without this step, victims of SEA in the host State cannot obtain justice.

Troop contributing countries (TCCs) are obligated to exercise criminal and disciplinary jurisdiction over peacekeepers for offences and crimes committed. This obligation is based on the status-of-forces agreement concluded between the host State and the UN as well as the doctrine of sovereign immunity. Simply put, peacekeepers are immune from host State jurisdiction; however, this should not mean impunity for their actions because their home State is obligated to hold them accountable for their actions.

For TCCs to hold peacekeepers accountable for SEA committed, legislation must be enacted that achieves the following aims. Firstly, enacted legislation must prohibit and criminalize the scope of conduct contained in the UN SEA definition. Two specific challenges come to mind. A lacuna between the two could perpetuate impunity because a peacekeeper who commits SEA will not be liable for a crime but at best disciplinary action for breach of internal rules. Also, while the UN SEA definition categorizes all sexual relations with persons under the age of 18 as sexual abuse, the age of consent varies across the globe. This variation may reflect the traditions, religion, culture and history of a particular country. However, States must be reminded of their obligations in terms of Article 34 of the nearly universally ratified Convention on the Rights of the Child, which obligates them to undertake all appropriate national, bilateral and multilateral measures to protect the child from all forms of sexual exploitation and sexual abuse. Secondly, enacted legislation must have extraterritorial application. Meaning the legislative provisions apply to citizens who commit offences outside the State's boundaries.

South Africa, whose greatest asset lies in the power of its example, has enacted legislation that fulfils its obligations as a TCC. The Sexual Offences and Related Matters Amendment Act (Sexual Offences Act) covers "all matters relating to sexual offences". It criminalizes "all forms of sexual abuse and exploitation". Chapters 2 to 4 of the Act set out broadly defined categories of offences which adequately covers the scope of conduct in the UN SEA. Section 61 of the Sexual Offences Act provides for the extraterritorial application of the Act. Therefore, other States can draw from this example by ensuring their national legislation effectively criminalizes sexual offences and applies extra-territorially. The SDG framework provides the much-needed space to address impediments to sustainable development. However, challenges within and between the goals need to be addressed to help fulfil the promise of leaving no one behind.

NTEMESHA MASEKA

References

Anderson, Letitia (2010). "Politics by Other Means: When does Sexual Violence Threaten International Peace and Security?", *International Peacekeeping* 17(2), 244–260.

Atuhaire, Pearl Karuhanga, Nicole Gerring, Laura Huber, Mirgul Kuhns, and Grace Ndirangu (2018). *The Elusive Peace: Ending Sexual Violence during and after Conflict*. United States Institute of Peace Special Report 437.

Bastick, Megan, Karin Grimm, and Rahel Kunz (2007). *Sexual Violence in Armed Conflict: Global Overview and Implications for the Security Sector*. DCAF – Geneva Centre for Security Sector Governance.

Ferstman, Carla (2013). "Criminalising Sexual Exploitation and Abuse by Peacekeepers", United States Institute of Peace, Special Report 335.

Institute for Economics and Peace (2019). SDG16+ Progress Report 2019 A Comprehensive Global Audit of Progress on Available SDG Indicators. Available at: https://www.kpsrl.org/sites/default/files/2019-03/SDG16Progress-Report-2019-web.pdf.

Levy, Marc A. and Michelle Scobie (2015). "Promote Peaceful and Inclusive Societies for Sustainable Development, Provide Access to Justice for All and Build Effective, Accountable and Inclusive Institutions at All Levels", International Science Council Review of Targets for the Sustainable Development Goals: The Science Perspective.

Malone, David (2018). "ON SDG 16: Peace, Justice, Strong Institutions", Freedom from Fear 14, 174–179.

Nordås, Ragnhild and Siri C.A. Rustad (2013). "Sexual Exploitation and Abuse by Peacekeepers: Understanding Variation", International Interactions 39(4), 511–534.

Winkler, Inga T. and Carmel Williams (2017). "The Sustainable Development Goals and Human Rights: A Critical Review", The International Journal of Human Rights 21(8), 1023–1028.

World Bank (2011). *World Development Report 2011: Conflict, Security and Development*. World Bank.

60. Philanthropic Institutions

Philanthropy can be defined as a voluntary private funding of the production and provision of public good for public benefits. A philanthropic organization is different from a government actor because the latter is a public initiative for the public good. It is also different from corporate institutions which are for-profit private initiatives for the private good. Philanthropy varies in institutional forms, types and purpose ranging from charitable donations, private foundations, corporate social responsibility, and donor-advised funds. However, to be classified as a philanthropic actor, the organization must (a) not be profit-oriented, (b) not be part of the public sector, (c) use their own financial resources, (d) be led by an independent body, and (e) aim to tackle issues for the common good. Though not a prerequisite characteristic, the assets of a modern philanthropic foundation are usually set aside in a permanent, donor-directed and tax-advantaged private trust.

Philanthropy is also not a new concept; acts of giving are as old as antiquity. In ancient times, religion underscored the obligation to give to the needy and poor. Judaism and Christianity, for instance, emphasize one's duty and responsibility to give alms as a way of imitating God and good gesture towards fellow humans. In Islam, the Qur'an advises adherents to help in fulfilling the needs of the poor and less privileged, and for the rich to give away a portion of their surplus wealth. The latter, known as the *awqaf* (or Muslim endowments) have fulfilled social development purposes for hundreds of years within and outside Muslim communities and are a precursor to the modern institutional philanthropy we know today.

The root of modern, organized and institutionalized philanthropy can be traced to foundations created by business tycoons John D. Rockefeller and Andrew Carnegie in the early twentieth century. In an 1889 essay 'The Gospel on Wealth', the steel magnate Andrew Carnegie preached that the rich should channel their fortunes for societal good by supporting systematic social investments. Specifically, Carnegie believed that for capitalism to not only survive but thrive, it must embrace the strategic practice of gift-giving. For him, philanthropy's greatest 'gift' was to provide a means of lifting communities out of poverty whilst at the same time instilling habits of self-reliance. Also, to prevent the dangerous tension as a result of growing inequality, it was necessary to manage the pace and direction of national and global social change. This, Carnegie believed, would reduce possible peasant insurgency and destabilizing class tensions. To this end, he created, in 1910, the Carnegie Endowment for International Peace, which became one of the leading foreign policy think-tanks in the USA. In the following year, he founded the Carnegie Foundation of New York with an endowment of US$125 million, making it the largest single philanthropic trust established at that time. The Carnegie Foundation focused on education via the establishment of public libraries throughout the United States, Britain, Canada and other English-speaking countries, as well in the arts and cultural initiatives.

Following in the footsteps of Carnegie, John D. Rockefeller established the Rockefeller Foundation in 1913 after the US Supreme Court anti-trust ruling, which ordered John D. Rockefeller's Standard Oil Company to be broken up into smaller companies. The Rockefeller Foundation focused on medicine, public health such as the eradication of diseases such as hook worm, scientific research, and agriculture such as the Green Revolution. The Green Revolution invested in domestic and international agricultural reform and modernization with the objective, according to Nally and Taylor, of 'aligning rural values with market relations' (Nally and Taylor, 2015). Two decades after the creation of both the Carnegie and Rockefeller Foundations, the charitable sector in the US saw a proliferation of institutional and organized philanthropy from wealthy families and business magnates. The earliest ones include the Kresge Foundation created in 1924 by Sebastian Kresge to expand opportunities in arts, and culture, education and environment; the Ford Foundation in 1936 by Henry Ford with a focus on national politics supporting voter registration drives, school decentralization initiatives and advocacy groups; and the W.K. Kellogg Foundation in 1930 by the breakfast cereal pioneer W.K. Kellogg for the promotion of childhood welfare and development. Outside the US, Sir Rata Tata Trust was established in 1919 in India for the advancement of India and catalysing transformational change among her myriad peoples. The Wellcome Trust – founded by the English pharmacist Sir Henry Wellcome in 1936 – focuses on research to improve human and animal health and is one of the oldest philanthropic organizations outside the US.

The global era

Globalization coupled with mobility and increase in finance capital has seen a worldwide increase in the number of philanthropic foundations both in developed and developing countries. Today, there are more than 200,000 foundations in the world. Over 86,000 foundations are registered in the USA, 85,000 foundations in Western Europe and 35,000 in Eastern Europe (Jens Martens and Karolin Seitz, Philanthropic Power and Development: Who Shapes the Agenda? (2015), available at https://www.globalpolicy.org/images/pdfs/GPFEurope/Philanthropic_Power_online.pdf accessed 15 August 2019).

In the Global South, there are approximately 10,000 foundations in Mexico, nearly 2,000 in China and at least 1,000 in Brazil according to the Global Policy Forum (Jens and Seitz, 2015, above). Even though institutional philanthropy is a recent phenomenon in Africa, the continent is seeing a rise in the number of formalized structures of giving with notable foundations. Prominent examples include the Mo Ibrahim Foundation established in 2006, which focuses on governance, education and leadership, as well as the Aliko Dangote Foundation, which focuses on tackling malnutrition in children.

Despite the recent rise of philanthropic foundations in all parts of the world, the Bill and Melinda Gates Foundation (BMGF) is today by far the most prominent. Established in 2000 by Microsoft founder Bill Gates and his wife Melinda, and with an endowment of US$42.9 billion, the BMGF is the largest philanthropic actor in international giving and plays an incredibly strong role in shaping and directing policies at the highest echelons of international decision-making in the sphere of global development. For instance, its spending on global health exceeds the combined assessed contributions to the World Health Organization (WHO) by Member States and it is the second largest contributor to the WHO after the US. Like the Rockefeller and Carnegie Foundations a century prior, the donations and investments of BMGF in various sectors have fundamentally shifted how development is viewed and delivered in the last ten years and underscores the growing influence of philanthropic foundations in shaping agendas both at home and abroad. Guided by the principle of 'harnessing of advances in sciences and technology to help all people lead healthy, productive lives', the BMGF is involved in sustainable development solutions, global health, public education, agriculture and nutrition. It adopts a strategic approach in tackling complex social and development problems. This involves working with key established organizations already involved in the development space, strategic investing to attain measurable objectives, and a date-driven approach according to their own internal priorities. In this way, the BMGF is managing activities normally regarded as being the domain of the State or international organizations, participating, directly or indirectly, in the creation of norms and the production of knowledge on development.

Criticisms of philanthropic institutions

There is no doubt that with money comes power and influence, and the rising influence of global philanthropic actors and their largess has consequently raised questions about the generosity of the mega-rich. In the early days, philanthropists such as Rockefeller and Carnegie were reviled for their charitable giving, which was seen as exploitative of the working class. Commentators note that early philanthropists endowed their foundations from the profits of exploitative industries of the day such as oil, steel, railroad and manufacturing. These profits were made as a result of low wages, poor labour conditions, strike breaking and civil conflicts. Carnegie, for instance, presided over various labour strikes in the 1890s which led to the deaths of many striking workers. Thus, even though these philanthropies provide services for the public good, their capitalist practices essentially maintain social and economic failures that generate the very inequalities and injustices they wish to ameliorate. Moreover, scholars such as Linsey McGoey and Ann-Emmanuelle Birn contend that philanthropy has frequently served, directly or indirectly, to enhance donors' business and investment interests. For instance, the decision to create the Rockefeller Foundation was part of a larger ploy by John D. Rockefeller to shield some of his income and inheritance from taxation, as a way to polish his image, and to garner prestige and influence in the US and in world affairs.

Further, philanthropies are undemocratic and unaccountable in nature. Unlike government officials that can be voted off after poor performance or an executive that can be fired by its board, philanthropic foundations are not accountable to anyone. The leadership is usually made up of family members of the owners and answerable to no one. The Gates Foundation's board, for example, is Bill and Melinda Gates, William Gates Sr., and Warren Buffett. Similarly, smaller family foundations are made up of heirs and family-selected board members not answerable to the public or government. As a result, philanthropies do not have obligations of procedural accountability to the public or to the recipients of their generosity. Moreover, because the default legal time horizon of a modern institutional philanthropy is perpetuity, founders or trustees can direct and dictate the course or purpose of a foundation forever, without input from the public or those directly impacted from the actions of the foundation.

Third, the very tax-exempt status of foundations and tax-deductibility of philanthropic and charitable donations are seen as subsidizing the preferences of the rich. To be sure, the justification behind such tax exemption is based on the belief that such tax incentives will increase philanthropic giving, however, the downside is that such tax relief results in the loss of funds that would otherwise be tax revenues and sources for public development and welfare programmes. Seen this way, philanthropy – especially as practised in the developed countries – is not just benign voluntary activity of a donor but also drains limited public funds.

Philanthropies to the rescue

Regardless of the criticisms and apparent tension in the growing power of philanthropies, their presence and action are required and necessary. This is pertinent as dwindling government aid for welfare projects means loss in public goods. Philanthropies are stepping in and filling the vacuum caused by shrinking budgets by providing the needed development finance for the provision of basic public services. Seen this way, philanthropies are, therefore, funding public goods that are under-produced, or not produced at all by the State.

In addition, philanthropies are willing to take risks by investing in long-term projects. Unlike public officials that need to show results quickly from the expenditure of public funds in order to get re-elected or private corporations that must report to their boards and shareholders on their investment, philanthropies do not face such burdens. The undemocratic nature of its governance means their founders can embark on riskier, long-term projects without impatient investors or the vagaries of short-term election cycles. The legal time horizon as well as their protected endowment mean that philanthropies are well suited to engaging in high-risk, long-term policy experimentation and social reform required for finding solutions to market failures.

Undoubtedly, the growing divide between the haves and the have-nots as a result of capitalism means the influence of philanthropies will continue to grow. However, their rising presence and influence decry the need to interrogate what role they should have in democracies and in the constitution of international development. Also, given their exponential growth, there is an urgent need to develop a framework to hold philanthropic entities accountable and to prevent evasion of responsibility in cases of abuse or human rights violations to reduce possible negative outcomes of the power imbalances and ambiguities of charitable giving.

AMAKA VANNI

References

Aftyka, Leszek (2019). 'Philanthropy in Ancient Times: Social and Educational Aspects', Journal of Vasyl Stefanyk Precarpathian National University 6(1), 149–154.

Birn, Anne-Emanuelle (2014). 'Philanthrocapitalism, Past and Present: The Rockefeller Foundation, the Gates Foundation, and the Setting(s) of the International/Global Health Agenda', Hypothesis 12(1), 1–27.

Bishop, Matthew and Michael Green (2008). *Philanthrocapitalism: How the Rich Can Save the World*. Bloomsbury Press.

Cueto, Marcus (1994). *Missionaries of Science: The Rockefeller Foundation and Latin America*. Indiana University Press.

Hasan, Samiul (2015). *Human Security and Philanthropy: Islamic Perspectives and Muslim Majority Country Practices*. Springer.

Leat, Diana (2016). *Philanthropic Foundations, Public Good and Public Policy*. Palgrave Macmillan.

McCully, George (2008). *Philanthropy Reconsidered: Private Initiatives Public Good Quality of Life*. AuthorHouse.

McGoey, Linsey (2016). *No Such Thing as a Free Gift: The Gates Foundation and the Price of Philanthropy*. Verso.

Nally, David and Stephen Taylor (2015). 'The Politics of Self-Help: The Rockefeller Foundation, Philanthropy and the "Long" Green Revolution', Political Geography 49, 51–63.

Payton, Robert L. and Michael P. Moody (2008). *Understanding Philanthropy*. Indiana University Press.

AMAKA VANNI

61. Planetary Boundaries

Introduction

Since the industrial revolution human activity has built up such environmental influence that it has led to changes in the biophysical system Earth. The consequence of this human activity on the wider natural environment on which we as human species depend, has huge effects on how humans act and develop. It has led us away from the human friendly Holocene-epoch and into the new geological era of the Anthropocene, in which the environmental conditions are very likely to be catastrophic for the resilience of human societies and economies.

The planetary boundaries (PBs) concept is a framework that "defines a safe operating space for humanity based on the intrinsic biophysical processes that regulate the stability of the Earth system" (Steffen et al., 2015, 1259855-1). The aim of the PBs framework is to create a bridge between Earth science and policy governance (Rockström et al., 2009; Steffen et al., 2015). PBs introduce the concept of thresholds in order to provide a guide for law and policy-makers to respond and maintain a global environment in which human societies can develop and thrive, based on our evolving understanding of the functioning and resilience of the Earth system.

The PBs framework has attracted a lot of interest in both scientific, policy and business communities and has been much discussed since its publication. First this chapter sets out the content of PBs, second it sets out its link with international law, governance and policy, and lastly it addresses critiques and discussions on the concept.

Planetary boundaries

First published in 2009 (Rockström et al., 2009) and updated in 2015 (Steffen et al., 2015) the group of researchers behind the PBs concept emphasize the "urgent need for a new paradigm that integrates the continued development of human societies and the maintenance of the Earth System (ES) in a resilient and accommodating State" (Steffen et al., 2015, 1259855-1). As contribution to a new paradigm, the nine PBs set out in the research "provide a science-based analysis of the risk that human perturbations will destabilize the ES at the planetary scale" (Steffen et al., 2015, 1259855-1).

PBs are identified as thresholds for nine planetary biophysical subsystems or processes that determine the self-regulating capacity of the Earth System in a stable "Holocene-like" State: climate change, change in biosphere integrity (including biodiversity loss), stratospheric ozone depletion, ocean acidification, biogeochemical flows (among others nitrogen and phosphor), land system change (such as deforestation), freshwater use, atmospheric aerosol loading, and introduction of novel entities (such as plastic polymers and genetically modified organisms).

Two boundaries can be identified as operating at the level of the whole Earth System, climate change and biosphere integrity, since they are both highly integrated, emergent system-level phenomena connected to all the other PBs. If the limits of one of these core PBs are transgressed, they can already move the Earth System into a different state by themselves and could therefore be considered as hierarchically more important.

Others are sub-global or regional systems, such as land system change and freshwater use, that do not have a singular threshold at global level. Quantification of their "global" boundary is thus more difficult as it concerns river biomes, regional forest or marine ecosystems. Transgression of their threshold does not in itself lead to a new state of the Earth System, however, they generate feedbacks to the processes that do have large-scale thresholds. This is exemplified in the 2018 Hothouse Earth report that points out the interaction between regional ecosystems such as the Amazon rainforest, the Greenland and Antarctic ice sheets, and the permafrost when reaching their tipping points on a trajectory towards a "hothouse" Earth (Steffen et al., 2018, 8255). All in all it is important to acknowledge the interdependence of all nine PBs as well as addressing the interactions between them. Fernández and Malwé mention that "since each planetary boundary level has been determined by assuming that the other boundaries are not exceeded, it has been stressed that exceeding one boundary could lead to either a shift in the position or a transgression of other boundaries" (Fernández and Malwé, 2019, 49).

Three zones are identified for each PB: (1)

a safe zone, where the subsystems are considered to be in the safe zone, not yet subject to irreversible change; (2) a zone of uncertainty, where there is uncertainty of the precise position of the threshold; and (3) a zone beyond uncertainty where science suggests that tipping points have been transgressed towards a new state of the Earth System.

The PBs researchers apply the precautionary principle in setting the threshold at the edge of the safe zone as for the science to be useful for policy-makers. This "safe setting" allows policy-makers time to intervene in order to avoid transgressing the boundaries.

Kim and Bosselmann formulate it as follows:

> PB is intended to be used in defining the boundary between the safe Holocene and the Anthropocene, thereby conditioning the type and level of human activities upon respecting the earths subsystems or processes. The threshold levels of indicators are in essence a set of "Earths" minimum standards for safeguarding the planetary sustainability must haves which are absolutely essential for human survival and "sustainable development" of any kind. (Kim and Bosselmann, 2015, 96)

In sum, PBs are set up to delineate a safe operating space for humanity and inform and guide human activity and development, and in particular guide human decision-making.

Use of PBs in law and governance

Even though PBs are aimed at guiding human decision-making, they are explicitly not aimed at being political. In their main publication, Steffen et al.:

> do not suggest *how* to maneuver within the safe operating space in the quest for global sustainability. The PB framework does not as yet take into account for the regional distribution of the impact or its historical patterns. Nor does the PB framework take into account the deeper issues of equity and causation. (Steffen et al., 2015, 1259855-8, emphasis added)

As a first type of use, Kim and Bosselmann (2015) suggest to introduce the idea of planetary biophysical limits in international law, and more broadly, in the governance of States and corporations. They submit that PBs provide a scientific groundwork for a new ethic which could be used to ground new law and governance systems and function as a sort of *ius cogens* "grundnorm" of ecological integrity,

similarly to how human rights and rule of law play a function in national contexts.

This way PBs provide an overarching priority goal under which individual institutions and legal frameworks should operate in a mutually supportive manner in order to avoid trade-offs. At present, neither in the Sustainable Development Goals (SDGs), nor in international environmental law, is there an overarching goal or internal coherence between instruments. PBs can plug this gap by providing a scientific underpinning to an idea of "ecological integrity" used in international (environmental) law at planetary scale.

Second, from a global governance perspective, Biermann (2012) considers the PBs as an attempt at a quantified identification of the policy space's boundaries to remain in the safe operating space of humankind on planet Earth. In his opinion PBs define the overall target corridor that leaves ample space for different policy trajectories, naturally, under the normative assumption that the underlying objective is sustainable development.

Additionally, Fernández and Malwé point out that:

> the Agenda 2030 does not specify that what is at stake is the maintenance of the Earth system in a Holocene like State, which is the overarching purpose of the planetary boundaries framework. Furthermore, the Agenda does not make any reference to the scientific concern that this system may tip over abruptly and irreversibly toward another State, which would be unfavourable for humanity, if the ecological thresholds are transgressed as a result of human caused transformations. These omissions indicate the absence of important elements of the planetary boundaries framework in the Agenda. This absence is even more obvious in the Sustainable Development Goals, which do not make any reference at all to the planet. (Fernández and Malwé, 2019, 52)

PBs allow for creating a hierarchy in the SDGs and revisiting the classic paradigm of sustainable development. (Ibid.)

Thirdly, several scholars point out that the PBs framework is very useful in defining research questions on governance in both Earth sciences as social sciences and humanities. Coming from Earth sciences, the PBs are relevant for humanities and social sciences by providing a base to study the interplay between ecological and social systems.

Fourthly, PBs can be used in legal

instruments, governance and policy documents. So far, the uptake has been limited. The concept entered the international political arena when the UN Secretary General referred to PBs in his Synthesis report on the post-2015 agenda, however it was not taken up further in any other UN formal documents (Synthesis report of the Secretary General on the post-2015 Agenda: The Road To Dignity by 2030: Ending Poverty, Transforming All Lives and Protecting the Planet, 4 December 2015, A/69/700). At EU level, the 7th Environmental Plan of Action is the most important document where PBs are integrated (Decision No. 1386/2013/EU of the European Parliament and of the Commission of 20 November 2013 on a General Union Environment Action Programme to 2020 "Living Well, Within the Limits of Our Planet", Annex I, para. 8). However, no further steps of operationalization of PBs are included. It is important to mention that both documents use PBs within the classic vision of human dominated nature management and optimization and efficiency thinking, not considering the Earth as a complex dynamic system or taking into account resilience as a crucial element.

As a way forward, Fernández and Malwé (2019) make a proposal for integrating PBs into international law in the form of a framework convention on PBs that can address the uncertainties of such a complex dynamic system, but also the interdependence of the subsystems in one legal umbrella document.

Criticisms and challenges

This section lists five criticisms and challenges of the PBs framework, both on the PBs concept itself and on its usefulness in law and governance:

First, Biermann (2012) argues that the definition of some "planetary boundaries" is complex and politically problematic. The lack of precision of scientific bases for some boundary limits, the impossibility of reversibility, interlinkages and complexities such as environmental problem shifting between PBs, makes using PBs in political decisions difficult.

Secondly, Biermann points out that even if the idea of boundaries is normatively neutral, the exact definition and operationalization of them is not. For example, the land-use change boundary prescribing a maximum cropland conversion becomes very normative when famines are still prevalent. The translation from the assessment of natural processes into needs and proposed actions, is a political process that affects the political role of the scientists and thus also their scientific legitimacy. Thus, the assessment of PBs is inherently political, hence scientists become political actors.

A third criticism is the eco-centric character of the PBs framework, placing a greater importance on staying within the environmental ceiling than over the "social floor", nature before social equity. In line with this lies the criticism of developing countries that PBs infringe their right to development and to exploit natural resources to provide in their basic needs. Kim and Bosselmann (2015) reject that there is a conflict between the two and argue that it is only the current unjust economic order that forces countries to exploit their natural resources for poverty reduction. They maintain that a just international economic order is a prerequisite for ecological sustainability.

Related to the question of subordinance of social equity, Biermann throws up the question whether deliberative democracy and protection of human rights are prerequisites and inherent part of the strive for respecting PBs. This remains an open question.

Fourthly, Montoya et al. (2018) critique the existence of a "limited space" in which growth and ecological depletion are possible as long it does not reach the threshold. The PBs concept is created to show people the destructive relation of humans with nature, but only goes halfway, instead of aiming at building complete regenerative processes and activities. In the same vain Schlesinger questions whether thresholds are a good idea for pollution and argues that "waiting to act until we approach these limits merely allows us to continue with our bad habits until it's too late to change them". "Management based on thresholds, although attractive in its simplicity, allows pernicious, slow and diffuse degradation to persist nearly indefinitely" (William H. Schlesinger (2019). "Planetary Boundaries: Thresholds Risk Prolonged Degradation", Nature Climate Change 1, 112–113, 113).

Finally, PBs are difficult to use at national level. Authors of the PBs framework acknowledge that it is not meant to break down in small regional/national boundaries, nor that it is very useful in that context.

VINCENT BELLINKX

References

Biermann, Frank (2012). "Planetary Boundaries and Earth System Governance: Exploring the Links", Ecological Economics 81, 4–9.

Fernández, Edgar and Claire Malwé (2019). "The Emergence of the 'Planetary Boundaries' Concept in International Environmental Law: A Proposal for a Framework Convention", Review of European, Comparative and International Environmental Law 28(1), 48–56.

Folke, Carl et al. (2016). "Social-ecological Resilience and Biosphere-based Sustainability Science", Ecology and Society 21(3), art. 41.

Galaz, Victor et al. (2012). "'Planetary Boundaries' – Exploring the Challenges for Global Environmental Governance", Current Opinion in Environmental Sustainability 4(1), 80–87.

Kim, Rakhyun E. and Klaus Bosselmann (2015). "Operationalizing Sustainable Development: Ecological Integrity as a Grundnorm of International Law", Review of European, Comparative and International Environmental Law 24(2), 194–208.

Montoya, José M., Ian Donohue, and Stuart L. Pimm (2018). "Planetary Boundaries for Biodiversity: Implausible Science, Pernicious Policies", Trends in Ecology and Evolution 33(2), 71–73.

Rockström, Johan et al. (2009). "Planetary Boundaries: Exploring the Safe Operating Space for Humanity", Ecology and Society 14(2), art. 32.

Rockström, Johan et al. (2018). "Planetary Boundaries: Separating Fact from Fiction. A Response to Montoya et al.", Trends in Ecology and Evolution 33(4), 233–234.

Steffen, Will et al. (2015). "Planetary Boundaries: Guiding Human Development on a Changing Planet", Science 347(6223), 1259855-1–1259855-10.

Steffen, Will et al. (2018). "Trajectories of the Earth System in the Anthropocene", Proceedings of the National Academy of Sciences 115(33), 8252–8259.

62. Poverty

What is poverty?

A wise woman working and living amongst the poor in Port Elizabeth, South Africa, described poor people as "those who are without choices".

Many academics have tried to define poverty, but there is no one universally accepted definition. Definitions may favour an objective or a subjective evaluation of facts or ideals and are often clad in the definer's underlying world view, philosophy or school of thought.

It is possible to define poverty in purely economic terms, as the World Bank does by using an amount of US dollars available per person per day as a yardstick to define extreme poverty and moderate poverty. Seebohm Rowntree, a sociologist, who in 1901 published a study of his investigations in York, England, also at first blush uses monetary terms to calculate the minimum cost for food, clothing, fuel and household necessities. Rowntree found that a quarter of the poor people interviewed were impoverished because of no income, half of the people interviewed had an income, but their income was too low to sustain a healthy living, and the last quarter had sufficient income to purchase necessities, but their spending was unwise or unnecessary, causing them not to have enough for mere physical efficiency. A definition referring only to the amount of money one has is seen as an absolutist view of poverty as it only refers to the minimum needed to sustain life.

Peter Townsend, a socialist and academic professor who wrote extensively on poverty, disagreed with the use of an absolutist definition. In his 1979 book he argues that it was impossible to divorce the poor's physical existence from their psychological well-being and from the organization and structure of society. He sees poverty relative to the society in which the poor person lives. He defines poverty as a situation where a family's means are so far below those which are at the disposal of the average family that the poor family is effectively excluded from the ordinary living patterns, customs, and activities of that society. Townsend thus opts for an equality-based definition, which he calls objective and which regards people as poor if their income, even if adequate for survival, falls markedly behind that of the community.

A relative definition of poverty takes into account social expectations, which in turn affects the standing or dignity of persons within a society. This had already been recognized by Adam Smith in 1776 when he opined that there are objects or things which even the lowliest should have as the country's custom dictates it for credibility as a person. One such item that no person could be without, he suggested, was a cotton shirt. International human rights instruments, which recognize socio-economic rights as fundamental to a person's well-being and dignity, have since the days of Smith moved the relative definition to include the aspects of dignity and equality.

There is a correlation between poverty and inequality, but these concepts are not the same. Amartya Sen, one of the foremost academics on the topic and a Nobel Prize for economics recipient, states in "Poor, Relatively Speaking" that it would be absurd to call someone poor just because he had the means to buy only one Cadillac per day when others in that community could buy two each day. Sen further asserts that poverty and inequality are related, but independent. It is misleading to use one as a marker of the other. Although both concepts have historically been closely associated with an interest in economic and social change, they do not change at the same pace. Studies have indicated that they may even change in opposite directions.

One way to differentiate between inequality and poverty is to determine a poverty line with regard to the acceptable living standards of a community. Rowntree was reportedly the first person to suggest the use of a poverty line in 1901.

Poverty and quality of life also depend on the individual's personal and social capacity, argues Sen in his "capabilities approach" in *Development as Freedom*. It is not only a lack of resources, but also an individual's ability to use the income in a manner in which they can achieve the freedom to lead the kind of life which that person values. Sen thus provides a bridge between the absolute and relative theories of poverty. Sen in *Development as Freedom* sees deprivation of the personal and social capability as absolutes, whereas the resources needed to fulfil those capabilities are seen as relative to the society. Sen states that a person's capabilities are influenced by economic opportunities, political liberties, social powers and the enabling conditions of good health, basic education, and the encouragement and cultivation of initiatives.

Degye Goshu, a professor of Agricultural Economics at Haramaya University, Ethiopia, defines poverty as the human condition characterized by the sustained deprivation of resources, capabilities, choices, power and security necessary for an adequate standard of living, and other rights (Degye Goshu (2016). "The Dynamics of Poverty, Vulnerability, and Welfare in Rural Ethiopia", in Herman Musahara (ed.), *Inclusive Growth and Development Issues in Eastern and Southern Africa*. Organization for Social Science Research in Eastern and Southern Africa).

Although poverty may be interpreted and understood differently, definitions of poverty all involve a common element of material insufficiency, which translates into a lack of resources needed for survival to function as a full and active member with standing and dignity within that society. This implies that poverty is more than just a correlation between income and consumption. It is rather a multidimensional phenomenon which includes the measuring of living standards, health and education and freedom.

Correlation between poverty and human rights

In practice there is a correlation between poverty and human rights because poverty often influences a poor person's access or enjoyment of amenities of life and/or human rights. In the matter of Soobramoney v. Minister of Health (Kwazulu-Natal), the Constitutional Court of South Africa acknowledged in November 1997 that millions of people were living in deplorable conditions and in great poverty and in great disparity to others in South Africa, and that there was a need to transform the society so that there would be human dignity, freedom and equality in the new constitutional order. The Court specifically found that as long as disparity and poverty continue, the hope of the realization of human rights will have a hollow ring.

The court could nevertheless not assist Mr Soobramoney by ordering the State to provide him with kidney dialysis and he died soon after the judgment as he did not have money to access needed health care.

Poverty and access to justice

There is a correlation between poverty and justice and the rule of law. Danie Brand et al. write about a 2012 research project at the University of Pretoria, South Africa, on the relationship between law and poverty ("Poverty as Injustice", Law Democracy and Development 17, 273–297). Their starting point was the assertion that poverty is an injustice. The implicit reverse is thus that justice is the absence of poverty. They rejected the view of poverty as foremost being a social problem, as this obscured the political dimensions of poverty. However, if poverty is defined as inadequate access to basic living resources such as housing, food, water and health care, then the political dimensions of poverty are brought to the fore. Economic and political power determine access to the said basic resources.

There can be no access to justice in the face of poverty, unemployment and inequality. Any strategy to change this will be contingent on two factors, according to Yousuf Vawda, a law professor at the University of KwaZulu-Natal, South Africa (Yousuf Vawda (2005). "Access to Justice: From Legal Representation to the Promotion of Equality and Social Justice – Addressing the Legal Isolation of the Poor", Obiter 26(2), 234–247). Firstly, the government needs to have the political will and deploy the necessary resources to meet these challenges. Secondly, it will depend on people having the capacity to access their human rights. Access to justice, he states, is therefore the key to ensuring that both conditions are realized.

Causes of poverty

The causes of poverty are multi-faceted and include economic, social and political factors, as well as political system failures. Recessions, coupled with a weak rule of law and poor government investment, often preserve already existing poverty. Lack of education or ineffective education increase poverty. High levels of corruption weaken the ability and the efforts to make an impact on poverty. Lack of access to health care may cause poverty. Children receiving inadequate nutrition makes them less likely to break out of poverty or more likely to become poor as their ability to develop their full human capabilities is undermined. Even geographic factors such as lack of access to fertile lands, fresh water and minerals can increase poverty.

Causes of poverty have been classified as residual, pathological and structural. Residual poverty results when a few people are "left out" whilst most people are empowered when the economy grows. Pathological poverty regards people as being responsible for their own welfare and responsible to move themselves out of poverty, for example a jobless person is responsible for being unemployed. Structural poverty identifies the system as producing poverty and inequality.

Ongoing political and religious instability exacerbates the refugee crises and the large number of undocumented persons, which in turn are major causes for the increase and perpetuation of poverty.

Sustainable Development Goal 1

The Sustainable Development Goals (SDGs) were adopted by the UN General Assembly as part of its development agenda to guide global development efforts between 2015 and 2030. There are only ten years of this period remaining at the time of writing. The SDGs replaced the Millennium Development Goals (MDGs), which were in operation between 2000 and 2015.

SDG 1 aims to end poverty in all its forms everywhere. SDG 2 aims to end hunger. The UN estimates that more than 700 million people, or 10 per cent of the world population, still live in extreme poverty. They are surviving on less than US$1.90 a day and the majority live in Sub-Saharan Africa. Poverty affects children disproportionately resulting in one out of five children living in extreme poverty.

The UN declared the following targets to achieve SDG 1:

*   **1.1** By 2030, eradicate extreme poverty for all people everywhere, currently measured as people living on less than $1.25 a day;
*   **1.2** By 2030, reduce at least by half the proportion of men, women and children of all ages living in poverty in all its dimensions according to national definitions;
*   **1.3** Implement nationally appropriate social protection systems and measures for all, including floors, and by 2030 achieve substantial coverage of the poor and the vulnerable;
*   **1.4** By 2030, ensure that all men and women, in particular the poor and the vulnerable, have equal rights to economic resources, as well as access to basic services, ownership and control over land and other forms of property, inheritance, natural resources, appropriate new technology and financial services, including microfinance;
*   **1.5** By 2030, build the resilience of the poor and those in vulnerable situations and reduce their exposure and vulnerability to climate-related extreme events and other economic, social and environmental shocks and disasters;
*   **1.A** Ensure significant mobilization of resources from a variety of sources, including through enhanced development cooperation, in order to provide adequate and predictable means for developing countries, in particular least developed countries, to implement programmes and policies to end poverty in all its dimensions;
*   **1.B** Create sound policy frameworks at the national, regional and international levels, based on pro-poor and gender-sensitive development strategies, to support accelerated investment in poverty eradication actions.

Jeffrey D. Sachs, special adviser to the United Nations Secretary General on the MDGs and director of Columbia University's Earth Institute, wrote in 2005 that a world without extreme poverty may be attainable by 2025 if the developed world makes a sincere attempt to meet basic human needs on a global scale. To reduce poverty there will need to be a multifaceted approach. The perceptions of poor and the non-poor must be changed. National governments and the international community must champion change. However, SDG 1 does not, unfortunately, place any measurable obligations on developed countries.

Governments attempt to reduce poverty through social grants, work creation programmes, minimum wage legislation and other social legislation. However, the Carnegie Council on Ethics and International Affairs suggests that litigation may also be an effective tool to enforce human rights in order to hold the political powers accountable for alleviating poverty and to expose abuses linked thereto.

The impact of crime on the human dignity of especially the poor and vulnerable has also not, in the writer's opinion, received sufficient attention in the development of the SDGs as it must be accepted that crime increases poverty.

The writer hereof expresses the hope that the next ten years will bring visible and permanent alleviation of poverty to a world in much need of it.

LILLA CROUSE

References

Carnegie Council on Ethics and International Affairs (2000). "Litigating Human Rights: Promise v. Perils – Introduction", Human Rights Dialogue 2(2), 1–3.

Rowntree, Seebohm (1901). *Poverty: A Study of Town Life*. Macmillan.

Sachs, Jeffrey D. (2005). *The End of Poverty: Economic Possibilities for Our Time*. The Penguin Press.

Sen, Amartya (1982). *Choice, Welfare and Measurement*. Blackwell.

Sen, Amartya (1983). "Poor, Relatively Speaking", Oxford Economic Papers 35(2), 156–157.

Sen, Amartya (1999). *Development as Freedom*. Oxford University Press.

Smith, Adam (1776). *The Wealth of the Nations*, Book 5, Chapter 2, Part I.

Soobramoney v. Minister of Health (Kwazulu-Natal) (CCT32/97) [1997] ZACC 17; 1998 (1) SA 765 (CC); 1997 (12) BCLR 1696 (27 November 1997).

Townsend, Peter (1979). *Poverty in the United Kingdom: A Survey of Household Resources and Standards of Living*. Penguin Books.

Vandenhole, Wouter (2018). "De-Growth and Sustainable Development: Rethinking Human Rights Law and Poverty Alleviation", The Law and Development Review 11(2), 647–675.

63. Public Administration

"Public administration" is a wide range of activities and processes, including the conduct of officials responsible for the organization and implementation of government policies. Public administration is also defined as "public leadership of public affairs directly responsible for executive action" (Appleby, 1947) and "the management of public programs" (Denhardt and Denhardt, 2009). Public administration also refers to an area of study, a profession, or an institution concerning the formation and implementation of government policies (Vigoda, 2002).

Theories and Theorists: There are three broad theoretical approaches to public administration, including Classical Public Administration Theory (Wilson, 1887), New Public Management Theory (Hood, 1991), and Postmodern Public Administration Theory (Fox and Miller, 1995). A non-exhaustive list of key public administration theorists includes Max Weber, Woodrow Wilson, Frank Goodnow, Frederick Winslow Taylor, Luther Gulick, Mary Parker Follett, Herbert A. Simon, Christopher Hood, Laurence E. Lynn, Hugh T. Miller, and Charles J. Fox.

Public Administration and Law: In modern States, law defines the processes and requirements for the formation and implementation of government policies. Administrative agencies hear and adjudicate public administrative matters in quasi-judicial settings ("judicialization" of public administration), and courts, where independent of the executive regime, perform a judicial review of government actions and determine their legitimacy by adjudicating disputes arising from public administration. Constitutions provide an overall regulatory platform for public administration by defining the organization and powers of the government (and their limits). Statutes and regulations (e.g., public administrative law) further detail the processes and requirements for the organization and implementation of government policies. Scholars argue that public administration is law in action and mainly a regulative system (Vigoda, 2002).

Public Administration and Development: Public administration has a significant impact on the promotion of economic and social development. The role and focus of public administration may vary depending on the overall policy stance and economic rationale under which development policies are framed and implemented. Scholars identify the following "three movements" in which development has been promoted with a particular policy stance (Trubek and Santos, 2006).

Developmental State: Developmental States assume the critical role in economic development. The successful developing countries in East Asia in the 1960s through the 1980s, such as South Korea, Taiwan, Singapore, and more recently China, are examples of successful developmental States. In developmental States, public administration plays an active role in the promotion of development; public administrators develop and implement economic development plans, invest and manage key sectors, control foreign capital and international trade, relocate surplus, and suppress resistance.

Dissidents of developmental States criticize active public administration for its interference with the autonomy of individuals and private businesses associated with the implementation of State-led development policies. Advocates consider active public administration and promotion of the State-led development policies instrumental to economic development that has successfully lifted the most impoverished economies to economic prosperity.

The success of public administration in developmental States depends on the competence of personnel, organizational strength, financial and technical resources, and the integrity of administrators. The lack of these qualities in public administration of many developing countries resulted in weak public administration and unsatisfactory outcomes in economic development.

Neoliberal Reform: Neoliberal reform refers to a series of pro-market initiatives that began in the 1980s, which discouraged positive government interventions in the economy and promoted free market approaches, including privatization and trade liberalization. This approach has an impact on public administration, such as downscaling its size, reflecting its emphasis on the private sector. Neoliberal reforms undertaken by public administration also focus on the measures supported by the Washington Consensus such as fiscal discipline; a redirection of public expenditure priorities toward areas offering both high economic returns and the potential to improve income distribution (such as primary health care, primary education and infrastructure); tax reform to lower marginal rates and broaden the tax base; interest rate liberalization; a competitive exchange rate; trade liberalization; liberalization of inflows of foreign direct investment; privatization; deregulation; and protection of property rights.

Neoliberal policies led economic reforms in the post-Soviet Eastern Europe, South America, and Africa, but the implementation of these policies failed to bring the promised economic outcomes. Institutional weaknesses, lack of the proper sequencing and poor oversight of policies have been cited as causes of this failure (Lee, 2019).

Holistic Approach to Development: A new movement, which adopts a more holistic approach to development, has emerged in the 1990s, shifting focus from economic development to a range of socio-political agendas. Public administration under this approach focuses on broader development issues, such as relief of poverty, environmental protection, gender equality, protection of labour, social inequality, the rule of law, and democratic governance. The Sustainable Development Goals (SDGs) initiated under the auspices of the United Nations incorporate this new approach and presents a number of development goals and targets. The massive financial requirements and the skills and disciplines required for the implementation of the SDGs present challenges for public administrators, particularly those in developing countries facing serious resource restraints. There is a substantial need for training and education.

General Theory of Law and Development: The impact of public administration (as "law in action") on development can be analysed by the "General Theory of Law and Development" (Lee, 2017; 2019), a generalized theory that attempts to set the disciplinary parameters of law and development and explains the causal mechanisms by which law impacts development ("regulatory impact mechanisms"). The regulatory impact mechanisms are comprised of three distinctive, but interrelated, categorical elements: "regulatory design", "regulatory compliance", "quality of implementation", and additional sub-elements as explained below.

Regulatory Design: The first element of the regulatory impact mechanisms, "regulatory design", concerns how optimally a law is designed to achieve its regulatory objectives. This assessment is potentially a complex task, and regulatory design is analysed in the following three categories (sub-elements): anticipated policy outcome, referring to the expected result of the policy advanced by the law; organization of law, legal frameworks, and institutions ("LFIs"); and adaptation to socio-economic conditions.

Regulatory Compliance: The second element of the mechanisms, "regulatory compliance", refers to the conduct of the general public in complying with law. Law would not be effective without compliance by the general public. The analysis of regulatory compliance is comprised of the assessment of two sub-elements: general regulatory compliance, which refers to the overall level of compliance with the law in any given jurisdiction, and specific regulatory compliance, which pertains to the strength of public compliance with a particular law. Effective public administration seeks to improve the level of general regulatory compliance through public education and proper monitoring and enforcement of law across the board, and specific regulatory compliance by aligning the requirements of the law with relevant public demands and interests.

Quality of Implementation: The third and final element of the mechanisms is "quality of implementation". It assesses the degree to which a State meets the requirements of law and undertakes the mandates under the latter to fulfil its objectives. A State implements law through legislation, judicial decisions and administrative actions. This implementation, when it poses political challenges, also requires a degree of political will. Thus, two outstanding factors, State capacity and political will, determine the quality of implementation. Public administration is relevant to both factors.

State Capacity: A State must have the due capacity to implement law. State capacity refers to its financial, technological and administrative capabilities, including internal controls against corruption, the ability to achieve enforcement of laws and fulfil regulatory objectives. Since the State implements its policies through public administration, the strength of public administration is a determinant of State capacity.

Recruitment of Public Administrators: The quality of public administrators determines the strength of public administration. To ensure the quality of personnel, governments often adopt a competitive application process to recruit public administrators and also determine promotions and job assignments based on the evaluation of their performance. The private sector is a source for recruitment; senior administrators may be recruited from private corporations, non-governmental organizations (NGOs), and academia. Career public officials form the main corpus of public administration, but the government may also delegate certain public administrative tasks (e.g., operation of public transportation services) to private enterprises. Developing countries with resource constraints face challenges in recruiting competent public administrators. Good governance, as advocated by the 2030 Agenda, will require recruitment of competent public administrators. Cultural factors are relevant; for example, a cultural factor that enabled the successful developing countries in East Asia to recruit highly disciplined and devoted public officials, despite initial financial constraints (i.e., modest government salary), was the Confucian tradition that encouraged educated elite individuals to seek government positions with the notion that service to the State in the position of a government official is a personal and family honour.

Political Leadership: Effective political leadership is conducive to creating political stability essential for economic development (Lee, 2017; 2019). Political leadership that presents a clear vision for development and practical plans for its implementation guides, streamlines, and coordinates public administration and reinforces its effectiveness. Political leaders also emerge among both elected and non-elected career public administrators. Political leadership with extensive experience in public administration is often effective in the development and implementation of policies and the LFIs that facilitate economic development.

Democracy, Development, and Public Administration: The proper system of governance and the role of public administration are important in the context of development. While democratic governance ("good governance") is considered a development goal, the deliberative and elective nature of democracy presents challenges when the government faces a long-term development decision that may require voters to make an immediate sacrifice, particularly in the early stages of economic development when resources are limited and difficult choices have to be made. In addition, a change of regime, which is an inevitable outcome in

elective democracies, can also lead to a shift in development policy and even in development objectives. Some of these changes are for political reasons rather than for development, and they may be adverse to the development interests. For these reasons, a level of development may realistically be necessary before a democratic system of governance operates efficiently and continues to promote development (Lee, 2017, p. 455; Trebilcock and Mota Prado, 2014, p. 123). A working democracy requires economic and social resources, such as public education, access to information, and the rule of law, which may not be achievable without economic development in place. Thus, in the pursuit of democratic governance, public administration is required to facilitate conditions necessary for a working democracy, often under challenging socio-economic conditions, by providing public education, promoting open access to information, supporting the rule of law, and maintaining active channels of communication and cooperation between the government and the non-governmental sectors.

YONG-SHIK LEE

References

Appleby, Paul (1947). "Toward Better Public Administration", Public Administration Review 7(2), 93–99.

Denhardt, Robert B. and Janet V. Denhardt (2009). *Public Administration: An Action Orientation*. 6th edition. Thomson Wadsworth.

Fox, Christopher J. and Hugh T. Miller (1995). *Postmodern Public Administration: Bureaucracy, Modernity, and Postmodernity*. University of Alabama Press.

Hood, Christopher (1991). "A Public Management for All Seasons?", Public Administration 69(1), 3–19.

Lee, Yong-Shik (2017). "General Theory of Law and Development", Cornell International Law Journal 50(3), 415–471.

Lee, Yong-Shik (2019). *Law and Development: Theory and Practice*. Routledge.

Trebilcock, Michael J. and Mariana Mota Prado (2014). *Advanced Introduction to Law and Development*. Edward Elgar.

Trubek, David M. and Alvaro Santos (2006). *New Law and Economic Development*. Cambridge University Press.

Vidoda, Eran (ed.) (2002). *Public Administration*. CRC Press.

Wilson, Woodrow (1887). "The Study of Administration", Political Science Quarterly 2(2), 197–222.

64. Regulating Multinational Corporations

Alternative narratives

Descriptions of attempts at regulating multinational corporations (MNCs) are generally characterized as political and/or economic disagreements on whether corporate conduct should be regulated at the domestic or international level, or altogether structured through self-regulation rather than through legal standards establishing obligations directly applicable to MNCs. As demonstrated by Pahuja and Saunders (2019), however, the historical struggle over the corporation and its relationship with the State and international law itself, engage both questions of authority and of legal form. Historically, with the framing of the struggle over the corporation in terms of identifying the appropriate fora for the regulation of corporate conduct (characterized by disagreements which continue to this day), other fundamental questions about the constitutive and constituent nature of the corporation were implicitly neutralized. More specifically, the acceptance in 1975 that the UN Commission on Transnational Corporations (UNCTC) should be predominantly a forum to negotiate the relationship between MNCs and States and discuss future regulation of corporate actors through a Code of Conduct, meant that two outstanding disputes were implicitly settled: disputes over whether the corporation should be conceived as a private or political entity; and over whether and how it could maintain its legal personality across jurisdictional boundaries. Arguably then, what we are left with today is a debate which does not even begin to question the private nature of MNCs and their ability to transcend jurisdictional barriers; a debate primarily articulated within the specific terms of the business and human rights discourse, and centred on the procedural technicalities of *how* (rather than *by whom*) corporate conduct should be regulated.

Continuity and parallel projects in the regulation of MNCs

The current articulation of the debate within the framework of business and human rights means that the United Nations Guiding Principles on Business and Human Rights (UNGP), despite their shortcomings, represent the principal platform on which debates and reform proposals have been articulated since their adoption by the UN Human Rights Council in 2011. The UNGP were presented as completely separated, both conceptually and procedurally, from previous 'failed' efforts at regulating corporate conduct. It is possible, however, to draw an alternative genealogy of the UNGP, which contextualizes them as a continuation of previous attempts at regulating corporate conduct, including through the UNCTC, and in parallel with legal and political efforts aimed at facilitating market liberalization and at consolidating the rights of MNCs as fundamental market actors. This alternative narrative is useful to understand political and policy divergences which continue to underlie the debate, not least on the ongoing negotiations for a binding treaty on business and human rights.

Parallel continuities: From the UN Global Compact to a binding treaty on business and human rights

The UN Global Compact was announced by Kofi Annan on 31 January 1999 in his address to the World Economic Forum in Davos. It was presented as a call to 'embrace, support and enact a set of core values in the areas of human rights, labour standards, and environmental practices'. Launched in New York the following year, it aimed at supporting the business community in advancing UN goals and values through responsible corporate conduct. The UN Global Compact, in essence, was conceptualized as a learning platform, through which public private partnerships were promoted and various sets of self-regulating standards were elaborated, such as the Principles for Responsible Investment. Since the UN Global Compact and the UNGP were designed by the same architect, John Ruggie, it is not surprising to note a certain level of continuity and complementarity between the two. As Ruggie himself claimed, the UN Global Compact paved the way to the establishment of the UNGP, since it 'normalized' a specific corporate social responsibility discourse. But what did this 'normalization' entail and what was lost in the process of bringing the corporate social responsibility discourse to the core of the then nascent business and human rights project?

When the UN Global Compact was launched in 2000, the UN Sub-Commission on the Promotion and Protection of Human Rights was working on what later became the Draft Norms on the Responsibilities of Transnational Corporations and Other Business Enterprises with Regard to Human Rights (UN Draft Norms). The UN Draft Norms significantly departed from the parallel project of the UN Global Compact in that they attempted to identify obligations directly applicable to MNCs. The business world aligned against the UN Draft Norms and when they were presented to the UN Human Rights Commission in 2004 they were eventually rejected due to a lack of consensus. The Commission requested an in-depth study on 'the scope and legal status of existing initiatives and standards' on business and human rights, followed by the appointment of a UN Special Representative of the Secretary General (SRSG) mandated to 'clarify the roles and responsibility of States, companies and other social actors in the business and human rights sphere'. In 2005, John Ruggie was appointed to this role and, in 2008, at the end of his first mandate, the Human Rights Council (the successor of the Human Rights Commission) unanimously adopted the 'Protect, Respect and Remedy' framework developed by Ruggie and his team. The framework, in full alignment with traditional interpretations of international law and with the 'normalized' discourse of the UN Global Compact, confirmed that the duty to protect against human rights abuses caused by non-State actors, including companies, is vested primarily upon States; that companies do not have obligations under international human rights law but do have a responsibility to respect human rights; and finally that victims of corporate human rights abuse need strengthened access to effective remedies. The SRSG's mandate was extended until 2011 to provide further guidance on how to operationalize the framework, a task that Ruggie carried out through the development of the UNGP, which were then submitted and approved in June 2011. The Human Rights Council also established, as follow-up mechanisms, an annual stakeholder forum on business and human rights and an expert UN Working Group.

Based on the groundwork of the UN Global Compact, the UNGP were able to speak to diverse corporate, civil society and government actors, by adopting the language of normative and regulatory standards already familiar to the different audiences: the legal discourse on State obligations; the risk management discourse of corporate governance; and the civil society's advocacy discourse on remedial action. The UNGP were thus able to restructure existing standards in new policy objectives, whereby MNCs accepted 'responsibility' towards *non-binding* international human rights law. What was achieved through the UN Global Compact and the UNGP, however (and is perhaps not discussed enough in the existing literature), was the creation of what Ruggie described as a regulatory 'ecosystem' for human rights. A new 'pluralizing' system of global governance aimed at mobilizing different stakeholders (civil society, companies, etc.) to which ultimately the UN multilateral system would willingly delegate authority for both policy-making and policy implementation. Yet, whilst this multistakeholder ecosystem of governance consolidated itself within the business and human rights discourse, efforts at establishing binding obligations on corporate actors were reignited in June 2014, when the UN Human Rights Council adopted Resolution 26/9, proposed by Ecuador and South Africa, for the establishment of an open-ended intergovernmental working group mandated 'to elaborate an international legally binding instrument to regulate, in international human rights law, the activities of transnational corporations and other business enterprises'. Negotiations of this binding instrument are ongoing and it might be too early to predict how these negotiations will end but, for the purposes of our analysis of continuity and parallel journeys, it is not difficult to draw similarities between the UN Global Compact and the UNGP on the one hand, and the UN Draft Norms and negotiations for a binding instrument on the other. Whilst Ruggie insists on ensuring that work on the implementation of the UNGP continues in parallel with these negotiations, it is crucial to reflect on the key elements of, and structural transformations engendered by, the governance system underpinning the UNGP.

The promise of polycentric governance

Ruggie presented the adoption and implementation of the UNGP as an example of successful new governance system and theory. New governance theory is based on the premise that 'old' governance models (which would see States negotiating a legally binding treaty prescribing applicable norms and policies) are unsuitable to deal with today's global challenges. What this theory prefers, instead, is an engagement with a full range of actors to stimulate multistakeholder processes of informal cooperation and public private partnerships: what Ruggie described as an exercise in and a product of polycentric governance. The UNGP, so the argument goes, encompassed and aligned three governance systems (of public law and governance; of civil governance; and of corporate governance) to deliver 'cumulative change'. Thus, while as claimed by Ruggie the 'Protect, Respect and Remedy' framework addressed *what* should be done to achieve such cumulative change, and the UNGP indicated *how* things should be done, the dispute over *who* should be overseeing and guiding the process, ensuring for instance democratic accountability and transparency, was implicitly settled and became conceptually uncontested. Whilst States discussed the shortcomings of existing legal and policy measures relevant to responsible business in conflict zones, 'investment agreement negotiators helped shape proposals for better safeguarding human rights within the system of investor protection; human rights organizations and plaintiffs' lawyers advanced ideas for judicial reform. The various strands were brought together in multistakeholder consultations' (Ruggie, 2014: 10). In this process, I argue, everybody had the impression of having somewhat achieved their own specific objective, whilst ultimately losing sight of the bigger picture that in the meantime was clearly delineating itself in the background.

Similar to the way in which through the UNCTC process the private nature of MNCs and their ability to transcend jurisdictional barriers became implicitly accepted, through the UN Global Compact, the framework and the UNGP, the fact that corporate actors were active participants of a new political platform for global governance, de facto replacing multilateralism, also became 'normalized'. As emphasized by Gleckman (2018), multistakeholder platforms also have their own financing structures, capable of mobilizing private capital to achieve shared objectives (in the case examined by this entry, the implementation of business and human rights policies and standards to regulate corporate conduct). At a time in which government funding allocated to the

UN is at its lowest, the financial power of these multistakeholder platforms places them in a key position to set policy priorities towards the 'cumulative change' identified by Ruggie. They thus can and are, slowly but steadily, redefining the acceptable scope and direction of human rights standards regulating corporate conduct. The last chapter of this story, however, remains to be written, while history and its contrasting definitions and re-definitions are still far from settled, as we seek different answers to the questions that new governance theory will otherwise present as implicitly 'normalized'.

DARIA DAVITTI

References

Commission on Human Rights (2003). *Norms on the Responsibilities of Transnational Corporations and other Business Enterprises with Regard to Human Rights.*

Eslava, Luis, Michael Fakhri, and Vasuki Nesiah (eds) (2017). *Global History, and International Law: Critical Pasts and Pending Futures.* Cambridge University Press.

Gleckman, Harris (2018). *Multistakeholder Governance and Democracy: A Global Challenge.* Routledge.

Human Rights Council (2014). Resolution 26/9: Elaboration of an international legally binding instrument on transnational corporations and other business enterprises with respect to human rights. Human Rights Council.

Pahuja, Sundhya (2019). 'Corporations, Universalism, and the Domestication of Race in International Law' in Duncan Bell (ed.), *Empire, Race and Global Justice.* Cambridge University Press.

Pahuja, Sundhya and Anna Saunders (2019). 'Rival Worlds and the Place of the Corporation in International Law' in Jochen von Bernstorff and Philipp Dann (eds), *The Battle for International Law: South-North Perspectives on the Decolonization Era.* Oxford University Press.

Picciotto, Sol (2011). *Regulating Global Corporate Capitalism.* Cambridge University Press.

Ruggie, John Gerard (2014). 'Global Governance and 'New Governance Theory': Lessons from Business and Human Rights', Global Governance 20, 5–17.

Sornarajah, Muthucumaraswamy (2015). *Resistance and Change in the International Law on Foreign Investment.* Cambridge University Press.

UN Office of the High Commissioner for Human Rights (2011). *Guiding Principles for Business and Human Rights: Implementing the United Nations Protect, Respect and Remedy Framework.* OHCHR.

65. Resistance

Introduction

Resistance is one of the core concepts in critical theory, used by a wide range of writers to understand and explain the agency of social movements, and their capacity to act beyond the reach of hegemonic power and/or ideology. Generally, resistance can be seen as a relational category, because *to resist* means to function in opposition to a dominant power (Hollander and Einwohner, 2004). However, as will be explained in this entry, the diametrical relationship of resistance with power does not mean that resistance can only be defined in negative terms. To the contrary, in its contemporary use, resistance often illuminates the existence of viewpoints and lifestyles that are alternative to the hegemonic approach (Brighenti, 2011), which means that resistance can also be a productive category, capable of identifying new paths and horizons for political action.

Origins

Historically, the category of resistance had been used for a range of political aims and ideologies. It originated mostly in a context of war, as a way of describing an insurgent action by those who are on the opposite side of the imperial military power. For instance, one of the earliest analyses of resistance by Carl von Clausewitz concerned the struggle against Napoleonic warfare in the early nineteenth century (Caygill, 2013, pp. 15–29). This understanding of resistance as a tactical fight against standing armies was further popularized by the French Resistance against the Nazi rule, and it survives until the present day in the analysis of modern guerrilla warfare. The idea of resistance has also been crucial in anti-colonial struggles, for instance in Gandhi's movement against British rule, where Gandhi famously advocated peaceful resistance, rather than popular uprising based on violence against imperialist forces (Gandhi, 1997). Another realm where the notion of resistance had been crucial was the evolution of socialist thought and doctrine. For instance, Marx and Engels considered workers' resistance against capital owners as the necessary condition for enabling a global communist revolution – the propositions later developed by Lenin and Mao, amongst others (Caygill, 2013). However, in contrast to Ghandi, Mao was a strong proponent of armed, rather than peaceful, resistance against colonial powers.

The contemporary thought on resistance in many ways reflects these multiple pedigrees of resistance: it tends to be rooted in an anti-capitalist, anti-imperial, anti-military and anti-colonial thinking. However, differently to Gandhi's focus on the independence of an Indian State, or concerns of socialist thinkers with capture of State power through resistance, most contemporary resistance is aimed *against* the neoliberal State and its nationalistic development policies. One of the earliest social movements of this sort were the Zapatistas in Mexico (Caygill, 2013), followed by many others, mostly from the Global South (Santos, 2016), all of which see the modern State as a means of capitalist exploitation and a vehicle of violent globalization processes (Santos, 2008).

Relationship to power

Michel Foucault was a key thinker for those interested in resistance. He famously claimed that 'where there is power there is resistance, and yet, or rather consequently, this resistance is never in a position of exteriority in relation to power' (Foucault, 1998, p. 95). Foucault's notion of the biopower of the State, and also the idea that disciplinary power is not concentrated in one group or institution but is dispersed within and beyond the State, provided an important theoretical steppingstone for contemporary understandings of resistance (Brighenti, 2011). That is because Foucault's analysis broadened considerably the understanding of resistance – from a focus on political leadership and ideology, to everyday dispersed practices that discipline and condition individuals. With this broadened framework of analysis, Foucault also created a serious theoretical challenge to the very idea of resistance (Brighenti, 2011). That is because, if power is dispersed everywhere in a society disciplining individuals in their daily life, and if resistance can only be a reflection of power and never fully outside of it, then, even if successful, resistance is likely to become but another source of power, thus further increasing the capacity to discipline and punish.

It is not possible to capture in this short text

the full breadth of theoretical discussion that followed from this Foucauldian challenge. However, by and large scholars interested in resistance seem to agree that even in the context of Foucault's understanding of power, it is possible to hold a productive understanding of resistance; the one that starts as a reaction to power; but which might lead to alternatives *to* power, and also toward new ways of being (Brighenti, 2011). Put otherwise, resistance does not have to result in a power shift akin to revolution, as was expected by the earlier anti-capitalist thinkers such as Marx; or in new methods of disciplining society, as feared by Foucault. This shift of emphasis from anti-power to alternative thinking, particularly in the context of modernity and globalization, is also at the heart of contemporary resistance, as reflected in the writings of theorists of resistance such as Boaventura de Sousa Santos (Santos, 2008; 2016) or Balakrishnan Rajagopal (Rajagopal, 2003).

Repertoire of resistance

Foucault's reframing of power and resistance brought to light a range of questions about what actions qualify as resistance and why. Whilst originally resistance was understood as a type of warfare against violence of a dominant military regime; since Gandhi and his emphasis on peaceful resistance, the ideas of armed resistance have been increasingly discredited. To be sure, there exist arguments in the literature on moral philosophy that defend the right to resist – by force, if necessary – if subjected to a serious structural injustice or a violent and arbitrary coercion (e.g. Brennan, 2018). However, such arguments are not widely accepted. Particularly since 9/11, the use of force as counter-violence is more commonly associated with terrorism, rather than resistance. Generally, the rise of terrorism as a governance category at the global level had largely undermined the legitimacy of armed resistance and contributed to an idea that only States hold the monopoly over the armed use of force.

On the other end of the resistance repertoire, some actions are neither violent nor directly confrontational to power. In fact, they might be completely invisible to those in power. This type of resistance includes acts such as taking overly long breaks at work, strategic tax evasion, refusal to register assets or formalize land title, or refusal to engage with digitalized governance. Scott (1985) famously qualified these acts as everyday resistance because despite being 'invisible', they might be the only means of resistance available to those who wish to express their disagreement with the dominant order. As Scott and others writing on this topic had argued, such instances of everyday resistance have a central role to play in modern capitalism, precisely because the exercise of power by current dominant order so often affects our life and choices at the individual level. Here, the task of a researcher is to notice such 'everyday resistance', whilst at the same time not reading resistance into all acts of non-compliance or disobedience with the law.

In between violent and armed resistance, and the uncoordinated everyday resistance of multiple individuals, there are a range of actions and/or refusals to act, all of which can be considered a part of a rich repertoire of resistance. An important element that turns action or inaction of a particular group into resistance, can be time. Gramsci was one of the thinkers who observed that often resistance and its successes only become visible in a long-term perspective; as a set of interventions into political processes, rather than a clash of forces that directly oppose one another. Accordingly, resistance operates in a different timeframe than the politics visible in a daily life of modernity. This focus on a temporal element is a bedrock of indigenous resistance, which tends to emphasize a perspective that goes beyond the life of a single individual, but rather understands a life as a part of the wider collective process that stretches from the past via the present, to the future (Caygill, 2013).

Resistance in law and development research

All the features of resistance highlighted above create significant challenges for an examination of this category in law and development research. That is because focus on resistance usually aims to capture and articulate something that takes place beyond the dominant order, as well as alternatives to that dominant order. Whereas both development discourse and State-based law tend to be a part of hegemonic ideology and dominant structure of a modern State, i.e. central within the very logic that resistance aims to transcend.

This tension between institutionalized order and resistance and social movements has been an important focus of scholars writing in the tradition of Third World Approaches to International Law (TWAIL). For instance, Rajagopal had aptly noted that the problem with theorizing resistance in the context of international law, is that both the sources, and the traditional methods of international law, are ill-suited to capture the dynamic of bottom-up struggles (Rajagopal, 2002). In terms of sources, international law usually only recognizes State-made law and top-down rules of liberal international institutions, most of which tend to promulgate the narrative of development as a leading vision for the world (Rajagopal, 2002). Doctrinal methods of analysis too put the sources of institutionalized order at the centre of analysis, whilst potentially leaving the informal dynamics of social movements and those excluded from international decision-making at the periphery of research (Rajagopal, 2002). Rajagopal made these observations nearly two decades ago, during which international law had seen alternative methods becoming more visible, ethnographic observation being one of them (e.g. Eslava, 2015). However, Rajagopal's observations about sources of law and legitimacy based on State consent remains a key analytical force that makes resistance invisible to the mainstream research in international law.

Continuous emphasis on the State consent as sufficient condition for generating legitimacy also means that a number of policy-making initiatives continue to side-line social movements from the core debates about the future of human development. For instance, it is notable that the Sustainable Development Goals (SDGs) were debated and agreed upon within the high-level inter-State institutional fora. While this emphasis on the 'high-level' political agreement guarantees the visibility and acceptance of the SDGs by States and other powerful actors, it also means that SDGs could readily be perceived as a part of the hegemonic development agenda that advances certain interests while silencing others, and which might therefore become subject to resistance.

It is notable, however, that certain areas of law are perceived more favourably by resistance movements than others; for instance, human rights, or participatory mechanisms in environmental decision-making (Rajagopal, 2002). On the other hand, the capacity of rights – a concept of dominant liberal order – to provide space for alternative viewpoints and to challenge development ideology, has also been put under critical scrutiny (Chatterjee, 2004). It is therefore a matter of practice and further scholarly scrutiny to ascertain whether law and resistance can be mutually reinforcing and analysed together, or whether resistance is bound to operate always beyond the horizon and the reach of the law.

GIEDRE JOKUBAUSKAITE

References

Brennan, Jason (2018). *When All Else Fails: The Ethics of Resistance to State Injustice*. Princeton University Press.

Brighenti, Andrea Mubi (2011). 'Power, Subtraction and Social Transformation: Canetti and Foucault on the Notion of Resistance', Distinktion: Scandinavian Journal of Social Theory 12(1), 57–78.

Caygill, Howard (2013). *On Resistance: A Philosophy of Defiance*. Macmillan Publishers.

Chatterjee, Partha (2004). *The Politics of the Governed: Reflections on Popular Politics in Much of the World*. Columbia University Press.

De Sousa Santos, Boaventura (2008). 'The World Social Forum and the Global Left', Politics and Society 36(2), 247–270.

De Sousa Santos, Boaventura (2016). *Epistemologies of the South. Justice Against Epistemicide*. Routledge.

Eslava, Luis (2015). *Local Space Global Life. The Everyday Operation of International Law and Development*. Columbia University Press.

Foucault, Michel (1998). *The Will to Knowledge: The History of Sexuality*. Vol. 1. Penguin Books.

Hollander, Jocelyn A. and Rachel L. Einwohner (2004). 'Conceptualizing Resistance', Sociological Forum 19(4), 533–554.

Rajagopal, Balakrishnan (2002). 'International Law and Social Movements: Challenges of Theorizing Resistance', Columbia Journal of Transnational Law 41(2), 397–434.

Rajagopal, Balakrishnan (2003). *International Law from Below: Development, Social Movements and Third World Resistance*. Cambridge University Press.

Scott, James (1985). *Weapons of the Weak: Everyday Forms of Peasant Resistance*. Yale University Press.

66.   Right to Development

Historical evolution

The Right to Development (RTD) has become recognized as the most controversial human right of our time. Bound in international politics and suppressed by hegemonic structures, the RTD has arguably made little progress since its adoption in 1986. On one side, proponents of the right assert its vital role in giving a voice to the need for global restructuring; on the other sceptics (and rejectionists) see the right as an amalgamation of existing human rights serving no additional purpose. Over the last 30 years the RTD has generated a vast array of political debate and academic interest, yet such discussions have done little to progress the right politically or conceptually.

The RTD has always represented the disparity between the 'developed' and the 'developing', the Global North and the Global South. In 1967 at the first Ministerial Conference of the G77 in Algiers, where members stood for economic and social development and the establishment of a new world order, Keba M'baye, Foreign Minister of Senegal, declared:

> Our task is to denounce the old colonial compact and to replace it with a new right. In the same way that developed countries proclaimed individual rights to education, health and work, we must claim here, loud and clear, that the nations of the Third World have the right to development.

The statement by M'baye was representative of the argument made by developing nations throughout the 1960s and 1970s; that sovereign equality was essentially meaningless if it was not met with more equitable distribution of economic resources. This was encapsulated by the international development discourse for the creation of a New International Economic Order (NIEO) and further illustrated by prominent aspects of the RTD contained within the Charter of Algiers in 1967. The Charter stated, inter alia, that the international community had an 'obligation' to rectify 'unfavourable trends' and create conditions within which all nations can enjoy 'economic and social well-being'.

In 1977 the UN Commission on Human Rights commissioned a study on the subject of the RTD and after a number of studies and reports, the RTD was formally adopted by the UN General Assembly on 4 December 1986 in the Declaration on the Right to Development (Resolution 41/128) by an almost unanimous vote. The single dissenting vote was cast by the United States and the eight abstentions were developed countries, including a number of countries from the European Union: representative of the division in opinion along economic lines.

Many years of discussion regarding the normative content and legal status of the right followed, leading to the formation of a new consensus at the Second World Conference on Human Rights in 1993 and the Vienna Declaration and Programme of Action. The Vienna Declaration reaffirmed the RTD as a universal and inalienable right and an integral part of the fundamental human rights framework, and further committed the international community to engage in cooperation for its realization. In order to expand understanding of the RTD and monitor implementation the UN Commission on Human Rights established an open-ended intergovernmental working group and appointed an Independent Expert (1998–2004). The Working Group was also supported between 2004–2010 by a High-Level Task Force (HLTF) and, more recently, the Human Rights Council appointed a Special Rapporteur on the RTD for a period of three years from September 2016.

Content of the right

The Declaration contains 16 preambular paragraphs and ten Articles which set out definitions, rights and duties, a commitment to eliminate human rights violations, and the need for international peace and security. The RTD is defined as an 'inalienable human right' which entitles every person and all peoples to participate in, contribute to, and enjoy development in which human rights can be fully realized (Article 1). No specific definition of 'development' itself is given, however meaning can be derived from its description as a 'comprehensive' and multi-faceted 'process' which contains social, cultural, political and economic aspects (Articles 2(1), 4(2) and 8(1)).

The RTD differs from traditional human rights frameworks in its attempt to marry individual and collective rights, looking not only at the State, but at the individual as a recipient of development. Article 2(1) places the human person at the centre of development as both an 'active participant' and a 'beneficiary'. Emphasis is also placed on ensuring that women have an active role in the development process (Article 8). The RTD requires all States and the international community to formulate 'appropriate national development policies' (Article 2(3)). Although what is deemed 'appropriate' is not defined, it is inferred that policies should be in line with the progressive realization of the RTD, as well as other human rights. The planning of developmental activities must be 'active, free and meaningful' (Article 2(3)) in order to achieve 'eradication of social injustices' through 'appropriate economic and social reforms' (Article 8). States are obligated to create conditions in which development can thrive by removing any obstacles resulting from 'failure to observe civil and political rights as well as economic, social and cultural rights' (Article 6(2)). References to other human rights throughout the declaration demonstrate the interdependency, indivisibility, and mutual reinforcement of the frameworks; but equally feed into rejectionist ideology that the RTD represents an amalgamation of existing human rights.

The obligation to cooperate in 'ensuring development and diminishing obstacles to development . . . in such a manner as to promote a new international economic order' is included within Article 3(3) and pays homage to the historical context within which the RTD emerged. Article 4(2) continues that such international cooperation should be part of 'sustained action' to promote 'rapid development of developing countries', igniting critical views from the Global North that such provision moves towards the creation of an obligation on what is considered discretionary international development cooperation. The RTD does not, however, provide any reiteration of specific obligations regarding development assistance or international debt.

The RTD is not legally binding, existing within the realms of soft law due to its proclamation within a Declaration. While many of its substantive aspects, such as the reference to civil and political, economic, social and cultural human rights, are derived from the United Nations Declaration of Human Rights of 1948 (Articles 1, 55 and 56), another soft law instrument, they also link to the 1966 International Covenant on Civil and Political Rights (ICCPR) and the International Covenant on Economic, Social and Cultural Rights (ICESCR), both of which are legally binding hard law instruments. Principles such as State sovereignty and non-discrimination are also part of customary international law and are therefore binding upon all States.

The RTD represented a huge breakthrough in the relationship between the Global North and the Global South. The right emphasizes the need for equity and the indivisibility of human rights and places focus on inclusive participation, all of which are seen within modern development frameworks such as the Sustainable Development Goals (SDGs). The right has been reaffirmed in a number of instruments including inter alia the Millennium Declaration, the outcome document of the UN Conference on Sustainable Development 'The Future We Want' (2012), the Addis Ababa Action Agenda of the Third International Conference on Financing for Development (2015), and the aforementioned SDGs. Still, despite members of the UN having agreed to implement the Declaration, no agreement has been made on the nature of the obligation.

The RTD has also gained recognition within regional instruments, first enshrined in Article 22 of the African Charter on Human and People's Rights (1981) prior to the UN Declaration. The provision declared that all peoples shall have the right to 'economic, social and cultural development' with due regard to 'freedom and identity' in the 'equal enjoyment of the common heritage of mankind'. Article 22(2) continued that States shall have 'the duty, individually or collectively, to ensure the exercise of the right to development'. The provision remains the only hard law document containing the RTD specifically, however a women's right to 'sustainable development' is contained within Article 19 of the Protocol to the African Charter on Human and Peoples' Rights on the Rights of Women in Africa (2003). The RTD was also included in the ASEAN Human Rights Declaration (Articles 35–37) illustrating the continued relevance of the right through a contemporary formulation with multiple linkages made to the sustainability of such development.

Obstacles to implementation

Underdevelopment of normative content

Literature on the RTD has expanded definitions of the right but with no progressive clarity and no demonstration of its normative force. The majority of rigorous debate has been conducted from a legal human rights stance with little consideration of its normative force vis-à-vis non-State actors, donors or international financial institutions. In 2010 the HLTF released a report providing detail on the 'core norm' of the right to development, identifying three aspects of the norm: comprehensive and human centred development policy; participatory human rights processes; and social justice in development. However, this further elaboration was not matched by consensus from all States. Further, the persistent viewpoint from the Global North of the RTD as an amalgamation of all individual rights dilutes potential for the development of normative character.

Persistent North-South divide

In line with opinion at its formation, interpretation of the RTD continues to be divided along economic lines. The Global South places emphasis on the need for radical change of the global system, including greater participation of developing countries in global decision-making, and focusing on the RTD as a collective right of the people; emphasizing what is wrong with the continuing hegemonic structure and resisting the need for domestic reform. Conversely, the Global North focuses on increasing good governance, enhancing democracy, and improving economic management within developing countries, ignoring the need for structural adjustment at the international level and the extraterritorial obligations contained within the RTD. As stated by Bonny Ibhawoh (2011), the RTD has been used as 'both a sword and a shield in the battle for high moral grounds on some of the most important human rights issues that confront our world today'. Ibhawoh refers to the right being invoked as a justification for greater international development assistance, as well as for deflecting criticism for continued human rights violations, or as the rationale behind continued high emissions.

Lack of linkages with Global Development Agenda

The fulfilment of the RTD requires policies and programmes which will allocate resources to ensure its implementation. Linkages between international development and human rights have been illustrated through the progressive use of the rights-*based* approach to development, as opposed to the right *to* development: further demonstration of the reluctance of the Global North to recognize the extraterritorial aspect of the RTD. Further, despite increasing recognition of the structural issues present within aid, illustrated through the Paris Declaration (2005), Accra Agenda for Action (2008), and the Busan Partnership for Effective Development Cooperation (2011), reference to the RTD is not contained within any of the documents aiming to improve aid effectiveness. The realization of the RTD and the way in which aid is conducted are intrinsically linked, therefore without recognition of this relationship, it is unlikely that significant progress in implementation of the RTD will take place.

Future prospects

Discussions on the future of the RTD have focused on translating the right into a legally binding convention or 'Development Compact' which would take the form of an agreement establishing reciprocal obligations between developing countries, the UN system, international financial institutions and bilateral donors. In September 2018 the UN Human Rights Council requested that the Working Group on the RTD develop a draft legally binding instrument on the RTD (UN HRC Resolution 39/9). The vote in relation to the resolution was 30 in favour and 12 against, with five abstentions. Once again, votes were divided along economic lines, with many EU countries voting against. Given this continued divide those drafting the treaty will be faced with a decision between the creation of a treaty with clear obligations to the satisfaction of developing countries or the creation of an instrument which is vague and largely focuses on principles, rather than obligations, in an attempt to gain a greater level of support.

Critical viewpoints on the RTD are often based on the limited progress made in developing 'tangible' outcomes, such as the creation of a binding legal instrument or enforcement mechanism, often overlooking the intangible outcomes of the discourse. The RTD has played a significant role in the substantive framing of development by opening up space within which to mobilize dialogue and work towards building consensus. However, as non-State actors, international financial institutions, and transnational corporations continue to gain power, the extra-territoriality of the RTD becomes increasingly poignant in order to keep pace with development in a globalized world. Attention must be paid to the implementation of the RTD at both a national and international level; failure to do so will likely see the RTD continue to stagnate. As progress towards a legally binding instrument is now underway the RTD is at a pivotal stage in its development. Whether this process can close the gap between developing and developed countries through the formation of a well-supported instrument, creating a new era for the RTD, is a question which will likely be answered in the near future.

JULIE GIBSON

References

Arts, Karin and Atabongawung Tamo (2016). 'The Right to Development in International Law: New Momentum Thirty Years Down the Line?', Netherlands International Law Review 63, 221–249.

Ibhawoh, Bonny (2011). 'The Right to Development: The Politics and Polemics of Power and Resistance', Human Rights Quarterly 33(1), 76–104.

Marks, Stephen (2004). 'The Human Right to Development: Between Rhetoric and Reality', Harvard Human Rights Journal 17, 137–168.

Marks, Stephen and Rajeev Malhotra (2017). 'The Future of the Right to Development' (working paper). Available at: https://cdn1.sph.harvard.edu/wp-content/uploads/sites/134/2018/06/Marks-Malhotra-The-Future-of-the-Right-to-Development-2017.pdf.

Rajagopal, Balakrishnan (2013). 'Right to Development and Global Governance: Old and New Challenges Twenty-Five Years On', Human Rights Quarterly 35(4), 893–909.

UNGA (2010). Report of the High-Level Task Force on the Implementation of the Right to Development on its Sixth Session. UN Doc A/HRC/15/WG.2/TF/2/Add.2.

Vandenbogaerde, Arne (2013). 'The Right to Development in International Human Rights Law: A Call for its Dissolution', Netherlands Quarterly of Human Rights 31(2), 187–209.

Villaroman, Noel G. (2010). 'The Right to Development: Exploring the Legal Basis of a Supernorm', Florida Journal of International Law 22(2), 299–332.

Villaroman, Noel G. (2011). 'Rescuing a Troubled Concept: An Alternative View of the Right to Development', Netherlands Quarterly of Human Rights 29(1), 13–53.

67. Rights of Nature

The recognition of nature as a subject of rights is a process that is taking place in several regions of the world. It was a discussion in different periods and started to regain importance in 2008. In that moment, this recognition became a new strategy for nature protection in the context of larger alternatives to global capitalism, known as *sumak kawsay* (good living) or *suma qamaña* (live well). The constitutional and legal proposals in Ecuador and Bolivia represent the first cases where nature is explicitly recognized as a legal entity: as *Pachamama* in the Constitution of Ecuador (2008), and as *Madre Tierra* in the Mother Earth Rights Act (2010) and the Framework Act on Mother Earth and Holistic Development to Live Well (2012) in Bolivia.

The Ecuadorian Constitution affirms in its Seventh Chapter, entitled "Rights of Nature", that Nature, or *Pachamama*, where life is reproduced and occurs, has the right to integral respect for its existence and for the mainte- nance and regeneration of its life cycles, struc- ture, functions and evolutionary processes. It also established that Nature has the right to be restored. For its part, the Bolivian legisla- tion, in the Mother Earth Rights Act (2010) defines the list of rights for Mother Earth: to life, to diversity of life, to water, to clean air, to balance, to restoration, and to live free of pol- lution. Two years later, the 2012 Act explicitly connects this legal recognition with the *suma qamaña* (live well), incorporating, in its sixth Article, a list of principles of living well: to be able to grow, to be able to eat well, to be able to work, to be able to dance, to be able to com- municate, to be able to dream, to be able to listen, to be able to think. In those regulations some monitoring mechanisms are also pre- sent as the Bolivian Mother Earth Defender, the Plurinational Council for Living Well in Harmony and Balance with Mother Earth, and the Plurinational Authority of Mother Earth.

Nevertheless, many tensions and contradic- tions arise in both countries, especially in how proposals that affect ecosystems are handled. This is a central problem in territories rich in natural resources, which in many cases are a central base of their economies.

This recognition is presented as very innova- tive. Until the recognition of legal rights for nature in Ecuador and Bolivia, only physical or legal persons were considered as subjects of rights. This is a legal concept that works as an ideal basis for deriving rights and legal obli- gations. The idea of the recognition of rights beyond those of humans has been a theme in animal and environmental ethics for several years as well as among law professors. Since the 1970s, the first articles from Christopher Stone in the United States asking for the legal stand- ing of trees as well as Marie-Angèle Hermitte in France about the legal status of biodiversity and Godofredo Stutzin in Chile affirming the importance to recognize these rights, among others, began to generate a field of discussion that is currently expanding in many law schools around the world.

The language of rights assumes, then, a cen- tral place in these debates and strategic judicial claims and could be presented as an opening point that, recently, has been translated into some legal systems. As described above, these translations are part of the legal systems in Ecuador and Bolivia and imply an interchange between the Western language of the recog- nition of rights and non-Western concepts, ideas, worldviews. Connecting the constitu- tion, a symbol of modernity, with words and expressions from ancestral worldviews in one central text became an interesting and powerful challenge.

The recognition of rights beyond those of humans today permeates the agenda not only in Latin America. It has begun to become visible in other regions and internationally. In the 2012 United Nations Conference on Sustainable Development that took place in Rio de Janeiro, Brazil, known as "Rio+20", the final document written under the title "The Future We Want" in its paragraph 39 affirms that some countries are recognizing these rights. During this confer- ence a proposition for a Universal Treaty on Rights of Mother Earth was widely promoted and presented as a series of independent col- lective agreements produced by representatives of major groups and stakeholders of civil soci- ety. For its part, the United Nations started in 2009, under the leadership of the Plurinational State of Bolivia, the Harmony with Nature Initiative. For the last decade, this strategy has been developing and brings together professors and researchers from all over the world work- ing on the topic and contains resolutions of the

General Assembly of the United Nations as well as annual reports of its Secretary General. It also updates the information about law, policy and education on rights of nature in different areas of the world, which facilitates observing how quickly this idea has been proliferating in the most diverse latitudes.

In this same period, many other documents on the topic were produced. These include, for example, the International Declaration on Mother Earth Rights signed by 35,000 persons in 2010 in Cochabamba in Bolivia, the citizen proposal for a European Union Directive where this recognition is a central point, or the Declaration of the Alternative World Water Forum, developed in Marseille, France, in 2012, which recognized the rights of ecosystems and species to exist, develop, reproduce and perpetuate. Also since 2015, the International Tribunal on Mother Earth Rights has been operating periodically; sometimes in parallel to the climate change Conference of the Parties (COPs) that have been taking place.

In parallel, a growing number of cities around the world are including the rights of nature in local regulations, for example, in Argentina, Australia, Brazil, France, Mexico, Uganda and the United States. There are also instances of special concessions. In New Zealand, legal personhood rights were recognized for the Whanganui River in an historical agreement between the Crown Government of New Zealand and the Iwi of the Whanganui River. Similar experiences are observable in New Zealand in relation to the Te Urewera national park that was removed from the national park system and was legally recognized as a legal entity or the Mount Taranaki, today also recognized as a subject of rights.

In addition, an increasing number of judicial decisions from different countries are focusing on the juridical status of nature. The first one in Ecuador refers to the right of a river not to be diverted from its natural course, the likely consequence of the expansion of a road. It is the Vilcabamba River in Loja Province in the south of Ecuador that gave rise to the first legal case in which a judge settled a dispute on the basis of the rights of nature on 30 March 2011. In applying, for first time, Article 71 of Ecuador's new Constitution, the Provincial Court of Loja ruled in favor of nature.

An important number of subsequent decisions based on the rights of nature are related with the legal status of rivers, especially in India, Bangladesh and Colombia. In this last country, from 2016 until now, several rivers have been recognized as subjects of rights as a consequence of judicial actions related with harm to rivers caused by mining, deforestation and water pollution. In this same period, two different judicial decisions declared that the Colombian Amazonia and the Pisba Highlands have this same juridical character. The case related with the Amazonia is also the first one about climate change in Latin America and introduces the idea of an intergenerational pact to decide about the future of the Amazonia and its deforestation.

With these types of decisions another path opens to the rights of nature. Even in countries where nature is not explicitly recognized as a subject of rights, courts begin to interpret current legislation from a less anthropocentric perspective. This recent strategy is gaining visibility during the last four years introducing new arguments, in some cases related with the recognition of indigenous rights. This is clear in the case of Colombia, where the rights of indigenous people, already part of their legal system, became the gateway to the rights of nature and allowed the development of the idea of *biocultural rights*. From this perspective, the Constitutional Court introduced as an argument that the conservation of biological diversity should include the protection of the lifestyles and the cultures.

More than one decade after the constitutional recognition in Ecuador, the increasing number of regulations, judicial decisions and local policies place in a distant past the discussions about whether to recognize or not nature as a subject of rights. These judicial cases, innovative institutions, alternative projects, documentary and propositional compendiums of regulations show that a non-anthropocentric worldview is beginning to gain importance, permeating and propelling some legal consecrations that have a sort of "equality" between the human and non-human. Not only do human beings have rights, but Mother Earth and *Pachamama* also do: right to restoration, to life, to the integral respect of their existence, to life diversity, to balance, to be free from pollution, to water, to clean air.

Today, other issues on the topic seem to be more crucial, for example, how have these new legal tools started to be mobilized? In which ways could this process represent a way to democratize the environmental law concepts, perspectives and tools? What is the jurisprudence necessary to make effective the rights of Mother Earth? What are the institutional innovations required for this process? In which way is the nature as a legal entity related to an alternative worldview construction? How has this idea begun to cross frontiers?

It is difficult to predict the result for nature protection of this perspective, available legal tools, judicial decisions and new institutions. Even so, it is possible to generate a series of reflections and contributions to the legal-institutional scaffolding for the protection of nature from eco-centric perspectives from different latitudes of the world starting with two South American countries that have special and heterogeneous worldviews. It may be that this process of recognizing the rights of nature is "re-coloring" our perspectives of "green" and these types of contributions can enrich the ethical, social and environmental debates and the issues that belong to the legal field, thus channeling more appropriate arguments for the defence of the natural world and identifying agendas and challenges of undeniable relevance for the present and future.

MARÍA VALERIA BERROS

References

Acosta, Alberto and Esperanza Martínez (2009). *Derechos de la Naturaleza: El futuro es ahora*. Abya Yala.

Belloso Martín, Nuria (2018). "El debate sobre la tutela institucional: generaciones futuras y derechos de la naturaleza", Cuadernos Democracia y Derechos Humanos 14.

Berros, Maria Valeria and Anna Leah Tabios Hillebrecht (eds) (2017). "Can Nature Have Rights? Legal and Political Insights", RCC Perspectives: Transformations in Environment and Society 6.

Bétaille, Julien (2019). "Rights of Nature: Why it Might Not Save the Entire World?", Journal for European Environmental and Planning Law 16(1), 35–64.

Boyd, David (2017). *The Rights of Nature: A Legal Revolution That Could Save the World*. ECW Press.

Carman, María (2017). *Las fronteras de lo humano: Cuando la vida humana pierde valor y la vida animal se dignifica*. Siglo XXI.

Gudynas, Eduardo (2015). *Derechos de la naturaleza: Ética biocéntrica y políticas ambientales*. Tinta Limón.

Hermitte, Marie-Angèle (2011). "La nature, sujet de droit?", Annales Histoire Sciences Sociales 1, 173–212.

Stone, Christopher (1972). "Should Trees Have Standing? Toward Legal Rights for Natural Objects", Southern California Law Review 45, 450–501.

Stutzin, Godofredo (1984). "Un imperativo ecológico: reconocer los derechos de la naturaleza", Ambiente y Desarrollo 1(1), 97–114.

68. Rule of Law

Introduction

The notion "Rule of Law", "Rechtstaadt", "Estado de Derecho" or "État de Droit" has a long and varied history. Nevertheless the "thread that has run for over 2,000 years, often frayed thin, but never completely severed, is that the sovereign, and the State and its officials, are limited by the law" (Tamanaha, 2009, p. 114).

In order to explain this notion and to understand its scope we are going to take into account: (1) its history; (2) its *desiderata*; (3) the debate about if it is an ideal that legal systems aspire to fulfill or a set of minimum requisites that must be fully accomplished by every legal system; (4) the discussion over whether its standards are or are not morally neutral; (5) its importance in nation-building; and (6) the arguments against it.

History of the rule of law

As Waldron has explained, the "Rule of Law has been an important ideal in our political tradition for millennia, and it is impossible to grasp and evaluate modern understandings of it without fathoming that historical heritage" (Waldron, 2016, p. 3). The history of this ideal began with Plato's advice that government should be "slave of the laws" (360 BCE). Aristotle continued this idea and claimed that it is better to be ruled by the best laws than to be ruled by the best man because laws are made after long consideration and are general and impartial (350 BCE). In the Middle Ages Aquinas remembered Aristotle's practical reasons to prefer the government of rules over the government of man and explained in which way political authorities should be submitted to legal precepts (1274 CE).

In the modern age Locke (1689) criticized absolutists' ideas and explained that the governance of laws which are established, promulgated and known by the people is much better than extemporary arbitrary decrees. Specifically, Locke claimed that people need a social contract to solve their insecurity problems mainly related to the lack of judges that

enforce natural law. But this social contract supposes a limited, divided (between executive and legislative branch) and revocable delegation of power, to limited purposes. Some years later, it was Montesquieu (1748) who completed the doctrine of the separation of powers, adding to executive and legislative branches the need to have an independent and legalistic judicial branch.

It was Dicey in his *Introduction to the Study of the Law of the Constitution* (1888) who offered a modern formulation of the rule of law in the context of a democratic system. In his words, the rule of law established that: (1) "no man is punishable ... except for a distinct breach of [pre-existing] law established in the ordinary legal manner"; and (2) "not only that with us no man is above the law, but (what is a different thing) that here every man whatever be his rank or condition, is subject to the ordinary law ... and ... ordinary tribunals".

In the twentieth century, after the Second World War, Lon Fuller (1969) reintroduced the debate on the importance of the rule of law to guarantee the freedom and dignity of those addressed by law. Apart from defending a link between the rule of law and justice, he also offered a list of *desiderata* detailing how positive law should be (Fassò, 2016, I and II).

The rule of law *desiderata*

Fuller's enumeration of the requirements or *desiderata* of the rule of law is the most widely accepted among legal theorists nowadays. Accordingly, it is usually accepted that legal rules (1) must have a minimum degree of generality in relation to the people and situations to which they are applied; (2) must be promulgated in order to be known by those whose conducts the rule intends to guide; (3) must be prospective or non-retroactive; (4) must be clear and precise (though this does not suppose that all rules must be precise to their greatest extent, leaving no room for legal principles or standards); (5) must be coherent with one another; (6) must enable their observance; (7) must have some sort of stability that allows them to be known by citizens; and (8) must be applied and obeyed by the public authority (Fuller, 1969, pp. 46–91).

All these requirements must be regarded not only by legislators or laws, but also by the State's institutions and processes, as the rule of law *desiderata* actually refers to the qualities they should possess. What is more, some of these attributes can only be assured by judges, and therefore, courts must also direct their acts according to these requirements. Particularly, judges must bear these *desiderata* in mind whenever interpreting and applying law. Some authors even propose a series of additional *desiderata* which are specific to the judicial activity: independence, public procedures, power of judicial review, accessibility, etc. (Finnis, 1980, p. 271).

The rule of law and the concept of law

If the rule of law is to be considered a conceptual requirement of rigid observance, the connection between the concept of law and the rule of law would be such that the social practices which do not fully accomplish those requirements could not be considered as law. On the contrary, if the rule of law is depicted as an ideal instead of a minimal requirement, we must ask ourselves two questions: (1) which is the relationship between the concept of law and the ideal of the rule of law?; and (2) does considering the rule of law as an ideal imply acknowledging that it has a moral content?

Most authors that deal with the issue of the rule of law often present it as an ideal, a value or a standard of excellence, and not merely as a minimum disjunctive requirement of every kind of law. In this sense, Raz states that it is not necessary for a set of rules to accomplish all of the requirements of the rule of law in order to be considered a legal system. "Conformity to the rule of law is a matter of degree. Complete conformity is impossible (some vagueness is inescapable) and maximal possible conformity is on the whole undesirable (some controlled administrative discretion is better than none)" (Raz, 1979, p. 223).

Is the rule of law morally neutral?

Against Lon Fuller's opinion, Hart claimed that the rule of law standards of excellence are morally neutral, since they do not guarantee that the rules, which respect the latter, will be justified. For Hart, it is not difficult to notice that even a tyrannical government can respect the requirements of the rule of law (Hart, 1958, pp. 593–629).

This comment sparks a debate about whether a "thin" or "formal" and "procedural" conception of the rule of law should be replaced by a "substantive" or "thicker" one. Dworkin was one of the first authors to support a substantive or thick conception of rule of law. He called this conception of the rule of law: "the 'rights' conception". Dworkin connects this vision with an understanding of the law according to which citizens have moral rights and duties towards each other and political rights against the State. In this conception the rule of law "is the ideal of rule by an accurate public conception of individual rights". He also thinks that this conception does not distinguish between the rule of law *desiderata* and the requirements of justice. This conception also requires that rules "capture and enforce moral rights" (Dworkin, 1980, p. 262).

Some authors nevertheless consider that it is more explanatory not to equate the concept of the rule of law with justice or with the substantive dimension of the concept of law. Instead, it is more enlightening to conceive the concept of the rule of law as an ideal that mainly focuses only on a part of the dimensions of law: the one that helps rules be more effective in their capacity to guide conduct and that justifies that it is better to be ruled by the best laws than to be ruled by the best man. This distinction can help spot the tensions between the formal and substantial dimensions of law, instead of hiding them behind a singular concept that does not distinguish the different elements that define it (Etcheverry, 2018, p. 126).

The latter does not mean that the rule of law standards of excellence are morally neutral, because what defines the moral content of a certain set of requirements is not that they guarantee a good result, or a good use of the laws that respect these requirements, but that they pursue a valuable end. For some authors, the confusion of those who deny that the requirements of the rule of law have an orientation to a valuable end might be due to the fact that they presume that the only specifically moral aspiration law has is to be fair. As a result, when proving that such purpose is not necessarily guaranteed by the requirements of the rule of law, they consider the latter to be morally neutral.

It is possible to think that the immediate objective of the requirements of the rule of law is not to guarantee justice. Instead, the aim of the rule of law *desiderata* is to accomplish other valuable purposes that constitute a necessary – though insufficient – condition for the justice of the laws that respect the requirements of the rule of law. Specifically, the aim of these requirements is not only for rules to be more effective in their capacity to guide and coordinate conducts, but mainly that they do this in a certain manner: (1) by guaranteeing some reciprocity between the authority and those who respect it; (2) by assuring a certain type of impartiality among those who apply the law; and, as a result, (3) by respecting in some fashion human autonomy. And this is sought by assuring the foreseeability of laws, the separation of State powers, and the rule of law, among others. The self-discipline required by the rule of law whenever it demands the authority to obey the rules and processes established by law implies the values of reciprocity, impartiality and, ultimately, the respect for human autonomy. All this is despised by a tyrannical government. That is why it is a mistake to conceive the rule of law merely as a technique either for good or for evil, depending on how it is employed. Actually, the rule of law is so valuable in itself that many times it has been presented as a limit to political maneuvering, in order to restrict arbitrary governments. Nonetheless, the rule of law *desiderata* are just a part of the requirements of justice; they do not guarantee every aspect of common good – in fact, not even its substance – since those who do not seek common good can still adhere to the values related to the rule of law to avoid losing popularity, for instance (Finnis, 1980, p. 273).

The rule of law and development

As it was explained before, the history of the relationship between the rule of law and development is far from new. In recent years, policymakers have placed increasing emphasis on the "rule of law" as a necessary ingredient in any development strategy. "In the 1990s, there was a massive surge in development assistance for law reform projects in developing and transition countries. These projects involved investments of many billions of dollars" (Trubek, 2006, pp. 74–94). In the words of the United Nations General Assembly: "the advancement of the rule of law at the national and international levels is essential for sustained economic growth, sustainable development, the eradication of poverty and hunger and the full realization of all human rights and fundamental freedoms" (UN General Assembly, The Rule of Law at the National and International Levels, A/RES/61/39 4 December 2006). More recently, the United Nations General Assembly

confirmed this guideline, establishing the "rule of law" as one of the goals (16.3) of its 2030 Sustainable Development Agenda (UN General Assembly, Transforming Our World: The 2030 Agenda for Sustainable Development, A/RES/ 70/1, 21 October 2015).

Although the importance of the rule of law in development strategy is rather clear, it is only a dimension of sustainable development that encourages sustained economic growth, the eradication of poverty and the full realization of human rights.

Opposition to the rule of law

Although both in the past and recent years the ideal of the rule of law is well valued, along history it also gathered many detractors. The young Plato (385 BCE), Thomas Hobbes (1681) and Carl Schmitt (1923) are among some of the authors that offered arguments against limiting governments by the rule of law. In more recent history, others have challenged the ideal of the rule of law, denouncing that it works as a tool of domination. Instead of considering it as a way of limiting a government in benefit of citizens, they have claimed that it works as a tool to limit majoritarian democracies in favor of the powerful. For this conception "the rule of law can prevail only when the relation of political forces is such that those who are most powerful find that the law is on their side" (Maravall and Przeworski, 2009, p. 3).

JUAN BAUTISTA ETCHEVERRY

References

Dworkin, Ronald (1980). "Political Judges and the Rule of Law", Proceedings of the British Academy 23(3), 259–287.

Etcheverry, Juan Bautista (2018). "Rule of Law and Judicial Discretion. Their Compatibility and Reciprocal Limitation", Archiv für Rechts- und Sozialphilosophie 104(1), 121–134.

Fassò, Guido (2016). *Storia della filosofia del diritto.* Vol. I-II. Laterza.

Finnis, John (1980). *Natural Law and Natural Rights.* Clarendon Law Series.

Fuller, Lon L. (1969). *The Morality of Law.* Yale University Press.

Hart, H.L.A. (1958). "Positivism and the Separation of Law and Morals", Harvard Law Review 71(4), 593–626.

Maravall, José María and Przeworski, Adam (eds) (2009). *Democracy and the Rule of Law.* Cambridge University Press.

Raz, Joseph (1979). "The Rule of Law and its Virtue" in Joseph Raz, *The Authority of Law*. Clarendon Press.

Tamanaha, Brian Z. (2009). *On the Rule of Law. History, Politics, Theory*. Cambridge University Press.

Trubek, David (2006). "The 'Rule of Law' in Development Assistance: Past, Present, and Future" in David Trubek and Alvaro Santos (eds), *The New Law and Economic Development: A Critical Appraisal*. Cambridge University Press.

Waldron, Jeremy (2016). "The Rule of Law", Stanford Encyclopaedia of Philosophy. Available at: https://plato.stanford.edu/entries/rule-of-law/#HistRuleLaw accessed 10 September 2020.

JUAN BAUTISTA ETCHEVERRY

69. Security

Definitions of security

Security refers to macro, meso and micro level conditions which sustain a safe and predictable existence of individuals, communities and societies. Current academic definitions of security have several origins, such as (neo)realism, world systems theory, constructivist and critical security studies, which have influenced the way that security and the role of the State is understood and approached. In international relations between governments, the development of international law, particularly after the Second World War, consolidated the security policy architecture, which forms the basis for practical cooperation. In this architecture, the United Nations Security Council is the only international organization with jurisdiction to maintain international peace and security at a global level, on the basis of the Charter of the United Nations (1945).

International law identifies States as the principal, sovereign actors in the international legal system. Cold War time politicians and academics, who followed the ideas of foreign policy realism, concentrated on the State and its relations vis-à-vis other States (e.g. Cox, 1981). Security was seen as a balancing act between States, each having its own national interests. Military security and foreign policy relations dominated political security agenda, and the threat of nuclear war and its prevention through such instruments as the Non-Proliferation Treaty (1970), were in focus.

Realism was challenged by world systems theory, which underlined macroeconomic structures in the construction of national interests, thus widening the understanding of factors which are relevant for security. Since the end of the Cold War, a critical outlook has expanded the concept of security to include challenges related to a wide range of issues in social, health, educational and environmental sectors. Organizations under the United Nations and regional institutions have been established to find transnational solutions to these challenges. Questions related to human rights have gained prominence in international relations.

Security includes several overlapping components. Military security concerns the armed offensive and defensive capabilities of States, and States' perceptions of each other's intentions. Political security concerns systems of government and institutional stability. Economic security concerns access to the resources, finance and markets necessary to sustain acceptable levels of State functions and economic growth. Societal security concerns the ability of societies to sustain and increase welfare, preserve their culture, religious and national identity and customs. Environmental security concerns the maintenance of the local and the planetary biosphere on which all other human enterprises depend (Buzan, 1984). This expansion of security conceptions includes not only the States, but various security entities inside of States, networks between States and regions, as well as transnational governance systems (Cox, 1981), where security policy and legal developments are closely linked to each other.

Human security and comprehensive security

Human security and comprehensive security are concepts which widened the scope of security after the unravelling of the two-pole superpower arrangement. They emerged at the time when a "civilizational" struggle between Global North and Global South, expanding militarization, regional armed conflicts, and the view that societal questions are security matters arose in the international political agenda.

In past decades, a more multi-polar system of international relations has begun to take shape and collectives comprising of individual States, such as the EU or the African Union, have assumed a role in security policy (Flockhart, 2016). Permanent human security issues have formed a complex system of relations where the balance of power is much more dispersed and unpredictable. Globalization has lowered and moved physical borders, and such topics as transnational crime and terrorism have acquired importance.

Human security places the individual and the people at the centre of security. In international law, the roots of human security are most of all in the United Nations' Universal Declaration of Human Rights (1948) and in the Geneva Conventions (1949), which established the rules of conduct during war and conflict. Even as the State is the main guarantor of security from military security to daily safety, the strengthening of security depends on the conditions and possibilities of individuals and communities. It should be noted that in comparison to the definition of security, which includes questions from global and regional security architecture to inter-organizational networks and local policing, safety here refers to conditions preventing individual injury and loss. Civilian crisis management, civil-military coordination and conflict prevention have been important areas for the practical development of human security policy-making and implementation.

Human security is closely linked with the level of good governance, measured by, for instance, the Worldwide Governance Indicators of the World Bank, which reports regularly on six broad dimensions of governance. The Worldwide Governance indicators (voice and accountability, political stability and absence of violence, government effectiveness, regulatory quality, rule of law and control of corruption) are also in line with the United Nations Sustainable Development Goals (SDGs). These 17 goals are based on the 2030 Agenda for Sustainable Development, which was adopted by UN Member States in 2015. Among the goals are reduction of poverty and eradication of hunger, provision of good health, social and educational services, promotion of gender equality, clean water and affordable energy, climate action, preservation of nature and strong institutions.

If human security stresses the fundamental question of what we are trying to protect, then comprehensive security covers security policy planning and implementation transcending administrative and geographical boundaries and implies taking into account both micro and macro level security issues across policy sectors and borders. It includes the idea that security policy must have a cross-sectoral and cross-border character, and include global perspectives and regional cooperation.

Comprehensive security is most visible as an incentive for institutional choices, such as the development of networked cooperation nationally and across borders. An example of such practical interconnectedness at a regional level is the work of Frontex, the European Border and Coast Guard Agency, established in 2016, which has aimed at creating harmonization in legislation and practices in member countries. Other examples include the United Nations Office on Drugs and Crime (UNODC) with its field and liaison offices in four continents, and Interpol, which works in its 194 member countries and is regulated by its 1956 Constitution.

Recently, the importance of migration to societal transformation resulted in the adoption of the Global Compact by the majority of UN Member States in 2018. The Global Compact established the first inter-governmentally negotiated non-binding agreement, covering all dimensions of international migration. It presents a new tool aimed at improving the governance of global migration, addressing its challenges through international cooperation, providing policy options for governments, and strengthening the contribution of migrants and migration to sustainable development.

Both human security and comprehensive security include the idea that international law and international organizations play a dominant role in States' security policy. This notion, however, is contested by a good number of States emphasizing their sovereignty in matters pertaining to internal affairs. There are two opposing views in the application of international law. One supports a universalistic understanding of the scope of international law, while the other promotes a selective view on international treaties and institutions. This division, or national variation, has been most visible in the areas of human rights, migration and refugee policy, as well as international crimes.

National security

Contemporary national security is understood as a form of a strategic culture connecting internal and external security with the overall resilience of a society. National security is linked with the government's and responsible authorities' assessment of security threats, the birth of societal risk positions, definitions of vital societal interests and decisions concerning proper action. Defined in this manner, the concept of national security is a neutral term.

In recent decades, the political significance of national security has increased as a result of globalized phenomena and interaction that cuts across traditional spheres of interests and shapes the limits of State sovereignty. Tackling global security risks often leads to critical evaluation of the effectiveness of regional security cooperation and re-evaluation of national security policies. National security is an actively used tool for political changes in authoritarian States but its popularity is not limited to any political culture or region of the world. Everywhere, legislative changes and organizational reforms in the security sector have been justified with more attention to national security.

Comprehensive security thinking may be embedded in national security documents, typically in security strategies and adjunct legislation, which aim to create an efficient administrative and legal system for security policy planning and implementation. For instance, in both the United States and the Russian Federation, national security strategies have a prominent role in legislative and organizational developments of the government. The United States Department of Homeland Security oversees the planning and implementation in major internal security sectors, based on the Homeland Security Act of 2002, Intelligence Reform and Terrorism Prevention Act of 2004 (Public Law, pp. 108–458) and Implementing Recommendations of the 9-11 Commission Act of 2007 (Public Law, pp. 110–153). In Russia, the Security Strategy (Ukaz Presidenta RF ot 31 dekabrya 2015, No. 683 "O Strategii natsional'noi bezopasnosti Rossiiskoi Federatsii") is used as an all-encompassing framework for governmental policy-making.

If comprehensive security refers to the way of organizing security management, and national security to the political framework of security policy-making, then securitization is the by-product of heightened political attention to security risks. This attention to national security can emerge in conditions where political decision-making is particularly challenging, as is the case during internal upheavals or external shocks. In such a situation, information is flowing, but it does not produce a balanced reflection for the development of legislation and institutions. Internal competition for different policy lines often increases in the government. Political consensus may be underlined as a requirement for an effective solution (Beck, 1992).

Historically, securitization has taken place in the aftermath of political transitions, coups or revolutions, or abrupt changes in a country's social and economic environment. Examples of the latter include the financial crisis of 1998 in the Russian Federation, or large-scale migration to Europe in 2015. The framing of social and cultural questions as possible security threats has increased enormously in the post 9/11 world and led to the development of various new mechanisms to follow the movement of people, goods and communication across borders. When societal questions became a part of national security, this affects their management, norms for management, and ways of thinking in involved organizations.

Ideally, comprehensive and human security should be linked through good governance and the development of security administrations and self-understanding of people working in security professions, also promoted by the SDGs. However, securitization is a process, which leads to increasing control in the public sphere and affects definitions of public service accountability.

Several institutional factors promote securitization. Among these are the development of planning and coordination of security governance at global, regional and local levels, as well as digitalization of both internal and border security. In national contexts, interconnectedness has increased network governance and constant evaluation of quantitative effectiveness. Newly framed threat assessments, along with existing organizational and political pathologies, often foster securitization. Paradoxically, increasing societal security and everyday safety in communities requires comprehensive security planning and implementation, often requiring and legitimizing the expansion of rights for authorities, sometimes at the expense of human rights protection.

Heightened attention to anti-terrorism has presented a significant challenge to the rule of law, upholding human rights in criminal investigation and increased securitization of migration regimes. Anti-terrorism action has led to legislative changes across the globe, and technological development of international cooperation in anti-terrorism action under the umbrella of national security has reduced transparency.

Modernization of security profession practices and ways of thinking are a constant challenge everywhere, but particularly in transitional, authoritarian and weak States, where organizational boundaries may be very rigid, while unofficial rules and corruption dominate in actual decision-making. Efficient protection of human and civil rights can be difficult due to wide or obscure discretionary rights of authorities, weak position of judges, corruption in the public sector and overall widespread informality. These problems are relevant to understanding legal and administrative challenges in the Global South, but also in societies in the Global

North, where legal sovereignty is increasingly emphasized and authoritarian politics are practised under the umbrella of national security.

Securitization can have long-term effects on a country's legal and administrative culture. It can instigate divisions between various social groups, divert political attention away from social, economic, educational and health issues to national security risks and in this manner further increase alienation and marginalization of individuals and groups. The responsible implementation of national security includes well-functioning organized channels for political representation, freedom of information, professionally monitored network governance, security cooperation based on the rule of law, and putting the individual's circumstances in the focus of attention. Finding a balance of human, comprehensive and national security lies in the hands of legislators and government officials and requires constant dialogue at all levels of the society.

ANNA-LIISA HEUSALA

References

Bauman, Zygmunt (2000). "Social Uses of Law and Order" in David Garland and Richard Sparks (eds), *Criminology and Social Theory*. Oxford University Press.

Beck, Ulrich (1992). *Risk Administration: Towards a New Modernity*. SAGE Publications.

Buzan, Barry (1984). "Peace, Power, and Security: Contending Concepts in the Study of International Relations", Journal of Peace Research 21(2), 109–125.

Cox, Robert W. (1981). "Social Forces, States and World Orders: Beyond International Relations Theory", Millennium: Journal of International Studies 10(2), 126–155.

Ferreira, Rialize and Dan Henk (2009). "'Operationalizing' Human Security in South Africa", Armed Forces and Society 35(3), 501–525.

Flockhart, Trine (2016). "The Coming Multi-Order World", Contemporary Security Policy 37(1), 3–30.

Kaldor, Mary (2003). *Global Civil Society – An Answer to War*. Polity Press.

O'Brien, Karen, Asuncion Lera St. Clair and Berit Kristoffersen (eds) (2010). *Climate Change, Ethics and Human Security*. Cambridge University Press.

Stern, Eric K. (1995). "Bringing the Environment In: The Case for Comprehensive Security", Cooperation and Conflict 30(3), 211–237.

Van Aerschot, Paul and Patricia Daentzer (eds) (2014). *The Integration and Protection of Immigrants: Canadian and Scandinavian Critiques*. Ashgate.

70.   Social Protection

Social protection as a core component of global poverty reduction

Over the past two decades, it has become generally accepted that the establishment of social protection systems plays a crucial role in achieving some core socio-political and development policy objectives. In its Report on the World Social Situation 2018 the UN Department of Economic and Social Affairs has made clear that "(s)ocial protection is a key policy tool for addressing poverty, inequality and social exclusion. No country has been able to reduce poverty and improve living conditions on a broad scale without putting comprehensive social protection systems in place" (UN DESA, 2018, p. 1). Of particular importance in this context is the concept of "social protection floors" – that is, social protection measures that guarantee access to at least basic income security and basic medical care for all inhabitants (International Labour Organization (ILO), 2017, p. 8). According to *Philip Alston*, UN Special Rapporteur on extreme poverty and human rights, the

> Implementation of the right to social protection through the adoption by all States of social protection floors is by far the most promising human rights-inspired approach to the global elimination of extreme poverty . . . No other operational concept has anything like the same potential to ensure that the poorest 15 to 20 % of the world's people enjoy at least minimum levels of economic, social and cultural rights. (Report of 11 August 2014, UN Doc. A/69/297, para. 2)

The 2030 Agenda for Sustainable Development, adopted by the United Nations in 2015 (UN Doc. A/RES/70/1), states under the heading "Ending poverty in all its forms and everywhere" that governments are requested to "[i]mplement nationally appropriate social protection systems and measures for all, including floors, and by 2030 achieve substantial coverage of the poor and the vulnerable" (Sustainable Development Goal (SDG) 1.3). This goal has a bridging function within the new Agenda because social protection programmes are not only important components

of poverty reduction and risk prevention strategies (SDGs 1.1, 1.2, 1.5), but also of health and food security (SDGs 1.5, 2.1, 2.2, 3.4, 3.8); they promote social cohesion (SDG 10.2) and help to reduce inequality – not least also with regard to gender relations (SDGs 4.5, 5.1, 5.4, 10.1, 10.4); beyond this, social protection contributes to getting people back into work (SDGs 8.5 and 8.6) and enables children from poor households to attend school (SDGs 4.1 and 8.7). Not only the UN and other globally active international organizations have recognized the added value of social protection measures, but also organizations of the Global South are committed to the expansion of social protection systems. Relevant recommendations can be found, for example, in the Social Policy Framework for Africa (of 31 October 2008, AU Doc. CAMSD/EXP/4[I], para. 2.2.3), in the Social Charter of the Americas (of 20 September 2012, OEA/Ser.P AG/doc.5242/12 rev. 2, Article 14), and in the ASEAN Declaration on Strengthening Social Protection (of 9 October 2013).

According to a definition of the ILO, social protection can be described as:

> the set of policies and programmes designed to reduce and prevent poverty and vulnerability throughout the life cycle. Social protection includes benefits for children and families, maternity, unemployment, employment injury, sickness, old age, disability, survivors, as well as health protection. Social protection systems address all these policy areas by a mix of contributory schemes (social insurance) and non-contributory tax-financed benefits, including social assistance. (ILO, 2017, p. 1)

In line with this wide-ranging approach, the ILO has adopted numerous conventions and recommendations aiming to raise the level of protection in the various areas of social protection worldwide. The most important treaty document drawn up by the ILO in this field is the Social Security (Minimum Standards) Convention of 1952 (210 UNTS 131). It lays down minimum requirements for all relevant social risks that are considered to require State (or State-guaranteed) protection, and establishes principles for the good governance of these systems. However, the treaty has been meanwhile ratified by only 59 countries, mostly belonging to the Northern hemisphere. Although the Convention contains flexibility clauses which allow the ratifying ILO members to limit their contractual obligations to specific branches of social security and to a certain percentage of the population, many States are reluctant to undertake these commitments.

The second key document in this area is the 2012 Social Protection Floor (SPF) Recommendation (ILO Recommendation No. 202). Against the background that especially those people who do not have a formal employment relationship are mostly not reached via the "classical" contributory forms of social security (according to the latest World Bank estimates, 60 per cent of the working age population in South Asia works in the so-called informal sector, more than 50 per cent in Latin America and even more than 70 per cent in Sub-Saharan Africa; see World Bank, 2019, p. 94), the ILO has expanded its concept and recommended – as already mentioned – "social protection floors" providing basic guarantees for the entire population. Nevertheless, governments are requested not to leave their programmes at this comparatively low standard of protection, but to continuously raise it to the level of the ILO social security conventions. Even though the SPF-Recommendation is merely a soft law document, it is nevertheless of great importance for current global debates – on the one hand because the International Labour Conference adopted it almost by consensus, and on the other hand because it is now also one of the main reference documents for SDG 1.3 ("including floors").

So while a broad agreement exists on the general potential of social protection programmes, especially for poverty reduction, there are differences on many details (see for an overview Gentilini and Omamo, 2011). This is already starting with the question of whether social protection in countries with a large informal sector should primarily take the form of social assistance programmes (including cash transfers and in-kind transfers, such as food assistance – the World Bank also uses the term "social safety nets" in this context) or whether social insurance schemes (mainly financed by earnings-based contributions) can also be successfully implemented here. When cash transfers are paid, the question arises as to whether these should be linked to certain conditions or whether only specific population groups should benefit from them; closely related to this is the debate on whether it makes sense to support the idea of a universal basic income (UBI) in low- and middle-income countries (see World Bank, 2019, p. 109). Moreover, in many developing countries informal social protection is still widespread; it is usually provided by families or by village or district communities. The challenge for these countries is to find the most efficient ways of linking their traditional informal protection systems with the newer formal programmes. Furthermore, there has recently been much discussion about how social security can be guaranteed in fragile States or in conflict or post-conflict situations. Not least the question also arises as to what significance climate change has for this issue, i.e. what an "adaptive social protection" concept could look like (see World Bank, 2018, p. 84).

The rights-based approach to social protection in the Global South

Social protection is not only a development goal, but also a human right. The right to social security is guaranteed both in Article 22 of the Universal Declaration of Human Rights and in Article 9 of the International Covenant on Economic, Social and Cultural Rights of 1966 (993 UNTS 3), as well as in several other global and regional treaties. Many low- and middle-income countries have also adopted the right to social security in their constitutions. The wording varies in scope and level of detail: some provisions are quite concise and contain no more than the statement that every person or citizen has the right to social security (or that the right to social security is guaranteed). However, there are also countries, particularly in Latin America, where more detailed versions of this right have been included in the constitution. Other constitutions do not explicitly mention the right to social security, but refer to the international human rights obligations to which the country is generally bound.

For the implementation and enforceability of the right to social security, the commentary work of the Committee on Economic, Social and Cultural Rights (CESCR) has proved very helpful. In its General Comment No. 19, issued in 2008 (UN Doc. E/C.12/GC/19), the CESCR suggests – similarly to the ILO approach – a broad interpretation of the term "social security". Measures covered by it primarily include contributory (insurance-based) and non-contributory schemes (e.g. social assistance), but also privately run programmes, self-help measures and community-based or mutual schemes. A major obligation of governments is now to ensure, by means of such programmes and schemes, adequate protection in the areas of health and old age provision, in the event of unemployment or occupational accidents and diseases, in the area of family and maternity protection, as well as protection of disabled persons, widows and orphans. In organizational terms, General Comment No. 19 leaves the States parties a large margin of flexibility, but they are at least obliged to design their social security systems in such a way that access to them is guaranteed for all people in the country, which in particular has consequences for the affordability of social benefits or insurance contributions.

This commitment to non-discrimination (including support for particularly vulnerable population groups) is one of the key demands of the "rights-based approach to social protection" (see Sepulveda and Nyst, 2012; Kaltenborn, 2017, pp. 250). The concept also requires that entitlements to social benefits have to be anchored in the national legal system and that the population is adequately participating at all levels of implementation (legislation, executive programme specification, individual case decisions). In addition, civil society actors, and in particular those affected themselves, must be provided with monitoring mechanisms and complaint procedures that allow them to detect implementation deficits at an early stage and, if necessary, to defend themselves against them. Legal regulations that fall within the area of social protection exist in almost every country in the world. However, the regulatory scope is very heterogeneous. In many low- and middle-income countries there are statutory pension schemes, but coverage is usually limited to selected groups of workers in the rather small, formal economy. To a lesser extent, some countries of the Global South also provide country-wide social health services on a legal basis. The health insurance laws of Ghana, Thailand, Indonesia and China are important examples, some of which also serve as models for other countries. There are far less legal regulations for social assistance; notable exceptions are the social assistance laws in South Africa, Chile and Brazil, to name a few.

Usually, the right to social security is implemented via the public social welfare system. The State's "obligation to fulfil" – elaborated in detail in General Comment No. 19 – requires formulating a social security strategy, including an action plan, and the establishment of relevant programmes, taking into account the aforementioned rights-based approach. However, to the extent that the State itself does not provide social protection in a particular sector, but relies on the services of third parties (e.g. private health or pension insurers), it must comply with its "obligation to protect" and therefore take appropriate regulatory measures to ensure that no individual population groups are disadvantaged by inadequate restrictions on access to benefits.

Although these obligations linked to the right to social security are meanwhile clearly defined, the global community is still a long way from achieving its universal realization. The ILO estimates that 71 per cent of the world's population, i.e. about 5.2 billion people, have to live without any or without adequate social protection (ILO, 2017; see also ILO, 2019). So, hardly any other human right is violated as frequently each day as the right to social security. This is where the international community's obligation to assist comes in. The "extraterritorial obligation" contained in Article 2 para. 1 of the International Covenant on Economic, Social and Cultural Rights (ICESCR) states that the States parties to the Convention must also take an active part in the implementation of the Convention's obligations beyond their territory. As far as their financial means permit, the richer members of the international community must therefore support the poorer States in their efforts to ensure the full realization of, inter alia, the right to social security. Even if there is no binding definition of which specific States are obliged to provide assistance and to what extent, the political leaders of the Global North should be aware that they also have a substantial contribution to make in order to achieve the objectives of SDG 1.3 in the near future.

MARKUS KALTENBORN

References

Barrientos, Armando (2013). *Social Assistance in Developing Countries.* Cambridge University Press.

Gentilini, Ugo and Steven Were Omamo (2011). "Social protection 2.0: Exploring Issues, Evidence and Debates in a Globalizing World", Food Policy 36(3), 329–340.

International Labour Organization (ILO) (2017). World Social Protection Report 2017-19: Universal Social Protection to Achieve the Sustainable Development Goals. ILO 2017.

International Labour Organization (ILO) (2019). General Survey concerning the Social Protection

Floors Recommendation No. 202. ILC.108/III/B ILO 2019.

Kaltenborn, Markus (2017). "Overcoming Extreme Poverty by Social Protection Floors – Approaches to Closing the Right to Social Security Gap", Law and Development Review 10(2), 237–273.

Leisering, Lutz (2019). *The Global Rise of Social Cash Transfers*. Oxford University Press.

Sepulveda, Magdalena and Carly Nyst (2012). *The Human Rights Approach to Social Protection*. Ministry for Foreign Affairs of Finland.

United Nations Department of Economic and Social Affairs (UN DESA) (2018). Promoting Inclusion through Social Protection. Report on the World Social Situation 2018. Available at: https://www.un-ilibrary.org/children-and-youth/the-report-on-the-world-social-situation-2018_5ef37a49-en accessed 8 November 2020.

World Bank (2018). *The State of Social Safety Nets 2018*. World Bank.

World Bank (2019). *World Development Report 2019: The Changing Nature of Work*. World Bank.

71. South-South and Triangular Cooperation

Origins and definition

South-South cooperation (SSC or Technical Cooperation among Developing Countries) is an international development promotion tool introduced in the 1970s by "non-aligned countries". In its origins, it relied on the notions of solidarity and collective self-reliance between developing countries for attaining agreed development goals. While geopolitically oriented, SSC does not form a single institutionalized model or trade arrangement. The term can be used to refer to technical cooperation, knowledge sharing, training and technology transfer.

Nonetheless, significant changes on the international and political economy landscapes in the last decades have broadened the possibilities for SSC. The rise of South-South trade flows – as well as financial aid – and the emergence of new powerbrokers in the Global South – especially China, and, on a smaller scale, BRICS and others – have demanded new tools in the international arena.

SSC moves beyond conventional North-South trade and aid arrangements, and yet it is not a substitute to them, functioning rather as a complement as emphasized by the Addis Ababa Action Agenda, and endorsed by the UN's General Assembly Resolution 69/313. In this sense, SSC aims to structure international trade relations as a process of consensus and collective building, so that elements such as trust, mutual benefit and equity are considered constitutive of development partnerships. It shifts towards horizontal and cooperative relationships, fostering the exchange of solutions and skills, rather than vertical top-down interaction. For instance, the transfer of financial assistance would not involve macroeconomic and political conditionalities – it would rather be based on the alignment of interests. In that sense, peer-to-peer learning, mutual knowledge exchange, and sustainable investments in long-term partnerships can be seen as key features of SSC, albeit present in other cooperation models.

Triangular development cooperation (TrC or trilateral development cooperation), on the other hand, is another instrument built for the new international arena. It attempts to make compatible two historically different forms of interaction: North-South and South-South cooperation. In TrC, Northern traditional donors or multilateral organizations would support Southern-driven partnerships. One developing country would act as the provider (pivotal or emerging donor), and another would be the beneficiary (recipient). As they share (or would have shared at some point of their history) similar development challenges, the pivotal country's expertise would in theory fit the recipient's context and specificities. Potential geographic, cultural and linguistic bounds could facilitate the delivery of development assistance among them. Traditional donors would bring expertise in development projects, funding resources and institutional capacity.

Beyond this initial framing, TrC can accommodate a great variety of labor division and parties' roles. However, the tool relies on the premise that all parties must be engaged in a given project, including traditional donors. It is a means of bringing experience and expertise to development cooperation, and it works better when it involves learning and active engagement on all sides. As such, it should not be confused with direct support to SSC through "hand-off" funding. TrC intends to combine strengths of each partner while developing plural international trade arrangements. Similarly to SSC, TrC can be employed in several sectors, such as education, food security, agriculture, environment, health, governance, research, development, conflict and post-conflict resolution, security and risk management.

Adaptable as they are, both instruments can support and foster the 2030 Agenda and the Sustainable Development Goals (SDGs), as already acknowledged by relevant international documents, such as the Report of the second High-level United Nations Conference on South-South Cooperation. Aware of this potential, the United Nations (UN) system has developed operational guidelines in order to ensure their dissemination, as well as to identify potential roles the UN may have in these cooperation instruments. The UN Secretary General note (SSC/19/3) provides detailed tools as entry points, thematic priorities, indicators and roadmaps for the UN organizations and agencies in all levels (national, regional and global). It ambitiously attempts to mainstream the use and evaluation of SSC and TrC for development.

Challenges for SSC and TrC

Despite its actual uses and promises, SSC and TrC remain umbrella concepts without sufficient institutionalization in the international sphere. The Global South is hardly a homogenous place and hierarchies can play from within (China, for instance, has a bargaining power that is obviously different from smaller countries). Thus, the overarching use of SSC may ultimately blur its explanatory precision unless context – history, legal system, institutional setting, trade strategy and political system – is taken into account. Parties' roles and mechanisms of cooperation should be defined in view of these particularities. Furthermore, key variables that ultimately describe the substance of SSC and TrC – partners, projects, products, services, processes, identities – have to be better evaluated. The lack of evidence and rigorous information about SSC and TrC scope, scale and impact prevents further analysis on these modalities of regional and interregional integration. Also, the challenge of data collection across governments, agencies and all possible stakeholders in SSC and TrC impairs the assessment of the tools' main actors' strengths and fragilities.

In addition, SSC and TrC do not replace the traditional politics of development. Crucial disagreements over the nature and path chosen to achieve development are invariably hidden below the surface of the debates. As SSC and TrC rhetoric can be used to conceal interests (State or private) under the veil of solidarity, the "South-South" or "triangular" discourse ultimately bear the risk of being used by convenience by powerful players to gather support for their own interests, including to dismantle other initiatives or types of collective voices or alliances. That is, the strict focus on consensus-building language and homogenous "South" arguably makes it harder to analyze who wins and who loses within such power agreements.

Some of the questions related to SSC apply to TrC, but the latter has additional layers of complexity. The presence of more than two parties leads to an increased problem of coordination (legal, institutional and diplomatic). Transaction costs may also increase due to the existence of multiple procedures, longer negotiations, difficulties on reaching common grounds, planning and arranging the division of roles and responsibilities among the actors. Coordination and its legal face (form and function), in other words, presents an important and still ill-discussed challenge to the law and development scholarship.

Political economy also matters and is to be seriously considered, as relationships inside the triangle are not necessarily balanced. Pivotal and beneficiaries' policies can still be subject to the traditional donors' preferences. Depending on the case, traditional donors and pivotal States can have closer interests rather than an alignment between pivotal and beneficiary countries. Plus, the recipient potential ownership over development projects and programs is a cause for precaution. TrC's impact is improved when all partners play their roles with attention to national ownership, sovereignty, independence, equality, non-conditionality and non-interference principles.

To effectively develop the role of catalyst and promoter of SSCs and TrC, the UN system can play critical roles as advocate, knowledge broker, partnership builder and analyst, for instance. Yet, these roles are not given, nor a necessary remedy for other power asymmetries. They will only prove to be meaningful as long as the UN organizations and agencies can build innovative, resilient and enduring SSC and TrC projects, including ambitiously scaling for whole-of-government approaches.

Lastly, recent shifts on foreign policy context resulting from the emergence of nationalists or populists including in the Global South (as the Bolsonaro right-wing government in Brazil) makes South-South cooperation even less stable. That injects an extra layer of challenging uncertainty to the SDGs, once these critical players may easily disengage from the international sphere. And on a larger scale, the current debate on the future of multilateralism in the twenty-first century is also a variable to be considered and further tackled by the law and development scholarship. The threats of dominance, competition, as well as the proliferation of bilateral arrangements can weaken multilateral agreements, TrC included, and that, also, certainly deserves critical analysis for law and development scholars.

RAQUEL DE MATTOS PIMENTA, LÍVIA GIL GUIMARÃES AND DIOGO R. COUTINHO

References

High-level Committee on South-South Cooperation (2016). Framework of Operational Guidelines on United Nations support to South-South and triangular cooperation. Note by the Secretary General SSC/19/3. Available at: https://digitallibrary.un.org/record/826679 accessed 10 September 2020.

Jules, Travis D. and Michelle M. de Sá e Silva (2008). "How Different Disciplines have Approached South-South Cooperation and Transfer", Society for International Education Journal 5(1), 45–64.

Lin, Yuefen (2018). "Assessment of South-South Cooperation and the Global Narrative on the Eve of BAPA+40", South Centre Research Paper 88.

McEwan, Cheryl and Emma Mawdsley (2012). "Trilateral Development Cooperation: Power and Politics in Emerging Aid Relationships", Development and Change 43(6), 1185–1209.

Muhr, Thomas (2016). "Beyond 'BRICS': Ten Theses on South-South Cooperation in the Twenty-First Century", Third World Quarterly 37(4), 630–648.

United Nations (2015). Addis Ababa Action Agenda of the Third International Conference on Financing for Development. Available at: https://www.un.org/esa/ffd/wp-content/uploads/2015/08/AAAA_Outcome.pdf.

United Nations (2019). Report of the Second High-Level United Nations Conference on South-South Cooperation. Available at: https://undocs.org/en/A/73/L.80 accessed 10 September 2020.

United Nations Development Programme (2019). Southern Development Solutions for the Sustainable Development Goals. Available at: https://www.latinamerica.undp.org/content/rblac/en/home/library/poverty/southern-development-solutions-for-the-sustainable-development-g.html accessed 10 September 2020.

United Nations General Assembly. Resolution 64/222 of 23 February 2010 (66th Plenary Meeting endorsing the Nairobi outcome document of the High-level United Nations Conference on South-South Cooperation, 2010). Available at: https://undocs.org/en/A/RES/64/222 accessed 10 September 2020.

United Nations Office for South-South Cooperation and the United Nations Development Programme (2019). South-South Cooperation: A Theoretical and Institutional Framework. Network of Southern Think-Tanks, Research and Information System for Developing Countries.

72. Sovereign Debt

Introduction

Sovereign debt has multiple faces, all interconnected by historical, economic, legal and political contexts that mainly matter when a debt crisis occurs. Multiple institutions intervene in sovereign debt regulation, defaults and restructuring; however, the International Monetary Fund (IMF) still plays a leading role. Sovereign debt also displays multiple modalities (public and/or private loans, official bilateral debt, multilateral debt, bonds, debt export credits, investment-related debts, etc.) (Ilias Bantekas and Cephas Lumina (eds) (2018). *Sovereign Debt and Human Rights*. Oxford University Press). Sometimes, sovereign debt has been challenged, e.g. when it becomes "odious debt", this is, when governments request a waiver on previous governments' debt based on legitimacy arguments mainly related to post-colonial or post-war periods. Moreover, many debt restructuring processes in developing countries are confronted with the role of "odious creditors" who obstruct their development policies and/or peace and democratization processes (Tom Ginsburg and Thomas S. Ulen (2007). "Odious Debt, Odious Credit, Economic Development, and Democratization", Law and Contemporary Problems 70(3), 115–136; Jeff King (2016). *The Doctrine of Odious Debt in International Law*. Cambridge University Press). From a Law and Development perspective, sovereign debt encounters the following problems:

Firstly, the fragmentation of the global finance architecture is partly explained by the lack of an international legal framework on sovereign debt crises. As a result, governance of global finance is also fragmented, led by the IMF without a specific mandate. Other international organizations (IOs) also intervene without clear mandates, such as the Bank for International Settlements, the United Nations General Assembly (UNGA) and the UN Conference on Trade and Development (UNCTAD). Besides these IOs, non-institutional actors such as the Paris Club (of sovereign (mainly developed) creditors) or the London Club (of commercial banks) also intervene, as well as other IOs that grant financial support, such as the World Bank and regional development banks. Other IOs forecast restructuring or failure risks and rank the debtor's ability to comply with its financial obligations, such as the Organization for Economic Cooperation and Development (OECD), the World Economic Forum (WEF), and credit rating agencies (Klabbers, 2016). Moreover, the multiple faces of creditors, including bondholders, and the use of sovereign debt not only as a financial instrument but also as a foreign policy strategy to achieve leverage over sovereign debtors, complicate the design of an international legal framework and a coordinated governance of global finance (Anna Gelpern (2016). "Sovereign Debt: Now What?", The Yale Journal of International Law 41(2), 45–95).

Secondly, the political economy of IMF programmes has also shaped national economic policies by linking credit lines with macroeconomic and structural conditionality and by means of policy advice. IMF conditionality refers to economic policies and institutional reforms suggested, agreed or imposed by the IMF to borrowers. It aims at reaching macroeconomic stability (e.g. tax efficiency, public expenditure control, monetary and exchange rate equilibrium) and institutional efficiency of economic sectors (e.g. via trade liberalization, regulation of financial, corporate and labour issues). It has progressively covered other topics such as restructuring of public enterprises, privatizations, including of social security (Lizarazo-Rodríguez, 2011). IMF conditionality has been associated with the Washington Consensus that promotes private law approaches to reduce the role of the State in the economy, which does not focus on the protection of human rights (Stubbs et al., 2020). The IMF conditionality model has been replicated by other regional and global financial institutions ("IFIs") to guarantee reimbursement and to increase their policy leverage (Stubbs et al., 2020). IMF conditionality is an intermediate soft law construction between the total absence of legal commitments and a formal legal agreement, as borrowers accept structural adjustment programmes to obtain credit lines, whose non-compliance would result in financial and monetary marginalization, but without having an international contractual character and without being ratified by the parliament, published or registered (Erik M. Denters (1996). *Law and Policy of IMF*

Conditionality. Brill Nijhoff). The argument that IMF conditionality constitutes an undue interference in the internal affairs of States is contested by arguing that governments agreed on it, even if law-makers do not intervene and its non-compliance cannot be enforced before courts. The comprehensive evaluation of IMF conditionality has been a major challenge because the Monitoring of Fund Arrangements (MONA) database of IMF programmes lacks detailed information (Stubbs et al., 2020) and the IMF policy advice even more, because its identification and assessment is difficult (Dreher et al., 2015). Moreover, the low compliance rate of IMF conditionality reported by various empirical studies prevents any conclusion as to its correlation with macroeconomic results, sovereign debt reimbursement levels or with other social consequences. For instance, some studies argue that IMF debt restructuring programmes that target fiscal or monetary policies may worsen social expenditure (Stubbs et al., 2020). In contrast, a wide assessment of focalized budgetary conditions concluded that they might foster long-term social and public investment expenditures (Sanjeev Gupta, Michela Schena and Seyed R. Yousefi (2018). "Expenditure Conditionality in IMF-supported Programs", IMF Working Paper 18/255). Other studies argue that the prolonged use of IMF arrangements responds rather to ineffective IMF programmes, extended for political strategy or seeking results instead of imposing sanctions for non-compliance (Dreher et al., 2015). Moreover, an empirical assessment found a strong correlation between the number of IMF conditions and the number of granted waivers for non-complied conditions, justified by their difficult implementation (Stubbs et al., 2020). Another finding is that besides the main goal of IMF arrangements of reaching macroeconomic stability and avoid default, borrowers also use them to impose unpopular policies, to overcome domestic opposition, to increase credibility or to attract international capital (Dreher, 2018). This can be explained because IMF arrangements are concluded by governments despite many structural conditions needing legislative approval and/or judicial review, and because there is evidence that many conditions are part of the borrowers' agenda rather than the IMF's agenda (Axel Dreher, Silvia Marchesi and James Raymond Vreeland (2008). "The Political Economy of IMF Forecasts", Public Choice

137(1-2), 145–171; Lizarazo-Rodríguez, 2011). Although creditors also support fiscal adjustment proportional to the size of the borrower's fiscal deficit (Bernardo Guimaraes and Carlos Eduardo Ladeira (2017). "The Determinants of IMF Fiscal Conditionalities: Economics or Politics?", CFM discussion paper series (CFM-DP2017-03). Centre for Macroeconomics), some studies found that major IMF shareholders privilege access to funding or better conditions to their strategic borrowers, even when they do not comply with conditionality and independently of the technical evaluation. This has been demonstrated for borrowers that are temporary members of the UN Security Council, or strategic partners of the US in the UNGA (Dreher, 2018; Guimaraes and Ladeira, 2017, above; Dreher et al., 2015). This discretionary use of IMF conditionality linked to debt restructuring raises economic (Dreher et al., 2015) and human rights concerns because conditions seeking budgetary austerity limit the policy space of borrowers to allocate resources to social services. Borrowers are increasingly asked to ensure that adjustment programmes are compatible with their human rights obligations (Denters, 1996, above; Stubbs et al., 2020; Guzman and Stiglitz, 2015). However, it has not been possible to demonstrate a clear correlation among IMF conditionality, its influence on borrowers' policy space and human rights deterioration (Stubbs et al., 2020), as impacts of budgetary austerity on human rights can result from difficult economic conditions that motivated the entry into structural adjustments (Abouharb and Cingranelli, 2017). The main conclusion is that in-depth country assessments are necessary, but the low level of compliance with conditionality complicates the possibilities of causally linking conditionality with human rights deterioration (Abouharb and Cingranelli, 2017; Lizarazo-Rodríguez, 2011).

Thirdly, default and debt restructuring involve financial and political interests, as they are part of the sovereign creditors' foreign policy. Bondholders are also key players but not necessarily coordinated or empowered to express their will. Three debt restructuring approaches can be identified: The private contractual approach, mostly containing collective actions clauses (CACs), seeks to allow majoritarian bondholders to bind all of them to the restructuring terms. This approach does not guarantee a fair and impartial negotiation between sovereign borrowers and creditors

(Guzman and Stiglitz, 2016) and privileges New York bankruptcy law and jurisdiction that disregard the risk for sovereign borrowers, as occurred when volute funds challenged Argentina's restructuring (Giuseppe Bianco (2017). "How Neutral is the Law of Sovereign Debt Restructuring?", European Society of International Law (ESIL) 2017 Research Forum, Granada). In contrast, the statutory approach advocates for the regulation of international bankruptcy with a specialized court for settling related disputes. Several IOs have backed this initiative, but the main lender countries and other actors of global finance oppose because the role of the IMF would diminish (Stephanie Blankenburg and Richard Kozul-Wright (2016). "Sovereign Debt Restructurings in the Contemporary Global Economy: The UNCTAD Approach", The Yale Journal of International Law, 41(2), 1–7), although in practice, it has happened with the emergence of new creditors (Gelpern, 2016, above). A third hybrid approach proposes a (soft law) framework for the contractual approach that preserves IMF's leading role (Asonuma and Trebesch, 2016) and provides a framework to recognize the sustainability of debt restructuring (compatible with human rights law) as a principle of international law (Bohoslavsky and Goldmann, 2016; Guzman and Stiglitz, 2015; Gong Cheng, Javier Díaz-Cassou and Aitor Erce (2018). "Official Debt Restructurings and Development", World Development 111, 181–195). The "Tilburg Guideline Principles" (2003), the Maastricht Principles on Extraterritorial Obligations of States in the Area of ESCR (2011), or the UNCTAD Roadmap and Guide (2015) sought to define the human rights duties of IFIs and emphasize that States cannot accept arrangements that obstruct their compliance with international human rights law. The UN Independent Expert on the effects of foreign debt of States on the enjoyment of all human rights has released several recommendations and guidelines aiming at contractual approaches to debt restructuring guaranteeing fair negotiation that protects the policy space of borrowers without violating creditors' rights, aligning market practices with the international legal order and assessing the impact of loan conditionality on human rights (Guzman and Stiglitz, 2015). The Basic Principles on Sovereign Debt Restructuring Processes (UNGA A/69/L.84/2015) suggest that IFIs cannot be complicit in human rights

violations in the context of retrogressive economic reforms, and promote *ex ante* and *ex post* gender-sensitive impact assessments of austerity measures, IFIs' policy advice and loan conditionality on human rights (see also UNGA A/74/178/2019). The new version of these guiding principles (A/HRC/40/57/2018) further develop that States (all levels of State governments), IFIs and creditors should conduct human rights impact assessments as a main instrument to guarantee that economic reforms linked to debt restructuring respect human rights. Regarding borrowers, they should guarantee a progressive realization of human rights by allocating the maximum available resources without retrogression and should provide access to information and justice, when the implementation of economic policies undermines human rights.

Fourthly, courts play a key role in sovereign debt restructuring or default mainly in two scenarios: At the constitutional level, some courts have enforced human rights in structural adjustment processes, such as in Colombia (Lizarazo-Rodríguez, 2011) or Portugal (Francisco Pereira Coutinho, 2016). "Austerity on the Loose in Portugal: European Judicial Restraint in Times of Crisis", Perspectives on Federalism 8(3), E-105-132), but the IMF considered those judgments as an obstacle to budgetary adjustment. However, courts could play an important role by limiting the space of governments when negotiating debt restructuring to respect the constitutions and therefore, human rights treaties ratified by the State. In civil courts, holdout litigation challenges debt restructuring agreements, affects the balance between *ex ante* and *ex post* restructuring (Kartik Anand and Prasanna Gai (2019). "Preemptive Sovereign Debt Restructuring and Holdout Litigation", Oxford Economic Papers 71(2), 364–381; Lee C. Buchheit and G. Mitu Gulati (2017). "Restructuring Sovereign Debt after NML v. Argentina", Capital Markets Law Journal, 12(2), 224–238), disregards the doctrine of sovereign immunity of borrowers supported by the UNCTAD and UN soft law framework (W. Mark C. Weidemaier and Mitu Gulati (2015). "The Relevance of Law to Sovereign Debt", Annual Review of Law and Social Science 11, 395–408), and may affect debt negotiations in good faith. Holdout litigation has mainly developed through three channels: the private contractual litigation, mainly under US bankruptcy law as occurred in NML v. Argentina (Buchheit and Gulati,

2017, above; Bianco, 2017, above). Arbitration, which has not been successful (e.g. most cases brought before the International Centre for Settlement of Investment Disputes (ICSID) against Argentina did not conclude and the award that decided the claim against Greece held that sovereign debt cannot be treated as investment protected by bilateral investment treaties (BIT), because of its social and political significance (ICSID, Poštová banka, a.s. and Istrokapital SE v. Hellenic Republic, 2015; Goldmann, 2016). The human rights litigation option was rejected by the European Court of Human Rights. It held that debt restructuring does not violate the rights to private property or to equality and non-discrimination, States have a wide margin of appreciation to manage defaults and debt restructurings, and bonds investment is not a risk-free investment (ECtHR, Mamatas and Others v. Greece; Mathias Audit (2016). "Legal Engineering for the Creation of an International Centre for the Financial Safeguard of States", ICSID Review-Foreign Investment Law Journal 32(1), 227–257). Complementary measures have been proposed, such as the registration of holdout bondholders to identify litigants who have acted in good faith in past restructurings, the design of indicator benchmarks to promote pre-default restructuring (Asonuma and Trebesch, 2016), or the recognition of a standstill principle on abusive holdout litigation to protect the integrity of sovereign debt restructuring (see the Belgian Anti-vulture Act (2010) or the Debt Relief (Developing Countries) Act 2010; Goldmann, 2016).

Conclusion

Global finance covers multiple activities of State and non-State actors and multiple jurisdictions. The lack of an international legal framework and the fragmentation of its governance complicates the understanding of sovereign debt and the related policy space of debtors, creditors' rights and human rights protection in times of financial crises (Bantekas and Lumina, 2018, above). The claim to hold creditors, borrowers and IFIs accountable for the consequences of defaults and debt restructuring on human rights is rightful, although empirical evidence shows that tracing the responsibility is difficult. Moreover, human rights violations in times of austerity do not necessarily result from debt restructuring but

from the precariousness of borrowers' public finances, their lack of institutional capacity to allocate scarce resources and the political interests at stake when concluding debt restructuring arrangements. The UN guidelines point towards the human rights responsibility of States and IFIs in financial crises but disregard the role of non-institutionalized actors such as bondholders and volute investors. Holdout litigation remains a major challenge for sovereign debt restructuring as it benefits from the lack of an international legal framework and disregards the UN soft law framework that recognizes State immunity and the policy space of debtors to comply with human rights. National assessments, regulation and complementary measures in this respect are necessary to tackle sovereign debt challenges.

LILIANA LIZARAZO-RODRÍGUEZ

References

Abouharb, M. Rodwan and David L. Cingranelli (2017). "The Human Rights Effects of Participation in Program Lending Versus the CESCR" in Elena Sciso (ed.), *Accountability, Transparency and Democracy in the Functioning of Bretton Woods Institutions*. Springer.

Asonuma, Tamon and Christoph Trebesch (2016). "Sovereign Debt Restructurings: Preemptive or Post-Default", Journal of the European Economic Association 14(1), 175–214.

Bohoslavsky, Juan Pablo and Matthias Goldmann (2016). "An Incremental Approach to Sovereign Debt Restructuring: Sovereign Debt Sustainability as a Principle of Public International Law", The Yale Journal of International Law 41(2), 13–43.

Dreher, Axel (2018). "Political Influences in IMF and World Bank operations: Lessons for the Design of European institutions" in Nauro F. Campos and Jan-Egbert Sturm (eds), *Bretton Woods, Brussels, and Beyond*. CEPR Press.

Dreher, Axel, Jan-Egbert Sturm and James Raymond Vreeland (2015). "Politics and IMF Conditionality", Journal of Conflict Resolution 59(1), 120–148.

Goldmann, Matthias (2016). "Putting Your Faith in Good Faith: A Principled Strategy for Smoother Sovereign Debt Workouts", The Yale Journal of International Law 41(2), 117–140.

Guzman, Martin and Joseph E. Stiglitz (2015). "Creating a Framework for Sovereign Debt Restructuring That Works" in Martin Guzman, José Antonio Ocampo, and Joseph E. Stiglitz (eds), *Too Little, Too Late: The Quest to Resolve Sovereign Debt Crises*. Columbia University Press.

Klabbers, Jan (2016). "On Functions and Finance: Sovereign Debt Workouts and Equality in

International Organizations Law", The Yale Journal of International Law 41(2), 241–261.

Lizarazo-Rodríguez, Liliana (2011). "The Legal Scope of IMF Conditionality: Empirical Analysis of the Case of Colombia 1999–2006", Revista de Derecho Público 27, 1–42.

Stubbs, Thomas, Bernhard Reinsberg, Alexander Kentikelenis, and Lawrence King (2020). "How to Evaluate the Effects of IMF Conditionality", The Review of International Organizations 15, 29–73.

73. Sovereignty

In his excellent *International Law*, Jan Klabbers warns the reader that 'sovereignty itself does not signify very much' (Klabbers, 2017, p. 74). A short entry should therefore suffice!

At its minimum core, sovereignty signifies the capacity to exercise supreme authority and to ensure compliance.

In public international law, sovereignty is distributed on a territorial basis. A defined territory is an attribute of Statehood. The Montevideo Convention on the Rights and Duties of States (1933) thus provides that the State 'has the right to defend its integrity and independence, to provide for its conservation and prosperity, and consequently to organize itself as it sees fit, to legislate upon its interests, administer its services, and to define the jurisdiction and competence of its courts' (Article 3). The 2030 Agenda for Sustainable Development remains in line with this statement: World leaders, notwithstanding their pledge to engage in common action across the broadest universal policy agenda ever, reaffirm 'that every State has, and shall freely exercise, full permanent sovereignty over all its wealth, natural resources and economic activity' (GA Resolution 70/1, para. 18). In the 2030 Agenda, sovereignty equals State sovereignty, and its exercise by the State is full and free and continuous as long as the State exists.

How the exercise of sovereignty is allocated internally, i.e. within the State, is left largely to constitutional law: constitutions determine what State organs exercise sovereignty internally and the conditions under which they do so, e.g. whether assent by those living under State sovereignty is required (compare Philpott, 1995, p. 357). As to the external dimension of sovereignty, in the United Nations Charter, sovereign equality of States serves as a foundational principle (as expressed in Article 2(1) of the United Nations Charter). As States are legally equal, and each is entitled to exercise sovereignty, sovereignty offers a shield against external interference by other States. At least at the conceptual level, all States have a reciprocal interest in respecting each other's sovereignty.

In the context of decolonization, State sovereignty was gained by formerly non-self-governing territories as a result of conquering independence, often at considerable cost. The governments of the newly independent States finally gained the political authority to freely rule their territory and population, and were entitled to protection against external interference by other States, most notably by the former colonial powers.

In 1962, the UN General Assembly (UNGA) in its renowned Resolution 1803 (XVII) on permanent sovereignty over natural resources, also confirmed the economic authority of the new States. At the same time, the resolution reflected tensions around the interpretation of the notion of sovereignty that remain with us until this day. Although the preamble of the resolution refers to the inalienable right of all States to freely dispose of their wealth in accordance with their national interests, the first operative paragraph of UNGA Resolution 1803 (XVII) speaks of 'the right *of peoples and nations* to permanent sovereignty over their natural wealth and resources' (emphasis added). This right of peoples and nations was to be exercised 'in the interest of their national development and of the well-being of the people of the State concerned'.

The State/people ambiguity echoes the protracted debate on whether domestic sovereignty is located in the people or in the sovereign. If sovereignty resides with the people, State institutions merely exercise sovereignty on its behalf. The State exercise of sovereignty is functional, i.e. subservient to ensuring the well-being of the people.

In addition, and remarkably, rather than dwelling on economic sovereignty as such, UNGA Resolution 1803 (XVII) deals at length with the protection of foreign investment: the newly independent States are entitled to set their preferred policy with regard to foreign investment, but the conditions for nationalizations of foreign investments, including the payment of appropriate compensation, are defined in international law (compare Pahuja, 2011, p. 95).

Subsequent instruments adopted at the time when developing countries were arguing in favour of the establishment of a new international economic order, shed the ambiguity about the locus of sovereignty. In the 1974 Charter of Economic Rights and Duties of States, every State freely exercises full permanent sovereignty over all its wealth, natural resources and economic activities (Article 2,

UNGA Resolution 3281 (XXIX)), and State sovereignty now included exercising authority over foreign investment in accordance with *domestic* law. Developed States objected and maintained that only UNGA Resolution 1803 (XVII) reflected customary law.

In contrast, post-colonial human rights instruments bolster the idea of popular sovereignty. Common Article 1 of the international covenants on human rights (1966) provides that peoples have a right to freely dispose of their natural wealth and resources. In addition, they should 'in no case, be deprived of their own means of subsistence' (International Covenant on Civil and Political Rights and International Covenant on Economic, Social and Cultural Rights, common Article 1(2)). In human rights instruments, the State is not a holder of rights, but a bearer of duties that it owes to rights-holders. The people hold the right to decide how the natural wealth and resources on the territory should be used, and it is protected against State interference when government measures deprive the people of their means of subsistence. In 1970, the Friendly Relations Declaration added requirements on the nature of government: in order to be able to invoke sovereignty as a shield against external interference, the State needed to possess 'a government representing the whole people belonging to the territory without distinction as to race, creed or colour', and thus to act in compliance with the right to self-determination (UNGA Resolution 2625, 1970, principle 5).

At the time of the adoption of the UN Declaration on the Right to Development (UNGA Resolution 41/128 (1986)) the concept of people was primarily understood as referring to the entire population of a State (compare Article 2(3) of the Declaration). Since that time, however, international law has evolved, under the influence of the increasing recognition of indigenous rights at the global, and regional and domestic levels (particularly in Latin America) and the jurisprudence at the African Commission and Court on Peoples' Rights. In the UN Declaration on the Rights of Indigenous Peoples (UNGA Resolution 61/295 (2007)), indigenous peoples have the right to determine and develop priorities and strategies for the development or use of their lands or territories and other resources. States have the duty to consult and cooperate in good faith with the indigenous peoples concerned through their own representative institutions in order to obtain their free and informed consent prior to the approval of any project affecting their lands or territories and other resources, particularly in connection with the development, utilization or exploitation of mineral, water or other resources (Article 32). In the African Charter on Human and Peoples' Rights – that contains a peoples' right to dispose of wealth and natural resources (Article 21(1)) – peoples include indigenous peoples, but also 'marginalized and vulnerable groups in Africa' that are 'not accommodated by dominant development paradigms, victimized by mainstream development policies, and have their basic human rights violated' (the leading case is African Commission on Human and Peoples' Rights (ACHPR), Centre for Minority Rights Development (Kenya) & Minority Rights Group International on behalf of the Endorois Welfare Council v. The Republic of Kenya, 2009, para. 148).

According to the recently adopted Declaration on the Rights of Peasants and Other People Working in Rural Areas (UNGA Resolution 73/165 (2018)) peasants and other people working in rural areas have the right to determine their own food and agriculture systems 'recognized by many States and regions as the right to food sovereignty' (see Article 15(4)). According to the Declaration, food sovereignty includes the right to participate in decision-making processes on food and agriculture policy and the right to healthy and adequate food produced through ecologically sound and sustainable methods that respect their cultures (ibid).

A harmonious interpretation of these various sources of international law suggests that, under current international law, sovereignty still rests primarily with the State, but that State institutions exercising sovereignty need to meet an increasing number of requirements. Not only does sovereignty have to be exercised with a view to achieving development and serve the well-being of the population, it also brings with it State responsibilities to enable peoples to freely dispose of their natural wealth and resources, and not to deprive them of their means of subsistence. Ensuring the active, free and meaningful participation by people(s) involved in or affected by the exploitation of natural resources in both decision-making processes and benefit sharing is also a requirement in an increasing number of international instruments.

KOEN DE FEYTER

Sovereignty and responsibility have equally become intertwined in international environmental law. The Convention on Biological Diversity (22 May 1992) offers a nice example. In the preamble to the Convention, the reaffirmation that States 'have sovereign rights over their own biological resources' is immediately followed by a provision adding that States are consequently 'responsible for conserving their biological diversity and for using their biological resources in a sustainable manner'. Similarly, the UN Convention on the Law of the Sea (10 December 1982) combines in a single provision (Article 193) the sovereign State right to exploit natural resources and the State duty to do so in a way that protects and preserves the marine environment.

The preamble to the Biodiversity Convention in addition perceives of the conservation of biodiversity as a common concern of humankind. States retain sovereignty, but there is an expectation that they exercise sovereignty in such a way that the common interest of the international community as a whole is well protected. Werner Scholtz has suggested the term 'custodial' sovereignty: the State on whose territory global environmental resources are located that are needed by the world community as a whole is expected to act as the custodian of the interests of all peoples.

In international peace and security law, the best-known example of the linking of sovereignty and responsibility is the Responsibility to Protect doctrine. In the World Summit Outcome Document (UNGA Resolution 60/1 (2005)), sovereignty implies the responsibility of each State to protect its populations from genocide, war crimes, ethnic cleansing and crimes against humanity. This responsibility entails the prevention of such crimes, including their incitement, through appropriate and necessary means. The World Summit Outcome Document adds, perhaps more controversially, that the international community through the United Nations also has such a responsibility to help protect populations, in accordance with the variety of means that the United Nations Charter provides (see in particular World Summit Outcome Document, paras 138–139).

State sovereignty remains valuable, because it protects the domestic policy space that is necessary to create economic well-being, ecological sustainability and social justice as understood locally, i.e. as reflecting the preferences of the people(s) living within the territory. As Kingsbury puts it: sovereignty protects 'some autonomy in decision-making and hence some space for difference' (Kingsbury, 1998, p. 621). Even in an international legal system that rightly aspires to protect global common interests, the need for plurality remains, and State sovereignty based on territory can at least potentially achieve this function.

KOEN DE FEYTER

References

Anand, Ram Prakash (1987). *International Law and Developing Countries*. Nijhoff.

Besson, Samantha (2011). 'Sovereignty' in *Max Planck Encyclopaedia of Public International Law*. Oxford University Press.

Kalmo, Hent and Quentin Skinner (eds) (2014). *Sovereignty in Fragments: The Past, Present and Future of a Contested Concept*. Cambridge University Press.

Kingsbury, Benedict (1998). 'Sovereignty and Inequality', European Journal of International Law 9(4), 599–625.

Klabbers, Jan (2017). *International Law*. Cambridge University Press.

Pahuja, Sundhya (2011). *Decolonising International Law*. Cambridge University Press.

Pandiaraj, S. (2016). 'Sovereignty as Responsibility: Reflections on the Legal Status of the Doctrine of Responsibility to Protect', Chinese Journal of International Law 14(4), 795–815.

Philpott, Daniel (1995). 'Sovereignty: An Introduction and Brief History', Journal of International Affairs 48(2), 353–368.

Pourmokhtari, Navid (2013). 'A Postcolonial Critique of State Sovereignty in IR: The Contradictory Legacy of a "West-centric" Discipline', Third World Quarterly 34(10), 1767–1793.

Scholtz, Werner (2008). 'Custodial Sovereignty: Reconciliation of Sovereignty and Global Environmental Challenges amongst the Vestiges of Colonialism', Netherlands International Law Review 55(3), 323–341.

74. Sustainability

Sustainability seems to have become a polyseme. Its interpretations are extremely diverse, from encouraging green growth to requiring de-growth and radical change in ethics. This entry briefly recalls the legal origin of the notion of sustainability several centuries ago. It then attempts to differentiate three concepts that are often presented as merged: sustainability, sustainable development and the Sustainable Development Goals (hereinafter SDGs). Sustainability is associated with the preservation of the environment for future generations, while sustainable development and the SDGs, at core, support the integration of environmental concern within economic growth. The entry will argue that there is a crucial choice to be made on the merging or differentiation of the three concepts; law is a privileged instrument to further this choice.

Sustainability's international legal origins

As a normative concept, sustainability in Europe can be traced as far back as the fourteenth century (Bosselmann, 2017). It is generally linked to a realization of the finite quantity of forests and pasture, which should be managed so that future generations can benefit. Therefore, the necessity to preserve the environment for future generations has been associated with the notion of sustainability for centuries. However, the association of economic development with sustainability is more recent. Indeed, the pressure on resources intensified with the industrial revolution and the geographic expansion of the agricultural system. The adverse effects of economic development on the environment became increasingly evident. In 1972, the Declaration of the United Nations (UN) Conference on the Human Environment in Stockholm (or Stockholm Declaration) declared that environmental protection was a major issue, affecting well-being and economic development. The integration of development into the concept of sustainability was finally coined as "sustainable development" in 1987 in the Brundtland Report (Bürgi Bonanomi, 2012). It was defined as "development that meets the needs of the present without compromising the ability of future generations to meet their own needs", now the most commonly cited definition of sustainable development. As a consequence, sustainable development is usually understood as being composed of an economic, a social and an environmental pillar. In 1992, the Rio Declaration on Environment and Development restated the objective of economic growth in Principle 12. The international community endorsed the importance of the principle of integration in the Declaration's Principle 4, which declares that "[i]n order to achieve sustainable development, environmental protection shall constitute an integral part of the development process and cannot be considered in isolation from it". The principle of integration was declared part of international law by the Permanent Court of Arbitration in the Arbitration regarding the Iron Rhine: "international . . . law require[s] the integration of appropriate environmental measures in the design and implementation of economic development activities". In 2012, when the timeframe for the Millennium Development Goals (hereinafter MDGs) was soon to end, the UN Conference on Sustainable Development in Rio de Janeiro called for a new international development roadmap. Geared towards sustainable development, the 2030 Agenda for Sustainable Development was adopted by the UN in 2015, extending the concern for the environment through its whole framework, which encompasses 17 global goals, the SDGs.

Sustainability from three different perspectives

The international efforts described above seem to indicate that there is a consensus in the international community whereby the concepts of sustainability, sustainable development and SDGs shall now be understood as equivalent. However, the idea of sustainable development, namely that sustainability focuses on the concern for future generations and should be integrated into economic development, generates vivid debate. So does the idea that sustainability should be implemented through the SDGs (Kotzé, 2018). In these debates, three groups can, very broadly, be distinguished.

(1) Development without environment / No sustainability

The first group rejects the concepts of sustainability, sustainable development and the

SDGs outright. The argument rests, for some, on the belief that human activity cannot have an important and longstanding impact on the planet. Others consider that the protection of the environment cannot constitute an integral part of the development process: economic growth should be unaltered and any attempt to regulate markets, even for the protection of the environment, is negative. Some proponents of this approach argue that Global South countries simply cannot afford to comprehensively implement sustainable development nor the SDGs until they have developed economically (Lee, 2017). Finally, others argue that economic development is necessary for the elimination of poverty and for social justice, which should be prioritized over environmental protection. These perspectives are often accompanied by the view that sustainability is infused with neo-colonialism. Indeed, environmental protection policies can be seen as imposed by the Global North, responsible for most contamination, on the Global South, while this may hinder the latter's economic and social development. This standpoint is grounded in the public international law principle of the sovereign equality of States, which prohibits intervention in foreign States' political affairs. It is recognized in Article 2 of the UN Charter. The principle is also established in several international instruments, such as the "Declaration on the Inadmissibility of Intervention in the Domestic Affairs of States and the Protection of Their Independence and Sovereignty" and the "Declaration on Principles of International Law concerning Friendly Relations and Co-operation among States . . ." of the UN General Assembly. It is reiterated in numerous texts, such as the 1974 Declaration on the Establishment of a New International Economic Order, which demands the respect of the right of every country to choose its economic and social policies. According to the "grow now, clean up later" approach, environmental protection should be postponed until a certain level of economic development is reached, which is not determined in its characteristics or in its timing. Until that moment, natural resources are to be extensively exploited.

(2)   Integration of environment and development / weak sustainability

The second group believes in the possibility to protect the environment and continue economic growth; they are often identified as supporters of "weak sustainability". Their perspective is grounded in the acceptation that levels of natural capital decline, as long as the losses are offset by gains in other forms of capital, such as human-made capital. Generally, proponents of "weak sustainability" support sustainable development and the international effort towards the SDGs. They understand the notion of sustainable development as encompassing green growth. However, the resistance to an imposition of policies from the Global North on the Global South, which would limit the latter's development, is also present within weak sustainability. It was first made clear in Principle 11 of the Stockholm Declaration, which states that "[t]he environmental policies . . . should . . . not adversely affect the present or future development potential of developing countries, nor should they hamper the attainment of better living conditions for all. . .". The concept of sustainable development was in fact later formulated by the Brundtland Report with the very objective to reconcile both perspectives by proposing an environmental protection framework that would also consider the Global South's needs. Indeed, it was determined that sustainable development entails the sustainable use of natural resources and equity between generations – or intergenerational equity – as well as the equitable use and distribution of the outcomes of development within one generation – or intragenerational equity – (Barral, 2012). Apart from the obligation not to cause environmental damages beyond the limits of national jurisdiction, as it is sometimes understood, the strive for intragenerational equity is very much directed at the relationship between the rich and the poor, between Global North and Global South. With their broad consultation phases and their inclusiveness, the SDGs were also formulated with the objective to reconcile Global South and Global North perspectives. The same can be said of the 2015 Paris Agreement under the UN Framework Convention on Climate Change, where each country determines its national contributions to the reduction of global warming. "Weak sustainability" is per se anthropocentric, because it represents a people-centered balance of the three sustainable development pillars, as opposed to being an eco-centric, nature-centered approach.

(3)   Environment without development / "strong sustainability"

Finally, the third group, often classified as "strong sustainability" proponents, rejects the compatibility of sustainability and economic development. It also dismisses the centrality of future generations and rejects the SDGs as an instrument for sustainability's implementation, mainly because of their grounding on economic development and their anthropocentric nature. This perspective has been largely influenced by Indigenous Peoples' philosophies (Berros, 2019), such as the Andean *sumak kawsay*. Interestingly, the urge towards a more eco-centric vision had emerged in the UN 1982 World Charter for Nature, which places the protection of nature at the center of its purpose. Nowadays, "strong sustainability" supporters' arguments also rely on the findings of environmental scientists on planet systems and the Anthropocene. Indeed, according to them, the planet relies on nine systems, each with a certain threshold that cannot be crossed, which is defined as a planetary boundary. These nine systems are climate change; land system change; the rate at which biological diversity is lost; biogeochemical nitrogen; ocean acidification; stratospheric ozone; global freshwater use; chemical pollution; and atmospheric aerosol loading. Anthropogenic pressure, increasing dramatically since the Second World War, has caused the transgression of the first four of the systems' boundaries. The magnitude of this planetary alteration has brought us into a new geological epoch, the Anthropocene, which marks a rupture in the earth system. The transgression of planetary boundaries and its catastrophic consequences make "sustainable development" an oxymoron (Adelman, 2018), unless the definition of development as growth is abandoned. In this context, it has been proposed to revise the definition of sustainable development, as "development that meets the needs of the present while safeguarding Earth's life-support systems, on which the welfare of current and future generations depends" (Griggs et al., 2013, p. 56). The concept of Anthropocene is now adopted by many scholars, not only in geology and biology but also in anthropology, law and business, who advocate a turn from anthropocentrism towards eco-centrism (Salleh, 2016). The "strong sustainability" view is endorsed by ecofeminists, who criticize the exploitive essence of capitalism as built on sexism, racism and ecological destruction (Gaard, 2015). The role of law in the Anthropocene is then to define and support a change of ethics towards eco-centrism (Adelman, 2018). International and national law-making shall abandon the strive towards the SDGs, separate sustainability from economic development and reject capitalism, and finally widen the focus on the concern for future generations to supporting the protection of planet systems.

Conclusion

Sustainability has been associated with environmental protection and the concern for future generations for centuries. However, despite the wording of UN international declarations, the concepts of sustainability, sustainable development and SDGs should not necessarily be understood as interchangeable. The merging of these concepts has its roots in the last century's efforts to preserve economic growth and the failed attempt to spread growth's benefits for the Global North to the Global South. However, in the decision to merge or differentiate these concepts in the international and national law-making that follows lies the responsibility for the planet's future. Three options are offered to us. One is to opt for economic development without sustainability, and continue exploiting the natural resources for the benefit of capitalism while ignoring the dire planetary consequences. Alternatively, one can decide that "we can have it all" and attempt to integrate the protection of the environment into economic development and further sustainable development with the SDGs as a roadmap. Finally, one can acknowledge that the last decades have assisted the transgression of four out of nine planetary boundaries and the entry into the unstable Anthropocene epoch. This demonstrates sustainability's incompatibility with development as growth. If economic growth is considered a part of sustainable development, then this concept is a contradiction *in terminis* and the SDGs a path to nowhere. In addition to the abandonment of the growth paradigm, the Anthropocene epoch requires shifting the focus of sustainability from the concern for future generations to a concern for planetary systems.

STÉPHANIE DE MOERLOOSE

Acknowledgment

Funding for this research was provided by the Swiss National Science Foundation (SNSF).

STÉPHANIE DE MOERLOOSE

References

Adelman, Sam (2018). "The Sustainable Development Goals, Anthropocentrism and Neoliberalism" in Duncan French and Louis J. Kotzé (eds), *Sustainable Development Goals Law, Theory and Implementation*. Edward Elgar.

Barral, Virginie (2012). "Sustainable Development in International Law: Nature and Operation of an Evolutive Legal Norm", The European Journal of International Law 23(2), 377–400.

Berros, María Valeria (2019). "Rights of Nature in the Anthropocene: Towards the Democratization of Environmental Law?" in Michelle Lim (ed.), *Charting Environmental Law Futures in the Anthropocene*. Springer.

Bosselmann, Klaus (2017). *The Principle of Sustainability, Transforming Law and Governance*. Routledge.

Bürgi Bonanomi, Elisabeth (2015). *Sustainable Development in International Law Making and Trade: International Food Governance and Trade in Agriculture*. Edward Elgar.

Gaard, Greta (2015). "Ecofeminism and Climate Change", Women's Studies International Forum 49, 20–33.

Griggs, David et al. (2013). "Sustainable Development Goals for People and Planet", Nature 495, 305–307.

Kotzé, Louis J. (2018). "The Sustainable Development Goals: An Existential Critique Alongside Three New-Millennial Analytical Paradigms" in Duncan French and Louis J. Kotzé (eds), *Sustainable Development Goals Law, Theory and Implementation*. Edward Elgar.

Lee, Yong-Shik (2017). "General Theory of Law and Development", Cornell International Law Journal 50(3), 415–471.

Salleh, Ariel (2016). "Climate, Water, and Livelihood Skills: A Post-Development Reading of the SDGs", Globalizations 13(6), 952–959.

75.   Tax and Development

Introduction

Development, especially in developing countries, can be looked at from different viewpoints; prudent public expenditure is one means of advancing the development agenda. Effective mobilization of revenue is another crucial aspect. The latter can be achieved through the establishment of a sound tax system, which would subsequently lead to a drop in the rate of dependence on foreign aid for the receiving States going forward. So, in effect what this means is that taxation can be considered as a tool for development by all stakeholders especially as an item on the international tax and development agendas including the realization of human rights, the global financing for development process, and the processes surrounding Addis Ababa Action Agenda and the Sustainable Development Goals. More recently there has also been the High-level Panel on International Financial Accountability, Transparency and Integrity (https://www.factipanel.org/about accessed 10 September 2020).

In several developing countries, e.g. Kenya, there has been a trend of improved service delivery in several sectors of the government including in education as well as health services over the years (Waris, 2013). For example, the government has subsidized education in public institutions and this can directly be correlated to a significant improvement in collection of revenue. Therefore, what this brings out is that whereas closely monitoring government expenditure can write a story about development in a country, the other side of the coin is to carry a study on the role of revenue in enabling the government to carry out its work. In the recent book *Financing Africa* Waris mapped out all publicly available data on the continent about the continent canvassing both tax and development, select human rights and their linkages and relationships (Waris, 2019; UNODC, 2016, p. 14). The data is now housed at the University of Nairobi and allows one to look at a snapshot of African countries one by one to understand their fiscal systems (https://cfs.uonbi.ac.ke/Africa%20Revenue%20%26%20Expenditure%20Map accessed 10 September 2020).

Tax and development can be further analysed from a variety of perspectives. There are several factors that support the advancement of the concept of the use of tax to achieve development. Some of these factors are discussed in the next sections.

Positive factors

Creating a compliant tax base

This begins with the creation of a State-society trust (Waris, 2013). This is in turn crucial as far as increasing a country's tax base and building taxpayer compliance is concerned. However, the possibility of achieving this is hampered by several prominent factors, which include poor legal and regulatory frameworks in place that often create a conducive environment for crimes like tax evasions and illicit financial flows, among others. This is more often than not coupled with State inefficiencies and resultant menaces like widespread corruption. It is then not hard to see that the taxpayers would eventually develop mistrust in the government, which would in turn negatively affect their compliance.

However, these can be remedied. The first step is by demonstrating to the taxpayers that their money is being used by the State to actually better their lives. This can be done through a development policy that clearly links this improvement in service delivery to the collection of taxes. Compliance of the taxpayers is built by the trust the society has in the State and in the absence of this, the fiscal legitimacy of the State is undermined and damaged and would in time undermine the role of tax in development of a nation (Waris, 2018).

Establishing the principles of taxation

A good tax system is often built and established on the standards of certain principles (AICPA, 2017). Some of these principles include: equality, which contends that taxpayers should pay taxes based on their different economic capabilities (Waris, 2013); certainty, which prescribes that taxpayers should be held to a publicly known standard as far as the amount they are required to pay is concerned; convenience, which requires that the whole system surrounding payment of taxes should be designed with the convenience of the taxpayer in mind; flexibility, which requires that a tax system should be responsive to the economy; efficiency, which dictates that the collection and administration of tax should reflect efficiency; and simplicity, which contends that the tax system should be easy and inexpensive to administer.

Keeping with these principles is aimed at realizing the objectives of a good tax system that would in turn enable development.

Taxation in State building

In a State, taxation is not just about raising revenue but is also very much concerned with social development (Waris, 2013). This is in the context of the welfare State where the State seeks to cushion its citizens through social security programmes funded through taxation. All this is made possible through the concept of a social contract between the individuals and the State.

The State needs to protect the fiscal base of the country through various measures aimed at achieving taxpayer compliance in paying taxes as well as combating crimes like evasion in order to achieve its duty to contribute to State building through taxation. Studies suggest that income redistribution through taxes is more efficient for poverty reduction than even economic growth (Dagdeviren, 2001). Therefore, it is important to clearly point out the link between tax and public service in any discussion aimed at improving public service delivery in a country. This makes taxation an important factor in the endeavour of State building and to this effect tax has a crucial role in development.

Sound tax system

A sound tax system is critical as far as tax and development is concerned since it is an important indicator of the development of the fiscal State (von Kommer and Waris, 2011). To this end, it is necessary for States to establish fiscal legitimacy (Waris and Latif, 2015). This can be done through a number of ways, including: enhancing transparency and accountability in public policies; demonstrating improved public spending; expanding the tax base; increasing fairness in the tax systems; and improving the capacity as well as enforcement structures of the relevant bodies. These are some of the pillars upon which a good tax system can be built. Once it is put in place, a sound and effective tax

system is a clear indication of the growth of the fiscal State and a firm foundation for development through taxation.

Fiscal social contract

In most States, every constitution has a set of articles that set out how the State will finance itself. These provisions together are called the fiscal social contract and / or the fiscal constitution. The language in the fiscal articles in constitutions tend to be rights-based or power-based. However some have no clear constitutional provisions at all. When fiscal constitutions do not take into account the right or power of government to tax, and other modalities like the amount to be taxed as well as how it could be spent, the discretion of the government of the day is unchecked (Attiya Waris (2015). 'Delineating a Rights-Based Fiscal Social Contract Using African Fiscal Constitutions', East African Law Journal 1). This can in turn result in proliferation of various related crimes such as tax evasion and outright theft due to an absence of a clear legal framework.

A tax State is one where taxes are collected but spending is not on social goods and services, whereas a fiscal State actively spends State revenue on the improvement of the living standards of its residents. For a tax State that seeks to achieve the level of a fiscal State, there are some approaches that should be taken into consideration in order to achieve this. Firstly, there should be a fiscal interaction between the system of government and its outer environment, which includes taxpayers and beneficiaries of public revenue. Secondly, States should develop an approach on the redress of economic disparities that exist within its borders through taxation. Thirdly, States, especially in developing countries, should look into the role of taxation to support a welfare State as opposed to a State dependent on foreign aid. A fiscally self-sufficient State which decides on its own revenue and spending priorities can focus on improvement of living standards instead of the aid conditionalities which may not be aligned with national development plans, and this could in turn lead to alleviation of poverty. Once all this is taken into consideration, the resultant fiscal State would be able to draw the link between taxation and development.

Foreign exchange regulation

Foreign direct investment has been a major force behind government policies in most developing countries worldwide. This notwithstanding, the tax system addressing this area has not been given the necessary attention that it deserves in most of these countries. Failure to progressively address the tax laws in this area is likely to result in massive loss in tax collections due to factors like companies reporting foreign exchange losses (Attiya Waris (2005). 'An Analysis of Section 4A of the Kenyan Income Tax Act and a case for Reform: KRA Assessments and the Claiming Foreign Exchange Losses.' East African Law Journal).

Therefore, it is necessary for countries to analyse and clarify their laws regarding the treatment of foreign exchange gains and losses in order to avoid losing significant proceeds of taxation that could be channelled to development projects.

Negative factors

On the other hand, there are factors that undermine the use of tax to achieve development.

Loss of foreign exchange

This is mainly occasioned by lack of comprehensive framework in place to combat it. Foreign exchange losses often have a huge negative effect on the ability of the country to raise its targeted revenue for the period that has been set out (Adeniran et al., 2014). This will in turn result in loss of significant revenue that would otherwise have contributed to development in the country.

Illicit financial flows

Illicit financial flow is a very serious menace and for it to be fought, some measured steps need to be taken. They are as follows: enough knowledge needs to be built on the issue. This acquired knowledge needs to be widely shared and implemented in the public spaces at all times. Thereafter a debate needs to be instituted on the magnitude and impact of the menace being witnessed. Once all these steps are successfully implemented, change can then be brought about through the concerned institutions and these changes would often include reform in laws, policies and regulations.

The impact of illicit financial flows especially in developing countries cannot be underestimated. This is because there have been studies in the past that have highlighted a link between illicit financial flows and something as critical as the ability of these States to maintain security. It is therefore clear that illicit financial flows not only lead to loss of revenue in a country but also have other ripple effects that pose great risks on the country. Reforms need to be put in place to help combat this menace and to prevent significant losses in revenue that would otherwise be needed for development.

Tax evasion

Tax evasion is a global phenomenon that affects different States and individuals (Kemme et al., 2020). One of the ways in which this is done is through manipulation of image rights which is a contract that protects the publicity rights of prominent figures worldwide often registered with a company. This manipulation could be caused by complexities of cross-border taxation in some instances as well as deliberate tactics by professional enablers in other scenarios.

Image rights can easily be misused through tax havens that would enable the individuals in question to avoid paying taxes (Attiya Waris and Dick Osala (2018). 'Lionel Messi: Image Rights, International Financial Flows, Tax Havens and its Impact on Africa and Kenya' The Advocate). Sometimes, the offshore companies with which these rights are contracted pay relatively low corporation taxes or no taxes at all. This in turn deprives tax authorities of significant amounts that would have been payable to them in tax. These illegal flows of revenue out of the country will in turn hamper development efforts that would otherwise have been realized using these resources.

Misuse of rules by multinational enterprises

Every year, developing countries are losing a lot of capital through illicit capital flight, which is ever on the rise. This is especially significant considering the fact that most of these countries are faced with dangers of financial crises, high levels of poverty, as well as huge public debts.

Multinational enterprises usually adopt a variety of mechanisms to illegally evade taxes, some of which include: misuse of transfer pricing rules and false invoicing. This is further made possible by the prominence of international transfer of goods and services within multinational companies in global trade. These multinationals often have subsidiaries located in tax havens where none or rather insignificant tax is being paid. Intra-trading within these multinationals, which accounts for a huge percentage of international trade, is the means employed to further enable these illicit flows by the multinationals. This certainly leads to massive loss of revenues in the concerned States and subsequently loss in development opportunities. Legislation can be used to remedy some of this by ensuring that all transactions be lodged domestically through law and that all entities operating in a country be registered domestically.

Conclusion

In order to realize the links between taxation and development, it is important to take into consideration prudent management of resources, accountability, transparency and responsibility by the State towards its citizenry, and most importantly the improvement of the well-being of the society by the State through social welfare. It is very critical for the link between raised revenue and their expenditure to improve the lives of the people to be clearly established. Discussions around tax and development should not just be limited to enhancement in tax collection but should also go beyond this to capture tax distribution with an aim of achieving the fiscal redistribution policy especially in the developing countries.

ATTIYA WARIS

References

Adeniran, J.O., S.A. Yusuf, and Olatoke A. Ademeyi (2014). 'The Impact of Exchange Rate Fluctuation on the Nigerian Economic Growth: An Empirical Investigation', International Journal of Academic Research in Business and Social Sciences 4(8), 224–233.

AICPA (2017). Guiding Principles of Good Tax Policy: A Framework for Evaluating Tax Proposals. American Institute of Certified Public Accountants, available at: www.aicpa.org/Advocacy/Tax/.../Tax_Policy_Concept_Statement_No.1.doc.

Dagdeviren, Hülya (2001). Redistribution and Growth for Poverty Reduction. ILO.

Kemme, David M., Bhavik Parikh, and Tanja Steigner (2020). 'Tax Morale and International Tax Evasion', Journal of World Business 55(3).

UNODC (2016). High Level Conference on Illicit Financial Flows: Inter-Agency Cooperation and Good Tax Governance in Africa Tax and Good Governance Overview of the Project Pretoria.

Von Kommer, Victor and Attiya Waris (2013). 'Key Building Blocks for Effective Tax Systems in Developing Countries Utilizing the Theory of the Development of the Fiscal State' Bulletin for International Taxation 65(11), 620–636.

Waris, Attiya (2013). Tax and Development: Solving Kenya's Fiscal Crisis through Human Rights: A Case Study of Kenya's Constituency Development Fund. LawAfrica.

Waris, Attiya (2018). 'Developing Fiscal Legitimacy by Building State-Societal Trust in African Countries', Journal of Tax Administration 4(2), 103–118.

Waris, Attiya (2019). Financing Africa. Langaa.

Waris, Attiya and Laila Abdul Latif (2015). 'Towards Establishing Fiscal Legitimacy Through Settled Fiscal Principles in Global Health Financing', Health Care Analysis 23(4), 376–390.

76. Terrorism

There is no universal definition of terrorism. While political scientists may use the term for aggravated forms of political violence, legal approaches usually combine an objective element of the commission of certain categories of violent crimes, and a subjective element of terrorist intent. At United Nations' level the latter element is usually expressed as either an intent to create fear among (i.e., "to terrorize") the population or segments of it, or to compel the government to specific conduct (such as the releasing of prisoners or the withdrawal of troops from a conflict zone). Only deadly or otherwise very severe forms of violence, typically against ordinary members of the civilian population or segments of it such as a minority, or a threat of lethal violence through hostage-taking, would qualify as the objective element. Notably, for legal purposes it is not a conceptual element of the notion of terrorism that the perpetrator acts pursuant to a political, religious or ideological aim, even if in practice most acts of terrorism are committed by individuals or groups that are characterized by being inspired, usually fanatically, by such aims. For existing legal definitions of terrorism, reference is made to the 1999 Terrorism Financing Convention, UN Security Council Resolution 1566 (2004) and the model definition proposed in 2010 by the UN Special Rapporteur on the protection and promotion of human rights while countering terrorism (see UN document A/HRC/16/51).

Even if isolated terrorist attacks in the Western or Northern world tend to generate much media attention and policy responses, most acts of terrorism and most deaths through them occur in the developing world. According to the 2019 Global Terrorism Index, early twenty-first century terrorism is concentrated in three regions: the Middle East, South Asia, and Sub-Saharan Africa, jointly accounting for 93 per cent of terrorism fatalities in 2002–2017. Of all deaths from terrorist acts in 2018, 87 per cent took place in only ten countries, none of which is a Western State: Afghanistan (alone 46 per cent), Nigeria, Iraq, Syria, Somalia, Pakistan, Mali, Democratic Republic of Congo, India and Yemen.

In the twentieth century, several nations were tormented by domestic terrorism, often by political or religious groups. Gradually, and in particular in the first two decades of the twenty-first century, terrorism has become increasingly international in nature. Consequently terrorism, or at least international terrorism, has been identified as a threat to peace under the United Nations Charter. Between a 1970 convention against the seizure of airplanes and a 2005 convention against nuclear terrorism, a whole range of international treaties and protocols against various forms of terrorism have been drafted and adopted, while work towards a comprehensive convention against terrorism has so far not produced an outcome. The UN Security Council has adopted a number of resolutions to counter terrorism, often under Chapter VII of the UN Charter and thereby legally binding upon States. Some of the most important Security Council resolutions in the field are Resolution 1267 (1999) on listings and sanctions against certain terrorist individuals or entities; post-9/11 Resolution 1373 (2001) that established a range of legal obligations of States as well as created a Counter-Terrorism Committee; Resolution 1566 (2004) that comes closest to defining terrorism; and Resolution 2178 (2014) on measures to combat the phenomenon of foreign terrorist fighters. None of these resolutions authorizes the use of force across borders by any State. In many cases, Security Council resolutions have been used as a rapid way of legislating on State obligations in issues where there is no international treaty or the universal ratification of a treaty has progressed slowly. Such use of Security Council powers, which under the Charter are aimed at responding to urgent threats to peace and security, has been criticized as being ultra vires but by and large tacitly or even actively accepted by States. Likewise, terrorist listings by the Security Council for purposes of sanctions such as a travel ban and the freezing of assets, have been criticized as usurpation of powers that are ultimately of judicial nature and therefore not suitable for a political body to exercise. Piecemeal measures to add elements of due process into the listing and delisting procedures have been added but still no independent judicial review of them exists.

Many human rights bodies and experts, as well as non-governmental organizations, have, particularly after States' responses to the terrorist attacks of 11 September 2001, raised concerns over the adverse effect of counter-terrorism measures upon human rights. Initially such concerns were related to practices such as torture, arbitrary detention without trial and extraordinary rendition that affect primarily individuals who, rightly or wrongly, are suspected of terrorism. However, gradually human rights concerns have widened to cover negative impacts of insensitive counter-terrorism measures upon all human rights. In 2005 the UN Commission on Human Rights (succeeded in 2006 by the Human Rights Council) created the mandate of a Special Rapporteur on the protection and promotion of human rights and fundamental freedoms while countering terrorism. The resulting reports have mapped the human rights impact of counter-terrorism on, inter alia, the right to asylum, the right to privacy, economic and social rights, the right to a fair trial, and the right to non-discrimination (through the phenomenon of profiling), as well as the gendered human rights impacts of counter-terrorism. In 2006 the UN General Assembly, through Resolution 60/288, adopted a Global Counter-Terrorism Strategy that identifies human rights violations as a major contributing factor of terrorism. In the development context it is significant that the Strategy identifies, among conditions conducive to the spread of terrorism, "lack of the rule of law and violations of human rights, ethnic, national and religious discrimination, political exclusion, socio-economic marginalization and lack of good governance". As one of its four so-called Pillars, the Strategy affirms that measures to ensure respect for human rights and the rule of law should be seen as the fundamental basis of the fight against terrorism.

The role of respect for human rights in a strategic approach to countering terrorism, coupled with the identification of human rights violations among the structural causes of ("conditions conducive to") terrorism, represent an important official acknowledgment by States that human rights and countering terrorism are not mutually exclusive objectives, or even aims that would need to be "balanced" against each other. Rather, securing all human rights to all and making sure that human rights are not violated through counter-terrorism measures represent an effective and sustainable approach to combating terrorism. Various dimensions of this approach are reflected in the volume *Using Human Rights*

to Counter Terrorism (Nowak and Charbord, 2018). Under such an approach, the alternative to abstract "balancing" is insistence on the legality, necessity and proportionality of any concrete counter-terrorism measure.

Acknowledging compliance with human rights as strategic choice in the fight against terrorism is a lesson that is also of utmost importance in the development context. Development that secures the effective enjoyment of all human rights, including economic, social and cultural rights, to everyone, is not only in the interest of the people concerned but also furthers peace and security on the global level, including as a long-term strategy against terrorism. Against this background, the UN Special Rapporteur on human rights and counter-terrorism has consistently warned about two negative trends in development cooperation that may have the opposite effect. A first negative trend visible since 9/11 of 2001 is the securitization of development cooperation where short-term achievements in counter-terrorism are sought through shifting resources to development projects that have an immediate security objective, including training programmes related to countering terrorism. Triggered by a country study on Australia, the Special Rapporteur in 2007 recommended ensuring that technical or other assistance in the counter-terrorism field is not provided at the expense of development assistance, including programmes aimed at promoting economic, social and cultural rights:

> The Special Rapporteur recommends that development cooperation be furthered, keeping in mind the strategic importance of the promotion of economic, social and cultural rights in preventing terrorism and the need to avoid undermining that potential by shifting resources from such programming to short-term capacity-building and technical assistance in the field of counter-terrorism. (UN document A/HRC/6/17, para. 72 (b))

A second negative trend is related to overly broad measures to combat the risk that humanitarian aid, development cooperation or remittances sent to developing countries might be used, directly or indirectly, towards the financing of terrorism. Organizations or individuals involved in such activities may have been subjected to sanctions such as the freezing of their assets, or to criminal prosecution. Governments, in turn, may have turned

MARTIN SCHEININ

away from cost-effective and human-rights-promoting forms of development cooperation such as small projects by non-governmental organizations, to prioritizing large-scale projects run by profit-making corporations and often controlled by the recipient government. Tighter governmental controls may address the risk of terrorist organizations benefiting from development cooperation but often they come with the downside of reduced human rights benefits for the vulnerable and lower cost-efficiency.

In the above-mentioned 2007 report, the UN Special Rapporteur on human rights and counter-terrorism warned that the application of government measures to curtail charity work because of a perceived risk that the funds might end up in support of terrorism was unlikely to be effective because they do not rely on the reality of charity work: "They can . . . undermine general confidence in charities and encourage less transparent ways to transfer funds, thereby producing counterproductive effects" (UN document A/HRC/6/17, para. 46). In this context the Special Rapporteur (in para. 48) made reference to the Al Barakaat case, where soon after 9/11 the main organization for remittances into Somalia and also the country's largest private sector company was subjected to counter-terrorism listings and sanctions, resulting in a statement by the United Nations Development Programme that the closure of Al Barakaat had had a destabilizing effect on the economy of Somalia and a great humanitarian impact on the population of Somalia, who were unable to receive money from their relatives. Some years later, in the case of Humanitarian Law Project, the challenged US legislation criminalized "material support" to foreign terrorist organizations. The Humanitarian Law Project sought to provide to the LTTE in Sri Lanka and the PKK in Turkey training on how to use humanitarian and international law peacefully to resolve conflicts, to petition United Nations bodies and to engage in peaceful political advocacy. As these two entities had been listed as foreign terrorist organizations by the US Government, the US Supreme Court upheld the ban in June 2010.

Since then, the same negative trend has continued. In a 2019 report, the Special Rapporteur summarized that "[s]ince 2001, civil society space has been shrinking around the globe". She referred to severe risks of securitization or instrumentalization in development, education,

good governance, democracy and human rights promotion and further drawing humanitarian actors into a security-driven political agenda (UN document A/HRC/40/52, para. 64). This report also addresses the securitization of aid since 2001 and the increased conflation of humanitarian and political agendas (para. 119). In another 2019 report, the Special Rapporteur specifically addressed the role of the Financial Action Task Force, an international cooperation body largely operating outside the structures of international law, which defines itself as "the global standard-setter for combating money-laundering, terrorism financing and the financing of proliferation of weapons of mass destruction", and has been criticized for having a chilling effect upon humanitarian work and for restricting civic space. On a positive note, the Special Rapporteur was in 2019 able to state that the Task Force had lately responded to such criticisms and revised its recommendations in order to respect the vital role played by non-profit organizations to ensure that legitimate charitable activity continues to flourish (UN document A/74/335, paras 34–35).

As Nowak and Charbord (2018, p. 76) put it: "the ability of civil society actors to be effective in countering terrorism . . . depends in part on their ability to engage with communities in the proximity to a terrorist threat". Measures to prevent their involvement through reallocation of public funding, financial sanctions, or prosecution, will only be counter-productive.

MARTIN SCHEININ

References

Annual Reports by the Special Rapporteur on the protection and promotion of human rights and fundamental freedoms while countering terrorism (2005–2011): Martin Scheinin (2011–2017); Ben Emmerson and Fionnuala Ní Aoláin (2017). Available at: https://www.ohchr.org/EN/Issues/Terrorism/Pages/Annual.aspx accessed 10 September 2020.

Institute for Economics and Peace (2019). Global Terrorism Index 2019: Measuring the Impact of Terrorism. Institute for Economics and Peace.

International Legal Instruments (Conventions and Protocols) against terrorism. Available at: https://www.un.org/counterterrorism/international-legal-instruments accessed 10 September 2020.

Nowak, Manfred and Ann Charbord (eds) (2018). *Using Human Rights to Counter Terrorism*. Edward Elgar.

Resolutions by the United Nations General Assembly or the Security Council on countering terrorism.

Available at: https://www.un.org/counterterrorism/un-documents accessed 10 September 2020.

Saul, Ben (2008). *Defining Terrorism in International Law*. Oxford.

Saul, Ben (ed.) (2020). *Research Handbook on International Law and Terrorism*, 2nd edition. Edward Elgar.

Scheinin, Martin (ed.) (2013). *Terrorism and Human Rights*. Edward Elgar.

United States Supreme Court, Holder v. Humanitarian Law Project (561 US 1), 2020.

MARTIN SCHEININ

77. Traditional Authorities

(with a focus on Sub-Saharan Africa)

Traditional authorities, traditional leaders, chiefs, are all terms that refer to leaders whose legitimacy is rooted in history and culture, often combined with religious, divine or sacred references. Despite the term 'traditional', these leaders should not be seen as a residual of something authentic, as some traditional leadership positions resulted from colonial era acts of 'imagination' – a term denoting that the creation of new leadership positions and structures was done in dialogue, albeit often an unequal one, between colonial rulers and local society, particularly male-elderly elites. Such acts of imagination later often became lost to memory and the imagined institutions part of new constellations of power and authority.

Diversity marks the world of traditional authorities. Pre-colonial societies ranged on a continuum from largely acephalous societies with loosely linked segmentary lineage systems to extremely hierarchical societies with militarized forms of kinship or chieftaincy. Colonial and post-colonial histories, including modes and structures of governance and their relations with traditional authorities, were also highly varied. Under indirect rule policies, existing chiefs or new chiefs were integrated into the colonial administrative apparatuses by placing them between the local colonial administrators and the population. In direct rule policies, colonial governments preferred local administration to be done by civil servants selected for their skills, language proficiency, and compliant attitude towards the colonial endeavour. In practice, the differences between direct and indirect rule policies were much less stark, with both colonial policies making use of chiefs, where these were available and cooperative, and imposing others as chiefs or civil servants elsewhere. The main difference between chiefs in French and British colonies lay in the fact that the former were not allowed any autonomy or initiative as continuation of local self-government, whereas the latter were. This difference denotes the formal structure, though, and not necessarily the full reality on the ground.

Colonial governance had a profound impact on the balance of power in traditional governance. In pre-colonial societies, chiefs' powers were circumscribed by their council of elders, who represented the major factions of the community, and who could dismiss a chief and have him replaced by a rival. Abundance of land furthermore allowed people and groups who were dissatisfied with the way their chief ruled to move elsewhere. Under colonial rule, chiefs became dependent on colonial recognition, which transferred the downward accountability of chiefs towards their communities into upward accountability towards the colonial government. Chiefs were also given new, often unpopular, tasks such as tax collection and organizing compulsory labour and compulsory crop cultivation, which decreased the legitimacy of chiefs and increased their dependence on the colonial State.

Traditional authorities and their customary justice systems were expected to disappear with modernity, but are undergoing a resurgence in various regions of the world, such as in Indonesia, the Pacific, and Canada and Australia. Sub-Saharan Africa is a prime example. While in the first decades of independence a possible role for chiefs in processes of development and democracy in contemporary African states was largely overlooked, from the 1990s many African states have enhanced the position of traditional leaders and customary courts in constitutions and legislation, often alongside democratic local government institutions. Scholars link the 'resurgence of tradition' – itself a contested notion due to its suggestion of a return of the past, dehistoricizing the process and ignoring the continual development and agency of the institution – and the concomitant rise of identity politics, to processes of democratization, decentralization and liberalization. Liberalist policies, strongly connected to conditionality in foreign aid, debt relief and loan provisioning, placed many functions of the State with the private sector and the chiefs gained ascendancy as the representatives of such private actors, namely rural communities. The distancing of the State from the people also furthered tradition as an alternative mode of identification.

Around the same time as African states, the international community also started demonstrating a renewed interest in traditional leadership institutions. Prompted by developments in international law towards recognition of indigenous peoples' rights, 'group rights' and 'rights to culture', they increasingly saw 'traditional communities' as semi-autonomous development agents and their leaders as suitable, legitimate counterparts with the capacity to mobilize their population. As a result, international organizations and donor agencies started to pay more attention to traditional leaders at their conferences and in their development programming. In some instances, development aid was directly deposited into traditional leaders' funds, bypassing the central government.

This recognition of traditional communities and traditional leaders as actors in the development field also led to a growing donor attention to customary justice systems and an increasing engagement with these systems in donor programming in the field of rule of law building as well as transitional justice. This engagement was not unproblematic. Donors were not particularly well-versed in customary justice and often did not put in the amount of research needed to decode an unwritten, flexible system with much local diversity. They often approached projects as technical undertakings with limited eye for local power dynamics. Their often uncritical acceptance of traditional authorities as community representatives and custodians of customary law tended to overlook contested versions of customary law in the locality and lead to the adoption of a male-elderly elite representation of customary law. As such, donor engagement often profoundly affected the nature and functioning of customary justice systems.

While the relationship between States and chiefs has sometimes been analysed as a sort of 'zero-sum' relationship in which both are competing for (a delineated amount of) power and respect, in this new constellation it seems that both States and chiefs hope to augment their power and authority through cooperation and association with the other – resulting in relationships of dependency as well as competition. Through enlisting chiefly support, governments may seek to enhance State governance, hope to bring in the rural vote, and aim to gain access to natural resources on customary land. Governmental recognition of chiefs at the same time serves to increase or cement the power of the State over chiefs. Recognition, also in the post-colonial period, always includes conditions or exceptions, and is intertwined with questions of political power and control.

Chiefs in their turn, may attempt to use policies of State recognition to consolidate and expand their power. Opportunities to do so manifest themselves particularly when no attention is given in recognition and regulation processes to the relationship between traditional leaders and community members and to the role of councils, councillors and other customary structures at various geographical levels in decision-making and controlling the exercise of chiefly power. Summing up, interactions between traditional authority and the State lead to complicated two-way reconfigurations and to new processes of reordering and transformation, which can severely impact on local power divisions.

Traditional authorities are now to function in modern States, where their functioning is often subject to a State's constitution and its bill of rights. Constitutional or international human rights are often invoked in court against customary laws, prominently against unequal inheritance rights of men and women. Occasionally, constitutional and international human rights are also invoked to promote the evolution of the institution of traditional authority itself. A well-known example is the Shilubana case in South Africa, which concerned the question whether the chief of the Valoyi traditional community in Limpopo could be succeeded by a woman (CC of South Africa, Shilubana and Others v. Nwamitwa, 2009, para. 66).

A profound difference compared to the pre-colonial settings in which traditional authority institutions emerged, is the context of capitalism and high-value investments on the land of 'traditional communities'. This has in many places led to complex relations between States, chiefs and citizens. Changing values of land have led to struggles to redefine customary land tenure through the reimagining of chiefly authority and decision-making power. This has increasingly concentrated control of land revenues in the hands of chiefs, often in close cooperation with governmental and business elites. This sometimes involves a corporatization of traditional authority or tribal governments where for-profit Native corporations are created to lay the groundwork for development schemes in the name of traditional communities, but in fact often only profiting a small elite within that community as well as outside actors from both the business and government sector.

Another much-debated question is the compatibility of traditional governance systems, structured on the hereditary devolution of male power, with democracy and gender equality.

Traditional institutions commonly include direct participation of all adults or a system in which the major factions of a community are represented in the traditional council and have a say in important community matters. This is sometimes described as an African form of democracy. Recent literature, however, describes a breakdown of such mechanisms when money-making opportunities from customary land increase. This is particularly problematic if chiefly 'subjects' are denied a choice to opt out of traditional governance or customary courts. Some communities have introduced elections for traditional leaders. In other areas, however, traditional leaders are trying to do the reverse, for instance in the Eastern Cape province of South Africa, where chiefs are imposing headmen on villages with a long history of electing their own leaders.

Scholarly voices diverge in their assessment of the coexistence of traditional and elected local government structures, possibly because of their different geographical focus. Chiefs are, for instance, reported to improve the responsiveness of elected representatives and to facilitate the provision of public goods to the locality by the government, due to their intermediary position which enables them to mobilize local communities. Others rather find that the co-existing government structures lead to ambiguity and conflicts regarding their respective roles and responsibilities. Competition for popularity has furthermore been seen to diminish chiefs' willingness to enforce and sanction governmental rules, leading to a widespread reduction in compliance with laws.

While most traditional authority structures still have an overwhelmingly male bias, among some groups there is an evolution towards more 'gender-inclusive' traditional authority, including more female traditional leaders, enhancing the role of women in traditional courts, and changing customary norms detrimental to women. Another modernization of chieftaincy lies in the increasing professionalization of the institution. Where there is a choice from various candidates for a chieftaincy position, increasingly the candidate with the best education, skills and national and international contacts curries favour with the community. In Ghana, there is even a recent practice of electing 'development chiefs' – candidates wholly unrelated to the royal family, sometimes even foreigners, to assist the chief in bringing development to the area.

All of the above reiterates what Van Rouveroy and Van Dijk (1999, p. 7) wrote more than two decades ago: 'Chieftaincy is rapidly turning itself into a perplexing new phenomenon which appears capable of negotiating and modifying modern institutional arrangements to its own ends.'

JANINE UBINK

References

Baldwin, Kate (2016). *The Paradox of Traditional Chiefs in Democratic Africa*. Cambridge University Press.

Buur, Lars and Helene Maria Kyed (eds) (2007). *State Recognition and Democratization in Sub-Saharan Africa: A New Dawn for Traditional Authorities?* Springer.

Chanock, Martin (1985). *Law, Custom, and Social Order: The Colonial Experience in Malawi and Zambia*. Cambridge University Press.

Comaroff, Jean and John Comaroff (eds) (2018). *The Politics of Custom: Chiefship, Capital, and the State in Contemporary Africa*. University of Chicago Press.

Mamdani, Mahmood (1996). *Citizen and subject: Contemporary Africa and the Legacy of Late Colonialism*. Princeton University Press.

Ntsebeza, Lungisile (2005). *Democracy Compromised: Chiefs and the Politics of the Land in South Africa*. Brill Academic Publishers.

Oomen, Barbara (2010). *Chiefs in South Africa. Law, Power and Culture in the Post-Apartheid Era*. James Currey / University of KwaZulu-Natal Press.

Ubink, Janine M. (2008). *In the Land of the Chiefs: Customary Law, Land Conflicts, and the Role of the State in Peri-Urban Ghana*. Leiden University Press.

Van Rouveroy van Nieuwaal, B.E. Adriaan and Rijk van Dijk (eds) (1999). *African Chieftaincy in a New Socio-Political Landscape*. LIT Verlag.

Zenker, Olaf and Markus Virgil Hoehne (eds) (2018). *The State and the Paradox of Customary Law in Africa*. Routledge.

78. Transfer of Technology

Overview

Transfer of Technology (ToT) refers, within the global political economy, to the transmission of technologies owned by companies and States in industrialized countries to the Global South, in order to facilitate and enable their "catch-up", in a leapfrog strategy. In this sense, ToT is a distinctively developmental concept embedded in the second half of the twentieth century, including its shortcomings. It highlights not only the ever-growing technological gap between countries, but also how technology has been seen as a necessary condition for any development project.

Intellectual Property (IP) Rights (IPRs) are arguably the most relevant part of the debate, as most ToT is now related to IP protected knowledge. For its defenders, IP provides legal clarity, restricts free-riding and facilitates transfer and diffusion due to the clear boundary of rights. For its critics, the very same IP system creates monopolies and converts ToT into formalistic contractual transfers. While ToT is conducted mostly through licensing agreements, it is well-known that any successful ToT policy requires efforts related to infrastructure, skilled professionals and an enabling innovation ecosystem, among others.

Over the decades, a number of international proposals have been promoted to enhance ToT, with little success. Current international trade law rules (WTO, bilateral and regional trade agreements, but also global private contracts) drastically reduced the policy space for ToT policies that are not based on voluntary contractual agreements – the very same policies once widely utilized by now industrialized countries.

ToT has lost much of its original geopolitical momentum, which is largely explained by the neoliberal global order that considers any industrial policy to be outlawed and/or inefficient and by the advent of the global IPRs regime, which in theory would suffice to provide knowledge dissemination without the need for more interventionist policies.

The rise of protectionist unilateral policies by countries like the United States, instead of reopening the way for a critical and development-oriented ToT, strengthened the pressure against measures considered to be ToT, such as those successfully enacted by China.

Despite all of this, ToT remains a crucial debate for developing countries and a good entry point to understand long, yet still relevant, struggles between the Global South and North.

Background

ToT originally gained force as an international geopolitical issue with the decolonization of Africa and Asia, on one hand, and the economic heterodox Structuralism associated with the United Nations Economic Commission for Latin America and the Caribbean (ECLAC) in Latin America, on the other. Industrialization was a key element for all Global South development projects, wherein "advanced" technology was a premise. During the 1950s–1960s, ToT was a major demand by developing countries to correct structural economic asymmetries within the system. Starting from the 1970s, however, ToT became intertwined with the debate on IPRs (Gehl Sampath, 2019, p. 40). In 1975, at UN Conference on Trade and Development (UNCTAD), a famous report launched a discussion on how to amend the international patent system to complement other national development policies (UNCTAD and WIPO, 1975). Subsequently, a draft text on an International Code of Conduct was negotiated. An agreement was never reached, but broadly set the agenda for the decades to come, and has influenced the Trade-Related Aspects of Intellectual Property Rights (TRIPS) Agreement in 1994.

Overall, the ToT as a developing world agenda never gained prominence enough to become an international effective system. As a conclusion, the current ToT system is more a reflection of the global economic order rather than its subversion. The only countries which have managed to benefit from internalization of foreign technologies in the past decades are the ones who adopted other strategies, such as China.

ToT as a modern industrial concept (and its discontents)

ToT presupposes notions that are rooted in the twentieth-century global political economy. First, it entails a certain notion of what "technology" means: a set of tools that are to be converted into industrial application. Second, it has as a premise the notion that ideas (actually its expressions) can be appropriated, i.e., ideas are not common public goods and may have owners, which is a theoretical development directly related to the affirmation of IPRs. Accordingly, technology can be transferred, traded away and exchanged. Third, ToT presupposes a relatively linear path of development – the Third World is expected to replicate what others have done before.

These elements pose theoretical and concrete challenges to assessing the concept of ToT in contemporary terms. As to the first, "technology" tends to be seen more as a co-producing element, rather than a tool. It creates its users as much as it is created, and it is anything but neutral. As to the second, while the appropriation of the intangible is more accepted than ever before, it is also clear that transferring a set of information is not enough for the proper implementation of a certain technology or to a country's effective development. Infrastructure, skilled professionals, capacity-building and the broader "innovation ecosystem" are just as relevant. Therefore, the "technology" as a contractual object – as much as the invention description in a patent application – is not much more than an artefact that cannot be turned into an effective "know-how". This means that ToT entails much more than its hegemonic contractual and formalistic form. Finally, and no less important, it provides little or no room to alternative strategies – be it the once established imitation, the recent "degrowth" anti-capitalist strategies, or even the creation of new economic paths by developing countries.

ToT and IPRs

ToT deals directly with, and overlaps, IPRs, particularly after the 1970s. The intellectual property system is based on a theoretical balance between the private interest of the inventor/creator, to whom a temporary monopoly is granted, and the public interest at large, corresponding mainly to the access to the knowledge/technology therein after the monopoly expires. Although ToT policies are undertaken with the same public goal in mind, the overall assumption is that the IP regime would be sufficient to do so, rendering ToT irrelevant in this aspect.

Moreover, as any valuable set of knowledge is protected by IPRs (by establishing exclusive rights or by punishing unfair competition), ToT licensing means most of the time the licensing of one or more IPRs, such as patents. ToT is in this sense the macroeconomic dimension, while IPRs compose the microeconomic feature of the same phenomenon. Different countries adopt different policies regarding ToT and IP. For instance, in a country like Brazil, all ToT contracts need to be registered at the National Institute of Industrial Property. Such policy aims at increasing transparency and augmenting the dissemination of technologies. However, the same policy is also highly criticized by advocates of a more liberal economy for being bureaucratic and imposing mandatory information to be provided by foreign firms.

The TRIPS Agreement (1994) considers ToT an objective of the treaty (TRIPS, Article 7). It also recognizes the States' policy space to adopt measures to "promote the public interest in sectors of vital importance to their socio-economic and technological development" (TRIPS, Article 8.1). Article 40.2 allows Members to specify licensing practices that might be an abuse of IPRs and to adopt measures against them, which also reflects the interaction of the two systems.

Article 66.2 of TRIPS mandates developed countries to "provide incentives to enterprises and institutions in their territories" in order to promote and encourage ToT to least developed countries (LDCs). The provision is a remainder of the debate of the previous decades, but now incorporated into a treaty that reflects a different context, one that is much less open to the idea of industrial policy of any kind. Again, it is not surprising that the utilization of this provision is radically limited since its inception. Developed countries argue that they are committed to ToT as a development assistance – now, a sort of grace granted by industrialized nations to "less developed" ones – but also reaffirm that they cannot force any mandatory ToT, especially those owned by the private sector.

Furthermore, the increased role and enforcement of IPRs and associated rights, including the recent strengthening of trade secret and foreign investment legislations in the United States and the European Union, largely limit the possible scope of ToT initiatives. Maybe as a consequence of the voluntary and contractual-based model, the most effective ToT occurs through joint ventures and public private partnerships.

In the pharmaceutical sector, for instance,

VITOR HENRIQUE PINTO IDO, SHEILA C. NEDER CEREZETTI AND JULIANA KRUEGER PELA the Productive Development Partnerships (PDPs) in middle-income countries are an increasingly adopted model for the local production of medicines between domestic firms and public laboratories in partnership with transnational companies. PDPs are criticized for benefiting transnational companies (and the indirect interest of the States where such firms are based) more than domestic firms and laboratories, as their licensing agreements maintain both ownership and control of the technologies transferred in the hands of technology providers. They may nonetheless be more successful in achieving effective ToT to developing countries, as they usually include skills, manufacturing-related knowledge and other necessary procedures/technologies. The Covid-19 pandemic has revamped the debate on the need for ToT policies for manufacturing of vaccines, treatments and other health products, and the limits of IP-based models. India and Brazil seem to be cases of ToT under this model for Covid-19 vaccine candidates.

ToT and the neoliberal contemporary world order

The main basis of technology development by the now industrialized countries was not ToT, but rather imitation and assimilation. Germany and the USA, and then Japan and South Korea in the twentieth century, are prime examples of this strategy. The USA, for instance, did not protect copyrights for foreigners until the end of the nineteenth century. Some argue that industrial espionage was at the origins of the industrial revolution in the United Kingdom and later elsewhere, such as in France, Italy, and the USA, bringing foreign technologies to the respective nascent industries. Many countries favoured national companies through legal incentives (lax IPRs, for instance) and innovation policies of various kinds throughout the twentieth century. All sorts of strategies were vastly utilized and overall considered to be a legitimate national strategy.

However, starting from the consolidation of neoliberal governments in the 1980s onwards, the advent of notions of free trade and IPRs, theoretically justified on Ricardo's comparative advantages theory and fully institutionalized with the creation of the WTO in 1994, produced a major legal transformation in this regard. The policy space for countries drastically shrank and this also meant, for developing countries, requesting or demanding technology under much more difficult conditions. In the current global order, most of industrial policy is not allowed under international economic law, which includes more incisive ToT policies. Therefore, unlike the strategy deployed by most developed countries in their development projects, ToT denotes a more diplomatic, voluntary and contractual approach. It is based on the knowing, and relatively consensual, sharing of information.

A main challenge to ToT in the current global economy lies in the understanding that the only path for development is that of liberalization of markets and structural reforms. As hinted before, this is responsible for converting ToT into a pariah within the international system. Although discussions still take place in numerous intergovernmental spheres, including the WTO, the World Intellectual Property Organization (WIPO), and the Forum on Science and Technology and Innovation for the Sustainable Development Goals (STI Forum), they are framed as a marginal issue. Most middle-income countries abandoned the agenda altogether, as no country wants to be perceived as opposing the global liberal economic order. A notable exception can be found in the realm of Financing for Development (FfD), particularly through the Addis Ababa Action Agenda of the United Nations (2015), which highlights ToT prominently, but, given its relatively limited reach, confirms the norm.

Finally, the recent protectionist trends rendered evident by the United States and China trade dispute originated in 2018 shed a new light on ToT as an allegedly intrinsic illegal practice. Again, the discourses of intellectual property and ToT are intertwined: China is essentially criticized for supposedly forcing ToT of foreign technology, which would then violate "American IP". Paradoxically, the whole Chinese model was based on the *voluntary* legal model of contracts to which all foreign investors agreed. This debate highlights how ToT is inevitably related to development strategies and, as such, claims of global economic nature. But it also shows that, instead of paving the way for new development-oriented ToT policies for developing countries, the current protectionist trend tends to further limit the policy space of the Global South against the rules of international economic law.

VITOR HENRIQUE PINTO IDO, SHEILA C. NEDER CEREZETTI AND JULIANA KRUEGER PELA

Conclusion

All things considered, ToT should remain as important as ever before. With the advent of the fourth industrial revolution, developing countries have been promised to be able to leapfrog to high-skilled and technology-intensive digital industries without going through heavy industrialization. However, as the digital gap only increases, and as a small group of huge technology industries created a global oligopoly, this may actually mean a much worse off environment for developing countries. The global legal order, composed of IPRs, WTO and free trade agreement trade rules, global contracts enforced by private arbitration adjudication and unclear and insufficient licensing agreements, enhances – rather than counters – the disparity of powers within this system. Despite its shortcomings as a concept, ToT, if adequately deployed, would be at least a form of compensation (yet insufficient) to this imbalance.

VITOR HENRIQUE PINTO IDO, SHEILA C. NEDER
CEREZETTI AND JULIANA KRUEGER PELA

References

Amsden, Alice (2001). *The Rise of "The Rest": Challenges to the West from Late-Industrializing Economies.* Oxford University Press.

Branstetter, Lee G., Raymond Fisman, and C. Fritz Foley (2006). "Do Stronger Intellectual Property Rights Increase International Technology Transfer? Empirical Evidence From U.S. Firm-Level Panel Data", Quarterly Journal of Economics 121(1), 321–349.

Correa, Carlos (2010). "Can the TRIPS Agreement Foster Technology Transfer to Developing Countries?" in Keith E. Maskus and Jerome H. Reichman (eds), *International Public Goods and Transfer of Technology Under a Globalized Intellectual Property Regime.* Cambridge University Press.

Furtado, Celso (1964). *Development and Underdevelopment.* University of California Press.

Gehl Sampath, Padmashree (2019). "Intellectual Property and Technology Transfer: Why We Need a New Agenda" in Carlos Correa and Xavier Seuba (eds), *Intellectual Property and Development: Understanding the Interfaces – Liber Amicorum Pedro Roffe.* Springer.

Kim, Linsu (1997). *Imitation to Innovation: The Dynamics of Korea's Technological Learning.* Harvard Business Review Press.

Patel, Surendra, Pedro Roffe, and Abdulqawi Yusuf (2000). *International Technology Transfer, The Origins and Aftermath of the United Nations Negotiations on a Draft Code of Conduct.* Kluwer.

UNCTAD (2001). Transfer of Technology, UNCTAD Series on issues in international investment agreements. Available at: https://unctad.org/en/docs/psiteiitd28.en.pdf.

UNCTAD and WIPO (1975). *The Role of the Patent System in the Transfer of Technology to Developing Countries.* United Nations Publication.

World Intellectual Property Organization (2007). *WIPO Development Agenda (Cluster C – Technology Transfer, Information and Communication Technologies (ICT) and Access to Knowledge).* WIPO.

79. Transitional Justice

Overview

Transitional justice is defined by the United Nations as the full range of processes and mechanisms associated with a society's attempt to come to terms with a legacy of large-scale past abuses, in order to ensure accountability, serve justice and achieve reconciliation. At its core, then, transitional justice is a response to systematic, widespread violations of human rights. These violations are often so grave that normal State justice mechanisms are unable to provide an adequate response to them. Transitional justice is concerned with finding responses to massive human rights violations which will be viewed as legitimate on the local, national or international scale, at a time of immense political and social fragility in a country. This is of enormous importance in the aftermath of violence, when both legal and political institutions are often weak, heavily politicized and significantly under-resourced.

To understand the contexts in which the need for transitional justice arises, the phrase is best understood by splitting it into two parts: transition and justice. 'Transition' relates to the measure of time in the evolution of a country in which it is moving toward peace and stability after emerging from conflict and repression. The time it takes for a country to undergo this transitionary period varies according to context. Transition can take many weeks, months or even years. 'Justice' is best understood in relation to the institutional mechanisms of transitional justice, designed and implemented to promote a holistic sense of justice. In addition to ensuring criminal accountability for grave human rights abuses, transitional justice mechanisms, in putting victims and their dignity first, provide access to justice for serious human rights violations, but also recognize and acknowledge experiences of affected communities in order to rebuild social trust, thus ensuring that atrocities are never repeated. 'Justice' in this sense is not only 'top-down' justice, but also 'bottom-up', responding to the needs of those communities affected on the ground. In doing so, transitional justice not only provides access to justice for the most vulnerable, but also ensures that root causes of conflict are addressed, promoting a legacy of peace and establishing a basis for reconciliation.

Mechanisms

Scholarly consensus exists that the mechanisms of transitional justice fall into the following categories:

Criminal Trials and Tribunals: judicial investigations of those responsible for international crimes including genocide, crimes against humanity and war crimes. A central pillar of transitional justice, it has roots in the Nuremberg Trials and the less well-known Military Tribunal for the Far East in Tokyo. Such trials were not seen again until after the end of the Cold War, when the International Criminal Tribunal for the former Yugoslavia (ICTY) at The Hague and the International Criminal Tribunal of Rwanda (ICTR) in Arusha, Tanzania, took place, and the phenomenon of the hybrid court or tribunal arose composed of both international and domestic justice actors. Today, the International Criminal Court (ICC) is a vital mechanism of transitional justice as an international judicial body that can investigate, try and convict individuals of serious international crimes, namely those considered 'the most serious of international concern', as per Article 1 of the Rome Statute of the International Criminal Court. The ICC is a court of last resort in those cases where transitional countries are unwilling or unable to prosecute.

Truth Commissions: as non-judicial commissions of enquiry, truth commissions focus on the testimony of victims of atrocity, which in turn provide acknowledgment of suffering and survival to those most affected. Commissions make recommendations that contribute towards criminal justice, reparations and institutional reform processes to remedy this abuse and prevent repetition. These recommendations provide an opportunity for divided societies to begin the process of rebuilding trust among citizens in the institutions which serve them. To do so, truth commissions generate discussion amongst the wider population on crucial issues of transitional justice; a significant contribution towards building capacity for active citizenship and democratic process.

Reparations: refers to remedying the damage or harm caused by an unlawful act. The sole purpose of reparation is to re-establish the situation that existed before a 'harm' occurred, either to an individual or a group of people. Reparation initiatives are often State sponsored and a mixture of material and symbolic reparations, based on the right to reparations for victims of gross human rights abuses and war crimes in international law. Studies on the effectiveness of reparations have shown that the most effective programmes are those which adopt a mixture of both types of reparation.

Gender Justice: concerned with the gendered impact of human rights violations. Women and girls, and men and boys, are subjected to sexual violence and forcibly taking part in hostilities. Both genders deal with severe emotional consequences from their experiences. However, there are distinctive differences on the impact of the same violation on both genders and the response to them in their communities. To address different gender experiences is crucial to counter stigmatization and community rejection faced by survivors of both genders. As such, gender justice is of vital importance in challenging impunity for sexual and gender-based violence against women and girls and, increasingly, men and boys.

Institutional Reform: the rebuilding and reforming of State institutions through the process of reviewing and restructuring, so that they respect human rights, preserve the rule of law, and are made accountable to the population they serve. Institutions that undergo reform are usually public, such as the police, military and judiciary, which may have been involved in the violation of human rights. To focus on the transformation of those institutions complicit or responsible for past violations allows the reform process to focus on building civic trust and to prevent similar violations from happening in the future.

Memorialization efforts: these take place in diverse and contextual ways, and can include the setting up of museums, exhibitions or monuments, giving public testimony, storytelling, narrative, collating an archive collection, taking part in local/traditional justice processes, creating murals, artwork or music. Memorialization efforts aim to preserve the public memory of victims and prevent such abuses from ever happening again. Memorialization efforts can also reinforce the mandates and outcomes of truth commissions, reparations and institutional reform.

The mechanisms outlined do not represent an exhaustive list. Many societies have developed their own local and traditional justice approaches to past abuses. Moreover, it is vital to view all mechanisms of transitional justice as interdependent and not as alternatives to one another. Each mechanism has a specific function, but more than one can be implemented at the same time and in the same context. In doing so, transitional justice can be a catalyst for peace, reconciliation and democracy. This could not be more vital at a time when confidence in the State to guarantee the rights of its citizens has been severely damaged.

Critical perspectives on the terrain of transitional justice

Although the UN definition of transitional justice is the most widely recognized, transitional justice is in fact a term with a multiplicity of understandings. Indeed, even the UN has noted that various definitions and understandings exist even among their own closest partners in the field. From a cross-disciplinary standpoint there is no single, authoritative definition of transitional justice. Instead, the way that transitional justice is defined and evaluated is very much dependent on its relationship as a 'field' with other 'fields'.

Given its conceptual origins, it is no surprise that transitional justice is dominated by the plethora of research and scholarship of international law. Yet, this dominance of legalism has been said to be at the detriment of scholarship and practice. An over-reliance on legalism as the foundation of understanding transitional justice hinges on understanding it as a set of measures that ensure strengthening the rule of law remains central to the project of transitional justice, even though legal mechanisms are not always the appropriate response. This has led to transitional justice being described as divorced from the wider political, social or cultural contexts which produced violence in the first place. It is the author's position that in order to function effectively, a pluralistic, inter-disciplinary approach to transitional justice is necessary. Other transitional justice scholars in favour of this approach argue that transitional justice can, and should, extend past the legal framework to engage with other injustices outside of the sphere of human rights, particularly those of a structural or societal nature that enable or facilitate human rights violations. It is for this reason that scholarship has challenged the tendency to impose a one-size-fits-all approach to transitional justice by the international community, particularly in the way that such an approach leads to de-contextualized solutions. With mechanisms viewed as rigid, inflexible and harder to relate to changing conflict and post-conflict situations, there is a significant risk of a lack of legitimacy with the very people they are designed to assist. Critics of international law as a singular 'way of knowing' transitional justice suggest that viewing it through this lens is to merely provide a means of categorizing abuses; it is international law, therefore, which decides on the parameters for what 'type of harm' warrants a response from transitional justice mechanisms. Viewing transitional justice in this way imposes very generalized rules, norms and outcomes on societies undergoing transition.

However, the 'universe' of transitional justice is growing. It has been noted that a 'critical turn' in scholarship has emerged, whereby the mechanisms and processes of transitional justice are being scrutinized and questioned more than ever before, taking place primarily from fields outside of international law. Transitional justice today is constantly evolving across a wide range of disciplines, moving away from its theoretical beginnings in international human rights. A growing body of scholarship exists that promotes transitional justice as a field which should now be moving beyond legalism, and instead towards a 'thicker' understanding of its interdisciplinary application. To do so is not to dismiss the influence of international law on transitional justice, yet to understand the new interdisciplinary landscape that transitional justice is part of, it is important to engage with different 'ways of knowing' about transitional justice processes, to provide an entry point for discussion and exchange. It is for this reason that scholars have called for caution in the blind promotion of the rule of law in understanding transitional justice. This is set against some considerable resistance, as there are those who argue that an ever-widening interdisciplinary approach to the field has led to it being over-extended, and that in fact, a narrower definition is more desirable. The author argues that limiting the scope of transitional justice to those who have suffered a specific type of harm creates a 'general blindness' to other experiences and the needs of those who suffered them. This provides a vital entry point for discussion and exchange on the link between transitional justice and sustainable development, moving away from a purely ontological, definitional

debate towards an epistemological approach, grounded in context. This in turn allows for the core assumption and purpose of transitional justice (to deal with the past in order to build a stable future) to be not only reflexive, considering questions such as whose stories are told, how are they heard and accepted, and under which circumstances are they legitimized (or delegitimized), but also forward-looking and progressive, planning for how to meet the needs of the present without compromising the ability of future generations to do the same.

What is certain, however, is that a new terrain is being forged for transitional justice where multiple interdisciplinary voices exist. This a far cry from its conceptual origins in international law, yet an important 'transition' in the evolution of transitional justice.

JEANNETTE FRANCESCA RODGERS

References

Bell, Christine (2009). 'Transitional Justice, Interdisciplinarity and the State of the 'Field' or "Non-Field"', International Journal of Transitional Justice 3(1), 5–27.

Carden, Fred (2009). Knowledge to Policy: Making the Most of Development Research. IDRC SAGE.

Chambers, Robert (2014). 'Knowing in Development: A Radical Agenda for the Twenty-First Century', Forum for Development Studies 41(3), 525–537.

Jones, Briony (2020). 'The Performance and Persistence of Transitional Justice and its Ways of Knowing Atrocity', Cooperation and Conflict, 1–18. Available online.

Mani, Rama (2008). 'Dilemmas of Expanding Transitional Justice, or Forging the Nexus between Transitional Justice and Development', International Journal of Transitional Justice 2(3), 253–265.

McEvoy, Kieran (2007). 'Beyond Legalism: Towards a Thicker Understanding of Transitional Justice', Journal of Law and Society 34(4), 411–440.

Mukua, Matau (2015). 'What is the Future of Transitional Justice?', International Journal of Transitional Justice 9(1), 1–9.

Nagy, Rosemary (2008). 'Transitional Justice as Global Project: Critical Reflections', Third World Quarterly 29(2), 275–289.

Palmer, Nicola, Briony Jones, and Julia Viebach (2015). 'Introduction: Ways of Knowing Atrocity: A Methodological Enquiry into the Formulation, Implementation, and Assessment of Transitional Justice', Canadian Journal of Law and Society 30(2), 173–182.

Teitel, Ruti (2005). 'The Law and Politics of Contemporary Transitional Justice', Cornell International Law Journal 38(3), 837–862.

80. United Nations

The United Nations (UN) is the only universal international institution based on sovereign equality with broad competences in the field of development. In theory, this makes the UN a privileged forum and actor for development policy and law-making. In practice, the UN struggles with the triple challenge of fragmentation, managerialism and unilateralism: How to coordinate different specialized institutions, regimes and rationalities? How to combine technical and legal expertise with political legitimacy? And how to keep national egoisms and global hegemons in check? This entry uses these challenges as a foil to analyse three dimensions of the UN in the development process: its functions in that process, its institutional law, and its law reform activities at country level.

The functions of the UN system in the development process

When the UN Charter entered into force in 1945, it conferred upon the UN not only the grand mission to maintain peace and security and to protect human rights, but also the broad mandate to promote "higher standards of living, full employment, and conditions of economic and social progress and development" (Article 55). It charged the General Assembly (GA) and the Economic and Social Council (ECOSOC) with implementing this mandate and required Member States and specialized agencies to cooperate with one another to achieve these objectives (Articles 56–60). Since then, development operations have become the main activity of the UN system. They account for the majority of staff and 60 per cent of the annual budget, and they have contributed significantly to the global flow of finance, knowledge and norms towards developing countries (Stokke, 2009). Over the decades, the UN has performed (more or less well) three crucial functions in the process of international development: multilateral politics, institutionalization and norm-setting.

With its broad mandate, universal reach and inclusive structure, the UN provides a privileged forum for the multilateralization of global politics. It has lived up to this promise during the period of decolonization, when the GA became a political battleground in the struggles for a New International Economic Order (NIEO) and the reform of international law (Bernstorff and Dann, 2019). While developing countries ultimately gained political control of the GA, ECOSOC and the UN development system, the UN as a whole lost relevance as industrialized countries redirected funding and political support to the World Bank, the International Monetary Fund and other specialized agencies, to regional organizations like the European Union (EU) and Organization for Economic Cooperation and Development (OECD), and to informal venues like the G7/G20. As a result, institutional and legal fragmentation came to characterize the global approach to development governance. This fragmentation, as well as Cold War rivalry, US-American exceptionalism and new geopolitical competition, have hampered the UN's ability to multilateralize global development politics. The 2030 Agenda or the Financing for Development forum are attempts at overcoming some of this institutional fragmentation and integrating views from North and South on a consensual basis.

A second function which the UN has performed better is the institutionalization of development at the international level. Since its founding, the UN founded or midwifed significant new institutions like the United Nations Development Programme (UNDP), the United Nations International Children's Emergency Fund (UNICEF), the World Food Programme and the United Nations Conference on Trade and Development (UNCTAD) and performed an important coordination function for the plethora of specialized agencies, regional organizations and other institutions in the development sector (Stokke, 2009; Murphy, 2006). This institutionalization aligned with Member States' interests in channelling some of their aid through multilateral institutions and was driven by a self-reinforcing dynamic of bureaucratic growth. At the same time, the growth of the international development bureaucracy has been accompanied by constant calls and reforms for higher efficiency and effectiveness (Weinlich, 2011). This focus has contributed to a managerial culture that improved the performance of the UN system but also depoliticized development policy and operations to some extent.

A third function of the UN in the development process is norm-setting. Here the record is mixed. Norm-setting in the area of development has been intensive but often remained in the area of soft law or internal administrative law. GA resolutions on the NIEO, the 0.7 per cent-of-GDP-aid target, the Millennium Development Goals (MDGs) and the Sustainable Development Goals (SDGs) have shaped global discourse and UN practice but lack the judicial enforcement mechanisms that evolved in international economic law. In the area of human rights law, the UN succeeded in establishing foundational treaties that have become an important source of norms applicable to situations of poverty and underdevelopment, especially in the area of economic, social and cultural rights and the right to development. Yet, fragmentation between development and human rights communities remains an issue, while the increasing juridification of development also poses risks of depoliticization and expertification (Alston, 2005).

Unilateralism has been a constant challenge to the UN with respect to all three functions. Whether in the guise of Cold War superpower rivalry, humanitarian intervention, US-American exceptionalism, European agricultural and migration policy, or recent waves of populist nationalism, unilateralism has limited the capacity of the UN system to realize its potential as a universal and egalitarian forum and actor in the development process.

The institutional law of the UN development system

The three challenges also shape the institutional law of the UN development institutions, which form the UN development system. The system comprises 36 UN subsidiary organs, funds and specialized agencies active in the development sector. Its annual budget has risen to almost US$30 billion in 2016, roughly 20 per cent of worldwide Official Development Assistance (ODA), but remains largely dependent on voluntary and earmarked contributions from Member States subject to the threat of unilateral withdrawal. The system has evolved a body of primary and secondary law that is characterized by two distinctive normative features. First is the principle of sovereign equality. All Member States have the same voice, and there is no weighted voting or veto power as in the multilateral development banks (MDBs) or the Security Council. This shapes the institutional structure and outputs of the system, which tend to be more representative

of recipient States. Especially the UNDP has come to be known as the development organization of the developing countries, in which decisions tend to be made in decentralized country offices. The downside is that some industrialized countries have turned to other multilateral institutions or unilateral action (Murphy, 2006, pp. 15, 21, 139). In conflict-affected areas, the impact of the Security Council and its veto powers on development policies also remains considerable.

Partly as a consequence, the second feature of the system is its particularly intensive reliance on technical assistance, knowledge exchange and information governance. UN development institutions lack the financial clout of MDBs or the normative instruments of the UN human rights institutions. Consequently, advisory services, research and reports, statistics and indicators, network-building and the diffusion of ideas are important instruments with which they fulfil their mandate. This is exemplified by the concept of "human development" or more recently by the SDGs and the accompanying indicators (Stokke, 2019, pp. 343ff; Murphy, 2006, pp. 17–19, 199–208). The emphasis on technical assistance and exchange of expertise reflects a long-time preference of developing countries, but suffers from regime fragmentation (e.g. with respect to intellectual property and technology transfer) and requires a complex legal structuring of the nexus between knowledge, power and politics.

The institutional structure of the UN development system is marked by a separation of the political level and implementing functions. Political guidance and control lie with the GA and ECOSOC, which establish global goals (currently the SDGs) and pass periodic resolutions to establish policy and coordinate implementation. Implementation remains decentralized among subsidiary organs and specialized agencies but most of them are organized in the UN Development Group (UNDG), a consortium of 32 institutions tasked with inter-institutional coordination. At the country level, UN development institutions are present in 166 countries and have formed joint "UN Country Teams" led by a "UN Resident Coordinator" (usually the UNDP country director). Within this structure, individual institutions retain their legal and organizational autonomy but increasingly integrate administrative tasks, moving closer to a form of global composite administration that reduces fragmentation within the system while preserving some advantages of technical specialization.

The UNDP performs a particularly important role as central UN development administration and coordinating node within the system. Founded in 1965 by a GA Resolution that merged pre-existing programmes, the UNDP has become the largest donor of the UN system with a near-universal participation of 175 States (Schoiswohl, 2013). In its political organ, the Executive Board, developing countries hold a majority of 20 out of 36 seats and votes. Its Administrator heads a bureaucracy of over 6,400 staff members, of which 5,300 work in 135 country offices. This distribution indicates the decentralized nature of the UNDP, which is a hallmark of the institution and distinguishes it from more centralized organizations like the World Bank. Decentralization creates a network-like structure appropriate for a knowledge-based, learning organization, but also embeds UNDP deeply in local contexts and politics – a tension between two rationales that is not always productive (Murphy, 2006, pp. 51ff).

In its activities, the UNDP has contributed significantly to the evolving understanding of the concept of development and its implementation on the ground. In its body of administrative law, the UNDP has increasingly emphasized country-led programming and execution as well as transparency, social and environmental safeguard policies. Its Human Development Report and index, launched in 1990, popularized a multidimensional understanding of development against economic growth-focused structural adjustment policies. In its advocacy work and technical assistance activities, the UNDP has championed the cause of disadvantaged and vulnerable groups and a human rights-based approach to development, stretching its mandate and the requirement of political impartiality to its limits (Darrow and Arbour, 2009).

Law in UN operations at country level

Since the 1990s, UN operations at the country level have increasingly incorporated human rights-based approaches (HRBA), legal reform strategies and rule of law promotion activities. The UNDG committed to a HRBA in 2003 and has since then used human rights both as substantive objectives and procedural principles for its operations, emphasizing inter alia economic, social and cultural rights, non-discrimination and the participation of beneficiaries and affected groups. In parallel, UN institutions have increasingly engaged in rule of law promotion and law reform projects. This has been particularly relevant in post-conflict situations, where the UN has been heavily involved in constitution-making and State building efforts (Grenfell, 2013). With the adoption of SDG 16, rule of law and access to justice have been further mainstreamed in all types of operations (Arajärvi, 2018).

The HRBA and rule of law work address crucial challenges of the development process and tend to empower disadvantaged groups. At the same time, they can be strategies of institutional self-empowerment and remain contested concepts. Neither human rights nor rule of law are a panacea for resolving practical trade-offs and distributive choices, which remain an essentially political decision that cannot be legitimized by reference to human rights alone (Birkenkötter, 2020). There thus remains an important role for processes of democratic deliberation and parliamentary decision-making. Improving democratic embedding and cooperation with national parliaments remains an important task for the UN at country level, and possibly a worthwhile strategy against populist nationalism, managerialist depoliticization and country-level fragmentation.

MICHAEL RIEGNER

References

Alston, Philip (2005). "Ships Passing in the Night. The Current State of the Human Rights and Development Debate Seen through the Lens of the Millennium Development Goals", Human Rights Quarterly 27(3), 755–829.

Arajärvi, Noora (2018). "The Rule of Law in the 2030 Agenda", Hague Journal on the Rule of Law 10, 187–217.

Bernstorff, Jochen von and Philipp Dann (eds) (2019). *The Battle for International Law. South-North Perspectives on the Decolonization Era*. Oxford University Press.

Birkenkötter, Hannah (2020). *Rule of Law as a Power-Conferring Tool within the UN System: Unpacking United Nations Rule of Law Assistance* (forthcoming).

Darrow, Mac and Louise Arbour (2009). "The Pillar of Glass: Human Rights in the Development Operations of the United Nations", The American Journal of International Law 103(3), 446–501.

Grenfell, Laura (2013). *Promoting the Rule of Law in Post-Conflict States*. Cambridge University Press.

Murphy, Craig (2006). *The United Nations Development Programme. A Better Way?* Cambridge University Press.

Schoiswohl, Michael (2013). "United Nations Development Programme (UNDP)" in Rüdiger Wolfrum (ed.), *Max Planck Encyclopaedia of Public International Law*. Oxford University Press.

Stokke, Olav (2009). *The UN and Development: From Aid to Cooperation*. Indiana University Press.

Weinlich, Silke (2011). *Reforming Development Cooperation at the United Nations. An Analysis of Policy Position and Actions of Key States on Reform Options*. Deutsches Insitut für Entwicklungspolitik.

MICHAEL RIEGNER

81. Water and Sanitation

A commodity and a right

Water and Sanitation (WATSAN) are seen both as commodities to be traded and as human rights. International trade in water intensive products (e.g. water footprint labelling) and water supply and sanitation services can be subject to WTO rules. In addition, the involvement of private actors in this sector creates additional opportunities and challenges for managing WATSAN as a commodity. The Dublin Statement on Water and Sustainable Development 1992 highlights that it is important to consider water as an economic good for the sake of "efficient and equitable use", but also, that WATSAN should be recognized first as a human right that is available at affordable prices (Principle 4). In this entry, WATSAN is analysed primarily from a human rights and development perspective.

The right(s) to water *and* sanitation

The Right(s) to safe and clean drinking Water and Sanitation (RTWS) is one of the many rights that spring from the fountain of the rights to life, human dignity and adequate standard of living (ICCPR, Article 6; ICESCR, Articles 11(1), 12; CEDAW, Article 14(2)h; CRC, Articles 24, 27(3); CRPD, Article 28). Sanitation is a distinct right (UNGA Resolution A/RES/70/169) but is often addressed together with the right to water. In content and practice, RTWS is linked with health and hygiene and relates to the rights to life, health and adequate standard of living (ICESCR, Articles 11 and 12). "Access to equitable sanitation and hygiene" is included as a target under SDG 6. Water, Sanitation and Hygiene (WASH), then, is the defining goal of countless civil society and governance interventions. Discussions on RTWS focus not only on definitions and standards but also on the role of the State in management of water facilities and methodologies on measurement and monitoring of RTWS goals and actions. The role of non-State actors in administering RTWS, whether in partnership with the State or without, has not gone unnoticed either. The emerging impact of climate change on RTWS (consequently on other human rights) and the importance of RTWS for development, makes it an urgent global law and governance issue.

Content and standards

The work of the UN Special Procedures and the UN Committee on Economic, Social and Cultural Rights (CESCR) on the RTWS has been seminal in the development of RTWS. In 2003 the committee published General Comment (GC) 15, a comprehensive document that includes freedoms and entitlements regarding the right to water and both positive and negative obligations for States. The content of the right and the obligations depend upon a set of factors vis. sufficiency, safety and acceptability, availability, quality, and accessibility (physical and economic). In 2010, Resolutions of the UN General Assembly and UN Human Rights Council reaffirmed the importance of RTWS for all human rights (UNGA Resolution A/RES/64/292, 3 August 2010 and UNHRC Resolution A/HRC/RES/19/9, 6 October 2010). RTWS, like other economic and social rights, is further guided by the principles of (1) progressive realization of minimum legal thresholds up to the maximum available resources; and (2) non-retrogression, i.e. prohibition of deliberate retrogressive measures unless they can be justified (GC 3). RTWS also finds place in regional human rights instruments (African Charter on the Rights and Welfare of the Child, Article 14(2)c; Protocol to the African Charter on Human and Peoples' Rights on the Rights of Women in Africa, Article 15; Arab Charter on Human Rights 2004, Article 39; Council of Europe's Recommendation 2001/14 adopting the European Charter on Water Resources; see also, European Commission's proposal to amend the Drinking Water Directive 98/83/EC). It has been internalized in the domestic legal system of States as a fundamental constitutional right or a legislative right in different ways. As the first UN Special Rapporteur on RTWS, De Albequerque (2014) clarified State obligations deriving from the international RTWS on the right to sanitation taking cue from the obligations on the right to water regarding sufficiency, safety and acceptability, availability, quality, and accessibility (both physical and economic). While there are not any binding international standards for these obligations, the World Health Organization (WHO) guidelines are considered to monitor the implementation of RTWS. WHO guidelines on drinking water quality contain advice on water quality standards, management and monitoring (WHO 2011). In the area of sanitation WHO guidelines exist on the Safe Use of Wastewater (WHO 2006), Recreational Water Quality (WHO 2003) and Promotion of Sanitation Safety (WHO 2005) and most recently, on Sanitation and Health (WHO 2018), which include recommendations for the health and safety of sanitation workers and public sanitation behaviour change.

The monitoring of SDGs including SDG 6 also depends on quantitative indicators

The Inter-agency and expert group on SDG indicators (IAEG-SDG) places six out of 11 SDG 6 indicators in Tier I, which means at least 50 per cent of Member States regularly provide data relevant to the indicator (IAEG-SDG 2019). Even though standards for measuring access to RTWS and SDGs are not legally binding on Member States, they are valuable for influencing behaviour and governance on WASH issues. Despite the limitations of quantitative indicators for measuring fulfilment of human rights, they encourage disclosure of information by States on the implementation status of SDGs, which influences domestic and international governance on RTWS, investment and aid decisions and personal choices of people (Murthy, 2018).

Human rights are interrelated and interdependent and the RTWS is no exception to this principle. Initiatives towards RTWS have an impact on the right to life and human dignity, equal treatment and non-discrimination, right to adequate food, to a healthy environment, adequate standards of living, right to work and the right to education and vice versa. This can also be seen in the SDGs as WATSAN connects with other goals (SDGs 1–5, 10, 11, 13–15). Moreover, RTWS has been included in International Labour Organization (ILO) conventions dealing with rights of employees at the workplace (Occupational Health Services Convention 1985 No. 161; ILO Recommendation No. 115 of 1961 on Workers Housing; Hygiene (Commerce and Offices) Convention 1964 No. 120).

Access to WATSAN has been an important goal for sustainable development. The resolutions and statements of the UN bodies (UNESC 2010 E/C.12/2010/1; 2010 A/HRC/RES/19/9;

Dublin Statement on Water and Sustainable Development 1992; Agenda21 Rio Declaration on Environment and Development 1992; Report of the Special Rapporteur on the human right to safe drinking water and sanitation A/HRC/24/44, 11 July 2003; Goal 7, Millennium Development Goals; International Decade for Action: Water for Sustainable Development 2018–2028) reflect this conclusion. The rights-based approach to development (RBA) considers the fulfilment of human rights as a means to achieve human development. RBA requires integration of human rights principles of equality and non-discrimination and good governance at all stages of the development process (Emilie Elmer Wilson (2005). "Human Rights-based Approach to Development: Right to Water", Netherlands Journal of Human Rights 23, 213–243). In practice, it demands rights awareness amongst the community and an enabling legal infrastructure where violations can be effectively addressed.

While the primary responsibility to respect, protect and fulfil RTWS is on the States, GC 15 also promotes the **obligations of actors other than States** (Part VI). These include international organizations, transnational corporations and international financial institutions (IFIs) who financially contribute to WATSAN infrastructure and service delivery and are also users of water resources. The water sector received Official Development Assistance, i.e. concessional and non-concessional loans reaching US$9 billion between 2000–2016 especially in the Sub-Saharan Africa and South and East Asia regions (UNESC, E/2019/68). As per the World Bank PPI database 2017, the water and sewerage sector received US$76 million between 1990–2018 which is only 3 per cent of all private infrastructure investment from the private sector. This is way below the OECD estimated need of US$500 billion per annum (HLPW Outcome report 2018) and US$6.7 trillion by 2030 (OECD (2018). Financing Water: Investing in Sustainable Growth, OECD Environment Policy Paper No. 11, p. 5, available at https://www.oecd.org/water/Policy-Paper-Financing-Water-Investing-in-Sustainable-Growth.pdf). The reasons cited for this financing gap are undervaluing of water as a resource, its conception as a free resource and the low financial viability of water projects (OECD, 2018, above).

The importance of **aid and investment for RTWS and development** cannot be understated.

At the same time the obligation of external support agencies to *respect* RTWS and the obligation of States to *protect* it is of critical importance. Development cooperation and investment instruments can themselves contribute to human rights violations including RTWS. These are often coupled with conditionalities that interfere and even defeat the primary purpose of providing access to RTWS, e.g. control over the State service delivery system that can later lead to unaffordable user charges for water and influence over. They can interfere with the State's WASH policies, e.g. water privatization in Dar Es Salaam in 2003; or grant of project approvals without a human rights impact assessment or an environmental impact assessment, e.g. World Bank funding for the Sardar Sarovar Dam Project in India, from which the bank later withdrew in the face of citizen protests and two negative evaluations from independent reviews appointed by the bank itself. At the level of IFIs and other donor agencies, their own policies can include human rights protections and measures for project-affected individuals to ask for redress. The World Bank Environment and Social Framework adopted in 2018 requires governments to fulfil certain conditions to be eligible for investments and this includes an environmental and social impact assessment, which includes human rights principles to a limited extent (e.g. participation of "project-affected groups"). The World Bank can be considered as a leader when it comes to policy-setting as other IFIs and donor agencies often follow the policies and investment strategies of the World Bank (De Moerloose, Public lecture, University of Antwerp, 2019). This highlights the need for clear and effective preventive tools that can protect RTWS.

International soft law instruments such as the UN Global Compact, UN "Protect, Respect and Remedy" Framework 2011, the ILO tripartite declaration of principles on multinational enterprises and social policy and OECD guidelines for multinational enterprises offer a framework and create expectations for WASH responsibilities of companies for their employees in the entire supply chain as well as for engagements in service delivery and infrastructure building in the WASH sector and the implementation of corporate social responsibility projects. Ninety-two per cent of all private infrastructure investment projects in the water and sewerage sector, currently active, are public private partnerships

(PPPs) (World Bank PPI database, 2017). PPPs in the public service delivery sectors such as WASH as well as privatization of WATSAN services have been under fire for human rights violations arising from the conflicting motivations of State (service provision) and corporations (profit generation and commercial viability). In the absence of binding international treaties governing responsibility of businesses towards human rights and multilateral aid, there is a lack of accountability mechanisms for human rights abuse that results from PPPs, privatization and privately funded projects. In cases of disputes between private investors and States, the Convention on the Settlement of Investment Disputes between States and Nationals of Other States (ICSID) is applicable. The role of investments on RTWS can be seen in ICSID arbitration cases such as Suez and Vivendi v. Argentine Republic (ARB/03/19), involving privatization of water distribution and waste water treatment systems in Buenos Aires; Aguas Del Tunari v. Bolivia (ARB/02/3), where protests erupted in reaction to privatization of water distribution services leading to cancellation of a concession contract by Bolivia; and Biwater v. Tanzania (ARB/05/22), involving multilateral funding by the World Bank, African Development Bank and the European Investment Bank for a project to expand the Dar Es Salaam water and sewerage infrastructure on the condition that a private operator is in charge. These cases highlight that State accountability for RTWS is not enough. While private investments are crucial for WATSAN, these should be coupled with a human-rights-based multi-stakeholder approach.

Leaving no one behind

International law recognizes the specific vulnerabilities of marginalized groups in the WATSAN sector. GC 15 highlights the obligations of States towards vulnerable populations vis. children, persons with disability and women. Other groups deserving a special focus are indigenous peoples (ILO Convention No. 169, 1989, Article 15), the (growing number of) people residing in areas threatened by climate change, populations in the midst of a humanitarian crisis (see, UNESC: Concluding Observations, Israel, E/C.12/1/Add.90; Report of Special Rapporteur on right to water and sanitation, A/73/162) and lastly, victims of all sorts of discrimination.

Water is indispensable for life on the planet, not only for humans but for global ecosystems. Yet, approximately 2.1 billion and 4.5 billion people lack access to safe water and sanitation services respectively (WHO and UNICEF (2017). "Progress on Drinking Water, Sanitation and Hygiene: 2017 Update and SDG Baselines", available at https://www.unicef.org/publications/index_96611.html accessed 25 September 2020), and more than 80 per cent of the world's wastewater returns to the environment untreated (UNESCO (2017). "UN World Water Development Report, Wastewater: The Untapped Resource", available at http://www.unesco.org/new/en/natural-sciences/environment/water/wwap/wwdr/2017-wastewater-the-untapped-resource/ accessed 25 September 2020). However, the inclusion of WATSAN in the SDGs and in the context of the International Decade for Action, Water for Sustainable Development 2018–2028 is an impetus for WATSAN and has rekindled the discussion on the importance of RTWS.

DEVANSHI SAXENA

References

Baietti, Aldo and Peter Raymond (2005). Financing Water Supply and Sanitation Investments: Utilizing Risk Mitigation Instruments to Bridge the Financing Gap. Water Supply and Sanitation Sector Board Discussion Paper Series No.4. World Bank.

Clark, Christy (2017). "Of What Use Is a Deradicalised Human Right to Water?", Human Rights Law Review 17(2), 231–260.

De Albequerque, Catarina (2014). Realising the Human Rights to Water and Sanitation: A Handbook by the UN Special Rapporteur Catarina De Albequerque. UN Special Rapporteur on the human right to safe drinking water and sanitation.

Filmer-Wilson, Emilie (2005). "Human Rights based Approach to Development: Right to Water", Netherlands Journal of Human Rights 23(2), 213–241.

Heller, Leo and Colin Brown (2017). "Development Cooperation in Water and Sanitation: Is It Based on the Human Rights Framework?", Ciência and Saúde Coletiva 22(7), 2247–2256.

Muller, Mike and Christophe Bellmann (2016). Trade and Water: How Might Trade Policy Contribute to Sustainable Water Management? International Centre for Trade and Sustainable Development (ICTSD).

Murthy, Sharmila (2018). "Translating Legal Norms into Quantitative Indicators: Lessons from the Global Water, Sanitation and Hygiene Sector", William and Mary Environmental Law and Policy Review 42(2), 385–446.

Nhamo, Godwell et al. (2019). "Is 2030 Too Soon for Africa to Achieve the Water and Sanitation Sustainable Development Goal?", Science of the Total Environment 669, 129–139.

UN Department of Economic and Social Affairs (2018). Making Every Drop Count- High Level Panel on Water Outcome report. Available at: https://sustainabledevelopment.un.org/content/documents/17825HLPW_Outcome.pdf.

WWAP (UNESCO World Water Assessment Programme) (2019). The United Nations World Water Development Report 2019: Leaving No One Behind. UNESCO.

Index

Printed and bound by CPI Group (UK) Ltd, Croydon, CR0 4YY

17/04/2025

14658902-0001